# TAKE ME TO A CIRCUS TENT

## THE JEFFERSON AIRPLANE FLIGHT MANUAL

Photo
Courtesy Of:
Herb Greene

Craig Fenton

Cover to the book by kind permission of Herb Greene and may not be reproduced without the written consent of Herb Greene. Doesn't the cover to *Surrealistic Pillow* look terrific when not reduced to the size of a CD? From the Herb Greene collection. Herb Greene photographer. This is from a bunch of photos done around the time of the recording of some of *Surrealistic Pillow* circa 10/31/66-12-31/66. In the index this page is referred to as P1.

**One of two of the rarest Jefferson Airplane photos you will ever see. The other will be found later on during our flight to *Rock And Roll Island*, and is equal in historical value.**

**Photo by kind permission of Tim Lucas. From the Tim Lucas collection. Not to be reproduced without the written consent of Tim Lucas. Photographer unknown. The J. A. circa late 1965.**

**A special thanks for Tim (From 2400 Fulton Street) for contacting me and willing to share such a trophy.**

**These are his words about the photo:**

"I don't know if it's too late to include this in your book, but I am sending a very rare Airplane shot from 1965. I bought this from someone about six years ago, who got it signed by the band circa 3/26//66- 3/31/66 (Exact date unknown) at the Civic Auditorium in San Jose California. I've never seen this shot anywhere else, and I don't know who the photographer was. It's a rarity in that it's <u>signed by Skip and Signe,</u> who looks absolutely adorable. **It was so early in their autographing days that Paul signed it "Paul Airplane," and Skip signed it "Love, Alex Airplane."** Signe drew a little smiley face next to her first name and added "Smile." I wish the photo wasn't so dark so that the signatures stood out better. You have to angle the still against the light in order to see a couple of them. (Skip signed right under his chin)."

**In the index this page is referred to as P2.**

ISBN 0-7414-3656-6

Published by:

INFINITY
PUBLISHING.COM

1094 New Dehaven Street, Suite 100
West Conshohocken, PA 19428-2713
Info@buybooksontheweb.com
www.buybooksontheweb.com
Toll-free (877) BUY BOOK
Local Phone (610) 941-9999
Fax (610) 941-9959

*Printed in the United States of America*

*Printed on Recycled Paper*

*Published June 2007*

# "Take Me To A Circus Tent" (The Jefferson Airplane Flight Manual)
# Table of Contents

A) Airplane Terminology- Explanation of terms, and words found in the book.

B) Members aboard the various flights- This will tell you which of the Airplane musicians were included in the concerts, or studio recordings being discussed.

C) High Flying Birds 1965-1972- This is an alphabetical look at the studio vaults.  The treasures consist of alternates, demos, *jams*, rehearsals, rough mixes, etc.  There weren't any studio gems from 1989, but there were some small packages of value from the live performances.  The actual chapters of the book will cover the information in detail.

D) High Flying Birds 1965-1972 Live- This is an alphabetical look at the titled *jams*, live songs, improvisations, and riffs that have been documented to have taken place on stage.  The first and final appearance of the entry is listed as well.  The actual chapters of the book will cover the information in detail.

E) High Flying Birds 1989- The old plane looks pretty good!  This is an alphabetical look at the titled *jams,* live songs, improvisations, and riffs that have been documented.  The actual chapter of the book will cover the information in detail.

F) Hot Tuna Served Fresh 1989- This is an alphabetical look at the titled *jams,* live songs, improvisations, and riffs that Hot Tuna performed on stage during the reunion tour.  The actual chapter of the book will cover the information in detail.

G) The Final Flight Of The J.A. - A look at the 1996 Rock And Roll Hall Of Fame (Rehearsal), and (Performance).  The actual chapter will cover the information in detail.

H) Looking At The Flight-Logs And Those That Occupied A Seat 1965-72, 89 & 96- Each of the original studio albums of the J.A. are listed.  There are notations for the songs that were performed on stage at least once and those that never made it out of the studio.  There is also a year-by-year list of all tunes performed at least once.

# THE FLIGHT LOG'S CHAPTERS COME FROM THE FOLLOWING:

**When you see ^ it is to signify documentation that landed after November 2006.**

Enjoy the flight and please visit my sites for the latest happenings with the book, and updated music, video, and photo files for you fine J.A. fans. www.takemetoacircustent.net Web Site.

http://craigtheairplaneman.wordpress.com/ Blog.

# "Take Me To A Circus Tent" (The Jefferson Airplane Flight Manual)

# GETTING THE PLANE OFF THE GROUND

The most comprehensive look at the live history of the Jefferson Airplane ever compiled. A total of 121 performances, 110 different songs, 33 *jams*, and a combination of 36 improvisations, riffs, and vocal teases are examined. This includes one poem recited by Paul. The first and last appearance of the song is documented, as well as the Jefferson Airplane personnel of the era. Every track played from each studio album is listed, along with the songs performed each year. There is an alphabetical listing of all the verified material that was played live, separate documentation of 121 stage appearances (Including the only documented sound check), and information on many previously listed incorrect dates, and venues. The documentation also includes special guests and any unusual occurrences during the song, or performance. How does a 25:22 *jam* with Jerry Garcia and Mickey Hart from the Grateful Dead sound? Is the first live version of *Good Shepherd* with Grace, and Paul singing intriguing? What did *Mau Mau*, and *Starship* sound like, when played by the Jefferson Airplane? We'll fly back in time to 1962 when Jorma appeared as Jerry Kaukonen, discover some Marty Balin studio treasures from the same era, and when he left the J.A., take a look at Grace Slick & The Great Society's live (Including the 2002 reunion of sorts, without Grace), and studio recordings, many never released on LP, or CD! During the flight we'll even tell you how Grace and Jerry Slick were involved in a project for Sesame Street! Are you ready to feast your eyes on the 1965 Signe Anderson, and Skip Spence home music tape? By the way that includes a cover of the Rolling Stones song *I Can't Get No (Satisfaction)*.

This is the most comprehensive look at the studio vaults of the Jefferson Airplane ever compiled. A combination of 60 unreleased, alternate, excerpts, *jams*, demos, rehearsals, and rough mixes are dusted off, and explored for their historical value. **This includes the earliest authenticated studio recording, the demo for Columbia Records (That is correct) circa 8/65.** The legendary recording sessions of *Martha* are dissected, a *Fat Angel* studio version is unlocked, Jerry Garcia plays guitar on *Trial By Fire*, censored songs are discussed, and there is analyzation of some J.A. radio spots, and all the Levis Jeans commercials.

**The second section is 266 questions, and answers, regarding the Jefferson Airplane, Hot Tuna, Jefferson Starship, KBC Band, SVT, and Wooden Ships.** These aren't the same ones you have read over and over. Why not satisfy your curiosity, and find out which members of the Airplane did Signe Anderson play with at least one time after she left the band, why did Jorma use a second guitar-player on the *Yellow Fever* record, was there a version of the Jefferson Starship song *Jane* with an original Airplane member singing, and what song did both Paul Kantner's Wooden Ships, and Emerson, Lake, & Palmer perform as an encore?

**The third section is interviews from Jefferson Airplane, Hot Tuna, Jefferson Starship, and San Francisco friends. These are in depth, covering the artist's musical resume, and we remember Skip Spence, Spencer Dryden, and Chester Leo Helms (Chet Helms the famous promoter).** Discover the member of Led Zeppelin that was a tremendous help to Skip Spence during a difficult time, the J.A. musician that suggested Jorma play *Embryonic Journey* solo at the Rock And Roll Hall Of Fame, if Spencer Dryden wasn't physically able to perform at the Rock And Roll Hall Of Fame which drummer was waiting in the wings, what song the Great Society (Grace Slick) performed was rejected to be on a J.A. album, what two non Jefferson Airplane drummers played on the released studio version of *Feel So Good*, and which song did Marty feel would be the best video to release from the 1989 reunion record?

**The book is dedicated to my parents (You are missed more each day), sister, and two nieces. I extend the ultimate gratitude to every member of the Jefferson Airplane, for creating a sound not only of a generation, but a flight for eternity. Thank you for the past, present, and future.**

**Thank you for reading, and may you derive the same pleasure from the words, and pictures as I had researching, and archiving. Emailing me is easy if you please put "Jefferson Airplane" in the subject line at- <u>craigtheairplaneman@takemetoacircustent.net</u>.**

## Sources Of The Flight Log Manual:

I am very fortunate, and honored to be in possession of the music that is documented in the book. That is how I could substantiate the fact from fiction, and even provide the length of individual songs. **However!**

You can never have enough great help. **Thank you one million times:**

Art Cohen from Upper Darby, Pennsylvania. Art has helped uncover a lot of Airplane rarities over the years, and is an accomplished musician performing all over North America. Please check out his music at:
www.synkronosmusic.com (The Ministry Of Inside Things)
http://www.thegatherings.org/ (Ambient, electronic and space music)
http://www.menfromwhen.com (The Men From When)

Paul Crawford (The Marshall of Iowa) for uncovering a lot of buried Airplane treasure and archiving Paul Kantner's Wooden Ships shows.

Don Aters (Chet Helms best friend and the legendary photographer) for supplying many of the photos and contact information. www.haightstreetmusicnews.com

Herb Greene (The legendary photographer that took the photograph used for the *Surrealistic Pillow* album) for allowing his photographs to be used for the cover and inside the book. **A HEARTFELT** thanks for permission to be able to share with the readers so many pictures that have never been in book form.

Rick Martin (The legendary Airplane & Jefferson Starship fan hovering around Chicago) for setting up many of the interviews, even when working twelve hour days, and for sharing the same enthusiasm as myself during the entire writing of the book.

Mike Somavilla (Crest Of The Wave Productions) for supplying many of the photos and contact information. A true professional with a sense of humor!

You could never find six better individuals to call friends.

*All Music.com*- www.allmusic.com for allowing me to research the spellings of some of the musician's names and the composers of certain song titles. *All Music* is a great site if you are interested in learning about thousands of performers that have played on and or released albums over the years.

Collector's Choice Music- www.ccmusic.com for always having the Airplane Family releases for purchase by us old rockers. Gordon Anderson is not only a top flight executive but he is a true believer in rock and roll.

Dead Disc.com- www.deaddisc.com for helping with some of the catalog numbers of the original recordings and for having information on many of the San Francisco bands from the real era's (1960's and 1970's) of rock and roll!

Jefferson Airplane- www.jeffersonairplane.com for keeping the memories of the legendary band alive and for letting us old folks feel a bit younger.

Jefferson Starship- www.jeffersonstarshipsf.com for letting the fans know where the band will be playing and giving not only the normal but the eclectic information.

Jefferson Starship- http://www.geocities.com/SunsetStrip/Club/4220/index.html for being an amazing source of Jefferson Starship history. The effort must be recognized.

Steve Rowland- **Holding Together** (A terrific Jefferson Family publication that comes from a real fan and not a faceless corporation) can be purchased by contacting Steve at steveg.rowland@btinternet.com.

Richie Unterberger.com- http://www.richieunterberger.com/ Richie is often found reviewing albums on www.allmusic.com (Previously listed) but he also is an accomplished author.

Jefferson Airplane Base Version 2.4 from Scott Abbot 2000: This is actually a plug for the great work Scott did many years back. He put together a list of the other artists on the concert bill with the Airplane, and what venues they played from each of the fifty states. There was even information on the dates the Great Society performed with Grace Slick, birthdays of the members of the Airplane, and some information on film appearances. I haven't seen anything from Scott since the year 2000.

The ultimate thanks to those that have supported the Jefferson Airplane, Hot Tuna (Especially through 1977), and Jefferson Starship (The real J.S.). Please remember we may be old but we grew up with the best music ever!

Throughout the contents of the book you will notice enough photos that could have been made into a separate publication. For each photo **more than reasonable attempt** was made to find the actual photographer. Credit is given whenever possible and the thank you is continuous.

Promotional photos and flyers are "Fair Use" if being used for publication, publicity, research, and or documentation.

When deciding on the size of the index at the end of the book it was easy. The length makes it consumer friendly. Each reader may have a specific name that is important to them and to only list the most common bands and musicians would have been taking the cheap flight out and not offering you the luxurious Jefferson Airways to Rock & Roll Island.

Several people are referred to by two names during the written contents. The index will list them both . Here they are in advance (In case you're keeping score at home):

Jacky Kaukonen/Jacky Watts
Aaron Hurwitz/Professor Louie
Ron McKernan/Pigpen
Richard Penniman/Little Richard
Hugh Romney/Wavy Gravy
Joanie Simms/Joanie Sims

**Any capitalization of And, Of, or The** were done for the specific reason of annoying a couple of former English teachers. **Actually it is only to show emphasis.**

I tried to recreate the interview transcripts the way the artist spoke. There may be more commas on some of the interviews and others having less, but shorter sentence structure.

During the J.A. live portion of the book most times after the song and the time the line will end and the information will be underneath. There will be lines that look like the return key was hit early, but that was intentional.

Please note that **any change in the size of the print** was to ensure all passengers were able to get the maximum amount of both the photo allotment and page allocation.

**Signe Anderson get well soon!**

# INTRODUCTION:

There are times you take a path that is clearly chosen. Sometimes opportunities come along by circumstances becoming intertwined. When I started to passionately collect any music from the Airplane that I could procure, I noticed an amazing void in the accuracy of archival information. This was diametrically opposed to the Beatles, Grateful Dead, or Frank Zappa for example. As a life-long Beatles fan any question about a live or unreleased version of a song would be answered within seconds of posting on a Beatles Board or an email to one of the many Fab Four musical geniuses. When I would search for information about the Airplane's concerts, and studio sessions I would often encounter a question mark next to a song title. It perplexed me to no end how could somebody not want to know what they are listening to.

Countless times if the Airplane played a blues song it would be listed as a *jam*. The proper dating of the recording sessions and live shows more often then not were incorrect because of the dates being transposed. Since there isn't a universal (Why not I declare) way of writing month, date, and year, when information would be sent to archivists in and out of the U.S.A., it wasn't uncommon that songs were being listed as performed several months before they were written! Maybe worse than wrong information is no information. If fans don't make notations of special events at a show such as an extended *jam*, an unreleased song appearing for the first time, a special musical guest, and or some nuance during the vocals, how would one concert ever be differentiated from another?

Keeping with the same flight pattern if a bunch of phenomenal Airplane material from the vaults is only listed by song title, or a question mark, how would we ever be able to discuss the cover of the Rolling Stones song you will read about, the instrumental *Martha*, or the differences between the censored versions from the first album, and the originals intended for the record? That is why as far back as 1976, I started to write notes on any Airplane music that I could substantiate. I would listen intently for alternate lyrics, longer playing times, and information from different shows. I started to keep a journal of both musical information, and lesser known facts about the group.

In 1981 I began a nine year career as a radio disc-jockey. I would go back to broadcasting every now and then post 1990, but for the most part I ventured into a more stable job environment. (Then again maybe not. Writing isn't exactly the way to be firmly anchored). While working for various stations I would often get great questions asked from listeners both on the phone and at live promotions. Almost immediately after beginning my first announcing job I jotted down any questions I was asked about a specific band. A common theme at the three rock radio stations I called home during those years were a large amount of inquiries about 1960's and 1970's American bands and 1970's U.K. progressive music. As days turned to years I had countless inquiries about the Airplane Family. Additionally as computers became common in American homes I would answer emails from other Jefferson Airplane, Hot Tuna, and Jefferson Starship fans.

In the past few years I had given serious consideration to putting the documentation into book form. I thought the Airplane fan would enjoy having the information at their disposal. There was one segment missing. The reader of a book that spends hard earned money deserves something extra. The idea was to include one additional segment in the book. If I had a cross-section of interviews from the Airplane Family, it would enable the reader to find out where some of the former members have been and where they are now. Rick Martin has a long history of involvement in the San Francisco scene as a fan, an archivist of the Jefferson Starship music, and a friend to numerous musicians associated with the Airplane Family. Rick organized several interviews for me and those contents are proudly displayed in the final section of the book. Don Aters the amazing photographer contributed with his contacts as well, as did the "Fan Man" himself Mike Somavilla. **Thank you!**

There is no reason for repetition. I never aim to reinvent the wheels, or the wings in this case. There is a niche for everyone. The focus isn't on one musician dating another, and the break-up led to… **The central purpose is to explore where the plane hasn't stopped before.** The archiving of the live, and studio music, finding questions to discuss during the interviews that aren't the same ones that have been in print for forty plus years, and the question, and answer segment fly's into a good deal of uncharted air space.

6

# Pre-Flight:

## A) Airplane Terminology:

When I would be sitting miserably in high-school science classes deciding which album to purchase next, the teachers would often presuppose that every student possessed equal knowledge or passion. I have always made it a rule when writing or radio announcing to make sure I realized each of us are individuals and if a person is going to give me some of their valuable time, I can at least make sure they have pertinent information in a language that is distinguishable. The words below are how I am using them **in context to the book.**

> Symbol means without a pause. If you see a tune followed by >, it shows there weren't any pauses, and it went right into the next selection. It could also be after a tune-up the band went into a song.

*Acetate*- At one time it was uncommon for a musician to own a reel to reel machine and or a cassette player. When they wanted to listen to something at home that was recorded in the studio they were given a vinyl recording of the song.

*Airplane Family*- Any individual, or band project that came about as a result of at least one member having spent any length of time in the Jefferson Airplane, Hot Tuna, and or the Jefferson Starship.

*Alternate version*- This would be a different version of a song that has been recorded. It may be longer in length or without a specific instrument.

*Bonus Track*- A bonus track is a song put on a record or CD that was not there originally. Many times when a CD is reissued it will have additional material.

*Circa*- Is the approximate time frame. If you saw the band in 1967 but did not remember the exact month and date it would be listed as circa 1967.

*Coming out of*- If a song is ending but goes into another one I used those words to describe the transition. For example if *The Ballad Of You And Me And Pooneil* went right into *The House At Pooneil Corners* I may have in the comments that *The House At Pooneil Corners* started coming out of *The Ballad Of You And Me And Pooneil*.

*Composition*- Is another word for song or tune.

*Cut*- This means that the entire song was not available for documentation. The band may have played nine minutes of a specific tune but if all we have available is three minutes it has been cut. I mention this so if a song looked to be rather short it would not puzzle any of the readers.

*Demo*- A member of a band will often bring a tape of a song they started to work on for the other members to hear. It could be only a guitar and vocal. The band then decides if it is worthy of inclusion on the recording or even with additional work improper for the project.

*Ditty*- You will see a few notations of Jorma playing a *Guitar Ditty*. It is very short and catchy (Sounds like you have heard it before) but not something that is part of an existing song.

*Double-Track*- To get a fuller sound an artist may record a vocal and then record another vocal. You would have two vocal tracks recorded in the studio. The first can be the lead vocal. The second vocal track can be the exact same thing only lower (So it sounds as if there are two singers).

*False Start*- This is when the song is started incorrectly and stopped. The tune may have been written to start with a guitar but by mistake the drummer begins to play.

*Fill-in*- A guitar-player uses a few notes to enhance a specific part of a song. An example that comes right to mind would be the Steppenwolf anthem *Born To Be Wild*. If you listen to the song you will hear the guitar fills after certain words are sung.

*F & L*- When you see F, and or L, it is to show that was the first time the song was played, the last time played, or both the first, and last time played. I am going with **my documentation** on this because there have been times when people claim an obscure tune was performed live, and they could not back it up with either a description of the show, a full set list, and or a tape of the performance.

*Gig*- Another word for concert, performance, or show. It can also refer to getting the job.

*Improvisation*- This is something that is made up on the spot. There will be instances where Grace or Marty make up additional lyrics for an already existing song. There can also be improvisation from the instruments. Jack may add something to an already recorded piece of music when it is performed on stage.

*Jam*- This can be any length but it is the entire band playing instrumental music (There may be a segment of lyrics) that is made up on the spot. While improvisation may only be the addition of some lyrics, or music by an individual member the *jam* is the entire band playing together but creating each portion as they go along.

*Lip-synching*- A group being filmed on stage or in a studio but they aren't playing or singing live. The music being heard was pre-recorded.

*LP*- In the dark ages when I was young, CD's weren't invented yet. The music came on a vinyl record called LP for long-playing.

*Mix*- This is how the song sounds at the time you are hearing it. It may be the guitar is very high and you hardly hear the bass. In that case you would read that the guitar is mixed high and the bass low. If it is a good overall mix it means that the instruments and vocals are clear without one or more being muffled, too loud, or too low.

*Monitors*- The monitors help the band hear.

*Out-take*- When an album is finished there are almost always songs that were recorded but not included for one reason or another. If twelve songs were selected for an album, but fourteen were recorded the two that were left off become out-takes.

*Rehearsal*- If you read about a studio rehearsal it is the band practicing either a specific song or several of them during the time they are rehearsing.

*Riff*- Think of this as a catchy part of a song that sticks with you. If you listen to the beginning of the Beatles brilliant song *Day Tripper* or the start to the Rolling Stones classic *(I Can't Get No) Satisfaction* the notes being played by one of the guitars is the "riff."

*Session*- A studio session would be a period of time the band is booked into a recording studio to work on the writing, playing, listening to, and or recording of music.

*Set*- That is a reference to the performance. If a band played for ten songs somebody may refer to it as a ten song set. A band can have several sets. For instance if the Airplane played eight songs and took a break, Hot Tuna played five songs, and then the Airplane returned to the stage again, the Airplane would have a set one, and set two song list, and Hot Tuna only the one set.

*Take*- The band may have recorded multiple versions of a song. If they felt that the seventh try was the best, it may be called Take Seven.

*Track*- In a recording studio they use multiple tracks to put a song together. You may have one track for the bass, another for the guitar, one for the vocals, and one for the drums. The songwriter may feel the tune needs background vocals. This would mean another vocal track is added to the mix. It could also be another guitar, or a piano, etc. Track can also refer to a song. You may here somebody mention track four is the best one on the album.

*Tune*- Another word for composition or song.

*Tune-up*- This could be at the start or end of a song. The musicians are tuning their instruments to get ready for the next selection they will perform.

Venue- Is the place the band performed.

## B) Members aboard the various flights:

When you see the words *Line-up* followed by a number it will correspond to one on the list below. The members of the band at that time will be documented. Please note that since my list is for the archival history of live and studio works **I am not giving a number to the line-up prior to authentication of a live performance (An authenticated live recording).** That means when Jack Casady and Skip Spence became part of the group it is referred to as the initial live line-up. This isn't to discard the previous time period. It is with <u>sadness</u> we don't have live documentation (**Actual recordings**) from the days with Bob Harvey (Bass) and Jerry Peloquin (Drums). The listing is alphabetical and not attempting to place more importance on any particular member of the band. I am also listing the most noted instrument and if for the <u>most part</u> the musician was considered a vocalist or not.

<u>Line-up A</u>
**(Pre- record contract. There are no authenticated recordings of this line-up. Signe Anderson did absolutely confirm the band performed a song live called *Strawberries*).**
Signe Anderson- Vocals.
Marty Balin- Vocals.
Bob Harvey- Bass.
Paul Kantner- Rhythm guitar and vocals.
Jorma Kaukonen- Lead guitar.
Jerry Peloquin- Drums.

<u>Line-up B</u>
**(Still pre-record contract, but we do have documentation of the demo recorded for Columbia Records).**
Signe Anderson- Vocals.
Marty Balin- Vocals.
Bob Harvey- Bass.
Paul Kantner- Rhythm guitar and vocals.
Jorma Kaukonen- Lead guitar.
Skip Spence- Drums.*
**\*Skip Spence replaces Jerry Peloquin on drums.**

<u>Line-up 1</u>: **Called line-up 1 because it is the first line-up with documented live information.**
Signe Anderson- Vocals.
Marty Balin- Vocals.
Jack Casady- Bass.* **(\*Jack Casady replaces Bob Harvey on bass. This is the *Takes Off* line-up).**
Paul Kantner- Rhythm guitar and vocals.
Jorma Kaukonen- Lead guitar and vocals.
Skip Spence- Drums.

<u>Line-up 2</u>:
Signe Anderson- Vocals.
Marty Balin- Vocals.
Jack Casady- Bass.
Spencer Dryden- Drums.*
Paul Kantner- Rhythm guitar and vocals.

Jorma Kaukonen- Lead guitar and vocals.
**\*Spencer Dryden replaces Skip Spence on drums.**

Line-up 3:
Marty Balin- Vocals.
Jack Casady- Bass.
Spencer Dryden- Drums.
Paul Kantner- Rhythm guitar and vocals.
Jorma Kaukonen- Lead guitar and vocals.
Grace Slick- Vocals.\*
**\*Grace Slick replaces Signe Anderson on vocals.**

Line-up 4:
Marty Balin- Vocals.
Jack Casady- Bass.
Joey Covington- Drums and vocals.\*
Paul Kantner- Rhythm guitar and vocals.
Jorma Kaukonen- Lead guitar and vocals.
Grace Slick- Vocals.
**\*Joey Covington replaces Spencer Dryden on drums.**

Line-up 5:
Marty Balin- Vocals.
Jack Casady- Bass.
Joey Covington- Drums and vocals.
Papa John Creach- Fiddle and vocals.\*
Paul Kantner- Rhythm guitar and vocals.
Jorma Kaukonen- Lead guitar and vocals.
Grace Slick- Vocals.
**\*Papa John Creach is added to the line-up.**

Line-up 6:
Jack Casady- Bass.
Joey Covington-Drums and vocals.
Papa John Creach- Fiddle and vocals.
Paul Kantner- Rhythm guitar and vocals.
Jorma Kaukonen- Lead guitar and vocals.
Grace Slick- Vocals.
**\*Marty Balin leaves the group.**

Line-up 7:
Jack Casady- Bass.
Joey Covington- Drums and vocals.
Papa John Creach- Fiddle and vocals.
David Freiberg- Vocals, and rhythm guitar.\*
Paul Kantner- Rhythm guitar and vocals.
Jorma Kaukonen- Lead guitar and vocals.
Grace Slick- Vocals.
**\*David Freiberg is added to the band.**

Line-up 8:
John Barbata- Drums.\*
Jack Casady- Bass.
Papa John Creach- Fiddle and vocals.
David Freiberg- Vocals and rhythm guitar.
Paul Kantner- Rhythm guitar and vocals.

Jorma Kaukonen- Lead guitar and vocals.
Grace Slick- Vocals.
**\*John Barbata replaces Joey Covington on drums.**

Line-up 9:
Marty Balin- Vocals.
Jack Casady- Bass.
Paul Kantner- Rhythm guitar and vocals.
Jorma Kaukonen- Lead guitar and vocals.
Grace Slick- Vocals.

**With support from:**
Kenny Aronoff- Drums.
Tim Gorman- Keyboards.
Randy Jackson- Guitar, keyboards, and vocals.
Peter Kaukonen- Guitar (Contributed plenty on stage. A team player that didn't need the accolades).

## C) High Flying Birds 1965-1972:

A pre-flight breakfast for you. Yes, *Jefferson Airways* still gives you a great meal! The following are a list of the studio treasures that did not make the original studio albums. These may be alternates of songs that were included on the 1966-1972 records or material that didn't get released in any form. Some of the terrific reissue CD's have included some of the unreleased studio gems as bonus tracks. For full information about the listings please see the main contents of the book. The material is listed A-Z.

*And I Like It*
(Alternate long version) Circa 7/20/66 RCA Studios, Hollywood, California.

*Don't Let Me Down*
(Unreleased alternate long version) Circa winter 1967 RCA Studios, Hollywood, California.

*A Small Package Of Value Will Come To You, Soon*
(Two rough mixes) Circa winter 1967. Most likely Pacific High Studios, San Francisco, California.

*A Song For All Seasons*
(*Volunteers* album sessions) Circa 3/28/69- 6/30/69 Wally Heider Studios, San Francisco, California.

*Been So Long*
(Electric overdubs, instrumental) Circa 2/16/70 Wally Heider Studios, San Francisco, California.
This is a guitar only version of the song that was released on a Hot Tuna album *First Pull Up, Then Pull Down* 1971 RCA 4550. It would be their second release and second live affair.

*Bless Its Pointed Little Head*
2/69 *Bless Its Pointed Little Head* LP commercial (Long version).

*Broad Minded Men*
A bit of the song is part of the unedited out-take from *Crown Of Creation*. Please see that date in the main contents of the book for the information. Circa May 1968 RCA Studio A, Hollywood, California.

*Candy Man*
A bit of the song is part of the unedited out-take from *Crown Of Creation*. Please see that date in the main contents of the book for the information. Circa May 1968 RCA Studio A, Hollywood, California.

*Chushingura*
(Rough mix) Circa 2/68- 9/68 RCA Studios A and or B, Hollywood, California.

*Crown Of Creation* unedited out-take from the album sessions.
Circa May 1968 RCA Studio A, Hollywood, California.  This is often talked about as an untitled song.  It **isn't** a song, but the band having some fun in the studio.  Please see the date in the main contents of the book for complete information including song bits and the composers.

*Embryonic Journey*
Circa 12/16/65 RCA Studios, Hollywood, California.

*Eat Starch Mom*
(Instrumental) Circa 3/72-5/72 Wally Heider Studios, San Francisco, California.

*Fat Angel*
(Unreleased studio version) Circa 8, or 9/66 RCA Studios, Hollywood, California.

*Feel So Good*
(*Bark* session extended version) Circa 6/7/71 Wally Heider Studios, San Francisco, California.

*Frozen Noses*
(Demo) Circa 2/16/70 Wally Heider Studios, San Francisco, California.

*Good Shepherd*
1 (Rough mix) Circa 2/68- 9/68 RCA Studios A and or B, Hollywood, California.
2 Volunteers (Album sessions) Circa 3/28/69- 6/30/69 Wally Heider Studios, San Francisco, California.
3 Circa 4/17/69 Wally Heider Studios, San Francisco, California.
This is being listed twice because there is debate if this version got taken from the 1968 *Crown Of Creation* out-takes or rough mixes circa 2/68- 9/68 RCA Studios A and or B, Hollywood, California.

*Go To Her*
1 (Two alternate unreleased versions) Circa 11/17/66 RCA Studio A, Hollywood, California.
2 (Possible rough mix of the song) 10/5/67 Pacific High Studios, San Francisco, California.

*Greasy Heart*
1 (Rough mix) Circa 2/68- 9/68 RCA Studios A and or B, Hollywood, California.
2 1968 Promotional film of the song.

*Hey Fredrick*
(*Volunteers* album sessions) and (Rough mix).
Circa 3/28/69- 6/30/69 Wally Heider Studios, San Francisco, California.

*I Can't Get No (Satisfaction)* 10/5/67 Pacific High Studios, San Francisco, California.
The song is one of the Rolling Stones most popular and the J.A. had some fun in the studio with it!

*Ice Cream Phoenix*
1 (Rough mix) Circa 2/68- 9/68 RCA Studios A and or B, Hollywood, California.
2 (Demo) Circa late May through late June 1968 RCA Studios A or B, Hollywood, California.

*It's Alright*
This is often listed incorrectly as *It's So Fine*.
(Studio rehearsal) 10/5/67 Pacific High Studios, San Francisco, California.

*It's So Fine*
This is an incorrect name for the song titled *It's Alright*.  Please see that entry.

*Jam (Short) > Percussion*
Circa 2/10/68-6/5/68 RCA Studios, Hollywood, California.

*Jam (*Instrumental Blues Jam) Circa 3/72-5/72 Wally Heider Studios, San Francisco, California.

*J.P.P. McStep B. Blues*
1 (Alternate unreleased version) Circa 11/14/66 RCA Studio A, Hollywood, California.
2 (Album sessions) Circa 3/28/69- 6/30/69 Wally Heider Studios, San Francisco, California.

*Keep On The Sunny Side*
Circa May 1968 RCA Studio A, Hollywood, California.
A bit of the song is part of the unedited out-take from *Crown Of Creation*. Please see that date in the main contents of the book for the information.

*Lather*
(Rough mix) Circa 2/68- 9/68 RCA Studios A and or B, Hollywood, California.

*Let Me In*
(Uncensored version) Circa 2/26/66 RCA Studios, Hollywood, California.

*Levis Jeans Commercials* (Complete)
1967 listing of all four commercials. Since many have not heard the entire set of commercials, the information is listed in the main contents of the book.

*Long John Silver* (Radio commercials)
Circa summer 1972.

*Martha*
1 (Instrumental version) Circa 8/29/67 RCA Studio A, Hollywood, California.
2 (Rehearsal) 10/5/67 Pacific High Studios, San Francisco, California.
3 (Rough mix) Circa winter 1967. Most likely Pacific High Studios, San Francisco, California.

*Mexico*
(Demo) Circa 2/16/70 Wally Heider Studios, San Francisco, California.

*My Creole Belle* (Tease)
Circa 3/72-5/72 Wally Heider Studios, San Francisco, California.
Written and made popular by blues musician Mississippi John Hurt.

*On Top Of Old Smokey*
Circa May 1968 RCA Studio A, Hollywood, California.
A bit of the song is part of the unedited out-take from *Crown Of Creation*. Please see that date in the main contents of the book for the information.

*Pretty As You Feel*
(Extended) Circa 1/26/71 Wally Heider Studios, San Francisco, California.

*Rejoyce*
(Two rough mixes) Circa winter 1967. Most likely Pacific High Studios, San Francisco, California.

*Run Around* (Uncensored and mono version) Circa 2/26/66 RCA Studios, Hollywood, California.

*Runnin' Round This World* (Uncensored version) Circa 12/16/65 RCA Studios, Hollywood, California.

*Share A Little Joke*
(Rough mix) Circa 2/68- 9/68 RCA Studios A and or B, Hollywood, California.

*Spare Chaynge*
1 (Studio rehearsal) Circa 10/31/67 RCA Studio A, Hollywood, California.
2 (Rough mix) Circa winter 1967. Most likely Pacific High Studios, San Francisco, California.

*Starship*
(Rough mix) Circa 8, or 9/70 RCA Studios, Hollywood, California.

*Star Track*
(Rough mix) Circa 2/68- 9/68 RCA Studios A and or B, Hollywood, California.

*The Farm*
(*Volunteers* album sessions) Circa 3/28/69- 6/30/69 Wally Heider Studios, San Francisco, California.

*The House At Pooneil Corners*
(Demo) Circa late May through late June 1968 RCA Studios A or B, Hollywood, California.

*The Last Wall Of The Castle*
1 (Jorma demo) Circa 8/30/67 RCA Studio A, Hollywood, California.
2 (Rough mix) Circa winter 1967.  Most likely Pacific High Studios, San Francisco, California.

*The Man (The Bludgeon Of The Bluecoat)* With: Little Richard
Circa 4/26/71 to 9/71 Wally Heider Studios, San Francisco, California.

**The Other Side Of This Life**
Circa 8/65 Los Angeles, California (Studio not noted) Demo for Columbia Records.  **That is correct!  The demo is with Bob Harvey on bass!**

*The Saga Of Sydney Space Pig*
(Three segments, two are unreleased) Circa 5/31/68 RCA Studio B, Hollywood, California.

*Triad*
(Rough mix) Circa 2/68- 9/68 RCA Studios A and or B, Hollywood, California.

*Tuning-up*
Circa 3/72-5/72 Wally Heider Studios, San Francisco, California.

*Trial By Fire*
Three instrumental versions.  (Two with Jerry Garcia).
Circa 3/72-5/72 Wally Heider Studios, San Francisco, California.

*Turn My Life*
Circa 3/28/69- 6/30/69 Wally Heider Studios, San Francisco, California.
(*Volunteers* album sessions).

*Two Heads*
(Rough mix) Circa winter 1967.  Most likely Pacific High Studios, San Francisco, California.

*Volunteers*
(Album sessions) Circa 3/28/69- 6/30/69 Wally Heider Studios, San Francisco, California.

*Watch Her Ride*
(Rough mix) Circa winter 1967.  Most likely Pacific High Studios, San Francisco, California.

*We Can Be Together*
1 (*Volunteers* album sessions) Circa 3/28/69- 6/30/69 Wally Heider Studios, San Francisco, California.
(2) 1969 (*Promo* film) This finally got released to the mass market in 2004 on the *Fly Jefferson Airplane* DVD from Eagle Rock Entertainment 30065.

*White Rabbit*
(Promotional clip) Circa spring 1967.

*Won't You Try/Saturday Afternoon*
(Rehearsal) 10/5/67 Pacific High Studios, San Francisco, California.

*Wooden Ships*
(*Volunteers* album sessions) (Alternate take) With: Go Ride The Music > J.P.P. McStep B. Blues.
Circa 3/28/69- 6/30/69 Wally Heider Studios, San Francisco, California.

*Young Girl Sunday Blues*
1 (Rehearsal) 10/5/67 Pacific High Studios, San Francisco, California.
2 (Rough mix) Circa winter 1967. Most likely Pacific High Studios, San Francisco, California.

There were at the time fifty-six unreleased excerpts, *jams,* and songs. There isn't any documentation about the 1989 rehearsals, or unused material from the studio sessions. In 1996 for the Rock And Roll Hall Of Fame rehearsal there were three songs, and one *jam* that were documented.

The total for 1965-72, 1989, and 1996 are sixty unreleased excerpts, *jams*, and songs that will be examined in the main contents of the book.

## D- High Flying Birds 1965-1972 Live!

The <u>first</u> and <u>last</u> flights for all Jefferson Airplane songs, improvisations, and *jams* performed with titles. The provision for a listing must be <u>confirmation,</u> and not rumor, or speculation. At the conclusion of 1965-1972 please see 1989 (Hot Tuna songs performed on the tour are included for your enjoyment) and 1996. Any mention during our flight about a song's first or last appearance is **specifically talking about the <u>J.A version</u>.** Obviously countless songs that are documented would be played by Hot Tuna, the Jefferson Starship, Jorma solo, KBC, Wooden Ships, etc. Please note that throughout the book all songs are listed by the exact title. If a song begins with <u>"The"</u>, it will be in print that way. If the song title is a <u>number</u>, it will be found by how the number would be spelled out, such as "3" would be under "Three." Buckle-up please and enjoy the pre-flight festivities.

*Abraham, Martin And John*: The first, and only appearance of this was on the 11/25/70 Fillmore East, New York City show. Joey sang **one line** from the song. His voice was very faint in the background, before *3/5 Of A Mile In 10 Seconds*. The song was a Top 5 hit for Dion in 1968 and was written by Dick Holler.

*Aerie (Gang Of Eagles)*: The first live appearance was circa 1/21/72- 3/1/72 at the Capitol Theater, Port Chester, New York. The final time played was 9/22/72 Winterland, San Francisco, California.

*And I Like It*: 1/15/66, or 1/16/66 Kitsalano (Kits) Theater, Vancouver, Canada was the first appearance. 5/19/67 Men's State Polytechnic College, San Luis Obispo, California was the final appearance.

*A Super Jam*: 2/4/70 A Night At The Family Dog (TV Special), Family Dog At The Great Highway, San Francisco, California would be the only time the *jam* was performed. The Airplane were joined by members of the Grateful Dead and Santana on stage.

*Baby What You Want Me To Do*: The first appearance was on 1/15/66, or 1/16/66 at the Kitsalano (Kits) Theater, Vancouver, Canada. The final version performed until the 1989 reunion would be from 5/17/70 at the Assembly Hall, Bloomington, Indiana.

*Bear Melt*: This was performed for inclusion on the live album *Bless Its Pointed Little Head* released June 1969 on RCA Records LSP 4133. The band performed three nights 10/24/68-10/27/68 at the Fillmore West, San Francisco, California and three nights (six shows) 11/28/68-11/30/68 at the Fillmore East, New York City. There is no documentation how many of the nine performances *Bear Melt* were performed.

*Big Bad John*: David Freiberg sang **one line** from the song at the end of *Blind John* from the 9/3/72 Hollywood Bowl, Hollywood, California concert. The song was a 1961 (#1) hit by Jimmy Dean. The writers were Jimmy Dean and Roy Acuff. This was the only time the band used the line from the song.

*Blind John*: The first live appearance was circa 1/21/72- 3/1/72 at the Capitol Theater, Port Chester, New York. The final time ever performed was 9/22/72 Winterland, San Francisco, California.

*Blues From An Airplane*: The only appearance was on 2/1/68 at The Matrix, San Francisco, California. **1968 is correct!**

*Bringing Me Down*: The first time played was on 1/15/66 or 1/16/66 at the Kitsalano (Kits) Theater, Vancouver, Canada. 8/5/67 O'Keefe Center, Toronto, Canada was the final appearance.

*Brothers And Sisters*: *(Improvisational lyrics)* The only time Grace would improvise these vocals was from the 5/7/70 Fillmore East, New York City, show. As *Uncle Sam Blues* began Grace went into the improvisation.

*Bye Bye Baby*: The only time Marty would improvise these vocals was from the 5/7/70 Fillmore East, New York City concert. During *You Wear Your Dresses Too Short* Marty sang <u>one line</u>. Janis Joplin had been performing the song live during the same era. Composed by her band member Powell St. John this was the only time Marty used the vocal excerpt.

*Can You Hear Me*: The only appearance was during *Whatever The Old Man Does (Is Always Right)* with Joey singing from 8/24/70 Atlanta Municipal Auditorium, Atlanta, Georgia. This is not related to the next entry.

*Can You Hear Me Laugh*: Grace did the vocal improvisation this one time only at the 5/17/70 Assembly Hall, Bloomington, Indiana performance, coming at the end of *Greasy Heart*. This is not related to the previous entry.

*Chauffeur Blues*: 9/30/66 Winterland, San Francisco, California was the first appearance. 10/15/66 Fillmore Auditorium, San Francisco, California was Signe Anderson's final show and the last appearance of the song.

*China*: The only appearance of the song was 1/16/72 Public Hall, Cleveland, Ohio. This Is from Paul's 1971 album *Sunfighter*.

*Clergy*: Not a song but an opening for the *Bless Its Pointed Little Head* live album. Originally released June 1969 on RCA Records LSP 4133. The band performed three nights 10/24/68-10/27/68 at the Fillmore West, San Francisco, California and three nights (six shows)11/28/68-11/30/68 at the Fillmore East, New York City. There is no documentation how many of the nine performances *Clergy* was used for the opening.

*Come Back Baby*: The first time the song was ever played was on 3/4/67 at the Café Au Go Go, New York City performance. The final time was 9/22/72 Winterland, San Francisco, California until the 1989 reunion tour.

*Come Up The Years*: 9/30/66 Winterland, San Francisco, California was the first appearance. 10/15/66 Fillmore Auditorium, San Francisco, California was the final appearance.

*Comin' Back To Me*: 5/12/67 Fillmore Auditorium, San Francisco, California was the only time the song made an appearance.

*Crown Of Creation*: 9/10/68 Musikhalle, Hamburg, Germany, was the first time played. The final performance until the 1989 reunion tour was 9/22/72 Winterland, San Francisco, California.

*Diana*: The first live performance was on 1/16/72 at the Public Hall, Cleveland, Ohio. The final appearance ever of the song would be 9/22/72 Winterland, San Francisco, California. Paul used a hybrid version for the lyrics. Please see either of those dates for information.

*Down Home Blues*: The first performance of the song was 1/16/72 Public Hall, Cleveland, Ohio. It was also the first time Papa John got a lead vocal. The last time played was 9/22/72 Winterland, San Francisco, California.

*Don't Let Me Down*: 7/7/67 Fantasy Fayre, Los Angeles, California or 9/15/67 Hollywood Bowl, Hollywood, California most likely were the first, or last performance of the full song. Both dates have the same documentation. The final appearance which was a brief vocal by Marty during a *jam* with Dino Valente from Quicksilver Messenger

16

Service, can be found on the 12/31/67 Winterland, San Francisco, California show. Please note there is a listing for 1967 Live (Released 2003) by Collectors Choice Music. The playing time for the song is less on that recording but there is no documentation of a source.

*Don't Slip Away*: 9/30/66 Winterland, San Francisco, California was the first appearance. 3/11/67 Winterland, San Francisco, California was the final appearance.

*Dress Rap > You Wear Your Dresses Too Short*: The only time this was performed was at the final show 9/22/72 Winterland, San Francisco, California when Marty came back for the encore! Please also see *You Wear Your Dresses To Short* (Grace solo vocal improvisation) and *You Wear Your Dresses Too Short*.

*Drifting*: The first appearance was on 10/26/69 at Winterland, San Francisco, California. The song is often incorrectly listed as *Driftin'* and *Drifting Around*. The final appearance of the song was on 11/69 at the Municipal Auditorium, Utica, New York. The song ended up on the self-titled album by Bodacious D.F. (With Marty Balin) in 1973. It was reissued on CD by Acadia 8036 in 2002.

*Drum And Bass Short Ditty*: The only occurrence of this was at the 11/13/70 Capitol Theater, Port Chester, New York (Late show).

*East-West (Jam)*: 1/8/67 Webster Hall, New York City would be the only time ever played. This is often called *Blues* or *Unknown Blues*. The two writers of the song would not appreciate that. Paul Butterfield and blues musician Nick Gravenites are the composers. The title is actually *East-West*. The *jam* is mentioned because of the additional players on stage and the length of time. Two of the members of the Paul Butterfield Blues Band at the time Mike Bloomfield on guitar and Mark Naftalin on keyboards perform with the Airplane. Please also see *Hate To See You Go* for the same two musicians being involved.

*Easy (Jam with vocals by Grace)*: The only performance of the *jam* was on 5/17/70 at the Assembly Hall, Bloomington, Indiana.

*Eat Starch Mom*: The first time played was as an *instrumental* going into a *jam* at the 8/18/71 Gaelic Park, Bronx, New York show. The first time performed with vocals would be circa 1/21/72- 3/1/72 at the Capitol Theater, Port Chester, New York. The final time ever performed was 9/22/72 Winterland, San Francisco, California.

*Embryonic Journey*: The first and only time this was performed was on 1/17/96 at the Rock And Roll Hall Of Fame: Performance and induction, Waldorf Astoria Hotel, New York City. Jorma played the song solo!

*E Major Blues Jam*: 11/25/70 Fillmore East, New York City was the only appearance of the *jam*.

*Emergency*: The first performance was on 2/23/70 at the Fillmore West, San Francisco, California. The last time it was performed as a stand-alone was on 10/25/70 at an unknown venue, Wichita, Kansas. The last time the song was performed would be on 11/25/70 at the Fillmore East, New York City.

*Emergency (Grace pre-song lyrical improvisation)*: The only time this was done by Grace was 11/25/70 Fillmore East, New York City before the actual version.

*Eskimo Blue Day*: The first appearance of the song was on 8/17/69 at the Woodstock Music Festival, Max Yasgur's Farm, Bethel, New York. Nicky Hopkins played piano with the band during the festival. The first version with only the Airplane members was on 10/25/69 at Winterland, San Francisco, California. The last appearance of the tune was on 2/4/70 for the TV special A Night At The Family Dog, Family Dog At The Great Highway, San Francisco, California.

*Fat Angel*: The first appearance was on 9/30/66 at Winterland, San Francisco, California. 3/24/70 Capitol Theater, Port Chester, New York was the final appearance ever.

*Feel So Good*: 8/15/71 Wall Stadium, Wall, New Jersey, was the first time played. The final performance was on 9/22/72 at Winterland, San Francisco, California.

*Fishman Jam*: The only time performed was with vocals from Grace at the 10/25/69 Winterland, San Francisco, California show.

*Get Off Jam*: (Joey vocals). The first time performed was on 5/17/70 at the Assembly Hall, Bloomington, Indiana. The final appearance was on 8/24/70 Atlanta Municipal Auditorium, Atlanta, Georgia.

*Get Ready* (**Poem**): Recited by Paul. The only time ever done with the Airplane was on 1/17/96 at the Rock And Roll Hall Of Fame: Performance and induction, Waldorf Astoria Hotel, New York City. The poem was written by Rebecca Inez Bockelie. Paul let his son Alexander recite the poem during a Wooden Ships concert on 1/18/92 at the I-Beam, San Francisco, California.

*Good Lovin' (**Riff only**)*: 9/6/69 Family Dog At The Great Highway, San Francisco, California was the only time the riff was played. Near the end of *The Farm* Jorma plays the classic riff. The song was written by Rudy Clark and Arthur Resnick. It was a hit for the Rascals and the Grateful Dead did a well known version.

*Good Shepherd*: 5/7/69 Polo Field, Golden Gate Park, San Francisco, California (Afternoon show) was the first time performed, but with Grace singing lead and Paul background! 5/9/69 Soldiers & Sailors Memorial Hall, Kansas City, Kansas would be the first time Jorma sang the lead vocal! The final performance of the song until the 1989 reunion tour was 8/12/72 Festival Of Hope, Roosevelt Raceway, Westbury, New York.

*Go To Her*: 9/30/66 Winterland, San Francisco, California was the first appearance. The final appearance was on 2/1/68 at The Matrix, San Francisco, California.

*Go To Her (Solo excerpts by Grace)*: 8/5/67 O'Keefe Center, Toronto, Canada was the only time Grace sang a bit of the song by herself, before the actual song began.

*Got What You Want*: 5/7/70 Fillmore East, New York City, was the only time Grace performed the vocal improvisations during *Somebody To Love*.

*Greasy Heart*: The first time performed was at the 5/18/68 Northern California Folk-Rock Festival, Santa Clara County Fairgrounds, San Jose, California (Day show). The final time ever performed was on 8/25/72 at the Auditorium Theater, Chicago, Illinois show.

*Happy New Year (Marty vocal improvisation)*: 12/31/67 Winterland, San Francisco, California would be the only time this would be done by Marty. Coming out of *Ride This Train*, Marty sang the improvisation. This was part of a long segment of music with special guest Dino Valente (Quicksilver Messenger Service).

*Hate To See You Go*: 1/8/67 Webster Hall, New York City, would be the only time ever played. This is often called *Blues* or *Unknown Blues*. Obviously that would make the writer of the song Little Walter very unhappy. The most noted version is from the Paul Butterfield Blues Band. Two of the members at the time Mike Bloomfield on guitar and Mark Naftalin on keyboards joined the Airplane on stage. Please also see *East-West (Jam)* for another song these two musicians performed with the Airplane.

*Have You Seen The Saucers*: 2/23/70 Fillmore West, San Francisco, California would be the first appearance of the song. The 11/13/70 Capitol Theater, Port Chester, New York (Late show) had the final version of the song going into another tune (*Starship*). The final performance as a stand-alone song would be 9/22/72 Winterland, San Francisco, California.

*Have You Seen The Saucers (Grace vocal tease)*: 9/14/70 Fillmore West, San Francisco, California would be the first and only time Grace did a vocal tease of the tune. Grace teased the audience right before the band performed the entire song.

*High Flying Bird*: 1/14/66 Kitsalano (Kits) Theater, Vancouver, Canada was the first appearance. 2/1/68 The Matrix, San Francisco, California was the final appearance.

*High Flying Bird (Vocal excerpts by Grace)*: 8/5/67 O'Keefe Center, Toronto, Canada was the only time Grace sang a bit of the song by herself, before it started.

*Hollywood Jam*: The only appearance of this is either from the 7/7/67 Fantasy Fayre, Los Angeles, California show or from 9/15/67 Hollywood Bowl, Hollywood, California. Both dates have the same documentation.

*Honey Don't* (**Riff only**): During the 5/6/70 Fillmore East, New York City (Late show) Jorma played the riff for the only time. *Honey Don't* was written by Carl Perkins and most noted by the Beatles.

*I Can Tell*: The first performance of the song was 5/6/70 at the Fillmore East, New York City (Late show). The final time it would be performed was 11/25/70 at the Fillmore East, New York City.

*Ice Cream Phoenix (**Jam**)*: 2/1/68 The Matrix, San Francisco, California was the only appearance. Paul had a great comment before the song, "This is an instrumental so if you have words sing along."

*I Feel A Whole Lot Better*: 1/15/66, or 1/16/66 Kitsalano (Kits) Theater, Vancouver, Canada would be the only appearance. The song was written by Gene Clark of the Byrds.

*If You Feel*: 9/10/68 Musikhalle, Hamburg, Germany, was the first appearance. The final appearance was on 9/15/68 at the Concertgebouw, Amsterdam, Holland.

*I'm Going Home*: Marty sings **one line** from the Ten Years After song *I'm Going Home* during *The Other Side Of This Life* on the 10/25/69 Winterland, San Francisco, California show. The song was written by Alvin Lee from Ten Years After. It was the only time ever performed.

*In The Midnight Hour^*: 1/14/66 Kitsalano (Kits) Theater, Vancouver, Canada was the first documented appearance. The final time performed was 11/6/66 Fillmore Auditorium, San Francisco, California (Late show). Marty Balin told me the J.A. learned the song in case they had a show to play on New Years Eve. The song was written by Steve Cropper but most recognized by the Rascals and Wilson Pickett.

*In The Morning*: The first appearance was on 10/16/66 at the Fillmore Auditorium, San Francisco, California (Afternoon show). 11/25/66 Fillmore Auditorium, San Francisco, California, is the final appearance.

*In Time*: 9/10/68 Musikhalle, Hamburg, Germany, was the first appearance. 9/15/68 Concertgebouw, Amsterdam, Holland, was the final appearance.

*It's Alright*: 10/2/66 Fillmore Auditorium San Francisco, California (Afternoon show) is the only documented appearance. The song is often incorrectly called *That's Alright*.

*It's No Secret:* 11/6/65 Calliope Warehouse, 924 Howard Street Loft, San Francisco, California is the first appearance. The final appearance until the 1989 reunion tour was on 10/26/69, at Winterland, San Francisco, California.

*It's No Secret (Vocal tease by Grace)*: The only time this was done would be right before *It's No Secret* on 4/26/69 at the Swing Auditorium, San Bernardino, California.

*Jack Speaks*: 5/1/70 SUNY Athletic Field, SUNY Of Stony Brook, Stony Brook, New York was the first time Jack spoke on stage! The band had wires cut on stage, and Jack informed Grace. This would be the last time he would speak until 9/26/89 Fillmore Auditorium, San Francisco, California. Jack for only the second time spoke during an Airplane show! Grace had requested that he say something. Jack actually responded! "You look lovely tonight Gracie."

*Jam In The Key Of D*: The only time this was ever performed was 5/7/69 at the Polo Field, Golden Gate Park, San Francisco, California (Afternoon show).

*John's Other*: The first appearance of the song was 10/25/70 unknown venue, Wichita, Kansas and the final 9/22/72 Winterland, San Francisco, California.

*Jorma Cut His Bangs Short Jam*: The only time this occurred was on the 8/5/67 O'Keefe Center, Toronto, Canada performance.

*J.P.P. McStep B. Blues*: First time played was 11/25/66, Fillmore Auditorium, San Francisco, California. That is the only documented performance of the song being performed by itself. On 5/9/69 Soldiers And Sailors Memorial Hall, Kansas City, Missouri the song was played coming out of *Wooden Ships*. The final time the song would be seen from a live stage was 6/13/69 Family Dog At the Great Highway, San Francisco, California. There as well the song began coming out of *Wooden Ships*.

*Just Sit There (Grace vocal improvisation)*: The only time Grace did the improvisations was at the 5/7/70 Fillmore East, New York City concert.

*Lather*: The first, and last time the song would be performed until the 1989 reunion tour was on 11/10/68 on The Smothers Brothers Comedy Hour. It would seem very unlikely the song was performed 10/6/68 at Clarkson College, Potsdam, New York (It has been talked about). There has never been a complete set list furnished of that show and there never has been anybody to authenticate a recording. The Smothers Brothers would be the more logical debut. They could have recorded it several times for playback if they were worried about breaking in a song for the first time.

*Kansas City Blues (Move To Kansas City)*: 1/14/66 Kitsalano (Kits) Theater, Vancouver, Canada was the first appearance of the song. 2/1/68 The Matrix, San Francisco, California was the final appearance. Please see the entry 6/25/64 at Jorma's House, San Francisco, California, where Janis Joplin sings and Jorma plays the guitar. The song was composed by Will Shade and a well known version was from the Memphis Jug Band. The song is often incorrectly listed as *Kansas City* but that is a much different tune. That was written by Jerry Leiber and Mike Stoller. Popular versions of *Kansas City* were by the Beatles and Wilbert Harrison.

*Lawman*: 8/15/71 Wall Stadium, Wall, New Jersey would be the first time performed. The final appearance would be 9/22/72 Winterland, San Francisco, California.

*Lay Down Your Weary Tune*: The only appearance was on 1/15/66 or 1/16/66 at the Kitsalano (Kits) Theater, Vancouver, Canada. The tune was written by Bob Dylan, but most known by the Byrds.

*Leave You Alone*: 3/4/67 Café Au Go Go, New York City, was the first appearance of the song. It was played coming out of *Somebody To Love*. 3/12/67 Winterland, San Francisco, California was the final time played. It came out of a *jam*.

*Let Me In*: 10/16/66 Fillmore Auditorium, San Francisco, California (Afternoon show) was the first appearance. 8/5/67 O'Keefe Center, Toronto, Canada was the final appearance.

*Let's Get Together*: 1/14/66 Kitsalano (Kits) Theater, Vancouver, Canada was the first appearance. It was written by Dino Valente of the Quicksilver Messenger Service. The Youngbloods had tremendous success with the song several years later. 8/5/67 O'Keefe Center, Toronto, Canada was the final appearance.

*Long John Silver*: The first time performed was 7/72 William & Mary College, Williamsburg, Virginia and the final time would be 9/22/72 Winterland, San Francisco, California.

*Louie Louie*: Jack played a **couple of seconds on the bass** after a fan yelled it from the audience during the 9/15/68 Concertgebouw, Amsterdam, Holland concert. That would be the only time performed. *Louie Louie* was written by Richard Berry and it is one of the most covered songs in rock and roll history. The most well know version comes from the Kingsmen.

*Love Is Everywhere* (Marty vocal improvisation): The only time this would occur would be on the 5/7/69 Polo Field, Golden Gate Park, San Francisco, California (Afternoon show). Marty did the vocal improvisations during *Volunteers*.

*Martha^* : The first appearance was on 7/7/67 Fantasy Fayre, Los Angeles, California, 8/2/67 O'Keefe Center, Toronto, Canada (Late show) or 9/15/67 Hollywood Bowl, Hollywood, California. Both 7/7/67 and 9/15/67 have the same documentation. The final appearance was on 10/31/69 at the Los Angeles Forum, Inglewood, California.

*Mau Mau (Amerikon)*: The first appearance was on 8/10/69 at the Sheep Meadow, Central Park, New York City. The song would be part of Paul Kantner's *Blows Against The Empire* album from 1970. The final appearance of the song was on 10/25/69 at Winterland, San Francisco, California.

*Mexico*: Paul talked about the song on the 5/7/69 Polo Field, Golden Gate Park, San Francisco, California (Afternoon show), but there wasn't any music. The first time the song was played with documented music was on the 2/7/70 Anaheim Convention Center, Anaheim, California show. The 11/13/70 Capitol Theater, Port Chester, New York (Early show) was the final appearance of the song.

*Milk Train*: The first appearance was from 7/72 William & Mary College, Williamsburg, Virginia. The final time ever played was 9/22/72 Winterland, San Francisco, California.

*My Best Friend*: 10/16/66 Fillmore Auditorium, San Francisco, California (Afternoon show) was the first appearance. 3/12/67 Winterland, San Francisco, California was the final appearance.

*My Grandfathers Clock*: (Instrumental) 11/27/66 Fillmore Auditorium, San Francisco, California (Afternoon show) was the only appearance. The entire song was a little over one minute!

*My Grandfathers Clock^* : (Instrumental Tease) 11/6/66 Fillmore Auditorium, San Francisco (**The Real 11/6/66**) would be the first and last time played as a "Tease." 11/27/66 Fillmore Auditorium, San Francisco, California (Afternoon show) was the only actual appearance. The entire song was a little over one minute!

*Nothing (Jam with vocals by Grace)*: The *jam* originally surfaced as *Nothing* on 9/15/68 at the Concertgebouw, Amsterdam, Holland. It was called for one night *Tortoise Jam* on 6/13/69 Family Dog At The Great Highway, San Francisco, California. It would become known as *Same Old Phony Handshake* on 10/25/69 Winterland, San Francisco, California (When one line was sung). On 2/23/70 at the Fillmore West, San Francisco, California the first full version would be performed under that name. Only these three names are correct titles. It would be incorrectly listed as *Get Off* (Which is another *jam*), *Help Me*, *It's Easy*, *No Such Thing*, and *Thing* (Which is another *jam*). On 3/6/70 at the Municipal Auditorium, Dallas, Texas the *jam* was performed for the last time as a stand-alone song. On 5/7/70 at the Fillmore East, New York City the *jam* was performed for the last time ever coming out of *Whatever The Old Man Does (Is Always Right)*.

*No More War:* This was a vocal improvisation by Grace during *Have You Seen The Saucers* performed only once on 5/1/70 at the SUNY Athletic Field, SUNY Of Stony Brook, Stony Brook, New York.

*One Of These Days*: This was only performed on 5/9/69 at the Soldiers & Sailors Memorial Hall, Kansas City, Kansas. It was a *jam* with some vocal improvisations by Grace. Obviously this has **nothing** to do with the Pink Floyd song by the same name released on the *Meddle* album 11/11/71.

*Papa John Blues Jam*: **This entry is not for the J.A. This is for Hot Tuna**. It is included because of the number of fans that wanted the correct song information. The instrumentation was loosely based on *Every Time I Hear Her Name* from his self-titled 1971 Album. Papa John also sings a couple of improvised lines that are based on Robert Johnson's- *32-30 Blues* and Elmore James-*Early One Morning*. This can be found on the Hot Tuna set from 11/13/70 Capitol Theater, Port Chester, New York (Late show).

*People Got To Be Free (**Song and skit**)*: 11/10/68 The Smothers Brothers Comedy Hour is the only time ever done. It is performed as both a song and part of a skit with the Smothers Brothers, Pat Paulsen, and Kate Smith. The song was a worldwide hit for the Rascals and was written by band member Eddie Brigati. Pat Paulsen was a well known comedian from the 1960's and 1970's. Kate Smith recorded what many people feel is the finest version of *God Bless America* ever. The song was written by Irving Berlin.

*Philly Jam*: The only appearance of the *jam* was on 11/16/68 at the Electric Factory, Philadelphia, Pennsylvania.

*Plastic Fantastic Lover*: The first appearance was on the 10/16/66 Fillmore Auditorium, San Francisco, California (Afternoon show). The final appearance was on 8/24/70 at the Atlanta Municipal Auditorium, Atlanta, Georgia.

*Pretty As You Feel*: 11/13/70 Capitol Theater, Port Chester, New York (Early show) was the first time the song was played. The final appearance was 1/16/72 at Public Hall, Cleveland, Ohio.

*Ride This Train*: The first and only appearance of this song was 12/31/67 Winterland, San Francisco, California. Dino Valente a one time member of Quicksilver Messenger Service plays guitar on the song. The vocals were done by Marty. The songs that have been released with this title are not the same. This seemed to be vocal improvisations by Marty. Dino also plays and does some of the vocals with Jorma on *Baby What You Want Me To Do* from the same performance!

*Rock And Roll Island*: 8/15/71 Wall Stadium, Wall, New Jersey was the first appearance. The final time performed was 1/16/72 Public Hall, Cleveland, Ohio.

*Rock Me Baby*: 3/4/67 Café Au Go Go, New York City, was the first appearance. 6/28/70 Bath Festival Of Blues And Progressive Music, Royal County Fairgrounds, Shepton Mallet, Somerset, U.K. was the final appearance until the 1989 reunion tour.

*Run Around*: 9/30/66 Winterland, San Francisco, California was the first appearance. 12/31/66 Fillmore Auditorium, San Francisco, California was the final appearance.

*Runnin' Round This World*: 11/6/65 Calliope Warehouse 924 Howard Street Loft, San Francisco, California was the first appearance. 5/19/67 Men's State Polytechnic College, San Luis Obispo, California was the last performance.

*Same Old Phony Handshake*: The *jam* originally surfaced as *Nothing* on 9/15/68 at the Concertgebouw, Amsterdam, Holland. It was called for one night *Tortoise Jam* on 6/13/69 Family Dog At The Great Highway, San Francisco, California. It would become known as *Same Old Phony Handshake* on 10/25/69 Winterland, San Francisco, California (When one line was sung). On 2/23/70 at the Fillmore West, San Francisco, California the first full version would be performed under that name. Only these three names are correct titles. It would be incorrectly listed as *Get Off* (Which is another *jam*), *Help Me*, *It's Easy*, *No Such Thing*, and *Thing* (Which is another *jam*). On 3/6/70 at the Municipal Auditorium, Dallas, Texas the *jam* was performed for the last time as a stand-alone song. On 5/7/70 at the Fillmore East, New York City the *jam* was performed for the last time ever, coming out of *Whatever The Old Man Does (Is Always Right)*.

*Share A Little Joke*: The only appearance was on 2/1/68 at The Matrix, San Francisco, California.

*She Has Funny Cars*: The first appearance of the song was circa 10/24/-10/27/66 at The Matrix, San Francisco, California. The final appearance until the 1989 reunion tour was on 5/18/68 at the Shrine Exhibition Hall, Los Angeles, California (Night show).

*Short Guitar Ditty*: 5/7/70 Fillmore East, New York City, would be the only time performed.

*Short Instrumental Ditty*: 11/13/70 Capitol Theater, Port Chester, New York (Late show) would be the only appearance.

*Short Jam #1*: The first and only time performed was going into *You Wear Your Dresses Too Short* at the 11/30/69 Pop Festival West Palm Beach Auditorium, West Palm Beach, Florida show.

*Short Jam #2*: The only time this was performed would be at the 8/24/70 Atlanta Municipal Auditorium, Atlanta, Georgia concert where it went into *I Can Tell*.

*Short Jam #3*: This was the only time performed at the 9/14/70 Fillmore West, San Francisco, California show. The *jam* went into *Starship*.

*Somebody To Love*: The first time performed was at the Fillmore Auditorium, San Francisco, California on 11/25/66. On the 9/14/70 Fillmore West, San Francisco, California concert the group used for the first and only time a marching band drum intro by Joey. The final time played until the 1989 reunion would be 9/22/72 Winterland, San Francisco, California.

*Somebody To Love (Eye Patch improvisation by Grace)*: The only time this was done by Grace was on the 10/4/70 Winterland, San Francisco, California show. You can see that date for the funny three lines she added.

*Somebody To Love Me, Somebody To Need Me*: The only time Marty performed the vocal improvisation was at the 11/13/70 Capitol Theater, Port Chester, New York (Early show) during *You Wear Your Dresses Too Short*.

*Somebody To Love (Paul's Talking Tease)^* : The only time Paul would talk some of the lyrics would be 8/2/67 O'Keefe Center, Toronto, Canada (Late show).

*Space Jam*: The only appearance of the *jam* would be 9/6/69 Family Dog At The Great Highway, San Francisco, California. Jerry Garcia and Mickey Hart from the Grateful Dead are part of the *jam*.

*Spare Chaynge*: 8/5/67 O'Keefe Center, Toronto, Canada would be the first and last appearance of the song as a full version. 12/31/67 Winterland, San Francisco, California, was the final time performed but only brief instrumental excerpts.

*Starship*: The first version was from 9/6/69 Family Dog, San Francisco, California when it came out of *The Ballad Of You And Me And Pooneil*. The first and only stand-alone version was performed on 9/14/70 at the Fillmore West, San Francisco, California. The final time performed was 8/15/71 Wall Stadium, Wall, New Jersey when it was played briefly in the middle of *Volunteers*.

*Star Track*: 5/18/68 Northern California Folk-Rock Festival, Santa Clara County Fairgrounds, San Jose, California (Day show), was the first appearance. 5/9/69 Soldiers & Sailors Memorial Hall, Kansas City, Kansas was the final appearance.

*String Jet Rock*: (Papa John instrumental with the band). 1/16/72 Public Hall, Cleveland, Ohio, is the only performance of the song. This is from Papa John's 1971 self-titled album. Often this has been erroneously reported as an untitled instrumental or *jam*.

*Take Off Jam*: The only time performed was on 10/7/66 at Winterland, San Francisco, California.

*That's Alright*: That is the incorrect title for *It's Alright*. Please see *It's Alright* for the proper information.

*The Ballad Of You And Me And Pooneil*: The first appearance of the song was on 5/19/67 at the Men's State Polytechnic College, San Luis Obispo, California. The first time it was played going into *The House At Pooneil Corners* was on 8/28/68 at the Falkoner Cenret, Copenhagen, Denmark. The last time the two songs would be performed one into the other would be on 10/10/69 at the Agrodome, Vancouver, Canada.

*The Farm*: The first appearance was on 5/7/69 at the Polo Field, Golden Gate Park, San Francisco, California (Afternoon show). The final appearance was on 9/6/69 at The Family Dog At The Great Highway, San Francisco, California.

*The House At Pooneil Corners*: The first appearance was on 8/28/68 at the Falkoner Cenret, Copenhagen, Denmark coming out of *The Ballad Of You And Me And Pooneil*. The first time it was played as a stand-alone song was on 11/1/68 at the Schuyler Hotel, 57 West 45th Street, New York City. The last time the two songs would be performed one into the other would be on 10/10/69 at the Agrodome, Vancouver, Canada. The final appearance of the song as a stand-alone would be on 10/31/69 at the Los Angeles Forum, Inglewood, California.

*The Man (The Bludgeon Of The Bluecoat)*: 9/14/70 Fillmore West, San Francisco, California was the first appearance of the song. 1/16/72 Public Hall, Cleveland, Ohio was the final appearance.

*The Other Side Of This Life*: The first time the song was performed would be 1/14/66 Kitsalano (Kits) Theater, Vancouver, Canada. The total playing time was a bit over three minutes! The last time the song was played until the 1989 reunion tour was 8/12/72 Festival Of Hope, Roosevelt Raceway, Westbury, New York.

*The Other Side Of This Life (Tease)*: The only time Grace ever did this was on the 9/14/70 Fillmore West, San Francisco, California performance before the start of the actual song.

*The Son Of Jesus*: The only appearance of this song was 9/22/72 Winterland, San Francisco, California.

*Thing^* : 10/16/66 Fillmore Auditorium, San Francisco, California (Evening show) was the first appearance. The final appearance was either 5/3 or 5/4//68 Fillmore East, New York City. Part of the performance was released in 1998 by BMG on the CD- *Live At The Fillmore East,* catalog number 67563. *Thing* is included on the CD.

*This Old Heart Of Mine*: 10/31/69 Los Angeles Forum, Inglewood, California would be the only time performed. Marty does a great vocal. The song was composed by Lamont Dozer, Brian Holland, and Edward Holland Jr. The Isley Brothers had a very popular version.

*Third Week In The Chelsea*: The first appearance was 8/15/71 at Wall Stadium, Wall, New Jersey. The final appearance was 8/18/71 at Gaelic Park, Bronx, New York. Hot Tuna performed the song during the 1989 reunion with Grace, and four times with Grace, and drummer Kenny Aronoff.

*3/5 Of A Mile In 10 Seconds*: The first appearance of the song was on 10/15/66 at the Fillmore Auditorium, San Francisco, California. The final appearance was on 11/25/70 at the Fillmore East, New York City until the 1989 reunion tour.

*Tobacco Road*: 11/6/65 Calliope Warehouse 924 Howard Street Loft, San Francisco, California was the first appearance. The last appearance was 5/19/67 Men's State Polytechnic College, San Luis Obispo, California.

*Today*: 11/26/66 Fillmore Auditorium, San Francisco, California, was the first appearance. 9/15/68 Concertgebouw, Amsterdam, Holland would be the final appearance until the 1989 reunion tour.

*Tortoise Jam*: The *jam* originally surfaced as *Nothing* on 9/15/68 at the Concertgebouw, Amsterdam, Holland. It was called for one night *Tortoise Jam* on 6/13/69 Family Dog At The Great Highway, San Francisco, California. It would become known as *Same Old Phony Handshake* on 10/25/69 Winterland, San Francisco, California (When one line was sung). On 2/23/70 at the Fillmore West, San Francisco, California the first full version would be performed under that name. Only these three names are correct titles. It would be incorrectly listed as *Get Off* (Which is another *jam*), *Help Me*, *It's Easy*, *No Such Thing*, and *Thing* (Which is another *jam*). On 3/6/70 at the Municipal Auditorium, Dallas, Texas the *jam* was performed for the last time as a stand-alone song. On 5/7/70 at the Fillmore East, New York City the *jam* was performed for the last time ever coming out of *Whatever The Old Man Does (Is Always Right)*.

*Trail By Fire*: 7/72 William & Mary College, Williamsburg, Virginia was the first time the song was played. The final time would be 9/22/72 Winterland, San Francisco, California.

*Turn Out The Lights*: This was played for inclusion on the *Bless It's Pointed Little Head* live album. Originally released June 1969 on RCA Records LSP 4133. The band performed three nights 10/24/68-10/27/68 at the Fillmore West, San Francisco, California and three nights (six shows) 11/28/68-11/30/68 at the Fillmore East, New York City. There is no documentation how many of the nine performances *Turn Out The Lights* was performed.

*Twilight Double Leader*: 1/16/72 Public Hall, Cleveland, Ohio is the first appearance of the song. The last time performed would be 9/22/72 Winterland, San Francisco, California.

*Triad*: The first appearance was on 8/28/68 at the Falkoner Cenret, Copenhagen, Denmark. The final appearance was on 9/10/68 at the Musikhalle, Hamburg, Germany.

*Two Heads^* : The first appearance was on 7/7/67 at the Fantasy Fayre, Los Angeles, California, 8/2/67 O'Keefe Center, Toronto, Canada (Early show), or 9/15/67 at the Hollywood Bowl, Hollywood, California. Both 7/7/67 and 9/5/67 have the same documentation. The final appearance was on 2/1/68 at The Matrix, San Francisco, California.

*Uncle Sam Blues:* 4/26/69 Swing Auditorium, San Bernardino, California was the first appearance. The final appearance was on 11/13/70 at the Capitol Theater, Port Chester, New York (Early show).

*Up Or Down*: The first appearance of the song was on 5/6/70 at the Fillmore East, New York City (Late show). The final appearance was on 11/25/70 at the Fillmore East, New York City. The song was written by Jorma's brother Peter.

*Vancouver Jam*: The only appearance of the *jam* was on 10/10/69 at the Agrodome, Vancouver, Canada.

*Volunteers*: 4/26/69 Swing Auditorium, San Bernardino, California is the first time played. The final performance until the 1989 reunion tour was 9/22/72 Winterland, San Francisco, California.

*Walking The Tou-Tou*: The first appearance was on 7/72 at William & Mary College, Williamsburg, Virginia. The last one was 9/22/72 Winterland, San Francisco, California.

*War Movie*: The only appearance of this song was on 8/15/71 at Wall Stadium, Wall, New Jersey.

*Watch Her Ride*: 10/14/67 Winterland, San Francisco, California was the first appearance. 11/16/68 Electric Factory, Philadelphia, Pennsylvania, was the final appearance.

*We Can Be Together*: The first appearance of the song was on 5/7/69 at the Polo Field, Golden Gate Park, San Francisco, California (Afternoon show). The first appearance where it would go into *Volunteers would be on* 6/26/70 at the Kralingen Pop Festival, Rotterdam, Holland. The last time it would be performed as a stand-alone was on 11/13/70 at the Capitol Theater, Port Chester, New York (Late show). The last time it would be performed was 11/25/70 at the Fillmore East, New York City going into *Volunteers*.

*Whatever The Old Man Does (Is Always Right)*: The first appearance of the song was from 5/6/70 Fillmore East, New York City (Late show), when it went into *You Wear Your Dresses Too Short*. On the 5/7/70 Fillmore East, New York City, show the song was played out of *Up Or Down*. On the 5/17/70 Assembly Hall, Bloomington, Indiana show the song was played by itself for the first and last time. The final J.A. appearance was 8/24/70 Atlanta Municipal Auditorium, Atlanta, Georgia, Joey added an improvisational vocal (That night only) *Can You Hear Me*.

*When The Earth Moves Again*: The first appearance of the song was 8/15/71 Wall Stadium, Wall, New Jersey and the final appearance was 9/22/72 Winterland, San Francisco, California.

*White Rabbit^* : The first appearance was from the "Real" 11/6/66 Fillmore Auditorium, San Francisco, California (Late show). The final appearance until the 1989 reunion was on 11/13/70 at the Capitol Theater, Port Chester, New York (Early show).

*Wild Turkey*: 8/15/71 Wall Stadium, Wall, New Jersey is the first appearance of the song. The final time played was 8/25/72 Auditorium Theater, Chicago, Illinois.

*Wild Tyme*: The first appearance was on 2/1/68 at The Matrix, San Francisco, California. The final appearance was on 10/26/69 at Winterland, San Francisco, California.

*Won't You Try/Saturday Afternoon*: The first appearance was on 5/12/67 at the Fillmore Auditorium, San Francisco, California. The final appearance until the 1989 reunion tour was on 8/19/70 at the Curtis Dixon Hall, Tampa, Florida.

*Wooden Ships W/Go Ride The Music*: The first time performed would be 4/26/69 Swing Auditorium, San Bernardino, California. The first time with J.*P.P. McStep. B. Blues* would be on 5/9/69 Soldiers & Sailors Memorial Hall, Kansas City, Missouri. The song was played coming out of *Wooden Ships*. The last time prior to the 1989 reunion that the tune was performed would be the 9/22/72 Winterland, San Francisco, California show. The 9/22/72 concert was the final time the J.A. would include *Go Ride The Music* as part of *Wooden Ships*.

*Young Girl Sunday Blues*: 5/19/67 Men's State Polytechnic College, San Luis Obispo, California was the first appearance. The final one was on 10/31/69 at the Los Angeles Forum, Inglewood, California.

*You Wear Your Dresses Too Short*: The first time ever performed was at the 5/28/69 Winterland, San Francisco, California show when it came out of *Thing (Jam)*. 10/26/69 Winterland, San Francisco, California, was the first time performed without being part of a *jam*. The 11/25/70 Fillmore East, New York City show would be the final time ever performed without any improvisation first. The final time ever played would be the 9/22/72 Winterland, San Francisco, California show which included *Dress Rap*.

*You Wear Your Dresses To Short (Grace solo vocal improvisation)*: The only time this was done by Grace would be from the 9/22/72 Winterland, San Francisco, California show prior to the start of *Dress Rap > You Wear Your Dresses Too Short*.  Please also see *Dress Rap* and *You Wear Your Dresses Too Short*.

Between 1965 and 1972 there were ninety-nine songs performed live, twenty-one titled *jams,* twelve untitled *jams*, and the ditty's, improvisations, riffs of songs, segments of songs, and vocal teases (Titled or not) equaled thirty-one.

In 1989 the band performed twenty-nine songs, no *jams*, two instrumental excerpts, and one vocal tease.  Of the twenty nine songs a total of ten were performed for the first time.

In 1996 for the Rock And Roll Hall Of Fame the band performed three songs.  Of the three only *Embryonic Journey* was the first time played live.  Jorma played the song solo.  Paul read a poem (*Get Ready*) solo as well.  The poem was by Rebecca Inez Bockelie.

For the entire live history of the band the total documented songs performed live were: one hundred and ten, the total amount of *jams* both titled and untitled were thirty-three, and the ditty's, improvisations, riffs of songs, segments of songs, and vocal teases (Titled or not) were thirty-six.  This includes the one poem recited by Paul.

## E- High Flying Birds 1989: <u>The old plane looks pretty good!</u>

Songs with a 1 were performed on the opening show on 8/18/89 at the Riverside Theater, Milwaukee, Wisconsin. The others are listed with the show number representing the first time played.  *Third Week In The Chelsea* and *Two Many Years* were part of the: Hot Tuna set and can be found at the end of the 1989 Airplane information.

*America* 1
(This was from the Kantner, Balin, & Casady Band (KBC) self-titled album from Arista Records A-8440 in 1986).

*Baby What You Want Me To Do*
Show number five 8/25/89 River Bend Music, Center, Cincinnati, Ohio.

*Come Back Baby*
Show number fourteen 9/6/89 Great Woods, Mansfield, Massachusetts.  **Yes** it was part of the J.A. set and as an encore!

*Crown Of Creation* 1

*Freedom* 1

*Good Shepherd* 1

*I Believe* (Five second Grace vocal tease).
Written by Sammy Cahn and made popular by Louis Armstrong.  Show number six 8/26/89 Post Pavilion, Columbia, Maryland.

*Ice Age* 1

*It's No Secret* 1
Not performed on show number nine 8/30/89 Radio City Music Hall, New York City because of time restrictions.

*Lather* 1
(First time played with 100 percent documentation since 11/10/68 The Smothers Brothers Comedy Hour).  It would seem **very unlikely** the song was performed at Clarkson College, Potsdam, New York (It has been talked about) on 10/6/68.

*Miracles* 1
(This was from the Jefferson Starship album *Red Octopus* originally released in 1975 on Grunt Records 10999).
Obviously first time played by J.A.

*Panda* 1
Grace performed the song on the piano by herself the entire tour.

*Peter Gunn* (Five second instrumental tease).
Show number six 8/26/89 Post Pavilion, Columbia, Maryland.

*Planes* 1

*Plastic Fantastic Lover* 1

*Rock Me Baby*
Show twenty-three 9/28/89 Fillmore Auditorium, San Francisco, California, played for the first time as an encore!

*She Has Funny Cars* 1
Show number eleven 9/2/89 Garden State Arts Center, Holmdel, New Jersey was the first time documented that the intro of the song had a guitar playing with the drums.

Show twenty-five 10/7/89 March For The Homeless, Washington, D.C.  The J.A opened with *Somebody To Love* for the first time and not *She Has Funny Cars*.  This was the final reunion show.

*Solidarity* 1

*Somebody To Love* 1
Show twenty-five 10/7/89 March For The Homeless, Washington, D.C.  The J.A. opened with *Somebody To Love* for the first time.  This was the final reunion show.

*Strawberry Fields Forever* (Marty sang <u>one line</u>).
Show number fifteen 9/8/89 Blossom Music Center, Cuyahoga Falls, Ohio, Marty starts *Won't You Try/ Saturday Afternoon* **with <u>the opening</u> of the Beatles classic!**

*Summer Of Love* 1

*The Other Side Of This Life* 1 (Only played opening night 8/18/89).

*The Wheel: With drum-solo* 1

*3/5 Of A Mile In 10 Seconds*
Show seventeen 9/10/89 Pine Knob Amphitheater, Clarkston, Michigan finally saw the first appearance of the song!

*Today* 1

*True Love* 1

*Volunteers* 1

*White Rabbit* 1
Show eighteen 9/16/89 Pacific Amphitheater, Costa Mesa, California, *White Rabbit* <u>did not</u> get performed!

*Won't You Try/Saturday Afternoon* 1

*Wooden Ships* 1 (*Go Ride The Music* was not performed during 1989).

The set list for the final 1989 show was:

10/7/89 March For The Homeless, Washington, D.C.

(22:56) (Line-up 9) **The real finale to the reunion tour!**

**Please see this listing in the main contents of the book for complete information.**

Somebody To Love
Crown Of Creation
Baby What You Want Me To Do (Jorma vocals).  Peter Kaukonen takes the last solo!
She Has Funny Cars
Volunteers

## F-Hot Tuna Served Fresh. Hot Tuna selections from 1989:

8/18/89 Riverside Theater, Milwaukee, Wisconsin was the opening show of the tour.  If a song has a 1 after it, it means it was performed on the first night.  Any other numbers next to a song indicate the first appearance.  The Hot Tuna set was with Jorma and Jack.  Grace would sing with them on *Third Week In The Chelsea*.  Kenny Aronoff played drums on *Third Week In The Chelsea* four times.  Any songs or oddities that occurred after the first performance are listed below the song title.  Please note this is only a list of the first time a song, or oddity appeared. Please see the actual contents of the set lists in the book for full show details.

*Been So Long*
Show fourteen 9/6/89 Great Woods, Mansfield, Massachusetts.

*Candy Man 1*

*Death Don't Have No Mercy*
Show nine 8/30/89 Radio City Music Hall, New York City.

*Embryonic Journey*
Show seven 8/28/89 New York State Fair, Syracuse, New York.

*Five Foot Two, Eyes Of Blue (Has Anybody Seen My Girl).*
9/9/89 Poplar Creek, Hoffman Estates, Illinois.
Show sixteen.  Jorma, Jack, and Grace!  The song was written by Ray Henderson, Sam Lewis, and Joe Young.  A popular version was by Jimmy Dorsey.  Singers will often change "Girl" to "Gal", or "Baby."  The song is often talked about without the "Five Foot Two, Eyes Of Blue", as being part of the title.  It is also called *Five Foot Two, Eyes Of Blue (Has Anybody Seen My Baby)* and *Five Foot Two, Eyes Of Blue (Has Anybody Seen My Gal)*.  It would have been out of the stratosphere if Jorma, Jack, and Grace played even one more minute of the tune!

*Freight Train*
Show five 8/25/89 River Bend Music Center, Cincinnati, Ohio.
With Grace vocals.  Only twenty-five seconds.  It is a shame they didn't keep playing!  The version they performed was written by Elizabeth Cotten, Paul James, and Fred Williams.  A well known version was recorded by Elizabeth Cotten.

*Guitar Ditty (Number 1)*
Show eleven 9/2/89 Garden State Arts Center, Holmdel, New Jersey.

*Guitar Ditty (Number 2)*
Show twenty-one 9/26/89 Fillmore Auditorium, San Francisco, California.

*Has Anybody Seen My Girl (My Baby) or (My Gal)*
The real title to the song is *Five Foot Two, Eyes Of Blue (Has Anybody Seen My Baby), (Gal) or (Girl)*. Please go to the listings under the letter "F" for the details.

*Hesitation Blues 1*

*I Am The Light Of This World*
Show two 8/19/89 Fox Theater, St. Louis, Missouri.

*I Know You Rider*
Show fourteen 9/6/89 Great Woods, Mansfield, Massachusetts.

*I'll Be Alright Someday*
Show nine 8/30/89 Radio City Music Hall, New York City.

*Instrumental Ditty*
Show eight 8/29/89 Radio City Music Hall, New York City. First time the *Ditty* is performed on the 1989 tour.

*I See The Light*
Show sixteen 9/9/89 Poplar Creek, Hoffman Estates, Illinois.

*Jack Speaks*
Show twenty-one 9/26/89 Fillmore Auditorium, San Francisco, California. Jack for only the second time spoke during an Airplane show! Grace had requested that he say something. Jack actually responded! "You look lovely tonight Gracie." The last time Jack was heard talking on an Airplane stage was 5/1/70 SUNY Athletic Field, SUNY Of Stony Brook, Stony Brook, New York. That night the band had wires cut on stage and Jack had to inform Grace.

*Jorma's Short Improvisational Ditty*
Show thirteen 9/4/89 Lake Compounce, Bristol, Connecticut.

*Keep On Trucking*
Show four 8/23/89 Finger Lakes Performing Arts Center, Canandaigua, New York.

*Killing Time In The Crystal City 1*

*Let Us Get Together Right Down Here 1*

*Mann's Fate*
Show three 8/22/89 Mann Music Center, Philadelphia, Pennsylvania.

*Never Happen No More*
Show sixteen 9/9/89 Poplar Creek, Hoffman Estates, Illinois.

*99 Year Blues*
Show two 8/19/89 Fox Theater, St. Louis, Missouri.
Show twenty 9/23/89 Concord Pavilion, Concord, California. Jack takes a bass-solo!

*Police Dog Blues 1*

*San Francisco Bay Blues 1*

*Sunshine Of Your Love (Tease).*
Show twenty 9/23/89 Concord Pavilion, Concord, California. Jorma plays the "riff" to the classic song by Cream while tuning-up!

*Third Week In The Chelsea 1* (Jorma, Jack, and Grace).
Show eight 8/29/89 Radio City Music Hall, New York City.  First time the song is performed with drums on the 1989 tour!

*Too Many Years*
Show twenty-one 9/26/89 Fillmore Auditorium, San Francisco, California.  Although this was on the 1989 Airplane reunion record it was only performed by Hot Tuna for the tour!

*Trail By Fire*
Show eleven 9/2/89 Garden State Arts Center, Holmdel, New Jersey.

*Trouble In Mind*
Show thirteen 9/4/89 Lake Compounce, Bristol, Connecticut.

*Uncle Sam Blues*
Show twelve 9/3/89 Saratoga Performing Arts Center, Saratoga, New York.

*Walkin' Blues 1*

**Please note there was no Hot Tuna set on the twenty-fifth and final show 10/7/89 March For The Homeless, Washington, D.C.**

During the 1989 reunion tour Hot Tuna performed twenty-three songs, a combination of seven improvisations, guitar ditty's, song excerpts, and Jack for only the second time on stage during an Airplane concert spoke (Once).

## G- The Final Flight Of The J.A.

1996: The old plane flies one last time.

### 1/16/96 Rock And Roll Hall Of Fame (Rehearsals), Waldorf Astoria Hotel, New York City

The band rehearsed:

Volunteers
Embryonic Journey (**Jorma plays the song by himself**).
Crown Of Creation
Jam (Short).
**Paul Kantner remembers the rehearsal as really a sound check from the same day as the performance 1/17/96. There are many that feel 1/16/96 is correct.**

### 1/17/96 Rock And Roll Hall Of Fame: Performance and induction, Waldorf Astoria Hotel, New York City

**Welcome back Spencer!  Grace is not there.**

1 Crown Of Creation
2 Embryonic Journey (F & L)
This was the first, and only time this was performed with the Jefferson Airplane.
**Jorma played the song solo!**
3 Volunteers

1 Induction by Phil Lesh, and Mickey Hart of the Grateful Dead .

2 Acceptance speeches by Jack, Jorma, Spencer, Marty, and Paul > Paul reads a poem (*Get Ready*) from an eight year old (When first written) girl living in Seattle, Washington.  The poem was from Rebecca Inez Bockelie.  For complete details on the 1/16/96 and 1/17/96 Rock And Roll Hall Of Fame, rehearsal, performance, and acceptance

speeches please see the main contents of the book. Paul let his son Alexander recite the poem during a Wooden Ships concert on 1/18/92 at the I-Beam, San Francisco, California.

## H- Looking At The Flight-Logs And Those That Occupied A Seat 1965-72, 89 And 96

The following is a list of the songs performed at least <u>one time</u> from the J.A. studio albums. These are all available for purchase on CD, many with great bonus tracks!

*1966 Takes Off*: **RCA 3584 on August 15, 1966.**

And I Like It (Performed prior to the album being released).

Blues From An Airplane (Performed in 1968 after the album was released).

Bringing Me Down (Performed prior to the album being released).

Chauffeur Blues (Performed in 1966 but after the album was released).

Come Up The Years (Performed in 1966 but after the album was released).

Don't Slip Away (Performed in 1966 but after the album was released).

It's No Secret (Performed prior to the album being released).

Let Me In (Performed in 1966 but after the album was released).

Let's Get Together (Performed prior to the album being released).

Run Around (Performed in 1966 but after the album was released).

Runnin' Round This World (Including because it was on the original pressing).
(Performed prior to the album being released).

Tobacco Road (Performed prior to the album being released).

**All eleven songs were performed at least one time.**

All songs **excluding** *Blues For An Airplane* were performed at least one time in 1966. **A *jam* is only listed if it were titled on <u>any</u> of the yearly set lists.**

The other songs performed at least once in 1966 were:

Baby What You Want Me To Do
(Never released on an Airplane album). It would appear on the 1975 Hot Tuna record *Yellow Fever* on Grunt records 11238. The song was composed by Jimmy Reed. It is also referred to as *You Got Me Runnin'*.

Fat Angel
(This never appeared on a studio album. It first was released June of 1969 on the *Bless Its Pointed Little Head* live record RCA LSP 4133).

Go To Her
(This never appeared on an original J.A. album. It first was released (LP) on the collection of non album tracks from 1974 *Early Flight* Grunt 10437).

High Flying Bird
(This never appeared on an original J.A. album.  It first was released (LP) on the collection of non album tracks from 1974 *Early Flight* Grunt 10437).

I'll Feel A Whole Lot Better
(This never appeared on any J.A. record.  The song was written by Gene Clark of the Byrds).

In The Midnight Hour
(This never appeared on any J.A. record.  The song was written by Steve Cropper but most recognized by the Rascals and Wilson Pickett).

In The Morning
(This never appeared on an original J.A. album.  It first was released (LP) on the collection of non album tracks from 1974 *Early Flight* Grunt 10437).

It's Alright
(This never appeared on an original J.A. album.  It first was released (LP) on the collection of non album tracks from 1974 *Early Flight* Grunt 10437).  It is sometimes incorrectly called *That's Alright*.

J.P.P. McStep B. Blues
(This never appeared on an original J.A. album.  It first was released (LP) on the collection of non album tracks from 1974 *Early Flight* Grunt 10437).

Kansas City Blues
(This never appeared on any J.A. record).  The song was composed by Will Shade and a well known version was from the Memphis Jug Band.  The song is often incorrectly listed as *Kansas City* but that is a much different tune.  That was written by Jerry Leiber and Mike Stoller.  Popular versions of *Kansas City* were by the Beatles and Wilbert Harrison.

Lay Down Your Weary Tune
(This never appeared on any J.A. record.  The tune was written by Bob Dylan, but most known by the Byrds).

My Best Friend

My Grandfather's Clock (Short instrumental).
(This never appeared on any J.A. record).

Plastic Fantastic Lover

She Has Funny Cars

Somebody To Love

Take Off Jam
(This never appeared on any J.A. record).

The Other Side Of This Life
(This never appeared on a studio album. It first was released June of 1969 on the *Bless Its Pointed Little Head* live record RCA LSP 4133).

3/5 Of A Mile In 10 Seconds

Today

*1967 Surrealistic Pillow:* **RCA 3766 released 2/67.**

Comin' Back To Me (Performed in 1967 but after the album was released).

Embryonic Journey  (Performed 1/17/96 at the Rock And Roll Hall Of Fame, Waldorf Astoria Hotel, New York City, for the first and only time. **<u>Jorma</u> played the song solo**).

My Best Friend (Performed prior to the album being released).

Plastic Fantastic Lover (Performed prior to the album being released).

3/5 Of A Mile In 10 Seconds (Performed prior to the album being released).

Today (Performed prior to the album being released).

She Has Funny Cars (Performed prior to the album being released).

Somebody To Love (Performed prior to the album being released).

White Rabbit (Performed prior to the album being released).

**Nine of eleven songs performed live.**

Not documented to have been played:

D.C.B.A.-25

How Do You Feel

Besides the eight songs from the album that were played in 1967 here are the rest that were performed at least one time that year:

And I Like It

Baby What You Want Me To Do

Bringing Me Down

Come Back Baby
(This never appeared on an original J.A. album).  It first was released (studio out-take 3/7/67) on the *Loves You* (Box Set) from 10/92 on RCA 61110-2.  The song was written by Lightnin' Hopkins.

Don't Let Me Down
(This never appeared on an original J.A. album.  It first was released on the *Loves You* (Box Set) from 10/92 on RCA 61110-2).

Don't Slip Away

Fat Angel

Go To Her

High Flying Bird

Hollywood Jam
(This never appeared on any J.A. record).

It's No Secret

Jorma Cut His Bangs Short Jam (This never appeared on any J.A. record).

Let's Get Together

Leave You Alone (This never appeared on any J.A. record).

Let Me In

Martha

Ride This Train
(This never appeared on any J.A. record).  The first and only appearance of this song was 12/31/67 Winterland, San Francisco, California.  Dino Valente a one time member of Quicksilver Messenger Service plays guitar on the song.  The vocals were done by Marty.

Rock Me Baby
(This never appeared on a studio album. It first was released June of 1969 on the *Bless Its Pointed Little Head* live record RCA LSP 4133.  It has been credited as a traditional song).

Runnin' Round This World

Spare Chaynge

The Other Side Of This Life

The Ballad Of You And Me And Pooneil

Thing
(This never appeared on a studio album.  It first was released on *Live At The Fillmore East* 4/28/98 RCA 67563.  That obviously is the release date and not the performance information).

Tobacco Road

Two Heads

Watch Her Ride

Won't You Try/Saturday Afternoon

Young Girl Sunday Blues

**1967 *After Bathing At Baxter's:* RCA 1511 released 12/67.**

Martha (Performed prior to the album being released).

Spare Chaynge (Performed prior to the album being released).

The Ballad Of You And Me And Pooneil (Performed prior to the album being released).

Two Heads (Performed prior to the album being released).

Watch Her Ride (Performed prior to the album being released).

Wild Tyme (Performed in 1968 but after the album was released).

Won't You Try/Saturday Afternoon (Performed prior to the album being released).

Young Girl Sunday Blues (Performed prior to the album being released).

**Eight of eleven songs performed live.**

Not documented to have been played:

A Small Package Of Value Will Come To You, Shortly

Rejoyce

The Last Wall Of The Castle

The rest of the songs performed at least once during 1967 are listed under the *Surrealistic Pillow section* because two albums were released that year.

**1968 Crown Of Creation: RCA 3797 released 9/68.**

Crown Of Creation (Performed prior to the album being released).

Greasy Heart (Performed prior to the album being released).

Ice Cream Phoenix (Performed prior to the album being released).
**(Performed as an instrumental *Jam*)**

If You Feel (Performed prior to the album being released).

In Time (Performed prior to the album being released).

Lather
(Performed in 1968 but after the album was released). There is no documented evidence of the song being performed 10/6/68 at Clarkson College, Potsdam, New York. There has never been a complete set list furnished of that show and there never has been anybody that has authenticated a recording.

Share A Little Joke (Performed prior to the album being released).

Star Track (Performed prior to the album being released).

The House At Pooneil Corners (Performed prior to the album being released).

Triad (Performed prior to the album being released).

**Ten of eleven songs performed live.**

Not documented to have been played:

Chushingura
(Although claim has been made this song was performed on 7/19/69 at the Aragon Ballroom, Chicago, Illinois, there has **never been** audio authentication or even a complete set list for any show it supposedly had been played).

Here are the rest of the songs documented to have been performed at least one time during 1968:

Bear Melt
(This never appeared on a studio album. It first was released June of 1969 on the *Bless Its Pointed Little Head* live record RCA LSP 4133).

Blues From An Airplane
(Although never documented to have been played 65-67, it did make **one appearance in 1968**).

Clergy
(This never appeared on a studio album. It first was released June of 1969 on the *Bless Its Pointed Little Head* live record RCA LSP 4133).  (**_Not a song_** but an opening to the show).

Fat Angel

Go To Her

Greasy Heart

Ice Cream Phoenix (**Performed as an instrumental *Jam***).

It's No Secret

Kansas City Blues

Martha

Nothing (Also known as *Same Old Phony Handshake* and *Tortoise Jam*).

People Go To Be Free
(This never appeared on any J.A. record).  Performed as a combination song and skit on the Smothers Brothers Show. The song was a major hit for the Rascals and written by group member Eddie Brigati.

Philly Jam
(This never appeared on any J.A. record).

Plastic Fantastic Lover

Rock Me Baby

She Has Funny Cars

Somebody To Love

Star Track

3/5 Of A Mile In 10 Seconds

The Ballad Of You And Me And Pooneil

The House At Pooneil Corners

The Other Side Of This Life

Today

Turn Out The Lights
(This never appeared on a studio album.  It first was released June of 1969 RCA LSP 4133, on the *Bless Its Pointed Little Head* live record).

Two Heads

Watch Her Ride

White Rabbit

Wild Tyme

Won't You Try/Saturday Afternoon

Young Girl Sunday Blues

**1969 Volunteers: RCA 4238 released 11/69.**

Eskimo Blue Day (Performed prior to the album being released).

Good Shepherd (Performed prior to the album being released).

The Farm (Performed prior to the album being released).

Volunteers (Performed prior to the album being released).

We Can Be Together (Performed prior to the album being released).

Wooden Ships (Performed prior to the album being released).

**Six of ten songs performed live.**

Not documented to have been played:

A Song For All seasons

Hey Fredrick

Meadowlands

Turn My Life Down

Here are the rest of the songs documented to have been performed at least one time during 1969:

Come Back Baby

Crown Of Creation

Drifting
(This never appeared on any J.A. record).  It ended up on the 1973 album by *Bodacious D.F.*.  The self–titled album by the band with Marty Balin as the vocalist.  The song was written by Jesse Osborne.

Fat Angel

Fishman Jam
(Never released.  This was not related to the song *Fishman* from Paul and Grace's 1973 album *Baron Von Tollbooth & The Chrome Nun*).

Greasy Heart

It's No Secret

Jam In The Key Of D
(This never appeared on any J.A. record).

J.P.P. McStep B. Blues

Martha

Mau Mau (Amerikon)
(This never appeared on an original J.A. album.  It was released 10/70 by Paul Kantner on *Blows Against The Empire* RCA 4448).

Mexico
(This never appeared on an original J.A. album.  It first was released (LP) on the collection of non album tracks from 1974 *Early Flight* Grunt 10437).

Plastic Fantastic Lover

Same Old Phony Handshake (One line only).
(Not found on any J.A. record).  Also known as *Nothing* and *Tortoise Jam*.

Short Jam #1
(This never appeared on any J.A. record).

Somebody To Love

Space Jam
(This never appeared on any J.A. record).
(With Jerry Garcia and Mickey Hart) 9/6/69 from the Family Dog At The Great Highway, San Francisco, California.

Starship
(This never appeared on any J.A. record).  (It was released 10/70 by Paul Kantner on *Blows Against The Empire,* RCA 4448).

Star Track

3/5 Of A Mile In 10 Seconds

The Other Side Of This Life

Thing

This Old Heart Of Mine
(This never appeared on any J.A. record.  The song was composed by Lamont Dozer, Brian Holland and Edward Holland Jr.  The Isley Brothers had a very popular version).

Tortoise Jam
(This never appeared on any J.A. record.  It is also known as *Nothing* and *Same Old Phony Handshake*).

Uncle Sam Blues
(Never released on any original J.A. album.  A live version from 8/17/69 Woodstock Music Festival, Max Yasgur's Farm, Bethel, New York can be found on the *Loves You* (Box Set) from 10/92 on RCA 61110-2).

Vancouver Jam
(Never released on any original J.A. album).

You Wear Your Dresses Too Short

Watch Her Ride

White Rabbit

Wild Tyme

Won't You Try/Saturday Afternoon

Young Girl Sunday Blue

## The next album wouldn't be released until 1971.

These are the songs that were performed at least once in 1970:

A Super Jam
(Not found on any J.A. record). This is from 2/4/70 during the TV special A Night At The Family Dog, Family Dog At The Great Highway, San Francisco, California. With members of the Grateful Dead and Santana.

Baby What You Want Me To Do

Come Back Baby

Crown Of Creation

Emergency
(Never released on any original J.A. album. This finally got released on the *Loves You* (Box Set) from 10/92 on RCA 61110-2).

Eskimo Blue Day

Get Off Jam
(Not found on any J.A. record).

Good Shepherd

Greasy Heart

Have You Seen The Saucers

I Can Tell
(Not found on any J.A. record). The song was written by Ellas McDaniel and Samuel Smith. Two noted versions are from John Hammond Jr. and Bo Diddley.

John's Other
(Not found on any J.A. record). (It is available live on the second Hot Tuna album, *First Pull Up, Then Pull Down*, from RCA Records- LSP 4550).

Mexico

Plastic Fantastic Lover

Rock Me Baby

Same Old Phony Handshake
(Not found on any J.A. record). Also known as *Nothing* and *Tortoise Jam*.

Short Jam #2
(Not found on any J.A. record).

Short Jam #3
(Not found on any J.A. record).

Somebody To Love

Starship

The Ballad Of You And Me And Pooneil

The Man (The Bludgeon Of The Bluecoat)
(Not found on any J.A. record).

The Other Side Of This Life

3/5 Of A Mile in 10 Seconds

Uncle Sam Blues

Up Or Down
(Not found on any original J.A. album.  It became available on the 1974 (LP) release *Early Flight* from Grunt Records 10437.  Written by Jorma's brother Peter).

Volunteers

We Can Be Together

Whatever The Old Man Does (Is Always Right)

White Rabbit

Won't You Try/Saturday Afternoon

Wooden Ships

**1971 Bark: Grunt FTR 1001 released 9/71.**

Feel So Good (Performed prior to the album being released).

Lawman (Performed prior to the album being released).

Pretty As You Feel (Performed prior to the album being released).

Rock And Roll Island (Performed prior to the album being released).

Third Week In The Chelsea (Performed prior to the album being released).

War Movie (Performed prior to the album being released).

When The Earth Moves Again (Performed prior to the album being released).

Wild Turkey (Performed prior to the album being released).

**Eight of eleven songs performed live.**

Not documented to have been played:

Crazy Miranda

Never Argue With A German If You're Tired Of European Song

Thunk

Here are the rest of the songs documented to have been performed at least one time during 1971:

Come Back Baby

Eat Starch Mom (Performed as an instrumental).

John's Other

Somebody To Love

Starship

The Man (Bludgeon Of A Bluecoat).

Volunteers

**1972 Long John Silver: Grunt FTR 1007 released 6/72.**

Aerie (Gang Of Eagles) (Performed prior to the album being released).

Eat Starch Mom (Performed prior to the album being released first as an instrumental and then with vocals).

Long John Silver (Performed in 1972 but after the album was released).

Milk Train (Performed in 1972 but after the album was released).

The Son Of Jesus (Performed in 1972 but after the album was released).

Trail By Fire (Performed in 1972 but after the album was released).

Twilight Double Leader (Performed prior to the album being released).

**Seven of nine songs played live.**

Not documented to have been played:

Alexander The Medium

Easter? (That is the actual title with the **?**).

Here are the rest of the songs documented to have been performed at least one time during 1972:

Blind John

China
(Never on any J.A. album.  This was released in 12/71 by Paul Kantner, on the *Sunfighter* album.  Grunt Records FTR 1002).

Come Back Baby

Crown Of Creation

Diana
(Never on any J.A. album.  On the 1972 Airplane tour Paul performed a hybrid version of verses one and two.  This was released in 12/71 by Paul Kantner on the *Sunfighter* album.  Grunt Records FTR 1002).

Down Home Blues

Eat Starch Mom (With vocals).

Feel So Good

Good Shepherd

Greasy Heart

Have You Seen The Saucers

John's Other

Lawman

Pretty As You Feel

Rock And Roll Island

Somebody To love

String Jet Rock

The Man (Bludgeon Of A Bluecoat)

The Other Side Of This Life

Volunteers

Walking The Tou-Tou (Instrumental)
(Never released on an Airplane record).  This ended up on Papa John's 1972 album *Filthy*.

When The Earth Moves Again

Wild Turkey

Wooden Ships

You Wear Your Dresses Too Short
**(With Marty Balin returning for the encore of the final performance on 9/22/72 at Winterland, San Francisco, California).**

Some statistical information on the album tracks that were played live. If you count the song titles from the first release (*Takes Off*) through *Long John Silver*, there were seventy-four tracks. Fifty-nine have been documented without question to have been played live at least 1 time. That is 79.73 percent.

The next stop on the flight is the 1989 reunion record.

**1989 Jefferson Airplane: Epic 45271 released 9/89.**

Freedom

Ice Age

Panda

Planes

Solidarity

Summer Of Love

The Wheel

Too Many Years* **This was played by Jorma and Jack during the <u>Hot Tuna</u> set.**

True Love

**Nine of thirteen songs played live.**

Not documented to have been played:

Common Market Madrigal

Madeleine Street

Now Is the Time

Upfront Blues

**After the 1989 tour sixty eight of eighty seven songs were played live from the studio albums. That is 78.1 percent. I didn't include the excellent 1974 compilation of cool oddities *Early Flight* because it is not an original studio album and was released posthumously.**

From the Don Aters collection.  Don Aters photographer.

It all starts and stops here.

# Enjoy the flight.

# Chapter 1: Circa 1962-1965
# "Some Will Come And Some Will Go"

*Please note* if you see F and or L next to a song or *jam* it is notating the first or last time it was performed. F is for the first time, L for the last, and F & L for first and last.

The information documented below is mostly Jefferson Airplane (Being the main focus of the book) however there will be some other lost treasures explored including **but not limited to** early Marty Balin, Jack Casady, Bob Harvey, Jorma Kaukonen, and a live and studio breakdown of the Great Society's (Grace Slick) material.

## Jorma Kaukonen-

1962 Offstage Music Theatre, San Jose, California

(40:42) **The solo acoustic concert billed as "Jerry Kaukonen."**

1 San Francisco Bay Blues 3:19
Jorma played the musical part the way you would think. His vocals were more indicative of the folk-rock style of that era.

2 Uncle Sam Blues 3:44
Jorma performed a slower version then future audiences would experience. The combination of folk and blues meshed very well.

3 I Belong To The Band 3:57
Jorma's vocal's sounded more in line with what you would hear further down the road. The instrumentation and the lyrics were delivered with strong confidence.

4 Another Man Done Gone 3:24
Those fortunate to have been seeing the young performer on stage were treated to a great version of the tune. The hands and the voice created a rendition crafted well enough to make those that sat in the venue wonder was there only one musician paid to play?

5 Poor Little Ellen 4:03
This was a traditional song that Jorma performed. The only noted versions that I could find were by Walter Forbes and Obray Ramsey (Thank you www.allmusic.com for the two listings). The song had earmarks of bluegrass, country, and folk. What was most fascinated about hearing Jorma's version was he didn't seem as confident during *Poor Little Ellen* as he did with every other selection. Of the ten documented tunes played *Poor Little Ellen* was the only that Jorma didn't bring with him to Hot Tuna and or solo.

6 Never Happen No More 3:25
The sounds that transpired both musically and voice related were solid. The confidence was redefined.

7 Follow The Drinking Gourd 3:35 Vocal version.
A tremendous version resonated from Jorma's acoustic guitar. This one I couldn't stop listening to. Over the years having gotten used to it as an instrumental the vocal version made it feel brand new. The selling point of the tune is with or without the words it is perfect for the folk or rock crowd.

8 Hesitation Blues 4:48
Jorma played the song in a slower fashion. The vocal pacing as well didn't have the fun or command that the Hot Tuna crowd would eat up in the 1970's.

9 Instrumental 4:54 **The birth of Embryonic Journey?**
Ever wonder what the feeling would be to discover a lost artifact? Without question this was an early taste of
*Embryonic Journey*! The complexity wasn't there but the premise for one of the finest instrumentals ever
created can be traced to this performance. The structure of the song at this juncture would have enabled Jorma
to consider adding words or keeping the music as the point of focus. He certainly found the proper road to
fruition. The tune is mostly chords and doesn't have the tremendous nuances that catapulted it to legendary
stature. By the reaction of the paying customers Jorma's drawing board version flew off the ground nicely!

10 Winin' Boy Blues 4:33
The last documented song from the performance was well done.

Jorma's arrangement of the music and vocals were less intense than further down the road but still showed his
tremendous ability that made any crowd feel the composition was his own.

## Jorma Kaukonen, Janis Joplin, and Steve Talbot-

12/62 Offstage Music Theatre, San Jose, California

(56:30)

The selection of songs was very good. The question of the century had to have been with Jorma and Janis on
stage how does Steve Talbot get to sing fifteen of twenty songs, Janis only five, and Jorma zero. **Steve's vocals
are unlistenable.** He puts on a bluegrass inflection no matter the style of the tune and fails during every note.

1 Tune-up > Little Birdie 3:41

2 Sugar Baby It's All Over Now 2:08
This has often been documented as two separate songs but it is one title only.

3 Ride Railroad Blues 2:56

4 (99 Year Blues) 2:49
Having Jorma be silent during this selection was inexplicable.

5 Instrumental 1:51
A typical folk influenced song with nothing memorable having transpired.

6 Amelia Earhart, Lady Of The Earth 4:02
Give exceptional credit for Jorma being able to block out the vocals and keep playing in the proper time
signature.

7 Instrumental 1:39
This one was bluegrass based and nothing but a race to the finish.

8 Instrumental 2:18
Same result as song number seven.

9 Janis Joplin intros the next song > Honky Tonk Angel 4:57 Janis vocals.
Before the song began Janis was arguing which key the tune should be performed. This wasn't the best stage
etiquette for a young performer and future star.

10 Empty Pillow 2:10 Janis vocals.

11 Tired Of Living Alone 1:57 Cut.
Ordinarily when a song is cut and you are an archivist it is very disheartening. Since Steve was singing the tune it was actual a gift.

12 Sloppy Drunk Baby 2:39

13 Ain't Got No 44 3:03
This selection had a great blues feel with the combination of Jorma's playing and a real vocalist.

14 Instrumental 1:53

15 High On The Mountain 4:58

16 Instrumental 1:50
This was close to how *Sally, Where's you Get Your Liquor From* sounded back then.

17 Red Mountain Blues 3:52
This is not the same song as *Black Mountain Blues*. Janis did a terrific job on the vocals. The crowd was enthralled by every second.

18 Ain't Got No Reason 2:27 Janis vocals.

19 My Mary Jane 2:21 Janis vocals.

20 Never Happen No More 2:48
*Never Happen No More* shouldn't have been performed if Jorma couldn't take the microphone away from Steve Talbot.

There is one part of the performance where people are asking that Jorma does more. Even as far back as 1962 he had developed a style that would command attention. The audience was highly into Janis's interpretation of the blues. There was no research available on Steve Talbot. That made supper digest more easily.

## Marty Balin-

Circa 1962 Demos (9:56) Hold on to your seats. Here is a message from Airplane Control Center and long time fan Mike Dolgushkin. **"*I Specialize In Love*" got some brief airplay on KYA in San Fransisco. The week of July 16, 1962 it made a brief appearance at number 59 on their Swingin' 60 survey.**

1 You Made Me Fall 2:01
If you take lyrics that fit with 1955-1962 rock and roll but think country you would have the theme of the song. The tune is catchy and without any superfluous extended instrumentation.

2 Nobody But You 2:21
The second tune is more in the mid-tempo rock and roll style from that era. The background vocals along with Marty's lead singing made for a good representation of what you would hear on the radio or in the local record shop.

3 You Are The One 2:20
This was a ballad. The tempo is slow and there is a bit of a country influence. The piano ending enhanced an already very marketable tune.

4 I Specialize In Love 1:00 Cut. This is the best of the four songs. When it first circulated for the Airplane collector we didn't have an opportunity to experience the second part of the song (It was cut off).

5 I Specialize In Love 1:57 Uncut.
Thanks to the always appreciated 1992 Box Set-*Jefferson Airplane Loves* You (RCA 61110-2) we all were able to hear the song uncut. The second half has a nice up-tempo beat and Marty's vocals were strong and full of confidence. The song is in the realm of the rock and roll numbers from that era with a sprinkle of country for extra flavor.

All four tunes would have been very marketable if Marty had been an established artist. The old story is you need a resume getting the music released, but how do you get the songs to the public if the record company doesn't give you the resume.

## Marty Balin & Town Criers –

<u>Unknown location circa 1963</u> (Live)

(3:48) **Marty told me he didn't remember this song**!

1 Hellbound Train 3:48 (**It was spelled as one word**). This was on a various artists CD *San Francisco Live*, released 11/18/97 Prophecy 12010. They made a mistake of the spelling of the band on the CD, by writing **Town Cryers**. Marty intros the song before it starts. The tune is not only a nice peak as to what Marty was doing at this time but an excellent song. The lyrics tell a story about a person having a bad dream. It was very common during the days of Top 40 radio the record companies preferred songs to be under three minutes. It would have been interesting if the song could have been edited and promoted would history have turned out differently?

## Jorma Kaukonen, Janis Joplin, and Billy Roberts-

<u>1963 Coffeehouse, San Francisco, California</u>

(25:05)

1 Old Gospel Ship 1:42
Billy lead vocals and Janis background.

2 Stealin' 1:58
Janis and Billy share the vocals.

3 Janis intros the next song > Leavin' This Morning 1:56
Janis takes the lead vocal.

4 Janis intros the next song > Daddy, Daddy, Daddy 2:32
Janis takes the lead vocal.

5 Janis intros the next song > Careless Love 3:55
Janis takes the lead vocal 3:55

6 Bourgeois Blues 2:21
Janis takes the lead vocals.

7 Janis intros the next song > Black Mountain Blues 3:21
This is not the same song as *Red Mountain Blues*.

8 Instrumental 1:06

9 Read My Letter 2:19 Billy Roberts vocals. This could be the highlight of the nine selections.

It is a shame that the recorded material that survived from the performance is so short but on the other hand we have to be thankful that such a great moment in time were captured. *Bourgeois Blues* was the best of the nine selections however Jorma played solid in a background role and Janis delivered the blues with gusto. Billy Roberts is sometimes credited as the writer of the legendary song *Hey Joe*. He copyrighted the tune in 1962. There are many that feel the song is traditional. There is some terrific information about **the controversy** at http://www.heyjoe.org/lyrics.html.

# Jorma Kaukonen and Pigpen-
# (Ron McKernan would become part of the Grateful Dead).

1964 Tangent, Palo Alto, California

(5:13)

1 Sweet Georgia Brown 1:57 (Jorma only).
This was done as an instrumental version. It sounded terrific. It would have been nice to hear a longer rendition and one with vocals.

2 Dupree's Diamond Blues 3:16 (Jorma with Pigpen on harmonica).
Jorma took the vocal helm for this one. There are much more favorable tunes Jorma performed during the pre-Airplane days.

# Jorma Kaukonen-

1964 Cabale Creamery, Berkeley, California

(49:52)

1 Jorma intros the next song > Great Change 3:42

2 Jorma intros the next song > Follow The Drinking Gourd (With vocals) 4:00
On this particular night the arrangement seemed better suited for the instrumental version.

3 Tune-up > Jorma intros the next song > Uncle Sam Blues 4:02
This particular version was much slower than future renditions. It lacked the energy you would expect.

4 Candy Man 2:59

5 Sally, Where'd You Get Your Liquor From? 1:50
It is often forgotten the song is from Reverend Gary Davis and had been played long before the Hot Tuna record *The Phosphorescent Rat*.

6 Pawn Shop Blues 2:49

7 Down And Out Blues 2:46
The song is known by its more common title *Nobody Knows You When You're Down And Out*.

8 Let Us Get Together Right down Here 2:47

9 Tune-up > Never Happen No More (False start) :28
This was very strange. Jorma starts to play the wrong song and decides to stop. He plays the tune he originally wanted to, but performs this one the song after!

10 Tell Me Mama 4:24

11 Jorma intros the next song > Never Happen No More 3:18

12 Jorma intros the next song > Trouble In Mind 3:56

13 Follow The Drinking Gourd (With vocals) 4:47
Jorma played the intro differently.  He strummed some chords before the normal interpretation started.

14 Tune-up > Improvisation > Keep On Truckin' 4:04

15 Lord, I'll Be With You 3:53
This could be related to *How Long Blues*.  The two songs would sound great together.

Jorma's set was very well received.  His guitar and voice were in fine form.

## Jorma Kaukonen and Janis Joplin-

<u>6/25/64 Jorma's House, San Francisco, California</u> (21:44**) Please note former KSAN personality Tom Donohue (While alive) and many fans feel Jorma's first wife Margareta is on the typewriter.**

**Janis sings the vocals and plays the typewriter as a musical instrument**.  The songs are both well performed and well sung.  Jorma is terrific with his technique and Janis is having fun.  Many times in both live settings and the studio environment you got the feeling singing was a job first to Janis.

1 Tune-up > Trouble In Mind 3:31

2 Long Black Train 3:49 (Often called incorrectly *Black Train*).

3 Kansas City Blues (False start) > Kansas City Blues 3:09
Jorma would sing this song in the Airplane.  The first documented time would be 1/14/66 at the Kitsalano (Kits) Theater, Vancouver, Canada.

4 Hesitation Blues 4:11
This track was released as part of the Hot Tuna promotional album *The Last Interview* from 1978 on Grunt DJL1-2852.  It's hard to picture Jorma holding a guitar and not singing any portion of the song.

5 Down And Out Blues > Jorma shows and sings to Janis the ending > Down And Out Blues (Ending) 3:23
The song is better known as *Nobody Knows You When You're Down And Out*.

6 Daddy, Daddy, Daddy 3:23

For the time period and the equipment available the fidelity of the recording was very good.

## Great Society (Grace Slick) -

<u>1965 Somebody To Love/Free Advice (North Beach Single 1001)</u>

(5:38)

Please also see 1966 for information on every <u>**verified**</u> Great Society live, studio song, and the **two** members of the band that have been constantly overlooked.  **Their full names are provided!**

Bard Dupont- Bass.  (Bard was on the studio recordings and Peter van Gelder on the live ones).

David Miner- (Also has been called David Minor) Rhythm guitar and vocals.

Darby Slick- Lead guitar.

Grace Slick- Vocals.

Jerry Slick- Drums (Married to Grace at the time).

1 Somebody To Love 3:06 (Originally known as *Someone To Love*) A-Side.

2 Free Advice 2:32 B-Side.
The flip-side was more psychedelic, and Grace handled the background vocals.  The intro sounded as if a bass and tuba came together.  The single deserved better fate!

# Jefferson Airplane-

Circa 1965-1966 RCA Records (Promo tape)

(20:09) (Line-up 1)

The story goes but never confirmed, in 1965 (Pre release of the LP), or 1966 RCA Records **allegedly** sent out the promo tape to radio, TV stations, record shops and publications.  There are a few things that seem to make it all a myth.  The opening announcer's voice has an obvious accent.  Those in advantageous radio and or TV voice-over jobs speak generically, where no regional accent should surface.  The second oddity is the dead-air between songs.  If you have ever worked in radio and or TV, one of the first lessons is how awful dead-air sounds to the listener.  It would seem impossible that a major label would not have flawless production.  The final and maybe most convincing event that makes people wonder if this is fact or fiction, at the very end of the tape there is a curse word.  In 1965 it would be highly strange for a corporation to allow any curse words in the promo.  Remember RCA wasn't too thrilled with the language on *Let Me In*.  Interestingly enough the parties responsible for the nice collectable did have enough knowledge of the band to add: *Lay Down Your Weary Tune* and *In The Midnight Hour*.

All songs are fragments: *Running Round This World, The Other Side Of This Life, Lay Down Your Weary Tune, In The Morning, Tobacco Road, High Flying Bird, My Best Friend, Chauffeur Blues, Embryonic Journey, Let's Get Together, In The Midnight Hour*, and outro.

# Skip Spence and Signe Anderson –

Circa summer 1965 The Home Music Tape from Skip Spence's home, San Francisco, California

(31:59)

Skip Spence- Vocals, acoustic guitar, and bass.

Signe Anderson- Vocals.

1 Instrumental 1:36
Skip plays a combination rock and roll and folk-rock piece.  It was pretty straight-forward, and sounded as if he wanted to get warmed up for the song that Signe would be singing shortly.

2 Chatter > Improvisation :30 Skip was still warming up, and mentioned the words *Lazy River*. Written by Sidney Arodin, and Hoagy Carmichael, there are hundreds of versions issued over the years. Bobby Darin and the Mills Brothers have recorded well known covers of the song. Skip's acoustic playing seems limited by having used a guitar that wasn't pleasant sounding or expensive.

3 Improvisation > Lazy River (Skip sang the first line only) 3:12 Signe vocals.

4 Instruction by Skip :15 Skip explained the verses Signe should sing.

5 Lazy River 2:15 Signe vocals.

6 Improvisation :08 Skip played some improvisation based on the *Lazy River* theme.

7 Chatter :06 Skip told Signe "Let's take it from the beginning."

8 Lazy River :09 Skip vocals.

9 Something Else :20 Skip vocals.
*Something Else* was written by Eddie Cochran and Sharon Sheeley. There have been numerous cover versions. Two that are noted are from the Move and the New York Dolls. Former Beatles drummer Pete Best did a version too!

10 Instrumental > Tobacco Road 2:45 Skip vocals. This version is very strong. Skip was making use of a lousy sounding guitar. The instrumentation had the feel of the Nashville Teens rendition. Another well done version was by Lou Rawls. The song was composed by John D. Loudermilk.

11 Chatter :15 The arrangement for Tobacco Road was talked about.

12 Tobacco Road (False start) > Tobacco Road 2:09 Skip vocals. Once again applause please. Skip kept the Nashville Teens sound in mind.

13 (I Can't Get No) Satisfaction 4:30 Mostly Skip vocals with some by Signe. This is one of the Rolling Stones most noted songs. The problem with the way Skip decided to approach the tune was he did not use the classic "riff" that makes it one of the most recognizable tunes anywhere. Skip played the song with all chords.

14 Skip put ice in his drink :05

15 Nadine 3:31 Skip vocals. This song was well known by Chuck Berry. He also composed it along with Alan Freed. Skip did a terrific version. His voice was not as hoarse as usual and he came through despite a cheap guitar!

16 Chuck Berry question by Signe (About his song arrangements) > Skip plays common Chuck Berry riffs > Chatter 1:33

17 Apparently I Go Crazy (I Lost My Mind) 3:52 (Skip vocals) With chord instructions by Skip. There is no documentation available about the song title. This seems to be a hybrid of an original composition by Skip with influences from the Ivory Joe Hunter song *I Almost Lost My Mi*nd. Pat Boone had a well known version of that tune.

18 Chatter :08 Skips tells Signe the ending of the previous song was strange.

19 Jeannie :15 Skip sang a cappella vocals.
Skip doesn't sing enough of the lyrics to decipher one hundred percent if it is an original song or the tune by the Cascades, written by John Gummoe and D. Stevens.

20 Bass playing in the background > Chatter > Bass playing 1:27

This was a fascinating look at two of the members of the Airplane having fun and being in a relaxed environment. Whenever you can experience musicians you listen to playing cover songs it gives an inside look at their influences and how those would help shape the songs they wrote and or played on.

# Jefferson Airplane-

1965 Unknown location

The one song that is often listed *Chauffeur Blues* could be 9/30/66 Winterland, San Francisco, California or 10/15/66 Fillmore Auditorium, San Francisco, California.

## 8/65 Studio unknown, Los Angeles, California, (Demo for Columbia Records)

(2: 24) (Line-up B) http://www.warriorrecords.com offers this song as part of a various artists CD called *Then & Now* Volume 1 (Warrior Records SFS23931). **They list Jack Casady on bass (It was Bob Harvey) and give the source as The Matrix, San Francisco, California, early 1965. The Matrix wasn't open until 8/13/65!**
Signe Anderson- Lead vocals.
Marty Balin- Harmony vocals.
Paul Kantner- Rhythm guitar.
Jorma Kaukonen- Lead guitar.
Bob Harvey- Bass.
**(Jack Casady is mistakenly credited on the: Various Artists *Then & Now* CD Volume 1 Warrior Records SFS23931).**
Skip Spence- Drums.

**1 The Other Side Of This Life 2:24**
The arrangement is superlative for the time. The band captures the folk-rock sound but Jorma's fill-ins are masterful. They perform a very upbeat and spirited version. The demo tape that survived all these years is actually a bit off speed (**Too fast by eight percent**)! There is so much confidence being shown that it should surprise no one that the J.A. was offered a deal but held out for a better one to come along! Bob Harvey made this available on a CD called *Bob Harvey's Music Compilation Of Songs Performed from 1956-2006 Promotional CD (2006),* which he gave to fans on a brief tour of the west coast, including the 7/21/06 show at The Avalon, Santa Clara, California. **The entire Bob Harvey CD is examined in great detail, found under the year 2006.**

10/16/65 Longshoreman's Hall, San Francisco, California
The band did play there on that night, but the information is erroneous. The main clue is *Fat Angel* is listed as one of the songs, and it wasn't written yet!

**This was to be Bob Harvey's last show, but became Jack Casady's first!**
**Welcome to the flight Jack.**

How is this for a rarity?  An Airplane flyer (No pun intended) from 10/30/65 Berkeley, California,
with both Bob Harvey and Skip Spence in the photo.
Sorry for the quality, but this was a must.  Did you notice the ticket price?
Not a bad evening for a buck!
Can you pick out the members aboard the flight?
From left to right: Bob Harvey, Jorma Kaukonen, Marty Balin, Signe Anderson, Paul Kantner,
and Skip Spence.


Flyer by kind permission of Bob Harvey.  From the Bob Harvey collection.

Flyer not to be used without the written consent of Bob Harvey.

Photographer not known.

Please excuse the quality, however historical value outweighs the resolution of the flyer.

11/6/65 Calliope Warehouse 924 Howard Street Loft, San Francisco, California

This was the first Bill Graham Production. The show was for the San Francisco Mime Troupe Appeal Party.

(11:29) (Line-up 1)

**This is the earliest documented set list for the Jefferson Airplane.**

1 It's No Secret (F) 3:46
**This was the first appearance.**

2 Tobacco Road (F) 4:54
The version performed was not as up tempo as most but very strong. **This was the first appearance.** Written by John Loudermilk, but most recognized from the Nashville Teens and Lou Rawls.

3 Runnin' Round This World (F) 2:49
**This was the first appearance.**

A lot can be said from eleven minutes. The three songs performed gave a peak at the bands diversification. *It's No Secret* shows how Marty can enhance the music with his magical voice and *Tobacco Road* may have been a cover song but the Airplane put their stamp on it. *Runnin' Round This World* is catchy but in no way simplistic. San Francisco the plane has taken off.

Circa 12/16/65 RCA Studios, Hollywood, California

**Studio session for Embryonic Journey. (This is one of the most forgotten gems from the J.A. vaults).**

(2:10) (Line-up 1) **Jorma playing solo.**

http://www.warriorrecords.com released this on *Then And Now Volume 2*, Warrior Records SFS23931. **The source is listed as The Matrix early 1965, but the club didn't open until 8/13/65. Crowd noise is inserted at the end.**

The introduction is different from the released version. Jorma is playing notes to make the guitar sound like a bass for the first five seconds. There are also some additional finger-picking parts. The unreleased version is thirty-two seconds longer. While the fidelity makes you think you are listening to an old cassette tape, from a musical stand point this could have easily been the take used for the album.

Circa 12/16/65 RCA Studios, Hollywood, California

Studio session for the uncensored *Runnin' Round This World*.

(2:34) (Line-up 1)

1 Runnin' Round This World 2:34 (Uncensored)
Originally this was going to be the last song on Side A of the *Takes Off* album. The record company did not approve of all the lyrics. The line "The nights I've spent with you have been fantastic trips" caused enough controversy that the song was removed after a small initial pressing of the album. It was originally intended to finish Side A after *Tobacco Road*. Even on the limited number of copies that were available to the public before the removal of the song, the record company had censored the track. The new lyric was "The times I've spent with you have been fantastic." After the word "*fantastic*", a sound effect was inserted in place of the word "*trips*." The song finally saw the light of day on the 1974 vinyl release *Early Flight* (Grunt 10437). The censored version is a few seconds longer, and the vocal mix is a bit lower.

Photograph by kind permission of Herb Greene and may not be reproduced without his written consent.

From the Herb Greene collection.  Herb Greene photographer.

Signe Anderson deep in thought, maybe after blowing up a $100,000 mixing board.  Yes it is true!

More about that later.

The picture is circa 12/16/65-2/28/66.

# CHAPTER 2: 1966 "I FEEL SOMETHING NEW"

## Great Society (Grace Slick) -

If you haven't been fortunate to have heard the material from the Great Society I hope you will give it strong consideration. They were one of the most underrated bands of their time period. Even if Grace had not become part of the Airplane my feelings would have been the same. If you took the sounds of a psychedelic and garage band from that era, mixed in the sound of the Music Explosion (*Little Bit O' Soul*), sprinkled the Mamas And The Papas (Especially the break during *California Dreaming*), and toped it off with some of the Beatles circa 65, and 66, you would get a general idea of the Great Society's music! Please check out www.sundazed.com to see about purchasing the excellent CD *Born To Be Burned* from 1996 (Sundazed 11027). It includes the single *Somebody To Love* (Known as *Someone To Love*), and the flip-side *Free Advice*, as well as many other studio tracks and alternate versions. To see if any of the CD pressings of the two live albums originally released in 1968 known as *Conspicuous Only In Its Absence* and *How It Was* are available please visit: www.ccmusic.com and www.gemm.com.

### Circa 1966

**The complete** live and studio information for **every verified** song from the band! Documentation about the single *Somebody To Love* (Called **Someone To Love**), and *Free Advice,* as well as a listing of the members of the band, are repeated from the 1965 entry. * **Means it is an unreleased song, or version.** Thank you to Richie Unterberger, (Author of several music books) of www.richieunterberger.com, for helping to document the Great Society did have a forgotten member named Oscar. Thank you to Darby Slick for acknowledging maybe for the first time in print that Jennie Piersol was a one time member.

Oscar Daniels- (Always remembered as Oscar, he replaced David Miner on Rhythm guitar the last few months of the bands existence). Peter van Gelder remembered Oscar's last name during my interview with him.

Bard Dupont- Bass (He was on the studio recordings).

David Miner- (Also has been called David Minor) Rhythm guitar and vocals.

Jennie Piersol- Vocals (An original member for a **very short** period of time. The band started with two female singers! She was the sister-in-law to Darby and Jerry). This may be the first time she has been documented as a member of the group. In the 1969 section you'll read about a project both Grace and Jennie worked on, but at separate times!

Darby Slick- Lead guitar.

Jerry Slick- Drums (Married to Grace at the time).

**Grace Slick- Vocals.**

Peter van Gelder- Bass and saxophone (He was on the two live recordings issued by Columbia Records in 1968. You may have seen him referred to as Peter van Der Gelder).

In the 1960's a San Francisco publication called *Cream Puff War* had interviews with members of the Great Society. The songs discussed but never released either live and or studio were *Deep Blue Sea, I'm A Woman, Proud Blues,* and *Shazam*. These tunes have unfortunately never surfaced, even in unreleased fashion. Darby Slick told me the first song he wrote for the band was *When I Get You Down To The Ocean*. Jerry Slick told me on the last show the band ever played they performed a song by the famous jazz trumpet-player Miles Davis (Jerry couldn't recall which one). It would have been fascinating as to the title and their arrangement.

Peter van Gelder told me they performed Bob Dylan's- *It's All Over Now, Baby Blue*. *When I Get You Down To The Ocean* and *It's All Over Now, Baby Blue* have never surfaced either in live and or studio form.

## L- Live only. S- Studio only. L & S- Live and studio versions.

## Studio material (52:46) 15 Studio songs, 2 alternates, and 2 never released.

1 Born To Be Burned 2:02 L & S
The intro was :16, Grace and David Miner split the vocals on a tune that could remind you of the Del Shannon record *Runaway*, at least the instrumentation. This was included on Born *To Be Burned*.

2 Daydream Nightmare 3:16 L & S
The intro was 1:01. David Miner was the lead vocalist. The tune felt like you were listening to a garage band from that era. This was included on Born *To Be Burned*.

3 Don't Mess With Me* 1:16 S
The intro was :04, and Ms. Slick took control of the vocals. The song got cut, but from the minute or so that was available it sounded like a slower *Chauffeur Blues*! This tune has not been released! This came from a tape I received at least twenty years ago simply marked *The Matrix* and 1966.

4 Double Triptamine Superautomatic Everlovin' Man 1:52 S
The intro was :05, and David Miner was at the helm for the vocals. At times the guitars sounded similar to the arrangement of the Beatles- *She's A Woman*. This was included on *Born To Be Burned*.

5 Father Bruce 3:06 L & S
The intro was :07, and the vocals were handled jointly by Grace and David Miner. The song sounded a bit like *Go To Her*. Lenny Bruce the comic from the 1950's and 1960's that tested the boundaries of free-speech numerous times was the subject of the lyrics. This was included on *Born To Be Burned*.

6 Free Advice 2:27 S (B-Side single version) North Beach 1001
The single mix has Grace on background vocals, David Miner on lead, and an intro of :21. If you can picture the sound crossing a bass with a tuba would create, you have the introduction down pat. It's a song typical of the period with the psychedelic and garage band flavor. The mix on the single was very well done. They deserved a better fate. This was a strong selection for the flip-side. It was under the three minutes that the record companies put in their constitution and showed the listener another portion of their musical diversity. You can find this on *Born To Be Burned*.

7 Free Advice 2:08 Alternate #1.
The intro was :13, and there appeared to be a mix-up with the drums and vocals at one point. It seemed they were a bit out of sync! This was included on *Born To Be Burned*.

8 Free Advice 2:05 Alternate #2
The intro was :14, and the start of the mix was muffled. This was included on *Born To Be Burned*.

9 Free Advice* 2:06 (No information)
The intro was :17, and the muffled sound that was present on Alternate 2 was prevalent here. This did not match –up exactly with any of the other three versions. This came from a tape I received at least twenty years ago simply marked *The Matrix* and 1966. The version has not been released.

10 Girl 2:08 S
David Miner took the vocals on this one. The song is not the one by the Beatles. The intro was :02, and the tune could fit into the realm of *Tobacco Road*, without a hook. It sounded as if it came from a sixties garage band. This was included on *Born To Be Burned*.

11 Heads Up 1:18 S
Talk about short and to the point. The intro was :05, and the music ended before I could even digest my notes. It was a blues based song, where Grace took the lead vocals. This was included on *Born To Be Burned*.

12 Love You Girl 3:04 S
The intro was :49, and David Miner was the singer. The tempo was slow, and the music reminds you of *Today*, and *Martha*. David Miner was overshadowed by Grace in terms of vocal ability as has been pointed out three million and forty-eight times. It is rather unfair to categorize his voice as insufficient for lead vocals. Comparing most singers of the time period to Grace wouldn't show them in their best light. This was included on *Born To Be Burned*.

13 Push You In* 3:59 S
The intro was :04, and David Miner was the singer on this tune. There were segments to the song that would have made a cool TV theme for a 1960's spy show. The blues influenced the instrumentation. This came from a tape I received at least twenty years ago simply marked *The Matrix* and 1966. The version has not been released.

14 Right To Me 3:02 S
The intro was :29, and the feeling of the song was bluesy. David controlled the vocals. If you could strip down the song *Statesboro Blues* (Obviously without the slide-guitar from the Allman Brothers version) it could be a distant cousin. This was included on *Born To Be Burned*.

15 Somebody To Love 3:00 L & S (**Someone To Love**)
(A-Side single version) North Beach 1001
The intro was :08, before Grace's vocals were present. The tempo was moderate and the guitars were more rhythm driven than full of fill-ins or clever leads. Grace did not sing the words "Someone to love", but that was the original title. Although Jorma's tasty guitar segment was missing, this version can stand on its own. The song was a terrific representation of the band, both in the studio, and in the live environment. This was included on *Born To Be Burned*.

16 Somebody To Love (**Someone To Love**)* 2:18
The intro was :08 on this version as well but the vocals are split between David and Grace. What made the composition of the song so fascinating was David being mixed higher than Grace. This is a down to the bone version. It is without any guitar thrills. If you could play this version, the Great Society single mix, and the Airplane's version it would show you the terrific progression of the song. Even in the second stage (The Great Society's single) it was a terrific tune, that deserved to visit more home audio systems. This came from a tape I received at least twenty years ago simply marked *The Matrix*, and 1966. The version has not been released.

17 That's How It Is 2:25 L & S
Grace and David had the responsibility of co-lead vocals. The intro was :05, and the sound of the song was reminiscent of The Mamas And The Papas (More musically than vocally). This was included on *Born To Be Burned*.

18 That's How It Is 2:18 Alternate
The mix sounded the same. The intro was identical at :05. This was included on *Born To Be Burned*.

**19 Where 2:06 S**
The vocals were split between Grace and David. The intro was :05. The song was a mix of psychedelic with a country flavor. It sounded in the same zip code as the Beatles version of *Act Naturally*. This was included on *Born To Be Burned*.

**20 Where 2:10 Alternate**
There were no noticeable changes from the other version of the song. The intro was :05, and the fidelity was the same. This was included on *Born To Be Burned*.

**21 You Can't Cry 2:29 L & S**
David Miner was on lead vocals for this one. His voice resonated from the left channel. The intro of the song was :39, and the harmonica and drums were most easily recognized. Grace handled the background vocals. This was included on *Born To Be Burned*.

## Live Material: The live songs with an * are from 3/15-3/19/66, and or 6/21-6/25/66 The Matrix, San Francisco, California.

**1 Any Time You Want* 2:42 L**
David Miner was the lead vocalist. The blues tune sounded in the realm of the Robert Johnson song made famous by Cream (*Crossroads*). Although electric guitars were used on *Any Time You Want*, it still sounded as if it could have been recorded in the Mississippi Delta with a couple of old acoustic guitars. *Any Time You Want* came from a tape I received at least twenty years ago simply marked *The Matrix*, and 1966. The version has not been released.

**2 Arbitration 3:58 L**
David Miner was the singer for the garage rock song. The bass was upfront in the mix and the overall result sounded faintly like *It's No Secret*. This can be found on *Conspicuous Only In Its Absence*.

**3 Born To Be Burned 3:13 L & S**
Grace had control over the microphone on a composition that would have been stronger if the intro was longer. The opening sounds were from Peter van Gelder's bass and should have been given a longer life. This can be found on *How It Was*.

**4 Bullfrog Blues*^ 3:02 L (Thank you Darby Slick for the correct title).**
David Miner was the singer on this tune. When I first saw the song title I thought it was a blues cover from the fifties or sixties. The closest match was to the song by the same name from Sonny Terry (Harmonica-player that started in the 1930's and had worldwide recognition for his ability to play the blues and traditional folk music). It is a very solid tune for the live audience to have experienced. This came from a tape I received at least twenty years ago simply marked *The Matrix* and 1966. The version has not been released.

**5 Darkly Smiling 3:08 L**
From the opening notes of the guitar the song had special written all over it. Grace's inflection made the vocals haunting . Her voice excelled as she hit the high notes and the band stayed in the background during the verses to let her have the spotlight. Many of the Airplane fans that discovered this song years later were genuinely impressed. Although this is similar to *Grimly Forming* all the accolades have strayed to *Darkly Smiling*. This can be found on *How It Was*.

**6 Daydream Nightmare 4:35 L & S**
Grace's vocals were heard on a song with an Indian influenced intro and improvisational section. When the spotlight focused on the verses the tune was very reminiscent of the Sir Douglass Quintet hit single *She's About A Mover*. *Daydream Nightmare* can be found on the album *How It Was*.

60

7 Didn't Think So 3:23 L
Prior to its release this song was often referred to by the incorrect names of *Like A Raven*, *Never More*, and *Never Thought*. Grace held down the lead vocals with a song that was stronger on the lyrical side than the musical. Her voice didn't stray to far from the vicinity of *White Rabbit*. This can be found on *Conspicuous Only In Its Absence*.

8 Everybody Knows 2:36 L
Grace had the lead vocals on a song that was reminiscent of many from the time period. The song had potential but the finished product was not surrounded by strong enough instrumentation or enough catchy words. This can be found on *How It Was*.

9 Father 6:35 L **(This song originated from the jam found under entry 14).**
This song has been confused with *Father Bruce*. There were no vocals on *Father*. It had an Indian influence but if you think *The Other Side Of This Life* without the lyrics you get the general idea. It is a well constructed instrumental. Of the unearthed Great Society songs this is the longest beating out *Sally Go 'Round The Roses* by a few seconds. *Father* can be found on *How It Was*.

10 Father Bruce 3:38 L & S
The songs strength was the words performed by Grace. The title led the enchanted ticket holders to have believed the next three and on half minutes were about religion. The "Bruce" referred to was 1950's, and 1960's comic Lenny Bruce. His no holds barred stage act often resulted in a legal debate over first amendment protection. This can be found on *Conspicuous Only In Its Absence*.

11 Get Out Of My Life Woman* 2:35 L
Grace and David shared the vocal spotlight. The tune is a cover by Allen Toussaint (Legendary New Orleans rhythm and blues artist). Jerry Slick mentioned to me in an email that the Great Society made Jerry Garcia aware of the song. There is a version that can be found on Jerry Garcia's- *Pure Jerry* album. This is another blues influenced song that had the right presence for the stage. This came from a tape I received at least twenty years ago simply marked *The Matrix* and 1966. The version has not been released.

12 Grimly Forming 3:54 L
This is the absolute twin of *Darkly Smiling*. It is a haunting song that combined the logical ingredients of a marching beat and Grace singing dark vocals. What resonated (Vocal style only) was in the neighborhood of *Somebody To Love*. There is a tremendous similarity between *Grimly Forming* and the Airplane's *The House At Pooneil Corners*. The bond they share isn't in the words, the music, or the length of the finished product. It comes from the Great Society faithful making *Darkly Smiling* one of their favorites, even though this could be a twin, and the Airplane fanatic treating *The Ballad Of You And Me And Pooneil* as a gold metal winner (Which it was), but *The House At Pooneil Corners* as one of the crowd. *Darkly Smiling* has been performed by both of the terrific female vocalists when a part of the Jefferson Starship, Darby Gould and Diana Mangano. The Great Society live version can be found on *Conspicuous Only In Its Absence*.

13 I Don't Want To Talk About It* 6:00 L
David Miner handled the vocals. A good dose of the song musically sounded like the Byrds- *So You Want To Be A Rock And Roll Star*. The mix of the instruments were much louder than the sound of the vocals. There was a false ending that enhanced the overall feeling. This came from a tape I received at least twenty years ago, simply marked *The Matrix*, and 1966. The version has not been released.

14 Jam* 2:44 L **(This would become the song *Father*. Please see entry 9).**
All one can say is they got right to it. From the second the guitar's turned up to eleven on a scale of one to ten, the band took off for a few minutes. There was a passionate and natural energy throughout the music. This came from a tape I received at least twenty years ago simply marked *The Matrix* and 1966. The version has not been released.

15 Often As I May 3:44 L
Grace had the lead vocal on a stereotypical tune of the time. While it had the garage sound listening to the song several times one got the feeling Grace would have liked to move the time machine forward and have an improvisational section. This can be found on *Conspicuous Only In Its Absence*.

16 Nature Boy 3:10 L
Grace's vocal was in the same territory as *Two Heads*. She told a story enhanced by the clarity and command of her voice. The only missing element to the composition was a musical hook or riff to match Grace's vocal expertise. The most popular version of the song comes from Nat King Cole. The tune was written by Eden Ahbez (A unique individual. If you go to www.allmusic.com, you can understand why). This can be found on *How It Was*.

17 Outlaw Blues 2:28 L
This is a terrific Bob Dylan cover (Found on *Bringing It All Back Home*), that enabled Grace to show another facet of her vocal expertise. Pete Sears told me that when he worked with Grace in the studio he found her to be a superlative blues singer. The shortness of the tune should not be misconstrued as a throw-away number. This can be found on *Conspicuous Only In Its Absence*.

18 Sally Go 'Round The Roses 6:32 L
The song was one of the longest the band would perform. They weren't known for extended instrumental passages or *jams*. When you combine the music with Grace's lead vocal the finished concoction is a few years ahead of its time. Grace's voice was similar to the vocal inflection during *Two Heads*. There are fans of the band that felt the usual formula for shorter arrangements would have made this an even stronger composition. There was validity to their thoughts but their words have not been etched in stone. Marty Balin told me that the Airplane rejected recording, or performing this song! This can be found on *Conspicuous Only In Its Absence*.

19 Somebody To Love 4:23 L & S
Grace had sole possession of the microphone. The tempo was moderate, and Grace's voice wasn't allowed to reach full altitude too frequently. Grace did not sing the words "Someone to love", but that was the original title. The Great Society version stood on its own. The ending further enhanced the grip on the audience. The notes played by Darby Slick gave a false sense a second guitar solo would be part of the songs construction. While the Airplane versions live and studio were the definitive, the Great Society's renditions were not conspicuously absent. This can be found on *Conspicuous Only In Its Absence*.

20 That's How It Is 2:39 L & S
This has often been listed incorrectly as *That's How It Was*. That is the name of one of the two live albums from the band. The title came from changing the song title from the present (*That's How It Is*) to the past (*That's How It Was*). Grace is given the lead vocal on a song that sounds as if you were listening to the Dave Clark Five performing *Catch Us If You Can*. The Dave Clark Five had numerous Top-40 entries in the 1960's. This can be found on *How It Was*.

21 What You're Looking For* 3:42 L
David Miner was the vocalist on this tune. David didn't handle the vocals well. He sounded strained and the words were rough. The song was blues based until the guitar solo when Darby Slick made the first of two guitar leads more country influenced. This came from a tape I received at least twenty years ago simply marked *The Matrix* and 1966.

22 White Rabbit 6:15 L
This is one of the best live highlights of the band and may actual stand at the top. If you haven't heard the Great Society version (Those that have no cheating please), what is your guess on the length of the intro before Grace utters one word? How about 4:23! The construction of the song is fascinating in its ability to take you in several directions, all of them proper. The instrumentation is strong enough to have been without vocals. There is an Indian music influence throughout the introduction. The unused path would have been to trim the intro,

and let Grace do her thing. The one chosen was to stick with the extended intro and have Grace come in after about two thirds of the song had expired! When Grace was handed the torch she had several opportunities to hit the high notes, and to make the lyrical segment on par with the musical. All in attendance knew how that turned out. This can be found on *Conspicuous Only In Its Absence*.

23 You Can't Cry 2:58 L & S
David Miner had the vocal responsibilities, and Grace the background. If you wanted to get a sample of a garage band sound from that era you didn't have to look any further. The three minutes aren't wasted. The driving force of the guitars were able to suck you in for the entire ride. There were many sides to the Great Society, and even if some were rough around the edges, they didn't hurt when touched. This can be found on *How It Was*.

## Great Society- Fast Flight Facts

**Did you know that on the early posters and flyers the band was spelled**

**Great! Society? There was an exclamation mark after the word Great.**

**That was the idea of the girlfriend (Michele) of band member Bard Dupont.**

**Did you know that Grace Slick played a bit of rhythm-guitar and bass during her membership**

**with the Great Society?**

**Did you know that on 12/10/65 at the Fillmore Auditorium the Great Society not only performed**

**on the same bill as the Grateful Dead, but with the Jefferson Airplane as well?**

**Bard Dupont passed away on 1/20/05 at the age of 64.**

**If you would like to see a terrific photo (In addition to the wonderful shots found here) of the**

**band please visit the excellent site**

**http://www.bay-area-bands.com/index.html and you can check them out,**

**as well as many other terrific groups from that era.**

**Photograph by kind permission of Herb Greene and may not be reproduced without his written consent.**

**From the Herb Greene collection.  Herb Greene photographer.**

**The Great Society circa 1966- Grace Slick, Jerry Slick, David Miner, Bard Dupont (Taking a step**

**forward.  He played bass on the studio recordings), and Darby Slick.**

The Great Society circa 1966- Darby Slick,
Grace Slick, Jerry Slick, and Peter van Gelder in the front (He played bass on the live recordings).

**Photograph by kind permission of Herb Greene and may not be**

**reproduced without his written consent. From the Herb Greene collection. Herb Greene photographer.**

**Grace and husband of the time Jerry Slick, both of the Great Society circa 1966.**

**Photograph by kind permission of Herb Greene and may not be reproduced without his written consent. From the Herb Greene collection. Herb Greene photographer. Grace and husband of the time Jerry Slick, both of the Great Society circa 1966.**

**Photograph by kind permission of Herb Greene and may not be**

reproduced without his written consent.  From the Herb Greene collection.  Herb Greene photographer.

**Grace of the Great Society circa 1966, the beauty resonates off the page.**

# Jefferson Airplane-

<u>1/14/66 Kitsalano (Kits) Theater, Vancouver, Canada</u>

(18:27) (Line-up 1)

1 The Other Side Of This Life (F) 3:15
**This was the first appearance.** Notice the minuscule playing time. The first mission was to perfect the songs used for the live repertoire. The start of more improvisation would be occurring in late September 1966.

2 Let's Get Together (F) 3:18
**This was the first appearance.** It was written by Dino Valente of the Quicksilver Messenger Service. The Youngbloods had tremendous success with the song several years later.

3 Kansas City Blues (Move To Kansas City) (F) 1:34 Cut. Jorma vocals.
**This was the first appearance and first verified J.A. vocal for Jorma.** The song was composed by Will Shade and a well known version was done by the Memphis Jug Band. This is often listed as *Kansas City* but that is a much different tune. *Kansas City* was written by Jerry Leiber and Mike Stoller. Popular versions of the song were by the Beatles and Wilbert Harrison.

4 High Flying Bird (F) 2:31 Not from the start.
**This was the first appearance.**

5 In The Midnight Hour (F) 4:01
**This was the first appearance.** Marty Balin however told me that the band originally learned the song in case they performed at midnight on 12/31/65. The Airplane did such imaginative cover versions it was a shame this would not experience more flight time. Written by Steve Cropper but most recognized by the Rascals and Wilson Pickett.

<u>1/15/66, or 1/16/66 Kitsalano (Kits) Theater, Vancouver, Canada</u>

(35:43) (Line-up 1)

1 Lay Down Your Weary Tune (F & L) 3:23 The start is cut.
(Written by Bob Dylan but most known by the Byrds). **This is the only documented version performed by the band.** The arrangement was so precise it sounded as if they had composed the song years back!

2 Tobacco Road 3:36

3 Runnin' Round This World 2:34

4 Baby What You Want Me To Do (F) 3:08 Jorma vocals.
**This was the first appearance of the song.** Here is another example of a tune that would lead you to believe it would be a couple of minutes longer. The philosophy of getting the flight right before making it long, was a strong attribute the J.A. possessed. The day would come when this song would be tripled in length during an Airplane performance.

5 Bringing Me Down (F) 3:02
**This was the first appearance.**

6 I'll Feel A Whole Lot Better (F & L) 2:21
Written by Gene Clark of the Byrds. **Unfortunately this would be the only documented version of a great cover tune.** The J.A. sound was very much suited for the borrowed folk-rock songs performed during the Signe era.

7 It's No Secret 3:44

8 High Flying Bird 3:39

9 And I Like It (F) 5:48
**This was the first appearance.**

10 Go To Her 4:21

Circa 2/19/66 RCA Studios, Hollywood, California

*And I Like It* (Long alternate version)

The long alternate versions of *And I Like It*, were actually recorded five months after the one that was selected for the *Takes Off* album!  Please see Circa 7/20/66 for the details.

Circa 2/26/66 RCA Studios, Hollywood, California

3:26 (Line-up 1)

Let Me In 3:26 (Uncensored version)
If ever a lesson can be learned about the dangers of censorship in two easy minutes its right here!  The line "Don't tell me you want money" was replaced by "Don't tell me it's so funny."  The original uncensored version is 3:26, and contains additional guitar at the end.  The censored version often called the single version is 2:53.  It isn't only the original lyrics that make the uncensored version better, it is the slightly longer playing time.  If the single version would have been the only one recorded it still was a terrific track.  Paul delivered the vocal with as much passion as if he were singing a political tune.   Please see the next entry for a false rumor of a censored song!

Circa 2/26/66 RCA Studios, Hollywood, California

(2:32) (Line-up 1) A tremendous amount of gratitude goes to Martin Hughes of the U.K. for finally solving the mystery.  Thank you!

1 Run Around^ (Uncensored and mono version) 2:32
The record company censored *Let Me In* (Please see the above entry and *Runnin' Round This World* (Please see 12/16/65).  The good news was "Walk with me and stay the night" somehow escaped the eyes and ears of the censors during the playback of *Run Around*.  This caused much confusion all these years because listeners would always see "Walk with me and stay the night" as part of the printed lyrics.  "Blinded by colors come crashing from flowers that sway as you lay under me" were the censored words.  They were replaced by "Blinded by colors come crashing from flowers that sway as you stay here by me."  The uncensored mono version also has a three second shorter guitar fade than the stereo mix.  The imperative CD remaster of *Takes Off* released 2003 on RCA 82876 50352 2 finally unlocked this from the vaults.  It is included as a bonus track.

**Circa 5/66 Spencer Dryden takes over for Skip Spence  (Welcome aboard the flight Spencer).**

SIGNE ANDERSON and MARTY BALIN

**7/4/66 Berkeley Folk Festival photo by Barry Olivier.**

**Photo by kind permission of Barry Olivier.  The photo is not to be used without the written consent of**

**Barry Olivier.**

**Photographer Barry Olivier.**

**From the Barry Olivier and Mike Somavilla collections.**

**A wonderful birthday gift to America!  The J.A. in concert at the Greek Theatre, Berkeley, California.**

**Please visit www.barryolivier.com and inquire about the Barry Olivier Guitar Workshop.**

(8:56) (Line-up 2)

1 And I Like It 8:56 (Alternate long version)
This version is even longer than the bonus track on the 2003 *Takes Off* reissue RCA 82876 50352 2.  It is interesting to note that the longer version was recorded five months after the one that was chosen for the first album.  This was not a case of the record company or band thinking a song is too long for the project.  When you listen to the version that is almost three times the one released it seems as if the band wanted to achieve a live in studio feel.  It would have been normal to play around with the song and see how the extended passages would go over in a concert setting.  There were a couple of reasons this did not last in the set list, it didn't have enough of a blues nature to extend the song and wasn't up-tempo enough to improvise as a rock and roll number.  On the album track the tempo changes a bit at 1:46, on the alternate version there is a change at 5:50.  Jorma takes two solos on the alternate and one on the released track.  The differences in playing times are 3:15 for the released version and 8:56 for the alternate. The song often was mistakenly called *This Is My Life*, but the proper title is *And I Like It*.

7/22/66 Avalon Ballroom, San Francisco, California

The band did play there on that night but information reported is from San Francisco shows 10/66, 2/67, and 3/67.

Circa 8, or 9/66 RCA Studios, Hollywood, California

*Fat Angel* (Unreleased studio version)

(4:55) (Line-up 2)

1 Fat Angel 4:55
This song requested frequently during the live performances **was never released as a studio version**.  The arrangement sounded live in the studio but there was something obviously missing.  Without an audience present the energy level isn't fully saturated.  Even in a truncated format (Compared to the playing times live) the song needed the enhancement of the crowds appreciation for the improvisational sections.  When *Fat Angel* finally showed up on vinyl it was for the first live record *Bless Its Pointed Little Head*, released 6/69 RCA LSP 4143.

8/7/66 Fillmore Auditorium, San Francisco, California

The band did not play on this date.  Reported information is from 10/7/66 Winterland, San Francisco California.  Please see that date for complete details.

9/66 The Matrix, San Francisco, California

The band did not play this venue during the month.  Reported information is from other San Francisco shows from 1966.

Photograph by kind permission of Herb Greene and may not be reproduced without

his written consent.

From the Herb Greene collection. Herb Greene photographer. The J.A. getting ready for the 9/3/66

Monterey Jazz Festival (Day show), Monterey, California. You always think of a Rickenbacker guitar

looking nice in Paul's hand, but this particular shot has Jorma satisfied with one as well.

Photograph by kind permission of Herb Greene and may not be reproduced without his written consent. From the Herb Greene collection. Herb Greene photographer. The J.A. performing at the 9/3/66 Monterey Jazz Festival (Day show), Monterey, California.

<u>9/3/66 Fillmore Auditorium, San Francisco, California (Night Show)</u>

The band did play here on this night, but the reported information is from 9/30/66 Winterland, San Francisco, California.  Please see that date for details.

<u>9/23/66 Winterland, San Francisco, California</u>

This is the Jefferson Airplane's first performance at Winterland.  The documented information is really from 9/30/66 Winterland. The 9/23/66 information has five songs reported with the same running time and before *It's No Secret* Marty announces the same acts that will be playing later on.  Please see the entry from 9/30/66 for details.

<u>9/30/66 Winterland, San Francisco, California</u>

(56:03) (Line-up 2)

It is possible the final song of the night may have been *3/5 Of A Mile In 10 Seconds* but more likely is a version from the 2/4/67 Fillmore Auditorium, San Francisco, California show.  This performance also has been reported incorrectly as 9/3/66 Fillmore Auditorium, San Francisco, California and 10/2/66 Fillmore Auditorium (Afternoon show).  Please see 10/2/66 for the real performance from that date.

1 The Other Side Of This Life 7:40
The band has sound trouble on stage.  You can hear the group getting more and more comfortable, not only with each other but with the audience.  **The birth of their improvisational technique has begun!**

2 Tune-Up > Tobacco Road 5:21
This song is often left off the documentation from the performance.

3 Kansas City Blues (Move To Kansas City) 8:05 Jorma vocals.
Jorma's fondness for the blues came shinning through.  The perfect combination of the inflection in his voice and the guitar in hand would be a prelude of greatness to come.  (*Kansas City Blues* is often left off the documentation from the performance).

4 Run Around (F) 2:52
**This was the first appearance.**

5 Marty intros two acts that will be playing later > It's No Secret 4:07

6 Go To Her (F) 4:10
**This was the first appearance.**

7 Runnin' Round This World 2:45

8 Don't Slip Away (F) 2:44
**This was the first appearance.**

9 Come Up The Years (F) 2:45
**This was the first appearance.**

10 Bringing Me Down 3:00

11 High Flying Bird 3:42

12 Fat Angel (F) 5:37
**This was the first appearance.** It would become an instant favorite.

13 Chauffeur Blues (F) 3:18
**This was the first appearance.**

There were six songs that made their live debut. This was an important show because the band had gained enough confidence in their stage ability to use almost fifty percent of the set to break-in new material. *Fat Angel* made its first flight and while it became legendary in the Airplane world, the brilliance of *Come Up The Years* could illuminate any venue without a light show!

10/2/66 Fillmore Auditorium (Afternoon show), San Francisco, California

(27:09) (Line-up 2)

Any recorded information showing additional songs are erroneously listing portions of 9/30/66 Winterland, San Francisco, California and or 10/14/66 Fillmore Auditorium, San Francisco, California.

1 Don't Slip Away 2:44

2 Come Up The Years 2:47

3 Kansas City Blues (Move To Kansas City) Jorma vocals. 7:42

4 It's Alright (F & L) 2:19
**This was the only documented appearance of the song.**
It is surprising that such snap judgment could be made about a tune. *It's Alright* would not be given a second chance in front of an audience!

5 And I Like It 7:52
Confidence can spread rapidly. The band is not only willing to take the chance of extending the blues oriented material but Marty is able to hold the audience throughout the journey with his heart, soul, and vocal ability.

6 It's No Secret 3:41

10/5/66 Winterland, San Francisco, California

The band did not perform on this night. Reported information is incorrectly listing other 1966 Winterland shows.

10/7/66 Winterland, San Francisco, California

(30:16) (Line-up 2)

1 Take Off Jam (F & L) 8:05 With Jack bass-solo.
**This was the only time performed.** This is a very important opening number for the band. Jack shows a tremendous confidence taking the bass-solo and the special chemistry with Jorma is beginning to escalate even further.

2 Go To Her 4:33

3 Don't Slip Away 2:48

4 And I Like It 8:15
Marty says "Talk to the people" before the solo but the ending is different than 2/4/67 Fillmore Auditorium, San Francisco, California. Marty would often do that before Jorma's solo. This has often caused confusion about the authenticity of shows that included *And I Like It* in the repertoire.

5 High Flying Bird 4:06

6 Fat Angel 2:29 Cut.
(Songs five, and six may be from 2/4/67 Fillmore Auditorium, San Francisco, California). Those that have documented a longer playing time are listing *The Other Side Of This Life* from 11/27/66 Fillmore Auditorium, San Francisco, California.

## Marty Balin- Fast Flight Facts

**Marty spells his given first name Martyn.**

**Marty once appeared in a stage version of the classic play West Side Story.**

**After the Town Criers his next musical journey was not the Jefferson Airplane, but a folk band**

**called the Gateway Singers.**

**Marty helped County Joe McDonald with vocals on his 1977 LP called**

***Goodbye Blues* on Fantasy 9525.**

**If you go here http://www.jbppresentsmartybalin.com/,**

**you can find the latest solo releases from Marty.**

**Thanks to his dad Joel Buchwald you can also find archival material at the same web site.**

**It looks like the Town Criers material with Marty Balin will finally land at**

**www.ccmusic.com before the end of 2006!**

**Collectors Choice once again helping the old rocker. Check out their great site and thank**

**Gordon Anderson for caring about 60's and 70's music.**

## Signe Anderson- Fast Flight Facts

**In 1970 Signe Anderson was asked to be part of which band?**

**A) It's A Beautiful Day**

**B) Fleetwood Mac**

**C) Steve Miller**

**D) Country Joe McDonald**

While you enjoy the flight please think it over.  The answer will be found later on.

Did you know that one of the rarest Airplane Family collectables is a poster that includes

Signe Anderson from Carl Smith & The Natural Gas Company, most likely circa 1974.

The performance was held at

the Coaster Theatre, Cannon Beach, Oregon?  You can view a picture of it by going to the

following site:

http://www.postergeist.com/lists/female_vocalists.shtml

This is K-Plane radio.  On the air when in the air.  Now back to our regularly

scheduled book.

**Photograph by kind permission of Herb Greene and may not be reproduced without his written consent.**

**From the Herb Greene collection.  Herb Greene photographer.**

**Herb remembers taking several photos of the band with Signe Anderson 7-10 days before**

**her final performance on 10/15/66 Fillmore Auditorium, San Francisco, California.**

**Here is photo 1.**

**Did you notice Jack foreshadowing the next two changes in the band?  His finger is pointed right at**

**Signe and Spencer.**

**Photograph by kind permission of Herb Greene and may not be reproduced without his written consent.**

**From the Herb Greene collection.  Herb Greene photographer.**

**Herb remembers taking several photos of the band with Signe Anderson 7-10 days before**

**her final performance on 10/15/66 Fillmore Auditorium, San Francisco, California.**

**Here is photo 2.**

**Jack and Jorma are clowning around (Jack is tugging on Jorma's jacket).**

Photograph by kind permission of Herb Greene and may not be reproduced without his written consent.

From the Herb Greene collection. Herb Greene photographer.

Herb remembers taking several photos of the band with Signe Anderson 7-10 days before

her final performance on 10/15/66 Fillmore Auditorium, San Francisco, California.

Here is photo 3.

**Photograph by kind permission of Herb Greene and may not be reproduced without his written consent.**

**From the Herb Greene collection. Herb Greene photographer.**

**Herb remembers taking several photos of the band with Signe Anderson 7-10 days before**

**her final performance on 10/15/66 Fillmore Auditorium, San Francisco, California.**

**Here is photo 4.**

<u>10/14/66 Fillmore Auditorium, San Francisco, California</u> ^

(61:08) (Line-up 2) When you see ^ it is to signify documentation that landed after November 2006.

Thank you to Bruce Orr for helping with the research on the "first set." These three songs are the only ones documented. Excellent energy from the band on songs one and three.
1 Take-Off (Prerecorded Intro) > Go To Her > Tune-up > 5:43^
2 Runnin' Round This World 2:43^
3 Tune-Up > Marty talks about Percy Shelly (English romantic poet born August 4th, 1792 and died July 8, 1822) > Let Me In > Tune-Up 4:16^

This is often listed as the "second set."
4 Bill Graham Intro :15
For the intro of the second set Bill Graham says "The Leader of the opposition, Jefferson Airplane." His intro on the first set was "The Haight-Asbury version of the United States Air Force, Jefferson Airplane."
5 The Other Side Of This Life 6:51
6 Tune-Up > Marty intros the next tune written by Dino Valente > Let's Get Together 5:11
This is often erroneously listed as being from 11/27/66 Fillmore Auditorium (Afternoon show), San Francisco, California.
7 Tune-Up > Bringing Me Down > Paul thanks the crowd and intros the next song as "*This Is My Life*" 4:01
8 And I Like It (The correct title of the song) 6:47
9 Tune-Up > It's Alright 3:18
10 Tune-Up > Jam 12:18
There is a lot of significance with the *jam*. It is the first time documented that the band would play over <u>ten minutes</u>. The metamorphosis came along quickly. Once the interaction between the musicians was at the desired level of excellence, winning over the audience with the extended *jams* was only a matter of time.
11 Tune-Up > Go To Her > Tune-Up > 5:49
12 It's No Secret 3:49

<u>10/15/66 Fillmore Auditorium, San Francisco, California</u> ^ (39:40) (line-up 2)

# This is the last concert with Signe Anderson as a member of the Airplane.
Not only is this show part of history but it was a strong J.A. performance. **Grace comes aboard tomorrow!**

**^The show opened with a Bill Graham intro and then a jam. After *And I Like It the* J.A. performed *In The Midnight Hour*, Marty made an announcement, and Signe was given a goodbye monologue. After *High Flying Bird* ended the performance Bill Graham talked about Signe. Only what is documented below is what has circulated to collectors as of May 2007. Thank you to Alan Bershaw (Wolfgang's Vault) for the information above.**

1 (3/5 Of A Mile In 10 Seconds) 5:48 Performed in moderate tempo with good results.
2 Runnin' Round This World 2:26
3 Tobacco Road 4:10
4 Come Up The Years (L) 2:30
**This was the last appearance.** Surprisingly to many people it never received a fair opportunity as a live song.
5 Go To Her 4:02
6 Fat Angel 6:35

7 And I Like It 6:47
8 Chauffeur Blues (L) 3:20
As it turned out the best reaction of the performance were to Signe's vocals on this song. **This was the last appearance.** Wouldn't it have been terrific to have heard Grace perform this song once?
9 High Flying Bird 4:00
There is a bit of irony that the last song documented from this concert would be *High Flying Bird*. The group was soaring a bit higher each month with their live performances. In reflection on the relatively limited documentation we have on Signe she had a perfect ability to pick her spots. She was never about ego or having to be heard on every verse. **If I may use an oxymoron, her voice was quietly powerful.** To the credit of the band they were able to replace her with the best possible candidate. While we have heard that there were only two major female voices in town (Grace and Janis Joplin), California is a large state! **Grace would come aboard tomorrow and the sound barrier would be broken.**
A quick side note. I was speaking with the legendary photographer Herb Greene about a specific Jefferson Airplane photo with Signe Anderson. Herb told me that he remembers taking pictures of the band with Signe about seven to ten days prior to the last show. All of a sudden Signe decided to leave and Grace was in the band. Herb was very comfortable photographing Grace because he had taken many pictures of the Great Society. You can easily tell both the Great Society and the J.A. enjoyed Herb as a person and a professional.

## 10/16/66 Fillmore Auditorium, San Francisco, California (Afternoon show) (43:45) (Line-up 3)

**Version 1 correct. First show with Grace Slick.** The plane will soon reach new heights. Welcome aboard!
1 Let Me In (F) 3:24 **This was the first appearance.**
2 Run Around 3:36
3 It's No Secret 3:52
4 In The Morning (F) 6:06 Jorma vocals. **This was the first appearance.** Jorma performed the song with precision. Although many thought this was a cover of a blues song, it was written by Mr. Kaukonen.
5 My Best Friend (F) 3:34 **This was the first appearance.**
6 Plastic Fantastic Lover (F) 4:14 **This was the first appearance.** Often lost in the history of this show was the first flight of *Plastic Fantastic Lover*. Obviously the focus was on the new singer, however *Plastic Fantastic Lover* would fast become a major song in the Airplane's stage arsenal.
7 Bringing Me Down 3:00
8 And I Like It 4:42 Cut.
9 Go To Her 4:15
10 Fat Angel 5:44 The version started with a very quiet approach and ended the same way. This was the best way to get Grace acclimated to the group. They performed in the afternoon and she handled the background vocals. Excluding a couple of thanks after a song ended she did not engage in any banter. If you look at the playing times from the set list the key focus would be on the arrangements and making sure Grace would be comfortable. This show often has been documented incorrectly as being from the Fillmore Auditorium 11/6/66.

## 10/16/66 Fillmore Auditorium, San Francisco, California (Afternoon show) ^ **Version 2 (Incorrect).**

(26:37) (Line-up 3) Please note this is a new find from 2/07. Although the original source is said to be from the Bill Graham Archives, the contents don't correspond with the date. There would be more validity if you want to claim this is either a single performance or a combination from the October 24-27 & 11/16/66 dates at the Matrix, San Francisco, California, and or the Fillmore Auditorium, San Francisco, California 12/16/66-12/18/66 +12/30/66 gigs.
*"Don't Let Me Down"* **WASN'T PERFORMED LIVE UNTIL** 7/7/67 Fantasy Fayre, Los Angeles, California or 9/15/67 Hollywood Bowl, Hollywood, California. If history is being made why is there not even one moment of the second set. The band did not open a show with *"The Other Side Of This Life"* when Grace was a member until 11/26/66 Fillmore Auditorium, San Francisco, California. There is also a gap between track three and four. There isn't dead air between the others. It seems as if so often happens with Airplane material it could be two or more shows combined. It still is an amazing find and looks good in the J.A. collection!
1 The Other Side Of This Life 6:08
2 Tune-up > Paul intros the next song > Let's Get Together 4:22
3 Paul thanks the crowd > Tune-up > Let Me In 3:38
4 Don't Let Me Down 4:35 (Slight gap between end of track 3 and start of track 4). **This is not from 1966! It is from 1967.**
5 Run Around 3:49
6 Marty tells the crowd this will be the last song of the first set > It's No Secret > Marty & Grace thank the crowd 4:02

10/16/66 Fillmore Auditorium, San Francisco, California (Evening show) ^ (42:55) (Line-up 3)

**GRACE'S 2<sup>ND</sup> SHOW (EVENING).** Please note this is a new find that became available 3/07. If the source of the show didn't come from Bill Graham's Archives with proper labeling on the master reel and if he hadn't mentioned in the introduction it being the last of the "Fillmore" shows of the month, nobody would believe this was **Grace's second performance.** What makes it hard to comprehend is coming only hours apart from her debut, she is ready, eager, and authoritative! **An imperative edition to any Airplane fans collection.**
1 Bill Graham Introduction > Tobacco Road 4:26 (Grace's vocals are emphatic)!
2 Tune-up > Marty intros Jorma as "King Kaukonen" and calls the next song "*Kansas City*" > Tune-up > Kansas City Blues 8:07
3 Tune-up > Bringing Me Down 3:09
4 Tune-up > Marty intros the next song > This Is My Life 6:30
5 Tune-up > High Flying Bird 4:08 Grace's vocals exude confidence.
6 Marty intros the next song > Tune-up > Thing (F) > Jack Bass-solo W/distorted effects > Thing 9:47 **This was the first appearance.**
7 Tune-up > 3/5 Of A Mile In 10 Seconds (Interesting mid-tempo arrangement). > Marty thanks the crowd 6:44

**Photo by kind permission of Herb Greene. From the Herb Greene collection. Herb Greene photographer. Not to be reproduced without the written consent of Herb Greene.**

JEFFERSON AIRPLANE

Exclusively on **GRUNT** Records

Manufactured and Marketed by **RCA** Records

**Photo courtesy of Mike Somavilla. From the Mike Somavilla collection.**

**Not to be reproduced without the written consent of Mike Somavilla.**

**Photographer unknown.**

**This is a J.A. promo picture from circa fall 1966.**

**Thanks to BMG.**

Circa 10/24/-10/27/66, The Matrix, San Francisco, California

(18:18) (Line-up 3)

1 She Has Funny Cars (F) 3:12
**This was the first appearance.** The intensity of the song from the opening note made it one of my favorites from the band. It was a pleasant surprise when it not only became part of the 1989 reunion but was the opening number!

2 And I Like It 5:04

3 Let's Get Together 5:34 (Cut).

4 High Flying Bird 4:28

10/26/66 The Matrix, San Francisco, California

The band did play on this date but the recorded information is from a combination of 1966 shows. One giveaway is the material documented had Signe singing on certain tracks and Grace on some of the other ones. That would have been terrific! The show is not found on the list since the material is located on the actual performances.

**Photograph by kind permission of Herb Greene and**

**may not be reproduced without the written consent of Herb Greene.**

**From the Herb Greene collection.  Herb Greene photographer.  This is from a bunch of photos done**

**around the time of the recording of some of *Surrealistic Pillow* circa 10/31/66-12-31/66.**

Photograph by kind permission of Herb Greene and may not be reproduced without

the written consent of Herb Greene.

From the Herb Greene collection. Herb Greene photographer. This is from a bunch of photos done

around the time of the recording of some of *Surrealistic Pillow* circa 10/31/66-12-31/66.

**Photograph by kind permission of Herb Greene and may not be reproduced without**

**the written consent of Herb Greene.**

**From the Herb Greene collection.  Herb Greene photographer.  This is from a bunch of photos done**

**around the time of the recording of some of *Surrealistic Pillow* circa 10/31/66-12-31/66.**

**Herb did a tremendous job on this photo.**

**The nuance of having Marty backwards, but still his face shows because of the mirror is an example of**

**great analytical minds at work (Marty and Herb).**

**Photograph by kind permission of Herb Greene and may not be reproduced without the**

**written consent of Herb Greene.**

**From the Herb Greene collection. Herb Greene photographer. This is from a bunch of photos done**

**around the time of the recording of some of *Surrealistic Pillow* circa 10/31/66-12-31/66.**

**Photograph by kind permission of Herb Greene and may not be reproduced without the**

**written consent of Herb Greene.**

**From the Herb Greene collection.  Herb Greene photographer.  This is from a bunch of photos done**

**around the time of the recording of some of *Surrealistic Pillow* circa 10/31/66-12-31/66.**

**Photograph by kind permission of Herb Greene and may not be reproduced without the**

**written consent of Herb Greene.**

**From the Herb Greene collection.  Herb Greene photographer.  This is from a bunch of photos done**

**around the time of the recording of some of *Surrealistic Pillow* circa 10/31/66-12-31/66.**

**What makes Jack so good is not only the ability to improvise on the bass but if there is no bass (As in the**

**above photo) he still can contribute.**

**Photograph by kind permission of Herb Greene and may not be reproduced without the**

**written consent of Herb Greene.**

**From the Herb Greene collection. Herb Greene photographer. This is from a bunch of photos done**

**around the time of the recording of some of *Surrealistic Pillow* circa 10/31/66-12-31/66.**

**Jack was very much a dedicated follower of men's fashion and takes a well deserved bow.**

**Photograph by kind permission of Herb Greene and may not be reproduced without the**

**written consent of Herb Greene.**

**From the Herb Greene collection. Photographer Herb Greene. Doesn't Spencer look dapper**

**(Excluding the pants)? Circa 1966.**

**Photograph by kind permission of Herb Greene and may not be reproduced without the**

**written consent of Herb Greene.**

**From the Herb Greene collection.  Herb Greene photographer.  This is from a bunch of photos done**

**around the time of the recording of some of *Surrealistic Pillow* circa 10/31/66-12-31/66.**

**Photograph by kind permission of Herb Greene and may not be reproduced without the**

**written consent of Herb Greene.**

**From the Herb Greene collection. Herb Greene photographer. This is from a bunch of photos done**

**around the time of the recording of some of *Surrealistic Pillow* circa 10/31/66-12-31/66.**

Photograph by kind permission of Herb Greene and may not be reproduced without the

written consent of Herb Greene.

From the Herb Greene collection.  Herb Greene photographer.  This is from a bunch of photos done

around the time of the recording of some of *Surrealistic Pillow* circa 10/31/66-12-31/66.

The photo already has Paul thinking of future songs *Starship* and *Planes*.

**Photograph by kind permission of Herb Greene and may not be reproduced without the**

**written consent of Herb Greene.**

**From the Herb Greene collection.  Herb Greene photographer.  This is from a bunch of photos done**

**around the time of the recording of some of** *Surrealistic Pillow* **circa 10/31/66-12-31/66.**

**Jorma is wondering if he can work in another blues cover to the live set.**

Photograph by kind permission of Herb Greene and may not be reproduced without the

written consent of Herb Greene.

From the Herb Greene collection.  Herb Greene photographer.  This is from a bunch of photos done

around the time of the recording of some of *Surrealistic Pillow* circa 10/31/66-12-31/66.

Jorma seems to be having a good time with the photo shoot.

From the Herb Greene collection.  Herb Greene photographer.  This is from a bunch of photos done

around the time of the recording of some of *Surrealistic Pillow* circa 10/31/66-12-31/66.

You would be happy too if you brought over two brilliant songs for your new band to record.

## Grace Slick- Fast Flight Facts

Grace's middle name is Barnett.

Did you know in 1988 Grace helped out Kenny Loggins with vocals on his album

*Back To Avalon* (Columbia CD CK-40535)?

Did you know that Grace appears on the 1998 CD soundtrack (Miramax 62082)

to the movie:

Crow- City Of Angels?

Did you know the song (*Knock Me Out*) Grace appears on is a duet with

Linda Perry of 4 Non Blondes (1990's alternative rock group)?

If you are curious about some of the artwork from Grace you can visit the following site:

http://www.peabodyfineart.com/slick/


We now continue with another photo.

Please enjoy Ms. Grace Slick on the next page.

**Photograph by kind permission of Herb Greene and may not be reproduced without the written consent of Herb Greene.**

**From the Herb Greene collection. Herb Greene photographer. Grace Slick circa 1966.**

11/6/66 Fillmore Auditorium, San Francisco, California The date is correct, but the documentation listed is from another performance, unless the tracks show the titles of the "**REAL**" 11/6/66 late show that finally surfaced in February 2007. The first ten tracks on the fake 11/6/66 gig are from Grace's first show (Version 1).  Please see 10/16/66 Fillmore Auditorium, San Francisco, California (Afternoon show) for the proper information.  The remaining six songs are from various 1965 and 1966 shows.

11/6/66 Fillmore Auditorium, San Francisco, California (Late Show) ^ (81:12) (Line-up 3) **THIS IS THE REAL 11/6/66 PERFORMANCE!**  All prior documentation to February 2007 of the 11/6/66 gig was actually the first Grace Slick performance with the band (Version 1) from 10/16/66 Fillmore Auditorium, San Francisco, California (Afternoon show).
1 Bill Graham Intro (Same As The 10/15/66 Fillmore Auditorium) "The leader of the opposition, Jefferson Airplane." :32
2 Prerecorded "Take-Off Intro :49, 3 She Has Funny Cars 3:07, 4 High Flying Bird > Grace thanks the crowd 3:58
5 Let Me In 3:23, 6 Paul intros the next song > Run Around 3:21, 7 It's No Secret 3:36
8 In The Morning 5:41 (Jorma vocals), 9 Paul intros the next song > Tune-up > My Best Friend 3:20
Tracks 1-9 make up the 1<sup>st</sup> set.
10 Jam (Low intro) 10:26 Not too far from what would become "*Bear Melt*" but without the vocals by Grace.
11 Grace talks with the band > Tune-up > She Has Funny Cars 5:39, 12 Tune-up > High Flying Bird 4:36
13 Tune up > Paul intros the wrong song ("*Run Around*") > Runnin' Round This World 2:58
14 Tune-up > Go To Her 4:22, 15 Tune-up > My Best Friend 3:23
16 Grace thanks the crowd > Marty intros Jorma > Tune-up > In The Morning 6:43
17 **White Rabbit (F)** > Grace thanks the Crowd > Paul intros the song as it starts to play 2:36 **This was the first appearance!**
18 Tune-Up **W/My Grandfather's Clock (Tease) (**F & L) 1:10
This was the first and only time done as a "Tease."  The first and only time the song would be played was 11/27/66 Fillmore Auditorium, San Francisco, California.
19 Fat Angel 5:35 Nice intricacies by Jorma.
20 Tune-up > Paul tells the crowd good night > **In The Midnight Hour (**L) 5:47 (Tremendous version).  **This was the final performance of the song.**  Tracks 1-11 make up the 2<sup>nd</sup> set.

Circa 11/14/66 RCA Studio A, Hollywood, California (2:32) (Line-up 3) **J.P.P. McStep B. Blues (Alternate unreleased version)**
1 J.P.P. McStep B Blues 2:32 Not only one of the greatest *Airplane* tracks ever it is one of the finest songs composed.  The tune did not make the *Surrealistic Pillow* album.  It first escaped the vaults for the April 1974 vinyl release *Early Flight*, on Grunt Records 10437.  There are two differences in the released version and the alternate.  The released has a better mix of Jack's bass and uses the extra fifteen seconds of playing time for more of the non-vocal segment.

Circa 11/17/66 RCA Studio A, Hollywood, California (8:29) (Line-up 3) **Go To Her (Two alternate unreleased versions)**
1 Go To Her 4:00
The first time the song would surface in the studio would be *Early Flight* on Grunt Records 10437, released April 1974.  It clearly shows the strength of the band as songwriters.  There were brilliant tracks being left on recording studio shelves because *Surrealistic Pillow* would contain only eleven songs.  This version was only a couple of seconds longer than the one found on *Early Flight*.  The noticeable difference was the sound is very dull on the brilliant collection from 1974.  The version gathering dust has more of a presence.

2 Go To Her 4:04
Alternate version number two of *Go To Her* is six seconds longer than the one released.  There is an alternate guitar mix that shows the difficulty the band and the record company must have had in selecting the most optimum recordings.  Even alternate versions from the Airplane during all stages of their career were often worthy of taking their place on the released LP.

11/25/66 Fillmore Auditorium, San Francisco, California (49:21) (Line-up 3) Any documentation showing longer time is including *Let's Get Together* as the last song but that version is from 10/14/66 Fillmore Auditorium, San Francisco, California.  There is no mention by any of the band members why Judy Hellington is getting the serenade.
**1 (3/5 Of A Mile In 10 Seconds) (F) 5:36 This is the first appearance of the song!**  The fans in attendance were treated to the first flight of one of the finest live or studio tunes in the bands repertoire.
2 Tune-up > Short Birthday Serenade for Judy Hellington (No information given about Judy). >
3 The Other Side Of This Life > Tune-up 8:22

4 Marty intros the next song > Tobacco Road 4:32

5 Grace thanks the crowd > Tune-up > Marty intros the next song >Tune-up > J.P.P. McStep B. Blues (F) > Tune-up 5:05
**This marks the first appearance of the tune.** It would next be performed coming out of *Wooden Ships* on 5/9/69 Soldiers & Sailors Memorial Hall, Kansas City, Kansas.
There are always songs by any major band that never got the credit they deserve. This would be an example for the Airplane. The words work so well with the instrumentation. When you are able to have a set list as strong as the Airplane it is impossible that every number can become a staple of the band. I had always wished this would have been the case.

6 Grace intros the next song and first gets part of the title incorrect > She Has Funny Cars 3:34

7 Fat Angel >Tune-up > Paul thanks the crowd 7:28

8 Paul intros the next song > Tune-up > Plastic Fantastic Lover > Tune-up 5:07

9 In The Morning (L) 6:09 Jorma vocals.
**This was the final appearance.** There was some great guitar moments by Jorma.

10 Paul intros the next Song > Somebody To Love (F) > Grace and Marty thank the crowd 3:34
**This would be the first time performed with the Airplane!**

How would you like to have been present at the Fillmore this night? If *3/5 Of A Mile In 10 Seconds* didn't captivate you there was always the Airplane debut of *Somebody To Love*.

11/26/66 Fillmore Auditorium, San Francisco, California

(43:50) (Line-up 3)

1 The Other Side Of This Life 6:42

2 Bringing Me Down 3:12

3 Paul intros the next song > And I Like It > Tune-up 6:31

4 Tune-up > Marty intros the next song > Go To Her > Grace thanks the crowd 5:25

5 Tune-up > Fat Angel 7:46

6 Tune-up > 3/5 Of A Mile In 10 Seconds 6:03

7 Tune-Up > Today (F) 4:46
**This was the first appearance.** Instantly one can hear this is a creation of the finest art.

8 Tune-Up > White Rabbit > Grace thanks the crowd 3:25

11/27/66 Fillmore Auditorium (Afternoon Show), San Francisco, California

(10:46) (Line-up 3)

1 My Grandfather's Clock (F & L) (Instrumental) 1:06
**This has only been documented to have been performed the one time.** On 11/6/66 Fillmore Auditorium, San Francisco (**The Real 11/6/66**) the band performed a "*Tease*" of the song. Even at about one minute it did give you the feeling of listening to a Grandfather's Clock. It was rather clever to go from a song about one minute in length to the next one being almost ten times the amount.

2 Tune-Up > The Other Side Of This Life 9:40
This was a very strong version. Any documentation of more songs being performed is incorrect. The version of *Let's Get Together* that is often erroneously reported to have been played is from 10/14/66 Fillmore Auditorium, San Francisco, California. This is made obvious by Bill Graham's introduction of the band from that date.

12/31/66 Fillmore Auditorium, San Francisco, California

(12:20) (Line-up 3)

1 Bringing Me Down > Tune-up 3:12

2 Running Round This World 2:27

3 Tobacco Road 3:38

4 Run Around (L) 3:02
**This was the final appearance.**

Those that show longer playing times are including the beginning of the 8/5/67 O'Keefe Center, Toronto, Canada performance. The main clue is Grace's announcement that Jorma cut his bangs and then they do a quick improvisation. The only songs that were logical for 12/31/66 are listed above. This is also sometimes listed incorrectly as being from Winterland, San Francisco, California.

## Chapter 3: 1967 "Tell The World What It Means To Love"

THE JEFFERSON AIRPLANE                    Exclusive **RCA** Recording Artists

Jorma
Kaukonen

Paul          Grace         Spencer        Marty          Jack
Kantner        Slick         Dryden         Balin         Casady

Photo by kind permission of Mike Somavilla.  From the Mike Somavilla collection.

Not to be reproduced without the written permission of Mike Somavilla.  Photographer unknown.

This is a J.A. promo picture from

circa fall 1966 or winter 1967.  Thank you BMG Music.

**The GI Joe lunchbox (Far left) which Paul is holding makes it that much cooler!**

## Spencer Dryden- Fast Flight Facts

Spencer played in a band called the Heartbeats

(Not to be confused with Mickey & The Heartbeats) circa 1956.

Roy Buchanan was a member of the group. Roy was a top flight blues player

who committed suicide on 8/14/88.

Often overlooked is the appearance Spencer made on the 1972 LP from the Mill Valley Bunch,

called Casting Pearls (Polydor 2310 300).

Some of the majors players on the record were:

Mike Bloomfield

Nick Gravenites

Lee Michaels (His 1971 Top 10 single *Do You Know What I Mean*

is still a major song on the classic rock stations)

Mark Naftalin

We miss you Spencer!

## Hot Tuna (Jorma and Jack) Fast Flight Facts

Did you know on 8/19/06 at Gathering of the Vibes, Mariaville, New York, Bob Weir helped Hot Tuna perform *Walkin' Blues*?

Did you know on 9/04/04 at the
Mystic Theatre, Petaluma, California, old friend Pete Sears appeared on
*San Francisco Bay Blues*?

Did you know on 11/30/01 at the
Colonial Theatre, Keene, New Hampshire, *A Life Well Lived* was dedicated to George Harrison?

Did you know on 2/13/94 at the SEVA Benefit, Masonic Auditorium, San Francisco, California one of the major highlights was Bob Weir joining Hot Tuna for a cover version of Al Green's *Take Me To The River* (Made popular by the Talking Heads)?

If you don't touch that dial and keep it on K-Plane Radio, later on you will learn about some classic period Hot Tuna buried treasure.

<u>1967 Avalon Ballroom, San Francisco, California</u>

The band did not play this venue during 1967. Recorded information is really from a combination of 1967 shows.

<u>1967 Bouton Rouge, French TV</u>

(2:55) (Line-up 3)

1 Somebody To Love 2:55
This was part of a promotional film and includes mostly film of the band on stage, but the audio being heard is from the record.

<u>Circa winter 1967 RCA Studios, Hollywood, California</u>

(5:42) (Line-up 1)

Unreleased alternate long version.

1 Don't Let Me Down (Unreleased alternate long version) 5:42
This song didn't surface until the release of the *Jefferson Airplane Loves You* Box Set in 1992 from RCA 61110-2. The record company put the short 2:57 version on the CD. The alternate has Jorma's guitar intro for :30, and not :18, two guitar solos instead of one, and a very strange broken ending. As the song gets to the last few seconds it seems the band is out of synch! It would have been most optimum to have included both versions. The short one serves the purpose of having the entire 2:57 extremely cohesive. The alternate has the better intro and the extended length of time.

<u>1967 Bill Graham Live Collection</u>

The information listed is from a compilation of San Francisco shows during 1967. The contents are not documented here, because the actual material can be found on the performances used.

<u>1967 KSAN-FM Radio, San Francisco, California</u>

The information listed is from a compilation of San Francisco shows during 1967. The contents are not documented here because the actual material can be found on the performances used.

<u>1967 Levis Jeans Commercials (Complete)</u>

(5:11) (Line-up 3) First two listings from the 1987 vinyl release *2400 Fulton Street: An Anthology* RCA 90036.

1 White Levis :58 Announcer > Grace sings about White Levis with the band improvising in the background.
The music is closest to *A Small Package Of Value Will Come To You, Shortly* (*After Bathing At Baxter's*).

2 Stretch Levis (Beautiful Girl) :44 Announcer talks the entire time about Stretch Levis and the band improvises in the background.
The music is closest to *A Small Package Of Value Will Come To You, Shortly* (*After Bathing At Baxter's*).

3 White Levis :57
This is the same as the first one, but this was prior to being cleaned up for commercial release.

4 White Levis (Duck) :50 Announcer > Band Improvisation > Announcer tells us "I am a duck and can't wear White Levis." > Band Improvisation

The music is closest to *A Small Package Of Value Will Come To You, Shortly* (*After Bathing At Baxter's*). Never released. This one is excellent for its comedic value.

5 Stretch Levis (Beautiful Girl) :42
(Same as the first one, but this was prior to being cleaned up for commercial release).

6 Stretch Levis (Fit Right Cool) :57 Announcer > Marty takes the lead vocal as the band plays something in the realm of *It's No Secret* > Marty tells us in a funny voice "The world would be an empty and shallow place without Stretch Levis."
Never released. This one is highlighted by the entire band performing as if Stretch Levis were one of their songs!

1967-1970 Live Compilation

This is the same as 4/15/70 Winterland, San Francisco, California. They both contain incorrect information. Not only did the band not play on that night but *Won't You Try/Saturday Afternoon* is introduced as a new song!

1967 Live (Released 2003) By Collectors Choice Music

(14:13) (Line-up 3)

www.ccmusic.com

These are two live songs from a location not noted. In 2003 Collectors Choice Music had a special limited time offer. When the first four Jefferson Airplane albums were reissued and remastered on CD with bonus tracks, they offered those that bought all four at once a limited edition special 2 track CD. The sound quality is excellent. All that is mentioned about the disc is previously unreleased material. The item is now out of print.

1 Don't Let Me Down 6:14

2 Fat Angel 7:59

1967 Something Else British TV

(11:00) (Line-up 3)

1 White Rabbit
While the band performs there are psychedelic slides being shown.

2 Two Heads
There is more of a focus on the band during this song.

3 The Ballad Of You And Me And Pooneil (Short version)
There are psychedelic slides shown, but not as numerous as on the first song. The version of *The Ballad Of You And Me And Pooneil* is listed as short because it is closer in playing time to the single that was released.

1/8/67 Webster Hall, New York City

(32:21) (Line-up 3)

**This would be the first concert for the band in New York City. The event was billed as a Press Party and Showcase. Songs four and five have special guests!**

1 And I Like It :58
This was the ending of the song. The rest was cut.

2 Go To Her 4:08

3 (3/5 Of A Mile In 10 Seconds) 4:58
Jack's bass playing was terrific.

**4 Hate To See You Go (F & L) 4:56**
This was the only time ever performed. This is often called *Blues* or *Unknown Blues*. Obviously that would make the writer of the song Little Walter very unhappy. The most noted version is from the Paul Butterfield Blues Band. Two of the members at the time Mike Bloomfield on guitar and Mark Naftalin on keyboards joined the Airplane for songs four and five.

**5 East-West (Jam) (F & L) 17:31**
The Airplane continued to extend the boundaries with their friends (Please see song 4) helping on this number as well. This too is often erroneously called *Blues* or *Unknown Blues*. The two writers of the song would not appreciate that. Paul Butterfield and blues musician Nick Gravenites are the composers. The title is actually *East-West*. The *jam* is mentioned because of the additional players on stage and the length of time. The musicianship is superlative on songs four and five.

The uniqueness of seeing these **two tunes performed as a one time affair**, must have made everlasting memories on those that were aboard the flight that night. As of this date the seventeen plus minutes would be the longest time of an Airplane song. Flight times are made to be broken, and this one will!

1/29/67 Bell Telephone Hour: The Sights And Sounds Of San Francisco

(2:36) (Line-up 2)

(NBC TV) Footage from the Fillmore Auditorium, San Francisco, California 7 or 8/66.

The film was black and white (Never looking better), and an amazing journey back in time. The footage shown was from the Signe Anderson period, and that alone enhanced a terrific couple of minutes. The footage looks very close to what can be viewed on the 1980's Bill Graham Documentary, but obviously doesn't contain the short interview with Bill Graham, and Carlos Santana, that were recorded for inclusion on the Bill Graham tribute. This got released in 2004 on the *Fly Jefferson Airplane* DVD from Eagle Rock Entertainment 30065.

1 It's No Secret 2:26
To get a look at the band from the early days, and glimpses of what the Fillmore Auditorium meant to a segment of the city is one history lesson you don't want to miss.

2/3/67 Fillmore Auditorium, San Francisco, California

The band did play the venue on that day but the recorded information is a combination of 9/30/66 Winterland, San Francisco, California and 2/4/67 Fillmore Auditorium, San Francisco, California. Please see those days for show details.

2/4/67 Fillmore Auditorium, San Francisco, California

(91:53) (Line-up 3)

There is an incredible amount of misinformation about this performance. The most commonly documented mistake is *Go To Her* having been performed. The version of *Go To Her* had Signe on vocals. Since she was out of the band in 1966 this would have been a difficult task.  Additional incorrect documentation would be the set list for the concert and the amount of songs performed.  It was often reported that the entire show had between seven and ten songs.  You can see that is not the case when you look over the contents.  What further complicated things were the reports that tracks eight through eleven were from 8/5/67 O'Keefe Center, Toronto, Canada.  The playing times are different.  A major culprit for additional errors in the archival history is the band would often perform different sets in one show.  There were times they repeated songs.  That will be shown below.  Finally if you ever see a listing for *Take Off Jam* ending the concert it is erroneous as well.  The source of the information either repeated one of the *jam's* performed, or is listing the one from 10/7/66 Winterland, San Francisco, California.

1 Somebody To Love 3:11 The opening notes were cut.

2 Let's Get Together > Marty thanks the crowd > Tune-up > 4:44

3 Let Me In > Tune-up > 3:52

4 Tune-up > And I Like It 7:23

5 Tune-up > White Rabbit 2:59

6 Paul intros the next song > Plastic Fantastic Lover > Marty lets the crowd know Quicksilver Messenger Service will be coming up > Marty intros the next song 5:24

7 She Has Funny Cars 3:25

8 Jam (With slight instrumental portions of Fat Angel) 12:16
There was a keyboard being played during the *jam* by Grace.  The sound was very similar to Ray Manzarek from the Doors circa 1967.

9 (3/5 Of A Mile In 10 Seconds) 5:36
Grace and Marty worked very well together during this version.

10 Fat Angel 7:09

11 Somebody To Love 3:04
This is not a repeat from the opening song!

12 The Other Side Of This Life 6:54

13 Bringing Me Down 2:50

14 And I Like It 6:14
This is not a repeat from song four.

15 It's Alright 2:04

16 Jam 10:55 Includes short bass and drum-solo.

17 It's No Secret 3:45

2/8/67 Fillmore Auditorium, San Francisco, California

Bill Graham's notes do not show the band played on this night. Recorded information is from other February 1967 shows at the Fillmore Auditorium.

2/14/67 Fillmore Auditorium, San Francisco, California

The band did not perform on this date. Recorded information is a mix of 9/30/66 Winterland San Francisco, California and 2/4/67 Fillmore Auditorium, San Francisco. There are also incorrect listings from this date being from an unknown location.

3/3/67 Fillmore Auditorium, San Francisco, California

(30:29) (Line-up 3)

This is often reported incorrectly as being from Winterland, San Francisco.

1 Jam 11:08 Includes a short Jack bass-solo and a short Spencer drum-solo.

2 (3/5 Of A Mile In 10 Seconds) 5:13

3 Fat Angel 6:57

4 Marty intros the next song > Somebody To Love > Grace thanks the crowd 3:25

5 High Flying Bird 3:43 The beginning, and ending were cut.

3/4/67 Café Au Go Go, New York City

(64:09) (Line-up 3)

**The more logical time period for this concert would be 6/67.** It would be very unusual in the 1960's for a band to play the Fillmore Auditorium, San Francisco, California, on the third, (Please see that entry) perform one night in New York City on the forth, and then play the Frost Amphitheater, Palo Alto, California on the fifth!

1 It's No Secret 3:05

2 Let's Get Together 5:02
This was a very strong version.

3 White Rabbit 3:22

4 Bringing Me Down 3:45

5 My Best Friend 4:09

6 Come Back Baby (F) 6:36 Jorma vocals.
**This was the first appearance of the song!**

7 And I Like It 5:24

8 (3/5 Of A Mile In 10 Seconds) 3:50

113

9 Somebody To Love > Leave You Alone (F) 8:04
This is often mistaken for an extra verse from *Somebody To Love*. That is not the case. It is an improvisational piece by Marty, and both the vocals and instrumentation were superlative. **This was the first appearance of *Leave You Alone*.** The last appearance of *Leave You Alone* comes out of a jam on 3/12/67 Winterland, San Francisco, California.

10 Tobacco Road 4:38

11 Runnin' Round This World 2:28

12 Rock Me Baby (F) 6:01 Jorma vocals.
Jorma sets the mood with a great opening to the song and the band contributes terrific energy. This is the first appearance. Jorma's influence and live fan base are expanding. New York City got treated to a double scoop of Jorma debuts, *Rock Me Baby* (Traditional) and *Come Back Baby* (Lightnin' Hopkins).

13 Today 3:00

14 High Flying Bird 4:38

3/5/67 Fillmore Auditorium, San Francisco, California

The band played Frost Amphitheater, Palo Alto, California on this date. Recorded information about 3/5/67 is really a truncated listing of the 8/5/67 O'Keefe Centre, Toronto, Canada performance.

Circa 3/7/67-10/31/67 RCA Studios, Hollywood, California

(6:52) (Line-up 3)

1 Instrumental 6:52
The music was loosely based on *The Other Side Of This Life*. It was often reported that the *Instrumental* was the band performing *The Other Side Of This Life* in the studio without vocals. **That information was totally erroneous.**

3/10/67 Winterland, San Francisco, California

(52:28) (Line-up 3)

1 And I Like It > Tune-up 5:55

2 Don't Slip Away (This version is more up-beat than the standard) > Marty intros the next song > Tune-up 4:35 >

3 Tobacco Road > Tune-up 4:09

4 Somebody To Love 3:11 >

5 Leave You Alone 3:00

6 High Flying Bird 4:29 The intro was cut. Tune-up > Marty intros the next song as written by Jorma >

7 She Has Funny Cars > Tune-up 4:20 >

8 Let Me In > Tune-up 4:59 >

9 My Best Friend > Marty will intro the next song over three nights as *Jorma's Blues* > Tune-up 3:56

10 Come Back Baby > Tune-up 6:14
Jorma played a hot solo during *Come Back Baby*, and handled the vocals.

11 White Rabbit > Grace thanks the crowd > Tune-up 2:47

12 (3/5 Of A Mile In 10 Seconds) > Marty thanks the crowd 4:53

3/11/67 Winterland, San Francisco, California

(71:00) (Line-up 3)

Recorded information from this performance often leaves out the listings of tracks five and seven.

1 My Best Friend > Marty as on the previous night intros the next song as being from Jorma and titled *Jorma's Blues* > Tune-up 4:15

2 Come Back Baby (Jorma vocals) > Tune-up > Jorma fools around on the guitar for a few seconds 5:52

3 Today > Marty thanks the crowd and intros the next song 3:33 >

4 Don't Slip Away (L) > Grace thanks the crowd 3:36
**This was the final appearance.**

5 Grace intros the next song > Tune-up > Plastic Fantastic Lover 4:30

6 The Other Side Of This Life 7:49

7 Tune-Up > Grace intros the next song > Lets Get Together 3:30 Cut.

8 Bringing Me Down > Tune-up 3:26

9 Today > Marty intros the next song > Tune-up 4:09

10 Runnin' Round This World > Marty intros the next song 3:13

11 (3/5 Of A Mile In 10 Seconds) 7:40 Tune-up >
Jorma plays a well crafted solo on song number eleven.

12 Marty intros the next song > Fat Angel > Tune-up 9:47

13 Thing 6:03 (F) Cut.
*Thing* was an excellent instrumental that would have been nice to hear in the range of ten minutes or longer.

14 It's No Secret 3:29

3/12/67 Winterland, San Francisco, California

(64:36) (Line-up 3)

1 It's No Secret > Grace thanks the crowd 3:33

2 Grace intros the next song > White Rabbit > Grace thanks the crowd > Tune-Up > Grace intros the next song 3:12

3 Bringing Me Down 2:42

4 Marty intros the next song > Don't Let Me Down > Marty thanks the crowd 9:45
This version had more lyrics and was longer than the ones documented from 7/7/67 Fantasy Fayre, Los Angeles, California or 9/15/67 Hollywood Bowl, Hollywood, California. The information on those two shows is the same. Please see those dates for details.

5 Jam 6:08 >

6 Leave You Alone (F & L) 7:02
What made songs five and six so fascinating were the blending of the *jam* into Marty's improvisational piece. The other versions of *Leave You Alone* were done coming out of *Somebody To* Love, the first being 3/4/67 Café Au Go Go, New York City. **This was the first and last appearance of *Leave You Alone* coming out of a *jam*. It is also the final appearance in any arrangement.**

7 Today 3:24

8 She Has Funny Cars > Tune-Up > Marty intros the next song as the first the band ever played 4:09 >

9 High Flying Bird > Grace thanks the crowd > Tune-up 5:03

10 And I Like It > Marty intros the next song 6:10

11 (3/5 Of A Mile In 10 Seconds) 4:52

12 Marty intros the next song > My Best Friend (L) > Marty for the third straight performance intros the next song as *Jorma's Blues* > Tune-up 4:03
**This was the final appearance of *My Best Friend*.** That wasn't an outlandish decision by any means. There were too many songs far better suited for the stage.

13 Come Back Baby 4:46 Cut. Jorma vocals.

Circa spring 1967 Promotional clip

(2:30) (Line-up 3)

*White Rabbit* (Promotional clip)

1 White Rabbit 2:30
Somebody decided to give the J.A. the day off, why? The studio version of the song is played as an unnamed female explores the water, sand, and rocks from a beach. The band isn't a part of their own promotional clip.

5/7/67 Smothers Brothers Comedy Hour

(17:30) (Line-up 3)

This was taped for broadcast on 6/25/67. It is possible there were two rehearsal songs not ever aired. When I listened to the original copy I had received of this show, I noticed that there were two additional tunes on the tape. The recording sounds as if it could be part of a rehearsal or TV taping. On song five near the beginning Marty's microphone is too low and at the end you can hear Grace's being turned off. On song number six the sound changes during the music. These imperfections led me to believe the band recorded more music for the TV taping.

1 Smothers Brothers intro of the Jefferson Airplane :25 >

2 Somebody To Love 2:45
The members of the band are featured evenly during the song.

3 Smothers Brothers intro of the Jefferson Airplane :33

4 White Rabbit 2:22
They filmed mostly Grace singing in front of psychedelic slides.

*Somebody To Love* and *White Rabbit* were recorded on 5/7/67 for airing on 6/25/67.

5 High Flying Bird 3:36

6 Today 2:07

It is very feasible that songs listed after the numbers five and six are unused segments from the 5/7/67 taping.

5/12/67 Fillmore Auditorium, San Francisco, California

The most commonly listed information about this show is actually from 10/14/67 Winterland, San Francisco, California. Please go to that date for the proper information. Please see the contents below for the real 5/12/67 performance.

(43:18) (Line-up 3)

This was the real 5/12/67 show. It was the first documented version of *Won't You Try/Saturday Afternoon*. There is no intro to the song and the arrangement is a work in progress. This is also the concert with one of Marty's best vocal performances during *Comin' Back To Me*.

1 The Other Side Of This Life 8:02

2 Runnin' Round This World 2:30

3 She Has Funny Cars 3:31
A very short and basic version.

4 High Flying Bird 3:59

5 Marty intros the next song > Tobacco Road 4:03

6 Marty intros the next song > Let's Get Together 4:01

7 White Rabbit 2:22

8 Grace thanks the crowd > Paul requests that the lights be turned down > Comin' Back To Me (F & L) 7:39
Marty's performance was captivating! This was the first and last time played. Paul helped set the mood for song number eight. There is no doubt he could sense something special. Marty's vocal was so mesmerizing it would have been possible to hear him without interruption on a landing strip.

9 Won't You Try/Saturday Afternoon (F) 7:05
**This was the first appearance of the song.**

5/13/67 Fillmore Auditorium, San Francisco, California

The band did perform on this date but any recorded information is the real 5/12/67 Fillmore Auditorium performance.  Please go to that date for show details.

5/14/67 Fillmore Auditorium, San Francisco, California

The band did perform on this date but any recorded information is the real 5/12/67 Fillmore Auditorium performance.  Please go to that date for show details.

5/19/67 Men's State Polytechnic College, San Luis Obispo, California

(89:31) (Line-up 3)

1 The Other Side Of This Life 8:44

2 Let's Get Together 5:24

3 She Has Funny Cars 3:27

4 White Rabbit 2:52 The band had feedback on stage for a couple of seconds.

5 Let Me In 4:15

6 Today 4:08

7 Young Girl Sunday Blues (F) 1:23 Cut.
**This was the first appearance of the song.**

8 Somebody To Love 3:23 The intro is cut.

9 The Ballad Of You And Me And Pooneil (F) 11:31
**This was the first appearance of the song.**  For the initial time the J.A played *The House At Pooneil Corners* coming out of *The Ballad Of You And Me And Pooneil* please go to the 8/28/68 Falkoner Cenret, Copenhagen, Denmark show.

10 Tobacco Road (L) 4:22
**This was the last time ever performed.**

11 Runnin' Round This World (L) 3:07
**This was the last time it was performed.**

12 And I Like It (L) 6:13
**This was the last time it was performed.**

13 Jam 9:44

14 Tune-Up For Won't You Try/Saturday Afternoon :51

15 Won't You Try/Saturday Afternoon 7:01
The song was still being solidified. The intro was shorter but the arrangement was coming together. The strength of the song was at any stage of life it sounded well crafted enough for stage and studio representation.

16 Come Back Baby 7:29 Jorma vocals.

17 White Rabbit 2:46

18 It's No Secret 2:45 Cut.

## 5/29/67 Winterland, San Francisco, California

There has never been confirmation the band played on this night. Recorded information is actually the 5/12/67 Fillmore Auditorium (The real one) performance. Please go to that date for the contents of the show.

## 5/30/67 Winterland, San Francisco, California

There is no confirmation the band played on this night. Some claim that the performance was part of a benefit for Halo (Haight-Ashbury Legal Organization). Recorded information is actually the 5/12/67 Fillmore Auditorium (The real one) performance. Please go to that date for the contents of the show.

## Circa 6/67 Tonight Show (TV)

It has been confirmed the Airplane performed *White Rabbit* and *Somebody To Love*. After the initial airing of the program the documentation of the performance seemed to have been erased from rock and roll history. The unfortunate reasons for this have ranged from the master tape being destroyed to the lose of the original master.

## 6/67 Café Au Go Go, New York City (Please see 3/4/67)

Although the band was much **more likely** to have performed at this venue in June of 1967 for travel reasons, 3/4/67 has become the date the performance is associated with. Please see 3/4/67 for the information on the concert.

## 6/3/67 American Bandstand ABC-TV Studios

(8:27) (Line-up 3)

The band lip-syncs to the studio tracks. There is also an interview with Dick Clark. I had to include this because there is some humor associated with the program. It was often erroneously reported that Jorma was the most unhappy person in the building that day. If you ever get a chance to see the cool looking black and white footage on the first track Grace, Marty, and Paul are not exactly all smiles. On the second song it is Marty and Paul that were not doing cartwheels. It must have been uncomfortable for all involved. American Bandstand had become one of the most famous shows in the world. The premise was to have on the hit-makers of the day. Even though the Airplane would have some success on the singles charts that was never their forte. The audience at most could name a couple of their songs. Those were the two they lip-synced.

1 Dick Clark asks a person in the audience "Have you ever been to San Francisco?" > Dick Clark intros the band and the song :56

2 White Rabbit 2:36

3 Dick Clark tells the viewers that was the first of two songs > Somebody To Love 3:12

4 Dick has Grace intro the band and she almost forgot Paul's name > Dick has questions for the band:

For Grace: "Why did the music take off?"

For Paul: "Are older people afraid of the band?"

For Jack: "Would a hippy take 100,000 dollars to cut their hair, and wear a suit, and tie?"

For Jorma: "What will be happening in San Francisco this summer?"

Total time 1:43

6/17/67 Monterey Pop Festival, Monterey Fairgrounds, Monterey, California

(38:45) (Line-up 3)

This performance finally got released on audio CD in 1995 as an import from the United Kingdom, called *Live At Monterey* (Magnum 74). When a band plays a large festival it can often be both advantageous, and restrictive. The exposure is certainly there when masses attend, but if you are known for your on stage ability, and have to keep your set under forty minutes, you are bound to give up something. What it amounted to when you look back on the concert was the inability to stretch out the selections, excluding the last tune.

1 Stage intro > Somebody To Love > Grace thanks the crowd 3:15
The original documentation did not mention there was a stage intro.

2 Grace intros the next song > The Other Side Of This Life 6:56

3 Grace thanks the crowd > Tune-up > White Rabbit 2:44

4 High Flying Bird 4:12

5 Today > Grace thanks the crowd 3:08

6 Tune-up> She Has Funny Cars 3:22
Jorma's playing stood out on this song.

7 Young Girl Sunday Blues 3:36

8 The Ballad Of You And Me And Pooneil > Grace thanks the crowd 11:26

6/18/67 Monterey Pop Festival, Monterey Fairgrounds, Monterey, California

The band performed the previous day 6/17/67. Any recorded information is from the 6/17/67 show. Please go to that date for complete information.

6/19/67 Winterland, San Francisco, California

The band did perform there on that night but recorded information is from 10/14/67 Winterland. Please go to 10/14/67 for show details.

6/25/67 Smothers Brothers Comedy Hour

This was the playback date of the taping from 5/7/67. Please go to 5/7/67 for complete information.

7/7/67 Fantasy Fayre, Los Angeles, California

(61:44) (Line-up 3)

The notes from the performance are the exact same as **9/15/67 Hollywood Bowl, Los Angeles, California**. The band did play at these two venues but twice Paul says "See you in the park tomorrow." Bill Graham makes the same comment as well. The band didn't have another gig until 9/23/67 Seattle Center Coliseum, Seattle, Washington. The previous show at Golden Gate Park, San Francisco, California was 1/14/67 and the next one 5/7/69. There is no way even if rained out it would have taken that long to get new permits and to work out the schedule for all parties involved. The songs fit into the 1967 concert configuration but it is possible there was one more performance from Southern California that did not get listed in any data base.

1 Somebody To Love 2:33  The intro was cut.

2 She Has Funny Cars > Paul thanks the crowd and intros the next song 3:19

3 Young Girl Sunday Blues 3:41

4 Martha (F?) > Tune-Up 5:16
**This may be the first appearance of the song.** Since the information on 7/7/67 Fantasy Fayre, Los Angeles, California, and 9/15/67 Hollywood Bowl, Hollywood, California is the same, it is listed on both shows as the possible first appearance. The first version could be from 8/2/67 O'Keefe Center, Toronto, Canada (Late show).

5 Two Heads (F?) > Grace thanks the crowd > Tune-up > Marty intros the next song 3:37
**This may be the first appearance of the song.** Since the information on 7/7/67 Fantasy Fayre, Los Angeles, California, and 9/15/67 Hollywood Bowl, Hollywood, California, is the same, it is listed on both shows as the first appearance. The first version could be from 8/2/67 O'Keefe Center, Toronto, Canada (Late show).

6 It's No Secret 3:42

7 Don't Let Me Down (F? or L?) 7:53
**This was the first and last fully documented performance of the song.** Since the information on 7/7/67 Fantasy Fayre, Los Angeles, California, and 9/15/67 Hollywood Bowl, Hollywood, California, is the same, it is listed on both shows as the first appearance. **The final appearance which was a brief vocal by Marty during a *jam* with Dino Valente from Quicksilver Messenger Service, can be found on the 12/31/67 Winterland, San Francisco, California, show.** Please go to that date for details. Please also see the listing for 1967 Live (Released 2003) by Collectors Choice Music. The playing time for the song is less on that recording but there is no documentation of a source. That is why there is a question mark next to song number seven, if was the first, or last time performed.

8 Grace tells the crowd "Back away from the monitors on stage." > Bill Graham asks the people to "Get off the stage because the excess weight could cause it to break." > Today 3:21

9 Hollywood Jam (F & L) 9:48
**This is the first appearance of the song.** Since the information on 7/7/67 Fantasy Fayre, Los Angeles, California, and 9/15/67 Hollywood Bowl, Hollywood, California, is the same, it is listed on both shows as the first appearance. There were no vocals or unusual occurrences during the *jam*.

10 Plastic Fantastic Lover 4:59

11 Paul intros the next song > The Ballad Of You And Me And Pooneil > Bill Graham requests the crowd to "Exit the proper way."> Paul tells the crowd "There will be a party in the park tomorrow." >

12 White Rabbit > Grace thanks the crowd 2:28 Between Paul and Bill Graham there were three mentions during the show that there would be a concert in the park tomorrow. In order to not be repetitious I only documented the last one.

7/31/67 & 8/1/67 O'Keefe Center, Toronto, Canada The band did perform on these dates but any recorded information is listing the 8/5/67 O'Keefe Center, Toronto, Canada concert. Please see that date for show information.

8/2/67 O'Keefe Center, Toronto, Canada^ The band did perform on this date but any recorded information is from the "REAL" 8/5/67 O'Keefe Center, Toronto, Canada (Afternoon show) concert unless it matches the tracks from the **new find of 2/07 which is mistakenly labeled as 8/5/67 Early & Late.** Please see these dates for proper documentation.

8/2/67 O'Keefe Center, Toronto, Canada (Early show) ^ (30:42) (Line-up 3) Mislabeled as 8/5/67 O'Keefe Center (Early show Version 2). This is a new find from 2/07. The "**REAL**" 8/5/67 Early show is one of the Jefferson Airplane tapes that were substantiated as far back as the middle part of the 1970's. The gig was always well known for the "*Jorma Cut His Bangs Short Jam.*" The venue is correct but the show most likely was recorded from the afternoon performance of 8/2/67. Grace reads a promo for the "Trips Underground Film Festival" running on Saturday and Sunday. Since 8/5/67 was a Saturday she most likely would have commented the festival is tonight. 1 Take Off- Prerecorded Intro (Ending only) > Somebody To Love 2:53, 2 Paul thanks the crowd & intros the next song > Marty wants the crowd to dance > Grace talks with the crowd > She Has Funny Cars 4:11 (Not the normal passion on this version from Jorma), 3 Grace thanks the crowd > Tune-up > Grace reads a promo for the "Trips Underground Film Festival" running on Saturday and Sunday > Two Heads (**F?**) 4:11 **This may be the first live version of Two Heads!** Since the 7/7/67 Fantasy Fayre, Los Angeles, California and 9/15/67 Hollywood Bowl, Hollywood, California performances have the same documentation if *Two Heads* were not played on 7/7/67 this would make it the initial live version! 4 Grace thanks the crowd & intros Marty & the next song > Young Girl Sunday Blues 4:20 Excellent mix of Grace on the organ. 5 Tune-up > Paul intros the next song > Tune-up > Fat Angel > Paul requests the lights to be turned down as the song starts 9:13, 6 Paul thanks the crowd > Tune-up > Come Back Baby (Jorma vocals). Terrific playing by Jorma. 5:52 (Fades out).

8/2/67 O'Keefe Center, Toronto, Canada (Late show) ^ (45:47) (Line-up 3) The date being listed as 8/5/67 late show on a new find from 2/07 is not right. The venue is correct but the show most likely was recorded from the evening performance of 8/2/67. Grace reads a promo for the "Trips Underground Film Festival" running on Saturday and Sunday. Since 8/5/67 was a Saturday she most likely would have commented about the festival being "Tonight" and maybe a conflict with the concert. Since the 8/5/67 early show has been authenticated for decades, it is highly unlikely the new find would have anything to do with the date of 8/5/67. You can clearly see how a box could be mislabeled with a 2 and a 5 not being too far off if the handwriting is like mine. 1 The Other Side Of This Life (Low intro and not from the start) 6:44 On one of the verses Paul comes in a bit early "I don't know what I'm doing." 2 Tune-up > Grace thanks the crowd & intros the next song > Let's Get Together 4:29, 3 Grace intros the next song > It's No Secret 3:29 Could be the most upbeat version! 4 Grace thanks the crowd > Tune-up > Grace reads a promo for the "Trips Underground Film Festival" running on Saturday and Sunday 1:06 > 5 Two Heads 3:15, 6 Grace intros the next song > Tune-up > She Has Funny Cars 4:11, 7 Tune-up > Grace intros the next song > Martha (**F?**) 5:43 **This may be the first live version of Martha!** Since the 7/7/67 Fantasy Fayre, Los Angeles, California and 9/15/67 Hollywood Bowl, Hollywood, California performances have the same documentation if *Martha* were not played on 7/7/67 this would make it the initial live version! 8 Grace thanks the crowd > Paul intros Jorma & the next song as blues by Jorma > Blues Improvisation (Short) :58 > 9 Rock Me Baby 7:44 Some lyric changes by Jorma. He starts off with "Roll me baby." 10 Tune-up > Marty intros the next song > Today 3:54, 11 Tune-up > Paul talks the words "Don't you want somebody to love" & Grace whistles a bit as well (**F & L**) :49 > **This is the only time Paul would talk the words to "*Somebody To Love.*"** 12 Somebody To Love 2:56, 13 Grace thanks the crowd and announces the next thing is planned > Feedback from the stage :49

8/3/67 O'Keefe Center, Toronto, Canada, 8/4/67 Nathan Phillips Square, Toronto, Canada (Afternoon show), and 8/4/67 O'Keefe Center, Toronto, Canada (Night show) The band did perform on these dates but any recorded information is listing the 8/5/67 O'Keefe Center, Toronto, Canada concert. Please see that date for show information.

8/5/67 Fillmore Auditorium, The Matrix, or Winterland, San Francisco, California
The band did not perform at any of these venues on this date. Any recorded information is from 8/5/67 O'Keefe Center, Toronto, Canada concert. Please see that date for show information.

8/5/67 O'Keefe Center, Toronto, Canada (Afternoon show) (77:12) (Line-up 3) **The "REAL" 8/5/67 performance**. There is no documentation of an evening show. A truncated version of this show is often incorrectly listed as 12/31/66 Fillmore Auditorium, San Francisco, California. For the "**REAL**"12/31/66 performance please go to that date. A new find that came out in 2/07 as the **Early & Late performances from 8/567 is most likely the Early & Late shows from 8/2/67.** Please see that date for proper information. 1 She Has Funny Cars 1:57 The intro was cut. 2 Bringing Me Down (L) 3:03 **This would be the final appearance of Bringing Me Down.** Grace intros the next song >

3 Grace sings a bit of *High Flying Bird (F & L)* by herself > High Flying Bird 4:51
**This was the only time Grace sang a bit of the song by herself before the actual song started.**

4 White Rabbit 2:43

5 Grace thanks the crowd > Come Back Baby 5:28 Jorma vocals.

6 It's No Secret 3:29

7 The Other Side Of This Life 7:47 The intro was cut.

8 Let's Get Together (L) 4:00
**This was the final appearance.** Many may argue that as the band needed to bring in the newer material and flex their muscles with improvisation, *Let's Get Together* needed to be replaced in the set list. The tune was so rooted in their history, and the message never clearer then the summer of 1967, it could have continued to fly at least another month.

9 Let Me In (L) 3:28
**This was the final time performed.**

10 Today 3:27

11 Grace informs the crowd Jorma cut his bangs >

12 Jorma Cut His Bangs Short Jam (F & L) :39 Grace intros the next song >
**This was the only appearance of the *jam*.** Grace will soon make it a more common occurrence to banter with the audience and become a legendary live entertainer to go with performer.

13 Grace does a bit of *Go To Her* (F & L) by herself > Go To Her 4:20
**This was the only time Grace sang a bit of the song before the actual tune would begin.**

14 Spare Chaynge (F & L) 11:55 With improvisation and a bit of instrumentation from *The Other Side Of This Life*. Not a *jam* as commonly documented. **This is the first and last performance of the song as a full version. The last appearance ever would be 12/31/67 Winterland, San Francisco, California where it appeared briefly as part of a *jam*.** Please see that date for details.

15 (3/5 Of A Mile In 10 Seconds) 5:31

16 Fat Angel 9:51

17 Tune-up > Marty intros the next song > Somebody To Love > Grace thanks the crowd 4:14

8/67 (Between 8/7 and 8/21) The Eastman, Rochester, New York

(2:18) (Line-up 3)

1 White Rabbit 2:18
This is the only song that has been documented from the performance.

Circa 8/29/67 RCA Studio A, Hollywood, California

*After Bathing At Baxter's* (Studio rehearsal)

(3:23) (Line-up 3)

1 Martha 3:23 (**Instrumental version**)
There has never been any version of this song that isn't legendary. While the vocals are the integral part of the composition the musical arrangement has always been superb.

Circa 8/30/67 RCA Studio A, Hollywood, California

*After Bathing At Baxter's* (Demo)

(3:23) (Line-up 3)

1 The Last Wall Of The Castle (Jorma demo) 3:23
*After Bathing At Baxter's* had numerous special moments. It often happens that certain tracks get forgotten when there is an album full of masterpieces. *The Last Wall Of The Castle* when placed as the sixth song on the LP was 2:41 with vocals and with the full band. Jorma's demo is 3:23. It is first offered to the group before any words were added. Jorma's guitar mix is high and there are a couple of false endings. This has been listed from time to time as being from 1968. That isn't correct.

9/5/67 Fillmore Auditorium or Winterland, San Francisco, California

Recorded details of this date are incorrectly listing the 10/14/67 Winterland, San Francisco, California performance. Please go to that date for details.

9/14/67 The Rock Scene: Like It Is, CBC TV Studios, Toronto, Canada

It has been confirmed that studio versions of the songs were used. There was lip-syncing, but Grace had a live microphone to talk with the audience when needed. Psychedelic images were used liberally. The three songs aired were *White Rabbit*, *Two Heads*, and *The Ballad Of You And Me And Pooneil*. 9/14/67 is the recorded date. The playback aired on 10/16/67.

9/15/67 Hollywood Bowl, Hollywood, California

(61:44) (Line-up 3)

**The notes from the performance are the exact same as 7/7/67 Fantasy Fayre, Los Angeles, California.** The band did play at these two venues but twice Paul says "See you in the park tomorrow." Bill Graham makes the same comment as well. The band didn't have another gig until 9/23/67 Seattle Center Coliseum, Seattle, Washington. The previous show at Golden Gate Park, San Francisco, California was 1/14/67, and the next one 5/7/69. There is no way even if rained out it would have taken that long to get new permits and to work out the schedule for all parties involved. The songs fit into the 1967 concert configuration but it is possible there was one more performance from Southern California that did not get listed in any data base.

1 Somebody To Love 2:33  The intro was cut.

2 She Has Funny Cars > Paul thanks the crowd and intros the next song 3:19

3 Young Girl Sunday Blues 3:41

4 Martha (F?) > Tune-Up 5:16
**This may be the first appearance of the song.** Since the information on 7/7/67 Fantasy Fayre, Los Angeles, California, and 9/15/67 Hollywood Bowl, Hollywood, California, is the same, it is listed on both shows as the possible first appearance. The first version could be from 8/2/67 O'Keefe Center, Toronto, Canada (Late show).

124

5 Two Heads (F) > Grace thanks the crowd > Tune-up > Marty intros the next song 3:37
**This is the first appearance of the song.** Since the information on 7/7/67 Fantasy Fayre, Los Angeles, California, and 9/15/67 Hollywood Bowl, Hollywood, California, is the same, it is listed on both shows as the first appearance.

6 It's No Secret 3:42

7 Don't Let Me Down (F? or L?) 7:53
**This was the first, and last fully documented performance of the song.** Since the information on 7/7/67 Fantasy Fayre, Los Angeles, California, and 9/15/67 Hollywood Bowl, Hollywood, California, is the same, it is listed on both shows as the first appearance. The final appearance which was a brief vocal by Marty during a *jam* with Dino Valente from Quicksilver Messenger Service, can be found on the 12/31/67 Winterland, San Francisco, California, show. Please go to that date for details. Please also see the listing for 1967 Live (Released 2003) by Collectors Choice Music. The playing time for the song is less on that recording but there is no documentation of a source. That is why there is a question mark next to song number seven if was the first, or last time performed.

8 Grace tells the crowd "Back away from the monitors on stage." > Bill Graham asks the people to "Get off the stage because the excess weight could cause it to break." > Today 3:21

9 Hollywood Jam (F & L) 9:48
**This is the only appearance of the *jam*.**
Since the information on 7/7/67 Fantasy Fayre, Los Angeles, California, and 9/15/67 Hollywood Bowl, Hollywood, California, is the same, it is listed on both shows as the first appearance. There were no vocals or unusual occurrences during the *jam*.

10 Plastic Fantastic Lover 4:59

11 Paul intros the next song > The Ballad Of You And Me And Pooneil > Bill Graham requests the crowd to "Exit the proper way." > Paul tells the crowd "There will be a party in the park tomorrow." >

12 White Rabbit > Grace thanks the crowd 2:28

Between Paul and Bill Graham there were three mentions during the show that there would be a concert in the park tomorrow. In order to not be repetitious I only documented the last one.

10/5/67 Fillmore Auditorium, San Francisco, California

Recorded information from this date is not correct, it is from 10/14/67 Winterland, San Francisco, California. The band was at Pacific High Studios, San Francisco, California. Please see 10/14/67 for the contents of the show. Please see the next entry for the information on the 10/5/67 studio rehearsals.

10/5/67 Pacific High Studios, San Francisco, California

After Bathing At Baxter's Studio Rehearsals.

(66:19) (Line-up 3)

This is an example of why a band as proficient as the Airplane should have a series of unreleased material made available. The documented contents are the proper sequences. There have been reports that have only listed up to and including the 27:05 sequence of *Martha*. There have been incorrect orders of the sessions as well.

**1 I Can't Get No (Satisfaction) :57**
The vocals are not through a microphone, but it sounds as if Spencer is singing and there may be help from Marty. The song is one of the Rolling Stones most popular. This is a short and wonderful off-the-cuff version. Jorma doesn't play the legendary "riff", but it sets the standard for a great hour or so.

**2 It's Alright (Ending only) > It's Alright (Complete) 4:12** This is often listed incorrectly as *It's So Fine*.

**3 Won't You Try/Saturday Afternoon 12:06 Including:**
Won't You Try > Stopped to talk about the arrangement > Saturday Afternoon
This was a good look how the two parts of the song sounded before they were combined. Alone the segments were good enough for release on album. When placed together there are so many positive musical and lyrical standouts, that the idea to blend one portion into the next was the best choice for the final presentation.

**4 Martha 27:05** Including: Non vocal segment > Start of the song (Cut) > Complete run through > False start > Ending > Working on an arrangement > Working on a riff ("She does as she pleases") > Back to the beginning > Stopped for discussion > Martha (From the start ) (Grace's use of the "recorder" is fantastic).
The *Martha* epic is one of the finest unreleased pieces I have ever heard. It is a shame that this did not become part of an archival series. Paul is very focused on what he wanted to do and say with the arrangement. After my first listening two thoughts immediately came to mind. The song was going to be terrific in any finalized fashion. The basic outline was so intense there would be no way by the time it came to fruition it wouldn't be a masterpiece. The second thing is Grace is playing rather well a musical instrument called a "recorder." It may be best described as a "flute" with a haunting whistle.

**5 It's Alright 1:25**
The version wasn't complete, the mix is lower, and the song is stopped after Jorma's guitar solo.

**6 Young Girl Sunday Blues 3:55**
A bit longer than the released version.

**7 Go To Her :53 Cut.**
There wasn't a lot to go on here. The mix sounded higher than the released version, but the segment of the song that is available did not contain any nuances.

**8 Won't You Try/Saturday Afternoon 8:51 Including:** instrumental run through of first four minutes > The song is run through again with vocals appearing at the four minute mark > The song is stopped for segment arrangement.
The first four minutes sound as if this could be another song. There was a major difference in the instrumentation during the studio sessions and what would be the final take.

**9 Martha 6:50 Including:** The start of the song with Paul telling the band to change the tempo > The band stopping to discuss the arrangement > The song is played straight through.
This portion of the rehearsal conveyed an interesting event. Paul had a vision as to what the tempo of the song should be and he had the task of getting the band to see it the same way. It became obvious on the version used for release that he was successful many times over.

<u>10/11/67 Fillmore Auditorium, San Francisco, California</u>

The band did play there on that night but the recorded information is from the 10/14/67 Winterland, San Francisco, California performance. Please go to that date for the details.

10/14/67 Avalon Ballroom, San Francisco, California

The correct venue is Winterland, San Francisco, California. Please go to that date and venue for the information.

10/14/67 Winterland, San Francisco, California

(39:57) (Line-up 3)

1 The Other Side Of This Life 8:58  There is a nice beginning to the song. It opens as if a *jam* is taking place.

2 Watch Her Ride (F) 3:16
**This was the first appearance.**  An example of a solid studio track that wouldn't transfer to the stage as well.

3 It's No Secret > Tune-up 4:22

4 White Rabbit > Tune up 2:42

5 The Ballad Of You And Me And Pooneil 12:09 Cut.

6 Tune-Up > Fat Angel 8:30
This is often overlooked when documenting this show. Any recorded information of a longer playing time is including *Crown Of Creation* from 6/13/69 The Family Dog, San Francisco, California. There is also those that have written the band played *Go To Her* and *Don't Slip Away*. I have not heard those two songs being part of this concert in any of my research.

This is the correct information for the 10/14/67 performance. Most documentation from 10/14/67 is actually:

5/12/67 Fillmore Auditorium, San Francisco, California. Please see that date for correct information.

6/19/67 Winterland, San Francisco, California. The band did perform on that night but there is no documented set list.

10/5/67 Fillmore Auditorium, San Francisco, California. The band was at Pacific High Studios, San Francisco, California. Please see that date for correct information.

10/11/67 Fillmore Auditorium. The band did perform on that night but there is no documented track list.

10/14/67 Avalon Ballroom, San Francisco, California (Wrong venue).

10/15/67 Pacific High Studios, San Francisco, California. The band played at Hughes Stadium, Sacramento, California on that date. Please go to 10/5/67 Pacific High Studios, San Francisco, California for the correct information.

10/16/67 The Rock Scene: Like It Is, CBC TV Studios, Toronto, Canada

This was the playback date for the show recorded on 9/14/67. Please go to that date for information.

10/19/67 Warfield Theater, San Francisco, California

The band did play that date but what is commonly listed is incorrect. The recorded information is a combination of 10/14/67 Winterland, San Francisco, California and 6/13/69 Family Dog At The Great Highway, San Francisco, California.

<u>10/31/67 Terrace Ballroom, Salt Lake City, Utah</u>

**There is a <u>great deal</u> of humor about recorded information on this date.**  Not only did the band not perform on 10/31/67 but how welcome do you think they would have been in Utah during the 1960's?

<u>Circa 10/31/67 RCA Studio A, Hollywood, California</u>

*After Bathing At Baxter's* (Studio rehearsal).

(24:09) (Line-up 3)

Spare Chaynge 24:09
When I first heard this version I was surprised that some that had privy to it were making it to be the greatest lost treasure from the Airplane vaults.  There were those that were disappointed the entire twenty four minutes did not get placed on *After Bathing At Baxter's*.  There were others that wanted the album to be reissued as a double CD.  Even if you could go back in time you would have to reconfigure the running order of the album. Having been placed in between *Watch her Ride* and *Two Heads,* the 9:15 released version was pushing it.  The only place it could fit would be after the final track *Won't You Try/Saturday Afternoon*.  Not to belabor the point but the longevity of the uncut studio rehearsal is not a *jam*.  There are a lot of esoteric parts that were deemed superfluous when it came to the final mix of the song.  Here is a little known fact, if you check the next entry there was actually a 2:33 rough mix of the song!  It is a nice listen to experience but if you want the treasure chest to be opened the entire sessions of, *Marth*a, *The Last Wall Of The Castle*, and *Won't You Try/Saturday Afternoon* would be one hundred light years superior for starters.

<u>Circa winter 1967  Most likely Pacific High Studios, San Francisco, California</u>

*After Bathing At Baxter's* (Rough mixes).

(30:18) (Line-up 3)

1 Two Heads 3:02
The released version was nine seconds longer and had a better mix.  The rough mix did have more bass and the acoustic guitar was very present.

2 Watch Her Ride 3:05
The released version was five seconds longer, the guitar fill's are more audible, and drums end the song, and not the bass as found on the rough mix.

3 Spare Chaynge 2:22
Notice how short this is!  The released version was 9:06.  The rough mix has higher bass but the music is only a portion of the album version.

4 Young Girl Sunday Blues 2:50
The released version was 3:31.  The rough mix contains only one vocal track and does not have the laughter at the start that was a continuation from the end of *A Small Package Of Value Will Come To You, Soon*.

5 Rejoyce 3:58 Version 1
The released version which is three seconds less has a piano opening.  The rough mix begins with Jack's bass.

6 Rejoyce 3:58 Version 2 Grace piano intro.
The released and rough mix both have the piano intro.  The vocal mix is very slightly higher on the rough mix version.

128

7 Martha 3:26 **"Roadrunner"** opening!
The released version is three seconds shorter, and on the second verse Paul is singing lead, and Grace can be heard in the background. On the rough mix the vocal track is different, and Marty can be heard, and not Grace during the second verse. The rough mix had a clever intro, almost inaudible is an imitation of the Roadrunner cartoon character's *"Beep Beep."* It wasn't the person that created the voice of the Roadrunner, but is immediately recognized! The only blemish on the released version of Martha is not having the *"Beep Beep"* sound.

8 A Small Package Of Value Will Come To You, Soon 1:35
The released version has the drums mixed more noticeably and has a set ending. The rough mix has a false ending, and is one second longer.

9 A Small Package Of Value Will Come To You, Soon 1:33
The differences are very slight. The released version has a better mix of the drums and is one second longer.

10 The Last Wall Of The Castle 2:37
The released version is two seconds less and the rough mix has a two second longer intro before the vocals begin.

1967 Unknown from late in the year

This is actually a compilation of 1966 and 1967 shows. The contents aren't listed because the songs can be found on the performances they were selected from.

12/31/67 Winterland, San Francisco, California

(93:26) (Line-up 3) **Dino Valente** (Quicksilver Messenger Service) is the special guest on tracks 11-13.

1 Martha 5:19

2 The Other Side Of This Life 10:19
This was a strong version with a fine improvisational section.

3 Today 2:54

4 Rock Me Baby 8:30 Jorma vocals.
An interesting version. The blues are a bit slower and Jorma takes some liberties with the lyrics!

5 Two Heads 3:12 The band ended the track very well.

6 Won't You Try/Saturday Afternoon 4:36

7 Young Girl Sunday Blues 3:29
Marty put everything into this version.

8 Watch Her Ride 3:03
The upbeat nature helped enhance the song.

9 White Rabbit 2:03 This was an excellent vocal by Grace.

10 She Has Funny Cars 3:12 Cut.

**11 Baby What You Want Me To Do 3:35 Jorma and Dino Valente vocals.**

**12 Jam  17:22 >**

**13 Ride This Train** (F & L) > Happy New Year improvised vocal by Marty (F & L) > Don't Let Me Down (L) short vocal segment by Marty > Spare Chaynge (L) very short instrumentation > Ride This Train 11:27
This is the only time *Ride This Train* was performed.  This was the last time *Don't Let Me Down* appeared.  There is a mystery on the first and last time played as a full song.  7/7/67 Fantasy Fayre, Los Angeles, California or 9/15/67 Hollywood Bowl, Hollywood, California most likely were the first or last performance of the full song.  There is a full version that can be found under 1967 Live (Released 2003) by Collectors Choice Music.  The playing time for the song is less on that recording but there is no documentation of a source.  This was the final appearance of *Spare Chaynge*.  It was only played briefly.  For the first and last long version of the song please see 8/5/67 O'Keefe Center, Toronto, Canada for details.

**Dino Valente from Quicksilver Messenger Service on stage with the Airplane, not a bad way to spend New Years Eve.**  An already great show is escalated with Dino Valente on guitar and vocals, joining the celebration on songs eleven through thirteen.  *Ride This Train* most likely was an improvisational song, because the released versions with that title are not the same.  The vocals were done by Marty.

# Chapter 4:1968 "Stability You Strive For"

Photograph by kind permission of Bob Harvey and may not be reproduced without his written consent.

From the Bob Harvey collection. Bob Harvey photographer. Bob Harvey took this picture of

Marty Balin circa 1968 at the Jefferson Airplane Mansion 2400 Fulton Street, San Francisco, California.

Photograph by kind permission of Herb Greene.  From the Herb Greene collection.  May not be reproduced without the written consent of Herb Greene.  Herb Greene photographer.  Jack Casady circa 1968.

The J. A. House (Mansion) 2400 Fulton Street,  San Francisco.
Photograph by kind permission of Don Aters.  From the D.A. collection.  May not be reproduced without the written consent of D.A.

<u>1968 Perry Como Christmas TV Special</u>

(3:26) (Line-up 3)

1 Martha 3:26
The band did not play live but fantastic video footage was aired. It looked exactly like the Beatles circa 1966. The video production was terrific. There is some nice editing as the members of the group are filmed around a tree, the grass, and in the water. The clip finally came out in 2004 on *Fly Jefferson Airplane* DVD from Eagle Rock Entertainment 30065. It would have been nice if the other song of the special *Watch Her Ride* made it for release as well.

<u>1968 Westpole TV Show (Essay 1) KQED, San Francisco, California</u>

(4:17) (Line-up 3)

1 Intro by host Ralph Gleason :44

Ralph Gleason gives the itinerary of the program that will discuss the San Francisco rock scene. Ralph Gleason is known for being a music critic for the San Francisco Chronicle and was an editor with Rolling Stone magazine.

2 Ralph Gleason talks about the Jefferson Airplane, the cultural revolution, and the Airplane being on the cover of Life magazine :14

3 Crown Of Creation 3:19 Studio version. The song fades-out.

<u>Circa 2/68- 9/68 RCA Studios A and or B, Hollywood, California</u>

(Crown Of Creation)

(32:00) (Line-up 3)

Labeled as out-takes, and rough mixes, they seemed to be rough mixes. For simplifying the explanations of the songs, when talking about the unreleased version it is understood that it is either an out-take or a rough mix.

1 Share A Little Joke 3:12
The playing times are the same between the album version and this one. The only difference is the released version has a better mix of the vocals.

2 Greasy Heart 3:47
The released version is :21 shorter, has a better mix of the guitar, and fades-out. The unreleased version contains a longer guitar solo and ends with a sudden stop. The unreleased version without question would have been fine to release with the simple task of raising the level of the guitar.

3 Good Shepherd 4:32
This is being listed twice because there is debate if this version got taken from a 1968 session or the one from 4/17/69 Wally Heider Studios, San Francisco, California. The released version is ten seconds shorter and contains background vocals that are highlighted by Grace singing "La la la la." The unreleased has no vocal overdubs and a lower vocal mix. It sounds even in the earliest stages that with a bit of polishing *Good Shepherd* would become synonymous with Jorma.

4 Lather 2:57
The playing times are exact between the released and unreleased versions. Grace's vocals are better mixed on the released version and you can hear the nuances in the background better on the album version.

5 Chushingura 1:18
The released version was three seconds longer and had a better separation of sound.

6 Triad 4:58
The released version is three seconds less but the mix is a lot cleaner. The guitar on the unreleased version sounds terrific but the rest of the instruments needed to be better accounted for.

7 Star Track 3:07
The playing times on both versions are equal. The album version has better sound. I had hoped this would have had greater differences. The song is so tremendous that we can't have enough versions!

8 Ice Cream Phoenix 1 (2:58)
The released version is five seconds longer and the vocal mix is perfect. The unreleased version needed to tweak the voice levels.

9 Ice Cream Phoenix 2 (3:06)
This is the better of the two versions. The released version is three seconds shorter and the intro is nine seconds less than the unreleased. The version that wasn't used for the album is very solid and could have been a fine addition to the LP. Any notes showing there is a Jefferson Airplane rarity of an *Ice Cream Phoenix Jam* for 17:45 is a mistake. **That was from Hot Tuna at The Matrix, San Francisco, California 1969.**

1968 Promotional film

(3:35) (Line-up 3)

*Greasy Heart* (Promotional film).

1 Greasy Heart 3:35
The band is seen playing live through a bunch of psychedelic images. While the images can often look cool there is not enough Airplane video where we can enjoy the band performing.

1968 Jonathan Winters TV Show

(8:58) (Line-up 3)

1 Today 3:17
Very slow version!

2 Somebody To Love 3:03

3 Crown Of Creation 2:38
It has often been overlooked that the band performed on the Jonathan Winters Show. The best of the three selections would be the slower paced version of *Today*. In any tempo it is one of the finest songs ever penned.

1/30/68 The Matrix San Francisco, California

The band did play at the venue on this night, but the recorded information is an exact clone of 2/1/68 The Matrix, San Francisco, California. Please see the entry from 2/1/68 for complete information.

134

(128:37) (Line-up 3)

Information from 11/2/69 Elysian Park, Los Angeles, California is really part of the documentation of this show. The band did play on 11/2/69 but there are no confirmed set lists.

1 Tune-up > Grace tells the crowd "The next song can be one of two." >  Somebody To Love 4:35

2 Young Girl Sunday Blues > Tune-up 4:58

3 She Has Funny Cars > Tune-up > Paul intros the next song 4:53

4 Two Heads (L) > Tune-up 4:53
This was the final appearance.  At least for a few more months the song deserved a better live fate.

5 Martha > Tune-up 4:44

6 Kansas City Blues (Move To Kansas City) (L) Jorma vocals > Tune-up > Paul intros the next song 7:28
**This was the last appearance of the song**.  Song six has often been left off the documentation from this show.

7 The Other Side Of This Life 7:56

8 Today 3:14
A stellar version!

9 Won't You Try/Saturday Afternoon > Paul thank the crowds crowd > Tune-up 6:43

10 It's No Secret > Tune-up > Grace thanks the crowd 4:08

11 Blues From An Airplane (F & L) > Tune-up 2:52
**This is the only time performed!**  Better late than never!  Song eleven is another that would have been nice to have been performed on a continuous basis.  It has never gotten the credit it deserves for the well composed lyrics.  As good as it sounded in 1968 it would have been even better if played when first born.

12 Watch Her Ride 4:10

13 Plastic Fantastic Lover > Tune-up 3:53

14 Tune-up > White Rabbit 2:34

15 (3/5 Of A Mile In 10 Seconds) > Grace thanks the crowd > Tune-up 6:38

16 Share A Little Joke (F & L) >
**(This is the only appearance of *Share A Little Joke)*.**  Paul announces "The next song (*Ice Cream Phoenix Jam*) is an instrumental and if you have words sing along." > Tune-up 5:00 >

17 Ice Cream Phoenix Jam (Instrumental) (F & L) 9:52 Cut.
**This is the only appearance.**  It was a surprise that such an intense piece of work would come and go in one night.

18 Tune-up > Fat Angel > Tune-up 8:52

19 The Ballad Of You And Me And Pooneil > Grace thanks the crowd 10:33
The improvisational segment of the show (Songs seventeen through nineteen) were one of the reasons to this day 2/1/68 is considered one of their ten best performances ever.

20 High Flying Bird (L) 4:37
**This was the final appearance.**  Another link to the past is broken.  A superb tune that served the band and the fans well.

21 Wild Tyme (F) > Marty thanks the crowd > Tune-up 3:49
**This is the first appearance.**

22 Go To Her (L) > Paul thanks the Crowd > Tune-up 4:37
**This was the final appearance.**

23 Rock Me Baby 7:38 Jorma vocals.
Very nice slow blues version!

Circa 2/10/68-6/5/68 RCA Studios, Hollywood, California

(2:38) (Line-up 3)

1 Short Jam > Percussion 2:38
The *jam* portion only lasted forty-eight seconds.  It sounded almost exactly like the segment from *Crown Of Creation* when "We are voices" was sung.  The *jam* goes right into a percussion segment.

**Photograph by kind permission of Don Aters and may not be reproduced without the
written consent of Don Aters.
From the Don Aters collection.  Don Aters photographer.
Grace Slick on stage with the J.A. circa spring 1968, Fillmore East, New York City.**

136

<u>5/3/68 Fillmore East, New York City</u>

Part of the performance was released in 1998 by BMG on the CD *Live At The Fillmore East*, catalog number 67563. This date or 5/4/68 Fillmore East, New York City was the last appearance of *Thing*.

<u>5/4/68 Fillmore East, New York City</u>

Part of the performance was released in 1998 by BMG on the CD *Live At The Fillmore East*, catalog number 67563. This date or 5/3/68 Fillmore East, New York City was the last appearance of *Thing*.

<u>5/13/68 In Sounds Army Promo (Syndicated radio show)</u>

(9:26) (Line-up 3)

1 Host Harry Harrison talks with a listener attempting to pick the next hit record :46

2 Army Promo: 39

3 Greasy Heart 2:29 The song is faded-out early and is played from the album *Crown Of Creation*.

4 Interview with Grace Slick (Comparing her to Mama Cass from the Mamas & the Papas) :32

5 Outro of the segment: 17

When I first listened to this sometime in the middle part of the 1970's the entire concept made no sense. One of the most anti-war bands would be the Airplane. Grace has always remained faithful to the hope there will be peace one day. The program was sponsored by the United States Army. Harry Harrison is one of the most noted disc-jockeys ever. At the time he was working for WABC radio in New York City. There was a syndicated show that would run all over the country, In Sounds Army Promo. A listener would pick what they felt would be the next hit record. To the credit of the program they were able to have guests on that relied more on album sales, such as Grace and Eric Clapton from Cream. Although the interview with Grace is very short she was very modest when asked about her singing ability compared to Janis Joplin. Grace replied "There is no comparison, Janis is better." Many of us don't see it that way at all.

<u>Circa May 1968 RCA Studio A, Hollywood, California (Unedited out-take from *Crown Of Creation*)</u>

(8:48) (Line-up 3)

For reasons that will never be known, this has been documented as being untitled. It isn't a song. The engineering and production team from the studio are looking for a specific guitar sound. It is a terrific few minutes.

1 Band conversation regarding On Top Of Old Smokey > Chatter > Jorma is asked what he is going to play (Camp Song) > Jorma is corrected and told it is Castle (Neither got played) > On Top Of Old Smokey (Excerpts with Jorma changing the words) > Keep On The Sunny Side (With the band fooling around) > Jorma is asked to play the Jimmy Brown thing (He was a 1950's country artist) > Jorma does a variation of the riff to Broad Minded Men (Jimmy Brown) > Jorma plays eight bars of the classic That's All riff > Jorma plays a variation of Candy Man 2x > Candy Man (Excerpts with vocals) fades out.

Some information about the songs mentioned. *On Top Of Old Smokey* is a traditional song and most noted is the version by the Weavers. Paul is a large fan of their music. There was no song titled at the time *Camp Song. Castle* was a song written by Arthur Lee from the band Love. The J.A. song with "Castle" in the title is *The Last Wall Of The Castle* (*After Bathing At Baxter's*). *Keep On The Sunny Side* is a song written by A.P. Carter and Gary Garett. The most famous version is from the Carter Family. One of Jorma's favorites, *Candy Man* was written by

Reverend Gary Davis and appears on the second Hot Tuna record, *First Pull Up Then Pull Down* released in 1971 on RCA Records 4550.

<u>5/18/68 Northern California Folk-Rock Festival, Santa Clara County Fairgrounds, San Jose, California (Day show)</u>

Please see the next entry for the night show.

(48:11) (Line-up 3)

1 White Rabbit 2:12

2 Plastic Fantastic Lover 3:33

3 Watch Her Ride 3:56

4 Today 4:06

5 The Ballad Of You And Me And Pooneil 10:01

6 Greasy Heart (F) > Grace thanks the crowd 3:15
**This was the first time performed.** An immediate impact was felt.

7 Fat Angel 6:52

8 Star Track (F) 5:56 Jorma vocals.
**This was the first appearance.** It has always been one of the most underrated of any Airplane Family songs. For some reason I always think of *Ice Age* as a updated version of this tune.

9 Won't You Try/Saturday Afternoon 4:56

10 Somebody To Love 3:22

It was a nice twenty four hours of music for fans of the band. They had an opportunity to hear them play at different venues on the same day.

<u>5/18/68 Shrine Exhibition Hall, Los Angeles, California (Night show)</u>

Please see the previous entry for the day show.

(44:18) (Line-up 3)

1 White Rabbit > Grace thanks the crowd 2:26

2 She Has Funny Cars (L) 3:47
**Sadly this was the final appearance until the 1989 reunion tour.**

3 Watch Her Ride 3:01

4 Today > Grace thanks the crowd 3:29

5 Paul intros the next song > Greasy Heart 3:11

6 Star Track 5:53 Jorma vocals.

7 Somebody To Love > Grace thanks the crowd 3:35

8 Fat Angel 8:26

9 Won't You Try/Saturday Afternoon 4:58

10 The Ballad Of You And Me And Pooneil 5:26
Notice how short compared to most versions of the song this one is. It is possible there were time restrictions because the show clocks in a bit under forty-five minutes.

<u>Circa late May through late June 1968 RCA Studios A or B, Hollywood, California, *Crown Of Creation* demos</u>

(8:21) (Line-up 3)

These have been called rough mixes from circa summer 1968 but that isn't the case.

1 Ice Cream Phoenix 2:51
The released version is twelve seconds longer and the presence of an acoustic guitar can clearly be heard. The demo is not mixed as well and the acoustic guitar is absent.

2 The House At Pooneil Corners 5:30
The released version has a thirty second intro before any vocals make an appearance. It is eighteen seconds longer in total time and fades-out. The demo has an introduction of twenty-six seconds and ends with a cold stop. Even in the beginning stages the song is haunting and spectacular. People can look at two closely related items and view them as worlds apart. Over the years *The Ballad Of You And Me And Pooneil* is a legendary song to the ears of the Airplane fan. *The House At Pooneil Corners* which is so similar never got the same accolades.

<u>Circa 5/31/68 RCA Studio B, Hollywood, California</u>

*The Saga Of Sydney Space Pig.*

11:48 (Line-up 3)

1 The Saga Of Sydney Spacepig 1:17 (Extended)
The first time I received a copy of this on a cassette tape the writing next to the song called it an "extended version." How great is one minute and seventeen seconds being extended? What would a short version be? This is a short *jam* without any memorable moments.

2 The Saga Of Sydney Spacepig 2:24
This is by far the best of the three segments. It is an outstanding blues *jam* . The band is very tight and the playing is stellar. This part of the "**Saga**" could have effortlessly been inserted into another song. The music is that strong.

3 The Saga Of Sydney Spacepig 8:07
There has been documentation that this was an instrumental or a *jam*. That is not correct. There are words in the song that poked fun at law enforcement. The lyrics would never have gotten through the record company sensors and the song would not have been worthy of release on any Airplane record. The very first time I got a copy of this was years before the excellent 2003 *Crown Of Creation* remastered CD (RCA 82876 53226 2), released it as a bonus track. For some reason they only put out one of the three segments. Those that have shown this to be over ten minutes long have added the playing time of the hidden bonus track that begins to play

a few seconds after *The Saga Of Sydney Spacepig* ends. The hidden track is Jorma working on an arrangement of *Candy Man*. The best way to describe the music from The *Saga Of Sydney Spacepig* is to take two Beatles songs *Revolution No.9* and *You Know My Name (Look Up The Number)*. The song was too outlandish for *Crown Of Creation* but in a scaled down fashion it could have been to that album what *A Small Package Of Value Will Come To You, Shortly* was to *After Bathing At Baxter's*. Its inclusion on a record would have needed a *Baxter's* style album for logistical purposes.

6/13/68 Avalon Ballroom, San Francisco, California

The band did perform on that date but recorded information is from several 1966 shows. The contents of that list are found on the actual shows they were taken from.

Circa summer 1968 RCA Studios A or B, Hollywood, California, *Crown Of Creation* (Rough mixes)

These are not rough mixes but demos. Please see the entry for circa late May through late June 1968 RCA Studios A or B.

8/9/68 Soldiers & Sailors Memorial Hall, Kansas City, Kansas

The band did not perform on that night. Recorded information is from the 5/9/69 Soldiers & Sailors Memorial Hall, Kansas City, Kansas concert. Please go to that date for the details.

8/28/68 Falkoner Cenret, Copenhagen, Denmark

(79:22) (Line-up 3)

1 Stage Introduction > It's No Secret > Grace thanks the crowd 3:35

2 Watch Her Ride 3:59 With feedback and false ending.

3 Tune-Up > White Rabbit > Grace thanks the crowd > Tune-up 3:21 >

4 Plastic Fantastic Lover (Excellent playing by Jorma) > Tune-up 4:10

5 Grace intros the next one as written by Jorma (Not exactly) and sung by Paul > Fat Angel > Paul thanks the crowd 9:39

6 Short Cool Band Improvisation > Paul intros the next song :30 >

7 Star Track (Jorma vocals) > Paul intros the next song > Tune-up 7:19 >

8 Triad (F) > Grace intros the next two songs > Tune-Up 7:26 >
**This was the first appearance.** What were your feelings how *Triad* sounded live?

9 The Ballad Of You And Me And Pooneil 12:10 (F) >

10 The House At Pooneil Corners (F) > Tune-up 6:35
**This is the first time *The Ballad Of You And Me And Pooneil* was performed going into *The House At Pooneil Corners*.** For the first time played and first stand-alone version of *The Ballad Of You And Me And Pooneil* please go to 5/19/67 at the Men's State Polytechnic College, San Luis Obispo, California. It is the first appearance of *The House At Pooneil Corners*. The first stand alone version of *The House At Pooneil Corners* was on 11/1/68 at the Schuyler Hotel, 57 West 45<sup>th</sup> Street, New York City. Please see that date for the

information. The two *Pooneils* segueing into each other sounded brilliant! For almost seventeen minutes the audience experienced the pure power and energy of the Airplane machine.

11 Today 4:05

12 Paul intros the next song as it starts > Greasy Heart >

13 Tune-Up > Paul intros the next song 4:08

14 Won't You Try/Saturday Afternoon > Paul thanks the crowd > Tune-Up > Paul intros the next song 5:50

15 Somebody To Love > Grace thanks the crowd 3:19

9/10/68 Musikhalle, Hamburg, Germany

(52:57) (Line-up 3)

1 Paul intros the next song > Watch Her Ride 3:10

2 Triad (L) 6:03
**This was the final appearance.**

**3 Crown Of Creation (F) 3:34**
Jack plays fabulous bass-lines. This was the first version performed!

4 If You Feel (F) 5:28
**This was the first appearance.**

5 In Time (F) 5:21
**This was the first appearance.**

6 White Rabbit 2:24

7 Jam (No vocals) Some parts based on *3/5 Of A Mile In 10 Seconds* 12:06

8 The Ballad Of You And Me And Pooneil (With Jack bass-solo 9:44) >

9 The House At Pooneil Corners > Grace thanks the crowd

There are some fascinating events that took place during the show. *Crown Of Creation* made its debut! The band performed *If You Feel* and *In Time* back-to-back. Playing on foreign soil they could have taken the approach of performing the most noted songs of the period. They did not. The fans got to hear two very strong but not stereotypical songs and they were played one after the other. There is documentation claiming the band performed *3/5 Of A Mile In 10 Seconds* and *Won't You Try/Saturday Afternoon*. There may be merit to that, although I have not heard this performance containing even one second of those two songs.

9/15/68 Concertgebouw, Amsterdam, Holland

(59:63) (Line-up 3)

This performance has often times been listed incorrectly as being from the Paradisco. There are those that feel *Greasy Heart* was in the set list. The chances are it wasn't. This concert was a radio broadcast in Holland. If the station decided to air only an hour there were more logical tunes they would have removed. Please see songs three, eight, and nine.  There is a great percentage of the playback of the concert not being in the proper running order.

1 Won't You Try/Saturday Afternoon 5:22

2 Rock Me Baby 9:40 Jorma vocals.
This version was powerful!

3 If You Feel 4:42
The band did this rather well.  A very underrated song!  This was the final appearance.

4 Crown Of Creation 3:31

5 Today (L) 3:58
**This was the final appearance until the 1989 reunion tour.**  Tough to see this out of the set list!

6 Somebody To Love 3:39

7 Plastic Fantastic Lover 4:33

8 Somebody from the crowd wants the band to perform *Louie Louie* (F & L) and **Jack plays a couple of seconds on the bass!**  Followed by:
Nothing (Jam with vocals by Grace) (F) 10:41
This would be the only time any portion of *Louie Louie* would be performed.  The *jam* originally surfaced as *Nothing* on 9/15/68 at the Concertgebouw, Amsterdam, Holland.  It was called for one night *Tortoise Jam* on 6/13/69 Family Dog At The Great Highway, San Francisco, California.  It would become known as *Same Old Phony Handshake* on 10/25/69 Winterland, San Francisco, California (When one line was sung).  On 2/23/70 at the Fillmore West, San Francisco, California the first full version would be performed under that name.  Only these three names are correct titles.  It would be incorrectly listed as *Get Off* (Which is another *jam*), *Help Me*, *It's Easy*, *No Such Thing*, and *Thing* (Which is another *jam*).  *Louie Louie* was written by Richard Berry and it is one of the most covered song in rock and roll history.  The most well know version is from the Kingsmen.

9 In Time (L) 4:27
**This was the final appearance.**

10 The Ballad Of You & Me & Pooneil 7:37 Cut

After the performance ends there is an interview with Grace.  It seems that the person Grace spoke with wasn't a fan of the band.  Interview with Grace:  She is called Grace Silk and then asked "Why is the Jefferson Airplane not as political as Country Joe & The Fish?" 1:42

9/28/68 Ed Sullivan TV Show, New York City

(8:58) (Line-up 3)

1 Won't You Try/Saturday Afternoon 3:07
This was done during a rehearsal for the program.  It was recorded with psychedelic images in the background.  Most of the time when major bands performed on a noted TV show, they were able to play two or three songs.  The band was given one song that would air on the program.  Ed Sullivan did mention the concert they would be playing the next day and the Airplane did receive national exposure.

2 Crown Of Creation 2:49
This version is referred to as the "Backing Film." It has psychedelic images and doesn't focus as much on the group. The audience would view what is listed below.

3 Ed Sullivan intros the Jefferson Airplane :06 "**And now for the youngsters.**"

4 Crown Of Creation > Ed Sullivan talks about the concert the band will be doing tomorrow in New York City 2:56 The Airplane would be performing in Central Park. This version is what the audience viewed. The Backing Film was present with the psychedelic images but there was also more of a focus on the band performing.

Circa late Summer or fall 1968 Westpole TV Show (Essay 1) KQED, San Francisco, California

(4:17) (Line-up 3)

1 Intro by host Ralph Gleason :44

2 Ralph Gleason talks about the Jefferson Airplane :14

3 Crown Of Creation 3:19 Fades-out.
The version of *Crown Of Creation* is the studio recording.

# Jack Casady with Jimi Hendrix-

10/10/68 Winterland, San Francisco, California

(15:45)

1 Killing Floor 9:00
If you never heard about the two songs Jack joined Jimi for, the first sounds like the Who was playing *Shakin' All Over*. It is everything you would expect and more. No games or thrills, only off the scale rock and roll.

2 Hey Joe 6:45
This failed tremendously in comparison to the first song. There isn't anything that would lead you to see or listen to this more then once if you didn't know the performers on stage. Normally *Hey Joe* sounds great in any rendition. Jimi Hendrix, Deep Purple, the Byrds and the Leaves did well know versions.

# Hot Tuna (Jorma, Jack, and Spencer Dryden) with Jerry Garcia and Mickey Hart-

10/21/68 Airplane House, San Francisco, California

**This date and venue isn't correct, nor is Jorma part of the *jam* session.** The Jefferson Airplane did not perform on this date either. Please see the entry for Mickey & The Hartbeats 12/16/68, The Matrix, San Francisco, California, for complete information.

# Jefferson Airplane-

10/26/68 Fillmore West, San Francisco, California

(42:08) (Line-up 3)

This was a special night for the band. The record company was looking for material to be included on the first live album, *Bless Its Pointed Little Head*. Of the songs performed on 10/26/68 only *Rock Me Baby* made the album.

1 Fat Angel 8:31
This was an excellent opening number. The improvisation sounded strong and got the flight off the ground safely.

2 Rock Me Baby 9:17  Jorma vocals.
The version starts as slow blues for the first half and picks up in tempo later on.

3 Somebody To Love 3:30

4 Won't You Try/Saturday Afternoon 2:29 The start was cut.

5 White Rabbit 2:56 A bit slower before "When The Men On The Chessboard."

6 The Ballad Of You And Me And Pooneil 9:32 >

7 The House At Pooneil Corners 5:48
*The House At Pooneil Corners* never became the signature song that *The Ballad Of You And Me And Pooneil* was and is, but it is a terrific tune. It escalates in value when it is played following *The Ballad Of You And Me And Pooneil*.

10/30/68 The Matrix, San Francisco, California

Recorded information from this date is actually from 2/1/68 The Matrix. Please go to that date for the current information.

10/31/68 The Matrix, San Francisco, California

Recorded information from this date is actually from 2/1/68 The Matrix. Please go to that date for the current information.

11/1/68 Schuyler Hotel, 57 West 45th Street, New York City (Filming for 1AM)

(7:40) (Line-up 3)

The House At Pooneil Corners (F) 7:40
**This is the initial time the song was played as a stand-alone.** The first time it appeared was coming out of *The Ballad Of You And Me And Pooneil* on 8/28/68 at the Falkoner Cenret, Copenhagen, Denmark. Please see that date for details.

The performance was being filmed for the Jean-Luc Godard film *1 AM*. This was a fantastic piece of footage. The band is playing on the rooftop of the hotel. They know that it would be only a matter of time before the festivities would come to a screeching halt! As you would expect the facial expressions of those on the street, in their apartment, and at work, is correlated to their ages! There has been talk all these years that a second song, *Somebody To Love* was performed. What caused confusion *Somebody To Love* did indeed get played (Thank you Paul Kantner for 100 percent verification), **but as the first tune**. The only footage that seems to have been captured was *The House At Pooneil Corners*. Paul Kantner remembers if the festivities were allowed to continue, the band was going to play *Crown Of Creation*.

<u>11/10/68 The Smothers Brothers Comedy Hour</u>

(11:00) (Line-up 3)

This has been incorrectly documented as having taken place on 12/15/68. Grace's face is all brown during all the Airplane segments.

1 Crown Of Creation
The cameras focus on the entire band.

2 Lather (F & L)
**This was the first and last appearance of the song until the 1989 reunion tour.** It would seem very unlikely the song was performed at Clarkson College, Potsdam, New York on 10/6/68. There has never been a complete set list furnished of that show and there never has been anybody that has authenticated any recording. The Smothers Brothers would be the more logical debut. They could have recorded it several times for playback if they were worried about breaking in a song for the first time. Mostly shots of Grace, some of the entire band, and there are psychedelic shots as well.

**3 People Go To Be Free (Song and skit) (F & L)**
**This was the only performance of the song and or skit.** The tune was a worldwide hit for the Rascals and was written by band member Eddie Brigati. Pat Paulsen was a well known comedian from the 1960's and 1970's. Kate Smith recorded what many people feel is the finest version of *God Bless America* ever. The song was written by Irving Berlin. *Born Free* was composed by John Barry, and Don Black, with the most noted vocal by Matt Monro.

Smothers Brothers start singing > Jefferson Airplane plays one line of the song > Pat Paulsen tells a joke > Spencer Dryden sings one line of the song > Smothers Brothers sing one line from the song *Born Free* > Kate Smith sings one line from the song > Two comedic actors have a short segment about eastern Europe > Kate Smith visits a jail > Jefferson Airplane and Kate Smith sing two lines > Smothers Brothers perform a short segment on the word "no" > Jefferson Airplane and Kate Smith sing two lines.

Although the theme is serious "being free" the message is conveyed with comedic antics. Over the years I asked some fanatical Airplane fans what they thought of the idea of the skit. It turned out to be an even split. The ones that liked it felt that they were able to witness something unique, the band performing part of a cover song, and being involved with the other guests of the program. The ones that weren't enthralled by the skit were in agreement that the comedic element isn't the way a band, writer, or entertainer should express their feelings on a serious issue. Both sides make concrete points. The ultimate idea would have been for the band to perform the song without any other guests being part of the segment.

<u>11/16/68 Electric Factory, Philadelphia, Pennsylvania</u>

(63:29) (Line-up 3)

There are those that feel part of the contents of this show are from the European tour of 1968. The archival information looks to be legit about this performance.

1 Tune-up > Stage intro > It's No Secret 3:53

2 Watch Her Ride (L) 3:18 Cut.
**This was the final appearance.**

3 White Rabbit 2:12

4 Won't You Try/Saturday Afternoon 5:51

5 Grace intros Jorma > Tune-up > Star Track 8:10 Jorma vocals.

6 Tune-Up > Plastic Fantastic Lover 4:13

7 Fat Angel 10:09

8 Greasy Heart > Grace thanks the crowd 4:24

9 Tune-up > Crown Of Creation > Grace thanks the crowd > Grace by mistake is about to intro *In Time* as the next song 3:32 >

10 Philly Jam (F & L) 11:12 **This was the only appearance of the *jam*.**
No vocals on the *jam*.

11 Marty intros the next song > Improvisation > 3/5 Of A Mile In 10 Seconds > Paul thanks the crowd 6:17
The improvisation fit nicely into the intro of *3/5 Of A Mile In 10 Seconds*.

<u>11/18/68 Electric Factory, Philadelphia, Pennsylvania</u>

There is no documentation the band played this venue on that date or any other. Please see the entry for 11/16/68 Electric Factory, Philadelphia, Pennsylvania for show information.

<u>12/15/68 The Smothers Brothers Comedy Hour</u>

The correct information can be found on the entry of 11/10/68 The Smothers Brothers Comedy Hour. Please go to that date for information.

Mickey & The Hartbeats (With Jack Casady and Spencer Dryden) -

<u>12/16/68 The Matrix, San Francisco, California</u>

(81:57)

This is often mistakenly listed as 10/21/68 Jefferson Airplane House, San Francisco, California. It is very easy to decipher why erroneous information is synonymous with this show. I can remember specifically getting a two tape copy of this in 1976. The tapes was labeled Airplane House 10/21/68 (Tape 1 and 2) and a list of five names appeared on the cases, they were Jorma, Jack, Spencer, Jerry Garcia, and Mickey Hart. A major clue that the date and venue were incorrect would be there is no documentation of Jorma, Jack, and Spencer playing outside the Jefferson Airplane with each other at the same time. What further complicated the issue was the tape started with what is often listed by Grateful Dead fans as *Jam 2*. The reason for that appears to be the original recordings were on two separate reels. When they were transferred to tape the second reel seemed to be transferred first. When CD's became recordable there was another situation that made authentication even harder. Some collectors split the *jams* at a point they thought was the end. For the two song *jam*, there have been CD's that circulated with anywhere from three to four *jams*. The additional material that is found on the second tape depending on what the collector has is either another Mickey & The Heartbeats show or Hot Tuna from one of The Matrix shows from 1969. Since Spencer is only on one of the two *jams* it turned out to be something that fans of David Getz (Drummer for Big Brother & The Holding Company) were happy to add to their collections.

Thank you to Art Cohen (A true Grateful Dead historian and archivist) for letting me know the titles to the songs that were teased slightly during the second *jam*. I am documenting the performance as the master reels did but not the original tapes.

**1 Jam 37:48 Mickey & The Hartbeats without Bob Weir and Pigpen, but with Jack Casady and Spencer Dryden.**

**2 Jam 44:09 Mickey & The Hartbeats without Bob Weir and Pigpen, but with Jack Casady and David Getz. The *jam* includes teases of *Creator Has A Master Plan* (Jazz song composed by Pharoah Sanders and Leon Thomas), *Dark Star*, *Clementine*, and *China Cat Sunflower*.**

146

# Chapter 5: 1969 "Change The Strings And Notes Slide"

## Jefferson Airplane-

<u>1/2/69 Elysian Park, Los Angeles, California</u>

The band did not perform on this night. Recorded information is from 2/1/68 The Matrix, San Francisco, California. Please see that date for details.

<u>2/69 Bless Its Pointed Little Head LP (Commercial) Long Version</u>

(5:11) (Line-up 3)

1 Bless Its Pointed Little Head (Commercial) Long version 5:11
Announcer > Plastic Fantastic Lover > Jorma is asked "Why did it take so long for a live album to be released?" > Plastic Fantastic Lover > Marty quotes from the movie *King Kong* > Plastic Fantastic Lover > Paul is asked "How did you select the material for the album?" > Marty and Jorma are asked "How do you like the live album?" > Plastic Fantastic Lover > Paul and Jack are asked "How do you like the live album?" > Spencer is asked "How do you like the live album?" > Announcer outro.

Any mention of *Plastic Fantastic Lover* would be quick excerpts from the live record. Did you notice a certain member not accounted for? Interesting that if Grace had commitments that day why they would not have tried to include her in some capacity at another time. This was very well put together. The quotes from the group are often a few seconds and the music sounds nice as it is inserted several times (Short bits).

<u>2/69 Bless Its Pointed Little Head LP (Commercial) Short Version</u>

The short version is really the long version being cut after Marty was asked about King Kong. Collectors have often listed a short version but it is an exact repeat of how the long version unfolds. The short version gets cut a little after 2:00.

<u>2/11/69 Elysian Park, Los Angeles, California</u>

The band did not perform on this night. Recorded information is from 2/1/68 The Matrix, San Francisco, California. Please see that date for details.

<u>Circa 3/28/69- 6/30/69 Wally Heider Studios, San Francisco, California</u>

*Volunteers* (Album sessions)

(72:59) (Line-up 3)

1 Volunteers (Take 18) 2:12

The released version is ten seconds shorter with a more forceful intro. The unreleased version is fascinating hearing Marty sing the words. You can tell from the vocals that he is still playing around with the lyrical phrasings in his head.

2 We Can Be Together (Longer intro, and lead guitar overdub) 6:14
The unreleased version is twenty-seven seconds longer. The lead guitar intro starts at one minute and eight seconds and not at the thirty-five second mark. The result is miraculous. If for no other reason but to let the Airplane fans experience Jorma's playing at the start of the song, this needs to be unlocked a.s.a.p.

3 We Can Be Together (Paul Kantner's- Acoustic demo) 6:10
The unreleased version is twenty-three seconds longer. This is one of the finest demo's ever created. Paul is alone on acoustic guitar. His vocals are not as authoritative as if he were holding an electric guitar and other musicians were present. Paul plays the chords very well. The tone of the instrument in conjunction with his rhythm made for a result that can rival almost any demo ever created. This isn't an overstatement. The finished product of the song needed to be electrified to enhance the lyrical content but if you could ever win a prize to the Jefferson Vault, walk right to the letter "w".

4 We Can Be Together (Lead guitar overdub, master take no. 75) 6:06
The unreleased version is nineteen seconds longer. It contains an intro of one minute and two seconds, as compared to the thirty five second version on the album. The intro isn't as long as the one minute and eight seconds that was documented above. The one flaw the unreleased version possesses is a muffled sounding mix.

5 Good Shepherd (Vocal overdubs on master take) 4:25
There aren't a lot of nuances to report. The unreleased version is three seconds longer and doesn't sound as well mixed as the album version.

6 Good Shepherd (Different vocal overdubs on master take) 4:28
The unreleased version is six seconds longer and there is a more relaxed vocal from Jorma. It makes for a nice alternate of a tremendous tune.

7 The Farm (Acoustic guitar overdubs on the master take) 3:00
The released version is eight seconds longer. The vocals are mixed better on the album version.

8 The Farm (Different acoustic guitar overdubs on the master take) 3:10
The unreleased version is two seconds longer than the album version.

9 Turn My Life Down (Demo, take no. 33) 2:59
The unreleased version is seven seconds longer. The vocal mix is lower than you would have anticipated but the acoustic guitar is more elevated.

10 Wooden Ships (Alternate take) With: Go Ride The Music > J.P.P. McStep B. Blues (Alternate take) With: Go Ride The Music 8:24
This is a buried treasure that should be in the hands of every Airplane fan worldwide. Once again the band looked at the possibility of putting *J.P.P. McStep B. Blues* on vinyl. This time it was going to be part of a medley. It is hard to believe this version which even got performed live didn't make it to the finish line. *Wooden Ships* by itself is six minutes and twenty-five seconds on the album. *J.P.P. McStep B. Blues* would have added between two and two and one half minutes. The alternate take of *Wooden Ships* did not have the very low intro as on the LP. *J.P.P. McStep B. Blues* had a sound effect added to the start of the song. The noise is the only thing that mares the entire medley.

11 Wooden Ships (First vocal take) > Go Ride The Music > J.P.P. McStep B. Blues (Instrumental version) 8:23
The noise effect is also present at the start of this version of *J.P.P. McStep B. Blues*.
This was interesting to see how *J.P.P. McStep B. Blues* would sound as an instrumental following *Wooden Ships*. The vocals are in their basic stages. The harmony line that repeats "Na" is absent. Since *J.P.P. McStep B. Blues* is without any lyrics the band decides not to tack on the *Go Ride The Music* portion during the instrumental segment. *Wooden Ships* on its own merit sails proudly. It would be hard in retrospect to want perfection tinkered with. At the time of creation if the version released would have had *J.P.P. McStep B. Blues* it would never have lost any of its greatness.

12 A Song For All Seasons 3:28 (Alternate vocal mix)
This version has been given erroneous information. There are not alternate vocals! There is an alternate vocal mix. Alternate lyrics would have made this an excellent newly found treasure. The words are the same as on

the album. Spencer's voice is set too low for a song that is carried by a story he is telling through the lyrics. The recording date has sometimes been listed as 8/28/69 that is not correct. The band did not have commitments that day. It also is out of the time frame that would have made sense for the recording process. The released version is two seconds shorter. The alternate contains a false ending.

13 Hey Fredrick (With lead guitar overdubs) Instrumental version 6:40
The released version with vocals was one minute and forty-seven seconds longer. The alternate has a cold ending, while the album version has a quick fade-out. The vocals enhance the song but hearing the instrumental version gives you the feeling of an entirely different element of the song.

14 Hey Fredrick (Different take with lead guitar overdubs) Instrumental version 7:10
The released version is one minute and seventeen seconds longer. Both versions fade-out. This seems more together than the version above and the playing is more intense.

If you are keeping score at home which two songs from the *Volunteers* album do we not have an alternate version to talk about? That is excellent! *Eskimo Blue Day* (One of the finest tracks from the band) and *Meadowlands*.

Circa 3/28/69- 6/30/69 Wally Heider Studios, San Francisco, California (*Hey Fredrick*- Rough mix)

(8:07) (Line-up 3)

1 Hey Fredrick 8:07
This version of the song does have the vocals in the mix. It is twenty seconds shorter than the album version. The most noticeable difference is the lower mix of the piano and guitar when they first make their appearance.

Circa 4/17/69 Wally Heider Studios, San Francisco, California

(4:32) (Line-up 3)

Out-take, or rough mix

1 Good Shepherd 4:32
This is being listed twice because there is debate if this version got taken from the 1968 *Crown Of Creation* out-takes or rough mixes, circa 2/68- 9/68 RCA Studios A and or B, Hollywood, California. The released version is ten seconds shorter and contains background vocals that is highlighted by Grace singing "La la la la." The unreleased has no vocal overdubs and a lower vocal mix. It sounds even in the earliest stages that with a bit of polishing *Good Shepherd* would become synonymous with Jorma.

4/26/69 Swing Auditorium, San Bernardino, California

(69:37) (Line-up 3)

1 Stage Intro > 3/5 Of A Mile In 10 Seconds 5:29

2 Somebody To Love > Paul intros the next song 4:45

3 Wooden Ships (F): With: Go Ride The Music > Tune-up 8:05
**This was the first time performed!** The first and only time played with *J.P.P. McStep B. Blues* would be 6/13/69 Family Dog, San Francisco, California.

4 Fat Angel 10:06

5 Uncle Sam Blues (F) 6:49 Jorma vocals.
**This is the first appearance.** The band has terrific energy going on as Jorma and his six strings do their thing.

6 Plastic Fantastic Lover > Tune-up > Grace does a couple second vocal tease of *It's No Secret* (F & L) 3:51 >

7 It's No Secret 3:53

8 Greasy Heart 5:24

9 Won't You Try/Saturday Afternoon (Not from the start) 2:42

10 Volunteers with some improvised lyrics by Grace (F) 5:03
**This was first time played!** The power and passion were present and the song would become one of the most important created in the Jefferson Family legacy of masterpieces.

11 Jam 3:14
The sound is somewhat similar to *The Other Side Of This Life*.

12 White Rabbit 3:02

13 The Other Side Of This Life 7:14

This show is often forgotten about. When history is traced it gave us both the debut of *Uncle Sam Blues* and *Volunteers*. Those two songs alone would have made for an unforgettable night of music.

# Jack Casady with Jimi Hendrix-

4/27/69 Oakland Coliseum, Oakland, California

(17:42)

1 Jimi intros Jack Casady > Voodoo Child (Slight Return) with band introductions.
**Jimi intros Jack Casady by mistake as Jack Bruce** (Cream) 17:42
It is the full scale blowtorch you would hope for. The only flaw in the construction of the song was the two times the tempo got slowed down. The intensity needed to stay at the same level. That is a minor gripe, because at least fifteen minutes were the magical moments that you could see on any given night in the 1960's.

# Jefferson Airplane-

5/7/69 Polo Field, Golden Gate Park, San Francisco, California, (Afternoon show)

(71:32) (line-up 3)

1 The Other Side Of This Life 6:36 There was an excellent Jorma guitar solo.

2 Grace thanks the crowd > Somebody To Love 4:14 Jorma's guitar at the beginning sounds like Hot Tuna circa 1975-1977 as it explodes with thunder.

3 The Farm (F) 2:59
**This is the first appearance.** *The Farm* was never performed all that many times live.

4 Greasy Heart 4:03

**5 Good Shepherd (F) 5:30**
**This is the first time performed.** 5/9/69 Soldiers & Sailors Memorial Hall, Kansas City, Kansas, would be the first time Jorma sings the song. Please go to that date for the information. Mostly Grace vocals with Paul very light background vocals! This is one of **the most unique occurrences during the bands live history**. As the vocals are ready to come in you are waiting for Jorma's voice. It never materialized! Grace is singing the lead and Paul is handling the background. Grace sings the song without any improvisational vocals and Jorma plays as if the band had been performing the song for ages.

**6 Plastic Fantastic Lover 3:58**
Jorma's intro to this is frantic and fantastic!

**7 Uncle Sam Blues 7:43** Jorma vocals.

**8 Tune-up > Grace does a couple of announcements for people that got separated from their friends or family >**
Volunteers with some improvised lyrics by Marty (*Love Is Everywhere*) (F & L) 5:12
This would be the only time Marty did the vocal improvisation.

**9 White Rabbit 2:35**

**10 Won't You Try/Saturday Afternoon 5:06 Cut.**

**11 Jam In The Key Of D (F & L) 10:25**
**This was the only time performed.**

**12 We Can Be Together (F) > Tune-up and some sound trouble > Paul intros the next song as *Mexico* 6:12**
There is no documentation available from this performance about *Mexico*. If *Mexico* was played, it would have been the first appearance. The first documented appearance was on 2/7/70 at the Anaheim Convention Center, Anaheim, California. This is the first appearance of *We Can Be Together*. Please see 6/26/70 the Kralingen Pop Festival, Rotterdam, Holland for the first time it would go into *Volunteers*. The phenomenal combination of *We Can Be Together* and *Volunteers* are ready to continue carrying the torches of greatness.

**13 Tune-up 3/5 Of A Mile In 10 Seconds 6:49**

5/9/69 Soldiers & Sailors Memorial Hall, Kansas City, Kansas

(60:37) (Line-up 3)

Any documentation showing longer playing time are erroneously counting three songs after *The Ballad Of You And Me And Pooneil* that were not part of the performance.

1 It's No Secret 3:02

**2 Good Shepherd (F) 5:24** Jorma vocals.
**This would be the second time the song is performed, and the <u>first</u> with Jorma taking on the lead vocals.**
The debut of the tune was 5/7/69 Polo Field, Golden Gate Park, San Francisco, California when Grace sang lead and Paul background. Please go to that date for the information.

3 Grace intros the next song > Watch Her Ride 3:03

4 The Other Side Of This Life 7:02

5 Martha 4:54

6 Crown Of Creation 3:01

7 The Farm 2:35

8 Won't You Try/Saturday Afternoon 4:55

9 Star Track (L) 4:34 Jorma vocals.
**This was the last appearance of the song.** Jorma had enough tremendous material to sing lead on several songs per show.  Since that wouldn't be the case a fantastic song gets retired.

10 Wooden Ships > Go Ride The Music > J.P.P. McStep B. Blues (F) > Go Ride The Music 6:54
You could never say enough how great it sounded when *Wooden Ships* had been performed along with *J.P.P. McStep B. Blues*.  **This is the first time the song was performed since 11/26/66 Fillmore Auditorium, San Francisco, California.**  The 11/25/66 show had *J.P.P. McStep B. Blues* as a stand-alone song.  This would be the first appearance of *J.P.P. McStep B. Blues* sandwiched between *Go Ride The Music*.

11 One Of These Days 10:28 Jam with Grace improvising the vocals. (F & L).
**This would be the only time ever performed.**  It is not the Pink Floyd song from *Meddle* released 11/11/71.

12 The Ballad Of You And Me And Pooneil 4:45 With Jack bass-solo.  The song was cut.

5/9/69 Soldiers And Sailors Memorial Hall, Kansas City, Missouri

Please See 5/9/69 Soldiers And Sailors Memorial Hall, Kansas City, Kansas.  The correct location of the venue is the state of Kansas.

5/28/69 Winterland, San Francisco, California

(90:34) (Line-up 3)

1 Won't You Try/Saturday Afternoon > Grace thanks the crowd 5:02

2 Somebody To Love 4:02

3 Young Girl Sunday Blues 3:48

4 Wooden Ships: With: Go Ride The Music 6:32

5 Paul intros the next song > Volunteers 3:52

6 Tune-up > Come Back Baby 7:17 Jorma vocals.
The intro had you wonder if they were going into a *jam*.

7 Tune-up > Fat Angel 8:39 Paul intros the next song > Plastic Fantastic Lover 5:05

8 Tune-Up > Grace intros the next song > Greasy Heart 4:41

9 Tune-Up > Grace intros the next song > Tune-up >

10 We Can Be Together 6:35 Tune-up >

11 Crown Of Creation 4:16

12 (3/5 Of A Mile In 10 Seconds) 5:30
The version is highlighted by terrific interplay between Jorma and Jack during the guitar break.

13 Grace intros the next song > Thing (Instrumental jam) > You Wear Your Dresses Too Short (F) 18:50
**This is the first time performed.** The initial time that it would be played without coming out of a *jam* would be 10/26/69 Winterland, San Francisco, California. Grace points out that everybody plays on *Thing* but her! Marty had a great vocal inflection during the part of the song when he sings *Sock It To Me Baby*. He could have been paying homage to Mitch Ryder with *Sock It To Me Baby* and or Otis Redding. The co-writers of *Sock It To Me Baby* were Russell Brown and Bob Crewe. Mitch Ryder & the Detroit Wheels are well noted for their version. Otis Redding was the composer of the song *Respect* and many performers have used that line. Aretha Franklin had an amazingly famous version.

14 Wild Tyme > Marty intros the next song as *The Ballad Of You And Me* and not *The Ballad Of You And Me And Pooneil*. 6:09
There is no recorded information about the version of *The Ballad Of You And Me And Pooneil* performed.

6/69 Avalon Ballroom, San Francisco, California

Recorded information about this date is really 6/13/69 The Family Dog, San Francisco, California. Please see that date for the information.

6/7/69 Winterland, San Francisco, California

The band did not perform on that night. Recorded information about this date is really 6/13/69 The Family Dog, San Francisco, California. Please see that date for the information.

6/13/69 Family Dog At The Great Highway, San Francisco, California

(73:06) (Line-up 3)

The documentation from this performance is one of the most incorrectly recorded in the history of the band. The Airplane did play this venue on the thirteenth, fourteenth, and sixteenth. The only show that has ever been authenticated is from the thirteenth. One of the original points of confusion was former legendary progressive rock station KSAN, San Francisco had broadcast the performance. When it was repeated music from other dates were included. Any notations that *Eskimo Blue Day* had been performed are not correct. That was from the 2/4/70 taping of A Night At The Family Dog. Further complicating the archival history of the show were listings of the songs as coming from 6/69 Avalon Ballroom, San Francisco, 10/19/67 Warfield Theater, San Francisco (The band performed on that night but there is no documentation of the correct songs played), and 6/7/69 Winterland. The band did not have a show on that night. The opening *Tortoise Jam* would only have the title during this performance. The *jam* originally surfaced as *Nothing* on 9/15/68 at the Concertgebouw, Amsterdam, Holland. It was called for one night *Tortoise Jam* on 6/13/69 Family Dog At The Great Highway, San Francisco, California. It would become known as *Same Old Phony Handshake* on 10/25/69 Winterland, San Francisco, California (When one line was sung). On 2/23/70 at the Fillmore West, San Francisco, California the first full version would be performed under that name. Only these three names are correct titles. It would be incorrectly listed as *Get Off* (Which is another *jam*), *Help Me*, *It's Easy*, *No Such Thing*, and *Thing* (Which is another *jam*).

1 Tortoise Jam (F & L) 13:59 >

2 Grace talks about almost every subject 3:13 >

3 Grace ends the stage chatter > The band gets ready for the next song :32

4 The Ballad Of You And Me And Pooneil 7:59

5 Paul welcomes the crowd and intros the next song by Freddie Neil > The Other Side Of This Life 6:21

6 Wooden Ships: With Go Ride The Music 5:55 (A bit more laid back) >

7 J.P.P. McStep B. Blues (L) > Go Ride The Music 2:33
**Unfortunately this would be the final time the song would ever be performed.**

8 Crown Of Creation 2:58

9 Greasy Heart 3:26

10 Good Shepherd 6:38 Jorma vocals.
Jorma's guitar playing is highly inspired throughout the song.

11 Fat Angel 9:13

12 Volunteers 3:41
Interesting version with improvisational lyrics.

13 The House At Pooneil Corners 6:32

### 6/14/69 Family Dog At The Great Highway, San Francisco, California

The band did perform on that night but recorded information is from the 6/13/69 Family Dog At The Great Highway, San Francisco, California concert. Please go to that date for the information. It is possible this night or 6/16/69 was the first time Joey Covington played with the Airplane. **Yes the Airplane**. **Welcome aboard the flight Joey.** Without question he performed with them on 8/2/69 Atlantic City Racetrack, Atlantic City, New Jersey. He also performed certain shows prior with and without Spencer!

### 6/16/69 Family Dog At The Great Highway, San Francisco, California

The band did perform on that night, but recorded information is from the 6/13/69 Family Dog At The Great Highway, San Francisco, California concert. Please go to that date for the information. It is possible this night or 6/14/69 was the first time Joey Covington played with the Airplane. **Yes the Airplane**. **Welcome aboard the flight Joey.** Without question he performed with them on 8/2/69 Atlantic City Racetrack, Atlantic City, New Jersey. He also performed certain shows prior with and without Spencer!

### 7/9/69 Winterland, San Francisco, California

There is no documentation the band performed on this night. Recorded information is from the 6/13/69 Family Dog At The Great Highway, San Francisco, California concert. Please go to that date for the information.

### 8/2/69 Atlantic City Racetrack, Atlantic City, New Jersey

There is no information about the songs that were performed this night. The entry is placed here because it is a great trivia question, who was the drummer for this show? **Excellent answer, it was Joey Covington.** It is very possible his first performance with the Airplane was 6/14/ or 6/16/69 The Family Dog, San Francisco, California.

8/2/69 Fillmore East, New York City, or Winterland, San Francisco, California

Recorded information with the above listings is incorrect. The band was playing at the Atlantic City Racetrack, Atlantic City, New Jersey. A great trivia question is to name the drummer? Very good! It was Joey Covington. Information furnished from that date is listed as Winterland, San Francisco, California 10/4/70. There is a lot of confusion if 10/4/70 was the date of the performance, or the date that San Francisco radio stations KSAN, and KQED, as well as KQED-TV broadcast the show. This very well could have been a playback date. There is not one hundred percent certainty that this was a date in the Bill Graham file. The band did perform at Winterland on 10/1/70 and 10/5/70. Since 10/5/70 was the first show with Papa John Creach and he is not mentioned in the documentation it is either from 10/1/ or 10/4/70 . Please go to 10/4/70 Winterland for details.

8/10/69 Sheep Meadow, Central Park, New York City

(78:33) (Line-up 3)

1 The Other Side Of This Life 6:35 Cut.

2 Won't You Try/Saturday Afternoon 5:04

3 The Ballad Of You And Me And Pooneil 8:23 The start was cut.

4 Come Back Baby 5:42 Jorma vocals. The start was cut.

5 Fat Angel 7:56 Including improvisational lyrics by Paul.

6 Plastic Fantastic Lover 3:03

7 Somebody To Love 3:33

8 Wooden Ships: With: Go Ride The Music 5:59

9 (3/5 Of A Mile In 10 Seconds) 5:24

10 White Rabbit 2:09

11 We Can Be Together 5:53

12 Volunteers 3:21

13 Mau Mau (Amerikon) (F) 15:31
**This was the first appearance.**
*Mau Mau* possessed a bit of *Feel So Good*, in fact at 9:30 Jorma played the riff and repeated it several times. When this song was changed around and completed it turned up on Paul's 1970 release *Blows Against The Empire*. During the performance Paul sang most of verse one, and all of verses three, and four. The band had a lot of confidence that this could be presented in an optimum situation. This was made obvious by having it as the final song of the gig. The results were intense. The lyrics by Paul in conjunction with fine guitar work by Jorma left a calling card that this song would be worthy of recording. (A shame not be the J.A.).

8/17/69 Woodstock Music Festival, Max Yasgur's Farm, Bethel, New York

(34:44) (Line-up 3, and **Nicky Hopkins** on piano)

One of the fascinating things about this event is how the set list appears incorrectly almost all the time. What you see below **is the way the show unfolded**. Those that have written information with the songs in a different order were mislead that any video shown of the performance was always in sequence.

1 Stage Intro :15 > Tune-up >

2 Grace talks to the audience :22 >

3 The Other Side Of This Life 1:41 Song fades out.
An amazing fact is with a half a million fans in attendance a complete version of this song <u>has never shown up</u>.

4 Plastic Fantastic Lover 4:20

5 Volunteers 2:46

6 Tune-up > Won't You Try/Saturday Afternoon 5:20

7 Tune-up > Grace talks to the audience > Eskimo Blue Day (F) >
**This was the first appearance of the song.** They certainly didn't choose an obscure concert for it! The first time with only J.A. members performing the song was on 10/25/69 at Winterland, San Francisco, California. Please see that date for information.

8 Grace thanks the crowd > Tune-up 6:47

9 Uncle Sam Blues 6:08 Jorma vocals.

10 Somebody To Love 4:19

11 White Rabbit 2:40

Woodstock will always be known as one of the most famous gatherings in the world. What has always been unfair to many of the performers is the festival as a whole overshadows some good rock and roll. This wasn't the best performance the band ever had but in no way was it without value. The set was very consistent with a chance to hear the music sounding a bit differently thanks to Nicky Hopkins. If you should have any portion of video and or audio of the concert, listen to the Airplane set twice. The first time focus on the music. The second time isolate the fine playing by Nicky Hopkins. There are incalculable reasons why he was always in such demand for session work and live performances. Nicky Hopkins could enhance a piece, play the basics, or handle the more complex improvisations.

After the 8/18/69 Dick Cavett Show, Nicky would not perform again with the Airplane in a live environment. You can find him helping out on the *Volunteers* LP, and the reunion record.

<u>8/18/69 Dick Cavett Show</u> (Recording date)

(16:40 ) (Line-up 3 and **Nicky Hopkins on piano** one last time live. Did I mention **David Crosby** sings background on *Somebody To Love*. Sorry I forgot. David Crosby sings background on *Somebody To Love*. Glad I remembered.

1 We Can be Together 6:25
The song is performed with psychedelic images in the background.

2 Volunteers 3:06

3 Somebody To Love (**With David Crosby background vocals**) 3:42

4 Jam (Cut) 3:57 (**David Crosby stays on stage to shake his tambourine**).

Considering the band performed at Woodstock the prior day, this was rather enjoyable. It is always cool when contemporaries of the Airplane share the same stage. David Crosby certainly was not only a contemporary but a close friend. All versions ever seen of the *jam* are edited and cut. The band starts to play and the show breaks for a commercial. When they come back there is no time left and the band plays as the program goes off the air. Why were so many commercials aired? The advertisements were better back then. It actually wasn't funny how little the appearance of the band meant to the higher-ups of the program, after the Airplane started to perform the *jam* they played all of two minutes and twenty-one seconds, and they went to commercials. They go back to the Airplane still playing, and thirty-three seconds later more commercials were aired. They come back for a minuscule one minute and three seconds, and the show ends! The uncut footage of the entire *jam* has never seen the light of day.

8/19/69 Dick Cavett Show

This was the playback date. Please see the previous entry 8/18/69 for the information.

9/1/69 International Speedway, Baton Rouge, Louisiana

The band did perform on that night. Unfortunately the information is mistakenly documenting the 9/6/69 Family Dog At The Great Highway, San Francisco, California performance. There hasn't been any verified set list from that night. Please see that date for details.

9/6/69 Family Dog At The Great Highway, San Francisco, California

(86:01) (Line-up 3)

There are many who felt that the band did not perform on this night and any information is from the 9/7/69 Family Dog At The Great Highway, San Francisco, California performance. I stand with the Airplane performing on this night and the Grateful Dead the next. Too many collectors of Grateful Dead music have the documentation the same way. Those that have documented information from 9/1/69 International Speedway, Baton Rouge, Louisiana, are actually listing the contents of this performance. The band did play on that night but there never has been a proper set list appearing for the fans to review.

**A couple of good friends show up later on!**

1 The Ballad Of You And Me And Pooneil (F) > Starship (F) 15:25
**This is the first time that *The Ballad Of You And Me And Pooneil* did not either stand-alone or go into *The House At Pooneil Corners*.** This is the first appearance of *Starship*. The only time it would be a stand-alone song would be 9/14/70 at the Fillmore West, San Francisco, California. Please see that date for details. Paul sings about fifteen percent of the lyrics but the band kept *The Ballad Of You And Me And Pooneil* theme going. The J.A. did a prodigious job with the transition from *Pooneil* into *Starship*. Paul handles the vocals with a lot of passion and the band was rather comfortable with the alternate finish to a great number.

2 Good Shepherd 7:02 Jorma lead vocals.

3 We Can Be Together 5:56

4 Drum Intro > Somebody To Love 3:50

5 The Farm (L) 3:03
Near the end of the song Jorma plays a "riff" from *Good Lovin (F & L)*. The song was written by Rudy Clark and Arthur Resnick. It was a hit for the Rascals and the Grateful Dead did a well known version. This was the only time the riff got played. This was the final appearance of *The Farm*.

6 Crown Of Creation 3:18

7 Come Back Baby 5:49 Jorma lead vocals.

8 Wooden Ships: With: Go Ride The Music 6:10

9 Volunteers: Including a short Spencer Dryden drum-solo 4:08

**10 Jam: With Jerry Garcia 5:49**

**11 Spencer Dryden Drum Solo > Space Jam 25:22 (F & L) with <u>Jerry Garcia and Mickey Hart from the Grateful Dead.</u> This is the only performance of the *jam*.** Look at the playing time of the *jam* with Jerry Garcia and Mickey Hart. **It is the longest time of an Airplane improvisation, *jam*, or song ever!** Hot Tuna will repay the favor the next night. Please see that entry for information and the legendary *Rock And Roll Jam*.

## Jorma, Jack, and Joey Covington, Jam with the Grateful Dead-

<u>9/7/69 Family Dog At The Great Highway, San Francisco, California</u>

**(27:41) Jorma, Jack, and Joey Covington, Jam with the Grateful Dead.**

**Rock And Roll Jam: With the Grateful Dead including:**

1 Peggy Sue 3:34 Jorma vocals.

2 That'll Be The Day 3:50 Jerry vocals.

3 Johnny B. Goode 3:43 Jerry vocals.

4 Baby What You Want Me To Do 4:55 Jorma vocals.

5 Pipeline (Instrumental) 1:45 >

6 Big Railroad Blues 3:44 Jerry vocals.

7 Louie, Louie 2:49 > Joey Covington vocals.

8 Twist And Shout 1:33 > Joey Covington vocals.

9 Blue Moon 1:43 Joey Covington vocals.

*Peggy Sue* was composed by Jerry Allison and made popular by *Buddy Holly*.

*That'll Be The Day* was composed by Jerry Allison and made popular by *Buddy Holly*.

*Johnny B. Goode* was composed and made popular by Chuck Berry.

*Baby What You Want Me To Do*, also called *You Got Me Running*, was composed by Jimmy Reed and made popular by Hot Tuna.

*Pipeline* was composed by Brian Carman and Bob Spickard, and made popular by the Ventures and Dick Dale.

*Big Railroad Blues* was composed by Noah Lewis, and made popular by the Grateful Dead, and Hot Tuna.

*Louie Louie* was composed by Richard Berry and made popular by the Kingsmen.

*Twist And Shout* was composed by Phil Medley and Bert Russell, and made popular by the Beatles, and the Isley Brothers.

*Blue Moon* was composed by Richard Rodgers and Lorenz Hart, and made popular by Elvis Presley, and the Marcels.

# Jefferson Airplane-

10/10/69 Agrodome, Vancouver, Canada

(107:17) (Line-up 3)

There has been recorded information listing *White Rabbit* as part of the concert and no mention of *The House At Pooneil Corners*. It is possible that *White Rabbit* did get performed but there isn't complete authentication. Any mention of the band performing longer then the 107:17 is incorrect. There have been erroneous listings of five additional songs after *The House At Pooneil Corners*.

1 Won't You Try/Saturday Afternoon 5:12

2 Somebody To Love 4:12

3 Young Girl Sunday Blues 4:18

4 Wooden Ships: With Go Ride The Music 7:06

5 Paul intros the next song > Volunteers > Tune-up 3:34

6 Come Back Baby 7:00 Jorma vocals > Tune-up

7 Fat Angel 9:37

8 Plastic Fantastic Lover 3:15

9 Grace chatters with a fan > Tune-up > Paul intros the next song 1:16 >

10 Tune-up > Greasy Heart > Grace intros the next song 4:25

11 We Can Be Together > Tune-up 6:42

12 Marty intros the next song > Tune-up > Crown Of Creation 3:32

13 Paul intros the next song as it starts > 3/5 Of A Mile In 10 Seconds 5:37

14 Vancouver Jam (F & L) > You Wear Your Dresses To Short 18:35
**Very well done. The *jam* leads seamlessly into the vocal. This was the only appearance of the *Vancouver Jam*.**

15 Wild Tyme 4:32

16 The Ballad Of You And Me And Pooneil (L) (With Jack bass-solo) 11:47 >

17 The House At Pooneil Corners (L) 5:38 Cut.
**This is the final time the two *Pooneils* would be performed with one going into the other.**  The last time *The House At Pooneil Corners* would be performed as a stand-alone song was on 10/31/69 at the Los Angeles Forum, Inglewood, California.  Please see that date for details.

<u>10/25/69 Winterland, San Francisco, California</u>

(93:55) (Line-up 3)

1 Tune-up > :11

2 Somebody To Love 4:09

3 Young Girl Sunday Blues 3:35

4 Wooden Ships: With: Go Ride The Music > Tune-up 7:07

5 Volunteers 2:59

Won't You Try/Saturday Afternoon > Tune-up > 5:56

6 Uncle Sam Blues 5:58 Jorma vocals.

7 Fat Angel 10:27 > Tune-up >

8 Greasy Heart 3:59
Jorma played exceptionally well during *Fat Angel* and the band was very energetic performing *Greasy Heart*.

9 Paul asks for more monitor > Tune-up > :19

10 Martha > Tune-up 4:58

11 Grace's stage chatter > The Ballad Of You And Me And Pooneil 10:10

12 Tune-up >:44

13 Tune-up > Eskimo Blue Day (F) > Tune-up > 6:14
**This is the first time the song was performed with only members of the band.**  Nicky Hopkins played piano on the very first appearance on 8/17/69 at the Woodstock Music Festival, Max Yasgur's Farm, Bethel, New York.  Please see that date for information.

14 (3/5 Of A Mile In 10 Seconds) 5:58
There was an excellent intro to the song.  It sounded as if Spencer is taking a short drum-solo.  After the first verse Marty was heard saying "I forgot the words."

15 Mau Mau (Amerikon) (L)
Paul changed some lyrics from verse one and sang some of the second > Grace tells the boys to bring it down to sea level > Fishman Jam (F & L) (With Grace on vocals) > Same Old Phony Handshake (Grace sings only that line) (F) > Fishman Jam (With more vocals by Grace) 14:36
**This was the final appearance of the song *Mau Mau (Amerikon)*.  This was the only performance of the *Fishman Jam*.**  This was not related to the song *Fishman* from Paul and Grace's 1973 album *Baron Von Tollbooth &*

*The Chrome Nun. Same Old Phony Handshake* originally surfaced as *Nothing* on 9/15/68 at the Concertgebouw, Amsterdam, Holland. It was called for one night *Tortoise Jam* on 6/13/69 Family Dog At The Great Highway, San Francisco, California. It would become known as *Same Old Phony Handshake* on 10/25/69 Winterland, San Francisco, California (When one line was sung). On 2/23/70 at the Fillmore West, San Francisco, California the first full version would be performed under that name. Only these three names are correct titles. It would be incorrectly listed as *Get Off* (Which is another *jam*), *Help Me*, *It's Easy*, *No Such Thing*, and *Thing* (Which is another *jam*).

16 The Other Side Of This Life 6:28 (With Marty singing one line from *I'm Going Home*).
Marty sings one line from the Ten Years After song *I'm Going Home*. (F & L). Written by band member Alvin Lee. **It is the only time Marty would do this.** *Mau Mau* ended up on the 10/70 Paul Kantner album *Blows Against The Empire*.

10/26/69 Winterland, San Francisco, California

(91:53) (Line-up 3)

1 Good Shepard (The intro is cut.) Jorma vocals > Tune-up 6:14

2 Wild Tyme (L) > Tune-up 3:40
This is the final appearance. Not surprisingly the live version has come to a finale.

3 Greasy Heart > Tune-up 4:59

4 We Can Be Together > Tune-up 7:48

5 Come Back Baby (Jorma vocals) > Tune-up 6:51

6 Martha 3:02

7 Plastic Fantastic Lover > Tune-up 4:07

8 Drifting (F) 4:34 (Also incorrectly known as *Driftin*, and *Drifting Around*).
**This is the first appearance.** It is also the proper title. This would end up on the 1973 album by *Bodacious D.F.* The self–titled LP by the band had Marty Balin as the vocalist. The song was written by Jesse Osborne.

9 It's No Secret (L) 3:38
**This is the final appearance until the 1989 reunion tour.** It is hard to imagine an Airplane performance without this song. It would be almost twenty years before the Airplane faithful could enjoy the tune again.

10 The Other Side Of This Life > Tune-up 8:40
The band excelled on this version with superlative craftsmanship on both the structured and improvisational segments.

11 Wooden Ships: With Go Ride The Music > Tune-up 6:59

12 Eskimo Blue Day 6:06
Many consider this the best live version of the song. Grace could sing this another one hundred times and it would be difficult to surpass the power and the passion.

13 You Wear Your Dresses Too Short (F) 13:56
**This was the first time ever performed without coming out of a *jam*.** The first time played was 5/28/69 Winterland, San Francisco, California, show, when it came out of *Thing* (Jam). Marty took charge from the opening note. It starts off as if it would be a slow blues tune and as it unfolds Marty throws in some rhythm and blues phrasing to the words. When the improvisational part comes he backs off and lets the band shine.

14 The Ballad Of You And Me And Pooneil 11:00 Cut.
The version enthralled the audience with a Jack bass-solo, and a bass, and drum improvisational segment.  The last half of the show is totally intense!

10/31/69 Los Angeles Forum, Inglewood, California

(142:43) (Line-up 3)

Recorded information of this show often incorrectly states the location as Los Angeles, when it was Inglewood.  An additional inaccuracy is this performance and 5/7/70 Fillmore East, New York City were one in the same.  The set lists are different.  Please compare both entries for yourself.  What confused a lot of fans was hearing Joey Covington during the Hot Tuna portion of the shows.  Joey was a member of Hot Tuna before the Airplane.  The contents below have the correct order of both the Airplane and Hot Tuna sets.  There has been erroneous information that *Plastic Fantastic Lover* did not get performed.  Often times the Hot Tuna set has been listed in no particular order.

1 Won't You Try/Saturday Afternoon 6:15

2 Volunteers > Tune-up 3:50

3 Good Shepard 8:39 (Jorma vocals) > Tune-up >

4 Uncle Sam Blues 6:25 Jorma vocals.
Not to be overlooked here is Jorma getting two songs in a row with lead vocals.

5 Martha 2:55 (L) The start was cut.
The band had sound trouble on stage.  This was the final appearance.  Doesn't it seem even before Marty's departure more and more top shelf material is being put to rest?

6 Plastic Fantastic Lover > Paul tells the crowd "The band is taking a break so the crew can fix the sound problems." 3:59

Hot Tuna: With Jorma, Jack, Marty, and Joey, performing for a bit under thirty minutes.  (27:27)

7 Come Back Baby 6:51 Jorma vocals.

8 True Religion 4:45 Jorma vocals.

9 Drifting 4:09 Marty vocals.

10 I Can Tell 5:21 (Cut) Joey vocals.
The song was written by Ellas McDaniel and Samuel Smith.  The  most noted version is by John Hammond Jr.

11 Up Or Down 6:21 Marty Vocals.
Peter Kaukonen (Jorma's brother) wrote this song.  The Hot Tuna set ended here.

Jefferson Airplane set continues:

12 This Old Heart Of Mine (F & L) 3:17
**The only time performed!**  This is not on any Airplane Family release.  The song was composed by Lamont Dozer, Brian Holland, and Edward Holland Jr.  The Isley Brothers had a very popular version.  Marty did a magnificent job of keeping the spirit of the rhythm and blues version but putting his own vocal stamp on the tune.

13 You Wear Your Dresses Too Short 12:00 The nice thing about this piece of music it allows Jorma and Jack to flex their musical muscles before the vocal segment comes in, and then Marty is handed the torch.

14 We Can Be Together 5:58

15 Greasy Heart > Tune-up > Paul talks about Wooden Ships 4:33

16 Wooden Ships: With: Go Ride The Music 6:08

17 Young Girl Sunday Blues (L) > Tune-Up > 4:03
This was the final appearance.

18 The Other Side Of This Life 9:26

19 Fat Angel 12:59

20 The House At Pooneil Corners (L) > Tune-Up 6:18
**This was the final time ever played.** The final time ever performed coming out of *The Ballad Of You And Me And Pooneil* was on 10/10/69 at the Agrodome, Vancouver, Canada. Please see that date for details.

21 Eskimo Blue Day 5:40

22 White Rabbit: 29 The entire song was cut excluding the ending.

23 The Ballad Of You And Me And Pooneil 7:21
Although not a long version there was a Jack bass-solo and a solid improvisational segment.

**Grace Slick (W/Production by Jerry Slick) -**

Circa 11/69 Public Broadcasting, Sesame Street (Jazzy Spies) 10 Voiceovers

(7:40)

**One of the most overlooked Airplane Family collectables** happens to be Grace Slick doing ten voiceovers during the first season of the world famous children's television show Sesame Street. The segments were titled *Jazzy Spies* and each lasted forty-six seconds. It is the nineteenth most asked question in universal history why the segments weren't forty-five seconds. All of the *Jazzy Spies* were part of teaching the numbers from 1-10 to the kids watching. The format is regimented. Grace would count the numbers one through ten and then emphasize the featured number. She made her voice fit nicely with the music in the background. (They did not use either Jefferson Airplane or Great Society material). As an added bonus Jerry Slick (Great Society) was involved with the production. Jerry has a well known company Slick Film that has been involved with all sorts of video work for a number of years. The music was by Denny Zeitlin.

**Here are two great historical facts from Jerry Slick:** "I was also able to do a commercial for Jr. Hot Shoppe, with music by Nicky Hopkins, vocal by Grace, rhythm section from Steve Miller. I did other Sesame Street with music by three former members of the Great Society- Darby, Peter on sitar, vocals by Jeannie Piersol, who rehearsed with the Great Society in the very beginning, but decided to be a mom instead. Sad, 'cause Grace really liked singing with her."

11/69 Municipal Auditorium, Utica, New York

(81:38) (Line-up 3)

The exact date was never documented but it was between November sixteenth, and the twenty-fifth. Although this was a radio broadcast there are songs missing. The band would not have opened with *Good Shepherd* and some of the songs clearly had edits between them. The performance was very strong and it would have been stupendous to have gotten documentation from the opening note to the last song.

1 Good Shepherd: 49  The entire song is cut excluding the ending.

2 Tune-up> Somebody To Love 4:30

3 Uncle Sam Blues 6:06 Jorma vocals.
This has been often documented incorrectly as *Rock Me Baby*.

4 Have You Seen The Saucers 5:28
There was an excellent tempo change near the end of the song.

5 Grace thanks the crowd  > Mexico 2:13

6 Wooden Ships: With: Go Ride The Music 5:57

7 The Other Side Of This Life 7:54

8 Nothing (Jam with vocals) > Tune-Up > Grace thanks the crowd 13:57

9 Fat Angel 12:43
One of the finest versions that including a lot of improvisation and a false ending.

10 Won't You Try/Saturday Afternoon 5:03

11 Drifting (L) 3:14 Marty vocals.
**This was the final appearance.**  The general consensus was this song had sounded equally strong when performed
by Hot Tuna and the Airplane.  Unfortunately the Airplane didn't stick with this number on stage.  *Drifting* has
always been associated with the early Hot Tuna sets more than with the Airplane.  Marty would finally record this on
the self-titled Bodacious D.F. record.  More on that later on!

12 Marty intros the next song as it starts > Greasy Heart 3:22

13 The Ballad Of You And Me And Pooneil 10:14

<u>11/2/69 Elysian Park, Los Angeles, California</u>

The band did play there on that night but the recorded material is from 2/1/68 The Matrix, San Francisco, California.
Please see that entry for complete details.

<u>11/22/69 Ritchie Coliseum, College Park, Maryland</u>

(57:41) (Line-up 3)

1 The Ballad Of You And Me And Pooneil 7:40

2 White Rabbit 2:05

3 Crown of Creation 2:52

4 Wooden Ships: With: Go Ride The Music 5:43

5 Good Shepherd 6:14 Jorma vocals. >

6 Come Back Baby 5:52 Jorma vocals (Cut) >
Here was another example of Jorma getting two songs in a row to pilot the flight.

7 The Other Side of This Life 5:38

8 You Wear Your Dresses Too Short 9:49

9 Greasy Heart 3:15

10 We Can Be Together 5:33 >

11 Volunteers 2:57

<u>11/30/69 Pop Festival West Palm Beach Auditorium, West Palm Beach, Florida</u>

(59:01) (Line-up 3)

Any documented listing of more playing time is mistakenly adding a song after *Volunteers*. This show was always known for being full of high energy throughout the performance.

1 We Can Be Together > Tune-up > Grace wants the middle microphone fixed > Stage adjustments 7:16

2 Somebody To Love > Tune-up 5:12
This was an interesting version. The intro is fast and Grace has some fun improvising the lyrics.

3 Paul intros the next song as it starts > The Other Side Of This Life > Marty asks the crowd "Can you hear through the sound trouble?" 6:52

4 Good Shepherd 7:14 Jorma vocals.

5 Short Jam #1 (F & L) > You Wear Your Dresses Too Short 11:50
**This was the first and only time the *jam* was performed.**

6 Marty Calls the next song *Pooneil 1* > The Ballad Of You And Me And Pooneil
(The fast tempo at times made this a strong version). > Grace talks about the sound trouble on stage > Tune-up 10:39

7 Greasy Heart > Grace thanks the crowd > Tune-up 4:13

8 White Rabbit 2:24

9 Volunteers 3:21

<u>12/6/69 Altamont Speedway, Altamont, California</u>

(30:14) (Line-up 3)

There will never be words that properly explain the emptiness this date leaves in the heart. It wasn't only sickening for those in attendance but for any fan that has read about the off stage horrors. Those on the premises would witness death, injuries, and questioning how events could be so different not even four months removed from Woodstock.

I didn't write about the non-musical aspects during the Airplane performance, because that isn't the scope of the book. Enough has been documented previously about the non-musical brutality.

Even with the crowd the size of the Altamont show, (300,000) there are three songs we know were performed but lack documentation. They were *We Can Be Together*, *Somebody To Love*, and *Volunteers*. It is believed in order they would have been the first, third, and last song performed.

1 Stage Announcement and re-introduction of the band :31

2 The Other Side Of This Life 4:02 Grace improvises some lyrics  > The song is stopped because of trouble on the stage, and in the crowd.

3 Paul, and Grace are asking everyone to let cooler heads prevail.

4 (3/5 Of A Mile In 10 Seconds) 5:48 Marty does some vocal improvisation at the end of the song.

5 Greasy Heart 3:59

6 White Rabbit 2:16

7 Come Back Baby 1:31 Cut. Jorma vocals.

8 The Ballad Of You And Me And Pooneil 10:42 With Jack bass-solo.

## Unknown 1969 & 1970 Live Locations

44:23 (Line-up 3)

Recorded information often mistakes this from being 2/28/70 Winterland, San Francisco, California.  That is not correct.  One of the giveaways is when Paul intros *Wooden Ships* as a new song.

1 Fat Angel 13:01
Jorma finishes the last minute of the song with a flurry!

2 Paul intros the next song as new > Wooden Ships: With Go Ride the Music > J.P.P. McStep B. Blues > Go Ride The Music 8:00

3 The Other Side Of This Life 6:46  The start of the song was cut.

4 Nothing (*Jam* with vocals) 14:25

5 Mexico 2:09 Cut.

## Unknown 1969 Live Location # 2

This is another compilation of information from a few different 1969 and 1970 performances.  The contents are not listed because the actual songs can be found on the specific shows.

## 1969 We Can Be Together (Promo film)

(5:47) (Line-up 3)

This finally got released to the mass market in 2004, on the *Fly Jefferson Airplane* DVD from Eagle Rock Entertainment 30065.  The beginning is interesting Grace and Paul are filmed by themselves on stage joking as they have a conversation that can not be heard.

# Chapter 6: 1970 "Do You Know The People Out There"

<u>1970 American television- Unknown date, and program</u>

Recorded information showing notes about an unknown television performance is talking about the 8/18/69 Dick Cavett Show. Please go to that entry for details.

<u>1970 Dallas, Texas</u>

Recorded information claiming documentation from a Dallas performance are using the notes from the 3/6/70 Municipal Auditorium, Dallas, Texas concert. Please see that entry for details.

<u>1970 Greek Theatre, Los Angeles, California</u>

The band did not perform at a venue with this name located in Los Angeles. Recorded information from that date are notes from a couple of 1970 Fillmore West, San Francisco, California concerts. The contents are not listed, since you can see the specific shows for the information.

<u>1970 Fillmore West, San Francisco, California</u>

Recorded information showing only the year and venue is from documentation gathered on various San Francisco concerts from 1968-1970. The contents are not listed since the actual documentation can be found on the specific concert.

<u>1970 Unknown location</u>

(8:52) (Line-up 3)

This is often mistakenly documented as part of a show from New Orleans, Louisiana. The band did not play there.

1 Mexico 2:01

2 The Other Side Of This Life 6:51
The band clicked on this version. Jack does a nice bass-solo to get the song moving off the ground.

<u>1970 Unknown location #2</u>

Recorded information showing an unknown location is from the 11/20/70 War Memorial, Rochester, New York concert. The reason for the debate is only two songs have been authenticated and neither of them had Papa John Creach as one of the musicians. He did not perform on every tune and that is why there is debate about the authenticity. Please go to that entry for details.

<u>1970 Unknown location #3</u>

Recorded information showing an unknown location is from the 9/14/70 Fillmore West, San Francisco, California performance. Please go to that date for details.

<u>2/4/70 A Night At The Family Dog, Family Dog At The Great Highway, San Francisco, California</u>

(22:31) (Line-up 3) **With Special friends!**

The recording date of the special was 2/4/70. It was broadcast on 4/27/70, and 12/13/70.

1 The Ballad Of You And Me And Pooneil 8:21

2 Eskimo Blue Day (L) 4:49
This is the final appearance of the song.  Even without taking up five minutes of stage time the feelings were
this didn't fit into the live repertoire.  There were many that held a different view!

**3 A Super Jam: (F & L) With Jerry Garcia, and Carlos Santana 9:21 Cut.**
The *jam* included members of the Airplane, Grateful Dead, and Santana on stage.
Jorma takes the first solo and Jerry Garcia the second.  There is a noticeable edit two minutes before the *jam* was
cut and the program ended.  The music was fairly standard and the members on stage were more outstanding
than the results of the legendary get together.  **This would be the only appearance of the *jam*.**

2/7/70 Anaheim Convention Center, Anaheim, California

(127:03) (Line-up 3)

The venue is often erroneously listed as Anaheim Stadium.  The performance is often incorrectly noted as being
from 6/6/70, 6/7/70, or 7/6/70.  Hot Tuna opens up the show.

The Hot Tuna portion includes Jorma, Jack, Marty, and Joey.

1 Baby What You Want Me To Do 5:14 The beginning of the song was cut.  Jorma vocals.

2 True Religion > Tune-up 5:40 Jorma vocals.

3 Tune-up > I Can Tell 8:16 Joey vocals.

4 Drifting 3:34 Marty vocals.
Some documentation has incorrectly reversed the playing order of songs three, and four.

5 New Song (For The Morning) 4:23 Jorma vocals.

6 Whatever The Old Man Wants (Is Always Right) 6:49 Joey vocals.

7 Come Back Baby 4:49 Jorma vocals.

8 You Wear Your Dresses Too Short 9:48 Marty vocals.

There has been recorded information about the Hot Tuna set that has left out three songs they performed.  Those
songs are numbers three, four, and six.

Jefferson Airplane set begins.

1 The Other Side Of This Life 7:07

2 Somebody To Love 4:18

3 Good Shepherd 7:27 Jorma vocals.

4 The Ballad Of You And Me And Pooneil 8:25

5 Mexico  > Grace thanks the crowd 2:12

6 We Can Be Together 5:42

7 Plastic Fantastic Lover 3:23

8 Uncle Sam Blues 6:06 Jorma vocals.

9 Wooden Ships: With: Go Ride The Music 6:44

10 Greasy Heart 3:38

11 Crown Of Creation 3:35

12 Volunteers: With Marty improvising some lyrics > Grace thanks the crowd 5:11

13 Encore: Won't You Try/Saturday Afternoon 5:40

14 Encore: White Rabbit 2:21

15 Encore: Paul intros the next Song > 3/5 Of A Mile In 10 Seconds > Short Spencer drum-solo near the end > 3/5 Of A Mile In 10 Seconds 6:28

This show is interesting because it is more known for the Hot Tuna performance. The Airplane set was fine, but there weren't any standout selections.

Circa 2/16/70 Wally Heider Studios, San Francisco, California

(14:40) (Line-up 3)

1970 sessions

1 Frozen Noses (Grace demo) 3:50
Grace approaches the song in the style of *Triad*. This was not a gem. The guitar, and vocals don't mesh well. If the song had not been abandoned there would have been considerable work to make this presentable.

2 Mexico (Grace demo) 2:22
This is with acoustic guitar. It is tremendous. The demo is actually sixteen seconds longer than the version released on the 1974 album *Early Flight*, from Grunt Records 10437.

3 Mexico (Full band) 2:16
The version with the full band is ten seconds longer than the one that would be released. The vocal mix is high, as is Jorma's guitar. It is a solid rendition of the song.

4 Been So Long (With electric overdubs, instrumental) 4:12
This is a guitar only version of the song that was released on a Hot Tuna album *First Pull Up, Then Pull Down* 1971 RCA 4550. It would be their second release and second live affair. The debut was acoustic but this was electric. The unreleased version is twenty-seven seconds longer than the Hot Tuna version from 1971. Jorma's configuration of the song at the time was already brilliant.

2/23/70 Fillmore West, San Francisco, California

(74:48) (Line-up 3)

Recorded information from this show has sometimes documented the venue incorrectly as Winterland. Those that have listed *Wooden Ships* and *Fat Angel* being part of the performance may be correct, but only the music found below has been substantiated. Erroneous information about the performance has omitted *Emergency* and

*3/5 Of A Mile In 10 Seconds*.  The order of the songs performed has been incorrect on a number of occasions.  There were not two *jam's* performed.  Those documenting *Thing* and *Same Old Phony Handshake* or *Same Old Phony Handshake* being performed twice are mistaken.

Please see the information below.

1 We Can Be Together 5:33 >

2 Volunteers 3:23

3 Good Shepherd 7:09 Jorma vocals.

4 Tune-Up > Drum Intro > Somebody To Love 4:53

5 Emergency (F) 1:26  The start of the song is cut.
This was the first appearance.  The song never became one of the most noted but they attempted to give it a large push.  It would receive national TV exposure on 3/26/70 for the Dick Cavett Show ABC TV Studios, New York City.

6 Uncle Sam Blues 6:07 Jorma vocals.

7 Tune-up > Have You Seen The Saucers (F) 8:07
**This was the first appearance of the song.**

8 Grace thanks the crowd > Mexico 2:18

9 The Other Side Of This Life 8:29

10 Same Old Phony Handshake (F) 13:59
The *jam* originally surfaced as *Nothing* on 9/15/68 at the Concertgebouw, Amsterdam, Holland.  It was called for one night *Tortoise Jam* on 6/13/69 Family Dog At The Great Highway, San Francisco, California.  It would become known as *Same Old Phony Handshake* on 10/25/69 Winterland, San Francisco, California (When one line was sung).  On 2/23/70 at the Fillmore West, San Francisco, California the first full version would be performed under that name.  Only these three names are correct titles.  It would be incorrectly listed as *Get Off* (Which is another *jam*), *Help Me*, *It's Easy*, *No Such Thing*, and *Thing* (Which is another *jam*).

11 Greasy Heart 3:37 Cut.

12 3/5 Of A Mile In 10 Seconds 7:51
There was a false ending to the song.  This was a long version with a good finale.

2/28/70 Winterland, San Francisco, California

The band did perform on this night but recorded information is not from this location.  One of the giveaways is Paul introducing *Wooden Ships* as a new song.  There has been documentation about what sources the songs came from but the playing times do not match up.  Please go to 1969 and 1970 Unknown Location #1 for information.

3/6/70 Municipal Auditorium, Dallas ,Texas

(108:15) (Line-up 3)

This is also often reported as Dallas 1970.

1 Tune-Up > We Can Be Together 6:17

2 Marty needs more stage monitor > Tune-up > Marty intros the next song > Somebody To Love 4:37

3 Tune-Up > Wooden Ships (False start) > Wooden Ships: With Go Ride The Music 7:19

4 The Ballad Of You And Me And Pooneil 10:42 With Jack bass-solo.

5 Paul tells the sound crew "I can't hear anything on stage." > Tune-up 1:08
There must have been a lot of sound difficulties for the band. In the Airplane days it was very infrequent that you would ever hear Paul complain about anything on stage.

6 White Rabbit 2:34

7 Emergency 4:24

8 Uncle Sam Blues 7:30 Jorma vocals.
It sounds as if Papa John Creach is playing fiddle on this track. Although he wasn't a member yet he could have been a guest!

9 Grace intros the next song > Tune-up 4:01

10 Paul intros the next song > 3/5 Of A Mile In 10 Seconds 5:46
There is a well thought out alternate ending. Marty counts from one to ten for the finish.

11 Marty thanks the crowd and intros the next song > Crown Of Creation 4:23

12 Nothing (L) (*Jam* with lyrics) Grace puts in one line from *Same Old Phony Handshake*.
**This is the last time the jam was performed as a stand-alone song.** For the final appearance ever please go to 5/7/70 at the Fillmore East, New York City. The *jam* was performed coming out of *Whatever The Old Man Does (Is Always Right)*.

13 Marty thanks the crowd and intros the next song > Greasy Heart 4:31

14 Tune-up > Won't You Try/Saturday Afternoon 6:39

15 Volunteers > Paul, and Grace thank the crowd 3: 57

16 Encore: Good Shepherd 7:27 Jorma vocals.
The strength of the bands version of this tune was so impressive it can fit into any spot in the set list.

17 Encore: Grace thanks the crowd > The Other Side Of This Life 9:16

**Photo courtesy of Mike Somavilla. From the Mike Somavilla collection.**

**Not to be used without written consent of Mike Somavilla.**

**Photographer unknown.**

**This is a promo picture of the J.A. with**

**new member Joey Covington. Circa 3/24/70. Thank you BMG .**

3/24/70 Capitol Theater, Port Chester, New York

(97:31) (Line-Up 4)

This show has been often documented as Joey Covington's first performance with the Airplane. In actuality he performed previously. It is documented without any question that Joey played at the 8/2/69 Atlantic City Racetrack, Atlantic City, New Jersey concert. It is very likely that he was on drums for the band on either the 6/14/69 or 6/16/69 The Family Dog, San Francisco, California show.

1 The Ballad Of You And Me And Pooneil 11:30

2 White Rabbit 2:27

3 (3/5 Of A Mile In 10 Seconds) 6:02 The band started to get real comfortable by the third song.

4 Wooden Ships: With Go Ride The Music 8:23

5 Come Back Baby 9:00 Jorma vocals.

6 Fat Angel (L) 12:32
An interesting arrangement to the song. At times Marty is talking the lyrics. **This was the last performance of the tune.** Time flies much too quickly.

7 Emergency 4:34 Cut. Documentation of this show has often left out *Emergency* being performed.

8 Have You Seen The Saucers 10:53

9 Good Shepard 9:59 Jorma vocals.
Excellent arrangement, with a fine bit of instrumentation before the opening vocal.

10 We Can Be Together 5:19 >

11 Volunteers 5:53
If ever two songs fit perfectly together from the band it would have to be ten and eleven.

12 Up Or Down > You Wear Your Dresses To Short 11:13 Cut

3/25/70 Suffolk Community College, Seldon, New York

(56:46) (**Line-up 4 but** <u>without</u> **Grace**)

The question came up if a main member of a band can't perform at a scheduled concert should the show go on? Grace had throat trouble and was not able to sing. It is a shame that the only documentation we have is a partial set list. In order to fully answer the question it would be good to have known what else was performed and did the band use improvisations and *jam's* to fill the void.

1 The Other Side Of This Life 6:50

2 Tune-up > Marty intros the next song > Wooden Ships: With: Go Ride The Music 7:22

3 Tune-up > Paul intros the next song > 3/5 Of A Mile In 10 Seconds  6:02 With short drum-solo at the end.

4 Tune-Up > Paul explains why Grace isn't on stage > We Can Be Together 7:55

5 Tune-up > Uncle Sam Blues 6:55 Cut.  Jorma vocals.

6 Tune-up > Emergency 5:18

7 Tune-up > Marty needs more stage monitor > Have You Seen The Saucers 7:36

8 You Wear Your Dresses Too Short 7:36

3/26/70 Dick Cavett Show ABC TV Studios, New York City

(15:44) (Line-up 4)

Although it is often reported that the Dick Cavett Show was taped the day before broadcast it would be unlikely for the Airplane performance.  Grace had throat trouble on 3/25/70.  She was unable to perform at the Suffolk Community College show.  It wouldn't be logical that she could have taped the program but not tried to perform at the concert.  Please see the entry of 3/25/70 for details.

1 Dick Cavett intros the band > Emergency 5:05

2 Dick Cavett interviews Grace 5:09

3 Grace tells Dick "This isn't the song we wanted to play but the sensor wouldn't let us perform our first choice." (She doesn't mention the first choice but hints it is *White Rabbit*). > Volunteers 5:30 Cut.

This was the exact same situation as the 8/18/69 appearance.  The band is performing and the attitude is clearly "We'll be back with a commercial after this brief song."  The Airplane plays a bit over four minutes of the tune and then it is time for commercials.  When they come back the Airplane is still playing as the show is ending.  Wouldn't it have been feasible to lesson the monologue or the useless jokes?

Although you don't think of *Emergency* as an Airplane song that would be performed on national TV it was a solid tune on stage.  There was so much material the band had created that worked well in a live environment we often take for granted how plentiful their catalog of songs were.

4/2/70 San Francisco Rock: Go Ride The Music (TV Special), Wally Heider Studios, San Francisco, California

(56:35) (Line-up 4)

This was the recording date of the program.  It would air 12/6/70.  To better enjoy a good evening of music if you have an opportunity to watch the video of the performance, or listen to the audio, omit the interviews until you have heard all the songs.  The idea of putting song, interview, song, broke up the continuity of the TV special.  A band that is known for their stage work, can't be fully appreciated with the start and stop mentality.

1 Tune- up > Chatter > We Can Be Together

2 Volunteers: With some improvised lyrics.

3 Marty interview

4 Jerry Garcia talks about the Airplane.

5 Mexico

6 Marty interview

7 Plastic Fantastic Lover > Tune-up

8 Somebody To Love

9 Emergency

10 Wooden Ships: With: Go Ride The Music

<u>4/15/70 Winterland, San Francisco, California</u>

Recorded information about this date is completely erroneous. The band did not perform on 4/15/70 and *Won't You Try/Saturday Afternoon* is introduced as a new song. The contents of the documentation can be found under 1967-1970 Live Compilation.

<u>4/27/70 A Night At The Family Dog ,The Family Dog At The Great Highway, San Francisco, California</u>
<u>(TV Special)</u>

This is the playback date for the recording that was done on 2/4/70. Please go to that entry for the information.

<u>5/1/70 SUNY Athletic Field, SUNY Of Stony Brook, Stony Brook, New York</u>

(127:14) (Line-up 4)

SUNY is short for State University, New York.

1 Grace makes a stage announcement > Tune-up > Volunteers 6:10
There was some lyrical improvisation. The song would be performed again later!

2 Joey is having sound trouble on stage > Somebody To Love 6:09
This song as well had some lyrical improvisation.

3 Grace thanks the crowd > Tune-up > Grace wants to know if the crowd can hear the band > Paul intros the next song as it starts > The Other Side Of This Life 11:49 Very consistent version.

4 Tune-up > Paul intros the next song > Mexico 4:04

5 Grace thanks the crowd > Tune-up > Grace intros the next song as it starts > Come Back Baby 9:25 Jorma vocals.
Jorma plays real well throughout the song and the extended time lets him perform one of the best Airplane versions of the tune.

6 Joey is having sound trouble on stage > Tune-up > Stage announcement > Tune-up > White Rabbit 4:48 Grace gets hoarse during the song!

7 (3/5 Of A Mile In 10 Seconds) 7:58

8 Tune-up > Marty jokes the problem with the sound is the vocals are too low! > Marty wants people to dance > Crown Of Creation 4:46

9 Tune-up > Marty intros the next song and Jorma > Good Shepherd > Tune-up 9:12 Grace does some vocal improvisation. Lead vocals by Jorma.

10 Jack tells Grace "Wires on the stage have been cut." (F) > Grace comments she never heard Jack speak on stage > Tune-up > Jam > Joey tells Paul about more sound troubles. **23:52 (21:25 of actual music).** When Jack speaks on stage it is a rarity. When Hot Tuna played together up to and including the 1977 tour you would always have at least one person per show asking Jack to say something. He would often put the choke sign around his throat and smile. **This would be the last time he would speak until 9/26/89 Fillmore Auditorium, San Francisco, California. <u>Jack for only the second time</u> spoke during an Airplane show!** Grace had requested that he say something. Jack actually responded! "You look lovely tonight Gracie."

11 The band is having trouble with the public address system > Tune-up > Have You Seen The Saucers (With extended lyrical improvisation) *No More War (F & L)* and instrumental improvisation 13:27 **This is the only time the improvisational vocal segment by Grace was performed.**

12 Joey is still having sound trouble: 44

13 We Can Be Together 5:44 >

14 Volunteers (2<sup>nd</sup> time played) With some lyrical improvisation 3:04

15 Encore: Grace thanks the crowd > Stage announcement > Tune-up > The Ballad Of You And Me And Pooneil 15:47 With Jack bass-solo.

When you look through the archives of the bands lives performances this stands out for being a show that had the potential for disaster. Grace sounds as if she may be sick and Paul as well. The sound trouble on stage further complicated matters. To top off the bad luck it was an outdoor show on a very cool night. This is where the professionalism kicked into overdrive. The band didn't throw their hands up and leave the crowd stranded. The *jam* was full of power and positive energy. It is always nice when they played *Volunteers* twice and they ended up with an explosive version of *The Ballad Of You And Me And Pooneil*.

<u>5/3/70 Central Park, New York City</u>

(74:22) (Line-up 4)

1 Somebody To Love 5:51

2 Wooden Ships: With: Go Ride The Music > Tune-Up 7:35

3 Paul intros the next song > Mexico 3:01

4 Paul intros the next song as it starts > The Other Side Of This Life 8:03

5 White Rabbit > Tune-up 3:25

6 Crown Of Creation > Tune-up 4:36

7 Come Back Baby 6:44 Jorma vocals.

8 Plastic Fantastic Lover 4:01

9 A fan passes Grace a note to perform a song by the New York Rock And Roll Ensemble > Grace tells the fan "The band has enough trouble playing our own songs." > Grace has always had a fantastic sense of humor. The spur of the moment reply to the fan was a great example of her stage persona.

10 Have You Seen The Saucers > Tune-up 8:20 With lyrical improvisation. This was a solid version both from a musical and vocal stand point.

11 Good Shepherd 7:10 Jorma vocals.

12 Greasy Heart > Marty thanks the crowd, the people associated with the Fillmore East, and Bill Graham for helping to put the show on > Tune-up 5:05

13 We Can Be Together 5:18 >

14 Volunteers 5:51 > Paul and Grace thank the crowd.

5/6/70 Fillmore East, New York City (Late show)

(179:54) (Line-up 4)

This performance has always been considered one of the best Airplane gigs ever!

1 Volunteers > Tune-up 3:51

2 Somebody To Love > Tune-up > Jack fools around on the bass 5:54 >

3 Good Shepherd (Jorma vocals) > Tune-Up > Grace intros the next song 9:10

4 Mexico 2:30

5 The Ballad Of You And Me And Pooneil 14:32

6 Wooden Ships: With Go Ride The Music 7:38

7 Uncle Sam Blues (Jorma vocals) > Paul intros the next song 7:07

8 Emergency 5:40

9 The Other Side Of This Life > Paul tells the crowd "There will be a short break to set up the stage for acoustic guitar work." 8:01

Acoustic Hot Tuna (Jorma and Jack).

10 Tune-Up > Feedback > Sea Child 8:06

11 New Song (For The Morning) > Tune-up 5:04

12 Hesitation Blues > Jorma intros the next song > Tune-up 5:20 >

13 Death Don't Have No Mercy > Tune-Up 6:14

14 Mann's Fate **(Hot Tuna set ends)** > **(J.A. set starts)** > Grace intros the next song and tells the meaning of the lyrics > Tune-up > Five second Joey drum-solo > Tune-up (long) 9:51 >

15 Have You Seen The Saucers 5:58

16 White Rabbit > Tune-up 3:11

17 We Can Be Together > Volunteers (Played for the 2<sup>nd</sup> time) 9:32

18 Greasy Heart 6:10

19 Won't You Try/Saturday Afternoon 5:19

20 Joey dedicates the next song to Bill Graham > I Can Tell (F) (Joey vocals) 10:11
(Erroneous information lists the song title as *I Know You Don't Love Me*). **This is the first appearance.**

21 (3/5 Of A Mile In 10 Seconds) > The crowd wants an encore 8:22

22 Encore: Tune-up > Up Or Down (F) > Tune-up 6:05
**This is the first appearance of the song.**

23 Encore: Baby What You Want Me To Do > Jorma plays the riff to *Honey Don't (F & L)* at about 2:40) >
Baby What You Want Me To Do 6:37
*Honey Don't* was written by Carl Perkins and most noted by the Beatles version. **This was the only time the riff got played!** What a shame!

24 Encore: Whatever The Old Man Does (Is Always Right) (F) (Joey vocals) > You Wear Your Dresses Too
Short > Bye Bye Baby (F & L) (Brief vocal excerpt by Marty) > You Wear Your Dresses Too Short 19:36
This is the first appearance of *Whatever The Old Man Does (Is Always Right)*. The next appearance on the
5/7/70 Fillmore East, New York City show the song was played out of *Up Or Down*. The first time it was
played by itself was on 5/17/70 at the Assembly Hall, Bloomington, Indiana. Please see those dates for details.
This was the only appearance of *Bye Bye Baby*. The version Marty took the lyric from was a song that Janis
Joplin had been performing live during the same era. The song was composed by her band member Powell St.
John. This was the only time Marty used the vocal excerpt.

5/7/70 Fillmore East, New York City

(120:30) (Line-up 4)

This show is often documented as 5/10/70 Fillmore East, New York City. The band performed that night at the
Kiel Auditorium, Saint Louis, Missouri. Recorded information listing *Rock Me Baby* and *Star Track* are
incorrect. The group hadn't performed a documented version of *Star Track* since 11/16/68 The Electric Factory,
Philadelphia, Pennsylvania. The two songs seem to have been taken from a Hot Tuna show 3/18/70, The
Family Dog, San Francisco, California. Coming off the legendary 5/6/70 performance it would be hard to equal
the brilliance on successive nights. The concert is a good one but more remembered for some of Grace's
outrageous stage comments.

Hot Tuna opens the show. (Acoustic Jorma and Jack).

1 Winin' Boy Blues 5:02 (The beginning is cut).

2 New Song (For The Morning) 4:41

3 Jorma thanks the crowd and intros the next song > Tune-up > Mann's Fate 5:43

Jefferson Airplane set begins.

4 Tune-up > 2:45 >

5 Have You Seen The Saucers 6:25

6 (3/5 Of A Mile In 10 Seconds) 7:31

7 We Can Be Together 5:18 >

8 Volunteers 3:29

9 Grace thanks the crowd > Tune-up 3:02

10 Won't You Try/Saturday Afternoon 3:26 Cut.

11 Somebody To Love: With Grace vocal improvisation: Got What You Want (F & L) (10:15) Grace explains the band are the people that the current generation is rising up against because they have the fancy limousine and a good income. **That is the only time Grace did the improvisation.**

12 Wooden Ships: With: Go Ride The Music and Grace vocal improvisation *Just Sit There (F & L) > Short Guitar Ditty (F & L)* 7:33 Grace wanted the people to move out of their seats. **This was the only time for both the vocal improvisation and the *Short Guitar Ditty*.**

13 Mexico 2:11
Grace gets hoarse during the song.

14 Uncle Sam Blues (Starts off with Grace's improvisational vocal *Brothers And Sisters*) (F & L) > Uncle Sam Blues (Jorma vocals) 7:12
**This was the only time that the improvisational vocal by Grace was heard.**

15 Emergency > Tune-up > Grace asks the crowd "To be Heard in Washington, D.C." 6:52

16 Crown Of Creation 3:00

17 The Ballad of You And Me And Pooneil: With Jack bass-solo > Grace thanks the crowd > Crowd wants an encore > Bill Graham compliments the light show and is upset over somebody in the audience cursing the band > Joey intros the next song as "Whatever The Old Man Does (Is Always Right)" but the band goes into another song! 15:37

18 Encore: Up Or Down (Only a couple of minutes played) > Whatever The Old Man Does (Is Always Right) (F) Joey vocals 6:15 >

19: Same Old Phony Handshake (L) (*Jam* with vocals) 13:52
**This was the first time *Whatever The Old Man Does (Is Always Right)* was played out of a song.** The first time it was performed was the 5/6/70 Fillmore East, New York City (Late show), when it went into *You Wear Your Presses Too Short*. The first time it was played by itself was on 5/17/70 at the Assembly Hall, Bloomington, Indiana. Please see those dates for details. **This is the last time the *Same Old Phony Handshake Jam* would be performed.** The last time it would be played as a stand-alone song was on 3/6/70 at the Municipal Auditorium, Dallas, Texas. Please see that date for details.

5/10/70 Fillmore East, New York City

Any recorded information about this venue on that date is mistaken. The band performed at the Kiel Auditorium, Saint Louis, Missouri. The documentation of the events is erroneously taken from the 5/7/70 Fillmore East, New York City concert. Please see that date for the information.

<u>5/17/70 Assembly Hall, Bloomington, Indiana</u>

(88:05) **(Line-up 4 without Marty)**

The venue has never been confirmed.  The date is correct.  Marty was not at that performance!  He had a situation that he had to take care of from the previous day.  This was the first time a live audience would get an indication what the band would sound like without him.

1 Tune-up > The Ballad Of You And Me And Pooneil 12:45 With Jack bass-solo.

2 Mexico 3:12 With Grace improvising lyrics at the end of the song.

3 Tune-up > Get Off Jam (F) (The real *Get Off Jam*) Joey vocals 15:34
**This is the first appearance.**

4 Greasy Heart 3:47 With: *Can You Hear Me Laugh* (F & L) vocal improvisation by Grace at the end of the song.  This would be the only time Grace used the vocal improvisation.

5 Tune-up > Uncle Sam Blues (Jorma vocals) Cut.

6 White Rabbit 2:29

7 Volunteers 3:54

8 Whatever The Old Man Does (Is Always Right) (F & L)  5:58 Joey vocals.
**This is the first and last time the song was played by itself.**  On the 5/6/70 Fillmore East, New York City (Late show) it went into *You Wear Your Dresses Too Short*.  That was the first time it was ever performed.  On the 5/7/70 Fillmore East, New York City show it came out of *Up Or Down*.  For the final time ever played, please see the 8/24/70 Atlanta Municipal Auditorium, Atlanta, Georgia performance.  Joey added an improvisational vocal (That night only) *Can You Hear Me*.

9 Easy (*Jam* with Grace vocals) (F & L) 15:00
**This is the only performance of the *jam*.**

10 Baby What You Want Me To Do (L) 10:20 Grace improvises some vocals and sings background to Jorma's lead vocals.  This is the last version of the song performed as the Jefferson Airplane until the 1989 reunion.  This is a very loose version of the song with a good result.

11 Somebody To Love 5:40

<u>6/70 Amsterdam, Holland</u>

Recorded information showing a performance in Amsterdam from June is from the 6/26/70 Kralingen Pop Festival, Rotterdam, Holland.  Please see that entry for details.

<u>6/6/70 Anaheim Convention Center, Anaheim, California</u>

The band did not play on that night.  Those documenting 6/6/70 have the wrong date.  The actual performance was 2/7/70.  Please go to that entry for information.

<u>6/7/70 Anaheim Convention Center, Anaheim, California</u>

The band did not play on that night.  Those documenting 6/7/70 have the wrong date.  The actual performance was 2/7/70.  Please go to that entry for the information.

6/26/70 Kralingen Pop Festival, Rotterdam, Holland

(48:26) (Line-up 4)

This also is erroneously documented as both 6/26/70 Kralingen Pop Festival, Rotterdam, Holland 6/70 and Amsterdam, Holland. Those that claimed *Volunteers* as being the first song are not correct. That was how a documentary *Stamping Ground* filmed in Europe, opened the edited version of the footage. *Volunteers* is actually the last song of the concert. *The Ballad Of You And Me And Pooneil* was not a short version as sometimes listed (3:01) it was an edited version shown on the *Stamping Ground* documentary.

1 Somebody To Love 7:35

2 The Other Side Of This Life 8:23
A nice consistent version!

3 White Rabbit 2:12

4 Won't You Try/Saturday Afternoon 5:12

5 Plastic Fantastic Lover 6:03

6 The Ballad Of You And Me And Pooneil 11:45
This was a great version because not only did it go over eleven minutes but Jack's bass is rather prominent in the mix.

7 We Can Be Together (F) 6:03 >

8 Volunteers 3:29
**This was the first performance with *We Can Be Together* going into *Volunteers*.** Please see 5/7/69 at the Polo Field, Golden Gate Park, San Francisco, California (Afternoon show) for the first stand-alone version.

6/27/70 Kralingen Pop Festival, Rotterdam, Holland

Recorded information on that date is actually the 6/26/70 performance from the same location. The band did not perform on 6/27/70. Please see the entry of 6/2/70 for the proper information.

6/28/70 Bath Festival Of Blues And Progressive Music, Royal County Fairgrounds, Shepton Mallet, Somerset, U.K.

(48:40) (Line-up 4)

1 Stage Introduction > Volunteers > Grace thanks the crowd 3:34

2 Somebody To Love 4:42 With some improvised lyrics.

3 Tune-up > Paul intros the next song as it starts > The Other Side Of This Life 7:16

4 Grace clowns around on stage > Won't You Try/Saturday Afternoon 5:01

5 (3/5 Of A Mile In 10 Seconds) 5:43

6 Tune- up > Grace talks with the audience and the band goes into a short Improvisational Instrumental 1:32

7 Rock Me Baby (L) 7:38 Jorma vocals.
The band performed a terrific version!  This was the last appearance of the song until the 1989 reunion tour.

8 The Ballad Of You And Me And Pooneil 9:54 With a Jack bass-solo.

9 Grace thanks the crowd for staying through the rain > Stage announcer thanks the Airplane for performing > Grace thanks the crowd a final time 1:16
This was a very classy move by Grace.  Countless times musicians can be out of touch with the audience.  Grace was truly appreciative that the large audience stayed through the inclement weather to see the band perform.

<u>7/6/70 Anaheim Convention Center, Anaheim, California.</u>

The band did not perform on this night.  Those documenting the show from Anaheim are listing the 2/7/70 concert.  Please go to that date for the details.

<u>Circa 8 or 9/70 RCA Studios, Hollywood, California</u>

(5:17) (Line-up 4)

Starship 5:17 Rough mix.

This would end up on Paul's *Blows Against The Empire*.  The album was released 10/70.  Excluding the fidelity the rough mix is better than the *Blows Against The Empire* version.  The LP mix had a thirteen second longer intro (:57 compared to :44), the change in tempo occurred at 1:33 on the album, and 1:18 on the rough mix, the guitar solo was twelve seconds longer on the record, and the album version ends at 7:02, with a cold stop.  The rough mix ends with a fade.  On the album version the song continues with a piano and guitar part.  The rough mix ends at a perfect 5:17.  The rough mix does sound muffled at times however the music is perfect.  What also enhances hearing the rough mix for the first time is having it as a stand-alone song.  On the LP *Starship* comes out of the ending of *X-M*.

<u>8/19/70 Curtis Dixon Hall, Tampa, Florida</u>

(83:47) (Line-up 4)

Joey's playing is very strong throughout the performance.

1 We Can Be Together 5:27 The band starts to have sound trouble at the end of the song.

2 Grace thanks the crowd, and asks "Is the sound okay?" Somebody To Love 3:42
With Grace improvising some lyrics.

3 Grace thanks the crowd > Tune-up > Won't You Try/Saturday Afternoon (L) 6:05
**This is the final appearance of the song until the 1989 reunion tour.**

4 Grace thanks the crowd and Paul intros the latest member of the group Joey Covington > Whatever The Old Man Does (Is Always Right) 6:35 Joey vocals.

5 Tune-up > Mexico 3:44

6 The Other Side Of This Life 8:09

7 Up Or Down 5:34

8 Uncle Sam Blues 6:01 The beginning of the song is cut.  Jorma vocals.

9 Tune-up > Paul intros the next song > Plastic Fantastic Lover 4:30
Less structured vocals by Marty during *Plastic Fantastic Lover*.

10 Grace intros the next song > Tune-up > Grace complains about a hum on stage and the band start the next tune anyway! > Crown Of Creation 4:41
(That was a rather funny moment).

11 Grace thanks the crowd > Tune-up > The Ballad Of You And Me And Pooneil 12:51
With Jack bass-solo and a false end.  This was not only one of the finest versions of the song ever performed but one of the highlights of their live shows.

12 An employee makes a stage announcement > Grace makes fun of the employee and how laid back he is > Volunteers > Paul thanks the crowd 5:25

13 Encore: White Rabbit > Grace thanks the crowd 2:25

14 Encore: 3/5 Of A Mile In 10 Seconds > Marty and Grace thank the crowd 5:51
The band had sound trouble on stage during the final song.

8/24/70 Atlanta Municipal Auditorium, Atlanta, Georgia

(108:14) (Line-up 4)

1 Somebody To Love 4:32 The openings notes were cut.

2 Tune-up > Crown Of Creation 4:25

3 Paul intros the next song > The Other Side Of This Life 8:52

4 Up Or Down 7:22

5 Tune-up > Mexico 4:21

6 Tune-Up > We Can Be Together 6:58

7 Marty thanks the crowd and intros the next song >

Whatever The Old Man Does (Is Always Right) 10:30 Joey vocals.  With: *Can You Hear Me* (F & L) vocal improvisational segment 10:30
**This was the last time played and the only performance with the *Can You Hear Me* vocal improvisation.**  For the first and only time played by itself, please see 5/17/70 Assembly Hall, Bloomington, Indiana.

8 Plastic Fantastic Lover (L) 8:00
This was an interesting rendition.  It was longer than the standard live version and less structured musically by all the band members. **This was the final appearance of the song until the 1989 reunion tour.**

9 Paul intros the next song and intros Jorma as well > Come Back Baby 7:22 Jorma vocals.

10 Have You Seen The Saucers 6:53 With Grace doing some vocal improvisation.

11 Grace thanks the crowd > Greasy Heart 4:30

12 Grace thanks the crowd > Good Shepherd 8:06 Jorma does the lead vocals, but after the last verse Grace does a bit of vocal improvisation.

13 Short Jam #2 (F & L) > I Can Tell (*Jam*) > I Can Tell (Improvisational lyrics by Joey) > I Can Tell (Standard lyrics by Joey) > Get Off Jam (L) (Joey vocals) 20:56
**This was the first and last time *Short Jam #2* was performed.  This was the last time the *Get Off Jam* would be performed by the J.A.**

14 White Rabbit 2:05 The first few seconds were cut.

15 Volunteers 3:13 The first few seconds were cut.

This was a show that you don't often here discussed but it was a solid performance.  Not only did the *I Can Tell* segment of the concert work out very well, the shorter selections were tight and full of energy.

9/14/70 Fillmore West, San Francisco, California

(124:02) (Line-up 4)

Any recorded information showing more songs and a longer playing time have documented some tracks incorrectly. They are actually from 10/25/69 Winterland, San Francisco, California.

1 We Can Be Together 6:26

2 Mexico 2:33

3 Crown Of Creation 3:34

4 Paul intros Joey > Joey needs more volume on stage > Whatever The Old Man Does (Is Always Right) Joey vocals. 5:55

5 Tune-up > The Ballad Of You And Me And Pooneil (L) 10:15
**This was the last time the song was performed.**  Didn't you wish for this in 1989?

6 Paul intros the next song: 11

7 Emergency 4:47

8 Come Back Baby 6:26 (Jorma vocals) Jorma playing is superlative throughout the song.

9 Marching drum beat intro > Somebody To Love > Grace thanks the crowd 6:55
Grace improvised many of the lyrics during *Somebody To Love*.  **This is the only documented performance where the song had the marching band drum intro by Joey.**

10 Wooden Ships: With: Go Ride The Music 7:29 During the song Jorma, Jack, and Joey had an improvisational section that worked rather well.  You can see very quickly when Joey was made a full member of the group he quickly established himself as a drummer that could handle the total spectrum of sounds the band had created and those that were on the runway awaiting take-off.

11 Paul intros the next song as being written by Jorma's brother > Tune-up >

12 Up Or Down 6:18

13 Uncle Sam Blues 6:45 Jorma vocals.

14 Have You Seen The Saucers (Tease of the song was sung by Grace) (F & L) > Have You Seen The Saucers 6:56
When Grace was teasing the song she put on a deep voice to sound like a strange man. **This was the first and only time Grace did the vocal tease.**

15 The Man (The Bludgeon Of The Bluecoat) 4:44 Joey vocals.
This is the first appearance of the song.

16 The Other Side Of This Life "Tease" of the song was sung by Grace (F & L) > The Other Side Of This Life 8:06
**This was the only time the tease of the song was done.**

17 Volunteers > Grace thanks the crowd 3:46

18 Grace asks for a faster tempo as the next song starts > Greasy Heart > Grace thanks the crowd 3:30

19 Grace wants to know what song is next :55

20 You Wear Your Dresses Too Short > Grace comments "The last song was strange." > Tune-up 11:05

21 Short Improvisation: 37

22 Short Jam #3 (F & L) :46 >
**This was the only time performed.**

23 Starship (F) 9:21
**This is the second time played but the first and only as a stand-alone song.** Please see 9/6/69 Family Dog, San Francisco, California for the first version when it came out of the end of *The Ballad Of You And Me And Pooneil*. This was one of the great highlights of the bands live performances. Paul does a fascinating arrangement of *Starship*. He sings the lyrics for verse one up to but not including *Hydroponic Gardens*, verse two he starts with *Dear Brumus*, verses three, and four he goes back to verse one, and finally on verse five he starts with *Hydroponic Gardens*.

24 Encore: 3/5 Of A Mile In 10 Seconds 6:53

9/15/70 Fillmore West, San Francisco, California  (Early show)

(50:22) (Line-up 4)

1 Somebody To Love 5:42

2 Crown Of Creation 3:37

3 Mexico 2:32

4 Whatever The Old Man Does (Is Always Right) 5:49 Joey vocals.

5 Have You Seen The Saucers 7:47

6 Uncle Same Blues 5:53 Jorma vocals.
Excellent instrumentation on this version.

7 Emergency 4:20

8 (3/5 Of A Mile In 10 Seconds) 6:28

9 We Can Be Together 5:05 The intro was cut.

10 Volunteers > Paul, and Grace thank the crowd 3:49

The first time I had an opportunity to listen to this performance the mix of the drums were high. This enabled me to get a good appreciation to what Joey was doing behind the kit. His playing is terrific throughout the set list.

<u>10/4/70 Winterland, San Francisco, California</u>

(78:21) (Line-up 4)

The date has been debated by Airplane archivists. There are those that feel there hasn't been enough evidence that the show actually took place 10/4/70 and that the band may have had an off night. I am in agreement with that side. The reason for my justification is the performance was a radio broadcast from two San Francisco stations KSAN, and KQED, and a TV broadcast on KQED. A live broadcast of a band the magnitude of the Airplane would have had a lot more conclusive evidence of the performance. The logical conclusion seems to be that the concert may have been taped on the first day of October at Winterland. Although the group also performed at the same venue on the fifth day of the month that was Papa John Creach's first gig. Since he is not heard on any of the songs that date can be ruled out. This show also circulates incorrectly as 8/2/69 Winterland, San Francisco, California. That is impossible since the band was playing at Atlantic City Racetrack, Atlantic City, New Jersey. Recorded information being from 12/31/70 Winterland is erroneous as well. That performance was Hot Tuna. Several of the songs from the concert had a great mix of Jorma's guitar.

1 Have You Seen The Saucers > Grace thanks the crowd 6:51

2 Crown Of Creation > Grace thanks the crowd 4:08

3 Somebody To Love 6:59 (**With Grace's famous <u>"Eye Patch"</u> vocal improvisation.  F & L**)
This was an example of Grace's quick wit. During the song she added the following words (Talking them and not singing): "Eye-patches should be warn on the left side of the face, regardless of which eye is injured, those are the hospital rules." **This would be the only time Grace would add the words to the song.**
In addition there was an excellent mix of Jack's bass during the tune.

4 Mexico 2:28

5 Paul intros the next song being written by Jorma's brother > Up Or Down > Paul intros the next song > Tune-up 7:36

6 Whatever The Old Man Does (Is Always Right) (Joey vocals) > Tune-up 7:18

7 Emergency 5:23

8 Wooden Ships: With: Go Ride The Music 6:38

9 The Man (Bludgeon Of A Bluecoat) Joey vocals > Tune-up 5:58

10 Greasy Heart 4:00

11 Tune-up > You Wear Your Dresses Too Short 7:35

12 Tune-up > We Can Be Together > Paul announces "Quicksilver Messenger Service is playing next" 5:37 >

13 Volunteers > Paul, and Grace thank the crowd 5:50

**10/5/70 Winterland, San Francisco California  (Welcome aboard the plane Papa John).**

There is no recorded documentation of the songs that were performed.  That is a major loss of history **because it is the first show with Papa John Creach.**

10/25/70 Unknown venue, Wichita, Kansas

(67:58) (Line-up 5)

This turned out to be an important show.  It is the first documented concert with accurate information on Papa John.

1 Come Back Baby 6:42 Jorma vocals.

2 Up Or Down 6:07 >

3 Whatever The Old Man Does (Is Always Right) 4:57 (Joey vocals) >

4 John's Other (F) 4:14

**This was the first appearance of the song.**  The audience got a taste of one of the songs that would be played with Papa John.  It was an instrumental number that went over very well.

5 Have You Seen The Saucers 5:16

6 Somebody To Love 2:52

7 We Can Be Together 5:32

8 Mexico 2:17

9 Crown Of Creation 4:04

10 Emergency 4:35 (L)
**This was the final time the song was played as is.**  Grace did some lyrical improvisation before the actual version on 11/25/70 Fillmore East, New York City.  Please see that date for the information.

11 Uncle Sam Blues (False start) > Uncle Sam Blues 6:27 Jorma vocals.

12 Jam 5:54 Cut.
This was a blues based instrumental *jam* that had Papa John up in the mix.

13 (3/5 Of A Mile In 10 Seconds) 6:40

14 White Rabbit 2:05

(74:32) (Line-up 5) Please also see the Late show.

1 Have You Seen The Saucers (Cut) 5:50

2 Somebody To Love 7:59

3 We Can Be Together 5:53

4 Crown Of Creation 3:41

5 Mexico (L) 2:25
**This was the final appearance of the song.**

6 Uncle Sam Blues (L) (Jorma vocals) 8:24
The band excelled while stretching this out.  This was the final appearance of the song.

7 Pretty As You Feel (F) 8:50
**This was the first appearance of the song.**

8 The Other Side Of This Life 9:12

9 White Rabbit (L) 2:37
**This was the final appearance, until the 1989 reunion tour.**

10 Volunteers > Paul and Marty thank the crowd > Papa John intros the band 5:37

11 Encore: You Wear Your Dresses Too Short 14:04 With some improvisational lyrics by Marty "*Somebody To Love Me*, "*Somebody To Need Me*." (F & L)
**This was the only time this was performed.**  The beginning set list of the show has never been documented. The final selection *You Wear Your Dresses Too Short* with the vocal improvisation by Marty was superlative! Please see the fantastic late show entry from the same night.

11/13/70 Capitol Theater, Port Chester, New York (Late show)

(172:56) (Line-up 5) Please also see the Early show.

Although it took a number of years for information to surface that two shows were performed on 11/13/70, the research seems to legitimatize the detective work.  The length of the performance does not match up with any other from that period of time and the **forth song** of the night is not found on any other documented Airplane performance. The show is nothing short of tremendous!

Hot Tuna opens the show.  Jorma, Jack, Marty, Papa John, Joey, and Will Scarlett.

1 Come Back Baby 8:03

2 Whatever The Old Man Does (Is Always Right) (Joey Vocals) > Tune-Up 6:31
Although no longer in the J.A. set, Hot Tuna continues to give it stage time.

3 Up Or Down (Cut almost at the start) > Tune-Up 2:24

**4 Papa John Blues Jam 10:23**
Instrumentation was loosely based on *Every Time I Hear Her Name* from his self-titled 1971 album. Papa John also sings a couple of improvised lines that are based on Robert Johnson's- *32-30 Blues* and Elmore James-*Early One Morning*. The band is cooking and it looks like it will be all instrumental but Papa John throws in some common blues lyrics.

5 Papa John intros the band > Get Off (Vocal *jam* with Joey on vocals) 9:53 (Still in the Hot Tuna set).

6 You Wear Your Dresses To Short > Tune-Up 18:55 (The end of the Hot Tuna set).

The Jefferson Airplane set starts here:

7 Have You Seen The Saucers (L) (With false ending) > Starship 18:21
This version would not be the last one ever that came on 9/22/72 Winterland, San Francisco, California. It would be the last one performed going into another song. Please see 9/22/72 for details. This is a logical transition from one tune to another but not an easy one. The band was flawless and Paul did an interesting thing with the lyrics. He sang almost the entire song but left out nine lines from "*America Hates Her Crazies*" to "*All The Years Gone From Your Age.*" This has been erroneously listed as *Hijack*.

8 (3/5 Of A Mile In 10 Seconds) 7:53
The tempo is a bit slower but there is nothing wrong with the rendition. Marty counts off the numbers one through ten which made for a great alternate ending!

9 Good Shepherd (Jorma vocals) > Tune-Up 10:00 > We Can Be Together (False Start) >

10 We Can Be Together (L) 8:00
**This is the last time the song would be performed as a stand-alone.** Please see 11/25/70 at the Fillmore East, New York City where it would be performed before *Volunteers*.

11 Pretty As You Feel > Short Instrumental Ditty (F & L) 10:20
*Pretty As You Feel* had a slower tempo during certain portions of the song but came off very strong. This was the only appearance of the *Short Instrumental Ditty*.

12 John's Other > Tune-up 8:43

13 Somebody To Love 9:04
Grace improvised a bunch of lyrics and this became one of the longest versions of the song ever performed!

14 Volunteers > The crowd wants an encore > Marty calls out the rest of the band > Drum And Bass Short Ditty (F & L) > Tune-up 11:07
**This is the only time the *Drum And Bass Short Ditty* occurred.**

15 Encore: Emergency > Marty says "Paul and Grace to come up on stage if you desire." 6:06

**From here until the last note of the show, it is credited as <u>Hot Tuna</u>.**

16 Encore: Peggy Sue (Jorma vocals) > Tune-up 6:12

17 Encore: Harmonica Intro > I've Been All Around This World (Will Scarlett vocals) > Tune-up 9:53

18 Encore: Baby What You Want Me To Do 10:57 Jorma, and Will vocals!

The encore segment was worth the price of admission! Please see the previous entry for the early show from the same date.

<u>11/20/70 War Memorial, Rochester, New York</u>

There is often debate if this date is correct.  Since the two tracks that have been documented from the performance do not include Papa John Creach it is hard to substantiate the information.  Papa John didn't appear on every song of the concert.

(13:46) (Line-up 5)

1 We Can Be Together 5:18

2 Somebody To Love 8:28
One of the most interesting renditions of the song.  While Grace is often improvising the lyrics Marty does an excellent background vocal.

<u>11/25/70 Fillmore East, New York City</u>

(124:41) (Line-up 5)

Information often listed as 11/26/70 from the same venue is incorrect.  The band did perform on 11/26/70 but all documentation is about this concert only.

1 Paul intros the first song > Mexico 3:00

2 Grace thanks the crowd > Tune-up > Joey sings the opening line from *Abraham, Martin &* John (F & L) :49
(This was a hit for Dion in 1968) If you have ever heard the performance this is very low in the background.  **It is the only time any part of the song had been performed.**

3 (3/5 Of A Mile In 10 Seconds) (L) 5:38
The band clicked on all cylinders.  **This was the final appearance of the song, until the 1989 reunion tour**.  When you have followed a bands activities for the entire flight it hard to believe the plane wouldn't travel *3/5 Of A Mile In 10 Seconds* (A song of such brilliance) until a seventeen year long hiatus ended.

4 Grace thanks the crowd > Grace does some lyrical improvisation from the next song (***Emergency***) and throws in a plug for Levis Jeans (Grace is a smart lady since the band recorded commercials for Levis). 1:42 >

5 Emergency 4:38 (L)
**This is the final appearance of the song.**  The last time it was played as is was 10/25/70 Unknown venue, Wichita, Kansas.  Please see that date for the information.

6 Tune-Up > False drum start for Greasy Heart > Greasy Heart 5:01

7 Grace intros Papa John > Papa John intros the next song > E Major Blues (F & L) (Jam: With short Joey drum-solo 19:31 (18:33 of actual music.  There were no vocals during the *jam*).  **This was the only appearance of the *jam*.**

8 Tune-up > Come Back Baby 7:19 Jorma vocals.  Excellent version.

9 Up Or Down 8:01 (L) >

10 Tune-up > I Can Tell (L) 16:35 With Joey vocals and a Short Bass, and Drum Segment
**This was the last time both *Up Or Down* and *I Can Tell* were performed.**

11 Tune-up > Joey intros Papa John > John's Other 8:43

190

12 Tune-up > You Wear Your Dresses Too Short (L) 10:46
**This was the last version performed <u>without</u> any improvisational parts done at the beginning of the song.** That is how the final version ever was performed at 9/22/72 Winterland, San Francisco, California. Please see that date for details.

13 Marty thanks the crowd > Tune-up > Have You Seen The Saucers 7:30
The audience reacted very well to the song.

14 Grace thanks the crowd > Tune-up > Somebody To Love > Long Improvisational Lyric Segment > **Somebody To Love 13:22**
The version was so long that it outlasted *You Wear Your Dresses Too Short* by almost three minutes. **It is the longest documented version of *Somebody To Love*.**

15 Tune-up > We Can Be Together (L) 7:52 >

16 Volunteers (Missing the opening notes) > Grace thanks the crowd 4:02
**This is the last time *We Can Be Together* would be performed.** Please see 11/13/70 at the Capitol Theater, Port Chester, New York (Late show) for the last time it would be played as a stand-alone tune. Hard to comprehend *We Can Be Together* would not fly again. This was another solid New York City performance. The improvisational sections along with the normal instrumentation, and lyrical approaches were stellar.

<u>11/26/70 Fillmore East, New York City</u>

The band did perform on this night but all documented information is from the 11/25/70 show at the same venue. Please see the previous entry for all the details.

<u>12/6/70 San Francisco Rock: Go Ride The Music (TV Show), Wally Heider Studios, San Francisco, California</u>

This was the playback date for the show originally recorded 4/27/70. Please see that entry for details.

<u>12/13/70 A Night At The Family Dog ,The Family Dog At The Great , Highway, San Francisco, California</u>
<u>(TV Special)</u>

This was the playback date for the show originally recorded 2/4/70. Please see that entry for details.

<u>12/31/70 Winterland, San Francisco, California.</u>

The band did not perform on that date. Hot Tuna did play the venue. Recording information about this performance is documenting the Winterland show of 10/4/70. Please see that entry for details.

# Chapter 7: 1971 "Straining Every Nerve"

Circa 1/26/71 Wally Heider Studios, San Francisco, California

(11:17) (Line-up 5)

*Bark* session, unreleased version.

1 Pretty As You Feel (Extended version 1971) 13:40
The released version was four minutes and twenty-six seconds.  The two versions have an introduction of thirty-five seconds.  The album version starts to fade-out and finally ends at four minutes and twenty-six seconds.  The extended version has a false ending at about four minutes and forty seconds.  It ends as a you are led to believe the music is finishing and the band goes into a *jam*.  The mix on both were excellent.  If the *Bark* album was released in a time period where CD's existed would the normal versions of *Pretty As You Feel* and *Feel So Good* have been the extended ones?  Please see the entry circa 6/7/71 Wally Heider Studios, San Francisco, California for the extended *Feel So Good*.

**Circa 4/71 Marty Balin leaves the plane.**  **(The flight would never be the same again).**

Circa 4/26/71 to 9/71 Wally Heider Studios, San Francisco, California

(7:47) (Line-up 6) *The Man (The Bludgeon Of The Bluecoat)* **With Little Richard.**

**Little Richard (Richard Penniman)** is known for his 1950's style of rock and roll and rhythm and blues.  His version of *Tutti Frutti* is legendary.  Joey Covington became friendly with his mom and that helped set up the session with Little Richard.  On both versions of *The Man (The Bludgeon Of The Bluecoat)*, Little Richard plays a piano part that is both typical of his style but also a perfect fit for the song.  It was obvious by title alone the song would not be released.  If the lyrics had been changed the music was very catchy.

1 The Man (The Bludgeon Of The Bluecoat #1 (4:06) With: Little Richard
The song was performed live by the band but never released.  The first version the piano comes in immediately and Joey is heard at one point during the song  saying "Go to C."  There is a false ending at 3:50.

2 The Man (The Bludgeon Of The Bluecoat #2 (3:41) With: Little Richard
Joey intros the song on this version.  The vocal track is different and that is evident when Joey says "C" and not "Go To C" as he did on the other version.

Circa 6/7/71 Wally Heider Studios, San Francisco, California

10:18 (Line-up 6)

*Bark* session, unreleased version.

1 Feel So Good 10:18 Extended version 1971

The released version was four minutes and thirty-four seconds.  This version starts off with the same instrumentation.  Did you remember the first instrument heard was the piano and not the guitar?  It is thirty-seven seconds before the vocals appear.  The mix on both is very strong.  What is fascinating about the unreleased version is there are additional vocal layers.  It sounds as when Jorma is singing at times his voice is double-tracked and other instances Joey is putting on a combination voice of fifties rock and roll and fifties rhythm and blues.  The out-take version takes off musically at three minutes and fifty seconds when a monster *jam* begins.  The ending is very sudden and takes you by complete surprise!

If the *Bark* album was released in a time period where CD's existed would the normal versions of *Feel So Good* and *Pretty As You Feel* have been the extended ones? Please see the entry of Circa 1/26/71 Wally Heider Studios, San Francisco, California for information on *Pretty As You Feel*.

8/15/71 Wall Stadium, Wall, New Jersey

(68:37) (Line-up 6)

Opening night of the 1971 tour. (**There were only five scheduled shows**).

1 Rock And Roll Island (F) 3:31
**This was the first appearance of the song.**

2 Tune-up > Feel So Good (F) 10:29 Jorma vocals.
**This was the first appearance of the song.**

3 Tune-up > Somebody To Love 4:12 Grace talks about nothing in particular > Tune-up >

4 When The Earth Moves Again (F) 4:28
**This was the first appearance of the song.**

5 Grace talks about nothing in particular > Tune-up > Pretty As You Feel 6:53 Joey vocals.

6 Lawman (F) 2:25
**This was the first time performed.**

7 Come Back Baby 7:32 Jorma vocals

8 The Man (Bludgeon Of A Bluecoat) 4:41 Joey Vocals >

9 Wild Turkey (F) > Grace thanks the crowd 7:16
**This was the first appearance of the song.**

10 Tune-up > Third Week In The Chelsea (F) 5:25 Jorma vocals.
**This was the first appearance.**

11 Tune-Up > Joey clowns around on the drum kit >

War Movie (F & L) 5:58
**This was the only appearance of the song.**

12 Tune-Up > Volunteers > Starship (L) (Brief vocal excerpts) > Volunteers 6:41
**This was the final appearance of *Starship*.**

Those that were the casual fan and attended this show were surprised to say the least. Their reaction to *Rock And Roll Island* as the opening song was a combination of shock and bewilderment. The long time fanatics weren't far behind in their reverberations.

A new era had begun. The live performances would change dramatically. A look at the stage would be met by two less eyes. Marty Balin had left and now the current configuration had to fly the plane with one less member. There were some good moments from the 8/15/71 concert. *Pretty As You Feel* is a tremendous song and *Third Week In The Chelsea* is not only one of Jorma's finest moments but a lyrical masterpiece that any writer would be honored to have created.

8/18/71 Gaelic Park, Bronx, New York

(91:22) (Line-up 6)

1 The band is checking the sound levels on stage > Lawman 3:14

2 Tune-Up > Feel So Good 12:32 Vocals Jorma.

3 Grace has some stage banter with the fans as if she is doing a football cheer > Rock And Roll Island 5:34

4 Tune-up > Joey requests more volume > Pretty As You Feel 7:20

5 Tune-up > Come Back Baby 8:37 Jorma vocals.

6 Tune-up > When The Earth Moves Again 5:57

7 Tune-up > John's Other 8:28

8 Tune-up > Grace asks somebody in the crowd "Are you a chick?" > 1:01

9 Third Week In The Chelsea (L) 4:50 Jorma vocals with background by Grace.
**This was the final appearance of the song. It would be performed on the 1989 reunion tour but during the Hot Tuna segment.**

10 Tune-up > Somebody To Love 4:41 Interesting version. Grace skips some of the beginning words and at times sings the lyrics as if the song was an improvisational number.

4 Tune-up > Wild Turkey 12:08

5 Volunteers 4:45

**6 Eat Starch Mom (Instrumental version) (F) > Jam 12:11**
**This is the first ever appearance of the song.** The first time played with vocals would be circa 1/21/72- 3/1/72 Capitol Theater, Port Chester, New York. Please see that show for details. This was the second show of the 1971 tour. Would you believe that Grace's vocals were heard on under half the performance. During over fifty-one minutes of the show Grace's voice is not present! The band did open with a stronger number *Lawman* and *Eat Starch Mom* worked very well as an instrumental.

**There were only five shows that were scheduled during 1971.** Unfortunately there isn't documentation on the other three concerts.

# Chapter 8: 1972 "Rollin' On, Won't Be Long"

## Jorma Kaukonen-

<u>Circa 1/72-4/72 Yerba Buena Avenue, San Francisco, California (Home Demos)</u>

Any documentation that shows this as 6/72 is erroneous. There are six of the nine songs from the *Burgers* album found on these demos. There would be no reason to be recording demos of songs for any album that was already complete and that Hot Tuna was performing live already. If there isn't a comment about the song it means there wasn't anything out of the ordinary that warrants documentation.

(137:58)

1 Instrumental 4:25
In the same style as *Follow The Drinking Gourd*. This wasn't a spectacular piece but with some retooling it could have been released.

2 How Long Blues 3:25

3 Walkin' Blues (Loosely based) Instrumental 3:26
You can hear the similarity to *Walkin' Blues* and also enjoy Jorma's own flavor. This should have been given room on some Jorma solo LP.

4 I Want You To Know 3:43

5 New Song (For The Morning) 5:38

6 Been So Long (Instrumental) 3:16
Jorma has the incredible ability to make songs with or without the vocals legendary. As pretty as the lyrics are to the song you would equally enjoy the beauty of the guitar on this version.

7 Instrumental 3:05
This is better than the instrumental listed under song number one. It too is in the neighborhood of *Follow The Drinking Gourd*.

8 Fool's Blues 3:25
This is a stellar version of a tune that sounded terrific during the Hot Tuna 1970's period.

9 Sea Child 4:09 Found on the *Burgers* album.

10 New Song (For The Morning) 4:20

11 Water Song 4:16 Found on the *Burgers* album.
This was fascinating to experience the first time I heard this around 1976. The intro to the song is different and **there is no harmonic** (Sound that Jorma makes at the end of the song that sounds so magnificent).

12 Been so Long (Instrumental) 1:41 Cut

13 Water Song 4:15 Found on the *Burgers* album.
This version as well had a different arrangement. It is not nearly as strong as the finished product but provides a solid understanding how the tune progressed. **No harmonic at the end.**

14 Been So Long 3:44
The intro is somewhat different. Jorma is singing but doesn't have a microphone.

15 Improvisation > Police Dog Blues 3:46
Jorma does a very spirited version. This is as good as I've heard him play the song by himself.

16 Instrumental 5:13
There are a couple of interesting items about this one. The song sounds rather close to *Killing Time In The Crystal City* and it appears Jorma is talking to Tom Hobson (Credited on the *Quah* album with Jorma).

17 New Song (For The Morning) 5:11

18 Improvisation > I Know You Rider 4:11
If you asked Jorma to play this another one hundred times it is possible this version would not be topped! It has a magical feel and Jorma is tremendously inspired throughout the tune.

19 (99 Year Blues) 3:45 Found on the *Burgers* album.

20 Been So long 4:10
It appears Jorma is attempting to find his way for the direction he wishes the song to take root.

21 Death Don't Have No Mercy 6:04
Jorma does a very relaxed version.

22 I Want You To Know 3:23

23 Highway Song 2:15 Found on the *Burgers* album.
This was one song I couldn't wait to check out. I was curious how a version without the help of David Crosby would sound. The instrumentation is real strong and Jorma doesn't sing all the words. It is in the developmental stage and is on the fast track to success.

24 Uncle Same Blues 3:38
It's hard to accept any version that doesn't have Jack's thunderous bass coming in at the start of the song.

25 Instrumental 4:27
This is *Hamar Promenade* with a softer approach. It sounded very releasable.

26 I Want You To Know 3:30

27 Keep On Truckin' 4:07 Found on the *Burgers* album.

28 Instrumental 3:25
This was rather well done. It is in the realm of the Beatles song *Get Back*.

29 Sunny Day Strut 4:49 Found on the *Burgers* album.

30 Water Song 4:05 Found on the *Burgers* album.
This one should be unearthed. It begins with Jorma playing the ending with the harmonic and when the song is over he finishes with the harmonic again.

31 Sea Child 5:34 Found on the *Burgers* album.

32 (99 Year Blues) 4:04 Found on the *Burgers* album.

33 Happy Turtle Song 1:49
The rather underrated instrumental would finally be released on the Hot Tuna album *Pair A Dice Found* in 1990.

34 Third Week in The Chelsea 4:32

Do you recall the three tunes from *Burgers* that are not found on the demos from 1972?
That was excellent to name them that quickly. *True Religion, Ode For Billy Dean,* and *Let Us Get Together Right Down Here* are not found on the thirty-four songs listed above.

# Jefferson Airplane-

1/16/72 Public Hall, Cleveland, Ohio

(79:59) (Line-up 6)

The 1972 tour opened on the fourteenth of January at the Crisler Arena, Ann Arbor, Michigan. There is no documentation as to what songs were performed.

1 Somebody To Love 4:50 First few notes were cut.

2 Tune-up > When The Earth Moves Again 5:29

3 Grace thanks the crowd > A cool dog starts to bark in the background > Twilight Double Leader (F) 3:19
**This was the first appearance of the song.**

4 Lawman 2:59

5 Tune-up > Feel So Good 10:08 With Jorma vocal and a Jack bass-solo.

6 Papa John intros the next song > Down Home Blues (F) 4:51
From his 1971 self-titled album. **This was the first documented show with Papa John performing the song and singing a lead vocal.**

7 Pretty As You Feel (L) 5:41 Joey lead vocals.
**This was the final appearance of the song.**

8 Tune-up > Rock And Roll Island (L) 4:01
**This was the last appearance of the song.**

9 Tune-up > Good Shepherd 7:33 Jorma vocals.

10 Tune-up > The Man (Bludgeon Of A Bluecoat) (L) Joey vocals. 4:50 >
**This was the final appearance of the song.**

11 Come Back Baby 7:27 Jorma vocals.

**12 China (F & L) 3:47**
This Is from Paul's 1971 album *Sunfighter*. **This was the only time the song was performed.**

13 Greasy Heart 3:53

**14 String Jet Rock (Papa John instrumental with the band) 5:54 (F & L)**
This is from Papa John's 1971 self-titled album. This has always been erroneously reported as an untitled instrumental, or *jam*. **It is the only documented time the song was performed by the Airplane.**

**15 Diana :53 (F)**
This is from Paul's 1971 *Sunfighter* album. Paul did a hybrid version of the two parts. The first four lines were from *Part 2*, as were the next four, and then the final two were from *Part 1*. **This is the first appearance of *Diana*!**

16 Volunteers 4:16

The performance was very strong and with many surprises. Although the days of the set list being from the classic period 1965-70 ended with Marty's departure, there are always strong moments you can pick out from the post Marty era. *When The Earth Moves Again* is a solid live song. Papa John does a nice job during *Down Home Blues* and *String Jet Rock* had the crowd hanging on every note. Paul did his share with a live taste of *China* and *Diana* from *Sunfighter*. The band would soon have replacement parts but the old plane could still reach the proper altitude during portions of the last tour.

Circa 1/21/72- 3/1/72 Capitol Theater, Port Chester, New York

(40:18) (Line-up 7) Welcome aboard David Freiberg!

The only documentation of the performance is the last half.

1 Tune-up > Trial By Fire 4:48 Jorma vocals.

2 Blind John 5:06 David vocals.

3 Tune-up > Have You Seen The Saucers 4:40

4 Tune-up > Aerie (Gang Of Eagles) (F) 3:45
**This was the first live appearance of the song.**

5 Eat Starch Mom (F) (Vocal version) 5:27
Excellent energy from the band. **This was the first time performed <u>with vocals</u>.** The first time played was as an instrumental going into a *jam* from 8/18/71 Gaelic Park, Bronx, New York. Please see that show for details.

6 Tune –Up > Twilight Double Leader 4:52
Even those that will never be happy with any post 1970 performances have given this song the thumbs up.

7 Tune-up > Diana 1:29
Paul did a hybrid version. The first four lines were from *Part 2*, as were the next four, and then the final two were from *Part 1*.

8 Volunteers 4:44

9 Tune-up > :26

10 Short Improvisation :10 >

11 Tune-up > When The Earth Moves Again 4:46
This song worked very well on the final tour. It is perfect in the five minute range and did not need to be retooled.

198

(38:49) (Line-up 7)

Joey Covington may have been a part of these sessions. Joey left April of 1972. John Barbata did not recall spending any of this time in the studio with the J.A. His only recollection of being in the studio when first joining the Airplane was to rehearse. Sammy Piazza (Hot Tuna) did not remember being present for the recording of the *Trial By Fire* sessions.

1 Instrumental Blues Jam  10:27
The music was slow blues with an increase in tempo roughly half-way through. There weren't any memorable segments that could have been used for insertions on other songs.

2 Tuning 1972  4:05
The members of the band are tuning-up and do so by playing a bit of the selection from the *Instrumental Blues Jam.*

3 Eat Starch Mom (Instrumental) 6:28
The unreleased version is one minute and fifty-six seconds more than the one on the *Long John Silver* album. On the instrumental version Jorma starts off with a short guitar solo. The bass and guitar are mixed a bit higher than the original vinyl version. This was very well done. There certainly were a couple of options. You could add the vocals or keep this as an instrumental. If the band and record company decided to use this version either as the master with the vocals being added or keeping it without the lyrics, no fan of the band would have found legitimate complaints.

4 Trial By Fire 1 (Instrumental) 5:20
The released version on the *Bark* album (With vocals) was forty-four seconds shorter. The instrumental has a very tasty acoustic guitar and a great mix of the bass. At the early stages the song already sounds as if a lot of care went into the craftsmanship but Jorma would make changes in the instrumentation as he went along.

5 Trial By Fire 2 (Instrumental) **With Jerry Garcia** 5:33
The second instrumental version with help from Jerry Garcia of the Grateful Dead is fifty-seven seconds longer than the *Bark* version. This started off with the testing of the sound of the drums. It appeared Jerry Garcia played a peddle steel guitar. The version has a very upbeat and well designed sound. There are more recognizable passages from what would be put down on the final mix but still some changes would occur.

6 Tuning with My Creole Belle tease 1:47
*My Creole Belle* is a song written and made popular by blues musician Mississippi John Hurt. While the musicians are tuning a small portion of the tune is played!

7 Trial By Fire 3 (Instrumental) **With Jerry Garcia** 5:09
This version is thirty-three seconds longer than the *Bark* album release. Jorma has added some fill-ins on the guitar and at about two minutes and thirty-five seconds the song begins to hold a stronger consistency to what the ears would discover when hearing the final production.

3/22/72 Wally Heider Studios, San Francisco California

(Recording session for *Revolutionary Upstairs Maid*)

When I interviewed Paul Kantner he did authenticate the legitimacy of the song. There isn't any other documentation available.

# Jorma Kaukonen-

<u>6/72 Yerba Buena Avenue, San Francisco, California (Home Demos)</u>

This date is not correct.  The Hot Tuna album *Burgers* was already getting reviewed and the band was performing the material prior to this date.  Please see Circa 1/72-4/72 for complete details.

# Jefferson Airplane-

<u>7/1/72 Auditorium Theater, Chicago, Illinois</u>

The band did not perform on this date.  Please see the entry from 8/25/72 for all the details.

<u>Circa summer 1972</u>

(2:08) (Line-up 7) Joey Covington was on part of the record (*Long John Silver)* but with the appearance of John Barbata on both the album and 1972 tour there was a change in the line-up.  The change is reflected on the next live entry which is from 7/72.

*Long John Silver Radio Commercials.*

1 Long John Silver (Radio commercial) (1) 1972 (1:05)

Announcer: "I walk into a room, it's nicely furnished." > Long John Silver > Announcer > Long John Silver
The beginning of the commercial is brilliant.  The spoken words have nothing to do with the album!  Only slight excerpts of the title track from the record are played.

2 Long John (Radio commercial) (2) 1972 (1:03)
Announcer: "Does the name *Long John Silver* ring a bell?" > Milk Train > Announcer: "Does the name Jefferson Airplane ring a bell?" > Alexander The Medium > Announcer with music from Alexander The Medium being played in conjunction with his voice.

The first short commercial is much better.  The second however did give the consumer two short song excerpts, and it did not repeat *Long John Silver* from the first one.  Only excerpts of the songs are played.

JEFFERSON AIRPLANE

Exclusively on **GRUNT** Records

Manufactured and Marketed by **RCA** Records

Photograph by kind permission of Mike Somavilla. From the Mike Somavilla collection.

Not to be reproduced without written permission of Mike Somavilla.

Photographer unknown.

This is a promo picture of the J.A. circa 7/72 with new member John Barbata.

Thank you BMG.

(83:23) (Line-Up 8) **First show with John Barbata.  Welcome to the flight John.**

1 Have You Seen The Saucers 1:51 The start of the song was cut.

2 Tune-up > Grace intros the newer members David and John > Aerie (Gang Of Eagles) 3:59

3 Tune-up > Feel So Good 11:39 Jorma vocals.

4 Tune-up 3:00

5 Lawman 3:19

6 Tune-up > Crown Of Creation 3:21
It was nice to see the band play another older tune (1968).

7 Tune-up > Paul intros the next song and intros David > Blind John 5:39 David vocals.

8 Paul intros the next song > Tune-up > Milk Train (F) 4:20
**This was the first appearance of *Milk Train*.**

9 Tune-up > Long John Silver (F) 6:53
**This was the first time played.**

10 Tune-up > Wooden Ships 2:50 Cut.

11 Improvisation > Greasy Heart 4:04

12 Grace thanks the crowd > Walking The Tou-Tou (F) (Instrumental) 7:03
This ended up on Papa John's 1972 album *Filthy*.  **It is the first documented version the band performed.**
With a catchy "riff" by Jorma it came off very well.

13 Trial By Fire (F) 3:47 Jorma vocals. Cut.
**This was the first appearance** of the song that would become heavily requested during any incarnation of Hot Tuna.

14 Twilight Double Leader 4:45 The start of the song was missing.

15 Eat Starch Mom 6:00 Vocal version.

16 Diana (Not from the start) :47
Paul did a hybrid version.  The first four lines were from *Part 2,* as were the next four, and then the final two
were from *Part 1.* >

17 Volunteers > Paul thanks the audience 5:26

18 Encore: When The Earth Moves Again 4:29  The band gave a lot of credence to this song on the 1972 tour.
Often documented as the encore!

<ins>8/10/72 Dillon Stadium, Hartford, Connecticut</ins>

(85:06) (Line-up 8)

There have been many false representations of the set list of this concert. The songs that has been omitted from documentation have notations below.

1 Tune-up > Have You Seen The Saucers > Grace thanks the crowd 4:28

2 Aerie (Gang Of Eagles) 3:02 The start of the song was cut.

3 Feel So Good 11:16 Jorma vocals and with a Jack bass-solo.

4 When The Earth Moves Again > Grace thanks the crowd 3:49

5 Tune-up > Crown Of Creation 3:47

6 Long John Silver 5:09 The ending was cut.

7 Blind John 4:42 Vocals David.

8 Trial By Fire 4:37 Jorma vocals.

9 Tune-up > Walking The Tou-Tou 7:03 No vocals. The playing time was longer, but the master recording had starts and stops during the song.

10 Tune-up > Twilight Double Leader 5:59

11 Tune-up > Lawman > Grace thanks the crowd 2:58

12 Eat Starch Mom 4:49 With vocals.

13 Wooden Ships 6:17 With: Go Ride The Music.

14 Tune-up > Band Improvisation :42

15 Volunteers 2:37
Amazingly short for a live version. The entire song didn't even last three minutes!

16 Paul thanks the crowd > Somebody To Love > Grace thanks the crowd 3:45

17 Come Back Baby 6:00 Jorma vocals .

18 Greasy Heart 4:05

**Songs twelve through eighteen are often left off any documentation of this performance.**

8/12/72 Festival Of Hope, Roosevelt Raceway, Westbury, New York

(84:19) (Line-up 8)

1 Tune-up > Paul intros John and David >

Paul intros the next song > Blind John 5:51 Vocals David. The ending was cut.

2 John Barbata briefly plays around on the drums > Tune-up > Paul intros the next song > Eat Starch Mom (With vocals) 8:00

3 Tune-up > Wooden Ships 8:47 With: Go Ride The Music

4 Tune-up > The sound crew is working on the stage trouble > The Other Side Of This Life (L) 8:28
**This was the final time the song would be played until the opening night of the reunion tour.** It wouldn't be performed again after the initial 1989 show. Would you like to know a secret just between you and me? This tune should have continuously shown up on the 1989 tour.

5 Tune-up > Good Shepherd 8:17 (L) (Cut) Jorma vocals.
Grace sang some improvisational lyrics. **This was the last time the song was performed until the 1989 reunion tour.**

6 Tune-up > Have You Seen The Saucers 5:16
There was a great reaction from the crowd.

7 Paul thanks the crowd > Tune-up > Paul intros the next song > Aerie (Gang Of Eagles) 3:59

8 Grace thanks the crowd > Feel So Good 12:36 Jorma vocals. There was a well done segment with a bass and drum-solo together.

9 Tune-up > Crown Of Creation 4:02

10 Tune up > Grace intros the next song > Milk Train 5:19

11 Grace thanks the crowd > Tune-up > When The Earth Moves Again 5:17

12 Tune-up > Paul intros the next song > Long John Silver > Grace thanks the crowd 8:21

When the band played the three classic period songs in a row *Wooden Ships*, *The Other Side Of This Life*, and *Good Shepherd*, it was terrific that the older tunes were not only performed, but twenty five minutes of the concert allowed people to go back in the time tunnel! That didn't lesson the bad news. *The Other Side Of This Life* and *Good Shepherd* would not be allowed to fly again until 1989.

8/15/72 Bandshell, Central Park, New York City

There is no data to support the band performed in New York City or any other location on this night. Please see the next entry 8/16/72 for details of the concert.

8/16/72 Bandshell, Central Park, New York City

(70:04) (Line-up 8)

1 Somebody To Love 3:55

2 Grace thanks the crowd > Bill Graham intros Papa John because he had forgotten to when the show started > Tune-up > Grace intros David and the next song > Crown Of Creation 4:06

3 Twilight Double Leader 5:38

4 Feel So Good 10:07 The start of the song was cut. Jorma vocals.
There was a nice combination bass and drum-solo segment.

5 Tune-up > Long John Silver (With short drum-solo) 6:44 Cut.
This is right up there with any live version of the song.

204

6 Tune-up > Blind John 5:07 David vocals.

7 Grace thanks the crowd > Have You Seen The Saucers 3:48

8 Grace thanks the crowd > Aerie (Gang Of Eagles) 2:06 Both the start and the end of the song were cut.

9 Trial By Fire 4:34 Jorma vocals.

10 Wooden Ships 6:14 With: Go Ride The Music. The intro was cut.

11 Diana :46 The intro was cut.
Paul did a hybrid version. The first four lines were from *Part 2*, as were the next four, and then the final two were from *Part 1*.

12 Volunteers > Paul, and Grace thank the crowd 4:08

13 Encore: Tune-up > Papa John says hello to the crowd, and intros the next song > John's Other 7:33 >

14 Encore: Eat Starch Mom (With vocals) > Paul and Grace thank the crowd 5:11
The blending of the two encores worked very well. Jorma was becoming more and more comfortable with *Feel So Good*.

Of the music that has been documented from this performance there weren't any *jam's*. In fact some of the songs were not long at all.

8/25/72 Auditorium Theater, Chicago, Illinois

(147:21) (Line-up 8)

This had often been mistakenly documented being from 7/1/72. The band did not perform on that day. Three songs from this performance were selected to be on *Thirty Seconds Over Winterland*. Those were *Crown Of Creation* , *When The Earth Moves Again*, and *Milk Train*. The August twenty-fourth show from the same venue was the source for *Trial By Fire*, for the live record.

1 Tune-up 3:39 >

2 Somebody To Love (L) 4:44
**This was the last time played until the 1989 reunion.** It is hard to close the airport to so many of the historic tunes. A piece of your heart and the engine of the plane have been removed.

3 Tune-up > Wooden Ships: With :Go Ride The Music 6:51

4 Tune-up > Milk Train 5:08

5 Tune-up > Long John Silver 6:03

6 Tune-up > Paul intros the next song > Blind John 6:22 Vocals David.

7 Tune-up > Papa John intros the next song > John's Other 7:13

8 Trial By Fire 5:25 Jorma vocals. Cut.

9 Tune-up > Lawman 4:29

10 Tune-up > Papa John intros the next song > Down Home Blues > Papa John thanks the crowd 5:31

11 Paul intros the next Song > Twilight Double Leader > Grace thanks the crowd 5:21

12 Tune-up > Crown Of Creation 4:11

13 Tune-up > Jorma tells a joke > Eat Starch Mom 5:53 With vocals.

14 Tune-up > Improvisation > Tune-up 6:50

15 Have You Seen The Saucers 3:42

16 Tune-up > Aerie (Gang Of Eagles) 4:23

17 Tune-up > Feel So Good 13:28 Jorma vocals. With bass and drum-solo, at the same time.

18 Tune-up > Greasy Heart (L) 4:18
**This was the last appearance of the song.**

19 Tune-up > Walking The Tou-Tou (Instrumental) 8:02

20 Tune-up > Come Back Baby 7:57 Jorma vocals.

21 Tune-up > Diana > Paul thanks the crowd for coming 1:09
Paul did a hybrid version of the song. The first four lines were from *Part 2*, as were the next four, and then the final two were from *Part 1*.

22 Volunteers > Paul thanks the crowd 4:53

23 Encore: Tune-up > Paul intros the next song 3:06

24 Encore: Wild Turkey (F) 9:06
**This was the last appearance of the song.**

25 Encore: Tune-up > When The Earth Moves Again > Paul thanks the crowd 5:09

26 Encore: Grace Improvisational vocal and conversation with the audience.
The band had left, but Grace stayed on stage and fooled around a bit with her voice, and talked with the crowd. 5:09

<u>9/3/72 Hollywood Bowl, Hollywood, California</u>

(35:20) (Line-up 8)

Only about a third of the show has been documented.

1 Tune-up > Trial By Fire 3:51 Cut.

2 Blind John 3:26 **With: *Big Bad John* ending!** (F & L) (The intro was cut).
David does a cool thing as the song ends he adds the words from the 1961 (#1) song by Jimmy Dean called *Big Bad John*. The song was composed by Jimmy Dean and Roy Acuff. **This was the only time the band used the line from the song.**

3 Tune-up > Have You Seen The Saucers > Grace thanks the crowd 4:28

4 David intros the next song > Aerie (Gang Of Eagles) 3:33

5 Tune-up > Grace thanks the crowd > Eat Starch Mom 5:11

6 Tune-up > Twilight Double Leader 4:33 Songs five and six had the best energy of the evening.

7 Tune-up > Diana 1:34
Paul did a hybrid version of the song. The first four lines were from *Part 2*, as were the next four, and then the final two were from *Part 1*. >

8 Volunteers > Grace thanks the crowd 4:36

9 Encore: When The Earth Moves Again 4:02

## 9/22/72 Winterland, San Francisco, California

(128:31) (Line-up 8) **An old friend helps say "Goodbye" on the encore!**

**Sadly this was the last Airplane show until the 1989 reunion. San Francisco radio station KSAN helped preserve history by making this a live broadcast. Thank you many times over.**

1 Bill Graham intros the band 1:14

2 Somebody To Love (L) > Tune-up > Grace intros the first song 5:21
**This was the last performance of the song until the 1989 reunion tour.**

3 Twilight Double Leader (L) 6:38
**This was the last time the song would be performed.**

4 Wooden Ships 6:45 With: Go Ride The Music (L) 6:45
**This was the last performance of the song until the 1989 reunion tour.** *Go Ride The Music* would not be included on the version played by the J.A. in 1989. Why not I declare?

5 Milk Train (L) > Grace intros the next song > Tune-up 4:30
**This was the last time the song was ever performed.**

6 Blind John (L) > Tune- up > 5:24
**This was the last time the song was ever performed.**

7 Tune-up > Come Back Baby (L) (Jorma vocals) > Tune-up 7:34
**This was the last performance of the song until the 1989 reunion tour.**

8 Grace fooling around on stage > Tune-up > The Son Of Jesus (F & L) 6:08
**This was the only performance of the song!**

9 Long John Silver (L) 5:24
**This would be the last time the song was ever played.**

10 When The Earth Moves Again (L) > Tune-up > 4:22
**This is the last appearance of the song.**

11 Down Home Blues (L) 5:25 Papa John vocals.
**This was the last time ever performed.**

12 Eat Starch Mom (L) 6:17 With vocals.
**This was the last time ever performed.**

13 John's Other (L) 6:22 >
**This would be the final appearance ever.**

14 Tune-Up > Trial By Fire (L) 5:55 Jorma vocals.
**This would be the last time the song would be performed.**

15 Lawman (L) 3:15
**This would be the final appearance ever.**

16 Have You Seen The Saucers (L) 4:27
**This would be the final appearance ever.** The 11/13/70 Capitol Theater, Port Chester, New York (Late show) had the final version of the song going into another tune (*Starship)*.

17 Aerie (Gang Of Eagles) (L) 3:43
**This was the final performance of the song ever.**

18 Feel So Good (L) 11:32 Jorma vocals.
**This was the final appearance.**

19 Crown Of Creation (L) 3:25
**This was the last time played until the 1989 reunion tour.**

20 Walking The Tou-Tou (L) 6:01 (Instrumental)
**This was the final appearance.**

21 Diana (L) :53
Paul did a hybrid version of the song. The first four lines were from *Part 2*, as were the next four, and then the final two were from *Part 1*. >
**This was the final appearance of the song ever.**

22 Volunteers (L) 4:25
**This was the final appearance, until the 1989 reunion tour.**

23 Grace Slick's: *You Wear Your Dresses Too Short Improvisation (F & L)* 1:24
Grace has some fun as she improvises the lyrics. **This was the only time performed.**

## Marty Balin returns!
24 Encore: Dress Rap (F & L) > You Wear Your Dresses Too Short (L) 13:01
**This was the only time the *Dress Rap* would be performed.** The 11/25/70 Fillmore East, New York City show would be the last time *You Wear Your Dresses Too Short* was performed without improvisation first. Please see that date for details.

An old friend returns. **Marty Balin** vocals on the final song of the final flight. In a fantasy world where every wish comes true the last concert of the band would have been a celebration of the years 1965-1972. Any member that was part of the group even for a day would have been able to sing or play on at least one song. If that couldn't happen the next hope would have been for more songs with Marty on stage. Only about a third of the show encompassed the material those that were fans of the group during the Marty Balin era would have wanted to experience. Bill Graham's intro and opening with *Somebody To Love* made for a nice take-off. Had this been an ordinary affair the show would have been very good for the post Marty Balin period. As the final notes bleared during the encore how many at Winterland or listening at home knew the plane would be grounded seventeen years?"

10/3/72 Winterland, San Francisco, California

The band did not perform on this date. Any recorded information from 10/3/72 is really the 9/22/72 final show at Winterland. Please see that entry for details.

# Marty Balin-

1973 Bodacious D.F. (With Marty Balin vocals) Rehearsal

(42:36) The rehearsal information is found after the LP listing.

The original self-titled LP looked like this:

1 Drifting 4:08
Marty performed this tune with the Jefferson Airplane and Hot Tuna. His vocals were terrific on the LP version and the band handled the music similar to how the Jefferson Starship (If recording in 1973) would have interpreted the arrangement.

2 Good Folks 7:35
This selection was between a ballad and a mid-tempo song. The bass and drums were most dominate.

3 The Witcher 6:34
Marty used a vocal parallel to the one on *Drifting*. This was a good rock and roll song.

4 Roberta 4:24
A bit of the blues surfaced on this composition. Marty sounded very focused and the band stayed enough in the background to let the words carry the tune.

5 Second Hand Information 4:56
This one is reminiscent of some of the older Airplane vocal improvisations Marty had done. The music isn't in the same realm but when Marty sang the words it seemed as if he wanted to make them up as the song unfolded.

6 Drivin' Me Crazy 7:11
If somebody listened with half an ear they may be convinced this was an early Jefferson Starship ballad.

7 Twixt Two Worlds 5:46
The track should never have fallen under the cracks. It has the terrific early 1970's rock sound and the approach Vic Smith used on the guitar were very clever.

Marty Balin- Vocals.

Gregory Dewey- Drums.

Mark Ryan- Bass.

Vic Smith- Guitar.

One of the guest appearances came from vocalist Anna Rizzo (Country Joe McDonald and Kingfish). She appeared on stage with Hot Tuna for a set on 8/25/86 at Pulsations, Media, Pennsylvania. Anna also worked with Marty on the 1972 self-titled LP by Grootna. Marty did not sing with the band but did participate in the recording as producer.

**The rehearsals looked like this:**

1 Tune-up > Roberta 4:19 Very low outro.
Marty takes a page from the Leon Russell vocal book and sings portions of the song the way Leon handled his famous tune *Tight Rope*.

2 Drifting Around 3:58 Very low outro.
The guitar intro was turned up a notch and the band did a solid version.

3 The Witcher 6:15
There was a strong intro of about one minute before you realized the song they would rehearse next was *The Witcher*.

4 Good Folks (False Start) > Good Folks 7:12
After a few seconds of the drums beginning the song the band realized it was a false start and started over. Mark Ryan's bass was high in the mix even during the guitar solo.

5 Drifting 3:40 Low intro.
For the second *Drifting* there is hardly any intro. It was interested that the song was presented in two forms. The first had about a twenty-five second intro and the second omitted it almost entirely.

6 Good Folks 7:40 Low intro.
The bass intro was almost reminiscent of some of the heavy metal of the time. Once the vocals kicked in it was back to a rock and roll number.

7 The Witcher 6:34
Gregory Dewey did some well conceived drumming and the entire band clicked. Throughout the rehearsals Marty was able to showcase different parts of his vocal repertoire.

# Hot Tuna (Jorma, Jack, and Bob Steeler) -

<u>1974 Wally Heider Studios, San Francisco, California (*America's Choice* out-takes)</u>

(33:42)

1 Hit Single #1 (5:20) No vocals.

2 Serpent Of Dreams 6:52 Vocals and long ending note.

3 Walking Blues 7:13 No vocals.

4 Invitation 9:58 No vocals and long fade.

5 Sleep Song 4:19 Vocals.

The songs without the lyrics were fascinating to hear in a different environment. The energy level was exceptionally high on all the selections and *Invitation* as you would expect was a blowtorch.

## Hot Tuna (Jorma, Jack, Bob Steeler, and Greg Douglass) -

<u>Circa Winter 1975 Studio Rehearsals</u>

(38:33)

1 Baby What You Want Me To Do 4:43

2 Come Back Baby W/Jam 7:37 Cut

3 Slow Blues Jam W/Improvisation 8:12

4 I'll Be Alright Someday 1:45 (Done as an instrumental).

5 Sally Where'd You Get That Liquor From? 1:41

6 Jam 14:23 Cut
The *jam* was loosely based on *Easy Now*. It was as compelling as you would imagine. Wouldn't it have been an even tastier sandwich if Greg were part of the band until at least the end of the 1977 tour?

## Hot Tuna (Jorma, Jack, and Bob Steeler) -

<u>1975 Wally Heider Studios, San Francisco, California</u> (*Yellow Fever* out-takes)

(26:29)

1 Song For the Fire Maiden 5:05

2 Free Rain 4:05

3 Bar Room Crystal Ball 6:19

4 Sunrise Dance With The Devil 4:55

5 Surphase Tension 3:49

6 Instrumental 3:49

All the songs are without vocals! The final selection has often been documented as *Watch The North Wind Rise* that **is not correct.** The instrumental versions further illustrate the meaning of power trio. It's so easy (Sorry Buddy Holly and Norman Petty) to take for granted the period of 1975-1977 and all the brilliance that came with it.

## Hot Tuna (Jorma, Jack, Bob Steeler, and Nick Buck) -

<u>7/77 Jorma's Basement rehearsal, San Francisco, California</u>

(72:15)

1 Thunderbolt Song 4:48 Instrumental

This sounds like the Who song *Eminence Front*. While the Who version came out after, it is the best comparison available. Without question with a bit of work this could have been presented for both the stage and recording studio.

2 Snow Gorilla 6:34 Instrumental
This is pure Hot Tuna metal. It is an all out assault of the senses. It is a miscarriage of justice this never became part of any live or studio album. Hot Tuna did perform this on the 1977 tour.

3 Tune-up for Bright Eyes :36

4 Bright Eyes 5:12 Instrumental
The exact words I wrote for *Snow Gorilla* should be cloned for *Bright Eyes*. It is a monster tune.

5 I Don't Know 8:43 Jorma sings but there isn't a microphone.
This sounded as if it was a *jam* and Jorma wanted to see how vocals would fit. It's a standard rock and roll based tune.

6 I Don't Know 3:47 Jorma sings but there isn't a microphone.

7 I Don't Know 7:48 Jorma sings but there isn't a microphone.

8 Wolves And Lambs 5:25 Jorma sings but there isn't a microphone.
This is a treasure that should not be guarded by the Rock And Roll Vault Commission. *Wolves And Lambs* sounds like a relative of *Watch The North Wind Rise*! The instrumentation is certainly in the same family!

9 Wolves And Lambs 1:16 Ending only. Jorma sings but there isn't a microphone.

10 Wolves And Lambs 5:56 Jorma sings but there isn't a microphone.

11 Jack's Tune 1:16
A short instrumental with Jack upfront in the mix.

12 Killing Time In The Crystal City 7:33 Jorma sings but there isn't a microphone.
Nothing of interest here. It sounded exactly like the way you thought it would.

13 Killing Time In The Crystal City 1:55 (Ending Only) Jorma sings but there isn't a microphone.

14 Killing Time In The Crystal City 1:57 (Ending Only) Jorma sings but there isn't a microphone. Jorma had a terrific sound on the guitar that totally enhanced the final section of the tune.

15 Lost In Time 2:31 Instrumental
This could be related to *Funky #7*. It is a little less funky but every bit as rock and roll. Here is another treasure that could have been worthy of being part of a studio and or live recording.

16 Swamp Life 6:33 Instrumental.
This is in the same style as *Snow Gorilla* and *Bright Eyes*, but a step below in terms of the result. This clearly showed how easily there could have been a superlative follow-up to *Hoppkorv*. The only thing missing from the rehearsals was a version of the *Party Song* which was played on the 1977 tour with Jack singing background vocals.

# Jefferson Airplane-

<u>Circa 1980's Bill Graham Documentary</u>

(2:11) (Line-up 2)

Before the plane makes its next stop in Milwaukee 1989, a quick word about the *Bill Graham Documentary*. This is very close to the 1/29/67 *Bell Telephone Hour: The Sights And Sounds Of San Francisco*. Filmed during either 7 or 8/66 (In amazing black, and white) at the Fillmore Auditorium, San Francisco, California. This presentation has short interviews with Bill Graham and Carlos Santana recorded during the filming of the documentary. A lot of the footage is similar to the program from 1/29/67 but does not show the stage where you can recognize Signe Anderson as one of the performers.

1 It's No Secret 2:11

# Marty Balin-

<u>1981 Hearts (Video)</u>

(4:16)

The video gives a further appreciation for the song. It's no secret (Sorry Marty) that most of the videos released during the heyday of music television were mind numbing, out of touch with the song, and generally forgettable. Marty was able to create a character in the video that enhances the tune. From the beginning the scope of the production isn't what your mind would presuppose. Marty is in jail and for most of the four plus minutes we get a peak inside his mind as how he feels about a certain young lady. There are segments of Marty and the woman on the outside but the simplistic setting of a jail cell, an acoustic guitar, and man torn from his true love is a great representation through images of a hit single and song known worldwide.

Jorma Kaukonen
Marty Balin

Grace Slick

Paul Kantner
Jack Casady

**JEFFERSON AIRPLANE**

Photo Credit: Lynn Goldsmith / LGI

**Photograph by kind permission of Mike Somavilla. From the Mike Somavilla collection.**

**May not be reproduced without the written consent of Mike Somavilla.**

**Photograph by Lynn Goldsmith.**

**This is a 1989 promotional photo.**

**Thank you Sony Music.**

# Jefferson Airplane-

<u>1989 Music Videos</u>

(8:10) (Line-up 9)

1 Planes 4:31

Without Peter Kaukonen, Tim Gorman, and Randy Jackson.  Kenny Aronoff is on the video for exactly one second!

Based on the vibrant footage of planes and rocket ships Paul Kantner had to have been involved with the project far more than just musically.  The video starts with moving clouds while a young boy is sleeping.  Throughout his dream you are told the story of the song.  An unidentified man leads him on a journey to realize his fantasy to explore the sky.  This was a well thought of sub-plot because the viewer thinks they know the man and most do.  The color footage of the band is simplistic as they are most commonly shown in an airplane hanger.  The black and white shots from the studio are excellent.  At the end of the video when the young boy is back in his bed we see the badge on the man from the dream and it reads H. Hughes.

2 True Love 3:39

Without Peter Kaukonen and Randy Jackson.
All involved with the making of the video did a very unappreciated job.  The final result was well constructed to the point even if you didn't like the song you could enjoy the production.  The theme of the video was a circus and side-show act.  When you first see the intro there is a sign that says *Tunnel Of Love.*"  That was the name of the hit album for Bruce Springsteen in 1987.  Marty is dressed as a ringmaster and Grace as a nun.  Kenny Aronoff is on drums and Tim Gorman handles the keyboards.  Randy Jackson and Peter Kaukonen are not seen.  Marty was excellent in the role of ringmaster and seemed genuinely into the entire festivities.  The Rickenbacker guitar Paul was using couldn't have fit anyone more deservingly.

Thanks to http://airplanestarship.tripod.com/index.html for being the one site on the internet to inform the J.A. fan where they can watch the Airplane and Jefferson Starship videos!  That would be http://music.aol.com/artist/jefferson-airplane/4603/video .

# 8/18/89 Riverside Theater, Milwaukee, Wisconsin

(149:58) (Line-up 9)

## The opening night of the reunion tour!  The plane is full of fuel, at least for a couple of months!  Doesn't it still look great?

1 She Has Funny Cars 5:22
If you didn't know the set list it was not only a great opening choice, but a gift!

2 Marty says "Hello Milwaukee" as the vocals are about to come in > Somebody To Love > Grace thanks the crowd 3:20

3 Plastic Fantastic Lover 4:12

4 Won't You Try/Saturday Afternoon 4:49

5 Today> Grace tells the crowd "It is about eighteen years since we played together." 3:32

6 Paul intros the next song > Good Shepherd 6:14 Jorma vocals.

7 Grace intros the next song > Lather 3:14
**First time played with 100 percent documentation since 11/10/68 on the Smothers Brothers Comedy Hour**.

8 Paul intros the next song > Solidarity 5:59

9 Wooden Ships > Paul and Grace thank the crowd 4:52
*Go Ride The Music* **would not** be performed during the 1989 reunion. Please don't throw anything at the stage.

10 The Wheel: With drum-solo 6:03 >

11 America 7:56

12 Paul intros the next song > Freedom > Paul thanks the crowd > Grace intros Randy Jackson and thanks the crowd 6:49

Hot Tuna set: Jorma and Jack. (36:48)

13 Hesitation Blues 5:20

14 Walkin' Blues 3:44

15 Let Us Get Together Right Down Here 2:36

16 Candy Man 4:16

17 San Francisco Bay Blues 4:16

18 Police Dog Blues 4:06

19 Killing Time In The Crystal City 6:00

20 Third Week In The Chelsea (**With Grace**) > Grace intros Jorma and Jack 6:30 > Grace intros the next song

(That was the end of the Hot Tuna set) >
**On all the shows Grace would join Jorma and Jack for *Third Week In The Chelsea*. It was one of the great parts of the concert. A phenomenal song escalated a bit higher.**

21 Panda 3:37 Grace solo on piano > Grace thanks the crowd.
Grace used the solo during the tour to talk about the love she had for pandas and the importance of helping them survive.

**22 Miracles 7:00 >**
**Obviously first time performed by J.A.** There were **many in shock** that Jorma and Jack would agree to play this song. It was also an interesting addition to the set list. You would think the songs would have been from 1965-1972 and the reunion record.

23 Paul intros the next song as it starts > Planes > Grace intros Kenny Aronoff 6:10
*Planes* was one of the three best tracks on the 1989 album (The other two being *Summer Of Love* and *Ice Age*), but it should have remained about where you see it in the set list. The song would actually become an encore!

24 Paul intros the next song > Ice Age 7:00 Jorma vocals > Tune-up

25 Summer Of Love 3:47
This had a lot of meaning to those on the stage and many that were old enough to have been there (1967 that is).

26 True Love 3:38

27 Short Improvisation > Crown Of Creation 2:47

28 White Rabbit 2:44
Grace did very well singing the high notes.

29 Grace thanks the crowd > Volunteers (With false ending as Marty thanks a bunch of people and organizations) > Paul thanks the crowd 5:18

30 Encore: Grace thanks the crowd and Marty tells them "We did the reunion not to go through life thinking what if." > It's No Secret 3:26

31 Encore: Paul tells the crowd "We first rehearsed this last night." (As the song starts) > The Other Side Of This Life 5:11
**This would be the only time the band performed *The Other Side Of This Life* during the reunion tour.**

What were your thoughts on the songs that were <u>not</u> included, such as *Fat Angel, 3/5 Of A Mile In 10 Seconds, The Ballad Of You And Me And Pooneil,* and *We Can Be Together*? The band also performed eight songs from the reunion record, one from the Jefferson Starship (*Miracles),* and one from KBC (*America*). By doing this obviously not all the legendary 1965-1972 tunes would make it to the stage. The newer material was clustered together. At one point four songs in a row were from the 1989 album and six in a row were non Airplane tunes. Hot Tuna performed eight songs during their set. The 1989 tour had four musicians not previously part of the live Airplane shows. Kenny Aronoff was known at the time for being the drummer for John Mellencamp, Tim Gorman had played keyboards with KBC, Randy Jackson was a member of Zebra, and on this tour played guitar, keyboards, and sang, and Peter Kaukonen (Guitar) had his own material as well as having played on but not limited to, Paul Kantner's album *Blows Against The Em*pire, *Sunfighter* and Grace's record *Manhole*. Peter's flight experiences includes (But not limited to) live stops with both Hot Tuna and the Jefferson Starship.

<u>8/19/89 Fox Theater, St. Louis, Missouri</u>

(140:46) (Line-up 9)

1 Drum intro > She Has Funny Cars 4:36

2 Somebody To Love 3:24

3 Grace thanks the crowd > Plastic Fantastic Lover 4:09

4 Won't You Try/Saturday Afternoon > Grace thanks the crowd 4:53

5 Today 3:42
On any tour this is pure genius!

6 Marty thanks the crowd > Good Shepherd 6:40 Jorma vocals.

7 Grace intros the next song > Lather 3:25

8 Solidarity > Grace intros Tim Gorman 6:17

9 Wooden Ships > Grace thanks the crowd 5:50
Very well played!

10 Grace intros the next song > America 8:13
Paul was very inspired during this song.

11 Paul intros the next song as it starts > Freedom >

Grace thanks the crowd > Grace intros Randy Jackson and Peter Kaukonen 6:45

Hot Tuna: (18:30)

12 Tune-Up > Hesitation Blues 6:13

13 Walking Blues 4:05

14 Tune-Up > 99 Year Blues > Jorma thanks the crowd 5:14 >

15 I Am The Light Of This World 2:58

16 Third Week In The Chelsea (With Grace) > Grace intros Jorma, and Jack 5:46
That was the end of the Hot Tuna set. They performed five songs.

17 Grace has a funny conversation with a fan that is about to become a dad > Grace informs the audience about pandas > Panda 6:08 Grace solo on piano.

18 Miracles 7:37

19 Grace intros the next song > Ice Age 7:28 Jorma vocals.

20 Paul intros the next song > The Wheel with drum-solo > Grace intros Kenny 7:32

21 Summer Of Love 4:33

22 True Love 4:08

23 Crown Of Creation 3:14

24 White Rabbit 2:51

25 Volunteers > Grace and Paul thank the audience 5:11

26 Encore: Grace thanks the crowd > It's No Secret 3:45

27 Encore: Planes > Paul, Grace, and Marty thank the crowd 5:53

During the Hot Tuna set *99 Year Blues* and *I Am The Light Of This World* are played for the first time. The playing time of the Hot Tuna set is cut in half. *Planes* was made an encore and *The Other Side Of This Life* was dropped for good. Show number two is over and the plane will take-off for Philadelphia, Pennsylvania now!

8/22/89 Mann Music Center, Philadelphia, Pennsylvania (Sound check)

(17:42) (Line-up 9)

The doors are open early for us. Relax and enjoy the Airplane's sound check. **This is the only Jefferson Airplane sound check that has been documented!**

1 Keyboard tune-up > Chatter > Level check > Keyboard tune-up > Sound crew adjust levels > Solidarity (Slight excerpts) > True Love (Excerpts) > Drum level check > Solidarity (Short keyboard excerpts only) > True Love (Excerpts) > Bass warm-up > Jack plays a bit of the bass-lines to *White Rabbit* > Peter Kaukonen guitar warm-up > Jorma guitar warm-up > True Love (Complete) > True Love (Excerpts)

8/22/89 Mann Music Center, Philadelphia, Pennsylvania

(133:13) (Line-up 9)

**It's time for the show. Hey, that's my seat.**

1 Drum intro > Paul welcomes the crowd > She Has Funny Cars 4:08

2 Somebody To Love 3:19

3 Grace thanks the crowd > Plastic Fantastic Lover 3:53

4 Won't You Try/Saturday Afternoon 4:59

5 Today 3:22

6 Grace intros Jorma > Tune-up > Good Shepherd 6:16 Jorma vocals.

7 Grace intros the next song and explains it is about a drummer turning thirty > Tune-up > Lather > Grace thanks the crowd 3:32

8 Solidarity 6:07
The version performed was the best of the first three nights.

9 Wooden Ships > Paul forgets some lyrics ,and Grace laughs! 5:54
This was well done by Grace. Paul had forgotten some of the words and Grace was able to joke about it and still delivered the correct lyrics.

10 The Wheel 7:19 With drum-solo > Paul intros Kenny 7:19

11 America 8:04

12 Paul intros the next song as it starts > Freedom > Grace thanks the crowd 6:52

Hot Tuna set: (19:19)

13 Tune-up > Walking Blues 4:26

14 Tune-up > San Francisco Bay Blues 3:52

15 Tune-up > Mann's Fate > Jorma thanks the crowd 5:26

16 Tune-up > Third Week In The Chelsea (With Grace) > Grace intros Jorma and Jack 5:35  This is the end of the Hot Tuna set.

17 Grace talks about the panda and intros the next song >

18 Panda 5:53 Grace solo on piano.

19 Miracles 7:09

20 Tune-up > Grace intros Jorma and the next song > Ice Age 7:17
Jorma vocals.  The band had a lot of energy on this version.

21 Grace intros the next Song > Summer Of Love 4:58

22 True Love 3:41  The intro is cut.

23 Grace intros Crown Of Creation 3:18
The band is getting more comfortable.

24 Paul thanks the crowd > White Rabbit 2:37

25 Grace thanks the crowd > Volunteers > Paul, Marty, and Grace thank  the crowd 6:01

26 Encore: Grace intros Peter, and Randy, and thanks the crowd > It's No Secret 3:17

27 Encore: Grace intros the next song > Paul thanks the audience > Planes > Paul and Grace thank the audience 5:43

For the third show Hot Tuna performed *Mann's Fate* for the first time on the tour.  The venue was the Mann Music Center so why not.  This performance is the best of the first three.  The crowd was very into the concert from the opening drum beat of *She Has Funny Cars* right through the last notes of *Planes*.

<u>8/23/89 Finger Lakes Performing Arts Center, Canandaigua, New York</u>

(134:45) (Line-up 9)

1 She Has Funny Cars 4:33

2 Somebody To Love 3:19

3 Plastic Fantastic Lover 4:16

4 Won't You Try/Saturday Afternoon 5:22

5 Today 3:36

6 Good Shepherd 6:32 Jorma vocals.

7 Lather 4:25

220

8 Solidarity 6:51

9 Wooden Ships 5:33
*The Wheel* was performed next but, there wasn't any recorded documentation available.

10 America 7:56

11 Freedom 6:35

Hot Tuna set: (17:22)

12 Keep On Truckin' 3:49

13 Walkin' Blues 4:10

14 San Francisco Bay Blues 3:51

15 (99 Year Blues) 5:32

16 Third Week In The Chelsea (With Grace) 5:30 Hot Tuna set ends here.

17 Panda 5:37 Grace solo on piano.

18 Miracles 6:28

19 Ice Age 7:23 Jorma vocals.

20 Summer Of Love 5:50

21 True Love 4:02

22 Short Improvisation > Crown Of Creation 3:21

23 White Rabbit 2:38

24 Grace thanks the audience > Volunteers 7:04

25 Encore: Funny Grace stage banter "This one is even before I was in the band, eighteen-hundred something." > It's No Secret 3:43

26 Encore: Planes 6:39

For the fourth performance Hot Tuna plays *Keep On Trucking* for the first time! Nothing out of the ordinary transpired. The band gets more and more at ease, at least through the eyes and ears of the audience.

8/25/89 River Bend Music Center, Cincinnati, Ohio

(130:44) (Line-up 9)

The venue of this show has been documented <u>incorrectly</u> as King's Island.

1 Drum intro > She Has Funny Cars 4:01

2 Hello from Grace > Somebody To Love > Grace thanks the crowd 3:21

3 Plastic Fantastic Lover 4:22
The band performed a very good version.

4 Won't You Try/Saturday Afternoon 4:51

5 Grace thanks the crowd and intros the next song > Today 3:22

6 Grace thanks the crowd >Paul intros Jorma > Good Shepherd 6:22
Jorma vocals.

7 Lather > Grace thanks the crowd 3:15

8 Grace thanks the crowd and intros the next song > Solidarity 6:07

9 Wooden Ships > 5:48
Smooth sailing all the way.

10 America 7:47

11 Paul intros the next song as it starts > Freedom > 5:56

Hot Tuna set (16:56)

12 Tune-Up > Hesitation Blues 5:13

13 Walking Blues 3:44

14 San Francisco Bay Blues 3:38

15 Tune-Up :31 >

**16 Freight Train :25 With Grace vocals.**
It is a shame they didn't keep playing!  The version they performed was written by Elizabeth Cotten, Paul James, and Fred Williams.  A well known version was recorded by Elizabeth Cotten.

17 Third Week In The Chelsea 5:35 With Grace.  The Hot Tuna set ends here.

18 Panda 3:32 Grace solo on piano.  During this performance Grace did not talk about the pandas being endangered.

19 Tune-up > Miracles 6:59
Many felt this may have been the best version of the tour.

20 Tune-up > Marty makes a joke about pandas > Ice Age 6:40
Jorma vocals.  The entire band put plenty of rock and roll into this one!

21 Grace intros Peter and Randy > Grace intros the next song > The Wheel (With drum-solo) 7:17

22 Summer Of Love 4:00 The start was slightly edited.

23 Grace intros the next song > True Love 4:02

24 Crown Of Creation 2:54

25 White Rabbit > Grace thanks the crowd 2:38

26 Grace thanks the crowd > Volunteers with a false ending > Marty calls Grace "Panda Woman" > Paul, Grace, and Marty thank the crowd 6:48

27 Encore: Paul thanks the crowd > Tune-up > Grace thanks the crowd and intros the next song > It's No Secret 3:02

28 Encore: Baby What You Want Me To Do 4:22 Jorma vocals.

29 Encore: Paul intros the next song > Planes > Grace and Paul thank the crowd > Paul thanks pandas as the song ends 5:04

The fifth installment of the traveling show had ended. Marty was in great spirits the entire performance. He joked about pandas a few times. The Hot Tuna off-the-cuff *Freight Train* was excellent. It was obvious Jorma and Jack would know the old folk-song, but give credit to Grace for having knowledge of some of the lyrics. This was the first time the band played three encores during 1989. *Baby What You Want Me To Do* was terrific. It was relayed to me there were a bunch of people that had discussed if this should be an encore or not. What do you think? It is certainly a powerful enough tune with a full electric band to place it anywhere on the set list.

8/26/89 Post Pavilion, Columbia, Maryland

(136:23) (Line-up 9)

1 Paul and Grace welcome the crowd > Drum intro > She Has Funny Cars 4:21

2 Somebody To Love 3:17

3 Grace thanks the crowd > Plastic Fantastic Lover > Grace intros Kenny 4:21

4 Won't You Try/Saturday Afternoon 4:48

5 Tune-up > Today 3:34

6 Paul thanks the crowd > Grace intros Jorma > Good Shepherd 6:10
Jorma vocals.

7 Lather > Grace thanks the crowd 3:24

8 Grace intros the next song > Solidarity 6:05

9 Grace thanks the crowd and intros the next song > Wooden Ships 5:48

10 Paul intros the next song > The Wheel 7:51 With drum-solo.

11 America 7:48

12 Paul intros the next song as it starts > Freedom > 6:17

Hot Tuna set: (21:28)

13 Let Us Get Together Right Down Here 2:42

14 Walking Blues 3:58

15 Tune-up > Mann's Fate 5:25

16 San Francisco Bay Blues > Jorma thanks the crowd 3:45

17 Tune-Up > Third Week In The Chelsea: With Grace > Grace intros Jorma and Jack 5:38
The Hot Tuna set ends.

18 Grace talks about pandas > Panda 5:32 Grace solo on piano.

19 Miracles 7:06

20 Tune-Up > Paul intros the next song > Ice Age 6:40 Jorma vocals.

21 Summer Of Love 4:57

22 Paul intros the next song  > True Love 3:51

23 Crown Of Creation 3:25

24 Grace thanks the crowd > White Rabbit 2:52

25 Grace thanks the audience > Volunteers > Marty and Grace thank the crowd 6:50

26 Encore: Paul thanks the crowd > **Peter Gunn (Five second instrumental tease) > Grace thanks the crowd
> I Believe (Five second Grace vocal tease) :10**

**Please see the notes after the final tune for information on the two "teases."**

27 Encore: Grace intros the next song > It's No Secret 2:35

28 Encore: Grace intros the next song > Planes > Grace intros Randy, Peter, and Paul > Marty and Grace thank
the crowd 7:24

Show number six of the tour comes to an end.  Nothing in the way of additions to the set list for either the
Airplane or the Hot Tuna segments.  The two teases before the encores were excellent.  The only regret they
were too short!  *Peter Gunn* was written by Henri Mancini and a fantastic version was done by Emerson, Lake
And Palmer.  *I Believe* was written by Sammy Cahn and made popular by Louis Armstrong.

8/28/89 New York State Fair, Syracuse, New York

(139:26) (Line-up 9)

1 Drum intro > Paul, and Grace welcome the crowd > She Has Funny Cars 4:27
The opening song's energy, and smoothness set the tone for the first 25:00.

2 Somebody To Love 3:24

3 Plastic Fantastic Lover (Real strong playing by Jorma) > Grace intros Kenny 4:29

4 Won't You Try/Saturday Afternoon 5:07

5 Grace thanks the crowd and Marty intros the next song  > Today 3:57

6 Grace intros the next song > Tune-up > Good Shepherd 6:08

7 Lather > Grace thanks the crowd 3:07

8 Grace intros the next song > Solidarity > Marty intros Tim 6:19

9 Grace intros the next song > Wooden Ships 5:19

10 Paul intros the next Song > The Wheel: With drum-solo > Paul intros Kenny 7:19

11 America 8:16

12 Paul intros the next song as it starts > Freedom > Grace thanks the crowd 6:11

Hot Tuna set: (18:09)

13 Walking Blues 4:22

14 Tune-up > Embryonic Journey 2:46

15 Tune-up > Hesitation Blues > Jorma thanks the crowd 5:31

16 Tune-Up > Third Week In The Chelsea (With Grace) > Grace intros Jorma and Jack 5:30 The Hot Tuna set ends.

17 Grace talks about pandas > Panda 5:00 Grace solo on piano.

18 Miracles 7:52

19 Tune-Up > Grace intros the next song > Ice Age 7:24 Jorma vocals.
There was a terrific feel of energy from the band during this version.

20 Grace intros the next song > Summer Of Love 4:23

21 Grace intros the next song > True Love 4:10

22 Crown Of Creation 3:12

23 White Rabbit 2:47 > Grace thanks the crowd.
The instrumentation and the vocals were terrific.

24 Volunteers > Paul thanks the crowd at the first false ending > Marty and Grace thank the crowd at the second false ending 8:25
The second half of the tune was very powerful.

25 Encore: It's No Secret 2:37

26 Encore: Baby What You Want Me To Do > Grace intros Randy and Peter 5:28

27 Encore: Planes > Paul and Grace thank the crowd near the end of the song 5:45
Jorma plays exceptionally well throughout the tune.

Show number seven was now history. The band had found it's way early in the performance. The Hot Tuna set contributed the first 1989 version of *Embryonic Journey*. That could enhance any segment of a live show. The three encores worked very well. Sometimes you take a chance, and it can work out well, and other times it may have been best left on the drawing board. When the band decided to not only put *Baby What You Want Me To Do* in the set but as an encore (8/25/89 River Bend Music Center, Cincinnati, Ohio) it wasn't only Jorma that came out with flying colors. It was a group effort to put so much energy into the arrangement. **Tomorrow night would be the long awaited return to New York City.**

8/29/89 Radio City Music Hall, New York City

(135:35) (Line-up 9) **New York City welcomes the Jefferson Airplane.**

1 Drum intro > Paul and Grace welcome the crowd > She Has Funny Cars 4:12

2 Somebody To Love > Grace thanks the crowd 3:14

3 Grace intros the next song > Plastic Fantastic Lover 4:06

4 Won't You Try/Saturday Afternoon 5:15

5 Grace thanks the crowd and Marty intros the next song > Today 3:13

6 Grace intros Jorma > Good Shepherd 5:52 Jorma vocals.

7 Grace intros the next song > Lather > Grace thanks the crowd 3:27

8 Grace intros the next song > Solidarity > Grace intros Tim 6:06

9 Wooden Ships 5:29

10 The Wheel: With drum-solo > Paul intros Kenny 6:55

11 America 8:08

12 Paul intros the next song as it starts > Freedom > Grace thanks the crowd 5:58

Hot Tuna: (17:54)

13 Hesitation Blues 5:13

14 Walking Blues 4:27

15 Tune-up Embryonic Journey 2:43

**16 Jorma's :46 Instrumental Ditty** > Third Week In The Chelsea:
**With Grace on vocals and <u>Kenny on drums</u> 5:38 First time of the tour performed with drums!**
The Hot Tuna set ends.

17 Grace intros Jorma and Jack > Grace talks about Pandas > Panda 5:35 Grace solo on piano.

18 Miracles 6:53

19 Tune-Up > Paul thank the crowd > Grace intros the next song > Ice Age 6:54 Jorma vocals.

20 Grace intros the next song > Summer Of Love 4:35

21 Grace intros the next song > True Love 3:54

22 Grace intros the next song > Crown Of Creation 3:05

23 White Rabbit 2:28

24 Volunteers: With false ending > Marty intros the entire band > Paul and Grace thank the crowd 8:12

25 Encore: It's No Secret 2:56

26 Encore: Baby What You Want Me To Do 5:32 Jorma vocals.  Good crowd reaction.

27 Encore: Planes > Paul thanks the crowd as the song is about to end > Grace and Marty thank the crowd 5:18

The eighth edition of the 1989 tour stopped in New York City.  This was the first appearance in the Big Apple since Central Park on 8/16/72.  The songs remained the same from previous nights.  There was an interesting event during *Third Week In The Chelsea*.  For the first time on the tour Kenny played drums on the song.  The prior seven concerts had only Jorma, Jack, and Grace on the stage.  Kenny handled this perfectly.  His playing was more in the background, and was able to keep the rendition at the superior level of the other shows.  Kenny told me that Jorma and Jack invited him to play drums on *Third Week In The Chelsea* whenever he wished.  Jorma did throw in a short *Guitar Ditty* during the Hot Tuna set.  The venue had both a great sense of anticipation and warmth for the band.  When it was all said and done the group had come off well and tomorrow would be even better!

8/30/89 Radio City Music Hall, New York City

(140:12) (Line-up 9)

1 Drum intro > She Has Funny Cars 4:41

2 Grace thanks the crowd > Somebody To Love 3:23

3 Grace thanks the crowd > Plastic Fantastic Lover 4:36
Jorma played really well throughout the song.

4 Won't You Try/Saturday Afternoon 5:02

5 Grace thanks the crowd and intros the next song > Today 3:16

6 Grace intros Jorma, and the next song > Good Shepherd 6:47
Jorma vocal.  The band played a very inspired version.

7 Tune-up> Lather 3:30

8 Grace intros the next song  > Solidarity 6:35  The crowd could feel the energy on this song.

9 Wooden Ships 5:16 The opening notes were cut.
The band played a high octane version.

10 Grace intros the next song > The Wheel 7:55 With drum-solo 7:55

11 America 8:52

12 Paul intros the next song as it starts > Freedom >Paul thanks the crowd 6:06

Hot Tuna set: (26:01)

13 Tune-up (Long) > San Francisco Bay Blues > 4:52

14 Tune-up > I'll Be Alright Someday 3:40

15 Tune-up > Jorma intros the next song > Death Don't Have No Mercy 5:53

16 (99 Years Blues) 5:38

17 Tune-up > Third Week In The Chelsea: With Grace and drums > Grace intros Jorma and Jack 5:56

18 Grace talks about Pandas > Panda 5:20

19 Miracles 7:13

20 Tune-up > Grace intros Jorma and the next song > Ice Age 7:07  Jorma vocals.
The guitar sounds on the song were a bit different than previous nights.  The version worked very well.

21 Grace intros the next song > Summer Of Love 4:21

22 Grace intros the next song > True Love 4:05

24 Grace intros the next song > Crown Of Creation 2:59 Good energy throughout the song.

25 White Rabbit 2:31

26 Grace thanks the crowd > Volunteers: With two false endings > Grace intros Kenny near the end of the song > Paul, Marty, and Grace thank the crowd 8:25
They didn't let New York City down with this version!

27 Encore: Grace intros the next song > Planes > Paul thanks the crowd as the song nears the end > Grace thanks the crowd 6:01

The ninth installment of the Airplane flight was a fantastic reunion performance.  The second and better of the two nights in New York City.  The crowd was even more upbeat than the previous evening.  Once again during *Third Week In The Chelsea*, Kenny helped out on drums.  The Hot Tuna set saw the first 1989 reunion performances of *I'll Be Alright Someday*, and *Death Don't Have No Mercy*.  Jorma and Jack got a bit more playing time than the last several shows.  The only fault you can find with the concert was the decision for the encore.  The time restrictions were very much etched in stone.  Grace let the crowd know before *Planes* started they only had six minutes of stage time left.  They played exactly six minutes and one second of the song.  In doing so *It's No Secret* would not be heard.  That is a not the type of tune you want removed from the set.

9/1/89 Jones Beach Theater, Wantagh, New York

(143:41) (Line-up 9)

The joke after this show was the additional member of the band **"The Wind"** was overly loud and annoying. Grace made a comment before *Good Shepherd* "The wind is blowing the band off the stage."

1 Drum intro > She Has Funny Cars 4:32

2 Somebody To Love 3:20

3 Grace intros the next song > Plastic Fantastic Lover 4:17

4 Tune-up > Grace intros the next song > Won't You Try/Saturday Afternoon 5:13

5 Today 3:17

6 Grace thanks the crowd and mentions "The wind is blowing the band off the stage." > Grace intros Jorma and the next song > Good Shepherd 6:54 Jorma vocals.

8 Tune-up > Lather 3:19

9 Grace thanks the crowd > Paul intros the next song > Solidarity 6:35

10 Grace intros Tim Gorman > Wooden Ships 5:49

11 The Wheel 7:31 With drum-solo.

12 America 8:13

13 Freedom > Grace thanks the crowd 6:24

Hot Tuna set: (20:47)

14 Tune-up > San Francisco Bay Blues 3:23 Not from the start.

16 I'll Be Alright Someday 3:35

17 Death Don't Have No Mercy 5:40

18 Tune-up > Embryonic Journey 2:37

19 Third Week In The Chelsea: With Grace.  Grace intros Jorma and Jack 5:42
This evening they performed the song the more common way with no drums.  The wind was so intense during the song it competed for the crowd's attention.

20 Grace talks about pandas > Panda 5:27  Grace solo on piano.

21 Miracles 7:11

22 Tune-up > Grace intros Jorma and the next song > Ice Age 7:17

Jorma vocals.

23 Summer Of Love 4:31

24 True Love 4:05 The opening is cut.

25 Crown Of Creation 2:51

26 White Rabbit 2:46

27 Volunteers > Grace thanks the crowd as the first false ending occurs > Grace thanks the crowd again and as they think the song is over the band played a bit more. 8:15

28 Encore: Paul thanks the crowd > Grace intros the next song > It's No Secret 3:01 Good to see it back in the proper spot!

29 Encore: Baby What You Want Me To Do 5:17 Jorma vocals. Excellent energy throughout the instrumentation by the band.

Encore: Grace intros the next song > Planes > Paul thanks the crowd as the song nears the end > Grace thanks the crowd 6:15

The band made it through show number ten! A good performance, thanks to the energy of the musicians. It wasn't easy work tonight. The wind was so loud that if you have ever heard a recording of the performance it sounds as if you are listening to a special on nature's elements and not a concert from a legendary rock and roll band! There weren't any changes in the set. Hot Tuna once again played both *I'll Be Alright Someday* and *Death Don't Have No Mercy*. *It's No Secret* was placed back in the set list as an encore.

9/2/89 Garden State Arts Center, Holmdel, New Jersey

(134:45) (Line-up 9)

1 Paul says "Hi." > **Drum intro (With some guitar) > She Has Funny Cars** 4:19

2 Grace thanks the crowd > Somebody To Love 3:14

3 Plastic Fantastic Lover > Tune-up 4:28 The intro to the song was a bit different.

4 Won't You Try/Saturday Afternoon 4:58

5 Today > tune-up > Grace thanks the crowd 3:23

6 Grace intros Jorma and the next song > Good Shepherd 6:25
Jorma vocals.

7 Grace intros the next song > Lather 2:59
There was sound trouble on the stage. Near the end of the song Grace said "Some of our speakers are over thirty years old." Grace never lost her sense of humor!

8 Grace asks the band to test the equipment > The band tests the equipment :25

9 Grace intros the next song > Solidarity 6:07

10 Grace intros Tim Gorman > Wooden Ships 5:22 Grace made a mistake at the end of the song with timing and the lyrics. She told the band away from the microphone she was sorry.

11 America 7:33 Grace and Paul come in a split second apart on the vocals!

12 Paul intros the next song as it starts > Freedom > Grace thanks the crowd 6:00

Hot Tuna set: (26:43)

13 Tune-up > Hesitation Blues > Tune-up > 5:32

14 Tune-up > Embryonic Journey > Tune-up 2:56 >

15 Tune-up > Trial By Fire > Tune-Up 4:31

16 Sound trouble on the stage 3:14

17 Candy Man 5:27 > Jorma thanks the crowd > Tune-up
Jorma's acoustic guitar sounded very good especially at the start of the song.

**18 Jorma's Instrumental Ditty :09**

19 Tune-Up > Third Week In The Chelsea 5:18 With Grace on vocals.

20 Grace talks About pandas > Panda 5:01 Grace solo on piano.

21 Miracles 7:31

22 Tune-up > Paul intros Jorma and the next song > Ice Age 8:13
Jorma vocals.

23 Summer Of Love 4:33

24 True Love 3:36

25 Grace intros the next song > Crown Of Creation 2:46

26 White Rabbit > Grace thanks the crowd 2:30

27 Volunteers > Paul and Marty thank the crowd during the false ending 8:25

28 Encore: Paul thanks the crowd > Tune-up > It's No Secret 2:57

29 Encore: Baby What You Want Me To Do 4:43 Jorma vocals. Very well done.

30 Encore: Grace intros Peter and Randy > Grace intros the next song > Planes 6:19

The eleventh show had some sound trouble creep in. The performance was good. There weren't standout moments. The guitar being part of the drum intro on *She Had Funny Cars* was the first documented time they arranged the song that way. *The Wheel* did not get performed. The Hot Tuna set was worth the price of admission with the first 1989 version of *Trail By Fire*. Jorma also had a short *Guitar Ditty* for us. Five of the last six songs played were from the classic period!

9/3/89 Saratoga Performing Arts Center, Saratoga, New York

(152:40) (Line-up 9)

1 Drum intro (The start was cut) > She Has Funny Cars 4:12

2 Paul says "Hi." > Somebody To Love 3:31

3 Grace thanks the crowd > Plastic Fantastic Lover 4:15

4 Won't You Try/Saturday Afternoon 5:38

5 Today 3:26

6 Grace intros Jorma, and the next song > Good Shepherd 7:16 Jorma vocals.
The band stretched out nicely the instrumentation on this version.

7 Tune-up > Grace intros the next song > Lather > Grace thanks the crowd 3:39

8 Grace intros the next song > Solidarity 6:41

9 Grace intros Tim Gorman > Wooden Ships 5:49 The last few seconds were cut.

10 America 8:02

11 Paul intros the next song > Freedom > Grace thanks the crowd 6:29

Hot Tuna set:(26:43)

12 Uncle Sam Blues 4:36 The intro was cut.

13 San Francisco Bay Blues 4:05

14 Tune-Up > Death Don't Have No Mercy 6:27

15 Tune-Up > Candy Man 5:53

16 Tune-Up > Third Week In The Chelsea: With Grace > Grace intros Jorma and Jack 6:42 Hot Tuna set ends.

17 Grace talks about pandas > Panda 5:46 Grace was real serious singing the tune.
Grace solo on piano.  Grace may have been the most passionate about her fight for the panda during this rendition.

18 Miracles 7:46

19 Grace intros Jorma, and the next song > Tune-up >  Ice Age 5:05 Cut.
Jorma vocals.  The band didn't have it together during the start of the song.

20 The Wheel: With drum-solo > Grace and Marty intro Kenny 8:00

21 Summer Of Love > Paul intros the song perfectly as if he were a disc-jockey talking up a record until the vocals came in 5:01

22 Grace intros the next song and mentions that bats are flying around > True Love 4:48

23 Grace intros the next song > Planes 5:26
Notice this was not an encore!

24 White Rabbit 2:53
Grace got hoarse during the song.

25 Grace thanks the crowd and intros the next song > Crown Of Creation > Paul and Grace thank the crowd 5:09

26 Encore: Tune-up > It's No Secret 3:23

27 Encore: Grace intros Jorma > Baby What You Want Me To Do > Grace intros Randy and Peter 6:47

28 Encore: Volunteers > Paul thanks the crowd right before the song ends > Paul and Marty thank the crowd 7:16
**Wasn't it great to see this as an encore!**

A dozen shows have now been performed. Hot Tuna treated the fans to the first *Uncle Sam Blues* of the tour! The encore segment was enhanced with *Volunteers* taking a spot from *Planes*. *Planes* still was performed but was moved a few songs before the encore segment.

9/4/89 Lake Compounce, Bristol, Connecticut

(139:25) (Line-up 9)

**The show is about to start and there is a slight problem, Marty isn't there. Not to worry, it's Hot Tuna to the rescue!**

Hot Tuna set: (35:34)

1 Jorma tells the crowd "Old Marty is late and it is up to Hot Tuna to save the day again." > Hesitation Blues 5:40

2 Walking Blues 3:55

3 Tune-Up > San Francisco Bay Blues 4:10

4 Trouble In Mind 2:42
This was a surprise. With all the songs Jorma and Jack could have performed you wouldn't think you would hear this in a short set.

5 Tune-Up > Embryonic Journey 2:46

6 Tune-Up > Trial By Fire 4:47

7 Tune-Up > Mann's Fate > Jorma thanks the crowd 5:57

**8 Jorma's Short Improvisational Ditty :40**

9 Third Week In The Chelsea > Grace intros Jorma, Jorma intros Grace, and Grace intros Jack 4:51 Hot Tuna set ends here.

10 Grace gripes about bugs and talks about pandas > Panda 4:51
Grace solo on piano. She did a very laid back version.

Jefferson Airplane takes the stage:

11 Drum intro > She Has Funny Cars 4:43

12 Somebody To Love 2:04 The start of the song was cut.

13 Grace thanks the crowd > Plastic Fantastic Lover 4:57

14 Won't You Try/Saturday Afternoon 5:27

15 Paul intros the next song > Today 3:31

16 Grace intros Jorma and the next song > Good Shepherd 6:42 Jorma vocals.

17 Grace thanks the crowd > Lather > Grace thanks the crowd 3:31

18 Grace intros the next song > Solidarity 5:49

19 Grace intros Tim Gorman > Tune-up > Wooden Ships 5:36

20 Grace intros Paul and the next song > America 7:53

21 Paul intros the next song as it starts > Freedom 5:55

22 Grace intros Miracles 7:11

23 Grace intros Jorma and the next song> Ice Age 7:11
Good version.

24 Tune-Up > Planes 5:18
Notice not an encore.

25 Summer Of Love 3:59

26 Tune-up > Grace intros the next song > True Love 4:34

27 Tune-up > White Rabbit 2:41

28 Grace thanks the crowd > Crown Of Creation > Paul and Grace thank the crowd 3:19

29 Encore: Grace thank the crowd > It's No Secret 3:14

30 Encore: Volunteers > Marty and Paul thank the crowd near the end of the song > Grace and Paul thank the crowd 5:33

Nothing unlucky about the number thirteen (The amount of shows played thus far in 1989) for the J.A. The concert would have the unique honor of being the only one of the 1989 tour to have **Hot Tuna open**. Marty was late and Hot Tuna performed over thirty minutes. The segment included the first appearance of *Trouble In Mind*. It was an interesting choice. While there were songs Hot Tuna played from the sixties and seventies that would have been preferable, *Trouble In Mind* came across very well. Jorma also throw in another short *Guitar Ditty*. The band omitted *The Wheel* because of the reconfiguration of the set list. The encore segment was perfect. *It's No Secret* and *Volunteers* are fine next to each other. Having archived Airplane material for so long it amazed me **this was the most uninspired Airplane crowd ever. They J.A. could have gotten the same reaction if they didn't show up.**

9/6/89 Great Woods, Mansfield, Massachusetts

(142:00) (Line-up 9)

1 Drum intro > She Has Funny Cars 4:36

2 Somebody To Love 3:30

3 Grace thanks the crowd > Plastic Fantastic Lover 4:16

4 Won't You Try/Saturday Afternoon 5:25

5 Today 3:32

6 Grace intros the next song > Tune-up > Good Shepherd 6:54 Jorma vocals.

7 Grace intros the next song > Lather 3:37

8 Grace talks about the reunion album and intros the next song > Solidarity 6:53

9 Grace talks about seeing one of the writers of this song on TV last night (David Crosby) > Grace intros the next song > Wooden Ships > Grace thanks the crowd 6:00

10 America 8:03

11 Paul intros the next song > Freedom > Grace thanks the crowd 6:06

Hot Tuna set: (20:55) (A couple of people don't shut up while Jorma and Jack perform).

12 Tune-up > I Know You Rider 4:04
It always will be magnificent.

13 San Francisco Bay Blues 3:51

14 Been So Long 4:21
This was great to have in the set!

15 Tune-up > Jorma thanks the crowd > Embryonic Journey 2:53

16 Jorma thanks the crowd > Tune-up > Third Week In The Chelsea (With Grace) > Grace intros Jorma and Jack 5:46  Hot Tuna set ends.

17 Grace talks about pandas > Panda 5:40
Grace solo on piano.

18 Miracles 6:30

19 The Wheel (With drum-solo) > Grace intros Kenny and manager Bill Thompson 7:55

20 Grace intros Jorma and the next song > Ice Age 7:08 Jorma vocals.

21 Grace intros the next song > Summer Of Love 4:50

22 Grace intros the next song >True Love 3:57

23 Grace intros the next song > Planes 5:17 The band was full of energy on this version.

24 White Rabbit 2:31 Excellent vocals by Grace.

25 Volunteers > Marty thanks the crowd during the false ending > Grace thanks the crowd 6:56

26 Encore: Tune-up > Come Back Baby 7:07 Jorma vocals.  Excellent energy from the entire band.

27 Encore: Tune-up > Grace thanks the crowd and then intros Peter and Tim > Grace calls Randy Jackson "Randy Gorman" and then corrected herself > Paul intros the next song > Crown Of Creation > Grace, Paul, and Marty thank the crowd 4:06

The fourteenth performance had all the members at the venue on time.  The crowd was very engaged and the band knew they were in a good atmosphere.  The Hot Tuna set gave us for the first time *I Know You Rider* and *Been So Long*.  The band did a couple of creative things.  *Come Back Baby* made it's first appearance on the 1989 tour, not part of the Hot Tuna set but as an encore for the Airplane.  *Crown Of Creation* felt right at home in the encore slot.  When discussing this with the moderate and hardcore fans the general consensus thought it came off well as an encore.

9/8/89 Blossom Music Center, Cuyahoga Falls, Ohio

(141:08) (Line-up 9)

1 Drum intro > She Has Funny Cars 3:56
Marty had a funny line after "Flash paradise", he said "What does that mean?"

2 Somebody To Love > Grace thanks the crowd 3:21

3 Plastic Fantastic Lover 4:05

4 Won't You Try/Saturday Afternoon 5:12 **Marty started the song with the first line from the Beatles, *Strawberry Fields Forever* -"Let me take you down cause I'm going to." This was one of the great moments in world history.**

5 Grace thanks the crowd and intros the next song > Today 3:18

6 Marty thanks the crowd and Grace intros the next song > Good Shepherd 5:55
Jorma vocals.

7 Grace intros Jorma > Tune-up > Grace intros the next song > Lather 3:31

8 Grace thanks the crowd and intros the next song > Solidarity 6:55

9 Wooden Ships 5:18

10 Grace intros the next song > America 8:25

11 Paul intros the next song > Freedom > 6:19

Hot Tuna set: (21:41)

12 Tune-Up > I Know You Rider 4:24

13 Tune-Up > Hesitation Blues 5:13

14 Been So Long 3:57

15 Tune-Up > Embryonic Journey 2:34

16 Tune-Up > Third Week In The Chelsea (With Grace) > Grace intros Jorma and Jack (5:33) Hot Tuna set ends.

17 Grace talks about pandas > Panda 5:05 Grace solo on piano.

18 Miracles 7:31

19 Paul intros the next song > The Wheel (With drum-solo) > Paul intros Kenny 7:30

20 Tune-up > Paul intros the next song > Ice Age 6:56 Jorma vocals.

21 Summer Of Love > 4:19

22 True Love 3:49

23 Planes 5:12
The band played very well throughout this version.

24 Paul thanks the crowd > White Rabbit 2:26

25 Grace thanks the crowd > Tune-up > Volunteers > Marty and Grace thank the crowd 6:20

26 Encore: Grace thanks the crowd > It's No Secret 2:45  A top flight version.

27 Encore: Tune-Up > Come Back Baby > Grace intros Peter and Randy 8:33
Jorma vocals.  Another quality version in the encore segment.

28 Encore: Crown Of Creation > Paul, Grace, and Marty thank the crowd 3:14

As the final notes were imprinted on concert number fifteen it showed the little things in life can make us happy. Marty telling a joke in the middle of *She Has Funny Cars* was rather funny and singing the opening line to *Strawberry Fields Forever* was an unexpected treat.  The band performed well.  The Hot Tuna set repeated from the previous show *I Know You Rider*, and *Been So Long*.  The response to *Crown Of Creation* as one of the encores continued to be very positive.

9/9/89 Poplar Creek, Hoffman Estates, Illinois

(135:01) (Line-up 9)

1 She Has Funny Cars 3:46 The drum intro was cut.

2 Somebody To Love > Grace thanks the crowd 3:28

3 Grace thanks the crowd > Plastic Fantastic Lover 4:25

4 Grace intros the next song > Won't You Try/Saturday Afternoon 5:17

5 Grace thanks the crowd > Today 3:33

6 Grace intros the next song > Good Shepherd 6:20 Jorma vocals.

7 Grace intros the next song > Lather 3:23

8 Grace thanks the crowd and intros the next song > Solidarity > Grace thanks the crowd 6:46

9 Wooden Ships 4:52 The intro was cut.

10 America 7:37

11 Paul intros the next song > Freedom 5:55

Hot Tuna set (20:19)

12 Never Happen No More 4:14  First time played during 1989.

13 San Francisco Bay Blues 3:51

14 I See The Light 6:09
This was a great choice and long overdue.

15 Tune-up > Embryonic Journey 2:52

**16 Tune-up > Five Foot Two, Eyes Of Blue (Has Anybody Seen My Girl) With Grace :34** The song was written by Ray Henderson, Sam Lewis, and Joe Young.  A popular version was by Jimmy Dorsey.  Singers will often change "Girl" to "Gal", or "Baby."  The song is often talked about without the "Five Foot Two, Eyes Of Blue" as being part of the title.  It would have been out of the stratosphere if Jorma, Jack, and Grace played even one more minute of the tune!

17 Tune-up > Third Week In The Chelsea 4:39 With Grace.  Hot Tuna set ends.

18 Grace intros Jorma and Jack > Grace talks about Pandas > Panda 6:44
Grace solo on piano.

19 Miracles 6:52

20 The Wheel (With drum-solo) > Paul intros Kenny 7:18

21 Tune-up > Paul intros the next song > Ice Age 7:14 Jorma vocals.

22 Tune-up > Summer Of Love > Grace thanks the crowd 4:19  The keyboard intro sounded especially nice on this version.

23 Grace intros the next song > True Love 5:12

24 Planes 4:51

25 White Rabbit 2:36

26 Grace thanks the crowd > Volunteers > Grace thanks the crowd 4:58

27 Encore: It's No Secret 2:55

28 Encore: Crown Of Creation > Grace, Paul, and Marty thank the crowd 3:06

The sixteenth show of the reunion tour had ended. *Summer Of Love* sounded particularly strong. The true highlights came from the Hot Tuna set. For the first time *Never Happen No More* and *I See The Light* were included. Right before *Third Week In The Chelsea*, Grace, Jorma, and Jack treated the audience to a half minute of *Five Foot Two, Eyes Of Blue (Has Anybody Seen My Girl)*.

9/10/89 Pine Knob Amphitheater, Clarkston, Michigan

(129:48) (Line-up 9)

1 She Has Funny Cars 2:25 Both the drum intro and opening notes were cut.

2 Somebody To Love 3:15

3 Grace thanks the crowd > Plastic Fantastic Lover 4:49  This was a very strong version.

4 Marty says "Hello."> Won't You Try/Saturday Afternoon 5:20

5 Grace thanks the crowd  > Today 3:26

6 Grace intros Jorma > Good Shepherd 6:21 Jorma vocals.

7 Grace intros the next song > Lather > Grace thanks the crowd 3:25

8 Grace intros the next song > Solidarity > Grace intros Tim 6:46

9 Wooden Ships 5:05

10 America 7:12

11 Paul intros the next song > Freedom > Grace thanks the crowd 5:55

Hot Tuna set: (20:32)

12 Tune-up > I Know You Rider 3:24 The start and middle of the song were cut.

13 Tune-up > Hesitation Blues 5:25

14 Tune-Up > Been So Long 3:59

15 Tune-Up > Embryonic Journey 2:34

16 Third Week In The Chelsea (With Grace) > Grace intros Jorma and Jack 5:10

17 Grace talks about pandas and intros the next song > Panda 5:53

18 Miracles 6:51

19 The Wheel 6:20 With drum-solo

20 Tune-up > Ice Age 6:51 Jorma vocals.

21 Summer Of Love > Grace thanks the crowd 4:39
There was nice guitar playing at the start of the song.

22 Grace intros the next song > True Love 3:49

23 Planes 4:36

24 White Rabbit 2:20 The first few notes were cut.

25 Grace thanks the crowd > Volunteers > Marty and Grace thank the crowd 5:30

26 Encore: It's No Secret 2:48
This was well played and helped set the tone for a good encore segment.

27 Encore: 3/5 Of A Mile In 10 Seconds > Grace thanks the crowd 3:37 The opening notes were cut. Finally one of the best songs ever written makes it onto the set list!

28 Encore: Crown Of Creation > Paul and Grace thank the crowd 2:53

The seventeenth performance finally brought us *3/5 Of A Mile In 10 Seconds*. How can anyone be disappointed? The song is timeless. It doesn't matter if it were the 1960's or the reunion tour, it is a pleasure to hear it performed. The strength of *It's No Secret* and *3/5 Of A Mile In 10 Seconds* provided an excellent one two punch. There were no additions to the Hot Tuna set.

9/16/89 Pacific Amphitheater, Costa Mesa, California

(134:33) (Line-up 9)

**They did not perform White Rabbit!**

1 Drum intro > She Has Funny Cars 4:18

2 Somebody To Love 3:10

3 Grace thanks the crowd and Paul welcomes everybody > Plastic Fantastic 4:04
The instrumentation was very strong throughout.

4 Won't You Try/Saturday Afternoon 5:10

5 Today 3:13

6 Paul thanks the crowd > Grace intros the next song > Tune-up > Good Shepherd 6:23 Jorma vocals. The band played a very spirited version!

7 Grace intros the next song > Lather > 3:22

8 Grace thanks the crowd and intros Tim Gorman > Solidarity > Grace thanks the crowd 6:21 The last few notes were cut.

9 Marty intros Tim > Grace tells that Stephen Stills and David Crosby helped Paul with the next song > Wooden Ships 5:14

10 America 8:03

11 Paul intros the next song > Freedom > Grace thanks the crowd 5:55

Hot Tuna set: (22:37)

12 Hesitation Blues 4:01 The start of the song was cut.

13 Tune-Up > Jorma intros the next song > Walking Blues 3:55

14 San Francisco Bay Blues 3:40

15 Death Don't Have No Mercy 5:15

16 Tune-up > Third Week In The Chelsea  (With Grace) > Jorma thanks the crowd > Grace intros Jorma and Jack 5:46  Hot tuna set ends.

17 Grace talks about pandas and intros the next song > Panda 5:29

18 Miracles 6:42

19 Tune-Up > The Wheel (With drum-solo) > Grace intros Kenny 7:53

20 Grace intros Jorma and the next song > Ice Age 6:41 Jorma vocals.

21 Summer Of Love 4:41

22 Tune-Up > Grace intros the next song > True Love 3:52

23 Planes 3:52 *White Rabbit* **did not get played next!**

24 Volunteers > Grace thanks the crowd during the false ending > Grace and Marty thank the crowd 6:18

25 Encore: It's No Secret 2:50

26 Encore: Grace thanks the crowd > 3/5 Of A Mile In 10 Seconds 4:08

27 Encore: Grace thanks the crowd  > Crown Of Creation > Grace and Paul thank the crowd 3:00

The eighteenth show of the tour was strange.  The band made its way to California and you would have expected some sparks.  The three encores were solid.  **In terms of notoriety the only noticeable event was the omission of *White Rabbit* from the set list.**  The Hot Tuna selections were all previously performed.  The Airplane is getting closer to San Francisco.

9/22/89 Greek Theatre, Berkeley, California

(136:08) (Line-up 9)

1 Drum intro > She Has Funny Cars 4:45  2 Grace thanks the crowd >

2 Somebody To Love 3:32

3 Plastic Fantastic Lover 4:24
The guitars sounded excellent during this version.

4 Grace intros the next song > Won't You Try/Saturday Afternoon 5:38
The guitars on this song as well were superlative.

5 Paul talks about his hope the band can play a free show at Golden Gate Park, San Francisco > Today 4:02

6 Marty thanks the crowd > Tune-up > Grace intros Jorma and the nest song > Good Shepherd 6:34 Jorma vocals.  The band did a tremendous job.

7 Grace dedicates the next song to Bill Graham and intros what is next > Lather 3:42

8 Grace thanks the crowd and intros the next song >  Solidarity > Grace intros Tim Gorman 6:39

9 Wooden Ships 5:30

10 Grace tells the crowd that Stephen Stills and David Crosby helped Paul with the previous song > Grace intros the next song > America 8:24

11 Paul intros the next song > Freedom 6:10

Hot Tuna set: (22:28)

12 Tune-up > Hesitation Blues 5:32

13 Walking Blues 3:59

14 Been So Long 3:54
Jorma and Jack put a lot into this version.

15 Tune-up > Embryonic Journey 3:07

16 Tune-up > Third Week In The Chelsea: With Grace and drums > Jorma thanks the crowd > Grace intros Jorma, Jorma intros Grace, and Grace intros Jack 6:16  (Hot Tuna set ends).

17 Grace talks about chewing gum > Grace talks about pandas and intros the next song > Panda 5:36 Grace solo on piano.

18 Miracles 7:00  The first few seconds were cut.

19 Paul intros the next song > The Wheel 6:47 With drum-solo.  The ending is cut.

20 Grace intros the next song > Ice Age 7:32 Jorma vocals.

21 Summer Of Love 4:30 The first few seconds were cut.

22 Grace intros the next song > True Love 3:44

23 Planes 4:52

**24 *White Rabbit* 2:46**
After not being performed during the 9/16/89 Pacific Amphitheater, Costa Mesa, California show, it was back!

25 Volunteers 6:10 The ending was cut.

26 Encore: 3/5 Of A Mile In 10 Seconds 4:22
This was a superior version.

27 Encore: Paul and Grace thank the crowd > Crown Of Creation > Paul thanks the crowd 3:22

The nineteenth installment of the 1989 Airplane tour had ended. The band would almost be ready for the return to San Francisco. *White Rabbit* **did get returned to the set list but** *It's No Secret* **did not get performed.** *3/5 Of A Mile In 10 Seconds* had the band clicking on all cylinders. The Hot Tuna segment did not hold any surprises. There was consistency during the performance and the band could feel the energy from the crowd.

9/23/89 Concord Pavilion, Concord, California

(138:15) (Line-up 9)

1 Drum intro > She Had Funny Cars (The song was performed, but there is no recorded documentation on the details).

2 Somebody To Love 1:12 The first half of the song was cut.

3 Grace thanks the crowd > Plastic Fantastic Lover 4:25

4 Won't You Try/Saturday Afternoon 5:00
The version performed was fantastic. The instrumentation at times was haunting.

5 Today 3:23
The band made a great transition and sounded equally fine on the slower tempo song.

6 Grace joked "I like the fact Jorma tunes his own guitar." > Grace intros the next song > Good Shepherd 6:37
Jorma vocals.

7 Grace intros the next song > Lather 3:22

8 Grace thanks the crowd and intros the next song > Solidarity 6:38

9 Grace intros Tim Gorman > Wooden Ships 5:37

10 America 8:08 The ending was cut during the keyboard outro.

11 Freedom > Grace thank the crowd 5:48 The opening notes were cut.
Grace's voice was in vintage fashion.

Hot Tuna set: (29:47)

12 San Francisco Bay Blues 3:58 The opening notes were cut.

13 Jorma thanks the crowd > Tune-Up > **Sunshine Of Your Love (Tease)** > I'll Be Alright Someday 4:02
(*Sunshine Of Your Love* was a major song from the band Cream).

14 Tune-up > Death Don't Have No Mercy 5:29

15 Jorma thanks the crowd > Tune-up > Mann's Fate 5:27

16 (99 Year Blues) Jack takes a bass-solo! 4:59

17 Tune-Up > Five Foot Two, Eyes Of Blue (Has Anybody Seen My Gal) With Grace (Sometimes singers use the word "Girl" or "Baby"). > Third Week In The Chelsea (With Grace) > Jorma thanks the crowd > Grace intros Jorma, Jorma intros Grace, and Grace intros Jack 5:42
Not since the 9/9/89 Poplar Creek, Hoffman Estates, Illinois show, had Jorma, Jack, and Grace performed the terrific few seconds of song number seventeen.

Hot Tuna set ends.

18 Grace talks about pandas and intros the next song > Panda 5:42
Grace solo on piano.

19 Miracles 6:39

20 Tune-up > Paul intros the next song >The Wheel (With drum-solo) 5:07
The last two minutes of the song was cut before the drum-solo started.

21 Tune-up > Grace intros Jorma, and the next song > Ice Age 7:24
Jorma vocals. Excellent version by the entire band.

22 Grace intros Randy > Summer Of Love 5:38

23 Grace intros the next song > True Love 4:02

24 Paul intros the next song > Planes 5:34

25 White Rabbit 2:53

26 Volunteers > Grace, Paul, and Marty thank the crowd 7:15

27 Encore: Grace intros the next song > Tune-up > 3/5 Of A Mile In 10 Seconds 4:38

28 Encore: Marty thanks the crowd > Grace intros the next song > Crown Of Creation > Paul, Grace, and Marty thank the crowd 3:25

Can you believe the twentieth show of the tour had ended already? This was a strong performance. The crowd appreciated the return of the band and the musicians were enjoying themselves. As you can tell *It's No Secret* was given a few days of rest and *3/5 Of A Mile In 10 Seconds* would be a staple of the California shows. The Hot Tuna set was filled with terrific playing and positive crowd vibrations. Jorma did a tease to the opening of the Cream classic *Sunshine Of Your Love*, Jack took a bass-solo during *99 Year Blues*, and for the first time since 9/9/89 Poplar Creek, Hoffman Estates, Illinois there would be the great few seconds of *Five Foot Two, Eyes Of Blue (Has Anybody Seen My Gal)* with Grace, Jorma, and Jack.

<u>9/26/89 Fillmore Auditorium, San Francisco, California</u>

(135:39) (Line-up 9) **Welcome home!**

1 Bill Graham intro > Drum intro (With guitar) > She Has Funny Cars 4:32
The version was terrific, having been solidified with the guitar being part of the drum intro.

2 Somebody To Love > Grace thanks the crowd 3:48

3 Plastic Fantastic Lover 4:35
Excellent vocals by Marty.

4 Won't You Try/Saturday Afternoon 5:08

5 Today 3:55

6 Grace intros Jorma and the next song > Tune-up > Good Shepherd 6:24 Jorma vocals.

7 Lather > Grace thanks the crowd and intros the next song 3:14

8 Solidarity 6:00

9 Wooden Ships 5:34
Real tight version.

10 Grace talks about the KBC Band and intros the next song > America > Paul intros the next song > Tune-up 8:23

11 Freedom 6:11

Hot Tuna set: (22:13)

12 Hesitation Blues 5:14

13 I'll Be Alright Someday > Tune-up 3:28

14 Death Don't Have No Mercy 6:00

15 Tune-up > Embryonic Journey 3:24

16 Tune-up > Too Many Years > Jorma thanks the crowd 4:07

**17 Jorma's :28 Ditty** > Grace Says "Say something Jack." > Jack says "You look lovely this evening Gracie."
Only the second time Jack would be heard on stage during an Airplane show. The prior time was 5/1/70 SUNY Athletic Field, SUNY Of Stony Brook, Stony Brook, New York when wires were cut on stage.

18 Third Week In The Chelsea (With Grace) > Grace intros Jorma and Grace talks about pandas 6:16 Hot Tuna set ends.

19 Panda 3:38

20 Miracles 6:56

21 Tune-up > The Wheel (With drum-solo) > Grace intros Kenny 8:23

22 Grace intros the next song and Jorma > Tune-up > Ice Age > Grace intros Peter and Randy 7:06

23 Summer Of Love 4:42

24 Paul Intros Next Song > True Love 3:35

25 Planes 4:40

26 White Rabbit > Grace thanks the crowd 2:35

27 Volunteers (With false ending) > Paul, Grace, and Marty thank the crowd 6:50

The band performed *It's No Secret* as an encore but there is no recorded documentation about the details.

The twenty-first performance was a return to the home land. The group was on stage at the Fillmore and there were some nice events. For only the second documented time the intro to *She Had Funny Cars* contained guitar and drums. All previous versions excluding the 9/2/89 Garden State Arts Center, Holmdel, New Jersey performance was drums only. The Hot Tuna set gave us the first appearance of *Too Many Years*. In actuality that brought the number of songs performed from the reunion album to nine of the thirteen tracks. Although it wasn't a full-band the song did get played. The tune felt good in the Hot Tuna set. Jorma gave us a twenty-eight second *Guitar Ditty*, and then the earth shook. It had nothing to do with the fault-line. Jack for only the second time spoke during an Airplane show! Grace had requested that he say something. Jack actually responded! "You look lovely tonight Gracie." The last time Jack was heard talking on an Airplane stage was 5/1/70 SUNY Athletic Field, SUNY Of Stony Brook, Stony Brook, New York. That night the band had wires cut on stage and Jack had to inform Grace. **A bit of a surprise was *San Francisco Bay Blues* not being part of the Hot Tuna selections.**

9/27/89 Fillmore Auditorium, San Francisco, California

(59:20) (Line-up 9)

The only documentation from 9/27/89 is the Hot Tuna set and some of the Airplane set that followed. The first set of the Airplane has been documented with the songs but not any further information.

1 She Has Funny Cars

2 Somebody To Love

3 Plastic Fantastic Lover

4 Won't You Try/Saturday Afternoon

5 Today

6 Good Shepherd

7 Lather

8 Solidarity

9 Wooden Ships

10 America

11 Freedom

Songs one through eleven do not have any recorded documentation, eliminating any chance for additional information.

Hot Tuna set: (29:19)

12 San Francisco Bay Blues 4:17

13 Tune-up > Uncle Sam Blues 4:36

14 Let Us Get Together Right Down Here 1:57

15 Mann's Fate 4:56

16 Tune-Up > Too Many Years 5:14

17 Embryonic Journey 2:23
This has been listed in the past as the last song performed by Hot Tuna but it would go against the previous format of finishing the set with Grace.

18 Tune-Up > Five Foot Two, Eyes Of Blue (Has Anybody Seen My Gal) 1:08 With Grace. Sometimes singers use the word "Girl" or "Baby."

19 Tune-Up > Third Week In The Chelsea (With Grace) 4:48 End of the Hot Tuna set.

20 Panda (Grace solo with piano).
There is no recorded documentation with information about this song.

21 Miracles
There is no recorded documentation with information about this song.

22 Tune-up > The Wheel (With drum-solo) > Grace intros Kenny 8:31

23 Ice Age 6:56 Jorma vocals.

24 Summer Of Love
There is no recorded documentation with information about this song.

25 True Love
There is no recorded documentation with information about this song.

26 Planes
There is no recorded documentation with information about this song.

23 White Rabbit 2:39

24 Volunteers > Grace Thanks Crowd 6:35

The Fillmore Auditorium once again was home base for the twenty-second appearance of the reunion. It is inexplicable to think that a show from San Francisco could not have complete documentation. It doesn't pay to guess what the encores may have been.  The Hot Tuna performance was solid.  Tonight the crowd did get to hear *San Francisco Bay Blues*.  *Uncle Sam Blues* was very good.  *Too Many Years* made another welcome appearance and we got the third quick snippet of *Five Foot Two, Eyes Of Blue (Has Anybody Seen My Gal)* with Grace, Jorma, and Jack right before *Third Week In The Chelsea*.

<u>9/28/89 Fillmore Auditorium, San Francisco, California</u>

(159:56) (Line-up 9) The third, and final night at the Fillmore.

1 Tune-Up > Bill Graham intro the bands > Drum intro > She Has Funny Cars 5:05

2 Somebody To Love 3:25

3 Plastic Fantastic Lover 4:31
This was a high energy version!

4 Marty thanks the crowd > Won't You Try/Saturday Afternoon 5:22

5 Today 3:59

6 Grace intros Jorma and the next song > Good Shepherd 5:59

7 Grace intros Jorma and the next song > Lather > Grace thanks the crowd 3:24

8 Grace thanks the crowd and intros the next song > Solidarity 7:16

9 Grace intros Tim Gorman > Wooden Ships 6:30

10 Grace thanks the crowd and intros the next song > America 9:07

11 Paul intros the next song > Freedom > Grace thanks the crowd 6:39

Hot Tuna set: (28:22)

12 Tune-up > I Know You Rider 4:25

13 Tune-up > Winin' Boy Blues 5:41

14 True Religion 3:54 The beginning of the song was cut.

15 Parchman Farm 4:30
Wasn't this an interesting choice?

16 Tune-up > Too Many Years 4:12

17 Tune-Up > Third Week In The Chelsea (With Grace and drums) > Grace intros Jorma and Jack 5:19
Hot Tuna set ends.

18 Grace's talks about pandas and intros the next song > Panda 5:46

19  Miracles 7:20

20 Paul intros the next song > The Wheel (With drum-solo) 8:16

21 Grace intros the next song > Tune-up >  Ice Age 7:24 Jorma vocals.
The energy increased as the song went along.

22 Grace intros Peter and Randy > Summer Of Love 5:10

23 Grace intros the next song > True Love 4:01

24 Planes 4:51

25 White Rabbit 2:53

26 Volunteers > Paul thanks the audience during a false ending > Paul thanks the crowd 8:06

27 Encore: Marty thanks the crowd and Grace intros the next song > 3/5 Of A Mile In 10 Seconds > Grace thanks the crowd 5:00
The band made sure the last version played on the reunion tour would be memorable.  Excellent energy throughout.

28 Encore: Rock Me Baby 7:51 Jorma vocals.
**The first appearance of *Rock Me Baby* was well worth the wait!**

29 Encore: Crown Of Creation >  Paul, and Grace thank the crowd 3:16

Show number twenty-three and the final of three nights at the Fillmore Auditorium was a memorable affair. *Plastic Fantastic Lover* was full of high octane and the band hit their stride rather early.  The encore segment had three songs that kept the audience focused and ecstatic.  Starting with a terrific version of *3/5 Of A Mile In 10 Seconds*, the band followed it up with the first *Rock Me Baby* of the tour!  One may have thought it would be part of a Hot Tuna set but had to be surprised by it landing as an Airplane encore.  Clocking in at almost eight minutes the instrumentation was stupendous.  Unfortunately all good things must come to an end, but at least it was on a great note.  *Crown Of Creation* was powerful and let the band walk off the stage knowing the final night of the Fillmore gatherings was the best!

9/30/89 Polo Fields, Golden Gate Park,  San Francisco, California

(159:33) (Line-up 9)

1 Bill Graham intros the band :06

2 Paul says "Hi." >Drum intro > She Has Funny Cars 5:03

3 Grace thanks the crowd > > Somebody To Love 3:24

4 Grace thanks the crowd > Plastic Fantastic Lover 4:29

5 Won't You Try/Saturday Afternoon 5:35

6 Grace intros the wrong song (*Good Shepherd*) > Paul and Grace intro the correct song > Today 3:28

7 Grace thank the crowd > Tune-up > Good Shepherd 6:13 Jorma vocals.

8 Grace intros the next song > Lather 3:16 Grace thanks the crowd 3:39

9 Grace thanks the crowd > tune up > Solidarity 6:43

10 Grace intros Tim Gorman > Wooden Ships 5:52

11 Marty talks about the local food bank > America 9:01

12 Paul intros the next song > Freedom > Grace thanks the crowd 6:14

Hot tuna set: (25:49)

13 San Francisco Bay Blues 3:54

14 Tune-up > Walking Blues 4:15

15 Tune-up > Death Don't Have No Mercy 4:13

16 I'll Be Alright Someday 3:18

17 Tune-up > 99 Year Blues 4:43

18 Jorma thanks the crowd, and intros Grace, and the next song > Tune-up > Five Foot Two, Eyes Of Blue (Has Anybody Seen My Baby) With Grace.  Sometimes singers use the word "Gal" or "Girl." :31

19 Tune-up > Third Week In The Chelsea 4:55 With Grace.

Grace intros Jorma and Jack as Hot Tuna .  She wanted to say something else (Hot F_ckin' Tuna), but Jorma's dad was at the show.  Hot Tuna set ends here.

20 Grace talks about Pandas > Panda 4:40 Grace solo on the piano.

21 Miracles 7:16

22 Paul intros the next song > The Wheel (With drum-solo) > Grace intros Kenny 9:01

23 Paul thanks all the people that helped the free concert take place 1:23

24 Grace intros Jorma and his dad > Ice Age 7:30

25 Grace intros Randy, Peter, and Jorma > Paul intros the next song > Summer Of Love > (5:35)

26 Grace intros the next song > Tune-up > True Love 4:08

27 Grace thanks the crowd and intros the next song > Planes 5:15

28 White Rabbit 2:51

29 Grace intros the next song > Volunteers > Paul, Grace, and Marty thank the crowd 6:51

30 Encore: Tune-up > It's No Secret 2:44
Nice to have the song back!

31 Encore: Rock Me Baby 6:41 Jorma vocals.

32 Encore: Grace intros the next song > Crown Of Creation 3:13

33 Encore: 3/5 Of A Mile In 10 Seconds > Paul and Grace thank the crowd > Bill Graham comes out to thank everyone involved with the show and to talk baseball 6:58 (Oakland A's vs. San Francisco Giants).

Can you believe it has been twenty-four shows already? The Airplane played a free concert in the park and they didn't disappoint the masses. They leave San Francisco having performed four excellent encores. It was nice that *It's No Secret* turned out to be one of them. *Five Foot Two, Eyes Of Blue (Has Anybody Seen My Baby)* got performed again, with Grace, Jorma, and Jack having some fun. It was only thirty-one seconds but a fine rendition. **Get away from the exit door! The Airplane hasn't landed yet. There is one more stop to go.** Relax, and watch the *Fly Jefferson Airplane* DVD as we head to Washington, D.C.

<u>10/7/89 March For The Homeless, Washington, D.C.</u>

(22:56) (Line-up 9) **The real finale to the reunion tour!**

1 Bill Graham intro of Wavy Gravy :20
Wavy Gravy (Real name is Hugh Romney) is a well known person in San Francisco. Besides being friends with the musicians, and dressing up in crazy costumes, he is a <u>very dedicated activist</u>, and <u>contributor to charities</u>.

2 Wavy Gravy talks about hunger 1:03

3 Bill Graham intros the Jefferson Airplane :13

4 Somebody To Love 3:24

5 Grace thanks the crowd > Grace intros the next song > Crown Of Creation 2:57

6 Baby What You Want Me To Do 4:49 Jorma vocals.
Peter takes the last solo.

7 Grace talks about money for the poor :28

8 She Has Funny Cars 3:55

9 Volunteers > Paul thanks the crowd near the end > Marty thanks the crowd 5:10
There was no false ending on *Volunteers*.

10 Bill Graham stage announcement :30

The final show of the reunion tour would be a short set. The band played twenty-five dates and gave many of those that had never seen the Airplane fly a chance to experience the live drama. The tour also had plenty of the older fans, and it seemed they enjoyed recapturing a bit of their youth. A wonderful attribute from a great rock and roll show is the ability to make time stand still for a few hours. Life especially after age thirty seems to accelerate at the speed of sound. To have been able to freeze the clock for a few hours felt rejuvenating. It was interesting that *She Has Funny Cars* was in the set, but for the first time not performed as the opening song (Excluding 9/4/89 Lake Compounce, Bristol, Connecticut when Marty was late). *Somebody To Love* is certainly a song that can fit anywhere. I have good and bad news. The bad is the Airplane would not fly again until 1996. The good is that we didn't have to wait seventeen years for it.

I would be remiss if I didn't give credit to Peter Kaukonen and his performance during the 1989 tour. Peter has exceptional ability but not an ego to match. Many times when he would have a solo or be playing some nice nuance on the guitar, he would be standing near or in back of an amplifier.

**Peter, thanks for your contribution!**

# Chapter 10: 1996-2006 "Their Lives Will Live In Books"

<u>1/16/96 Rock And Roll Hall Of Fame (Rehearsals) Waldorf Astoria Hotel, New York City</u>

(Paul Kantner remembers the rehearsal was actually a sound check from the same day). There are many that feel 1/16/96 is correct.

(26:48) (Line-up 3) **Spencer is back! Grace is not present.**

Grace had once mentioned at a book signing "Old people look silly playing rock and roll." That was the real reason she was not present for the rehearsal and induction. She was missed.

The rehearsal (Paul remembered it as a sound check only) took place at the Waldorf Astoria Hotel, New York City.

1 Improvisations > Volunteers > Improvisation 3:30

2 Chatter > Volunteers (False start) > Improvisation > Chatter > Improvisations > Chatter > Volunteers 8:17

3 Improvisations > Volunteers (False start) > Chatter > Embryonic Journey 3:52
**Jorma plays the song by himself!**

4 Improvisations > Crown Of Creation 7:25

5 Crown Of Creation > False start > Crown Of Creation 5:19

6 Chatter > Crown Of Creation 5:09

7 Chatter > Jam 3:04
The *jam* is short, but reminiscent of the ones from circa 1967-1968. **Well done guys.**

It was nice even for a day, Spencer would get to play with the Airplane again and the band could fly the old plane for twenty-four hours.

<u>1/17/96 Rock And Roll Hall Of Fame: Performance and induction, Waldorf Astoria Hotel, New York City</u>

(17:37) (Line-up 3) **Welcome back Spencer! Grace is not there.**

As mentioned in the previous entry, (The rehearsal) Grace was not present for any portion of the events.

1 Crown Of Creation 3:41

**2 Embryonic Journey (F & L) 2:44 (Paul suggested to have Jorma perform this solo).**
This was the first and only time performed with Jefferson Airplane members on stage. Jorma and Jack did play *Embryonic Journey* on the 1989 reunion tour, but in the Hot Tuna set.

3 Volunteers 3:56

1 Induction by Phil Lesh and Mickey Hart of the Grateful Dead 2:52

2 Acceptance speeches by Jack, Jorma, Spencer, Marty, and Paul > Paul reads a poem (***Get Ready***) written by Rebecca Inez Bockelie when she was eight, and living in Seattle, Washington. 4:24 (F & L)
**This was the only time the poem or any for that matter would be recited during a J.A. performance.**

The story told to appease those in attendance and the media was Grace had trouble with her back. Grace had stated during a book signing "Old people look silly playing rock and roll." I've always liked silly people (As long as they are old). What did you think? It would have been terrific if Grace performed. It was nice for a day that Spencer could be part of the J.A. Any reaction to the three songs that were played? What did you think of Jorma playing *Embryonic Journey* solo?

Three songs could never properly represent the body of work from the band. *Volunteers* was a choice nobody could argue with. *Crown Of Creation* is a tremendous song but would you have placed it above *It's No Secret*, *Plastic Fantastic Lover*, or *3/5 Of A Mile In 10 Seconds*? It is a tough call. What narrowed down the selection to choose from was the absence of Grace. There would be no way they attempt *Somebody To Love* or *White Rabbit*. *Wooden Ships* would have been problematic as well. It is imperative to never assume what you see on the surface is undeniable fact. Paul Kantner made a gracious and totally unselfish suggestion to Jorma, that he perform *Embryonic Journey* by himself and the other members of the band gave the consent. If we didn't know that, since the entire appearance was only a little over ten minutes one could make a valid point *Embryonic Journey* put more credence on a single part and not the entire plane. I thank Paul Kantner for setting the record straight during the interview found later on in the book.

The greatest of nights shouldn't contain any portions of sorrow. The band had not performed with Spencer since 1970 and the last Airplane show was 10/7/89 Washington, D.C. As they walked off the stage after *Volunteers* not only did the performance end, but the plane has sat abandoned, and "The electrical dust is starting to rust." (*Crown Of Creation*).

Great Society-

10/20/2002 San Francisco Civic Center, San Francisco, California (35th Anniversary Summer Of Love)

(33:52)

1 Intro of the band 1:06

2 White Rabbit (Low vocal mix) 4:49 Vocals Tessa.
The sound crew couldn't get the vocal levels correct until most of the song was over. The band sounded good, but you have to have empathy for Tessa, she looked forward to such a special moment and can hardly be heard during most of the song.

3 Sally Go 'Round The Roses 6:01
This came off nicely. The sound crew straightened things out and the band could concentrate on the music.

4 I Don't Want To Fall In Love > Tune-up 7:16
Written for Tessa by Darby. I was surprised that three of the six songs would be tunes the Great Society didn't perform originally.

5 I Need You More 4:46 Jor Slick (Darby's son sings).
Of the three post Great Society songs this one was the best. It had at times a more modern sound but in no way was it devoid of the necessary components from 1960's rock and roll.

6 Seven Years 4:11
Darby wrote this for the singer of the song Elizabeth McGill, her mom Allison Prival helped with the vocals. The tune wasn't anything out of the ordinary, however it was really nice that both mom and daughter could share the experience.

7 Somebody To Love 4:40 Vocals Elizabeth and Allison.
The arrangement was brilliant. It started with the Great Society rendition and ended with the Jefferson Airplane's version. This easily was one of the most overlooked live treasures of this decade.

## Great Society 2002:

Darby Slick -Lead guitar.

Jerry Slick- Rhythm guitar (He didn't want to play drums).

Peter van Gelder- Saxophone.

**With:**

Barry Flast- Keyboards (Jefferson Starship and Kingfish).

Paul Lamb- Bass.

Elizabeth McGill- Vocals on tracks 6 and 7.

Allison Prival- Vocals tracks 6 and 7 (Mother of Elizabeth).

Jimmy Sage- Drums.

Jor Slick- (Darby's son) Rhythm guitar and vocals).

Tessa- Vocals on tracks 2-4.

**Thanks to Barry Flast for the information on the show.**

## Great Society-

Special Diana Mangano vocal overdub for *White Rabbit* 2:58

There was hope that the Great Society performance from 10/20/2002 San Francisco Civic Center, San Francisco, California could be released as a DVD and or CD. When *White Rabbit* suffered from a low vocal mix **Diana was asked to sing the song in the studio and the attempt would be made to use her vocal track with the live version.** It turned out that the show did not get released but Diana did a splendid job. Near the end of the song you can hear both Diana and Tessa. Thanks to the magic of modern technology Tessa can honestly say she got to sing with Diana. I wonder if anybody told her.

I have great news. While you're waiting for your luggage please relax and enjoy the magical sounds of Marty Balin. Here are four CD's released through Marty's website http://www.jbppresentsmartybalin.com. **Thank you to Mr. Joe Buchwald for supplying the music.** More importantly thank you to Mr. Joe Buchwald for taking such an interest in the book and helping whenever he could! **You have earned every accolade ever given you!**

## Marty Balin-

In 2006 Marty and his dad decided to start to re-issue CD's, and release some of the lost treasures from the vaults for the first time. The original year the songs were recorded and the musicians aren't listed. Any duplicate songs from actual album releases are different versions. The material is impressive enough to enjoy with the knowledge that it is Marty Balin and well produced!

**Marty Balin (2000)**

1 Today 3:01 (Jefferson Airplane version from *Surrealistic Pillow* 1967).

2 Miracles 6:54 (Jefferson Starship version from *Red Octopus* 1975).

3 Hearts 4:17 (Version from the Marty solo album *Balin* 1981).

4 Atlanta Lady (Something About Your Love) 3:27 Original single that broke the Top 30 in 1981.

5 Do It For Love 3:12 Original single from 1983.

6 What Love Is 4:44 From the 1983 solo album *Lucky*.

7 There's No Shoulder 4:40 From the 1983 Japanese extended play single.
The song is a good introduction to what Marty often sounded like during the period 1981-1983. An extended play (EP) single contained more playing time than the standard (45 RPM).

8 Hold Me 5:59 (KBC version from the self-titled album 1986).

9 Sayonara 4:58 (KBC version from the self-titled album 1986). The most underrated KBC album track.

10 Camellia 3:46 Previously unreleased.
The song sounds very reminiscent of the KBC album. This would go over well in a live setting. There isn't any information available on the year the tune was written.

11 Valerie 3:53 Previously unreleased.
This isn't the song Steve Winwood covered and had massive airplay with. It is a slow in tempo and Marty is clearly the most integral part of the tune. There isn't any information available on the year the tune was written.

12 Candles 4:27 Previously unreleased.
The KBC Band performed this live and it is worthy of inclusion on a retrospective or studio release. There isn't any information available on the year the tune was written.

13 What's New In Your World 3:44 Previously unreleased.
Marty's voice is in solid form for the tune. It is well crafted and sounds like Marty from the 1980's. There isn't any information available on the year the tune was written.

14 What About Love 4:42 Previously unreleased.
This is one of Marty's strongest unreleased tracks. The bass and drums are so well meshed it is almost haunting. The song is constructed with an up-tempo beat and Marty sounds very strong.

**Marty Balin (2003)**

1 Don't Be Sad Anymore 3:21
Marty pays homage to the male vocal sound of the 1950's and 1960's.

2 City Lights 6:05
**One of the best tracks Marty recorded post Airplane. As a matter of fact this is one of the best post Airplane tunes by any Airplane Family member.** The arrangement is mid-tempo and is catchy to the point you hope the song goes on forever.

3 Free As A Bird 3:06
While it is not the John Lennon song the Beatles recorded, this is a nice bit of rock and roll. The band shadows Marty's vocal inflections perfectly.

4 L.A. Girls 3:27
Back to the 1980's Marty sound for this one.

5 Viva La Vida 4:04
This tune found its way to the Jefferson Starship stage. Long live life. You'll find the song being played over and over again on the CD player. The first listen will have you hooked.

6 Dance You Outta My Mind 3:42
Do you recall the Romantics hit *What I Like About You*? If you slow down the pace you got *Dance You Outta My Mind*.

7 Dance All Nite 5:10
The band plugs in for this one and gives a healthy dose of rock and roll.

8 Rockin' Blues 4:26
Marty shares the spotlight with a piano that has 1960's written all over it. The band is having fun and Marty is leading the way.

9 Time For Every Season 4:09
Another good rocker from Marty. If you enjoy the KBC song *It's Not You, It's Not Me*, you will immediately think this could be an equal twin.

**Nashville Sessions (2006)**

1 Rising From The Ashes 3:53
Marty did a wonderful job of putting a country music inflection into the vocals. The tune is enhanced by a piano playing southern rock style, but blending in seamlessly.

2 Lost Highway 4:03
The intro is rock and roll and then Marty brings us back to the 1960's sound of Creedence Clearwater Revival. John Fogerty would be proud to hear this one. It isn't a Fogerty composition, but his trademark is all over it.

3 Hide My Heart 3:29
If you can imagine a more upbeat *Hearts* you'll have this one down pat. Marty's voice brings you back to the 1970's. KBC played this tune live but Marty's studio version is stronger.

4 Count On Me 4:07
Yes is the answer. If the question was did Marty do another rendition of the Jefferson Starship song? There was a terrific approach to this arrangement. There is a tincture of country, but more prominent are Marty's mainstream and superb vocals. It often leaves a bad taste when an artist rerecords a well respected song, fortunately Marty was able to put a new stamp on an old envelope and send the song into an extremely good flight.

5 Nobody But You 5:23
This is a ballad from the opening note to closing vocals. The country style excluding the guitar break is innocuous.

6 Pieces Of The Rain 4:57
"Try living on the bottom if you think it is lonely on the top." The second Marty delivers those words it is picture perfect how profound the entire song is. The tune is full of exceptional imagery and to date one of the most underrated songs Marty has ever put on a record or CD.

7 Mercy Of The Moon 6:22
A pretty ballad that may remind you of hearing a Paul McCartney solo tune. The band is in the background for the majority of the composition, excluding a brilliant and articulate instrumental segment.

8 We Rise With Our Dreams 3:26
Another ballad, this one on the short side. Give this a couple of listens, it gains strength each time.

9 Hold Me 5:06
KBC played this song live. If you slowed down John Mellencamp's *Cherry Bomb*, you would be in the neighborhood of how the song is constructed.

10 Red Roses 3:53
Marty put the cowboy hat on for this one and delivered the vocals somewhat similar to the country sound of the 1960's.

The balance of doing what was in his heart (Nashville) and what the fan expects from Marty could have been a negative, but Marty made sure not only was there peaceful coexistence there was harmony as well.

**The Aviator- Lost Treasures (2006)**

1 Shape In The Night 3:32
Although reminiscent of *Hearts* to a degree this stands on its own rather well.

2 Breathe Away 4:12
Are you ready to dance?

3 Valerie 3:45
This isn't the song Steve Winwood covered and had massive airplay with. It is a slow in tempo and Marty is clearly the most integral part of the tune.

4 Shock Me 3:24
When you listen to a solid rock and roll song called *Shock Me* it may make you dislike the 80's Starship even more. (Maybe it was a dream and they never existed). Marty shows on this tune that not all 80's rock and roll has to leave you with acid reflux.

5 Devil Wears Lingerie 3:18
More straight ahead rock and roll from Mr. Balin. Isn't it always laughable when people that wouldn't know a rock from a roll have the audacity to think Paul McCartney and Marty Balin are only about the softer side of music?

6 Mary Ann 3:31
The background vocals are very similar to the style of the great three minute rockers from the 1960's.

7 You Know What I Like 3:48
Mix a danceable bass line with Marty circa 1986 and your ears will be perfectly in tune for this number.

8 I'm The One 3:32
You could sense Marty had fun with this one in the studio. The entire band shares the spotlight on an upbeat tune.

9 Viva La Vida 3:50
This tune found its way to the Jefferson Starship stage. Long live life. You'll find the song being played over and over again on the CD player. You'll be hooked after the first listen.

10 Free As A Bird 3:15
While it is not the John Lennon song the Beatles recorded, this is a nice bit of rock and roll. The band shadows Marty's vocal inflections perfectly.

11 City Lights 8:00
Did you notice the length of the song?  **One of the best tracks Marty recorded post Airplane.  As a matter of fact one of the best post Airplane tunes from any Airplane Family member.**  The arrangement is mid-tempo and is catchy to the point you hope the song goes on forever.

12 Yes, Yes, Yes  4:44
KBC performed this tune live.  It fit perfectly into Marty's sound in and around 1986.

13 Nothing To Lose 2:44
A good rocker that makes you feel your back in the 1960's or 1970's.  There is a portion of the tune that is in the same ballpark as the Byrds masterpiece *So You Wanna Be A Rock 'N' Roll Star*.

14 L.A. Girls 3:22
Back to the 1980's Marty sound for this one.

15 Always 3:48
Bits and pieces have the sound of a Stevie Nicks (Fleetwood Mac) solo tune.

16 Don't Be Sad Anymore 3:19
A simplistic arrangement that focuses on Marty's tale of a love song.

17 Someone 3:22
Marty's voice is in perfect form for a song to relax by.

18 Maybe For You 2:53
The band takes you back to years gone by.

## Bob Harvey-

Bob Harvey's Music Compilation Of Songs Performed from 1956-2006 Promotional CD (2006)

(71:27)

1 Bob Harvey intros his latest band Georgia Blue :41
Bob Harvey-Lead vocals, guitar and upright bass (Acoustic).
Alesia Chester- Auto Harp and vocals.
Zack Lanier- Lead guitar, banjo, mandolin, and vocals.
Lamar Hunter- Fiddle, mandolin, banjo, and vocals.

2 Bob Harvey talks about the first recording he ever made, a 78 RPM record in 1956.  He recorded *Be My Doll* in Manila, Philippines :30

3 Be My Doll 2:21
An upbeat combination of bluegrass and country.  The beauty of this is no attempt was made to alter the original sound quality.  The clicks, pops, and one skip are there for the listener's enjoyment!

4 Bob Harvey talks about his move to the west coast in 1960 and he intros the Slippery Rock String Band (1963):
Chuck McCabe- Banjo.
Lee Chaney- Guitar.
Mike Mindel- Fiddle.
Bob Harvey- Upright bass (Acoustic).

**Bob Harvey talks about meeting Marty Balin at the Drinking Gourd, San Francisco, California and intros the Jefferson Airplane personnel for the August 1965 demo for Columbia Records. (Recorded in Los Angeles, California).** *The Other Side Of This Life* 1:18

258

(Line-up B as introduced by Bob Harvey) http://www.warriorrecords.com offers this song as part of a various artists CD called *Then & Now* **CD Volume 1 Warrior Records SFS23931. They list Jack Casady on bass (It was Bob Harvey) and give the source as The Matrix, San Francisco, California early 1965. The Matrix wasn't open until 8/13/65!**

Jorma Kaukonen- Lead guitar.
Paul Kantner- Rhythm guitar.
Skip Spence- Drums.
Signe Anderson- Lead vocals.
Marty Balin- Harmony vocals.
Bob Harvey- Bass.

**5 The Other Side Of This Life 2:24**
The arrangement is superlative for the time. The band captures the folk-rock sound but Jorma's fill-ins are masterful. They perform a very upbeat and spirited version. **The demo is eight percent off speed (Too fast). There is so much confidence being shown that it should surprise no one that the J.A. was offered a record deal, but held out for a better one to come along!**

6 Bob Harvey talks about the same day auditioning for Capitol Records (Results never discussed), playing for producer Phil Spector (Please see the Bob Harvey interview for a funny story), and going to see a taping of the TV show Big Valley (With Barbara Stanwyck and Charles Bronson filming their parts). Charles Bronson tells the band not to be upset by a comment of one of the actors making fun of the length of their hair. Charles Bronson told the band "He's so low on the food chain he is hurting for people." Bob and Skip Spence later that night would write the song *Hurting For People*. **They did not record it (Our great loss)**. :55

7 Hurting For People 3:46
Bob doesn't discuss the version that is used for the CD but it is 2005 from San Francisco Blue called *Children Of The Wind*. He has played this song constantly over the years. It is a mixture of bluegrass music with the seriousness of a folk-rock tune. It is a strong candidate for the best song Bob Harvey has recorded. The version used for the CD has terrific production.

8 Bob Harvey talks about his time with the Jefferson Airplane and mentions the show at the Circle Star Theater, Santa Clara, California (The date is not given and this performance has been overlooked throughout the years. It had to have been between 8/14/65-10/2865. The Matrix, San Francisco, California 8/13/65 was the first gig the band played. Jack Casady's first performance was 10/30/65 Harmon Gymnasium, University of California, Berkeley, California) opening for Eric Burden & the Animals. Bob Harvey meets a reporter at the gig Carolyn Cravens and he writes a song for her *Black Velvet Soul*. :40

9 Black Velvet Soul 3:59
Bob Harvey came up with a superior formula for this one. The combination of a folk-rock sound and assertive lyrics paint very accurate pictures of his mind at the time. Bob Harvey doesn't specify which version was used for the CD. It is not the one from the 2005 Georgia Blue CD called *Seeds of Revolution*.

10 Bob Harvey talks about leaving the Jefferson Airplane in 1965, reforming the Slippery Rock String Band the same year, and the song from 1967 that got a fair amount of airplay in the Bay Area called *Tule Fog*. :22

11 Tule Fog (Dome Records 1967 A-Side) 1:55
The version is from the Slippery Rock String Band 1967. It sounds so much more realistic that the cracks and pops were left on the recording. The song is a cross of bluegrass and country and the result is a song that is fun to record. Bob's vocal sounds different than any other tune you can think of him singing. It is the most polished of all his releases.

12 Bob Harvey talks about his favorite song being the B-Side of the single *Sally Brought Him Home*. :17

13 Sally Brought Him Home (Dome Records 1967 B-Side to Tule Fog) 1:49
Lee Chaney wrote this track. Bob Harvey rerecorded a version on the live CD from San Francisco Blue released in 2005 called *Live On The Cartersville Express* (10/04) and on the 2005 Georgia Blue album *Children Of The Wind*. The version here is indeed the B-Side single from 1967. The recipe doesn't change, it is the upbeat bluegrass and country sound that Bob Harvey has perfected over the years. This particular track is meant to be funny. The original pops and clicks from 1967 never sounded better. I miss vinyl to this day!

14 Bob Harvey talks about the next song *Bugle Call Rag* :27

15 Bugle Call Rag 1:32
From 1967 the Slippery Rock String Band album called *Live At The House Of The Rising Sun*.
Did you ever wonder what a great armed forces bugle call would sound like bluegrass style? Here you go! An instrumental with plenty of kick.

16 Bob Harvey intros his favorite song from the ones recorded on *Live At The House Of The Rising Sun* called *Red Rocking Chair*. :06

17 Red Rockin' Chair 2:16
A typical bluegrass song with a high output of energy from the band.

18 Bob Harvey talks about the break-up of the Slippery Rock String Band, forming a new group Catfish Wakely, and recording a science-fiction song *Green World*. :26

Catfish Wakely:
Tom Lane- Lead guitar.
Ron Funk- Rhythm guitar.
Bob Harvey- Bass.

19 Green World 4:45
Written by Bob Harvey. The Catfish Wakely was influenced by the folk-rock scene. Bob should have gotten credit for how esoteric this track was for the time.

20 Bob Harvey talks about the East-Indian influences of Tom Lane and intros *Blowin' My Mind* from the Catfish Wakely. :10

21 Blowin' My Mind 4:54
Mix some psychedelic rock with folk and you have the idea. Another fairly esoteric arrangement.

22 Bob Harvey talks about being asked to write a song for a movie in early 1969 called *Bitter Cherry*. He wrote the title track.

Chuck McCabe- Lead guitar.
Homer Blake- Drums.
Tye Porter- Bass (Doobie Brothers).
Bob Harvey- Rhythm guitar and vocals.

23 Bitter Cherry 5:02
Imagine a dark screen with the audience feeling something will happen soon as a haunting piece of music is playing in the background. The general consensus of those that knew of the track were Bob Harvey was able to understand the difference between writing a song for a record album and creating a mood for a movie.

24 Bob Harvey talks about producing and writing music for a 1970 biker film called *Hard Ride To The Movies*. Don Preston (Frank Zappa & The Mothers Of Invention) is on the recording and Bob mentions other members of the Mothers were there too. He doesn't give the names. :14

25 Hard Ride To The Movies 2:45
The track is not much different than a strong early to mid-period Steppenwolf song. Bob takes the lead vocals and the band rocks on!

26 Bob Harvey talks about going back to college when he turned forty, being Entertainment Editor for Mother Trucker News, and writing a radio commercial for them called *Mother Trucker Blues*. :21

27 Mother Trucker Blues 5:24
This is obviously not the commercial version. Bob Harvey doesn't mention if they used the song for the commercial but if they had it would have been either thirty or sixty seconds. For the trucker looking for a bit of home-style bluegrass and country music, Bob Harvey is serving it up.

28 Bob Harvey talks about going to Saudi Arabia in 1990 and meeting mandolin-player Brian Fowler. They would form San Francisco Blue. Bob Harvey tells us his favorite song from the 2000 San Francisco Blue album *Idiot's Vision* is *It's High On A Mountain* :24

29 It's High On A Mountain 4:57
The vocal style doesn't sound distant from a solo Crosby, Stills, Nash & Young record if you sprinkled a dash of bluegrass.

30 Bob Harvey talks about the 2005 San Francisco Blue album *Hurting For People* and the version of *Bitter Cherry*. :13

31 Bitter Cherry 5:59
The version sounds more updated because band member Brian Fowler is a fan of the progressive-avant-garde group Hawkwind and he adds a little of their flavor to the bluegrass rendition.

32 Bob Harvey talks about going separate ways from Brian Fowler and recording a version of *Sally Brought Him Home* with Georgia Blue, from the 2005 album *Children Of The Wind*. :13

33 Sally Brought Him Home 3:41
The version although longer than the original (Please see track 13) certainly kept the recipe for success.

34 Bob Harvey talks about the next song *Eliminate The Steps* will be found on the next album he releases. :07

35 Eliminate The Steps 5:33
Although Bob Harvey introduced this as being unreleased it is actually a superb bluegrass style song found on the live CD from San Francisco Blue released in 2005 called *Live On The Cartersville Express* (10/04).

36 Bob Harvey talks about the Georgia Blue website www.georgiablue.us and thanks the listeners. :26

It should be noted what has given Bob Harvey the ability to perform bluegrass music so successfully over fifty years is having a talent for crafting an original or cover song that even if you are not a bluegrass or country music fan, you can listen to one of his released albums or see him live and be along for the entire ride.

# Chapter 11: Circa 1962-Present "I'll Smile And Say I Told You So"

**1965-Present: Jefferson Airplane, and Family questions, and answers. Including Jefferson Airplane, Hot Tuna, Jefferson Starship, SVT, KBC, & Paul Kantner's Wooden Ships.**

Please note I've attempted to put the questions in the most logical order, and in the section of the band they either refer to, or would be the closest fit at the time. **Thank you** for all the questions, ranging from phone conversations during the disc-jockey years, letters, emails, and through regular chatter with other Jefferson Airplane Family fans.

SVT (Jack Casady & Nick Buck) questions can be found after the Jefferson Starship questions conclude.

## Jefferson Airplane-

Q: "Did Jorma, Jack, or both have any recordings that were released prior to the *Takes Off* album?"

A: "In 1959 Jorma and Jack released a song called *Magic Key*. The band was called the Triumphs. It was put out as a 78 RPM. When 78 RPM's fell out of favor the 45 RPM would become the standard for a single and the 33 1/3 RPM would be for the LP. There is a site www.kaufman-center.org, that had some nice info on Jorma a few years back and they even mentioned the single."

Q: "Did Jorma play as a solo performer prior to the Airplane and did he use another name?"

A: "Jorma was a terrific solo performer playing folk and blues influenced material. There is documentation of shows from 1962-1964 in the main part of the book. On some of the performances he was billed as Jerry Kaukonen."

Q: "Jorma sometime in the early 1960's played with a guy named Billy Roberts. Is that the gentleman that wrote *Hey Joe*?"

A: "Billy Roberts is sometimes credited as the writer of the legendary song *Hey Joe*. He copyrighted the tune in 1962. There are many that feel the song is traditional. There is some terrific information about the controversy at http://www.heyjoe.org/lyrics.html. The Byrds, Deep Purple, and Jimi Hendrix are three examples of the song being released by major acts."

Q: "When Jorma was playing without a band before the Airplane did he play with any performers that would become famous as well?"

A: "Jorma not only was friends with Janis Joplin but played live with her in 1962 and 1963. They also played in Jorma's house in 1964. One song from the six song home tape with Janis (1964) appeared on Hot Tuna- *The Last Interview*, released 8/1/78 from Grunt DJLI-2852. That was a promo only LP, and contained *Hesitation Blues,* with Janis playing the typewriter as a percussion instrument. Jorma also played with Pigpen (1964), who would go on to be a keyboard-player with the Grateful Dead. You can see the songs they performed in the main part of the book."

Q: "I sometimes read on the internet about a folk group David Freiberg played in during the early 1960's. When they mention his female partner Michaela she never has a last name. Why does she not have two names?"

A: "David's partner was Michaela Conga. You are correct, no matter where you read her name it is always Michaela and never Michaela Conga. Thanks to David Freiberg for remembering."

Q: "Did Jorma perform a wonderful song right around 1964 with the words pawn shop in the title?"

A: "Jorma did play the song in 1964 called *Pawn Shop Blues*. It was written by Brownie McGhee."

Q: "Did Jorma try to get the original Airplane bass-player Bob Harvey out of the band so that Jack Casady could join?"

A: "It actually is a story that has <u>no</u> merit. Bob Harvey will tell you during the interview section of the book that Jorma had nothing to do with the change. Jorma even went with Bob to pick out a new bass. The record company wanted the band to have an electric folk-rock sound and they felt Bob's background was geared more to the old fashioned stand-up bass."

Q: "Did the recording contracts differ greatly from the San Francisco bands during the 1960's?"

A: "The contracts not only differed between bands but what a band was offered by two different companies. Bob Harvey the original Airplane bass-player told me that they had an offer from Columbia Records but management felt it was not the best deal out there. As it turned out that was a bold but wise move. The RCA deal did offer more for the band. Bob was kind enough to relay a fascinating side note. The song that the Airplane used to audition for Columbia was *The Other Side Of This Life*. Paul Kantner did an interview on 8/26/87 for WPYX-FM Radio (PIX 106) Albany, New York. The station was celebrating the 20th anniversary of the Summer Of Love. They were on location in San Francisco. One of the other guests was John Cipollina of the Quicksilver Messenger Service. Paul mentioned that "Quicksilver got the best deal of all of us." In the interview section of the book Peter Albin (Big Brother & The Holding Company) talks briefly about the first contract they had signed. The record company took a high percentage of the publishing rights and allowed only twelve takes per song, when they recorded the first LP. What he didn't bring up when the band needed to get from Chicago to San Francisco (The members had no money in their pockets) the record company not only wouldn't lend them money, they wouldn't give them an advance on future royalties. Many of the American bands were taken advantage of by the record companies. When your dream is a signature away you don't always look to see if you are selling your future for a song."

Q: "How far into the bands history did Jorma have to wait to sing a lead vocal live?"

A: " The first documented vocal was on *Kansas City Blues* 1/14/66 at the Kitsalano (Kits) Theater, Vancouver, Canada."

Q: "How many songs that were on the first album *Takes Off* were performed live prior to the release in September of 1966?"

A: "Six tunes have been one hundred percent documented as being part of the live attraction. They were: *And I Like It, Bringing Me Down, It's No Secret, Let's Get Together, Runnin' Round This World* (On the first pressing only), and *Tobacco Road*."

Q: "Am I thinking to much like a conservative, or were the cries of censorship of musicians, and entertainers in the 1960's unjustified?"

A: "February of 1966 would be an example of censorship that best defines how stringently the ropes were tied around the Airplane. You will find more information about this when you read the chapter on 1966. The short answer is the song "*Let Me In*" was deemed offensive, because of the following lyrics, "Don't tell me you want money." The line had to be rewritten to "Don't tell me it's so funny." Performers could be fined on stage for improper language as well."

Q: "How come when I search the internet for information on the song *Get Together* it only gives results about the group called the Youngbloods?"

A: "The Airplane which released the song years before the great version by the Youngbloods called the song *Let's Get Together*. Many websites require the search to be very word specific. Since the Youngbloods had the hit it is more easily associated with *Get Together*."

Q: "In 1965 or 1966 I was at an Airplane show, I asked the person next to me what was the name of the last song they played. The person told me "*Dino's Song*." It turned out it was *Let's Get Together*. The guy didn't seem to be making a joke. Why did he tell me the wrong name?"

A: "During several performances from 1965 and early 1966 Marty would introduce the tune as *Dino's Song*. The funny part of that was a song would surface on the first Quicksilver Messenger Service album called *Dino's Song*, but not be related to *Let's Get Together*. Dino Valente who would become a member of the Quicksilver Messenger Service was the songs composer and friend of the band."

Q: "If Signe Anderson stayed with the J.A. how differently would history have been written?"

A: "The group would not have had Grace's vocal dynamics, improvisational ability on stage, her tremendous persona, or *Somebody To Love*, and *White Rabbit* getting airplay all these years. It isn't that cut and dry. The quality folk-rock performers have had well deserved success for several decades in the U.S.A. and often abroad. The ground work was there on the *Takes Off* album. Maybe the stage would never have become a place for the outstanding *jams*, and extensions of the songs, however it is very possible there may have been more hit singles. The Byrds, Bob Dylan, and Simon and Garfunkel have been able to achieve ever lasting respect, and the possibility strongly exists the J.A. could have been there for the flight."

Q: "From the first day Signe Anderson left the Jefferson Airplane until now how many members if any has she played with on stage at least once?"

A: "On 11/27/85, Bill Graham Productions had their 20^th Anniversary, at the Fillmore Auditorium, San Francisco, California. On the bill was KBC. Signe and Spencer Dryden appeared on *It's No Secret* and *Plastic Fantastic Lover*. On that night alone she got to perform with four members, Paul, Marty, Jack and Spencer. On 2/27/88 at the Starry Night, Portland Oregon, Signe performed with Hot Tuna on *High Flying Bird* and *Chauffeur Blues*. Hot Tuna had Jorma, Jack, and Paul Kantner on the tour. Signe had now played with six members of the J.A. When Signe signed on for some 1993 shows with the Jefferson Starship she was able to play with Papa John Creach. It turned out rather nice. Signe would be on the same stage as seven former Airplane members."

Q: "Were there songs left off the *Takes Off* album that were good enough for release?"

A: "In order to properly answer the question I have to add one more variable. Songs good enough for release that also fit the theme of the first LP. Four tunes come to mind. If the band would have recorded a slower more folk oriented version (As compared to blues) of *Baby What You Want Me To Do*, it would have been a terrific addition. *High Flying Bird* was too brilliant of a song to have been put on the shelf, *I Feel A Whole Lot Better* (The Byrds), and Bob Dylan's, *Lay Down Your Weary Tune*, could have been brilliant pieces to the *Takes Off* puzzle. All those tunes were performed live by the Airplane prior to the LP's release."

Q: "During the early years of the band can you give me some of the other groups they played with that never became as large, but did make a dent in the music scene?"

A: "There were many that would fit that category. One of the earliest groups to be on the same bill as the J.A. was an outrageous act called the Fugs. Their repertoire including everything from folk to distorted out of tune rock and roll and from political rants to jug band music. Butterfield Blues Band never made a large dent in the album charts, but they deserve high accolades for bringing the blues to various cultures around the country. Two of the members of the band Mike Bloomfield and Mark Naftalin can be found in the 1967 portion of the book. They joined the J.A. for a couple of blues songs on stage in New York City. The Charlatans were never known for many extended songs (*Alabama Bound* was sometimes tinkered with for added length), but their folk sound with an appreciation for the blues made San Francisco and vicinity full of friendly faces when they appeared."

Q: "Are there forgotten tracks from the Skip Spence period that ended up getting released on a CD years later?"

A: "This question has surfaced because the second version of the Airplane live at the *Monterey Pop Festival* 6/17/67 CD put on some tracks that have no authenticity. The first clue how unethical this was, Skip wasn't even part of the line-up. The only version that every fan should own is on CD from Magnum (Thunderbolt) 74. This was made available in 1995. It is a legit release, with nothing but good attentions for the J.A. fan. Several years later a CD appeared with a slightly different name. It is best to not give any information about the title or catalog number. On that release the consumer was lead to believe the contents were the songs from the concert. Only some of the material is live. There are three songs that are credited to Jorma, Marty, and Skip. The titles were *What Your Askin'*, *Would You Love Me*, and *You're So Loose*. The music sounds closer to the Starship, and I don't mean Jefferson! Not only is the sound more eighties but in the days of censorship if the band had written a song about somebody being "loose" it would have gotten attention. There has never been documentation about a recording session for these tunes or information about them being performed live. It is horrible to take advantage of somebody that was either in search of the live recording of the Monterey show and or looking for Airplane treasure."

Q: "Did the Great Society with Grace ever record in the studio and or play live a Bob Dylan or Beatles song?"

A: "They did a cover of Bob Dylan's- *Outlaw Blues* live. Grace was the lead vocalist. It was put on one of the two live records that came out called *Conspicuous Only In Its Absence*. The other one was titled *How It Was*. In the main section of the book there is a complete list of verified studio and live material they performed."

Q: "Is there any music you recommend by Darby Slick after the Great Society? That is if it exists."

A: "*King Of The Fretless Guitar* is a CD that you can purchase from www.noguru.com. Darby is joined by his son Jor on the bass and Scott Matthews on drums. Darby uses a custom guitar (Designed by Darby and his son) and does a cover of Jimi Hendrix's *Red House*."

Q: "Is it true or false that the only reason the two live albums from the Great Society were released in the late 1960's were because of Grace's Airplane success?"

A: "While Grace was very marketable in 1968 (When the two LP's were released) the Great Society did have a major label offer to record a studio album. As it turned out the band broke up prior to doing so. It would have been interesting if given the opportunity which material (You can read about their music in the 1966 section of the book) would have been used for the album."

Q: "Is it possible that the date given for the show with the Airplane opening for the Rolling Stones is off by seven to ten days? I was at the performance and remember it being in July for sure."

A: "The two excellent Rolling Stones set list and tour date sites http://rocksoff.org/gazzassetlists.htm and http://www.frayed.org/index1.html are in agreement that the show did not take place on June 25th or June 26, 1966, as often reported. The date was 7/26/66 at the Cow Palace, Daly City, California. One of the ways to tell the Rolling Stones sites were correct is to look at the itinerary for the band. The Rolling Stones were on the east coast late June of 1966."

Q: "I understand that the performer Freddie Neil was an influence on Paul Kantner and many 1960's bands. What songs did he write that others may be more noted for?"

A: "*The Other Side Of This Life*, was a song that the Airplane turned into a tremendous live cover version, Harry Nilsson had a hit with *Everybody's Talkin* (To this day most people think he wrote the tune), and when Paul Kantner toured with Jorma and Jack as part of Hot Tuna they performed some nights *The Bag I'm In*. What is not brought up is Freddie Neil did a record in 1964 with Vince Martin. The title was *Tear Down The Walls*. Does that ring a bell?"

Q: "How was Bill Graham a positive force in helping to get the J.A. as much exposure as possible?"

A: "Bill Graham had a unbelievable eclectic eye and ear for music. By promoting shows with blues musicians such as Lightnin' Hopkins on the same bill as the J.A., he was able to often cultivate a new fan for the group. You may have wanted to go see rhythm and blues performer Percy Sledge but there could be several other bands on the bill. If you came out of the show enjoying only the artist you came to see at least he did his part in providing the musical diversity. An optimum conclusion to the evening's festivities would be that you walked out of the venue wanting to purchase at least one record from a performer you hadn't necessarily paid to watch. Although the band would get tired of the excessive touring from the amount of shows Bill Graham booked, they had exposure in most parts of the country. We lost Bill Graham on 10/25/91."

Q: "How did Chet Helms the promoter help the San Francisco bands?"

A: "The late Chet Helms (He passed away on 6/25/05) was the rarest of the rare. Although he promoted concerts he was a fan of the music first and even felt guilty that monies had to exchange hands to enter the venue. His legacy was the Avalon Ballroom in San Francisco. His final year of regular promotion 1970, would be the Family Dog in San Francisco. He was responsible for Janis Joplin coming to San Francisco. This meant he led to the formation of Big Brother & The Holding Company. Since Chet and Bill Graham were promoting shows with such diverse and high caliber acts the Bay Area became swamped with fans, and record company personnel that led to artists being signed, and the ability to continue to showcase their skills. It also built comradery between the groups. They may have had to compete for the dollar but most were happy to help other individuals and be part of a cultural scene that shook the globe. Chet Helms best friend photographer Don Aters remembers Chet in the interview section of the book."

Q: "When Skip Spence ended up in Moby Grape did he have any ill feelings toward the J.A.?"

A: "I asked Jerry Miller of Moby Grape (What a great credit to rock and roll and the human race) during the interview for the book if Skip had the feeling of having to keep up with the J.A.. Jerry told me that never once did Skip utter a bad word to him about any member of the Airplane or that he felt a competition with them."

Q: "Didn't the Moby Grape debut record do real well consider all the obstacles the band had to overcome?"

A: "What has been lost in the story of the ridiculous nonsense Skip and the band went through from squabbles with management, to the record company releasing multiple singles at once, the LP reached number 24 on the charts. If that doesn't sound impressive few bands would have had their determination to hurdle over the plethora of negative circumstances they faced and still be able to play in the yard of the big boys."

Q: "How many songs did Skip write for the first Moby Grape album? If he did write any how are they received?"

A: "Skip wrote two tracks. One called *Omaha* is often the listener's favorite song on the record, along with a non Skip tune called *8:05* (Yes that is the title). The other composition from Skip was *Indifference*. It is solid! He could be very proud if he only contributed *Omaha*, to have written a song as good as *Indifference* was gravy."

Q: "Is there some funny fact you learned about Skip Spence while working on the book?"

A: "Marty Balin and Jerry Miller (Moby Grape) often called Skip by the name Skippy when talking about their association with Skip. That may be known already but it sounds rather funny anyway. On the tragic side Marty told me how quickly the glow from Skip burnt out. The abuse of his body took its toll long before he passed away."

Q: "When Grace Slick joined the Airplane did she immediately bring the stage presence that would make her legendary?"

A: "Grace did not start being outrageous, funny, and master the vocal improvisations until the summer of 1967. You can point to a specific show on 8/5/67 at the O'Keefe Center, Toronto, Canada. It was during that performance she made reference to Jorma cutting his bangs and the band went into a very short *jam*. It was right there the stage persona would start to take root. As the 1968 shows approached she had succeeded at being a five-star singer and an A+ entertainer."

Q: "I picked up the *Takes Off* and *Surrealistic Pillow* CD's when they were first released. I was astonished not that both held up to any of the music of today but how much more mature the sound of the band had become in a short period of time. Would that be a correct view?"

A: "In roughly six months between releases of the two albums the music did grow to a more advanced level. *3/5 Of A Mile In 10 Seconds* and *Plastic Fantastic Lover* are examples from the Marty Balin side. Grace had contributed *Somebody To Love* and *White Rabbit*, and Jorma's *Embryonic Journey* would be able to speak volumes without words. A song by Paul that never got the credit it deserved was *D, C, B, A,-25*. Without even going through the other five songs, the musical I.Q. had exploded. In no way should that ever be a put down of the sounds of innocence. The first recording is an album that any band should be proud to have taken flight. The group felt the production on the second effort was a little over the top, and restrictive. When it came to recording *After Bathing At Baxter's*, the J.A. followed one path, their own."

Q: "Can you give an example as to why musicians and fans often feel record companies know less about music than a tree?"

A: "For the J.A., we can explore for a moment the second album *Surrealistic Pillow*. The first single released was *My Best Friend*. Very possibility the weakest tune on the record. It was also written by Skip Spence. Skip by this time is obviously out of the band. If we pretend the single sold well you are now promoting somebody that is on another record label. If the public enjoyed that style how will you recreate the song when the writer is with Moby Grape? Nobody could have predicted the well deserved success of *White Rabbit* but if you went through the LP for potential singles, *Plastic Fantastic Lover*, *Somebody To Love*, *Today*, and *White Rabbit* are light years better as an album track, single release, and or live tune. Marty Balin gave me a great example of a musician left scratching their head. Marty would come up with a song that the band liked and the record company would tell him it doesn't sound like an Airplane tune. Marty told me if he wrote the song, is in the band, and the people that play on the record are members of the band, how could it not sound like an Airplane song?"

Q: "Did Jerry Garcia contribute something to *Surrealistic Pillow* that has been debated for its authenticity?"

A: "We all knew that Jerry acted as a spiritual adviser, named the album, and played some uncredited parts on the recording. He also helped in changing the arrangement on *Somebody To Love*. I always wondered about that. Dennis McNally the Grateful Dead's publicist, is well acquainted with the facts, and fictions from that era. When he stated that was part of Jerry's input to the record during the interview I had with him, I take that as the final word."

Q: "When I bought the *Surrealistic Pillow* CD with the bonus tracks *Go To Her* became one of my favorite Airplane songs. Could it have been included on the original version from 1967?

A: "*Go To Her* is a tune that many J.A. fans have enjoyed both in the studio and from the stage. The difficulty with it being part of the original release was getting the eleven best songs on the record. If you go through the album the one song that it may outshine was *My Best Friend*. That would be a great debate. If we took one hundred people that purchased the record and gave them the choice of one or the other, which would win? I'll start the vote and cast one for *Go To Her*."

Q: "The first time I saw the Airplane live was February of 1968 in San Francisco. I focused primarily on the magic chemistry between Jorma and Jack. How far were they into touring before they would have such great comradery on stage?"

A: "There always seemed to be a musical connection, but the Fillmore Auditorium shows in San Francisco the end of <u>November 1966</u> were examples of the band able to use the strengths of Jorma and Jack by extended *Fat Angel* and *The Other Side Of This Life* during the set. Once it became the routine to have at least one ten minute song, or *jam* per show the reputation of the Airplane's lead guitarist and the bass-player continued to escalate."

Q: "How long did it take for the Airplane to tour outside of California?"

A: "It may not have been as quickly as you were thinking. If you discard playing two or three shows away from home the first time they would be outside the state of California for a week, or more was the summer of 1967. Some feel the first night of the tour was in Asbury Park, New Jersey on July 22nd (There is debate about that performance), or Toronto on July 23rd, and ending up at Expo 67 in Montreal on August 6th, 1967."

Q: "On 6/17/67 I attended the Monterey Pop Festival. What I thought would be a great setting for the Airplane was actually the shortest I ever saw them play. Were they selling the festival or the bands?"

A: "The Airplane didn't even perform thirty-nine minutes at the Monterey Pop Festival. The whole idea of several great bands playing the same day is much better on the drawing board than the real life application. If a band is worthy the idea is to enjoy them as long as possible. Countless multi-band concerts from the 1960's, · and 1970's gave the public the ultimate rock and roll, but not nearly enough of it!"

Q: "Were there songs the Airplane recorded that sounded very differently than the first time they were tried out on stage?"

A: "The first time they performed *Won't You Try/Saturday Afternoon* on 5/12/67 at the Fillmore Auditorium, San Francisco, California they didn't have an intro for the song and it was a work in progress. It still sounded good enough for release. On 5/7/69 at the Polo Field, Golden Gate Park, San Francisco, California (Afternoon show) they performed *Good Shepherd*, with Grace singing lead, and Paul background! Jorma didn't utter a word!"

Q: "Is there video available from the Airplane's appearance on the Tonight Show from the summer of 1967?"

A: "The band played *Somebody To Love* and *White Rabbit* during the appearance. It seemed when the question was brought up where is the archival footage the two answers are not what the Airplane fanatic had hoped to hear. The general consensus was either the master recording was destroyed or lost."

Q: "Did the J.A. have any ultra long songs on the original studio recordings?

A: "This may surprise you, but the longest track on a studio record was a bit over nine minutes. On the *After Bathing At Baxter's* release *Spare Chaynge* clocked in at 9:15."

Q: "When *After Bathing At Baxter's* came out what did the Airplane lose if anything for gaining so much control of the recording sessions?"

A: "When the original concept of the record started it was obvious that it could not match the sales of *Surrealistic Pillow*. The album was going to have to be strong enough to sell without the help of Top 40 radio. Normally you can fine fault with a record company, and sometimes producers, and engineers. In this case RCA Records, producer Al Schmitt and engineer Richie Schmitt gave the band the artistic freedom they deserved and earned. *Surrealistic Pillow* had cracked the Top 5 on the record charts. When it was all said and done, *After Bathing At Baxter's* broke the Top 20. They did lose in the pockets but if you can put a value on integrity they were millionaires."

Q: "Does Spencer Dryden say the words "He's a pinto" on the song *A Small Package Of Value Will Come To You, Shortly?*"

A: "That is funny. The words on the song from *After Bathing At Baxter's* are "He's a peninsula." It wasn't Spencer but a man who has been an assistant manager, road manager, and manager Bill Thompson. A Pinto was a car that first came on the market in the early 1970's."

Q: "Are there reviewers either past or present that didn't understand *After Bathing At Baxter's* didn't attempt to imitate, it was what it was because the band made it that way?"

A: "Here is an example of a mixed review. The overall rating was 3.5 out of 5. The criticisms were, "An intentional disaster, and incoherently poetic lyrics." The full review is on a website http://www.warr.org/jefferson.html. You can't be cynical of every intention an artist has. If *Surrealistic Pillow* was disliked for being too polished, and the songs sounded too structured, how could you take a swipe at *Baxter's* for not being conventional, produced without thought, and lyrics too complex?"

Q: "We always hear about how special 1967 was for rock and roll. What would solidify the comment (Keeping the answer to music and not politics)?"

A: "If you were an Airplane fan you would have had the great J.A. record *After Bathing At Baxter's* playing on the turntable. The Janis Joplin record is listed under the name of the band Big Brother And The Holding Company. Check out how impressive the list is of some other legendary recordings. I am only listing one record per band, and could have easily listed another group such as Love. This is in alphabetical order and not rating one over the other."

The Beatles- Sgt. Pepper's Lonely Hearts Club Band

Big Brother And The Holding Company- Big Brother And The Holding Company

Cream- Disraeli Gears

The Doors- The Doors

The Grateful Dead- The Grateful Dead

Moby Grape- Moby Grape

The Moody Blues- Days Of Future Passed

The Rolling Stones- Their Satanic Majesties Request

The Who- Happy Jack

The Yardbirds- Little Games

Do you enjoy the blues? There would have been:

The Blues Project- Live At Town Hall

Paul Butterfield Blues Band- The Resurrection of Pigboy Crabshaw

Jimi Hendrix- Are You Experienced

John Mayall- A Hard Road

If you want to see sixty choices listed by one music fan from 1967 please visit
http://rateyourmusic.com/list/csaunders9/60_best_albums_of_1967/. There is only one slight situation to be
aware of first. Inexplicably the person that gives their choices believes the Beatles- *Sgt. Pepper*, is overrated. I
reserved from commenting, because I am in shock somebody could state this. Help is on the way."

Q: "My second favorite Airplane song is *Martha* with the top choice being *Lather*. Does the *Martha* being
talked about in the song have a last name?"

A: "It reminds me of the question from the TV show *Get Smart*. Did Agent 99 have a first name? Martha Wax
was the name from the fabulous song on *After Bathing At Baxter's*."

Q: "One of the best shows ever was the Roundhouse in London, England on 9/6/68. Not only did I get to see
the Airplane, but the Doors too. I saw a film crew roaming around all through the festivities. Since there is
such cool Doors footage does that mean there is J.A video?"

A: "The J.A. performance did get recorded. There hasn't been any segment released. In fact there is very little
of the J.A. available to the public, either from the concert stage, or TV. It would have made for a stupendous
viewing experience to see *The Ballad Of You And Me And Pooneil* go into *The House At Pooneil Corners*."

Q: "Since *After Bathing At Baxter's* sold less than its predecessor what did the record company and band think
would be the best direction to follow for *Crown Of Creation*?"

A: "The band wasn't nearly as experimental with *Crown Of Creation*, but they did finish the record without the
feeling the production was too shiny as on *Surrealistic Pillow*. When *Pillow* is discussed as being too produced
that came more from the band and not most fans. The material came across as energetic, fresh, powerful, and
intense. *Crown Of Creation* in no way is a sell-out to the powers that be. The record's achievement of hitting
#6 on the charts has to do with the following the J.A. cultivated from the live performances and their track
record for having made three previously consistent albums. The title track, and *Greasy Heart* lunged at you
from the speakers, *Star Track*, *Ice Cream Phoenix*, and *The House At Pooneil Corners* were enthralling, with
their energy, and brilliance."

Q: "Can you think of a song written by the Airplane that they performed live after hitting it big where it didn't
seem right for the stage shows?"

A: "The first one that comes to mind is *Triad*, from *Crown Of Creation*. As a song in the set list it didn't have
the strength to be a ballad and wasn't full of energy to use for improvisation. They didn't even perform it for a
month before it was retired to the old tune home."

Q: "We always here about Grace's contributions (Writing or having brought over from the Great Society) with
*Somebody To Love*, and *White Rabbit*, but is there a song that she should have gotten more credit for in any
capacity?"

270

A: "*Greasy Heart* from *Crown Of Creation* should have been more synonymous with Grace. It worked well on stage, and had plenty of energy, and passion for the studio."

Q: "When the Airplane played on the roof 11/1/68 at the Schuyler Hotel, 57 West 45<sup>th</sup> Street, New York City, it is often talked about as being filmed for the Godard film. Is Godard the name of the film, the name of a company, or something else?"

A: "The film was *1 AM*, and person's name was Jean-Luc Godard. When the film came to fruition D.A. Pennebaker had taken over the project."

Q: "I was told that a record I once had by the American band Wings had the original J.A. drummer Jerry Peloquin. Is that true and can it be found on CD?"

A: "The terrific record from 1968 that had a very pleasant folk-rock and pop sound did contain the drumming of Jerry Peloquin. The bad news is the record never became a CD. The first time I spoke with Jerry I pleaded for him to rectify that! Maybe one day good fortune will occur."

Q: "I have listened to both the album and CD versions of *Bless Its Pointed Little Head* at least five hundred times and never get tired of it. Did most Airplane fans feel the same when it came out?"

A: "The general consensus was very positive. The record broke into the Top 20 on the charts and let the listeners hear the Airplane's ability to excel on stage. The one track over the years that didn't hold up was *Bear Melt*. The band had far better *jam*s and improvisations."

Q: "I purchased the Skip Spence album *Oar* in 1999 with the CD bonus tracks. I gave it at least ten listens on the CD player and found the material to be inconsistent. What were the general thoughts of the album when it was first released? If I can get in a second question please. Wasn't the reissue going to have a song that Skip did for the X-Files movie with Jack Casady?"

A: "In the spring of 1969 Skip was able release the record on a major label. Prior to the creation of the recording he had been through pure hell, which included some six months in a psychiatric hospital. The album sold very little, but there were those that thought the disjointed material created a tremendous result. If he had been able to sound as good as he did singing the song *Little Hands* it would have been an easier listen for most of the consumers. His vocals on *Little Hands* may have been as strong as any track he ever put on vinyl. The same could be said for *War In Peace*, then a track appears such as *Crippled Creek,* having a completely different and not nearly as presentable vocal. The folk-rock style would have been enhanced if there were some electric compositions added to the mix. www.sundazed.com (Sundazed Records) had reissued the album on CD, with the bonus tracks you mentioned. Anybody interested in making their own judgment can explore their fantastic website and see if it is still available for purchase. There has been total confusion about the Skip Spence song for the X-Files movie. The track called *Land Of The Rising Sun* did not make the movie soundtrack CD. It also wasn't put on the reissue of *Oar*. It ended up as a single B-Side to the song *All My Life* (Written in 1972.) Try the terrific site Freak Emporium to see if it is still in print."
http://www.freakemporium.com/site/list_label.cgi?label=Sundazed

Q: "I saw the Airplane a bunch of times and always thought that *We Can Be Together* and *Volunteers* sounded as good together as any two songs they played live. Could they have had them next to each other on the *Volunteers* album?"

A: "The record was made to use the power of the political songs as the opener and the final track. It would be hard to argue with the philosophy from such an outstanding piece of work. There was one more issue that would have been problematic. The two best songs suited to begin or close the album were *We Can Be Together* and *Volunteers*. *Good Shepherd* and *Eskimo Blue Day* are pure genius, but not optimum for the opening and closing tracks. The possible solution if it were your record would have been to use *Wooden Ships* as the first song and arrange the rest of the recording from there."

Q: "I saw the J.A. on 8/2/69 at the Atlantic City Racetrack, Atlantic City, New Jersey. The drummer was not Spencer. Was it Joey Covington, and why was he there? I enjoyed his playing very much."

A: "Joey was a great help in clarifying the period of time he started with the J.A. The band had thought of making a change in drummers. Reports that Joey wanted Spencer removed from the band were erroneous. Joey suggested the idea of going with two drummers. There were nights they played with double drums and there were shows that Joey played as a single drummer. His recollection is the first show he played with the J.A. was 6/14/69 or 6/16/69 at The Family Dog, At The Great Highway, San Francisco, California. Another point of confusion was Joey played with Hot Tuna before the Airplane."

Q: "If Spencer Dryden was proficient enough in the 1960's to be an Airplane drummer what made him deficient in the 1970's?"

A: "Spencer's strength's as a drummer were the ability to keep precise time, have a fantastic sense of rhythm, and not over-play. That formula worked many years for the band. As the music grew more complex, and the opportunity to extend songs and *jams* for the live faithful became necessary, they weren't playing to his strength's any longer. Spencer did not handle the three hour shows as well as Jorma and Jack. When Joey Covington came into the fold he brought the stamina for the live gigs, and the playing that was very well suited for the *jam's*, and improvisational pieces. This isn't a knock on Spencer's musicianship. It isn't unusual if you play drums, guitar, keyboards, or bass that you're not proficient in all facets of the instrument."

Q: "I attended Woodstock in 1969 and thought the piano playing of Nicky Hopkins made one of my favorite bands even more enjoyable. Why did he only perform with them one time?"

A: "Nicky Hopkins played with the Airplane two times. If you can get a hold of the Dick Cavett Show from the day after Woodstock he played with the J.A. one final time. He does session work for them on the *Volunteers* album and the reunion record as well. Nicky had health issues and passed away much to early (9/6/94). He found touring was too physically debilitating. He was in such demand as a session musician he has the honor of playing with the Beatles, the Rolling Stones, and the Who. On 8/30/89 Paul Kantner and Grace Slick were interviewed on WNEW-FM Radio, New York City. When the host of the show Pat St. John asked them about keyboards in the band, Paul responded by telling him Nicky Hopkins was with the Airplane about six months. When you listen to the live shows that are archived only the two mentioned above have Nicky on them. It was possible Paul meant Nicky spent six months with them in the studio (On and off) for *Volunteers* and the reunion album."

Q: "When I listen to the Crosby, Stills, & Nash version of *Wooden Ships* I don't feel the same intensity, but enjoy the vocal arrangements. What differences do you find from their studio interpretation, and the J.A.'s?"

A: "Both bands have won their own sets of fans over and many people appreciate the artistry of the two renditions. From the first time I listened to the CSN version I got the feeling the strength of the vocals (Their calling card) were of the most paramount importance, since that can often be their forte. When I first listened to the J.A.'s *Wooden Ships* the entire body of the song seemed more thorough. It wasn't only about the lead vocal or harmonies. The J.A.'s level of energy was higher and the song more captivating."

Q: "What was the longest song or *jam* performed by the J.A. live?"

A: "On 9/6/69 at the Family Dog At The Great Highway, San Francisco, California, Jerry Garcia and Mickey Hart joined the Airplane for the longest total time of any *jam* or song. The entire thing lasted twenty-five minutes and twenty-two seconds!"

Q: "When Papa John Creach became a member of the J.A. how did the fans react to a new instrument being part of the sound?"

A: "Papa John was well liked by the concert goers from the start. They appreciated his down to earth modesty, exceptional talent, the ability to improvise during the *jams*, and to enhance the construction of a song. If you should have any recordings of the concerts with Papa John, check out the response to *John's Other* and *Down Home Blues*."

Q: "I find the tune *Meadowlands* bizarre. Was there a reason for it on the *Volunteers* album?"

A: "Matthew Greenwald pointed out on www.allmusic.com, that Paul wanted the song to "snub the establishment" (It was loved by the Russian Red Army) and that it would be a nice piece of music before *Volunteers*." Since it was so short it may have been too innocuous to offend."

Q: "When people talk about Nicky Hopkins playing at Woodstock with the Airplane are they leaving out a *jam* session from late 1970 as another time he performed with the J.A. in front of an audience?"

A: "That is brought up often. The reason for the confusion is he did play with Jorma and Jack but it was part of a *jam* on or about 10/21/70. Although the venue is often listed as The Matrix, in San Francisco it is believed the *jam* was from Wally Heider Studios in San Francisco. Joey Covington and John Cipollina (Quicksilver Messenger Service) rounded out the musicians."

Q: "If Paul didn't want to record *Blows Against The Empire* in 1970, could the song *Starship* have fit on an Airplane release?"

A: "Without question it could have sounded very nicely on *Bark*. There would have been three avenues for the song to follow. It could have led off the record (*When The Earth Moves Again* was the opening song), it could have closed the album as a thought provoking tune, (*War Movie* ended the record), or could have been the second song, appearing right after *When The Earth Moves Again*. Even though fans may think of the song as part of a conceptual album, the song was performed live by the J.A. In a setting with an audience it sounded as if it could pass for an Airplane original."

Q: "I met my wife at the Airplane 11/25/70 show at the Fillmore East, New York City. There is no way I wouldn't remember the concert. When I tell people the J.A. played *Somebody To Love* for about fifteen minutes they claim I am rewriting history. Am I?"

A: "You are completely correct. The version of *Somebody To Love* performed on that night was thirteen minutes and twenty-two seconds. It is the longest documented playing time from the J.A. of that tune!"

Q: "When Bill Graham decided to close the Fillmore East in 1971 were escalation of costs the reason?"

A: "Bill Graham sent a letter filled with great articulation to a New York City weekly newspaper the Village Voice on April 29th, 1971. The letter appeared in print on May 6th, 1971. He provided a myriad of reasons for his decision. I found it fascinating that he was outspoken against the large festival concert idea from the start. He thought that prices would rise above the normal cost of inflation. Another point he expressed with dismay, there were those working behind the scenes to take the decision out of the hands of the promoter. When he dealt with certain managers, and representatives of an artist, or band, in order for the headliner to perform they often tried to manipulate the contract for other acts to share the bill. This could result in a group performing that was not deemed musically ready or necessary for the Fillmore."

Q: "Did the Airplane change any titles to songs that were originally considered to crude for airplay or even inclusion on a record?"

A: "The terrific song from *Bark* called *Pretty As You Feel* was initially known as *Shi_ _y As You Feel*. Thanks to Sean from Joey Covington's organization for the verification."

Q: "Now that it is many moons removed from the releases of *Bark* and *Long John Silver*, did the records get maligned unjustly by critics?"

A: "The albums should have been reviewed better at the time and deserved increased respect as the years have passed. Without an integral part of the machine (Marty) the *Bark* album still had five terrific songs, *Feel So Good*, *Lawman*, *Pretty As You Feel*, *Third Week In The Chelsea*, and *When The Earth Moves Again*. The final effort *Long John Silver* may not have had the same quality as its predecessor, but it did contain *Eat Starch Mom*, *Milk Train*, *Trial By Fire*, and *Twilight Double Leader* (One of the most underrated songs ever). Maybe when discussing an album we should review it two ways. The first is to compare the record to anything else the band has ever released. The second and maybe fairer approach is to judge it against any music ever created."

Q: "When Spencer Dryden started to play with the New Riders Of The Purple Sage in 1971 until his last session with them, how many Grateful Dead members appeared on the recording sessions?"

A: "There were four members that were once a part of the Grateful Dead (Any incarnation) that appeared on a studio New Riders Of The Purple Sage album when Spencer was part of the group. Jerry Garcia, Donna Godchaux, Mickey Hart, and Bill Kreutzmann."

Q: "Of all the singles the Airplane released through the end of the year in 1972, how many would you think the B-Side would have been stronger than the A-side?"

A: "Why don't we look at the American single releases, which song of the two were stronger, and which more marketable. There is a major difference at times! Thank you very much to www.deaddisc.com for the catalog numbers."

*It's No* Secret */Running Round This World*, 1966, RCA 8679.
The better song and choice was Side-A (*It's No Secret*).

*Come Up The Years /Blues From An Airplane*, 1966, RCA 8848.
The better song and choice was Side-B (*Blues From An Airplane*).

*Bringing Me Down /Let Me In*, 1966, RCA 8967.
The better song and choice was Side-B.

*My Best Friend /How Do You Feel?*, 1966, RCA 9063.
The better song was Side-B, the better choice was Side-A. *How Do You Feel* wasn't single material but a brilliant composition!

*Somebody To Love /She Has Funny Cars*, 1967, RCA 9140.
Two of the best songs ever written. Unfair to argue with this choice. The two songs are equal and the better choice was Side-A.

*White Rabbit /Plastic Fantastic Lover*, 1967, RCA 9248.
The better song and choice was Side-A.

*The Ballad Of You And Me And Pooneil /Two Heads*, 1967, RCA 9297.
The better song and choice was Side-A.

*Watch Her Ride /Martha*, 1968, RCA 9389.
The better song and choice was Side-B. Although *Martha* isn't the prototypical single, it is much stronger.

*Greasy Heart /Share A Little Joke*, 1968, RCA 9496.
The better song and choice was Side-A.

*Crown Of Creation /Triad*, 1968, RCA 9644.
The better song and choice was Side-A.

*Plastic Fantastic Lover /The Other Side Of This Life*, 1969, RCA 0150.
The better song was Side-B, the better choice Side-A.

*Volunteers /We Can Be Together*, 1970, RCA 0245.
This is an exact tie. They both are equal all around. Since *Volunteers* was shorter (More suited for airplay), can't argue the choice. One of the best singles ever released.

*Have You Seen The Saucers? /Mexico, 1970,* RCA 0343.
This was a tough choice. I have never touched a drug but think *Mexico* was the better song. The better choice was Side-A.

*Pretty As You Feel /Wild Turkey*, 1971, Grunt 65-0500.
The better song and choice was Side-A.

*Long John Silver /Milk Train*, 1972, Grunt 65-0506.
The better song and choice was Side-B.

*Twilight Double Leader /Trial By Fire*, 1972 , Grunt 65-0511.
I am in the extreme minority with this one. I have always liked *Twilight Double Leader* better. Side-B was the better choice, but Side-A the better song."

Q: "If Spencer couldn't be the drummer for the Airplane throughout their career I wish John Barbata could have. Did he play drums on a very early Linda Ronstadt record?"

A: "John Barbata appears on the 1969 Linda Ronstadt album called *Hand Sown...Home Grown*. The most noted tune on the LP was *Silver Threads And Golden Needles*."

Q: "The last time I saw the Airplane was in 1972 with John Barbata as the drummer. He was a true pro! Did he come from any group that I would know?"

A: "He was a member of a very successful American band the Turtles. They had several hits, but *Happy Together*, and *Elenore* are normally two that are recognized even by the casual fan. John Barbata played on two records for the Turtles, one was *Happy Together*, and the other *Battle Of The Bands*."

Q: "I thought the best period of the Airplane was obviously with Marty but the best drumming was with John Barbata. Are there a couple of more mellow albums he did work on that you can have me look for?"

A: "In 1971 John helped out a mellow rock band called Batdorf & Rodney. The album was called *Off The Shelf*. He played on the 1985 Everly Brothers record *Home Again*, both have the sound you are looking for."

Q: "I went to three shows in 1972, and besides missing Marty, I was disappointed that they didn't have any *jams* from the previous tours I attended. Was that my bad luck, or how the tour went down?"

A: "It was that way throughout the final months of the band. If you don't count *Dress Rap > You Wear Your Dresses To Short* as a *jam*, even the final performance was devoid of one of the calling cards of the band. It is shocking to a degree. Without a main cog of a wheel (Marty), you would of thought the group would continue with the strength of Jorma, and Jack's ability to extend *jams,* or songs, and keep them tasty."

Q: "I was told that Wally Heider who had the studio in San Francisco where the Airplane recorded some of the material worked with numerous musicians over the years. Is he still alive and what type of bands did he associate with?"

A: "Wally Heider died before the Airplane reunion tour of 1989 took off. Wally passed away in March of that year. He was an engineer or producer on an infinite amount of recordings. His metamorphosis was fascinating. He started working with jazz and big band musicians such as Art Blakey, Jimmy Dorsey, Duke Ellington, and Artie Shaw (Not in that order). When the Summer Of Love came in 1967 he would begin to work in the rock and roll world. Included from 1967 and on: Alice Cooper, Jimi Hendrix, Jefferson Airplane, and Frank Zappa (Not in that order), to name a few! Not a bad resume."

Q: "Are there writers or co-writers of Airplane songs that would be known to the music industry but not to even a life long fan (1965-1972)?"

A: "The Airplane did have five writers that wrote or co-wrote a total of six songs. Many would agree five of the six are pretty good. Gary Blackman gets a co-writing credit with Spencer Dryden and Bill Thompson (Manager, Assistant Manager, and Road Manager) on *A Small Package Of Value Will Come To You, Shortly*, a co-writing credit with Marty for *If You Feel*, and a co-writing credit with Paul for *The Farm*. Charles Cockey gets a co-writing credit with Jorma on *Ice Cream Phoenix*. Tom Mastin gets a solo credit for *How Do You Feel* and Roger Spotts, along with Grace, and Papa John Creach get co-writing credits for *Milk Train*."

Q: "If you were to take ten Airplane songs they recorded through *Long John Silver* to use as an introduction to the band which ten make the most sense? Do they have to be the ten best or is it a specific sound that you would seek?"

A: "The best way to introduce a listener to the band would be to take ten excellent songs, but make sure that you get a cross-section of the material and the different members are represented. It wouldn't be a true top ten, but would have the positive attributes of stellar songs and the diversity of the J.A. This is in alphabetical order and not placing more credence on one song.

A: *Embryonic Journey*- This would focus on Jorma's ability to say so much and not utter a word.

*Good Shepherd*- An ageless representation of genius. Jorma does the definitive version of a traditional song. This is good representation because we did not have the luxury of a released studio *Rock Me Baby* or *Uncle Sam Blues* to use for the time frame of 1965-1972 (In the studio).

*It's No Secret*- Not only a timeless composition but a great early introduction to Marty's vocal ability.

*Martha*- It is one thing to be esoteric and another to be sincere. Writing out of the stereotypical music handbook can often be creatively satisfying but a snooze-fest for the consumer. Paul was able to captivate the listener. The song formation was haunting at times, but the pure emotion had you spellbound.

*Somebody To Love*- Certainly an obvious pick. There are a couple of reasons for it. When you attempt to impress a potential new fan with a sampling of music having a couple of songs that are a bit commercial are often necessary. In this case *Somebody To Love* and *White Rabbit*, show the impressive vocal skills of Grace. If the newcomer can identify with the magical voice of the singer you already have the battle won.

276

*The Ballad Of You And Me And Pooneil*- Long before there were video games and the invention of mind-numbing videos of the 1980's, the attention span of the average person was still very short. If it took more then three minutes, the eyes, and ears may have been elsewhere. *The Ballad Of You And Me And Pooneil* is hypnotic. It could be the studio version, or a fifteen minute live journey, Paul had commandeered the flight, and nobody ever complained.

*Today*- If *It's No Secret* captured Marty excelling on a rock and roll number, it is only fair to offer equal time for a ballad. *Today* isn't only a song it is a masterful piece of art from the finest gallery.

*Volunteers*- What better way to showcase the band, then to have a song of political representation? This particular selection shows that two heads (Not the song) are better than one. Paul and Marty made this not only a well loved tune but for many an anthem.

*White Rabbit*- The reasoning here is exactly that of *Somebody To Love*.

*Won't You Try/Saturday Afternoon*- From the opening notes Paul had created a song that not only would represent *After Bathing At Baxter's* but further solidify his songwriting legacy."

Q: "If you were asked to pick a set list for the J.A. using any songs from 1965-72 but having the line-up of Grace, Jack, Jorma, Marty, Paul, and Spencer, what would your choices be? What would the order look like?"

A: "How about I answer that two ways please. The first is taking into consideration what most people would think is very fair. I also am using at least one choice from every studio album, including *Long John Silver*. The second will be to mention a bunch of songs if the fans wouldn't mind my taste."

*She Has Funny Cars*- Paul's idea to open with this in 1989 was pure genius.

*3/5 Of A Mile In 10 Seconds*- The song is perfect in any part of the show.

*White Rabbit*

*The Other Side Of This Life*- Blends well with *Fat Angel*.

*Fat Angel*

*Plastic Fantastic Lover*

*Crown Of Creation*- Paired with *Plastic Fantastic Lover* enhances a great tune.

*Rock Me Baby*- Jorma gets his first of three lead vocals.

*It's No Secret*

*Let's Get Together*- The two early tracks blend well.

*Wooden Ships > J.P.P. McStep B. Blues*

*Won't You Try/Saturday Afternoon*

*Today*- A Jefferson Airplane concert isn't right without this.

*Good Shepherd*

*Greasy Heart*

*Eskimo Blue Day*

*Third Week in The Chelsea*

*Martha*

*Twilight Double Leader*

*The Ballad Of You And Me And Pooneil*

*The House At Pooneil Corners*

*Somebody To Love*

*Encores:*

*We Can Be Together*

*Volunteers*

**There are several tunes that may be my selfish wishes, but I have strong beliefs in:**

*A Song For All Seasons*

*Blues From An Airplane*

*How Do You Feel*

*Ice Cream Phoenix*

*Star Track*

Q: "Is there a way to show my daughter and son the great concert posters of the J.A.?"

A: "The J.A. website www.jeffersonairplane.com has a great many of the terrific posters. Click on "Scrapbook", and they can experience the legendary artistry. If you go to www.wolfgangsvault.com, you can see numerous posters as well. They even play on the site live musical treasures from the 1960's!"

Q: "In a perfect world could the Airplane members have found a way to make solo records, but continue on as a band after 1972?"

A: "There were many logistical situations that didn't seem to have a positive solution. Even if every personality within the band coexisted, Hot Tuna never performed, and the grind of touring was a myth, what happens when it was time for a record to be finalized? The strength of having four people that could sing and write (Grace, Jorma, Marty, and Paul) can also be a dividing force. At the time there were no Compact Discs. Record albums averaged a little under forty minutes. If one song would be in the seven to eight minute range it may force a tune from another member to be off the finished product. You could be faced with a battle for valuable space on the LP. The theme of a record could be a difficult task to agree upon. If Paul wanted to explore space, Jorma felt the need to express his love of the blues, Marty wanted to chime in with either a straight ahead rocker or a terrific ballad, and Grace something esoteric, the end result may be very fragmented and disjointed."

Q: "When I would see the Airplane shows 1967-1972 I always thought it looked cool the way Jack would suddenly move around the stage. Was there a musical reason for that, or only how awesome it appeared?"

A: "Jack addressed that during one of the 1998 teaching sessions with Jorma at the Fur Peach Ranch. Jack is not only a brilliant bass-player, but his mind works in perfect harmony with those on stage. He explained that he moves around from time to time to hear how the sound of the band is for all the musicians (On all parts of the stage) and if there is a problem he can articulate it to them. During the sound check Jack doesn't simply walk on stage play a few notes and leave the building. He'll get a reading of what the band sounds like and will walk to different parts of the venue to encompass what the audience will hear. Listening to him discuss posture, blisters, or back pain that bass-players may experience was the same as consulting a musical encyclopedia. His knowledge of the instrument is not only in his hands, and heart, but engrained on the brain."

Q: "When Marty left the Airplane did he sit out a couple of years before he would be part of the Jefferson Starship?"

A: "Marty worked behind the scenes on the 1972 self-titled album by Grootna. The record was rock with some blues influence. One of the people that played on the session for the LP was Anna Rizzo (She also appeared on the Bodacious D.F. record). She would join Hot Tuna on stage for six songs on 8/25/86 at Pulsations, Media, Pennsylvania. In 1973 he was part of the group Bodacious D.F. The record had the same name. They did a version of *Drifting*, which the Airplane had performed in late 1969."

Q: "Did Marty ever mention when the band broke up in 1972 (Although he was gone sooner), his favorite place the Airplane played live?"

A: "I would have been curious if his answer in 1972 was the same as today. Marty told me that Winterland, San Francisco, was his favorite."

Q: "The live record *Thirty Seconds Over Winterland* is always nice to listen to. Did I read correctly that it didn't make the Top 40 album chart list?"

A: "The LP peaked at fifty-two on Billboard. The idea was to give a taste of the band at that time. The only gem from the 1960's was *Crown Of Creation*. *Thirty Seconds Over Winterland* is an enjoyable listen even today. The start of the record with *Have You Seen The Saucers*, put the plane on a proper course and landing with *Twilight Double Leader*, made for a safe return home."

Q: "Do I have this right or do people review J.A. albums without showing they know enough about the band to make a judgment? Even if they hate the record, shouldn't their be a litmus test to be able to name a song besides *Somebody To Love*?"

A: "You hit the nail on the esophagus. In a perfect world every critic would be knowledgeable about every J.A. album. It is a given right to not be a fan, however it is not the best journalistic approach to be in the dark about the band in question. There was a review done by a writer that criticized the song from *Early Flight* called *In The Morning*. The perplexing part was the song title was never mentioned, or an explanation as to why it was boring. If the band thrived on the ability to mix folk-rock, with blues, and sprinkle the exoteric elements why not at least point out what he sees as boring are what many clamored to hear more of."

Q: "Would *Git Fiddler* the instrumental on the Jefferson Starship album *Red Octopus* have been viable for the Airplane circa 1971, or 1972 on record, and or in concert, if it were an Airplane song?"

A: "That isn't outlandish to think about. The Airplane flavor is there to a degree. For the live audience it would fit right into the realm of *John's Other*. While *Git Fiddler* isn't as memorable, it is certainly worthy of live status. As for the studio the sound would have to change slightly. That would be more from the production angle. On the *Red Octopus* record it seems to have a sound too prototypical of the Jefferson Starship for the version to have been Airplane ready."

Q: "My favorite name for a record ever is *Baron Von Tollbooth & The Chrome Nun*. How did that name come about?"

A: "Many credit David Crosby for naming the record, because he called Paul by the name of Baron Von Tollbooth and Grace was The Chrome Nun. If you go to www.deaddisc.com and search for the name of the record they mention that it was David Crosby's nickname for Paul and Grace that led to the title of the LP."

Q: "Prior to the reunion of the Airplane in 1989 are there a couple of cases you can give me where several of the J.A. members are on stage together?"

A: "The most noted was on 3/4/88 at the Fillmore, San Francisco, California. It was billed as a Hot Tuna show with Jorma, Jack, and Paul Kantner. Throughout the night some special friends would join the guys. From the old days Will Scarlett (Hot Tuna), Papa John Creach, and Ms. Grace Slick. While they took turns on certain songs, Jorma, Jack, Paul, and Grace did perform together! To further solidify a night of greatness, Papa John played on one song with the four Airplane members. That brought the total to five J.A. members on stage at once. Marty wasn't there, but it certainly got the maintenance crew working on restoring the old plane. The other one that is often forgotten happened while KBC was playing. On 5/15/86 at the Berkeley Community Theater, Berkeley, California, Jorma joined the band on stage for *Plastic Fantastic Lover*! The one that is totally overlooked 11/27/85 Bill Graham Productions 20th Anniversary Thanksgiving Party, Fillmore Auditorium, San Francisco, California (Show was before the venue officially reopened). KBC was performing that night. On the last two songs Signe Anderson and Spencer Dryden come out for *It's No Secret* and *Plastic Fantastic Lover*!"

Q: "I purchased the Dinosaurs album when it came out in 1988. Spencer Dryden is my favorite Airplane member. Why didn't the record do better?"

A: "Your appreciation for Spencer is refreshing to hear. The Dinosaurs and or management from a marketing point of view did a few things wrong. If you have Spencer playing with John Cipollina why do you wait six years before you put out an album, why do you stay in California for most of the live shows, and why did the record sound poorly produced? They should have put out a live recording after the first round of shows. They could have wet the appetite of the old rockers. Peter Albin (Big Brother & The Holding Company, and the Dinosaurs) gave his reasons for waiting so long to release an album in the interview section of the book."

Q: "Did any Airplane members tell you of rehearsing songs for the 1989 reunion that did not get played live on the tour?"

A: "Tim Gorman was the one person that remembered they rehearsed the Jefferson Starship song from *Red Octopus* called *Fast Buck Freddie*, but did not play it during any of the reunion performances."

Q: "Why did the Airplane put out only one video from the 1989 album?"

A: "The J.A. actually put out two very good videos. The one that always comes to mind is *Planes*. They also did a video of *True Love*. What made that video so strong was it had the late 1980's production for the music fans that thought rock and roll began with the birth of music television, but had the terrific offbeat sense of humor you would expect from the group. If you please see the 1989 section of the book there is information on the theme of both videos."

Q: "My two favorite songs from the Airplane reunion record of 1989 were *Common Market Madrigal*, and *Madeleine Street*. My luck they didn't get played. Were they ever performed in front of an audience?"

A: "They were indeed. *Common Market Madrigal* was performed as a work in progress on 9/29/88 at the Great American Music Hall, San Francisco, California. Grace Slick joined Paul Kantner on stage, and according to Grace for the first time in her career she sang, and played piano by herself! Paul Kantner's Wooden Ships played *Madeleine Street* as one of the encores from a show on 7/22/91 at Stephen's Talkhouse, Amagansett, New York."

Q: "I was very impressed with Peter Kaukonen during the 1989 tour. I went to four of the shows. Why don't I see his CD's in the music stores even as special orders?"

A: "Peter did a great job playing guitar for the 1989 reunion shows. He sells his enjoyable recordings through the website www.peterkaukonen.com. There are several you can purchase and you wouldn't make a wrong decision with any. I highly recommend the one that is discussed in the interview section of the book *Going Home*. It is a wonderful tribute to his parents. For those that have felt the pain of losing one or both parents (My mom passed away in 2003), you could appreciate not only the idea of the CD, but the difficulty in achieving such breathtaking results. Peter's 1972 *Black Kangaroo* with bonus tracks is highly recommended as well."

Q: "I was so glad that if Spencer Dryden couldn't be part of the Airplane reunion in 1989 that Kenny Aronoff from John Mellencamp's band helped out. Are there any albums that he appeared on with other artists that come highly recommended?"

A: "Kenny has done an infinite amount of session and live work. Here are three CD's that you would enjoy. John Fogerty (Creedence Clearwater Revival) has a great live record from 1998 called *Premonition*, Richard Thompson (Fairport Convention) released a live record in 2003 called *More Guitar*, and Tony Iommi (Black Sabbath), and Glenn Hughes (Deep Purple) did a record in 2005 *Fused*, all give a different facet of Kenny's drumming."

Q: "If you took the shows that the Airplane performed from 1965 through 1972, and include 1989, are there fifteen to twenty that would be considered the elite?"

A: "It would be impossible to make an order of the Top 15 shows, however I can come up with that amount based on various factors that you can ascertain from the main section of the book. Those would entail any, or all combinations of special guests, the song selection, the instrumentation of the band, and or specific versions of certain tunes. I am putting these in order by date and not most significant."

1/8/67 Webster Hall, New York City

12/31/67 Winterland, San Francisco, California

2/1/68 The Matrix, San Francisco, California

8/28/68 Falkoner Cenret, Copenhagen, Denmark

4/26/69 Swing Auditorium, San Bernardino

6/13/69 The Family Dog, San Francisco, California

8/10/69 Sheep Meadow, Central Park, New York City

9/6/69 The Family Dog, San Francisco, California

10/10/69 The Agrodome, Vancouver, Canada

10/25/69 Winterland, San Francisco, California

10/31/69 The Los Angeles Forum, Inglewood, California

5/6/70 Fillmore East, New York City (Late show).

9/14/70 Fillmore West, San Francisco, California

11/13/70 Capitol Theater, Port Chester, New York (Late show).

11/25/70 Fillmore East, New York City

Q: "From all the shows the Airplane ever played in front of a live audience or recorded for a TV taping, how many had at least one special guest on stage?"

A: "The amount of special guests that have been verified and not rumored to have taken place are not that plentiful. Those occasions were memorable. You can see the information about the performances in the main section of the book. Here are the listing of the dates.

1/8/67 Webster Hall, New York City- Mike Bloomfield (Guitar) and Mark Naftalin (Keyboards) from the Paul Butterfield Blues Band.

12/31/67 Winterland, San Francisco, California- Dino Valente from the Quicksilver Messenger Service (Guitar, and vocals).

11/10/68 The Smothers Brothers Comedy Hour- Kate Smith (Singer), the Smothers Brothers, and Pat Paulsen (Comedian).

8/17/69 Woodstock Music Festival, Max Yasgur's Farm, Bethel, New York- Nicky Hopkins (Piano). Nicky was one of the most famous session musicians ever.

8/18/69 Dick Cavett Show- Nicky Hopkins (Piano) and David Crosby vocals.

9/6/69 Family Dog At The Great Highway, San Francisco, California- Jerry Garcia (Guitar) and Mickey Hart (Drums) from the Grateful Dead.

2/4/70 A Night At The Family Dog, Family Dog At The Great Highway, San Francisco, California- The Grateful Dead and Santana (Both the guitarist and his band)."

Q: "When the Airplane performed live from 1965 through 1972 and even the reunion shows of 1989, did they ever play a concert without a main member of the band?"

A: "There is one show they performed without Grace on 3/25/70 at Suffolk Community College, Seldon, New York. Grace had throat trouble. They played 5/17/70 at Assembly Hall, Bloomington, Indiana without Marty. He had a personal situation to take care of. There were several shows that Joey Covington played in place of Spencer (Before Joey was an official member), maybe the most noted would be on 8/2/69 at the Atlantic City Racetrack, Atlantic City, New Jersey."

Q: "Did Jack ever explain his idea for laying down a studio bass track, regarding making it good, but not stepping on other instruments?"

A: "Jack mentioned during one of the teaching sessions at Jorma's Fur Peach Ranch (1998) that the best idea is to have the other instruments already recorded. He then could put down the bass track, by picking the spots to shine, and the segments to lay low. The way he explained his rational was indicative of his high level of musical professionalism and intelligence."

Q: "Is there a show that could have been a complete disaster (Any year) for any number of reasons, but the Airplane instead of taking the easy way out fought through the difficulties?"

A: "On 5/1/70 at the SUNY Athletic Field, SUNY Of Stony Brook, Stony Brook, New York the J.A. had to overcome cut wires and constant sound trouble. If that weren't bad enough it was an outdoor gig on an unusually cool night, and Grace, and Paul sounded sick. You total up the negatives and would think it would be a concert to erase from existence. The band muddled through in a professional manner. When you look at the events of that night you will be impressed by their ability to play as well as they did, with the elements they faced."

Q: "Is there one funny Grace joke that stands out over time, you can include 1989?"

A: The funniest was also brilliant for its spur of the moment reply. On the 5/3/70 show from Central Park, New York City a fan passes Grace a note to perform a song by the New York Rock And Roll Ensemble. Grace tells the fan "The band has enough trouble playing our own songs."

Q: "I like some of the political Country Joe McDonald music. I would like to hear some other styles of his. Would there be an album with any Airplane or Jefferson Starship people helping Country Joe that would serve as a good introduction?"

A: "There is a compilation of music that Country Joe recorded in the 1970's, that came out in 1989. The title is *Classics*. The music has a solo Neil Young feel and Marty Balin is one of numerous people on the recording. There is a brilliant track *Save The Whales*. It came out on *Fantasy FCD-7709-2*."

Q: "Is the CD (1995) of the Monterey Pop Festival of 1967 a legit release?"

A: "It is a legal release and nice addition to the live collection. The CD of the performance from June 17, 1967 came out in 1995 (Magnum 74). What may have started the confusion about the legality were the original pressings that found there way into the record shops were from England, and the cover didn't seem to have the greatest of clarity."

Q: "What did you think of the song selection for the CD that came out in 1998 called *Live At The Fillmore East*?"

A: "The album is terrific and made excellent use of the eighty minutes that can fit on a CD. If you could still have (Couldn't be done) kept it as a single disc and traded *Wild Tyme* and *Watch Her Ride* for *The House At Pooneil Corners* and *Crown Of Creation*, it would have added another star to a well decorated release. Since those two songs were not performed in the time period used to capture the live music, the version we have is a fine representation of that era."

Q: "In 1999 did we have a Jefferson Airplane reunion that few realized?"

A: "If a reunion could be without the sounds of music, we sure did! The J.A. was inducted to the Bill Graham-Walk Of Fame in San Francisco, California. Jorma, Jack, Marty, and Spencer were in attendance. Only Grace was missing."

Q: "When Skip Spence passed away is it true that Spencer Dryden attending the funeral, even though he never played with Skip in the Airplane?"

A: "Not only did Spencer show the size of his heart but an incredible resolve to even be on the premises. Jerry Miller from Moby Grape told me how sick Spencer looked that day and what an effort it must have been to pay his tribute."

Q: "When I purchased the 1999 tribute CD for Skip Spence I was disappointed that almost all the artists weren't from his day. Doesn't that take away from the idea?"

A: "I always thought that way. Tribute releases should be from musicians that were around at the time of the artist being paid homage to. That is if the logistics are possible. On the 1999 *More Oar* tribute for Skip only Robert Plant (Led Zeppelin) and Tom Waits stick out as the important vocal contributors. You can make the point even Tom Waits career began after the 1960's (1973)."

Q: "When you hear about the words spoken or written regarding Spencer Dryden's death can you think of the tribute that was the most articulate?"

A: "Paul Kantner had some words that could have been used for a song. He wrote as only P.K. can. Check it out for yourself please at http://www.jeffersonairplane.com/tribute.html."

Q: "When Spencer Dryden was taken from us far too early it seemed that Jorma was honestly saddened by his thoughts in print. I'm glad that Spencer could leave the earth with a link to his past rediscovered. Are your thoughts the same or do you stand on another part of the ground?"

A: "I concur with how you feel. If you have taken any writing or speech courses it is easy to separate the sincerity of the tears from the ones they once called crocodile. If you visit the website mentioned in the previous entry you can digest the wonderful words."

Q: "With the terrible circumstances Spencer Dryden went through the last several years of his life, the destruction of his home, and the serious illness, did any Airplane members help him out?"

A: Many times charity is not publicized. From what we know Grace donated an original painting for auction, Jorma donated an original Airplane poster (Signed), Marty donated an original painting, and Jack a signed bass. For information about the charity show that was held 5/22/04 at Slim's in San Francisco please go to Peter Rowan's site http://www.peter-rowan.com/news.html."

Q: "Are there a few songs you can list that the Airplane, Jefferson Starship, and Hot Tuna have all performed at least once live? From all years are okay to use."

A: "There are a bunch of tunes that were played by the three bands. What would your guess be for the number of songs the three bands performed at least once? Would you vote in the 1-3 range, 4-6, 7-9 or 10+?"

*America*
*Chauffeur Blues*
*Down Home Blues*
*Good Shepherd*
*High Flying Bird*
*John's Other*
*Milk Train*
*Rock Me Baby*
*The Other Side Of This Life*
*3/5 Of A Mile In 10 Seconds*
*Volunteers*
*White Rabbit*
*Wooden Ships*

Q: "I decided to collect at least one CD of all the J.A. members, either as part of another band or doing session work. What do you recommend for Bob Harvey?"
A: "It is possible with all the wonderful bluegrass music Bob has put out over the years the finest work comes from his band Georgia Blue. The title is *Children Of The Wind*. Prior to its release in 2006 Bob sent me three tracks after they were completed. I was impressed on the first listening. When the album came out I gave it a good amount of time on the CD player. If you go to www.georgiablue.us you can check it out for yourself."

Q^: "Could you give me some information on the live Jefferson Airplane CD's that have come out since 2003?"
A: "***Cleared For Take Off*** " Acrobat (U.K.) ACMCD 4001 CD released 11/6/03 (Taken from the Winterland, San Francisco, California performances of 3/10-3/12/67). The sound quality changes throughout the CD and the pops come at no extra charge. Although the CD wasn't put together with the greatest respect to the band or fan (Some songs fade-out and have wrong titles), those that don't own the material will be interested. There should have been one version of everything played during the three nights. The CD doesn't include *"And I Like It"*, *"Let Me In"*, *"Fat Angel"*, or the jam. No information was given in the liner notes about the dates used for the songs so I have included that for you. *"3/5 Of A Mile In To Seconds"* 3/11/67, *"Don't Let Me Down"* 3/10/67, *"Don't Slip Away"* 3/10/67, *"She Has Funny Cars"* 3/12/67, *"Let's Get Together"* (Fades-out) 3/11/67, *"High Flying Bird"* 3/12/67, *"It's No Secret"* 3/12/67, *"Come Back Baby"* (Listed as *"Jorma's Blues"*) 3/12/67, *"Plastic Fantastic Lover"* (Intro cut) 3/11/67, *"Runnin' Round This World"* (Listed as *"Running Round The World"*) 3/11/67, *"Somebody To Love"* (W/*"Leave You Alone"* which was not listed) 3/10/67, *"The Other Side Of This Life"* 3/11/67, *"Thing"* (Fades-out) 3/11/67, *"Tobacco Road"* 3/10/67, *"Today"* 3/11/67, *"White Rabbit"* 3/12/67, *"Bringing Me Down"* (Listed as *"You're Bring Me Down"*) 3/11/67, and *"My Best Friend"* 3/12/67 (Listed as *"You're My Best Friend"*).

*"**Last Flight**"* Charly (U.K.) SNAD 555 CD released 2/19/07 (The final Jefferson Airplane show from Winterland, San Francisco, California 9/22/72). The sound quality is terrific but **inexplicability** left off the double CD is the encore with **Marty Balin**! There was plenty of time on the second CD and it is advertised as the complete concert. Below is the missing song and then the release where you can hear the encore with Marty. Grace Slick's: *You Wear Your Dresses Too Short Improvisation > Dress Rap > You Wear Your Dresses Too Short*. 1992 Jefferson Airplane Loves You (Box Set) RCA 61110-2.

*"**At Golden Gate Park**"* Charly (U.K.) SNAP 283 CD released 5/5/07 (The Polo Field-Golden Gate Park, San Francisco, California 5/7/69). The final song on the CD is listed as *"Mexico"* but is *"3/5 Of A Mile In 10 Seconds"* which is not mentioned. While the sound lacks a real punch it is a good quality recording. The show is a must for Jorma's guitar at the start of *"Somebody To Love"* and the first *"Good Shepherd"* with Grace taking the vocals. Please see pages 150-151 for complete details.

*"**Sweeping Up The Spotlight Jefferson Airplane Live At The Fillmore East 1969**"* RCA/Legacy 82876 81558 2 CD released 5/15/07 (Taken from the Fillmore East, New York City performances of November 28th and 29th of 1969). Why aren't we told which show each song is from? All the tracks were previously unreleased excluding *"Good Shepherd"* and *"Plastic Fantastic Lover"* which can be found on the expanded edition of *"Volunteers"* BMG Heritage 82876 61642 2 CD released 6/22/04.

Q: "How did you decide on the title of the book?"
A: "The title is from the J.A. song *3/5 Of A Mile In 10 Seconds*. Not only is it one of the finest songs ever written but the words are perfect for the carnival atmosphere we often witness from a rock and roll band."

**Some Hot Tuna questions (Including Jorma and Jack solo)-**

Q: "In April of 1969 one of the guys I work with went to the Matrix in San Francisco. He told me that Jorma, Jack, Joey, and Paul Kantner played that night but with a second drummer. He swears it was Aynsley Dunbar, is it true?"
A: "On 4/13/69 Aynsley did perform with the guys your friend mentioned. They played a combination of ten songs, *jams*, and instrumentals. Maybe the second most interesting part of the show besides Aynsley making an appearance was none of the material was geared toward Paul's style of music."
Q: "Isn't it wrong that people always think the first time Santana played on stage with Jorma and Jack was during an Airplane show from 2/4/70, A Night At The Family Dog, Family Dog At The Great Highway, San Francisco, California?"
A: "That is great detective work! While on 2/4/70 the Airplane, Grateful Dead, and Santana with his band had a *jam*, Jorma, and Jack played with Santana and his band on 8/10/69 at the Bandshell, Central Park, New York City. During the Santana set they performed *Jam > Uncle Sam Blues > Jam*."
Q: "In 1969 maybe 1970 I heard some material by a great band called Thing Dog. I was lucky because it was through a friend of the band. They were psychedelic and polished for an unsigned band. I am told the drummer was Bob Steeler. Is that true and did their music ever come out on CD?"
A: "It is fascinating to note that the music Bob Steeler recorded with Think Dog never got released during the time the band was together, or even when Bob was in Hot Tuna! They had at least two albums worth of material. A great record company Psychedelic Music did one of the coolest things possible. They got the rights to the second unreleased album (*Dog Days*) and put it out on vinyl only! They are putting it out on CD in the future." If you go to www.psychedelic-music.com you can purchase the record and check out some amazing bands of the past.

Q: "If we wanted to be overly technical is this a good trivia question? Prior to Greg Douglass in 1975 name the guy that played rhythm guitar for Hot Tuna during a couple of performances in Europe circa summer 1970. It was not during a *jam* session, but a paid admission concert."

A: "That isn't stretching things too much, since you pointed out it was only for two shows. When the Airplane played 6/26/70 at the Kralingen Pop Festival, Rotterdam, Holland and the 6/28/70 Bath Festival Of Blues And Progressive Music, Royal County Fairgrounds, Shepton Mallet, Somerset, U.K., joining Jorma, Jack, Marty, and Joey for the Hot tuna portion was a gentleman named Paul Ziegler. Check out page 429, for how long Jorma and Paul first played in the same circles."

Q: "Did Hot Tuna in the early days ever play an Airplane song that you may not have thought they ever would?"

A: "On 8/25/70 at L'Enfant Plaza, Washington, D.C., Jorma, Jack, Marty, and Joey played *Volunteers*! It was only a tad over three minutes, but how could one complain?"

Q: "In 1971 I first heard my favorite tune *I Know Your Rider* done live. It was an electric version. Do you think that the song is better done with somebody playing an acoustic guitar or plugged in and using the six string electric?"

A: "If it is Jorma he truly brings out the best of that song in either format. The electric version is excellent and sounds sincere enough to be put through a stack of amplifiers. Jorma's acoustic magic has it sounding brilliant as well."

Q: "When I saw Hot Tuna a few times in 1971 there was a song that I always identified with Will Scarlett (Harmonica). The name escapes me, but I know the Grateful Dead recorded a version."

A: "*I've Been All Around This World* is a traditional song that the Grateful Dead put on the live record *Reckoning*. Hot Tuna did an incredible live rendition with Willie Scarlett, but never put it on a live, or studio album."

Q: "Are there Hot Tuna fans that consider *Burgers* the last album they really were passionate about?"

A: "No doubt at all. When *The Phosphorescent Rat* first appeared at the local record shop there were a segment of fans to this day that didn't like the songs taking a harder edge. It is rather unfortunate. If you immediately decide that if a song has a certain decibel level it can't be well crafted, you are shutting yourself out from a good dose of rock and roll, and not helping the artist. Why there are stereotypes I'll never know. Loud isn't good, or bad, it should be judged on a case by case basis. It works the other way too. If somebody is into listening to fifteen minute *jams* with four guitars, it doesn't mean that a song on the mellow side of the tracks such as *Sea Child* isn't one of the finest creations on the planet."

Q: "It didn't hit me at the time but when I search my memory banks did Jorma's brother open some 1972 shows for Hot Tuna? I am thinking his band was the name of a strange animal?"

A: "Peter Kaukonen had a terrific record out called *Black Kangaroo*. It can be purchased from his website, with bonus tracks at www.peterkaukonen.com. His band did open several shows for Hot Tuna in 1972. There has never been any notations of the two brothers appearing on stage together on that tour."

Q: "Did Hot Tuna play an instrumental *Milk Train* or is my older brother trying to make me jealous?"

A: "An example of a show where they performed both *Eat Starch Mom* and *Milk Train* as instrumentals would be 4/73 at Princeton University, Princeton, New Jersey."

Q: "My favorite Hot Tuna member ever was Sammy Piazza. Can you tell me something that people may not be aware of?"

A: "Sammy had an opportunity to have been the drummer in ZZ Top. He has some fascinating stories that he shares in the interview section of the book."

Q: "For as long as I have been into Hot Tuna I have always heard something that I don't believe is the full story. Did Sammy leave the band because he was tired of the constant grind of the road?"

A: "It is amazing how that rumor got started. The truth is it was about money and the record company wanting to cut expenditures. Hot Tuna had an opportunity to continue on the road, but not having to pay Bob Steeler (Unfair to a quality individual) the same scale. Sammy discusses the situation in the interview section of the book."

Q: "I went to see Hot Tuna play seventeen shows with Sammy Piazza. There is one song that I never got to see performed, *Highway Song* from *Burgers*. Did this tune get played by any version of Hot Tuna?"

A: "Before I started writing the book I had heard at least three hundred and fifty live Hot Tuna performances. I had never come across even one second of the song live. I made it a point to ask Sammy Piazza about this. He told me they did play it. The reason it is factual he even recalled sitting backstage with Jorma one time and talking about a tempo change. Sammy's recollection of the Tuna days is impeccable."

Q: "Did Hot Tuna have a New Years Eve show 12/31/74 and if so anything special happen?"

A: "They didn't play 12/31/74, but they gave a nice holiday gift a bit earlier in December. On 12/18/74 they played Hjalmar Stromskolan, Stromsund, Sweden with drummer Esbjorn Jacobsen and on 12/28/74 they performed at Musiksalen, Vattudalsskolan, Stromsund, Sweden with Esbjorn on drums, Rolf Forsberg on guitar, and another unknown guitarist! One of the songs performed was an instrumental *Trail By Fire*. **Bob Steeler was missed!**

Q: "My favorite early Hot Tuna song is *Mann's Fate*. Is there a studio version that I can purchase somewhere?"

A: "*Mann's Fate* didn't make any of the Hot Tuna studio records. In 1975 a studio out-take with Jorma, Jack, and Bob Steeler was recorded, but never released. It ran a little over six minutes."

Q: "Of the fifty-two Hot Tuna shows I have attended my favorite was a 1975 concert with Greg Douglass in the band. Did it seem to you he was gone in the blink of an eye?"

A: "The best quote I heard about the superior magnitude of the shows with Greg was from a fan that called them "Epics." Greg performed with them from March 3 of 1975 through July 26, 1975. Greg did not want to be a rhythm guitarist. He preferred to be playing more leads, and Jorma was also looking for a specific rhythm style, and sound. It is a shame the combination of Jorma, Jack, Bob Steeler, and Greg didn't last. The caliber of each night couldn't ever be given enough accolades."

Q: "I got a tape of a Hot Tuna show that a bunch of us attended in Lenox, Massachusetts on 7/26/75. There was a song in the set that I am positive I heard the Airplane perform around 1970. Am I correct?"

A: "You got to attend the final show ever with Greg Douglass! The song you ask about is called *I Can Tell*. It was made popular by John Hammond Jr., and written by Ellas McDaniel, and Samuel Smith. You did indeed see the Airplane play the tune in 1970."

Q: "Did Hot Tuna have somebody help on guitar during the recording of *Yellow Fever?*"

A: For the 1975 album they used the services of John Sherman. Years later he would play with a rough sounding heavy metal band called Bad Wizard."

Q: "Why did Hot Tuna use an outside musician to play guitar with Jorma on the *Yellow Fever* record?"

A: "Bob Steeler had a great explanation that can be found in the interview section. If Jorma overdubbed one time, two, or ten, it is still Jorma playing. By bringing in an outside entity he was able to get a different sound to complement what he had contributed to the particular track."

Q: "In May of 1976 did Hot Tuna play a version of *Walking Blues* that lasted forty-five minutes?"

A: "That is a story that seemed to spread around the Tuna world throughout the mid to late 1970's. It wasn't *Walking Blues*, but *Funky #7*. At a show that remains one of their finest ever, on 5/4/76 at Lisner Auditorium, George Washington University, Washington, D.C., Jorma, Jack, and Mr. Bob Steeler played *Funky #7* for forty-two minutes and forty-two seconds. *Invitation* was the second longest tune of the evening clocking in at a short seventeen minutes and eight seconds!"

Q: "I got into Hot Tuna after 1977, and never got to see Bob Steeler play with them. When I listen to live tapes especially from 1976 he sounds great. Is there something if I saw him live back then I would appreciate that I can't get out of the recordings?"

A: "There would be two things at least. The first is his incredible stamina. He would play three, or more hours a night, and not be able to get out from behind the drum kit. He sounded as good on the last note as he did on the first. The other attribute is his total team player attitude. Bob has a rock and jazz background. He could play anything but often stayed low key to let Jorma, and Jack shine the most."

Q: "Were there tunes that Hot Tuna rehearsed in 1977 that did not get performed?"

A: "*Thunderbolt Song*, *I Don't Know*, *Wolves And Lambs*, *Jack's Tune* (Only about a minute of a song), *Lost In Time*, and *Swamp Life*. If you take those six rock and roll songs and add the three others that were performed *Bright Eyes*, *Snow Gorilla*, and *The Party Song*, there was enough material for a combination live/studio recording. When Jorma talks about 1975-1977 as "The Metal Years", we could have been listening to straight-ahead no holds barred very Hot Tuna!"

Q: "In 1977 I saw a few live shows and were wondering the names of the three songs that I didn't recall hearing previously and were they released?"

A: "Unfortunately the three fantastic tunes are gathering dust. *Bright Eyes*, *Snow Gorilla*, and *The Party Song* were the ones brought out for some of the 1977 shows. The first two mentioned were heavy enough to rock the foundation of any live venue. The third had the unique honor of Mr. Casady handling background vocals!"

Q: "I saw Hot Tuna forty-three times between 1972 and 1977. My favorite show was 11/11/77 at the Commack Arena, Commack, New York. Do I have some of this right, a guy unannounced with a guitar sang *Baby What You Want Me To Do*, and two blues tunes?"

A: "You were able to see one of the finest Hot Tuna performances ever. Not only did they perform almost four hours but the assistant road manager Jamie Howell joined them for *Baby What You Want Me To Do*, *Born In Chicago* (Written by Nick Gravenites, with a well know version by the Butterfield Blues Band), and *Looking For A Sign of life*. There isn't any documentation available about *Looking For A Sign of life*."

Q: "If you take every song Hot Tuna released on record up to and including *Hoppkorv* how many of the songs were never played on stage?"

A: "Hot Tuna being very fan friendly through 1977 performed every song live that they recorded through *Hoppkorv*. On the excellent *Burgers* album there was a tune *Highway Song* which has been often overlooked as ever being done in concert, but Sammy Piazza verified they did indeed play the *Highway Song* live."

Q: "If you took a poll of every Hot Tuna fan the day of the final 1977 concert and asked what is a better song *Embryonic Journey* or *Water Song*, which would win?"

A: "There wouldn't be a loser between those two. I can tell you first hand from seeing massive Hot Tuna performances that both titles were yelled out often at every show. By a slight edge *Water Song* had more requests."

Q: "On the final performance of Hot Tuna in 1977 did anything special happen on the last show?"

A: "I was very fortune to have attended the last performance of the 1977 tour. It was from The Palladium, New York City on 11/26/77 (Late show). Jorma announces near the end of the show that a San Francisco friend would be joining the band. Out comes Buffalo Bob Roberts to play the saxophone. He played on: *Rock Me Baby*, *Uncle Sam Blues*, *The Party Song*, and *Feel So Good*. *The Party Song* sounded very interesting with the saxophone. It was one of the best versions that they played (Performed only in 1977). The final song was *Invitation*, but that was without Buffalo Bob."

Q: "I always respected the playing of Bob Steeler. I was disappointed when the end of the 1977 tour came he didn't perform with Tuna again as a full-time member. Is there something you can tell me about Bob musically that may not be common knowledge?"

A: "Bob is a self-taught and an accomplished piano-player. He began to play at age twelve. It is with great hope that Bob will consider releasing some material in the next year."

Q: "I got to see Hot Tuna three times with Nick Buck and SVT five times with him. I respect greatly Nick as a person and a musician that doesn't look to be the general of a band, only enhance it. Would you say the Hot Tuna fans liked what he did on the 1977 tour?"

A: "Nick was very well liked for the reason you spelled out. He picked his spots when to shine and blended in really well with Jorma, Jack and Bob. Nick brought out a great point during my interview with him. He played on three Hot Tuna studio albums and that gave him credibility on the live tour."

Q: "On the 1977 tour did Hot Tuna play *Killing Time In The Crystal* City electric, or was it only performed by Jorma acoustically?"

A: "Hot Tuna did perform electric versions. The first documented electric performance was 7/8/77 at the Civic Auditorium, Santa Cruz, California."

Q: "When Nick Buck started to play live shows with Hot Tuna in 1977 did they do any songs which were not performed on the 1977 shows without him?"

A: "Hot Tuna performed *Bright Eyes*, *Easy Now*, *Genesis*, *Killing Time In The Crystal City*, *Party Song*, and *Winin' Boy Blues* once Nick joined the line-up. There hasn't been documented evidence of any of these songs played electrically in 1977 prior to Nick's arrival."

Q: "If you were attempting to show somebody the side of Hot Tuna that never got the credit it should (The studio albums through *Hoppkorv*) what songs would you take to solidify your point?"

A: "Hot Tuna should have received much more acclaim for the studio compositions. In order to sell the potential fan on the wide range of musical styles Hot Tuna explored I would take a bit of all of them. These aren't always my favorites, but strong compositions that could make an ear open wide. From the five studio albums I would take sixteen songs. It could be eighteen but *Bar Room Crystal Ball* and *Hot Jelly Roll Blues* weren't included. The attempt was to get the list to on or about fifteen.

*Burgers*:

*Keep On Truckin'*- The good time flavor that is perfect for a rock or folk version.

*99 Year Blues*- The right mix of blues, and rock, with a nice Jorma vocal.

*True Religion*- A perfect song that can always keep its folk roots, even when blended with rock and roll.

*Water Song*- One of the finest instrumentals ever recorded. It is timeless!

*The Phosphorescent Rat*:

*Easy Now*-  From the opening note it is a blowtorch!

*In The Kingdom*- Jorma's vocals and the music mesh perfectly. This was a mid-tempo song with brilliant results.

*I See The Light*- One of the most requested songs to hear live. It was superb the first time it went on the turntable and remarkable on CD as well.

*America's Choice*:

*Funky #7*- A lesson in how to improvise and expand your musical horizons. That was only in the studio. Live this song became an epic.

*Hit Single #1*- If for no other reason the title is too cool to not get a mention. On the serious side it is a prime example of straight ahead rock and roll Hot Tuna style.

*Invitation*- It didn't matter if the songwriter were Jorma or your fifth uncle twice removed. It is one of the finest songs created. Hearing it live only raised the level of intensity.

*Walkin' Blues*- Hot Tuna shows great appreciation for the blues with the cover from Robert Johnson. The studio version left a calling card for what this could do on a concert stage.

*Yellow Fever*:

*Baby What You Want Me To Do*- There could never be a version close to the Tuna studio or live rendition. The song was so well done that even people that weren't Hot Tuna fans would ask the title of this when they heard it during the progressive days of radio.

*Sunrise Dance With The Devil*- Jorma did like to call 1975-1977 "The Metal Years."

*Hoppkorv*:

*Song From The Stainless Cymbal*- If the majority of critics didn't have an anti-Hot Tuna bias this should have received legendary stature for its beauty.

*Watch The North Wind Rise*- This one has stayed a favorite of the long time Hot Tuna fan. The words and music are a creation of the highest magnitude."

Q: "Is it true on 11/24/78 at the Suffolk Forum, Commack, New York show Jorma played with drummer Bob Steeler, and no bass, or keyboards?"

A: "Jorma, and Bob Steeler did perform a few shows together, with no bass, or keyboards. Jorma played a normal acoustic set. When the electric music started the audience was in for a shock to the system. There weren't *Walking Blues*, or *Sea Child*, but *Happy Go Lucky Space Rats On Parade*, and *Happy Go Lucky Space Rats Go Underwater*. I happened to be at the performance you were referring to. If people had known what to expect it would have been a different reaction. I wanted to hear electric Hot Tuna, regardless of how many members were on stage. A couple of weeks later I listened to a recording of the gig and realized that there were a number of interesting compositions."

Q: "Is there a solo song from any of the Airplane members excluding Skip Spence that you would consider strange?"

A: "On the 1979 Jorma Kaukonen album called *Jorma*, the LP finished with a song called *Da-Ga-Da-Ga*. At the end of the song (It's only 1:27) Jorma starts talking about the words used for the title. The rest of the album was a normal record. It contained *Straight Ahead*, *Roads And Roads* and, *Vampire Woman*, etc."

Q: "Did Jorma play a very loose but cool version of *Volunteers* that you recall sometime between 1979 and 1980?"

A: "The version you are referencing that comes to mind was on 7/15/79 at Belmont Park, Elmont, New York. They did it a few times (Please see next question). He called the band Hidden Klitz and joining Jorma were Bob Steeler on drums and Denny Degorio on bass. They actually played the song over seventeen minutes!"

Q: "I was first getting into music at the time and was wondering did Jorma play a show where two other famous guitarists were with him on stage for an encore? One song sounded like a strange version of *Volunteers*."

A: "On 9/8/79 the show billed as Woodstock II, Parr Meadows, Shirley, New York, with (White Gland) Jorma, Denny Degorio bass, and Danny O'Brien drums. For the encore portion of their set they were joined by Stephen Stills from Crosby, Stills, Nash, and sometimes Young, as well as Leslie West from Mountain. The three songs performed, *Volunteers*, *Stormy Monday* (Written by T-Bone Walker, with a most memorable version coming from the Allman Brothers), and *Roll Over Beethoven* (Written by Chuck Berry, with a legendary version done by the Beatles), were terrific."

Q: "If we wanted to say that the great blues musician Nick Gravenites had three Hot Tuna members on his 1980 album *Blue Star*, would I be considered correct?"

A: "Even though Jorma and Jack didn't appear on the record your point would be well taken. Joey Covington, Greg Douglass, (Played on part of the 1975 tour), and Pete Sears all contributed to the album."

Q: "Did the Jorma album from 1980 called *Barbecue King* have a drummer who had an odoriferous name?

A: "Excellent vocabulary! John Stench played on the record. He was once a member of the band Chrome."

Q: "What was the album and title of a song that got some airplay for Jorma around 1980 or 1981? The hook had something to do with running with crowds of people."

A: "On the 1980 *Barbecue King* album the tune *Runnin' With The Fast Crowd* did receive some radio play. The record had some good material, such as *Man For All Seasons* and *Rockabilly Shuffle*."

Q: "I saw Hot Tuna in 1983 and am wondering what were the names of the drummer and other singer?"

A: "Shigemi Komiyama was on the drums, and Michael Falzarano played guitar, and did some of the vocals."

Q: "Can you give me some information on the 1983 Hot Tuna drummer Shigemi Komiyama? It seems as if he came out of nowhere and fell off the planet. I didn't think the earth was square. "

A: "Shigemi Komiyama is also known as Shig. One of his listed credits is playing with Yoko Ono on stage. Before being part of Hot Tuna, Shig performed in the USA with Thriller, Johnny Ace, Johnny Nitro, Fun Addicts, and Noh Buddies. Thank you to http://www.shig33.com/Bio.html for the information prior to 1983. He has been part of a number of bands after Hot Tuna, El Destoyo, Mach IV, Shig And Buzz, and the Shi-Tones. The music ranges are alternative, psychedelic, rock and roll, and surf. An interesting note is Shigemi also plays the bass. Does that mean Jack can play the drums?"

Q: "Did Bob Weir play with Hot Tuna on the 1983 tour?"

A: "On the 10/28/83 show at the Nassau Coliseum, Uniondale, New York, Bob Weir came out with Hot Tuna for the last song. They performed *White Rabbit*, with Bob Weir, and Michael Falzarano doing the vocals."

Q: "I saw Jorma perform acoustic in 1984. He played a song that the people next to us wrote down as *Junkies On Angel Dust*. Isn't that a line from the song and not the title?"

A: "*Man For All Seasons* is the name of the tune. It is one of the rock and roll songs that over time has been referenced by part of the song and not its real name. The record company thought *Man For All Seasons* would be a better title."

Q: "When Hot Tuna decided to play acoustic on the 1986 tour did that mean the show went back to Hot Tuna songs from the sixties and seventies?"

A: "The bulk of the songs were indeed from the classic period. Excluding when they appeared in 1986 with guests, such as Marty Balin's nephew Joey, David Bromberg, or Rick Danko from the Band, they only performed eight songs that you would not have heard Hot Tuna play in the 1970's. They are listed below."

Broken Highway

Follow The Drinking Gourd (Jorma played this as far back as the early 1960's).

I Belong To The Band (Jorma played this as far back as the early 1960's).

Ice Age

Too Many Years

Too Hot To Handle

Trouble In Mind

Vampire Women

Q: "I didn't get to see the 1986 shows with Joey Balin playing with Hot Tuna. Did Joey get to bring any songs with him for the group to play?"

A: "There were five tunes (Not performed each night) that Hot Tuna played in 1986 and 1987 with Joey on stage. They were *Hard Times*, *Judgment Day*, *New Time, New Day* (One title), *Ordinary Man*, and *Out Of My Hands*."

Q: "I went to seven shows from 1986, and 1987 with Joey Balin playing acoustic with Jorma and Jack. I enjoyed them opening note to encore. What ever became of Joey?"

A: "Joey Balin for many years produced rock and roll albums. He currently works as a stand-up comedian. You can check out his latest events at www.joeybalin.com."

Q: "In the summer of 1986 I was at the Hot Tuna show in Media. It was my favorite post 1977 concert. There was a female singer that came on the stage for what people called "set number two." I know the name from Airplane history. She is Anna Rizzo. Why do I know the name?"

A: "You have a great memory. Anna Rizzo is part of Airplane history, but not from the J.A. When Marty went solo, on the first two projects he had Anna associated with them. She did some vocals on the 1972 self-titled album by Grootna. Marty worked behind the scenes. She also helped with the singing on the 1973 self-titled LP from Bodacious D.F. Marty would handle the lead vocals. He even did a song the Airplane had played briefly in 1969 called *Drifting*, on the Bodacious D.F. record. Anne joined Hot Tuna on stage for six songs on 8/25/86 at Pulsations, Media, Pennsylvania."

Q: "I went to ten Hot Tuna shows in 1986. There was a show in the summer that Kingfish was on the bill (What a version of *Killing Time In The Crystal City*). Kingfish played a bunch of songs with Hot Tuna. One had a 1950's flavor and was the greatest thing ever, excluding my boss giving me a seventeen percent increase. Was the song called *I Have Pneumonia, So Give Me The Flu?*"

A: "If the person had pneumonia they wouldn't need the flu. The title to the song is, *The Rockin' Pneumonia And The Boogie Woogie Flu*. There is a tremendous live version by the Grateful Dead, on a CD called *Steppin' Out With The Grateful Dead: England '72*. This was released in 1992 by GDM/Arista 14084."

Q: "I went to see Jorma play a bunch of times over the years. I enjoy when he is with Jack or solo. One night he was with David Bromberg. Bromberg was singing some song about not being stupid or made fun of. The crowd was very into his theatrics. What is the title?"

A: "The title is *Will Not Be Your Fool*. One moment the crowd is totally silent for *Embryonic Journey*, and a moment later they are loud and proud for *Will Not Be Your Fool*."

Q: "My favorite Hot Tuna show post 1977 was the gig on 2/26/89 at the Riverside Church Theatre, New York City, with Danny Gatton. Jorma and Danny played as if they were in a band together for decades. I can't leave out Jack's thunderous bass. What happened to Danny?"

A: "Danny Gatton committed suicide in the fall of 1994. He never got the credit he earned. He had such diversity in his approach to playing the instrument. You mention how well he meshed with Jorma. Jorma's ability to play songs that are blues, folk, rock or country, brought out the best in Danny, on a cold winter night in New York City."

Q: "I saw a real fine Hot Tuna performance in winter 1989. Can you tell me about the drummer Joe Stefko and the keyboardist Lenny Underwood?"

A: "Joe Stefko has done work with Meatloaf and was part of a later (much) version of the Turtles. Lenny Underwood's history includes involvement with the hip-hop band the Beatnuts and session work with Whitney Houston and Madonna."

Q: "There was a guy that played with Hot Tuna on an encore in November of 1989. I was at the show and was impressed by the guys stage persona and how comfortable the guitar looked in his hand. Was his name Bill Goody?"

A: "You are very close. Billy Goodman was a roadie for the Jefferson Starship/Starship and on the 1989 Airplane reunion tour. He got to play some shows with Jorma (89-90) and Hot Tuna (89). The fans felt he handled himself very well. Billy is a very good guitarist. A song that went over well with the Hot Tuna crowd was called *Sweet*

*Home Chicago*. That was written by Robert Johnson. Billy has some funny stories in the interview section of the book and a website with his great CD's www.billygoodman.com."

Q: "I couldn't believe how good the Tuna show around 1989 with Billy Goodman was. It seemed and I have no knowledge that he and Jorma had a great stage chemistry."

A: "You have great insight. Billy was a roadie for Jorma and Jack on the 1989 Jefferson Airplane reunion tour. Billy and Jorma listen to many of the same artists such as the Reverend Gary Davis (Legendary folk musician) and Robert Johnson (Legendary Delta blues guitarist)."

Q: "I liked the 1990 Hot Tuna album *Pair A Dice Found*. I was glad that Harvey Sorgen was the drummer for many years. What can you tell me about his musical background?"

A: "In 1983 he was part of a group called Sorgen, Rust, Windbiel Trio. They put out an album of strange jazz and improvisation called *Outlet*. Harvey has played with Michael Falzarano in the Memphis Pilgrims, and has continued the bizarre sounding jazz and improvisations with the Fonda Stevens Group."

Q: "Was there a record in the early 1990's that both Jorma and Jack played on? It wasn't a band, but a guy that has put out many albums. All I remember he wasn't a blues musician."

A: "You were able to remember enough. The record was 1989. The performer was Warren Zevon and the album *Transverse City*, had Jorma, Jack, Jerry Garcia, and Neil Young, as well as many other well known musicians."

Q: "When I purchased the very inspiring and cool Hot Tuna- *Pair A Dice Found* CD in 1990, there was a song that seemed to be a hit when I was a youngster, *Eve Of Destruction*. Was that the case?"

A: "It was a major hit for Barry McGuire in 1965. The song was written by P.F. Sloan. It became a number one song in the USA and a Top 5 hit in the U.K. Hot Tuna played it live a few times but it didn't stick around for long. Both the studio and live versions are excellent."

Q: "I thought the Jorma record with Tom Hobson called *Quah* was the eleventh best album ever. When did he pass away and are there any nice words to read about him?"

A: "We lost Tom Hobson on 9/24/91. Please visit www.tomhobson.com. There are some wonderful words written about him including a great remembrance by Jorma."

Q: "In 1991 there was a Hot Tuna show I attended that had a song that I wasn't aware of before the concert. *Prison Blues* seems like the title. What can you tell me about the tune?"

A: "The title is *Folsom Prison Blues*. Hot Tuna does a great version of it live. Jorma's passion on the vocals makes it sound as if the song came right from his pen. The tune is from Johnny Cash. In 2004 Hot Tuna reissued *Live At Sweetwater 2* with bonus tracks. You can enjoy a terrific version. Check out www.allmusic.com and when you type in Hot Tuna you can click on the title I mentioned and even enjoy an audio sample."

Q: "I listened to a Hot Tuna show from 1992 that had a guy Roy Book Binder playing on two maybe three songs. Does he make albums?"

A: "One of the tunes Roy played with Hot Tuna on 1/4/92 at the Reach Resort, Key West, Florida, was *Statesboro Blues* (Written by Blind Willie McTell, but known by the great Allman Brothers version). Check out his 1988 album *Bookeroo*, for a version of the Jimmie Rodgers classic *Waiting For A Train*."

Q: "Did Hot Tuna have a surprise guest for a song or two that you were shocked to see on stage? Not for being good or bad, but because you don't think of the artist or band as somebody that would appear with them?"

A: "On 1/28/92 at Sweetwater, Mill Valley, California, Maria Muldaur played with Hot Tuna for two songs *Maggie's Farm* (Bob Dylan) and *I Belong To The Band*. Maria had a major hit with *Midnight At The Oasis*. Although her music is very varied from folk to country and gospel, I never knew one person that was into Hot Tuna and or Jorma solo that had any of her recordings. The same night the other performers were much more closely related to the Hot Tuna sound, Bob Weir, Pete Sears, and Happy Traum (Well known folk musician in the Woodstock, New York region)."

Q: "Is there a tune Hot Tuna performed that people were surprised at the low key nature of the arrangement?"

A: "One of the finest (If not the) blues tunes ever written is *Crossroads*, by Robert Johnson (Originally called *Cross Road Blues*). The definitive version comes from Cream. Eric Clapton's two solos are legendary. In 1993 Hot Tuna did a mid-tempo version. It would have been spectacular to have seen Jorma give it the *Walking Blues* (Also a Robert Johnson song) treatment!"

Q: "I know that Paul Kantner and David Crosby have appeared on stage together post Airplane days. Did David ever play with Jorma and Jack?"

A: "David Crosby appeared with Hot Tuna (Jorma, Jack, Pete Sears, and Michael Falzarano) at Lupo's Heartbreak Hotel, on 8/4/93 in Providence, Rhode Island. They played two songs *Drop Dead Mama* (David Crosby recorded the song for a record in 1989) and the traditional *Motherless Children* (Well known from Eric Clapton's version, but Paul Kantner did a terrific rendition during 1991 Wooden Ships tour)."

Q: "On 11/20/94 I was in the Guitar Center, Houston, Texas. I was so excited to see Jorma, Jack, and Michael Falzarano from a close proximity, that I didn't get the name of a song they played that Jimi Hendrix did. They didn't stretch the boundaries , but it was great as a non typical Hot Tuna choice. What was the title?"

A: "The guys played *Red House* from Jimi's *Are You Experienced*?"

Q: "There were three Hot Tuna fans the other day that mentioned a specific show from 1996 that most reminded them of the good old days 1975-1977. It was from Virginia. Was it a special guest or two that made them feel this way?"

A: "The show that was part of the Further Festival Tour, happened in Bristow, Virginia, at the Nissan Pavilion, on 6/26/96. The reason so many of the older fans liked this gig so much was during the set (Around forty-five minutes) they played eight songs, all that were performed during the real Hot Tuna days of 1968-1977. Since *Water Song*, *Ode To Billy Dean*, and *Baby What You Want Me To Do* were performed, you know the crowd was eating it up!"

Q: "I went to see Jorma in 1995 in Storrs, Connecticut, for the Guitar Summit Tour. I was attempting to think of the songs he performed the other night and I think I got everything but the opener. I can tell you it wasn't one that you would think in eighteen million years he would begin a show with."

A: "Jorma opened his portion of the show with *The Happy Turtle Song*, found on the Hot Tuna album *Pair A Dice Found*."

Q: "I went to see Hot Tuna seven times in 1996. The best was when they were joined by John Wesley Harding for one song. With a name like that was the tune a Bob Dylan original that they played?"

A: "John Wesley Harding obviously took his name from a Bob Dylan album. He joined Hot Tuna on stage for a terrific cover version of Dylan's *Rainy Day Women #12 & #35*. That performance was part of the Further Festival and that show in particular was very strong."

Q: "I think next to Jorma and Jack the person I like best to ever play in Hot Tuna was Michael Falzarano. Could you tell me if the 1996 Memphis Pilgrims CD would be good to own?"

A: "It would be well worth having a copy. *I Was The One*, *Love Gone Flat*, *Just My Way*, and *Judge, I'm Not Sorry*, are all songs you heard Michael perform. These four would be a great intro to the CD."

Q: "In 1998 I was at one of the Further Festival shows. There was a song Hot Tuna played called *Old Folks And Fools*. Why can't I find this anywhere?"

A: "The song often is incorrectly referred to *Old Folks And Fools*. This started as far back as the 1970's when it was performed by Hot Tuna. The correct title is *Fools Blues*. You can get a version of it on the Jorma CD called *Too Many Years* from 1998."

Q: "In the summer of 1998 I saw a Further Festival show with Hot Tuna playing a song with Rusted Root. Was it from the Who, Stones or some other famous 1960's U.K. band?"

A: "The tune you are describing comes from the Rolling Stones. The song is *You Can't Always Get What You Want*. It was performed a few times with Hot Tuna playing with Rusted Root."

Q: "Did Hot Tuna play a song sometime the end of 1999 that the Airplane played in the early days?"

A: "New Years Eve (12/31/99) at the Warfield Theatre, San Francisco, California, Hot Tuna along with Ratdog (Bob Weir), Bill Kreutzmann, and Mickey Hart, performed three songs. The first was *In The Midnight Hour*. The Airplane played the tune on 1/14/66 at the Kitsalano (Kits) Theater, Vancouver, Canada. The two other songs were *I Can't Get No (Satisfaction)* and *Not Fade Away*. There were actually three Grateful Dead members on stage with Hot Tuna, Bob, Bill and Mickey. *I Can't Get No (Satisfaction)* is one of the Rolling Stones most famous tunes. *Not Fade Away* was written by Buddy Holly. The Grateful Dead have a very well known version. Jorma (Jorma Kaukonen Band) has a live version that has been overlooked. It is available on the various artists live release called *Third Annual Gathering On The Mountain*, from music recorded on 5/8, and 5/9/98. The CD came out in 1999 on Relix 2099."

Q: "Can you recall any Allman Brothers playing with the J.A. or Hot Tuna on stage in the 1960's, or 1970's?"

A: "That would have been amazing to see. There are not concerts of the Allman Brothers on stage with J.A., or Hot Tuna, but there are Jorma, and Jack on stage with the Allman's 1999, and 2000. They played a total of four different songs. *One Way Out*, *Southbound*, *Statesboro Blues*, and *You Don't Love Me*. If you consider Warren Haynes a true Allman Brother, on 12/17/05 at the Asheville Civic Center, Asheville, North Carolina (A charity event), Warren joined Hot Tuna for *Rock Me Baby*. Greg Allman does appear with the Jefferson Starship at the House Of Blues, New Orleans, Louisiana on 3/18/95. Greg and the Jefferson Starship played *Rock Me Baby* and *Lord Have Mercy*. If that weren't enough, Randy California the guitarist from Spirit (Passed away 1/3/97) played with them as well!"

Q: "In the year 2000 I saw Hot Tuna at the Keswick Theatre, Glenside, Pennsylvania. It was close to Thanksgiving. This may have been my seventh favorite Tuna show out of sixty-eight. Can you tell me about the guy that played with them on the encore?"

A: "The special guest was Geoff Achison. He is a guitar-player, singer, and songwriter from Australia, known for his love of the blues. The show you mention was a good performance. Geoff played a tune called *24 Hours* with Hot Tuna. To learn more about him please visit his website at: www.geoffachison.com."

Q: "I am not into any San Francisco bands but Hot Tuna and the Airplane. I saw a Hot Tuna show in 2001 and a guy next to me almost jumped out of his skin when Buddy Cage played with them on a song called *Nine Pound Hammer*. It was a gig from 7/18/01 at the Stony Pony, Asbury Park, New Jersey. No sign of Bruce Springsteen."

A: "Buddy Cage is well known for his work with the New Riders Of The Purple Sage. He has done his share of session work, which includes playing in the studio with Bob Dylan."

Q: "In 2001 I was at a fun Hot Tuna show. A guy joined them for maybe ten songs that looked like the musician that wrote the song *Welcome Back* for the popular TV show called *Welcome Back Kotter*. Was that the same person with less hair?"

A: "The accomplished musician was John Sebastian. He did write the major hit for the TV show you mentioned. Long before that he was in a legendary 1960's band called the Lovin' Spoonful. He had played with Hot Tuna before. The concert you are talking about was at The Tabernacle, Mt. Tabor, New Jersey, on 11/24/01."

Q: "I saw Jorma perform in 2002. This particular show he was an opening act. He played two songs with Phil Lesh from the Grateful Dead. One I knew for sure. It was *Going Down The Road Feeling Bad*. The other song sounded as if it were a Grateful Dead tune or a Jerry Garcia solo. The title may have had the word rock or diamond."

A: "The tune is called *Dupree's Diamond Blues*. You can find a studio version of it from the Grateful Dead on *Aoxomoxoa*. If you go to www.allmusic.com, you can find some live versions that may interest you."

Q: "Can you tell me more about the Professor Louie and Michael Falzarano CD that came out in 2002 called *Flyin' High*?"

A: "It is a well received recording. It is actually listed as Professor Louie And The Crowmatix. It is an eclectic album. Louie has been friends with members of the Band. He will take you to the country one moment and give you a dose of roots rock and roll (A term for a style of rock and roll that is influenced by the blues) the next. There is a great version on the CD of a traditional tune that the Grateful Dead performed called *Jack-A-Roe*."

Q: "Although I tried to avoid him a former college classmate spotted me at a Jorma show in 2003. He told me he attended a gig on 2/1/03 at the Variety Playhouse, Atlanta, Georgia. He went on to claim Jorma was sick and did not sing. Is this true and did they play a bunch of songs that were instrumentals to begin with?"

A: "Jorma had laryngitis and for two nights was not able to sing. He didn't make the set list full of instrumentals. There were some but he gave the fans a chance to hear many songs without the vocals for the first time. I heard the show you were told about. *Hesitation Blues* and *Good Shepherd* were very unique without the words. The crowd was very respectful of Jorma's illness. The gig carried on and some history was made!"

Q: "I saw Jack Casady perform in 2003 and I thought the encore was the best song I've heard him do in years. The only problem was we didn't get the title. It was a blues song and sounded like a cover and not an original."

A: "Jack did a great version of a song called *Stop Messing Around*. The writer Peter Green was a former member of Fleetwood Mac during the early days."

Q: "I could listen to Bob Steeler play all day. Is there any band he associates with that plays some Hot Tuna?"

A: "Bob is a tremendous drummer. He plays a handful of shows a year with a Hot Tuna cover band called America's Choice. These guys are not run of the mill musicians. John Zabecki can play *Easy Now* one moment and show off his finger-picking expertise on *Embryonic Journey* the next. Steve Austin is a solid bass-player and Bob Steeler needs no introduction. Not only is it a real good band but the three guys are quality individuals."

Q: "A friend went to see Jorma in the winter of 2006. He was most impressed by a song he didn't recognize called *Praying On The Old Camp Ground*, is that a song that Jorma wrote, and is it unreleased?"

A: "The song is most popular by Mississippi John Hurt. It is a traditional tune that goes back prior to 1930. If you go to www.allmusic.com and type in the name of the song you can enjoy a brief audio portion. It is not available on a Hot Tuna or Jorma record. The good news is Jorma performed it during the spring of 2006 and Hot Tuna (Jorma and Jack) during the beginning of 2006."

Q: "Has Hot Tuna played the song *Genesis* in the past two years?"

A: " At the Merlefest, Wilkes Community College, Wilkesboro, North Carolina, on 4/29/06 they not only played one of the finest tunes ever recorded, but it was the encore."

**Photograph by kind permission of Don Aters. From the Don Aters collection. Don Aters photographer.**

**May not be used without written consent from Don Aters. Jorma Kaukonen from a Hot Tuna performance circa 2006.**

Q: "If you took any person that played with the Jefferson Airplane, how many appeared with Hot Tuna on stage for at least one song from 1968 to the present?"

A: The list is larger than one may think. The names are below."

Signe Anderson- 1/27/88 Starry Night, Portland, Oregon. *High Flying Bird* and *Chauffeur Blues*.

Marty Balin- Played with Hot Tuna on some 1969 and 1970 shows.

Joey Covington- Played with Hot Tuna on many of the 1969 and 1970 shows.

Papa John Creach- Played with Hot Tuna 1970-1973, and many times after.

Paul Kantner- Often forgotten is Paul did two shows with Hot Tuna on 4/3 and 4/13/69, both at The Matrix, San Francisco, California. He played a bunch of gigs with Hot Tuna in 1987 and 1988.

Peter Kaukonen- (Played with the Airplane in 1989) has performed with Hot Tuna several times. The earliest in 1969. He did a bunch of the post Airplane reunion shows in 1989.

Grace Slick- On the 1989 reunion tour performed *Third Week In The Chelsea* and some off-the-cuff material with Jorma and Jack. Please see the main section of the book for all the details."

## Some Jefferson Starship and solo questions-

Q: "Can you tell me where I should know the name Jack Traylor, besides he being friends with Paul Kantner?"

A: "In 1971 Jack's song *Earth Mother* appeared on Paul Kantner's record *Sunfighter*. In 1973 his composition *Flowers In The Night* was featured on the Paul Kantner, Grace Slick, and David Freiberg release *Baron Von Tollbooth And The Chrome Nun*. Jack sang the song as well. Another positive event for him the same year was making his own record with a band Steelwind. The album *Child Of Nature* had a former Airplane member and a future Jefferson Starship guitarist. David Freiberg former Airplane member and currently with the Jefferson Starship played keyboards and Craig Chaquico guitarist of the Jefferson Starship (Starting in 1974), helped out on the six string and even played mandolin. Diana Harris the vocalist, at certain times could get her voice to sound like Grace Slick. Jack Traylor also appeared on Grace Slick's 1974 album *Manhole* and co-wrote the song *Epic (#38)*. Jack Traylor has a website: http://www.kingtet.com/steelwind/."

Q: "Did Grace's 1974 recording *Manhole* fail on the charts because of the total lack of commercial potential?"

A: "Every track on the album seemed to have a different theme. From the subtle acoustic guitar on *Jay* to the Broadway musical style vocals on *Theme From The Movie Manhole*, to the blues of *Better Lying Down*. Grace deserves credit for letting the project be about creativity and not worrying about hit singles. The one flaw that many fans of the Airplane blamed for not purchasing the record or the CD later on was each song felt totally disjointed from the previous. It made *Manhole* sound like the LP was six in one. The number six were the total number of tracks released. In no way were they knocking an esoteric sound, they actually commended it. Their hopes were that the thirty seven minutes and forty seconds would have taken one similar route."

Q: "Did the Grace album *Manhole* get several Jefferson Airplane members together, at least in the studio?"

A: "If you count any amount of time spent with the band, five previous members, and one that was part of the 1989 reunion tour Peter Kaukonen. John Barbata, Jack Casady, David Freiberg, Paul Kantner, and Grace Slick, were all part of the sessions for the LP!"

Q: "Since the Jefferson Starship played shows before *Dragon Fly* got released what songs did they do in the very early days?"

A: "If you were seeing the Jefferson Starship in March of 1974 you would have seen these tunes listed below."

*John's Other*

*Milk Train*

*Volunteers*

*Wooden Ships*

From the 1970 *Blows Against The Empire* album (Paul):

*Sunrise > Hijack > Home > Have You Seen The Stars Tonite > X-M > Starship*

From the 1971 *Sunfighter* album (Paul):

*Diana*

From the 1973 *Baron Von Tollbooth And the Chrome Nun* (Paul & Grace):

*Ballad Of The Chrome Nun*

*Harp Tree Lament*

*Sketches Of China*

From the 1974 *Manhole* album (Grace):

*Better Lying Down*

*Come Again? Toucan*

*Epic (#38)*

*Them From The Movie Manhole*

Q: "When you bring up the record *Dragon Fly* the first thing that comes to mind is *Ride The Tiger*. Is there a song I may have overlooked that is worthy of discussion?"

A: "Maybe the most underrated Jefferson Starship tune, *Come To Life*. The production is very well done, and Craig Chaquico not only plays a very tasty guitar solo, but the sound of the instrument could not have been more perfect for the tune."

Q: "On the 1974 Jefferson Starship tour how many songs did they perform that the Airplane played, <u>regardless</u> if they were on Airplane albums?"

A: "A total of six songs were performed on the 1974 (From verified shows) tour including: *Diana, John's Other, Milk Train, Somebody To Love, Volunteers,* and *Wooden Ships. Diana* was never on an Airplane record. It can be found on Paul Kantner's *Sunfighter* (1971) album. *John's Other* as well was never on a J.A. record. That can be enjoyed on the Hot Tuna live record *First Pull Up, Then Pull Down* from 1971."

300

Q: "To this day I believe the best solo song by any Jefferson Airplane member is *Better Lying Down* from Grace Slick. Did the Jefferson Starship perform the tune in the early days?"

A: "They did play the song from Grace's *Manhole* album in 1974. Not only were they performing it, but the tune written by Grace and Pete Sears went from about three minutes in the studio to some nights over ten minutes on stage."

**Photo by kind permission of Mike Somavilla. From the Mike Somavilla collection.**

**May not be reproduced without the written consent of Mike Somavilla.**

**Photographer unknown.**

**Thanks to C.J. Strauss & Company.**

**This is a promo picture of Grace Slick circa 1974-1975.**

Q: "When *Red Octopus* got released in 1975 is it true that the rock radio stations played several songs from the album for almost two years?"

A: "*Fast Buck Freddie, Miracles, Sweeter Than Honey*, and *Play On Love* were on the radio as often as the sun comes up. Not only the album rock stations that were referred to as AOR (Album Oriented Rock), but the progressive rock stations played the songs often as well. A progressive rock station was one where the disc-jockey could select their own music, without the help of a play list, or consultant."

Q: "When *Spitfire* got released was it doomed before the first listening, because the predecessor had sold as well as it did?"

A: "It would have taken a Herculean effort to equal the accolades of the previous record. What has escaped the memory banks the album did break the Top 5. Besides *St. Charles* there was a terrific track called *Song To The Sun*. Portions of *Dance With The Dragon* were real good too."

Q: "On the 1976 record *Spitfire* was there a song that had potential but didn't seem to end up as strong as it could have?"

A: "*Dance With The Dragon*, could have been a relative of *Ride The Tiger*. There are segments of the song that are catchy and well crafted. The entire five minutes did not grade evenly."

Q: "In the late 1970's I thought I saw the coolest Jefferson Starship video. They were sitting on the floor and playing a song. I don't recall any other details. Was this a dream?"

A: "It exists. The video was from a British TV program Old Grey Whistle Test. The year was 1978, and the title was *Count On Me*. The group members were sitting on the floor and singing the song. It was terrific for its simplicity and not full of Hollywood's production claws. A funny side story is Jesse Barish who wrote the tune had never seen the video, until I sent him a copy."

Q: "Is there a record that Craig Chaquico did session work on that is overlooked?"

A: "The 1977 Commander Cody album *Rock 'N' Roll Again*, Craig plays some guitar. On that record as well was Nicolette Larson. She has a well know version of the Neil Young song *Lotta Love*. A friend of Craig Chaquico suggested her for Grace's replacement (After Grace decided to leave) in the Jefferson Starship!"

Q: "Is it true that before Marty unfortunately left the Jefferson Starship he did rehearse the song *Jane*?"

A: "There have been rumors about this for years. I asked Craig Chaquico to set the record straight. He had no memories of this happening, but Marty Balin thinks he did record an early version. It would have been a fascinating situation if it did come to fruition with Marty on vocals. Do you approach it as a rock and roll song, how about a ballad, or maybe a mid-tempo treatment would have been given to the tune. It is a sin we never got the opportunity to find out."

Q: "When *Freedom At Point Zero* came out and there were no Grace, or Marty, were there fans of the Jefferson Starship, and even of the J.A. that you remember reacting in a less than positive way?"

A: "There are a couple of memories forever etched in the brain. I was working part-time for a great collectable record shop in New York. They sold new and used albums. The day the album got released the first two people that purchased the record came back later and sold it back to the store for credit! A couple of weeks after the recording escaped lock and key a woman comes into the shop and asked me if she purchased a used copy of the album would it give her the right to do with it as she pleases? I informed her as long as she doesn't hurt herself, or any other person, by all means make yourself happy. She took a rock out of her pocketbook and scratched the album repeatedly for five minutes. When she was finished she proceeded to rip the cover into five hundred and eighty-nine pieces. Her final words were "I feel much better. Can I put this in your trash please?" I never saw her again."

Q: "I like the work of Aynsley Dunbar on the albums I have purchased over the years, from Journey to Frank Zappa, and the Jefferson Starship. He is the reason *Freedom At Point Zero* wasn't used as a salad plate. Can you give me a lesser known band he played with, I then can search for their music?"

A: "Aynsley got to replace Ringo Starr in the band Rory Storm & The Hurricanes. If you want to check out Aynsley Dunbar's Retaliation, you will find a blues-based band from circa 1968-1970. They had some interesting compositions. For electric blues many of them are short, but you'll like his playing. You can find some facts about Aynsley at both http://www.airplane.freeserve.co.uk and www.allmusic.com."

Q: "Did Marty Balin help a singer that had a few records in the 1980's with a first name of Jesse?"

A: "Marty worked with Jesse Barish on his albums in 1978 and 1980. Part of Jesse's resume was helping Marty on his self-titled 1981 record (Really called *Balin*), and was the composer for the Jefferson Starship songs *St. Charles* and *Count On Me*. For a more complete bio on Jesse please see my interview with him."

Q: "Is there any positive thing to say about *Modern Times* from 1981, except the joy experienced when the record ended?"

A: "Paul has a terrific track on the album called *Stairway To Cleveland (We Do What We Want)*. The only thing that put a blemish on such a fine song was not having it appear on an album worthy of Paul Kantner."

Q: "When Marty put out the *Balin* LP in 1981 wasn't there another hit single to go with the success of *Hearts*?"

A: "The tune *Atlanta Lady* broke the Top 30 for Marty. *Hearts* had cracked the Top 10."

Q: "I have seen the Airplane twenty-eight times and the Jefferson Starship nineteen. There is a show I attended that Pete Sears played a bass-solo that was so strong you would have thought it was a cross between Jack Casady and John Entwhistle from the Who. (John passed away on 6/27/02). The solo was fairly long and during a hot version of *Jane*. What may help narrow down the date is he did some theatrics with the instrument as well."

A: " On 9/2/84 at the Saratoga Performing Arts Center, Saratoga Springs, New York performance Pete may have played his finest solo. I was working as a disc-jockey in Florida and a guy and his girlfriend that I would often see at one of the local department stores had attended the show. They were talking about Pete's solo for twenty minutes. It must have been tremendous to witness."

Q: "Did Grace Slick sing on a Heart album around 1985?"

A: "Grace and Mickey Thomas, did make appearances on the 1985 album that Heart called *Heart*."

Q: "Can you give me an example of a Marty Balin album that should have been able to please the old fans and maybe make some new ones, but for one reason or another didn't?"

A: "In December of 1991 Marty released a solo album that should have been welcome by both Airplane and Jefferson Starship fans. The CD was called *Better Generation*. Marty's voice was in terrific shape. A song that KBC performed live called *Let's Go* can be found on *Better Generation*, with Marty's fantastic solo representation. Marty also did solo versions of *It's No Secret* and *Volunteers*. The CD finished off with a rendition of *Summer Of Love*. Marty handled his end of the recording perfectly. What did in the project was the production. It is robotic, which made it devoid of any human emotion. The work was the ultimate oxymoron. How can Marty be singing *Volunteers* and the sound be more tailored for some teeny-bopper appearing on a reality singing show? Even if it is one hundred years from today, let somebody take Marty's vocals from the album and get a band to rerecord the songs, with a production team that knows something about the 1960's and early 1970's."

Q: "I was played a tape of a Jefferson Starship gig from 6/14/92. The TLA (Theater Of Living Arts), Philadelphia, Pennsylvania. There was a song that was captivating. It was listed as *Genesis Hall*. Is that from a member of the group?"

A: "*Genesis Hall* is from one of the most respected British folk-rock bands ever, the Fairport Convention. The songwriter Richard Thompson has a large following as a brilliant guitar-player. If you can believe it the album from Fairport Convention came out in 1969 under the title *Unhalfbricking*. There are three Bob Dylan covers on the record, the best being *Million Dollar Bash*."

Q: "I went to a Jefferson Starship show July of 1992. The bass-player didn't look familiar to me. When I asked a few people, they shrugged their shoulders and walked away. Does he have a name and any interesting background?"

A: "He does have a name. David Margen was the bass-player for many years with Santana. He also played with Joey Covington's San Francisco Allstars."

Q: "In August of 1992 I saw the Jefferson Starship play a wonderful set of music. The drummer on stage puzzled everyone, since he was not recognizable to the fans."

A: "The drummer played at least two shows with the band that summer. His name was Jim Bailey. Thank you to Rick Martin for verifying my answer. Thank you to the **'Working Class Rocker'** – Darby Gould for informing me that Jim Bailey played drums in a group with her called Blind Tom."

Q: "I never got to see any of the 1993 Jefferson Starship shows with Signe Anderson. I think I would trade the twenty-two I have attended to go back in time for one with Signe. My question is did they play *Chauffeur Blues*? I am hoping you tell me no, or I'll be crying for at least six days."

A: "They did play *Chauffeur Blues* and *Blues For An Airplane* on some of the Signe gigs. You can pretend that never happened, or I do have a box of tissues handy."

Q: "One of my best memories was when I saw the Jefferson Starship perform in 1993 with Signe Anderson. Can you tell me on the shows she played that year how many songs were played that the Airplane did live, regardless of the year?"

A: "They performed a total of fourteen songs that the Airplane played live between 1965-1972 and 1989. Even if the song <u>was not found</u> originally on an Airplane recording, I am listing it. Looking over the tunes, I could see why it was an intense evening for you."

*America (*Performed by the J.A. in 1989).

*Blues From An Airplane*

*Chauffeur Blues*

*Crown Of Creation*

*High Flying Bird*

*John's Other*

304

*Let's Get Together*

*Miracles* (Performed by the J.A.. in 1989).

*The Other Side Of This Life*

*Papa John's Down Home Blues*

*Starship*

*Volunteers*

*When The Earth Moves Again*

*Wooden Ships*

Q: "I went to see the Jefferson Starship play on 2/6/93 at the Music Hall, Tarrytown, New York. They performed a fantastic song *Kisses Sweeter Than Wine*. What version of that extraordinary song is most noted?"

A: "The Weavers (A band Paul Kantner respects greatly) have the definitive version. Paul has always admired the vocals of band member Ronnie Gilbert."

Q: "I saw a Jefferson Starship show when Trey Sabatelli played drums and not Prairie Prince. What is Trey's background?"

A: "Trey has performed with the Jefferson Starship when Prairie had other commitments. Trey has worked with the Tubes and a 1990's metal band Gone Jackals."

Q: "Can you tell me something Paul Kantner did as a nice gesture during the Jefferson Starship days (Any period) that got overlooked?"

A: "Paul does a lot of charity work behind the scenes that goes unnoticed, but the gesture that comes to mind isn't about charity, but a class act. In 1991 an eight year old girl Rebecca Inez Bockelie wrote a poem called *Get Ready*. Paul took such a liking to her words that he recited the poem during Jefferson Starship and Wooden Ships live shows. He even read the poem at the Rock And Roll Hall Of Fame induction on 1/17/96. The Jefferson Starship played two shows at McCurdy Pavilion, Fort Worden State Park, Port Townshend, Washington, on 8/14/93. He let Rebecca read the poem before the encore started, on both the early, and late show."

Q: "When Jack Casady played in the Jefferson Starship in 1994 did they perform a healthy dose of Airplane material?"

A: "On a typical night the Airplane songs could run about fifty percent of the set. These were some of the great nuggets pulled out for a show on 5/28/94 at the Fillmore Auditorium, San Francisco, California. They are listed below."

*Crown Of Creation*

*Have You Seen The Saucers?*

*Lawman*

*Somebody To Love*

*3/5 Of A Mile In 10 Seconds*

*Today*

*Volunteers*

*White Rabbit*

*Wooden Ships*

Q: "Can you think of something nice the Jefferson Starship did for Papa John's family after he passed away?"

A: "The 1/21/95 Jefferson Starship The Next Generation concert from Los Angeles, California, was a benefit for the wife (Gretchen) of Papa John Creach. Grace Slick made a rare post 1989 stage appearance. No matter the difference in age, from the first time Joey Covington met him until Papa John was taken from us, the musicians were always respectful not only of his talent but of his friendship."

Q: "I have a braggadocios neighbor that wanted in the worst way to tell me something unusual Jack Casady did during the Jefferson Starship show from Tramps, New York City 2/23/95. I was bursting at the seems to find out but didn't want to give the loud and smelly neighbor any enjoyment. Could you fill me in?"

A: "At least the neighbor likes good music. Jack Casady played rhythm-guitar during the song *Triad*. Did you consider giving the neighbor a coupon for deodorant soap?"

Q: "I got to see several Wooden Ships shows and thought they were fantastic. I liked *Show Me The Way To Go Home* so much, that I had always hoped to see the Jefferson Starship perform it. I've seen them seventeen times with no luck. Can you give me a show that they played it?"

A: "There is a terrific venue in New Haven, Connecticut, called Toad's Place. On 3/1/98 during an acoustic gig they played the following during the encores: *When The Earth Moves Again, All Fly Away, Volunteers, Fat Angel*, and *Show Me The Way To Go Home*."

Q: "I went to see a Jefferson Starship show around 2002. They played a tune I enjoyed but know nothing about called *In A Crisis*."

A: "The song you liked can be found on the World Entertainment War (Darby Gould) CD called *Give Too Much*. It came out in the year 2000. To learn about the songs please go to www.amazon.com."

Q: "My favorite song ever is *D, C, B, A-25*. I never heard the Airplane perform it. Did the Jefferson Starship consider playing it ever?"

A: " Not only did they consider it they have done it live. A nice version of the song can be found on the 4/13/02 show from the Elks Club, Webster, Massachusetts. To make the evening even more special they performed *Hey Fredrick*. Any fan in attendance could have enjoyed two songs the Airplane never took to the stage!"

Q: "When Paul Kantner had some of the concerts with special guests circa 2003, what musicians could be found at the shows?"

A: "If we take a look at the 4/5/03 performance from the Marin Center Exhibit Hall, San Rafael, California, Marty Balin was playing with Paul during that period. They were joined by Signe Anderson and Spencer Dryden for *High Flying Bird* and *It's No Secret*. David Freiberg before becoming a full-time member of the band made an appearance for *Blind John*, and Darby Gould the former lead vocalist of the Jefferson Starship was on hand for a few songs as well. Darby has a terrific voice and a sincere appreciation for the past.

Rounding out the cast of characters were Jano Brown drums, Tim Gorman keyboards, Jack Traylor guitar, and vocals, and Bobby Vega on bass."

Q: "I always enjoyed Craig Chaquico as a musician during the Jefferson Starship days. What has he been up to these days?"

A: Craig has put out at least eight new-age/smooth jazz CD's for the label Higher Octave. His website will both catch you up to date and keep you posted on the current news. http://www.craigchaquico.com."

Q: "I was so turned off by the 1980's version of the Starship, I haven't even paid attention to any incarnation of the band the last twenty years. Have things improved the past several years? They didn't get worse I hope."

A: "You will be impressed with both the musicians and the songs Paul Kantner has put on the set lists the past few years. Slick Aguilar plays lead guitar, and sings, David Freiberg sings, Diana Mangano sings, and Chris Smith is on keyboards. The drummer was Prairie Prince, but he went to play on the New Cars reunion tour. (He'll be back). Currently Donnie Baldwin is handling the drums. David Freiberg's wife Linda Imperial sings as well. They often do a great version of *Rock Me Baby*! The songs listed below are not performed all the time, but they have been in the set list. Slick will often play a great instrumental version of the Beatles, *While My Guitar Gently Weeps*."

Count On Me

Darkly Smiling (This was the song the Great Society performed).

Fast Buck Freddie

Good Shepherd

Greasy Heart

It's No Secret

Lather

Lawman

Let's Get Together

Mexico

Plastic Fantastic Lover

Pride Of Man

She Has Funny Cars

The Ballad Of You & Me & Pooneil

Today

Triad

Volunteers

War Movie

We Can Be Together

When The Earth Moves Again

White Rabbit

Who Do You Love

Won't You Try/Saturday Afternoon

Wooden Ships

Q: "I thought *Alexander The Medium* was the greatest post 1969 Airplane tune. Is there a Jefferson Starship show in the past five years that they performed a live version?"

A: "You can find a live version on 5/3/05 from the Hudson Theatre, Hudson, New York. They performed a lot of interesting songs including *D.C.B.A.-25*, *Eskimo Blue Day*, *Sally Go Round The Roses*, and *Triad* (Not in that order)."

Q: "Did Jack Traylor pay homage to Jorma Kaukonen in some way during a Jefferson Starship show in fall of 2004 by playing such a nice version of *Follow The Drinking Gourd*, or does he dig the song?"

A: "Jack did perform *Follow The Drinking Gourd*, on the 10/2/04 concert at the Sweetwater Saloon, Mill Valley, California. Jack paid homage to those (Jorma included) that played folk music in the Bay Area circa 1961-1964."

Q: "I never got to see any of the Marty Balin shows with the Jefferson Starship in 2005. Did Marty sing any non typical songs of brilliance?"

A: "On the 2/19/05 PACC show from Webster, Massachusetts, Marty not only pulled from the vaults *Young Girl Sunday Blues* and *Comin Back To Me*, but the latter was an encore!"

Q: "I visited Germany in June of 2005. Two guys were talking about a Jefferson Starship show that I missed by two days. I couldn't make out the conversation, but it had something to do with the song *Hyperdrive*?"

A: "On 6/9/05 at the Haus Der Jugend, Osnabrück, Germany, Diana decided to sing *Hyperdrive* from the audience. (Thank you to Rick Martin and Jeff Hagen, Jefferson Starship super fans for great documentation of the European shows)."

Q: "Prairie Prince was my favorite Jefferson Starship drummer before going off to play on the New Cars reunion project. Can you tell me if he did any recording with the Grateful Dead?"

A: "Not with the entire band, but with a couple of former members. Prairie appeared with one time Grateful Dead keyboardist Tom Constanten on *Live From California* (The name of the band was Dos Hermanos and released in 1998) and the same year he played on the Missing Man Formation album with the late Vince Welnick (Former Grateful Dead keyboardist)."

Q: "Did The Jefferson Starship do anything special on 10/29/05, for the opening of the Jerry Garcia Amphitheater, McClaren Park, San Francisco, California?"

A: "They did indeed. Slick Aguilar handled the vocals for a great version of *Deal*, with a perfect Garcia inflection. Pete Sears played bass on the song as well as several others."

Q: "What does Mickey Thomas do these days and if it is musically related does he have any Airplane Family members involved?"

A: "Mickey tours with the Mickey Thomas Starship. He is using the former drummer from KBC, Darrell Verdusco."

Q: "Is it true that some hard to find Marty Balin material and maybe unreleased stuff as well, is finally going to be more easily traceable?"

A: "The great news is if you click on www.jbppresentsmartybalin.com, you will start to see the vaults being opened. Thanks to Marty's dad Joe Buchwald."

Q: "Over the past two years I went to see the Jefferson Starship five times. How do we get the word out to people that have the stigma of the 1980's version, that the songs are well done, and with Paul Kantner, Slick on guitar, David Freiberg, and Diana Mangano singing, the shows are full of a team effort and magnificent choices of songs?"

A: "It is imperative that people realize that 1980's Starship and the Jefferson Starship has nothing in common. In fact wasn't the Starship a dream? (A real bad one). There are people such as Paul Crawford, Jeff Hagen, and Rick Martin, that are letting the masses know that the latest Jefferson Starship is a must see. Posting positive messages on Jefferson Starship boards, informing Airplane Family fans of the set lists, and letting as many good folks know when they are playing, are all excellent ways to start breaking the unfair association to the 1980's. If you have a chance to inform any of the music groups on MSN, My Space, and Yahoo about the hard work and dedication the current Jefferson Starship band puts in to each show please do so. The members in the current Jefferson Starship are very down to earth and don't deserve any comparisons to the bad dream of the 1980's."

# Some SVT questions-

**Photo by kind permission of Mike Somavilla.  From the Mike Somavilla collection.**

**May not be reproduced without the written consent of Mike Somavilla.**

**Photographer Charly Franklin.**

**Thank you MSI Records.  This is a promo photo.**

**SVT circa 1981.  Left to right Paul Zahl, Jack Casady, and Brian Marnell.**

Q: "When did the first single from SVT get released?"

A: "The live single from 1979, featured the A-Side of *New Year*, and the B-Side of *Wanna See You Cry*."

Q: "Did history get rewritten when over the past decade or so fans decided that SVT stood for something medically related and not musically related?"

A: "History was rewritten incorrectly. When SVT first came on the scene, it was noted the name came from Jack Casady's bass amplifier and the set up of his equipment. One day it became a cool story to tell that SVT stood for Supra Ventricular Tachycardia. That is a medical condition for excessive heart beat and pulse rate."

Q: "When SVT first started I was positive there was a promotional poster with Bill Gibson (Huey Lewis & The News) as one of the members. When people talk about the group they only mention Jack, Nick Buck, Brian Marnell, and Paul Zahl."

A: "You are correct. Bill Gibson played on a couple of singles and then it was off to Huey land."

Q: "When did SVT put out their album?"

A: "In 1981 they released *No Regrets*, in 2005 it was reissued on CD, with four bonus tracks."

Q: "Did SVT record any well known cover songs on any of their releases?"

A: "The legendary Johnny Cash song *I Walk The Line* can be found on their release called *Extended Play*."

Q: "How was it to see SVT live, if you grew up with the Airplane and Hot Tuna?

A: "I went to see them at one of the many great venues that are no longer around, My Fathers Place, Roslyn, New York. If you went into the show hoping that all of a sudden they would become a new Hot Tuna, you were immensely disappointed. Those that understood the music would be completely unrelated enjoyed something different. The older crowd liked some of the songs and were so-so on the others. If you are interested in SVT's full discography the best place to visit is: http://www.bay-area-bands.com/bab00022.htm. The site did a tremendous job on all the releases of SVT with the proper song titles."

Q: "Did one of the members of SVT pass away?"

A: "Brian Marnell (Vocals, and guitar) died in 1983. It would be nice to keep Brian's memory alive and the bands as well. It is not without possibility that in the future some live shows may see the light of day. I asked Nick Buck about this in the interview section of the book."

# Some KBC Band questions-

Q: "I know the K, B, and C in the KBC Band, however what other people constituted the group?"

A: "Besides three Airplane members Paul Kantner, Marty Balin, and Jack Casady, the band was supported by Slick Aguilar on guitar, Tim Gorman on keyboards, Keith Crossan on saxophone, and Darrell Verdusco on drums."

Q: "How many songs from the album did the KBC Band perform live?"

A: "The band played every song from the self-titled 1986 record. *Mariel*, *It's Not You, It's Not Me* (That is one title), *Hold Me*, *America*, *No More Heartaches*, *Wrecking Crew*, *When Love Comes*, *Dream Motorcycle*, and *Sayonara*."

Q: "How did the KBC Band stretch out a set list with only one album?"

A: "If you can believe it they played twenty-seven non KBC album songs. It was really twenty-six, but I threw in the one time happy birthday for Jack!"

Birthday Serenade For Jack

Borderlands

Can You Feel The Heat

Candles

Crossfire

Dancing With The House On Fire

Girl With The Hungry Eyes

Give This Love A Try

Hide My Heart

I Don't Mind

In The Midnight Hour

It's No Secret

Keep On Rockin' And Rollin'

Let's Go (Available on a Marty solo album released 12/91 called *Better Generation*).

Michoacan

One Hundred Million

Planes

Plastic Fantastic Lover

Ride The Tiger

Solidarity

Spaghetti Western

Summer Of Love

Today

Too Late To Turn Back

Volunteers

Windows Of Heaven

Yes, Yes, Yes

Q: "Of the songs performed during the KBC Band tours, how many did the Airplane perform at least once from 1965-1972 and 1989?"

A: "*America*, *In The Midnight Hour*, *It's No Secret*, *Planes*, *Plastic Fantastic Lover*, *Solidarity*, *Summer Of Love*, *Today*, and *Volunteers*. The KBC Band played *Planes*, *Solidarity*, and *Summer Of Love* before they were put on the 1989 Airplane reunion album and played during the tour."

Q: "There was a great song I heard on the KBC Band tour called *Let's Go*. Is that a tune that Paul Kantner recorded for the *Blows Against The Empire* album?"

A: "That could easily confuse any fan. *Let's Go Together*, (*Blows Against The Empire*) can be remembered by the words "Wherever I go, I see you people." *Let's Go* (*Planet Earth Rock And Roll Orchestra*), can be remembered by the words "Dreamin' of freedom." The song *Let's Go* from KBC has the hook of the tune around the words "Come on let's go, let yourself go." Marty Balin did a great version on the solo album from 1991, *Better Generation*."

Q: "When KBC performed live did they properly mix the album songs, new material, and the classics?"

A: "I wish I could say "Yes, Yes, Yes." There was not enough of the Airplane songs thrown in during each performance. The ones listed a few questions earlier, were not played all in one evening. Even for the Jefferson Starship fans in attendance, *Ride The Tiger* received a thunderous ovation, but the thirst wasn't quenched for more of the same."

## Some Paul Kantner's Wooden Ships questions-

Q: "Am I reading an incorrect set list or did Paul play *Caroline* from the Jefferson Starship, at the 7/19/91 Bottom Line, New York City, early show?"

A: "Wooden Ships did indeed perform the song found on the Jefferson Starship album *Dragon Fly*. It was a nice touch, because Marty Balin is the solo composer of he song."

Q: "Did Paul play the great song *Stairway To Cleveland* during a Wooden Ships show in December of 1991?"

A: "That would have been worth the price of admission.  He did not perform the song on any of the Wooden Ships concerts.  The closest was on 12/14/91 at the IMAC, Huntington, New York.  Paul talked about music censorship and gave the crowd one vocal line from the tune."

Q: "What Airplane songs did Paul perform on the Wooden Ships shows?"

A: "He didn't play all of them at once, but at various shows *Crown Of Creation, High Flying Bird, Madeline Street, The Other Side Of This Life, Volunteers, We Can Be Together, When The Earth Moves Again, and Wooden Ships* were performed."

Q: "Did the audiences accept the newer material more, less or the same than from the KBC Band?"

A: "The fans that went to see Wooden Ships, were more willing to listen to the newer material.  KBC were three important members of the Airplane.  When Wooden Ships performed it was more of finding out what Paul would be playing at that juncture of his career."

Q: "Did Paul do anything on the Wooden Ships tours that were a bit different?"

A: "He read three poems fairly often.  Tim Gorman's keyboards would serve as a backdrop.  The response was very positive.  They sounded good, because of his belief and conviction.  The titles were: *For The Good Of Us All, Holocosto Optimista*, and, *The Police And The National Guard*."

Q: "During the Wooden Ship's tour I saw Paul twice play a fantastic song called *Show Me The Way To Go Home*.  What can you tell me about it?"

A: "Paul did such a tremendous job, it sounded as if he wrote it.  The tune was composed by Jim Campbell and Reginald Connelly.  The two best versions are from Emerson, Lake And Palmer (*Works Volume 2*) and Mr. Kantner.  Both Paul and ELP played the song as an encore.  Unfortunately Paul did not record his rendition for a CD."

Q: "Are there a couple of Wooden Ships shows that stand above the rest?"

A: "While the concerts were very well done on a nightly basis, two come to mind.  1/18/92 at the I-Beam, San Francisco, California.  The show started off with Paul and Tim Gorman.  Darby Gould joined them for *Shadowlands, All Fly Away, I'm On Fire, We Can Be Together, Volunteers*, and *The Other Side Of This Life*.  On 2/13/94 for the Seva Benefit, at the Masonic Temple, San Francisco, Wooden Ships consisted of Paul, Jack Casady, Diana Mangano, and Tim Gorman.  David Crosby helped them on *Have You Seen The Stars Tonite* and Paul's son Alexander lent a hand for *The Baby Tree*, and a poem (Alexander read this alone) called *Get Ready*.  That was written by Rebecca Inez Bockelie, when she was eight."

Q: "Was there a song on any Wooden Ships show that surprised people how strong it sounded live?"

A: "The tune that can be found on the Jefferson Starship album *Deep Space/Virgin Sky* called *I'm On Fire*.  It flowed nicely and Paul was able to convey his thoughts exceptionally well."

Q: "What song played during a Wooden Ships show may have been a surprise to a casual fan how well the crowd reacted to it?"

A: "*The Baby Tree*, which can be found on Paul's album *Blows Against The Empire*.  The reaction was always highly spirited."

Q: "I got to see eight Wooden Ships live dates.  I thought Tim Gorman worked amazingly well with Paul Kantner.  Does Tim have a record I may have overlooked?  I purchased his CD *Celtic Loop* already."

A: "His record from 1996 *Classical Daydreams* is often forgotten about. You can go to www.allmusic.com and listen to excerpts."

Q: "When over the years fans discuss the cool Wooden Ships gigs what seems to be their choice as the best song to have opened with?"

A: " The winner was three songs performed to start the festivities from *Blows Against The Empire*, referred to as the *Blows Against The Empire Suite*. That included *Hijack > Have You Seen The Stars Tonite > Starship*."

# Chapter 12: Interviews From 2006 "What I Say Is True"

It would be impossible to find the words to thank all those that were kind enough to have consented for an interview during the writing of the book. **I have never and will never take it for granted how fortunate I am.**

In a utopian society the interviews would have been equal in length and all those that had spoken possess the same gift of gab. In no way should a short answer be misconstrued for being uncooperative, aloof, and or indifferent.

We often forget the musicians we listen to, and the athletes we cheer are not insusceptible from illness, loss of a loved one, and or exhibiting human emotions. **I bring this to the surface to better illustrate why the premise of the book was to focus on the voluminous masterpieces created by, and performed by members of the Airplane Family, and their San Francisco friends.**

It has never been my intention to create a Supermarket Rag Sheet. While I am all too aware of the Airplane Family's tragedies such as divorce, substance abuse, and accidents, the reason why all of us have taken the flight to *Rock And Roll Island* are to recapture the phenomenal memories of the past, discover some new artifacts, and to preserve them in the most fortified time-capsule ever.

I've often read articles or books where the writer acts as if the spoken word is a private conversation between them and their guest, making it impossible to follow a story if you aren't supplied the pertinent information. During the interviews I have made sure if a name or band isn't familiar to give some short information. Enjoy the history lesson from the artists themselves, as they turn the clock back, and articulate sometimes with quick or dry wit how they helped build an island of rock and roll that is ceaseless.

**Slick Aguilar- Jefferson Starship, KBC Band, and Paul Kantner's Wooden Ships.**

Photograph by kind permission of Don Aters and may not be reproduced without the written consent of

Don Aters.

From the Don Aters collection.  Don Aters photographer.

Circa 2005 from a Jefferson Starship performance.

Craig: "Slick, it is nice to spend some time with you today. Thank you for willing to shed some light on your history."

Slick Aguilar: "You're welcome."

Craig: "The first time we were scheduled to speak, you were stuck with the Jefferson Starship in a snow storm. Glad every member is okay."

(Slick laughs and is ready to begin the interview).

Craig: "A constant that has always been talked about is your diversity with the guitar. Does that come with having been in such a wide range of bands from K.C. & The Sunshine, Buddy Miles (played with Jimi Hendrix), David Crosby to Marty Balin in 1984?"

Slick Aguilar: "That is part of it. I also listened to a lot of jazz players. Early on, the likes of Joe Pass and Larry Carlton."

Craig: "You enjoyed the sound of the Crusaders (Larry Carlton)?"

Slick Aguilar: "Definitely. I also enjoyed Lee Ritenour. I tried to get my hands on every recording I could. Do you remember a singer Maria Muldaur?"

Craig: "In 1974 *Midnight At The Oasis* was selling all over the globe."

Slick Aguilar: "She worked with a guitar-player that was incredible. His name was Amos Garrett. He played with a bunch of people, like Elvin Bishop and Paul Butterfield. She introduced me to Amos. I recorded a tape of nothing but his guitar solos. I listened to it over and over again. All these things would benefit me later on. Another guy that was a prodigy and teaching a class at seventeen was Pat Metheny. I was told that there is a player that I had to check out. He was on the campus of Miami-Dade (College) and there are two guys sitting on a bench. I walk over and introduce myself as Mark and ask which one of you is Pat Metheny? It turns out I get to sit in on his classes for a couple of years."

Craig: "Not a bad way to spend time in school. How about Pat not having a drivers license, but having the ability to teach a college class?"

Slick Aguilar: "That's funny Craig. Since it was free for me, it was that much better. The thing about Pat was the sound and the melody that would come out of the guitar."

Craig: "Slick going back to the 1970's, you were in a band that is legendary in Florida. I was a disc-jockey in the West Palm Beach market 1983-1986, and there were countless people that would talk about the group Tattoo. What were your memories of the group?"

Slick Aguilar: "The memories were excellent ones. I didn't want to play the Top 40. Tattoo was one of the first *jam* bands in the region. We had a solid reputation. As a matter of fact, we were joined on stage by members of Pure Prairie League (Country-rock band that had major success with a song called *Amie*) when they were in town. There was the Grateful Dead influence of being able to extend the songs. One of the places we played all the time was The Hut."

Craig: "Word had gotten out that you were something special. Didn't this lead to you joining David Crosby's band?"

Slick Aguilar: "He had seen us play previously. I think it was almost two years later he needed a guitar-player and he remembered me."

Craig: "When a decision has to be made to leave a band, in this case Crosby only needed you, is there a certain selfishness that has to win out over friendships?"

318

Slick Aguilar: "It was a no-brainer. If you ask any of the guys or any musicians, there was only one way to go. Anyone would want that chance."

Craig: "Have there been any projects you have been involved with that come to mind where they may not have been commonly known, but were both fun and rewarding in a musical sense?"

Slick Aguilar: "There is a guy named Rick O'Berry. He was a trainer for Flipper."

Craig: "Luckily the cool dolphin, not the band."

Slick Aguilar: (Slick laughs). "He was big into saving the whales. There were shows that I did with Timothy Schmit (The Eagles) and Richard Bell (Janis Joplin). It wasn't a major tour, or anything, but it was nice."

Craig: "Are there disappointments that the KBC Band (Kantner, Balin & Casady) didn't get the commercial reaction they should have; especially with three key Airplane members?"

Slick Aguilar: "Clive Davis, who has an amazing talent for going with the flow, flew out to see us. I was told that he rarely does this, and if he is seeing you he believes in the project. He had dealings with the Grateful Dead, Whitney Houston, and Billy Ocean. We did have our moments. The video of America was number nine on MTV and the first single, *It's Not You, It's Not Me* was number five on the AOR (Album Oriented Rock) charts. We weren't able to deliver the second album."

Craig: "Marty did a fantastic job on one of the tunes that would sometimes be an encore, *Sayonara*. There was the unique version of the Airplane tune *Plastic Fantastic Lover* done live with the horn arrangement."

Slick Aguilar: "That idea was mine. If you go listen to the Little Feat record, *Down On The Farm*, the title cut has a lick that inspired the horn arrangement for *Plastic Fantastic Lover*." (Slick hums the part (very well).

Craig: "I'm sure Lowell George (Their guitar-player who died 6/29/79) is smiling at you from heaven. What do you think most readily led you to becoming a member of the Jefferson Starship?"

Slick Aguilar: "I had the connection with Marty from 1984. I also had two things that Paul Kantner liked. I played with his good friend David Crosby and was friends with a guy that he admired a lot, Freddie Neil."

Craig: "Those two things are true, but you are being modest. It didn't hurt that you could play the wide range of music that would be in the nightly sets."

Slick Aguilar: "I appreciate that."

Craig: "When you joined the Jefferson Starship were there songs you looked forward to playing on stage?"

Slick Aguilar: "The last one. Just kidding! We joke with one of the roadies and ask his favorite song of the show and he'll reply "The last one." Seriously, you have to make every note count. All the tunes in the set list have to be given equal treatment. There are a couple of ones that come to mind. *Pooneil (The Ballad Of You And Me And Pooneil)* and *The Other Side Of This Life* by Freddie Neil."

Craig: "*The Ballad Of You And Me And Pooneil*, has such energy and the ability to stretch out on the improvisational section. *The Other Side Of This Life*, is another example of a song you are able to change around from gig to gig."

Slick Aguilar: "Freddie Neil for a couple of years was the man in the Village (A section of New York City)."

Craig: "It is a shame we lost him in 2001 (7/7/01). Did you and Paul ever discuss how others in his genre, seemed to get more commercial attention? He certainly had amazing respect from his peers."

Slick Aguilar: "I have never talked with Paul about that. As a person that knew Freddie, he wasn't willing to compromise his privacy. It was impossible to get him on stage to even play a song with his friends during the 1970's. He put it something like this, "Why should the ex-wife get half.""

Craig: "Paul gives a nice tribute, anytime *The Other Side Of This Life* is performed and in 1987 when Paul joined Hot Tuna for some shows, he did a wonderful *That's The Bag I'm In*."

Slick Aguilar: "Freddie was an influence in Paul's career and many others of his time. Another great song by Freddie is *Everybody's Talkin*."

Craig: "Not only a fantastic song, but a perfect example of a tune people think somebody else wrote. When you bring up the song, it is always Harry Nilsson's version they think of. What are your recollections of the 1998 record with long time friend Kevin Hurley, *Brothers By Other Mothers*?"

Slick Aguilar: "We were an eleven piece band. Not exactly right for going out on the road."

Craig: "Slick's very own orchestra!"

Slick Aguilar: "We had solid players. Darby Gould (Jefferson Starship), Donny Baldwin an excellent drummer that played in the Jefferson Starship and has filled in for Prairie Prince now and then, we had the horn section from Elvin Bishop's group and Tim Gorman (keyboards) who played with Paul Kantner in both Wooden Ships and the Jefferson Starship. He also played with the Jefferson Airplane on the 1989 reunion tour. There was money behind the project and we were able to do our own thing. In the end there were some decisions that didn't go right, representation for one. The record never got released."

Craig: "To this day it has never seen any commercial distribution?"

Slick Aguilar: "None at all."

Craig: "That is a good lead-in to the next question. Have you considered with all the archival material you are sitting on from Tattoo, Kevin Hurley, and the Slick Aguilar Band, to release the music by either mail order and or to sell it at the shows?"

Slick Aguilar: "That isn't a bad idea. I appreciate that the fans want to hear every note. I'm that way with Pat Metheny. I'll listen to an album and then want to know what the music sounds like live. Maybe I can work on that."

Craig: "Hope you go through with it, and I am happy to write the liner notes."

Slick Aguilar: "I'll have to remember that."

Craig: "Would Paul consider some archival Airplane being released? The other day I was talking with a fan and we both think it is a shame some of the brilliant gems are not available for the masses. The New York City January 8, 1967 show with Mike Bloomfield playing with them on *East West Jam*. Only a handful of people have been able to hear this."

Slick Aguilar: "I'm with you, man. I have certain people that I play with that want every note recorded. If I burp it is on one of their tapes. In order for that to happen, we have to get Paul to listen to music."

Craig: "Paul doesn't listen to music?"

Slick Aguilar: "In the car, he'll read a book. That's why we don't ride with him. (Slick chuckles). Once in a great while he puts on a Weavers tape."

320

**Photograph by kind permission of Don Aters and may not be reproduced without the written consent of**

**Don Aters.  From the Don Aters collection.  Don Aters photographer.**

**Circa 2005 from a Jefferson Starship performance.**

Craig: "You are always getting compliments on the message boards and at the live shows for two amazing covers. The first is the October 29, 2005 dedication of the Jerry Garcia Amphitheater, where you performed *The Deal*. The instrumentation and the vocal inflection was one of the finest covers ever."

Slick Aguilar: "Thanks, man that is really nice."

Craig: "How did you decide for that night to perform *The Deal*?"

Slick Aguilar: "I had done it in the past and loved the change from the first to the third major. There were the great lyrics by Robert Hunter. I noticed a lot of nice messages on the boards after that show."

Craig: "Another great part of the gig was having Pete Sears a former Jefferson Starship member, sit in during some of the set."

Slick Aguilar: "That was excellent. He played bass! It's nice to have a rock and roll band with a bass-player."

Craig: "We always root for Jack Casady to find time. The other cover is the instrumental of the Beatles, *While My Guitar Gently Weeps*. How did that end up in the set?"

Slick Aguilar: "George Harrison is one of those great players that can use melody in his solos. There were a lot of his tunes to consider. I thought about *While My Guitar Gently Weeps* as an instrumental. When we rehearsed it, it sounded fine. I like to throw in bits of songs that have instrumental appeal. "I do a couple of Jeff Beck bits.""

Craig: "*Cause We Ended As Lovers*."

Slick Aguilar: "The other is *Freeway Jam*. I hope if I ever make a true solo album, Jeff could play on it."

Craig: "Yes to both. Make a solo record and get Jeff to be on at least on track." (There is a chuckle by Slick). Did Paul Kantner have any thoughts of Prairie Prince playing drums for the New Cars reunion?"

Slick Aguilar: "Yes. He said, "When is he coming back?""

Craig: "You have to respect a man of few words. Does Paul have a drummer in mind for the Jefferson Starship?"

Slick Aguilar: "Paul asked me the other night about my thoughts. I told him that Donny Baldwin who played with the band in the past and did some gigs when Prairie had other commitments, would be the right fit for the band."

Craig: "Since he played with the group in the past, why not keep it in the family?"

Slick Aguilar: "Exactly my thoughts. Keep it in the family, man."

Craig: "How much longer do you think the *Jefferson Starship* can fly?"

Slick Aguilar: "I asked Paul, do you have a retirement fund? He told me yes, when he drops dead!"

Craig: "Isn't it fantastic after over forty years, he stills has the energy and passion. Instead of going through the motions, he's picking out songs that he didn't play on, such as *Darkly Smiling* from the Great Society."

Slick Aguilar: "Isn't that a fantastic song man? It's a good one for Diana Mangano."

Craig: "Let's hope you guys keep soaring for many years. Thank you very much for your time and I wish you the best for the band and your other projects."

Slick Aguilar: "You're welcome. Nice talking with you."

# Signe Anderson- Jefferson Airplane and Jefferson Starship.

Craig: "Signe, thank you for joining me tonight. I hope better times are ahead with your health."

Signe Anderson: "Thank you for letting me be part of the book."

Craig: "When you were singing at the Drinking Gourd, San Francisco, was it Marty, or Paul that first heard you?"

Signe Anderson: "It was Marty."

Craig: "Were you performing with a band?"

Signe Anderson: "I just sat in with anybody that would let me. We were playing folk oriented music."

Craig: "Did it appear that Marty got interesting in your ability the first time he watched you, or do you think he may have checked you out on more than one occasion?"

Signe Anderson: "I never asked him! My brother John Toly was the bartender, Larry Vargo (Once the bass-player in the Town Criers) had the music shop next store. Larry, and Marty worked together with the New California Singers. Marty would hang out at both the music shop and the Drinking Gourd. He had heard me and one night somebody told me that Marty was interesting in talking with me. Marty basically said to me that he wanted to start a band and wanted to know if I were interested. I said that I love music and would love to do it. It wasn't a planned thing. That was about it. We just said let's do it."

Craig: "Was there any audition for the band?"

Signe Anderson: "No, I never had to audition for anything. He heard me sing and that was good enough. You can play any tune, or change keys, I would follow anyone at anytime, with any harmony. I didn't do like solo work. I am a filler, you know. Granted all my life I have done solos, but my love was to make the harmony. I could follow anybody, they could change keys on me six times in one song, and I would still follow them. That was a main reason that Marty's ears paid attention."

Craig: "When Marty asked you to join the band were Bob Harvey (Original bass-player) and Jerry Peloquin (Original drummer) already hired?"

Signe Anderson: "Marty had talked to me about a band forming. Marty had a friend Paul Kantner that was in San Jose at the time. There was a time frame before I met Paul. I think that Jerry and Bob were working with Marty already. At the time it was very casual. Nobody thought of going on to great things. We loved music and wanted to play. Paul recruited Jorma and we were on our way."

Craig: "Do you recall performing any songs with Bob Harvey and Jerry Peloquin that you didn't play once they left the band?"

Signe Anderson: "I did a tune that Marty brought to the band called *Strawberries* (A traditional song with rhythm and blues singer Jerry Butler having the most well known version. You can hear a clip of the song at www.allmusic.com. Under choice select song, and type the title). It wasn't one of our songs. One line goes like this, "Love has a fresh strawberry taste." The tune was long gone when Jerry, and Bob had left. That makes me think we had an album worth of material in the can after we did the first one."

Craig: "It was a shame that all the great tunes didn't get released until the band had broken up. Finally in 1974 *Early Flight* got issued."

Signe Anderson: "RCA pulled a lot of things out. Later on they used the music. You have *Early Flight* for example and the *Jefferson Airplane Loves You* box set."

Craig: "When the final line-up was in place for the recording of *Takes Off*, did you have a feeling the band was something special?"

Signe Anderson: "I knew it. The combination between my voice and Marty made good music together. You know what Craig, they'll never put me in rock and roll history, or the Rock Hall Of Fame."

Craig: "Signe, those in the know have always been aware of your talents and contributions in the early days. *Chauffeur Blues* doesn't sound right if it didn't come from your voice."

Signe Anderson: "Grace Slick is considered the first vocalist of the Jefferson Airplane. As far as most people are concerned Grace was the first. The reason the J.A. got to be J.A. and later the Jefferson Starship was because of what we started in 1965. I spent my honeymoon September 18, of 1965 in the house in the Hollywood hills with my husband and all the boys in the band."

Craig: "What memories do you have of recording the *Takes Off* record, and was it nerve-racking, and a feeling of elation?"

Signe Anderson: "The record company didn't know what to do with us. Marty kept saying did you check our levels? They would say yes each time. He would tell them that I didn't sing in rehearsal and when it is my turn I will be louder than you have the settings. I ended up blowing up a one hundred thousand dollar board at RCA."

Craig: "They wouldn't listen. Did that happen during one of the takes of *Chauffeur Blues*?"

Signe Anderson: "It was during *Chauffeur* Blues, all that money down the tubes." (Signe laughs).

Craig: "Did you go into the studio with a formula?"

Signe Anderson: "I wanted to record my vocals as the band played. I wasn't interested in tracks being put down on top of other tracks. We had songs in the can, but they would want something else."

Craig: "The first time you heard a completed take of one of the songs such as *Let's Get Together*, did it sound pleasant to you?"

Signe Anderson: "Absolutely. It was good. Now with remastered CD's, it's beautiful. We were pioneers in many ways. What we performed live we would sound three times better than what you heard in the studio. We didn't overdub the record an immense amount. You know a lot of the groups of that time when they made the recordings they made them sound so much fuller and had so many tracks. With the J.A. there were six people that didn't embellish the constant overdubs. We didn't strive to make it sound like we had forty musicians, with fifteen vocalists. We were clear on the recording we wanted. When you saw us in concert the show was ten times better than the recording. Some of the other bands it was the other way around, and it sucked."

Craig: "Would that be one of the reasons the Airplane built such a faithful concert audience?"

Signe Anderson: "Sure. We could take what you heard on the vinyl recording and not only duplicate it but better it many times over."

Craig: "Do you have favorite tracks on the *Takes Off* record besides *Chauffeur Blues*?"

Signe Anderson: "I loved everything we ever did. There isn't one that you would throw away. I'm happy they finally released the songs on *Early Flight* that they wouldn't in the 1960's. I love all that music. Every bit of it was lovely."

Craig: "When you decided to leave the band to raise a family, had your path crossed with Grace Slick?"

Signe Anderson: "We would say hello to each other."

Craig: "Did you have any interesting offers to perform when you were watching your kids grow up?"

Signe Anderson: "In 1970 when I was pregnant with my second child, Steve Miller contacted me. He wanted to know if I would sing with a band that he was going to put together. I said this isn't a good time. He really wanted me to be the female vocalist. I was pregnant and told him that I have to say no. I love the fact he thought of me, but the family came first. My other daughter just turned forty and I was so glad to spend the last three days with her. She is a nurse."

Craig: "That is tremendous. You had told me how much you looked forward to seeing her."

Signe Anderson: "It was wonderful. She pampered me."

Craig: "When you left the Airplane did you keep an ear out when they released a record?"

Signe Anderson: "I always did. In fact here is a story for you. Years later the Jefferson Starship was putting together the "Red" album. What was the title?"

Craig: "*Red Octopus*."

Signe Anderson: "That's right it had *Miracles* on it. I only go by colors for album titles. I had been playing in Portland with Carl Smith & The Natural Gas Company. They were a big band with all horns. I saw Marty Balin. He played *Miracles* for me. I loved it. I told him what you really need to do is put horns on the song. If you put horns on the song it would wow the record buyer. When the album came out, he sent me a special copy. I influenced that, and am thrilled he listened."

Craig: "That is great that Marty listened to the suggestion. What was your impression the first time you heard *Surrealistic Pillow*?"

Signe Anderson: "I liked it. Honestly I liked everything they did. I wished Grace was not as afraid as she was when she performed. She and I in the years that followed talked about this. She was afraid of the audience and I took a step up in front of the audience. I loved performing live. It is possible that fear caused her to have some problems with drugs and alcohol. We talked during a concert that the Starship performed in Portland. Mickey Thomas dedicated the show to my youngest daughter and let her sit on a speaker the entire show. She loved that. Grace and I talked about the fact she was afraid to perform live. It was never comfortable for her. I was most happy on the stage."

Craig: "That is an interesting view on why Grace may have unfortunately had problems with substances."

Signe Anderson: "I think so. I am convinced of it. If she felt comfortable in her space, you may have seen more from her. She is a talent that is unbelievable."

Craig: "When the kids got older, did you ever think that it would be nice even if for the summer only to offer help on a recording session, or be part of a mini tour?"

Signe Anderson: "What I would have liked to do here in Portland, was find a piano-player that I loved so much and loved me so much that I can sit in a piano bar and sing my heart out. I would have done songs from the 1920's-1990's. I have always said I am a singer of songs. I am not a rock, soul, folk, or blues singer. I can sing anything. I rather sing music than do anything. Now I don't have the chops for it. I was intended to be a dancer. I broke my neck at nineteen. The next best thing to dancing was to sing. It has always been about the music."

Craig: "One of the great nights in rock and roll was when you showed up with Spencer Dryden for the KBC show at the Fillmore Auditorium, San Francisco, on 11/27/85. (Bill Graham Productions 20th Anniversary). Which person contacted you, and what was it like singing *It's No Secret* and *Plastic Fantastic Lover*?"

Signe Anderson: "Bill Graham contacted me. When it was time for *Plastic Fantastic Lover* I was out of my element. I know nothing and stood there. It was out of my ballpark. It is better to not do it at all, if you don't do it right."

Craig: "How much time were you given that Bill Graham wanted you at the show?

Signe Anderson: "It was done by the seat of my pants. I can do that very well."

Craig: "Prior to that were you working with any bands on a steady basis?"

Signe Anderson: "In the 1970's I worked with Carl Smith & The Natural Gas Company. It had to be from about 1973-1978. I left but would go back and do a few things with them. We were a ten, sometimes twelve piece band with a lot of horns."

Craig: "The next Signe appearance was for a Hot Tuna show 2/27/88 at the Starry Night, Portland, Oregon. That was during the time Paul Kantner was playing with Jorma and Jack. You got to sing *High Flying Bird* and *Chauffeur Blues*. How did that come about?"

Signe Anderson: "When they were coming to town they let me know. It was nice to see everybody."

Craig: "In 1993 you were part of a terrific tour with the Jefferson Starship that had Paul, Jack, and Papa John. How did you decide to go back on the road for a few months? What was it like to work with Papa John?"

Signe Anderson: "I loved Papa John dearly. He loved me too. We had a good rapport. To answer your question I was asked to be part of the band. Nobody had asked before."

Craig: "If you could go back in history would you have volunteered to be part of some of the Jefferson Starship tours?"

Signe Anderson: "I would never have volunteered."

Craig: "Did Paul Kantner call you in late 1992 to see if you were interested?"

Signe Anderson: "It was going to be a big chunk out of the year. I talked it over with the family. My second husband and I have now been married thirty years. It was an important decision to decide if the road would be the right choice. I am so fond of my husband, that I couldn't take off and go do my thing, without discussing the situation with him. I have always been family oriented."

Craig: "The fans were happy to see you back. What was it like performing Airplane songs that you hadn't done prior such as *Wooden Ships* and *Volunteers*?"

Signe Anderson: "I loved it. We did a bunch of good things. We also played things that Grace hadn't done, but Darby Gould and Diana Mangano had. All of it I wouldn't change. I have no regrets. I did the best I could do. Some of the songs sounded great, some may have sounded terrible. I had three days to memorize the lyrics of songs I hadn't done. Paul sent many of the songs to me to learn. When I got to San Francisco to see the band, we had to pull it off in three days. I think we did."

Craig: "When you finished your commitments for the 1993 tour, had you considered staying on for the next tour?"

Signe Anderson: "I hadn't thought of going any further. You know after all time goes on. I had to move on."

Craig: "You must have been so proud and touched when your daughter Onateska (Often misspelled Oneteska) was on stage singing *High Flying Bird* with you at the Waterfront Park, Portland, Oregon show on 8/13/93. How did that come about?"

Signe Anderson: "I was very proud. It was a wonderful evening for the family. Both Marty and Paul suggested she sing one song with me. I'll never forget that. She is the younger daughter."

Craig: "There was another tremendous moment on the 1993 tour. Paul had always loved a poem written by Rebecca Inez Bockelie. The poem was titled *Get Ready* and she was eight when she first had written it. On the 8/14/93 performance at McCurdy Pavilion, Fort Worden State Park, Port Townshend, Washington, Paul let Rebecca recite the poem prior to the encore on both the early, and late show. Paul was so touched by the poem he even recited it at the Rock And Roll Hall Of Fame inductions. Do you remember the show?"

Signe Anderson: "I absolutely remember the night. It was beautiful."

Craig: "What were your thoughts of meeting Darby Gould and Diana Mangano?"

Signe Anderson: "I have always been fond of the work they have done and the things they have done. They were wonderful to me. They made me feel good."

Craig: "On 1/17/96 when the Jefferson Airplane was inducted to the Rock And Roll Hall Of Fame, at the Waldorf Astoria Hotel, New York City, were you contacted to be part of the festivities, especially when Grace didn't want to be there because she thought old people looked silly playing rock and roll?"

Signe Anderson: "No I was never contacted."

Craig: "Was that a surprise that none of the band members made overtures to have you be a part of the induction?"

Signe Anderson: " It was a surprise, it also wasn't. It seemed it wasn't until many years later that they considered there were two female vocalists during the bands history."

Craig: "When you performed live for the final time on 4/5/03 at the Marin Center Exhibit Hall, San Francisco, was the feeling one of happiness, or sorrow?"

Signe Anderson: "It was happiness. Slick Aguilar played his heart out. Spencer Dryden played his heart out, and I sang mine out (*High Flying Bird* and *It's No Secret*). I have to point out that I hit every note! (Signe laughs)."

Craig: "Signe, it is hard to put into proper words how special of a person you are to talk with me for the book with all that is going on. May the coming months bring you and family the best of health. Thank you for your wonderful insight today."

Signe Anderson: "Thank you for the kind words. Best of luck with the book."

**I have to point out that Signe is one in a million! She is recovering from breast cancer (Please contact me about helping with her medical expenses) and didn't want to miss being part of the book.**

**Please make it known you are wishing her well and would like to help.**

The Airplane Man thanks you all.

# Kenny Aronoff- Jefferson Airplane drummer on the 1989 reunion tour.

Craig: "It is a pleasure to finally be able to speak with you."

Kenny Aronoff: "Thanks for letting me be a part of the book. I wanted to speak with you sooner, but the schedule has been unbelievable."

Craig: "That's actually a good thing. You finished a session with Rod Stewart, and are playing with John Fogerty (Creedence Clearwater Revival). We can talk a bit about the demand on your time later on. When the Airplane decided to fly again for the 1989 tour, how long before the first show were you contacted to play with them live?"

Kenny Aronoff: "I was asked originally if I would like to be part of the reunion record (*Jefferson Airplane*). When the record was being made the band wanted to know what my schedule would be for the coming months. They needed to have a drummer for the live shows. We began if I remember correctly making the record in the early part of the year. As for an exact date that I was able to agree to the tour, nothing is coming back to me."

Craig: "Were you surprised originally when you were asked to play on the record and perform on tour that Paul and Grace would go outside the Jefferson Family for a drummer?"

Kenny Aronoff: "The first thing was how excited I became. When I was a little kid that was one of the bands I listened to. I loved hearing *White Rabbit* on the radio. I bought *Surrealistic Pillow* and loved it. I wasn't surprised about getting the call, but was grateful to be able to do it! Spencer Dryden had health issues. The band reached outside the Airplane Family for that reason."

Craig: "I found it fascinating how badly they wanted one specific person and that person was you. Paul talked so glowingly about you during the interview. He seemed determined to have you on stage with the Airplane."

Kenny Aronoff: "That is cool. Coming from Paul Kantner how could I not appreciate those words. The only sad thing was the thing didn't keep going. The tour should have lasted forever. I was so into being part of that band. Walking on stage and seeing the hippies and the older fans waiting for the first notes of *She Has Funny Cars* was so cool. Getting to play *White Rabbit*, *Somebody To Love*, and *Crown Of Creation* was amazing. Then you have Grace Slick singing up there. The fun goes on with Marty Balin, and Paul, and the Hot Tuna set. I got to play at a rally for food in Washington, D.C."

Craig: "That was the final night of the flight. October 7th of 1989, it was the March For The Homeless."

Kenny Aronoff: "I got to talk with Bill Graham (Legendary promoter, and one time manager of the band). Bill had a meeting in the hotel room. They allowed me in. It was cool. Then people tell me it was like going back in time. Really great stuff."

Craig: "When the rehearsals started for the tour did things come together quickly for you?"

Kenny Aronoff: "For guys like Randy Jackson (Zebra) and I it came together quickly. We both had done heavy studio session work. It was like dude show up and know your parts and the other guys had played the songs so long they were fine. It came together quickly. All the dynamics were jelling quickly. That is an interesting group of people. I liked the way they did things as a democracy. Each person can voice their own opinion. If you consider that all the members had their own lawyers and crew, it was great that each voice got time to be heard."

Craig: "Did you rehearse any songs that didn't get played on the tour?"

Kenny Aronoff: "I don't recall any that didn't get played."

Craig: "I had asked Paul this question and he wasn't sure. After the opening night of the tour *The Other Side Of This Life* didn't get performed again. Any circumstances come to mind?"

Kenny Aronoff: "Wow, you got all sorts of data in your brain. I'm not sure of anything specific. The good thing was the band was head strong about what would work on stage. I mean that in a great way. They wanted it to be good. They really cared. These are super intelligent people in the band."

Craig: "For four of the shows on the tour you did something rather interesting. Grace would always come on stage for the last Hot Tuna song. Jorma, Jack, and Grace would play *Third Week In The Chelsea.* On a few of the gigs you joined them on drums. How did that come about?"

Kenny Aronoff: "Jorma and Jack told me if I ever wanted to come out and play on the song to go for it. A few nights I did."

Craig: "It was nice that you blended in during the song, but enhanced it as well."

Kenny Aronoff: "Thanks. They wanted me to join Hot Tuna. I had too much stuff already scheduled. I couldn't do it. I wanted to do it. I would have loved to have been in the Hot Tuna home."

Craig: "Michael Falzarano had mentioned that Hot Tuna wanted you for the 1990 live shows. He thought very highly of your playing."

Kenny Aronoff: Wow! Wow! That is so cool to hear. It is really cool, that these people are saying such nice words. As the new guy it was nice to be able to talk with Paul Kantner, Grace, and Marty. Paul has the best debating skills. He can do it better than anybody."

Craig: "One night on the tour 9/16/89 Pacific Amphitheater, Costa Mesa, California, *White Rabbit* didn't get played. Did something strange occur for that to have been left off the set list?"

Kenny Aronoff: "*White Rabbit* didn't get played. Holy whatever. That makes no sense. You can't skip that tune. I don't remember."

Craig: "Any special memories of the 1989 Airplane tour?"

Kenny Aronoff: "Grace had a hilarious sense of humor. You could tell her anything. The entire band was like that."

Craig: "Did it appear to you during the tour the band was having fun on stage?"

Kenny Aronoff: "I did get the feeling they were having fun. It was a short tour, but something that made many people happy."

Craig: "In 1990 you worked on the Bob Dylan CD *Under The Red Sky*. Do you have any interesting tales?"

Kenny Aronoff: "The first session was four different days. I worked with Stevie Ray Vaughan (Well respected guitarist that passed away 8/27/90) and his brother Jimmie Vaughan (Fabulous Thunderbirds)."

Craig: "You didn't get to meet George Harrison?"

Kenny Aronoff: "I didn't meet him. The first day I show up for the sessions I introduce myself to Bob Dylan. He says "I'm Bob". That was the last time he spoke with me the entire time."

Craig: "You did better than Slash from Guns 'N' Roses. He went the entire session without any words being said."

Kenny Aronoff: "It's strange. Bob was very reclusive in the studio. The record was amazing. I kept all the recordings of the sessions."

Craig: "When you did a session for Tony Iommi the guitarist for Black Sabbath in 2000, did you get to meet Ozzy Osbourne (Black Sabbath's singer) and (Bill Ward, the drummer for Black Sabbath)?"

Kenny Aronoff: "Tony had me on the tracks with Billy Corgan (Smashing Pumpkins). Since the schedules were different I didn't meet the two guys from Sabbath."

Craig: "Tony has always been an interesting character. Do you remember any events from the sessions?"

Kenny Aronoff: "He is a funny guy. I couldn't believe how funny he was. He was telling me about some of the things Black Sabbath did. When they wanted something they went all out."

Craig: "In 2001 you got to work with Mick Jagger on *Goddess In The Doorway*. Did you get to play with Pete Townshend and Bono (U2)?"

Kenny Aronoff: "I didn't play with Pete, or Bono. I had won an audition to appear on the record. There were days they wanted me, but I couldn't do it. There was one day I was able to give. Jagger was super cool. I may have recorded four songs. I don't remember if it were four, or less. I had played on the Stones album *Bridges To Babylon*. That was crazy. I was working days on a session and at night would record with the Stones. The day gig was in the studio with John Fogerty."

Craig: "You got to play on a tremendous live John Fogerty record *Premonition*. What was the feeling when you were playing some of the most legendary recordings such as *Proud Mary*, *Fortunate Son*, and *Down On The Corner*?"

Kenny Aronoff: "It was unbelievable. I was reading comic books and listening to *Born On The Bayou* when I was younger. I thought to myself if the Hulk could sing, he would have John Fogerty's voice. The Hulk looked like he would have that type of amazing voice. I thought back to the comic books, because I played with him on the Tonight Show, with Jay Leno."

Craig: "On the Cars reunion (New Cars), how did it work out that you and Prairie Prince got involved in the project?"

Kenny Aronoff: "I play on the new single. I was asked to record three songs with them. I believe two made the record."

Craig: "Why didn't the band either use you for the studio and live dates, or Prairie?"

Kenny Aronoff: "I was asked to join the band. I was told that I had to give a year. It was nice that they wanted me, but I had too many things on the table."

Craig: "Did any of the New Cars members tell you why Rick Ocasek didn't want to be part of the project?"

Kenny Aronoff: "I can't remember who told me that Rick didn't want to go on the road that long."

Craig: "How did things go on the sessions with Rod Stewart?"

Kenny Aronoff: "It was great. Rod is singing great. He had great songs for the album. It is going to be such a cool record. He is doing covers of Bruce Springsteen, John Fogerty, Bob Dylan, Van Morrison, and Bob Seger. He is doing the Elvin Bishop hit song *Fooled Around And Fell In Love*. There are nineteen songs recorded. He has to pick about thirteen for the CD."

Craig: "When you are asked to fill the drum seat for somebody that would be considered an integral part of the band (Jefferson Airplane as an example), do you try to be both Spencer Dryden and Kenny Aronoff to some degree?"

Kenny Aronoff: "Absolutely. If I try to be too much like Spencer I can play the parts but it would still sound like me because of my feel and power. I can bring things up to date, or make it more powerful."

Craig: "Did you ever get to meet Spencer?"

Kenny Aronoff: "I didn't get to meet him."

Craig: "Thank you very much for your time. I know that you have a show to do. It would have been great to get into all the session work and the years with John Mellencamp. Hopefully next time."

Kenny Aronoff: "Dude you're welcome. It was a pleasure. When the book comes out make sure you send me a copy."

## Marty Balin- Jefferson Airplane, Hot Tuna, Jefferson Starship, and the KBC Band.

Craig: "It is great to be able to get your inside view of almost forty-five years in the business. Thanks for joining me today."

Marty Balin: "Craig, you're welcome. I'm sorry we couldn't do this yesterday, but I had just gotten home from a few days playing with Slick Aguilar."

Craig: "We'll talk about that nice combination much later. Why don't we go back to 1962 or 1963. You had done some demos that I talk about in the book, *You Made Me Fall*, *Nobody But You*, *You Are The One*, and *I Specialize In Love* (That one was on the Jefferson Airplane Box Set, *Loves You*). Do you recall anything about the songs?"

Marty Balin: "I remember being a dancer at the time. I was asked to record some tracks. *I Specialize In Love*, was a song I wrote in the studio. It came together pretty quickly. There was a country feel to them. I believe that they may have gotten released on a small level. It was a blast being in the studio at that time. In fact they did get released, because I got a call from a rhythm and blues radio station in Oakland. They were playing one of the songs. It was strange that it ended up being played, but I was excited when they wanted to interview me for about five minutes. I had fame for a short time." (Marty Laughs).

Craig: "What do you remember from the song *Hellbound Train*, that came out on a various artists CD (*San Francisco Live*, released 11/18/97 on Prophecy 12010) when you were with the Town Criers?"

Marty Balin: "Did that really come out Craig? I don't remember much of the song."

Craig: "It had intriguing story of a guy in the bar, having a bad dream."

Marty Balin: "There are many things I have played on, or written that I don't recall. I tend to be weird, but I have never listened to a record after it came out. I always want to catapult forward and not be in the past. Craig, before I forget I have to tell you something that shows how history gets changed around. You were talking with my dad, (Joe Buchwald) about how managers can often have a different view of the way things really happened. One time myself and Bill Thompson (Manager of the J.A.) are in a limousine. I'm not sure of the year. The driver wanted to put on a tape of the Jefferson Airplane greatest hits. It was called *The Worst Of The Jefferson Airplane*. The driver was telling us how much he loved the album title and the band. I asked that he put something else in the tape deck. I don't listen to my own music. Bill Thompson tells him that he thought of the title. I tell Bill what are you talking about. I came up with the title for the album. Bill tells the driver that he was mixed up and it had to be some Jefferson Starship album he had something to do with the title. I'm sitting right next to the guy for crying out loud."

Craig: "Don't you love all the revisionist history of the band, especially when you were there?"

Marty Balin: "Man, at least with Bill Graham and Chet Helms they did love the music."

Craig: "If you look at the eclectic mix of shows Chet and Bill put on (Separately), it made people experience seeing the Airplane with, Junior Wells (Blues) or Dizzy Gillespie (Jazz)."

Marty: "We even played I believe Matrix gigs in San Francisco with Russian poets. You got a good education in music."

Craig: "Do you recall any songs that you performed when Jerry Peloquin was the drummer, and Bob Harvey the bass-player, which did not get played once Skip Spence and Jack Casady replaced them?"

Marty: "We did play many things, but I don't recall a specific tune that we dropped."

Craig: "When you ask ten people this you get a split in opinions. Do you feel when the drummer Skip Spence went to Mexico he told either Matthew Katz (Manager at the time), or any of the band members?"

Marty: "I believe he didn't, and that is one thing you can't forgive. I was walking down the street going for breakfast and I guy stopped me and asked if I heard that Skip went to Mexico with a couple of women?" I knew nothing about this, none of us did. I went to the bank and made sure his next check was cancelled. That's the one thing you can't do man. You can forgive and forget a bunch of crap, but when it means missing a gig it has to be dealt with. He was fired and Spencer Dryden came into the band. It is a shame what happened with Skippy. When I first saw him he was a glowing God. There was a light that would shine all around him. I went up to Skippy with a couple of drum sticks and told him that he was my drummer. He told me that he was a guitar-player. I told him he was my drummer. I had him take the sticks home and told him try playing for a week. After a week we got together and he was good. He played fine. The chicks loved him. It worked out in the end. He got to go to Moby Grape and play guitar and we got Spencer. The saddest day was when the glow was all gone. Moby Grape had played a show that may have been at the Fillmore Auditorium in San Francisco. They were done and were coming up a flight of stairs. I was about to go down the stairs. I hear a voice saying "Marty, you don't say hello?" It was Skippy. I couldn't recognize him. The glow was gone already. Even the voice seemed different."

Craig: "The tragedy with Skip was how early the sun would set, even before he passed away. If you look at some of the pictures of Moby Grape on stage in the early days, he already had the glassy-eyed look permanently engraved."

Marty Balin: "He really did burn out fast. When he released the solo record, what was that called?"

Craig: "The album was titled *Oar*."

Marty Balin: "That was it. He had some good stuff. The material was strange and maybe not together, but there was good stuff on it."

Craig: "The Airplane did three brilliant cover tunes that didn't make any of the LP's, *In The Midnight Hour* (Written by Steve Cropper, but most noted by the versions from the Rascals and Wilson Pickett), *Lay Down Your Weary Tune* (Bob Dylan), and *Feel A Whole Lot Better* (The Byrds). What do recall about them?"

Marty Balin: "I remember that *In The Midnight Hour* was a song every band knew. It may have been rehearsed to play at the Fillmore Auditorium, San Francisco if we had a New Years Eve show on 12/31/65. *Lay Down Your Weary Tune*, I recall that for some reason Matthew Katz (J.A.'s first manager) may have gotten a hold of a Bob Dylan song that wasn't released at the time. (The Byrds released it on *Turn! Turn! Turn!* 12/12/65). We played that live, but it never was recorded in the studio. I don't remember anything about *Feel A Whole Lot Better*."

Craig: "I was surprised that Paul found the censorship that went on during the recording of the first record (*Takes Off*) silly and not frustrating. His point of view was any publicity the band got was good. What were your feelings of *Let Me In* having to be rerecorded to change the line "Don't tell me you want money", to "Don't tell me it's so funny?""

Marty Balin: "It was ridiculous. What was worse was when *Runnin' Round This World* bothered the record company because of the word trips."

Craig: "When the first record was finished and you look back on some of the wonderful tracks that you were a big part of, *Blues For An Airplane*, *It's No Secret*, and *Tobacco Road*, what were your feelings? *Blues From An Airplane* is one of the most underrated songs ever recorded."

333

Marty Balin: "Thanks. *Blues From An Airplane* is a really good song. I did it a few times with the latest Jefferson Starship in the past few years. *It's No Secret* I had written with the hope that Otis Redding would record it. He never did. The song took off for the Airplane. All those years' people wanted to hear it. *Tobacco Road* is a song that I still perform. I put a different slant on it. I like to change."

Craig: "Any reason that *Blues From An Airplane* only got played one time, and that was in 1968 and how did you feel about the Lou Rawls and Nashville Teens versions of *Tobacco Road*?"

Marty Balin: "The reason that *Blues For An Airplane* only got performed one time, is we did a bunch of Paul songs and I didn't speak up. I would normally stay in the background and not cause a scene. There were times I did blow my stack. The majority of the times I was happy to sing. So many years removed from the time, I don't recall the two versions of *Tobacco Road* you asked about. I also liked the Valente tune that we recorded (*Let's Get Together*, by Dino Valente)."

Craig: "Do any stories that have been forgotten from the first recording sessions come to mind?"

Marty Balin: "You could tell early in the game how screwed up the business was. There was something that Jack may not have at the time. It may have been a union card, or some documentation. The recording studio didn't want Jack to appear on the record. We weren't going to have a record recorded without our bass-player. It was something miniscule and everything becomes a grand production. Luckily the nonsense was put to rest."

Craig: "What were your thoughts when you had to make a change in vocalists and Signe was out and Grace was in?"

Marty Balin: "We needed to play places besides California. The band had to get heard. Signe had plans for a family. The top choices were Grace, or Janis Joplin. Janis was a blues singer, and we thought that Grace would be the best fit. It turned out that was the right way to go."

Craig: "Over the years do you feel the national music publications excluding the San Francisco and New York City based writers had an anti-San Franciscan band mentality?"

Marty Balin: "I can't say, because I wasn't one that ever read reviews. My attitude was that every person on earth has an opinion. I would make a record and go on to the next one."

Craig: "As we fast forward to the recording of the second LP *Surrealistic Pillow*, what do you remember about one of the greatest songs the band would ever put on vinyl, *Today*?"

Marty: "There is a story behind that one. Thanks for the compliment. The group was at RCA Studios. On one side were the Rolling Stones and on the other Tony Bennett. Everybody wanted to see the Stones, I wanted to see Tony Bennett. I had written the song *Today* with the hope that he would record it. He didn't, but it got included on the record. I always had trouble trying to get my songs on the albums. There would be producers, engineers, or record company personnel that would tell me it's a good song, but it doesn't sound like the Jefferson Airplane. I would normally sit in the background, but when this came up I would explode. How could a song not sound like the Jefferson Airplane if it is written by a member of the band and recorded by the entire group?"

Craig: "Thankfully one of the best tunes the band ever recorded made it to the album. What about your remembrances of *Plastic Fantastic Lover*?"

Marty Balin: "That came together very quickly. I was watching television one night and the words started to flow. I had it done expeditiously."

Craig: "Do you recall the tune you and Jorma wrote, *She Had Funny Cars*, which opened the 1989 reunion tour."

Marty Balin: "That was Jorma and I fooling around. It was one of those things that got done quickly and sounded good."

Craig: "Did Grace bring any songs from the Great Society besides *Somebody To Love* and *White Rabbit*?"

Marty Balin: "What is the title of the song that has *Sally* as the first word?"

Craig: "*Sally Go 'Round The Roses*."

Marty Balin: "That one we didn't record."

Craig: "When it was time to record *After Bathing At Baxter's*, did you have more songs to offer besides *Young Girl Sunday Blues*?"

Marty Balin: "I was always writing. I don't recall other titles, but it was the same situation that I heard with *Today*. The song doesn't sound like a Jefferson Airplane song. I write the song, I play in the band, I perform it on stage, but the bleeping song isn't right for the Airplane. Go figure that one out."

Craig: "When *Crown Of Creation* got released I was always puzzled how did The *House At Pooneil Corners* not get the same recognition as *The Ballad Of You And Me And Pooneil*? The songs could be twins."

Marty Balin: "I haven't thought of that in a number of years, but *Pooneil Corners* was a well written song. Not being a person that paid attention to reading reviews, or comparisons of albums, once the record got done it was on to something else. I was always in constant motion."

Craig: "One of the most noted songs and albums to come out of the San Francisco scene had to be *Volunteers*. Any stories come to mind when you were writing the title track?"

Marty Balin: 'Sometimes fate can play a role in the creation of a song. I looked out my window and there was a garbage truck, with the writing *Volunteers Of America*. When it was first written it didn't have the political statement that I actually enjoyed. It took on a different life, I'm glad it did. It has a message that stays current throughout the generations."

Craig: "What were your memories of playing with Spencer Dryden?"

Marty Balin: "He could be a pain in my ass. We had to have a meeting to get rid of this guy. He could be a pain in the butt. We told Grace that if she didn't want Spencer to go, she could leave too. Spencer was a cool guy. I found out that Spencer was a light jazz drummer. When we got to the harder sound that Jorma and Jack wanted, they needed a kick-ass drummer. Spencer was fun, he was a funny guy. He was a fun friend, but as a musician he let me down many times. In fact a quick story for you Craig. One time we are playing *It's No Secret* at a show, at the side of my eye I see him drop a drum stick. Instead of grabbing another stick and coming right in, I see him out of the corner of my eye and I'm feeling the lack of power under me. I turn around and he is sitting down and about to light up a cigarette, instead of just coming back in. I turned around man and did a high kick. It hit his base drum and knocked him down. It was hilarious. I told him to never let me down again in front of an audience. I don't remember the year. These things happen, there were good times too."

Craig: "When you look back on the early shows you did with Hot Tuna in 1969 and 1970 what are your impressions?"

Marty Balin: "They were great. I enjoyed the mixture of songs. In fact I was asked to record a Hot Tuna record with Jorma, Jack, and Joey Covington. We were going to do it in Jamaica. I told the guys before we left that if you want me to do the album when we get there it has to be business. After we arrived I could never find Jorma and Jack. The people were really nice there. We may have played one show. I find out that RCA Records was paying Hot Tuna more because I was going to sing. Nobody informed me about that. I finally got so disgusted that I told Jorma I'll see you at the next Airplane gig. I believe it was in Holland (Kralingen Festival) 6/26/70."

Craig: "In 1970 when you decided to leave the Airplane, how did you get involved with the band Grootna (1972) and besides producing the album did you lend any vocal support."

Marty Balin: "I like to think I was seducer. I can be very tough on musicians in the studio, but I wanted to work the band hard, so they would succeed. I didn't sing at all on the record."

Craig: "In 1973 you worked with a band Bodacious D.F., on the self-titled record. What does the D.F. stand for and what made you decide to put the song you had done with Hot Tuna and a couple of times with the Airplane on the record, *Drifting*?"

Marty Balin: "Did I put that on the record. I would like to hear that."

Craig: "You can do that very easily. I gave you, and your dad a copy of the Bodacious D.F. rehearsal with *Drifting* done twice."

Marty Balin: "I like that song. I would like to play that live again. Thanks for reminding me. That would sound great if Slick Aguilar and I played that. The reason it went on the Bodacious record I was in a soul and rhythm and blues mood. It sounded right the way the band put it together. As for what the D.F. stands for. When we were making the record if something went well we would all say bodacious. If something didn't turn out right we would say dumb f_ck."

Craig: "Good way to camouflage the words. When the Airplane did the last show on 9/22/72 at Winterland, San Francisco, what was it like for you when you performed on the final song *You Wear Your Dresses To Short*?"

Marty Balin: "Did I leave the stage after that?"

Craig: "Unfortunately the entire band left the stage for seventeen years."

Marty Balin: "Then it must have been a bummer day. (Marty laughs). I don't remember it. I do remember being sad when Winterland closed as a concert venue. That was my favorite place. That was a beautiful place, I loved that place."

Craig: "What were your memories of playing with Papa John Creach, both in the Airplane and the Jefferson Starship?"

Marty Balin: "One night Jorma, Jack, and a great player from England named Graham Bond (Played with Jack Bruce and Ginger Baker, before they went on to Cream) are jamming in the studio. Joey Covington and I are sitting around. Joey suggests we go see an old violin-player in Los Angeles. We go to the club and nobody is there. This old guy plays *Somewhere Over The Rainbow*, it was the most beautiful thing I had ever seen. So then we take him back to the studio. I insisted that he play with Jorma, Jack, and Grand Bond. (If only that tape circulated). He was funny. He told us all the time you guys are too loud. He couldn't stand the volume, none of us could. He was great, what an experience playing with him. One time I had a friend staying over the house from RCA Records. He was showing me stride piano (Mostly a jazz technique, that was invented in Harlem, New York City in 1919). One day Papa John comes over and brings Eubie Blake (A ragtime piano legend) along. He had to be in his ninety's at the time (He lived to one hundred). Eubie starts to play the piano. Papa

John had his fiddle. All day they are playing. Eubie would tell Papa John to slow down son. Nobody knew Papa John's real age. I should have recorded that. It went on all day."

Craig: "How did the overtures come to you, to be part of the Jefferson Starship for the *Dragon Fly* album?"

Marty Balin: "We had a crazy thing. Everyone is running the band, but the band. We are all doing our own thing. During the time I had left, I watched the charts and could tell what was going to happen. It gets back to me that the interviews are stating that Paul is missing the days that Grace and Marty would sing together on stage. One day Paul gives me a call. He tells me that he has a song he would like me to write lyrics for. He gave me this thing that would become *Caroline*. I said cool. I was cracking myself up on each line of the song. If I could make myself laugh I knew it would be good. Each line kept building and then I finished it up. I gave it to Paul and the people in the room had their chins drop. They wanted to put it on the *Dragon Fly* album. At this point they had been touring with David Freiberg. They come back to me and tell me that Freiberg isn't right to sing *Caroline*. Would I come back and join the band? I tell them I got to do what I got to do. I want to do a groove with a love song kind of theme. They say okay Marty. They let me in the band."

Craig: "Is it is true that when you were writing *Miracles* you put the word baby in the lyrics about one hundred times, because Grace hated singing that type of love song?"

Marty Balin: "She did hate the word baby. I made her sing the words in the background. (Marty laughs). It was so funny. I got my goodies out of watching her having to sing it on stage."

Craig: "Besides the sales of the album, did *Red Octopus* feel good to you personally?"

Marty Balin: "I felt very good about things. The song (*Miracles*) is actually about an avatar in India, who is about an embodiment of love and consciousness. It is like the way the Persians wrote about women, but actually it was about God. That is basically what I was trying to say. I was trying to write a love song about the living God in India. That would be a man of miracles. During meditation the Baba would tell me to watch the charts, it will go up. It did and I loved it. The fulfillment in me, was the greatness in him."

Craig: "Did you find pressure to write material for *Spitfire*, since *Red Octopus* had been so entrenched on the charts?"

Marty Balin: "I can't do anything else but sing, or feel something. It has to be right. I can't always sing Paul's songs because I don't always understand them. I don't feel them. That is why when we play together I like when there is each of our songs to do. We both could feel them. I have too much to sing myself."

Craig: "You were able to contribute the timeless tune *St. Charles*."

Marty Balin: "That came about because I got involved in helping the American Indian. I wanted to do a movie. I was writing a screenplay. The Sioux Indians heard about what I wanted to do. They would stop by on the way to a powwow. They showed me films about them having to fight for the right to fish in their own river. I was shocked and began to learn about the Indian cultures. This young Indian poet comes over by the name of Warlance. Craig, it may have been Thunderhawk. He had written a poem by the name of *St. Charles*. I took the poem and told him hey man that is beautiful. Paul took the very first line of the poem. Then Paul wrote the rest of the lyrics, with some help from my friend Jesse Barish. Jesse is a prolific songwriter and nobody knows it."

Craig: "Is that how you got involved with Jesse's releases, the self-titled and *Mercury Blues*."

Marty Balin: "Yes, we were good friends and I helped him on those two albums. Bill Thompson wouldn't have thought of this, but I took a small percentage of the songwriting royalties, and my dad, and I put it in the bank. That was for using the one line of the poem. We left it there for many years. Many years later the Indians had come by for help. Thanksgiving was coming up. It was a week before, and they were on the way to a powwow. I told them I needed to look at something, but come by tomorrow. I checked on the bank account. There was between seven and ten thousand dollars. I get a check ready for them. When they came back I gave them the check to help them out. They were so touched. This blew them away. The little bit of money turned into enough to make Thanksgiving special for them. It was touching when they called me up to thank me. It was a fabulous feeling. They made me a brother and I can fish in their river."

Craig: "It's great to hear about the results of charity. Marty, for years there has been a story before you left the Jefferson Starship you recorded a very early version of *Jane*. Is that a rock and roll tale, or on the level?"

Marty Balin: "I think I was on that song when I left. The reason I left it was the summertime. The band kept rehearsing during the day. I wanted to go to the beach. They refused to rehearse at night. I told them they needed to find another singer. They had a guy in mind. Mickey Thomas was brought in and he could do the job better than I could. (**After I picked myself up from the fall, I had to let Marty know that millions don't agree with that**). Mickey had a commercial voice. He could do everything. He could even do Grace's parts."

Craig: "Did the record company wipe out your vocals and Grace's on a tune called *Things To Come*?"

Marty Balin: "It may have happened. I have no idea. Remember when the record company put out the box set?"

Craig: "*Jefferson Airplane Loves You*."

Marty Balin: "When they were getting it together, I got all these calls that I needed to contact them and help with the material. I said okay. When I did call, they didn't want any help. They did it themselves. They thought they knew what the Airplane was and what was in the vaults. In the mean time I am hanging out with the Doors, and they have ownership of their own masters. The music is beautiful. The poetry Jim Morrison did is wonderful. I wish we had that. The record company wanted nothing to do with the Airplane. That is very weird. To this day they only talk with Bill Thompson (Manager). Jorma, Jack, Grace, and Paul have rights to the name. I don't. I left the Airplane and told them they could have it all. I only wanted the book. It was a scrapbook from the first day to the last. It's in a vault. I looked at the book lately and thought it was great. I have to put it out someday."

Craig: "In 1981 you had a wonderful self-titled album *Balin*. It contained two hits, *Hearts* and *Atlanta Lady*. What do you remember about the record?"

Marty Balin: "When we had the trial going on with our first manager Matthew Katz, I wrote a goofy song called *Rock Justice*. A young lawyer comes by and asked what I was doing. I told him writing a song. At the time punk and new wave were big. He tells me that he has great people in San Francisco that could help with a record. I tell him that I need a guy from this band, and the girl from that band, and so on. He went out and he got all these people. At the time I owned a Church in San Anselmo, California. I told him to gather all the musicians and I would explain what is going on. We did some shows and they were fine, until ego got in the way. E.M.I. Records saw one and told me that I should do an album. I recorded the first song, which was *Hearts*. Some guy comes up to me and tells me that you should never record a hit as the first song. Then Bill Champlin of the Sons Of Champlin (San Francisco band from the 1960's) comes into the studio. Bill tells me that he wants to do a little background on the song. I knew how great he was. In the early 1960's the one band that scared the sh_t out of me was the Sons Of Champlin. They were that amazing. They never got popular, but they were heavy. People all over the globe loved the song *Hearts*. They always felt it fit their own culture. Craig, was *Atlanta Lady* a hit?"

Craig: "Marty, *Hearts* reached number eight on the charts, and *Atlanta Lady* peaked at twenty-seven."

Marty Balin: "I didn't know that it was even on the charts. No wonder why people like the song. I knew *Hearts* was big, but not the other one."

Craig: "How did the good idea to put Kantner, Balin, and Casady together come about in 1985?"

Marty Balin: "The Starship was going under. They had hit after hit, but they played in town and couldn't get two hundred people. I was playing with a band that did tunes the Starship, or Airplane would never do. They were dance grooves. This was at the Church. I told Paul to come up to the Church and rehearse with my guys. I thought with all that was going on with the Starship, it would ease his mind. We would play during the day, take a dinner break and then at night play with Paul. Almost immediately Paul goes out and gets us a record deal. We had released the album in 1986, and were playing and Clive Davis came to see us at some convention. He had all these heavy metal bands performing. Hair bands in those days. None of them communicated with the audience. I was amazed. We go on and the first song I had the audience rocking, people are dancing and he is on the stage. Clive tells us that we were pretty good. He signs us up and doesn't even know what we could do. He needed to pay attention to his people."

Craig: "Were you satisfied with the record?"

Marty Balin: "I never listened to it."

Craig: "Did you enjoy the live shows with Paul and Jack?"

Marty Balin: "We had a good band. It was a good band. My man Slick Aguilar was on guitar, what were the other players Craig?"

Craig: You had Darrell Verdusco on drums, Keith Crossan on saxophone, and Tim Gorman on keyboards."

Marty Balin: "Man, you are killing me. Keith Crossan was great. Jack was doing his thing on bass. I was in heaven with this band. One day we go to a meeting and Paul and Jack tell us we are breaking up the band. I was never let in as to why. It was good and Slick and I still play together."

KANTNER, BALIN, CASADY

MGMT: VINCENT LYNCH
(415) 546-7667

Photo by kind permission of Mike Somavilla.  From the Mike Somavilla collection.

Not to be used without the written consent of Mike Somavilla.  Photographer unknown.

This is a promo picture of the KBC Band circa 1985-1986.  Courtesy of Vincent Lynch Management.

Craig: "You had a chance to perform some of the Airplane tunes, the album songs, and unreleased material. One of the best tunes you have done opened some shows, *Let's Go*. It was perfect to get the crowd into the festivities."

Marty Balin: "I still want to record that. I still play that. I love that song. You are one of the few people that said that. I'm glad, I like that tune, live and in the studio. I wrote that tune and was hoping it would be used for the 1989 Airplane reunion. Paul and Grace loved it. They wanted to do it. The record company again said it was not an Airplane song. They had an idea in their minds what we should sound like. The other members were signed to a contract. I was only a hired hand. I had no power in the studio."

Craig: "One of the great KBC live shows was in Berkeley, California on 5/15/86. Jorma played on *Plastic Fantastic Lover*. You had four Airplane members on stage. What was it like playing with Jorma again?"

Marty Balin: "It was nice. I first saw Jorma in the 1960's. I told Paul that Jorma was a real good guitar-player and that was what we needed. I kept bugging Jorma, but he was such a musical purist. Finally we got him to play with us. He's the greatest. He is an underrated guitar-player. Jack is one of the best ever. I looked around on stage with some of the Jefferson Starship people, Slick (Guitar), Prairie Prince (Drums) before he went with the New Cars, and Paul Kantner, Diana (Vocals), and Chris Smith (Keyboards), how could I not love my gig?"

Craig: "On March 4, 1988 at the Fillmore, San Francisco, the prelude to the Airplane reunion occurred with Jorma, Jack, Paul, Grace, and Papa John all appearing on stage. Did you have an opportunity to be there?"

Marty Balin: "No, because at first I didn't know if they wanted me in the band. Grace insisted that I had to be part of it. Her insistence helped a great deal."

Craig: "What were your impressions of the 1989 tour?"

Marty Balin: "I thought that we were so strong and so good that we were able to pull everybody in. It seemed by the third concert Jack was with us and by the forth Jorma too. We could put on a good concert, I thought they were great. Then at the end they all walked away again."

Craig: "Why was that?"

Marty Balin: "They needed a leader. Without a leader, you don't have a vision. When you don't have vision you go nowhere."

Craig: "Why did Jorma have any bitterness at the beginning of the tour?"

Marty Balin: "I wish I knew. He was angry. Maybe he wanted to be a purist and play his thing, the Reverend Gary Davis music. It was always Jack, and Jorma, and then Paul, and Grace, and I'm running around between them. Live, it was Grace and I in the front, and the band followed us. In the studio we didn't necessarily make it fly the way it did live. In the studio we had to follow the band."

Craig: "How are things right now between you, and Jorma, and Jack?"

Marty Balin: "Things are fine. Jorma, has become really nice and Jack is a stellar individual. I haven't changed that much."

Craig: "How are things with you and Grace?"

Marty Balin: "I haven't talked to her since the Fireman's Benefit. It may have been 2002. She didn't want to sing any leads. When we started to sing, she whaled back. She still had the great voice."

Craig: "Any thoughts on the two videos that were released from the 1989 reunion album?"

Marty Balin: "What was the one song they did first, *Jet Airplanes*?"

Craig: "*Planes,* and then *True Love*."

Marty Balin: "*Summer Of Love* should have been a video. The song fit on the album well and the theme was perfect. It was easily understood. It was a summer tour and I had helped mix the song on the album. Originally I had gotten a phone call for the 20th Anniversary of the Summer Of Love. I was in one of those phases that I didn't feel like talking about the past. I grabbed a guitar, started to write and it felt like it took five minutes. The KBC live version went over real well."

Craig: "In 1991 you did a great vocal job on the solo record *Better Generation*. The production was really stale and impersonal. What went wrong with the musical part of the album? You finally had a chance to put *Let's Go* on a CD and you put three great remakes of Airplane tracks, *It's No Secret, Volunteers,* and *Summer Of Love*, on there as well."

Marty Balin: "The production was terrible. This was the time when the early version of Pro Tools was used in the studio. We cut the songs and when they were played back everything is out of synch. Sometimes pieces of the track would be missing. We tried it for awhile and I finally left. I never thought it would come out, but it did. Once you told me the songs that are on it, I'll have to listen to it."

Craig: "You did some great shows with Paul Kantner, when he had the Galactic Reunion tour and the regular Jefferson Starship band. 4/5/03 Marin Center Exhibit Hall, San Rafael, California, for example. That show had appearances by Signe Anderson and Spencer Dryden. Were they enjoyable to you and how was it to see Spencer and Signe again.?"

Marty Balin: "I loved the reunions, I wished Paul kept doing that. It's great to see these people again."

Craig: "Paul had good things to say about you and those shows. Would you work with him again?"

Marty Balin: "I would work with him anytime. I want to work with Paul Kantner. Paul and I could do an entire evening together. It would be great. How about if Paul and I played old folk songs and some Dino Valente tunes?"

Craig: "Tell me the city and date."

Marty Balin: "You see, it would be great. I would love to play with Jack, and Jorma, and Paul. I would play with Paul and Jack. I would love to play with Jorma and get to sing his songs. I love Jorma's songs. We could play the blues, folk, whatever. Can we do it my way? Now there aren't as many people that want to hear the music. I don't have time to promote it on a website. I'm busy writing my own songs, reading, and playing guitar."

Craig: "What has it been like performing with Signe Anderson, Grace Slick, Darby Gould, and Diana Mangano over forty plus years?"

Marty Balin: "Grace was great, I loved working with her. Darby blows me away. I love to work with her. She is a great talent. Diana is nice working with. I want to get her to write songs with me. Signe was a great singer when she was young, her voice was great."

Craig: "If only three Marty Balin songs could be saved for the time capsule which would you salvage?"

Marty Balin: "*Miracles, Comin' Back To Me,* and *It's No Secret*."

Craig: "I have to plug the website that your dad (Joe Buchwald) has put together. What a true gentleman. The website has some of the unreleased gems that your father was talking about releasing. If you go to www.jbppresentsmartybalin.com, there are rarities from Marty you can purchase, you can learn about future shows, and hear some audio clips."

Marty Balin: "My dad is great. He is smart, honest, funny, and an excellent traveler. I haven't seen the website, is it good?"

Craig: "As a famous and spectacular band from Liverpool said "It's getting better all the time."

Marty Balin: "I don't even know about all the computer stuff."

Craig: "We'll let your dad take care of that and you see about having something special in 2007, for the 40th anniversary of the Summer Of Love. Marty, it was a pleasure to be able to spend this much time with you. I hope that things are always good for you and the family. Paul and you need to play together soon. Thank you for being so gracious."

Marty Balin: "You're welcome. Craig, if you need anything else let me know. Best of luck with your book."

**Photograph by kind permission of Don Aters and may not**

**be reproduced without the written consent of Don Aters.**

**From the Don Aters collection . Photographer Don Aters.**

**The above photograph of Marty Balin circa summer 2006 from a**

**performance with Slick Aguilar.**

**Marty Balin and Slick Aguilar opened for the Jefferson Starship.**

**Photo from 8/11 or 8/12/06**

**B.B. King's, New York City.**

**Slick played both with Marty and with the J.S.**

# John Barbata- Jefferson Airplane and Jefferson Starship.

Craig: "John, it's great that I can have you share so many years of rock and roll drumming with the readers."

John Barbata: "Thank you Craig."

Craig: 'When we go back into the John Barbata time tunnel, did your history start with a band called the Sentinals and would you call them surf music?"

John Barbata: "They were really rhythm and blues. It seemed that the Sentinals were always booked with surf bands."

Craig: "There is a various artists surf music CD that has a Sentinals track *Big Surf*. The readers can check it out on www.allmusic.com, and hear an audio clip. When you moved on to the Turtles, what was it like working with Flo and Eddie?"

John Barbata: "They were great to work with. When I came in they got their first number one single, with *She'd Rather Be With Me*. They changed producers and brought in some new songwriters. There is a good story about Paul McCartney. The song *Happy Together* bumped off the Beatles hit *Penny Lane* from the number one position on the charts. Paul remembered that. He went to see the Turtles, and he came backstage to talk with us."

Craig: "It must have created a lifelong memory that not only did you get to meet Paul , but over the years all the Beatles."

John Barbata: "Craig, to take a phrase from my book, it was rock and roll heaven."

Craig: "One of your many sessions was with Lee Michaels in 1968 on his record *Recital*. Lee is known for the major hit *You Know What I Mean*, but has many other quality songs."

John Barbata: "The guy did well for himself. He owns five restaurants in Los Angeles. Lee was able to make good money in the sixties. He had shows back then that were paying him fifty grand a night. He did something really cool. He owed a record to the label A & M. He wanted out of the contract, so he records a *jam* session and hands it to them."

Craig: "That at least was nicer than Lou Reed recording *Metal Machine Music* (unlistenable repetition) in 1975. You were on an early recording of Linda Ronstadt (First one after the Stone Poneys), *Hand Sown, Home Grown*. Could you tell back then that she would have such a great career?"

John Barbata: "At one time I didn't get credit for that. I could tell. She had an incredible voice. Back then there weren't many better."

Craig: "You played on many of the works of Crosby, Stills, Nash, & Young, either for the band or the individual projects. What are some of the memories you have?"

John Barbata: "I did six or seven LP's in the early 1970's. There is a story behind Neil Young's album *Time Fades Away*. I get a call from Neil asking for me to help out on a tour. It turns out he wants me there the next day. We had a twenty minute rehearsal and then went out and played a ninety minute set. I didn't make a mistake. Graham Nash and Neil came up to me and wondered how I could do that. I told them I watched the bass-player for the cues and followed the guitar chords. That album didn't get released on CD for the longest time. That was because of the rough time the band went through. Danny Whitten had died shortly after being fired."

Craig: "When you compare playing on the CSNY, *Four Way Street* album to the Airplane days, what goes through your mind?"

John Barbata: "Man, they were a super group. They were one of the biggest in the world. When I was touring with them, I got a call about joining a band called the Eagles. I said I never heard of them. Glen Frey wanted me to join the band. Maybe if I joined Don Henley would have played the guitar."

Craig: "How did you end up replacing Joey Covington (He left the band) in the Airplane?"

John Barbata: "What happened was I knew David Crosby. He got me into the Airplane. They were real happy with me right off the bat. I got along well with Jack and Jorma. I jammed with the band, we jelled, and the next day I got the gig. Paul, and Grace liked me. At first Jorma and Jack were a little standoffish, but they warmed up quickly."

Craig: "Before you played the first show July of 1972 at William & Mary College, Williamsburg, Virginia, did you have any studio time with them?"

John Barbata: "There were rehearsals in the studio for the live shows. It turned out well. I was the only drummer of the Airplane to also play in the Jefferson Starship, both live and studio."

Craig: "When you joined the Airplane could you feel friction immediately in the band?"

John Barbata: "There was friction. Jorma and Jack wanted to start doing their thing full-time (Hot Tuna). They were into a different type of music and wanted to start playing more of the folk and blues. Paul was kind of running the show. The thing about the Airplane was they were like the Grateful Dead. When we walked on stage I had never been in a band that had that type of response. That carried over to the Jefferson Starship. Even though there were some that didn't like the Jefferson Starship, technically they had more success. They didn't have the mystique the Airplane had, but they certainly sold records. Much of my time in the band was the *Long John Silver* record and the live one, *Thirty Seconds Over Winterland*. The live one didn't sell as well as *Long John Silver*."

Craig: "*Long John Silver* made it to number twenty on the charts. The live record didn't break the Top 40. What was the final show for you like at Winterland, San Francisco, on 9/22/72, when Marty came on stage for the encore *You Wear Your Dresses Too Short*?"

John Barbata: "Marty had mentioned that he liked my drumming and that was one of the reasons he came back for the final song. It was great having Marty there. I was thinking that you may not have thought that the Jefferson Starship would have so many hits that were middle of the road style, but they sure did have a ton of success. Marty never felt that he got his just do. Even with *Miracles*, people would say that is the song Grace is on. Even though Grace was always the one people came to a full arena to see, I always called it the big three, with Grace, Marty, and Paul."

Craig: "Did you *jam* with Jorma, or Jorma, and Jack?"

John Barbata: "Jorma, Jack, and myself would *jam* almost after every show. We had a good time. We were good friends, it was great."

Craig: "What do you remember about playing with Papa John Creach?"

John Barbata: "Papa John was great. He was a real musician. He got on stage and could whale on the violin. The fans loved him. He would drive around with the Cadillac. It may not be known but I helped Papa John with his arrangements for the song *Milk Train*. I loved playing with him."

Craig: "Why was that not common knowledge?"

John Barbata: "I don't know. When I was part of the Airplane, I gave them the benefits of a studio drummer and how using producers in Los Angeles would be advantageous for the Jefferson Starship."

Craig: "Are the overall memories positive of the Jefferson Airplane experience?"

John Barbata: "For sure. In under a year we got to put out a studio record and a live one. It was great playing with them."

Craig: "When the band was winding down the final tour did you make any suggestions to any of the members about the future?"

John Barbata: "I did. Jorma and Jack were about to checkout of the band and go make Hot Tuna a full-time thing. I suggested to Grace and Paul that we replace the bass and the guitar, and we can carry on. There are other people out there. There are other fish in the sea (Very clever joke from John). I really like Jorma and Jack, but we had a really funny saying way back, only the best tuna gets to be Starship. They were great players, Jack may be the most gifted of all bass-players."

Craig: "You had the opportunity to play a song that both the Airplane and Crosby, Stills, Nash, and Young (Both CSN and CSNY) performed *Wooden Ships*. How did you feel about the two versions?"

John Barbata: "I think the Crosby, Stills, and Nash, version is better. In the studio it was much better produced. The Airplane version was real good too. The vocals were better on the Crosby, Stills, and Nash version."

Craig: "What are your recollections of playing on *Baron Von Tollbooth & The Chrome Nun* (Paul Kantner and Grace Slick), and Grace Slick's *Manhole*?"

John Barbata: "The music was esoteric and that gave me a good chance to show what I could do. The Airplane, their solo projects, and the Grateful Dead were really special. Grace was really professional in the studio. She had a great voice. Marty and Grace could really belt the vocals. Howard Kaylan from the Turtles could belt as well. The singers in Crosby, Stills, Nash, and Young weren't belters. Maybe sometimes Stephen Stills could belt. Neil Young can write unbelievable songs. He still has the drive."

Craig: "When you were in the Jefferson Starship which member were you most friendly with?"

John Barbata: "Craig Chaquico and I were the tightest in the band. He was a great guy."

Craig: "Craig Chaquico told me a story on how you showed him the importance of having the right equipment. You and Craig were in a music store because you needed either drum sticks, or cymbals. You tried two hundred before you found the right one."

John Barbata: "I even forgot about that. I'm glad you reminded me. I can use that quote for my next book. I should add that David Freiberg was very cool. He was quiet and got along with everyone. Pete Sears was a very good guy and never got the credit he deserved for his keyboard playing. I did an album called *L.A. Getaway* from Barbara Hill, and Chris Ethridge. We had Dr. John, Booker T., and Leon Russell. I'll tell you man, Pete isn't far behind those guys. Pete was great on the early Rod Stewart records."

Craig: "When you think of the difference between Jorma and Craig Chaquico what comes to your mind?"

John Barbata: "Craig was more melodic and Jorma was a great lead guitar-player. The combination of Craig's melodic playing and the hits Marty could write were important combinations. Isn't it funny that *We Built This City* was voted the worst song ever?"

Craig: "It's hysterical. At least now. When it came out it almost caused the end of civilization. It fell short of *Today*, *3/5 Of A Mile In 10 Seconds*, and every other Airplane, Jefferson Starship and garage band tune ever."

John Barbata: "I'm with you. The real tunes are from the Airplane and the Jefferson Starship. Don't forget to have people pick up the *Red Octopus* reissue CD with the bonus tracks. It sounds really good. That album was some of the best stuff I ever played on. Which reminds me, I brought in Larry Cox the producer and engineer for *Red Octopus*. The engineers in Los Angeles had stricter rules. They couldn't be smoking a joint in a Los Angeles studio. The records sounded better coming out of L.A. than San Francisco. At that time with a twenty-four track board you needed to be on top of things. There were no games to play. Graham Nash had used Larry Cox. I brought him in. The Airplane engineers were good, but I liked how Larry Cox did his business."

Craig: "When you finished the recording of *Red Octopus* did you know from all your years as a session drummer that the record would be a top seller, or at least close to it?"

John Barbata: "I can man. It's funny you ask that. I was on twenty hit singles. I was around many of the best producers and engineers in the business. You pick these things up man. To give you an idea how I could pick a hit, when Marty brought *Count On Me* into the group, Paul thought the song was too middle of the road. I jumped up immediately and said are you crazy, this is a hit single. You can't let this go by. It may not have gotten on the record if I didn't make the case for the song. I never brought that out. I'm glad you asked that. Thanks, man. Now if I reprint my book I have more things to add."

Craig: "When you had to follow-up *Red Octopus*, was there pressure in your eyes for the *Spitfire* release?"

John Barbata: "Absolutely man. The record company wanted us back in the studio as soon as possible."

Craig: "I hate bringing up the famous riot of 1978, but it is important that the fans know the road isn't all five star hotels and standing ovations. When Craig Chaquico told me the horror stories from the 6/17/78 Loreley Festival, Wiesbaden, Germany show, when the band had to cancel because Grace couldn't make it, I could see everything so clearly, as if I attended the concert. For somebody like yourself that was actually there, it must have been pure hell. David Freiberg risked his life to speak to the rioting crowd that the Jefferson Starship would come back for a free show and the promoter didn't bother to translate that part."

John Barbata: "First one of the roadies gets hit in the head with a bear bottle. The guy is minding his own business on stage and could have been killed. Craig told you about the amount of equipment that was destroyed. If you took his guitars and my new drum set alone, it was a fortune. The equipment was all secondary to the safety of the innocent people. Something that doesn't get brought up is if the riot never took place and Grace continued with the band, we were offered some incredible pay days to play more shows in Europe."

Craig: "We have to get a plug in for your book, *The Legendary Life Of A Rock Star Drummer*. I can't wait to read it. The stories you previously told me will make the readers realize how long you have played with the top rock acts and all the terrific session work. If they go to your website http://www.johnybarbata.com/, they can order the book. Not a bad ride, John. Both credited and unknown, you have played on about one hundred records. They can also pick up a couple of CD's you have done with your wife (Angie). Why don't we talk about them for a bit."

John Barbata: "First the book has great stories, it has sold nicely. It is a living resume. What I found out when I released the book I am getting the credit now. At the time I didn't do the things for the publicity. It is never too late. The website is great. My wife is an incredible singer and songwriter. She sounds like Bonnie Raitt and Linda Ronstadt. We did one album *Oklahoma Heartland* and sometime in the next few months we'll release *California*. I feel the title track will be a hit. My wife and I did all the vocals and all the writing. Another standout track will be *Long Distance Telephone*."

Craig: "John, we talked about one time you doing more drum clinics in 2007. How does it look for the fans to get to hear you play, and teach?"

John Barbata: "I am going to get that going. I have three companies talking to me. I've been offered a good deal. These are big outfits. I'll make up my mind soon. I'll get my name out there and see the fans."

Craig: "What drummers do you enjoy listening to?"

John Barbata: "I lived next to Booker T once and the drummer Al Jackson played on many Memphis recordings, I like Steve Gadd (Famous jazz session drummer, that has played with Simon & Garfunkel, Paul McCartney, and Steely Dan to name a few) and of course I enjoyed listening to Ringo Starr. Let me add Jim Keltner (Famous session drummer that has played with but not limited to John Lennon, George Harrison, and Bob Dylan). He's a great musician and a great guy. In all the years I've known him the only time he ever showed an ego was when he played on the John Lennon record *Imagine*."

Craig: "I appreciate that your career could be discussed for the book. Best of luck with the new album and I hope the drum clinics bring you to the east coast."

John Barbata: "Thanks buddy. Let me know when your book comes out, and if you need more information give me a yell."

**Jesse Barish-** Wrote the songs *Count On Me, Hearts*, and *Atlanta Lady* (To name a few), and Marty Balin and Jesse appear on some of each others recordings.

Craig: "It is great to be able to speak with you about the songs you have written for the Jefferson Starship and Marty, as well as your own recordings."

Jesse Barish: "Craig thanks for including me in the book. It is nice to talk about the songs."

Craig: "You played with David LaFlamme (He would be part of a band It's A Beautiful Day and one of their songs *White Bird* is considered one of the finest ever written) before you recording your first record. What was the name of the group?"

Jesse Barish: "I was in the original configuration of a band called the Orkustra^ (The spelling is correct) with David. I played the flute in that band. I am a flute-player as well as a singer and songwriter. After that I got a gig playing with John Phillips (Mamas & The Papas). He was promoting his record *John, The Wolf King Of L.A.* This was his first solo album. I was in a band called Trees. We were four male singers and songwriters. One of the guys in Trees knew John. He goes over his house to see if he would produce us. John instead offered to let us be his back up band, soon after I got signed by Shelter Records."

Craig: "What prevented the Orkustra from making it as a band?"

Jesse Barish: "It's hard to say. I left them after a few rehearsals that we had in a garage in the Haight-Ashbury section of San Francisco. They played a bunch of gigs and then they broke up. It's a shame they didn't go the distance. They had an upright bass, a cello, and an amplified oboe. It was a unique concept. They had the guitar and violin too. David is a great violin-player, a great musician, and a character."

Craig: "Any interesting stories when you played with another character John Phillips?"

Jesse Barish: "We go out on the road with John. There is a gig in New York. I think the club was called the Main Point. That may have been a club outside of Philadelphia. John thought the music was too loud for him. He fires two of the guitarists and the drummer. It was neat. John was a great guy. We played the Big Sur, California Folk Festival. That was excellent. Craig, before John passed away in 2001 (3/18/01) we were writing some songs together."

Craig: 'It is a shame that he is one of many of the great performers from the 1960's we have lost. After the tour with John Phillips you were able to record in 1972 an album *Jesse, Wolff, And Whings*. How did the project come together?"

Jesse Barish: "I was on the lot of A & M Records. I ran into Denny Cordell (Legendary producer that passed away in 1995. He produced the Moody Blues, Joe Cocker, and Leon Russell to name a few). I was excited because I had a few songs I wanted Joe Cocker to hear. Denny had produced the great record by Procol Harum, *Whiter Shade Of Pale*. I was real brave in those days; I would go up to anybody with my songs. He was really nice and instantly put me together with Joe Cocker. A few days later I got to play Joe Cocker a bunch of songs. Nothing happened with the songs I played for Joe. In the course of that I had made a demo. One day out of the blue Denny calls me. Denny told me he really liked the demo and wanted to sign me to a contract. I wasn't looking to get signed. Shelter Records was a really cool label back then. Leon Russell and J.J. Cale (Wrote *After Midnight* and *Cocaine*. He is a well respected musician that has recorded many albums over the years) were two of the artists. Denny ended up signing me."

Craig: "Did Joe Cocker tell you that your songs are good, but the style isn't a fit for what he is doing?"

(Thank you to Mike Somavilla for the proper spelling of the Orkustra).

Jesse Barish: "He wasn't receptive. He had just come off the Mad Dogs & Englishmen tour with Leon Russell. The last thing he wanted was to hear from another singer songwriter. It wasn't the right time and I didn't have the right songs for him."

Craig: "In 1972 you saw the release of *Jesse, Wolff, And Whings*. Did you get to play any live dates to promote the record?"

Jesse Barish: "We did gigs. In fact we got to go out with what they called Shelter Tours. That would be us and other Shelter Records artists. We played with blues legend Freddie King and with J.J. Cale. I also got to open shows for Leon Russell and Ike & Tina Turner. It was an odd record. It wasn't a great record."

Craig: "Shelter Records did see potential, they had the famous session pianist Larry Knechtel (A member of the band Bread, he also has done numerous sessions. He played one of the most famous piano parts in rock and roll history on Simon & Garfunkel's song *Bridge Over Troubled Water*) help out with the record."

Jesse Barish: "For some reason we ended up doing the record by ourselves. The record was done at Leon Russell's house. Every time that Denny scheduled somebody to be with us, he got sick or they got sick. For the most part the band and an engineer did the record by ourselves. We did a million takes and didn't have guidance. Working with Larry was great. We did it at Leon Russell's house. I remember the session. Leon had one of the first home studios. Larry showed up and that was a high point. As for the record it is disjointed and not a good representation of my work. I don't think anybody would think this was a good record. (Jesse laughs). It was a formative chapter in my life. The band ended up moving to Marin County, California. The band had lived in Hollywood, California but the gigs were in the vicinity of San Francisco. We got to open shows for John Cipollina's band Copperhead. We were the Monday night band at a club called The Keystone Berkeley. We played the Lions Share in San Anselmo, California. Then it turned into a duo with myself and Bill Wolff. I then decided around 1974 I wanted to go solo. I ended up in Mill Valley, California."

Craig: "Was this about the time you got introduced to Marty Balin?"

Jesse Barish: "That is right. Somebody told me that I should meet Marty. I was a huge Airplane fan. There are three albums I loved from the Airplane; they were *Surrealistic Pillow*, *After Bathing At Baxter's*, and *Crown Of Creation*. They are to me soundtracks to the sixties. Marty and I had a connection. We became good friends. Marty helped me in so many ways. Marty helped me to put a demo together of a few songs I wanted to get a record deal with. It now becomes 1976. There is a good story with the Jefferson Starship album *Spitfire*. There was a guy named Thunderhawk. He was an Indian friend of Paul Kantner. Thunderhawk had written something on a piece of paper that said "St. Charles sings." That was all he wrote. Paul had a piece of music in his head. He wanted to call it *St. Charles*. Paul gives it to Marty to write the lyrics. I guess that Craig Chaquico and Paul had done most of the music. Marty couldn't make anything out of it. Joey Covington had tried as well. Marty asked that I give it a try. I take the song home and I wrote the lyrics that night. I came back to Marty the next day. I sang it to Marty and he told me that was it! Marty changed a couple of things. The Jefferson Starship also did another song of mine on the record called *Love Lovely Love*. That was my introduction into that world."

Craig: "Did a musician introduce you to Marty?"

Jesse Barish: "It was a friend of mine Kevin Curran. He was a flute-player and he played the guitar. He has passed away. I met him in a second hand store. He had a flute in his hand. For many years Kevin did sound at The Roxy, Los Angeles."

Craig: "From the time you met Marty until the *Spitfire* record were you playing with a band?"

Jesse Barish: "I was kind of hanging out. I would work on songs, I didn't do any solo gigs. You could say I was out of the loop. I never networked the way other songwriters did. Meeting Marty was a very organic thing."

Craig: "Did Marty have a songwriting formula and advice to go with it?"

Jesse Barish: "Marty didn't talk about a formula. He encouraged me to do my thing."

Craig: "When the Jefferson Starship took the two songs for *Spitfire*, what did you feel inside?"

Jesse Barish: "It was unbelievable to me. Here is a guy that I admired all these years (Marty) and his band is taking two of my songs. As important my friend wanted two songs from me."

Craig: "You didn't stop there. On the Jefferson Starship album *Earth* you contributed three songs."

Jesse Barish: "Marty took me into Wally Heider Studios in San Francisco. I believe I did three songs. My version of *Count On Me* was one of those three tunes. I thought the demo was really good. I entered *Count On Me* in the American Song Festival. I got to be a quarter-finalist. I don't know if that was a big deal."

Craig: "Jesse, it was a big deal. The readers may be interested to know that you were competing with several thousand people."

Jesse Barish: "I don't remember if Paul had heard the song. The Jefferson Starship wanted to do *Count On Me*. I had a small band at the time. The musicians were very supportive of me, but some didn't like the idea of giving the song to somebody else. I had to decide if I save it for myself, there is no guarantee I get a hit. If I give it to the Jefferson Starship there is a real good chance they will have a hit. RCA Records is offering me a deal for the self-titled album I did. Marty had walked me into RCA and they signed me. I started to work on the record. It was nice. They didn't restrict me. I had a great feeling for *Count On Me*. I had to let it go and let them record it. They did a great version of it."

Craig: "Did the song come to you quickly?"

Jesse Barish: "It was very fast. I had it done in thirty minutes. There are songs I can finish that fast. It isn't always the case."

Craig: "For the record you recorded your own version of *Count On Me*. What was it like working with Marty on the record?"

Jesse Barish: "It was one of the high points of my life. The record (Jesse's self-titled fro m1978) wasn't rock and roll. It had a bunch of love songs. It was a very creative thing. There was something special in the air. As it turned out it didn't fly."

Craig: "You also got two more songs on the *Earth* album, *Crazy Feelin'* and *All Nite Long*. What do you remember about those two tracks?"

Jesse Barish: "This was funny. Somebody had to mention to me that I wrote *All Nite Long*. I didn't recall that. Marty loved *Crazy Feelin'*."

Craig: "Did you offer the band more then the three songs?"

Jesse Barish: "There was a period of time I would go to Marty's house everyday. I would play him the songs I wrote. He would tell me if they were worth taking to a Jefferson Starship rehearsal."

Craig: "If somebody wants to record your song, do you care how they record it? Are you able to cut the attachment to the arrangement you had in mind?"

Jesse Barish: "I like the people to stick to the melody as much as possible, at least for one verse and one chorus. I understand they want their own sound for the song."

Craig: "Have you ever seen the fantastic video for *Count On Me*? It was from the terrific U.K. television program the Old Grey Whistle Test. The band is sitting around the floor of a hotel room and playing the song."

Jesse Barish: "Really? Do you have a copy of that?"

Craig: "I sure do. You can have it in three days."

Jesse Barish: "Can it be a VCR thing? I would be thrilled to see that."

Craig: "I am happy to make sure you get a copy. Jesse, since you want a video of it, can I interest you in the eight track tape of *Red Octopus*?"

Jesse Barish: "Hey man, I'm VCR ready. I don't go much for the new stuff. I haven't had a computer in four months."

Craig: "Marty did two excellent songs of yours, *Hearts* and *Atlanta Lady*. He forgot that he had a hit with *Atlanta Lady*. When we talked he started to sing some of the song. *Atlanta Lady* made it to number twenty-seven on the charts."

Jesse Barish: "You are really informed Craig about the music."

Craig: "That is because I am a fan of his and of yours. If you ask me a science question I would get it wrong even if you gave me the answer." (As I did throughout every exam).

Jesse Barish: "On the self-titled Marty record from 1981, I had three songs. The two you talked about and *Music Is The Light*. Recently we had that come up. Marty called me and wanted to know if I had the chord changes for the song. I haven't remembered them yet. I sent Marty a song today called *Love Is*. I hope he likes it. I thought it came out great."

Craig: "Can you tell when you send Marty a song how he will normally react?"

Jesse Barish: "I can't. It is a crapshoot. Some he really loves and others he thinks are okay."

Craig: "What are the memories of writing *Hearts* and *Atlanta Lady*?"

Jesse Barish: "*Hearts* has a great story in a way. I was at a friend's house and having a hard time emotionally. I am in Los Angeles. By the way one of the guys from Jesse, Wolff & Whings was Kevin Kelley. Kevin was the drummer on the Byrds album *Sweetheart Of The Rodeo*. I'm at Kevin's house. I usually write the music first. I had a parking stub in my pocket. The type you get when you leave your car in a garage. I pull out the stub and wrote "Is everything alright." I was able to write a verse and a chorus on the parking stub. I now have that framed on my wall. I didn't know I saved it. I came across it one day and had it framed. I was able to finish the song in a couple of days. I didn't know it would be a hit, but did feel it was successful. The chord changes and the melody were strong. It didn't have a hook, but it had something. It caught a great moment. Marty's voice is unreal. Marty captured the moment. I remember I played the song for Marty and he wasn't that knocked out. The first time I played it he felt it was okay. The producer of the album John Hug liked it. John also produced a record of mine called *Mercury Shoes*. John and Marty became friends. John was able to convince Marty to sing the song. I was in Maui, Hawaii and I got a call from the studio. Marty and John are playing the recording of the tune for me. That was the first time I heard the song with music. I don't know if it was the final mix. Bill Champlin (Sons Of Champlin) did background vocals on the song."

Craig: "Marty told me that he thought Bill was terrific and in fact always liked the Sons Of Champlin."

Jesse Barish: "When they played the song for me on the phone I knew it was a hit. I was closing a chapter of my life. My marriage had ended and I wanted to make a fresh start. I left Mill Valley, California for Los Angeles. I have been here ever since."

Craig: "What do you remember about *Atlanta Lady?*"

Jesse Barish: "There aren't vivid memories of *Atlanta Lady*. I thought it was a great song. Marty liked that one more than *Hearts*."

Craig: "It is fortunate that Marty had an open mind."

Jesse Barish: "It is gratifying for me. I'm glad he still performs *Hearts*."

Craig: "What do you remember about your musical tastes in the 1960's?"

Jesse Barish: "I loved the Airplane as I mentioned and the Beatles. I would sit by the record player and listen to *Revolver*, and *Sgt. Pepper* by the Beatles and Dylan's *Blonde On Blonde*. Time would stop when those records came out. What do you have now? Music had a spiritual dimension. *Surrealistic Pillow* was the album I listened to over and over."

Craig: "What was your reaction to the album you did in 1980 *Mercury Shoes?*"

Jesse Barish: "I was in a messed up place. There are a few moments that are good. The album before was better. I thought it would put me on the map. We had gigs and a great band. I didn't come through."

Craig: "Do you consider yourself somebody that writes songs for other people?"

Jesse Barish: "I never considered it that way. I write songs all the time. I have friends that write songs that are used all the time. I had a couple of hits. I had *Count On Me* used in a movie fairly recently. It's in *The Family Stone*. They called either Marty or his dad for permission."

Craig: "What have you done the past several years musically?"

Jesse Barish: "I did an acoustic album with my son. We called it *Farther Son*. I did a folk-rock album called *Cherry Road*. I didn't try to market them. In the last year I did an instrumental CD called *Flute Salad*. It is a smooth jazz record but more funk. It is a style they have in Europe."

Craig "I hope you consider marketing the CD's. We have a mutual friend that will be happy to do the leg work for you. Jesse, it was a pleasure to hear the stories of the songs you wrote and I thank you for your time."

Jesse Barish: "Thank you. Let me know when the book is ready to come out."

**(An added note, Marty Balin was <u>very impressed</u> with Jesse's latest song *Love Is*).**

# Nick Buck- Hot Tuna and SVT.

Craig: "I really appreciate spending time with you today. Thank you for being part of the book."

Nick Buck: "Thank you. I'm sorry I have been so busy of late."

Craig: "Prior to the session work with Peter Green (Guitarist for Fleetwood Mac in the early days), what was going on for you musically?"

Nick Buck: "My family moved around when I was growing up. I spent my formative years in New Orleans. I played on Bourbon Street with a band called Face The Wall. They became White Fox. Then there was an opening in a band called Nectar and I joined. (Not to be confused with the progressive rock band that spells their name Nektar). I was about sixteen at the time. Nectar played both covers and original tunes. (The guitarist Bill Gregory went on to play with the band It's A Beautiful Day). We liked to play Bobby Blue Bland songs. (He was a legendary 1950's and 1960's blues singer). We sounded in the style of the Allman Brothers Band. There was heavy use of the guitar and the organ. In 1969 we opened a show for the Jefferson Airplane either in or around New Orleans. (Most likely 9/1/69 International Speedway, Baton Rouge, Louisiana). That was the first time I got to meet the band. They made an off handed comment about looking them up if we should ever get to San Francisco. Being young and naïve we took that as an open invitation to come live with them in their house. A few months go by and I pack up my stuff and drive from New Orleans to San Francisco. I knock on the door and they're like what are you hear for? To make a long story short I got to live in the Airplane House for awhile. Spencer Dryden was still living there and they had management offices as well. I still had a band but they disintegrated over time. That's how I got to meet Jorma and Jack as well. I got a call from a friend to audition for a band that had Henry Vestine (Henry was once a member of the blues band Canned Heat, known for the songs *On The Road Again* and *Goin' Up The Country*) as part of the group. I passed the audition but we never got past the rehearsal stage. Unfortunately Henry had some personal problems. Henry and Bob Hite (Henry was a guitarist and Bob Hite a singer. Bob was a member of Canned Heat at one time as well) had a phenomenal collection of music. Between the two of them they had most likely amassed the largest pre-war collection of blues music. They had country, Cajun, and doo-wop. They had 78's and 45's, it was an endless body of music. That was a great period for me. I stayed in Henry's house and was able to listen to all this phenomenal stuff. While this is going on I'm still keeping tabs on the music scene. Many years prior maybe when I was fifteen, a girlfriend and I took a bus from New Orleans to Miami for the Pop Festival. We wanted to see Fleetwood Mac. We got to meet Peter Green. In a bit of an odd circumstance we didn't have a place to stay. They invited us to stay with them in their hotel room. It was literally all the members of Fleetwood Mac in one room and my girlfriend and me sleeping on the floor in the other room. That is how I met Peter Green. I had affection for the music. I liked him and his sound. Now we fast-forward to Southern California. Fleetwood Mac was going to play the Whisky A Go-Go in Los Angeles. I got myself to the show and got back stage. I reacquainted myself with Peter Green. Peter told me that I should consider going to England. I could hang out with him and maybe there would be some musical stuff for me to do. Nothing was happening in California. I sold my equipment and went back to New Orleans to tell my parents what I was doing. I bought myself a plane ticket and went to England. I was able to live with Peter. That is how I got to play on the Peter Green record *The End Of The Game* (Released in 1970). Country Joe McDonald was working on an album in the same studio when Peter was recording *The End Of The Game*. I got to play on a couple of tracks on Country Joe's album *Hold On, It's Coming*, as did Peter. If I am not mistaken the first ten years the album was out they couldn't identify that Peter played on the LP. Finally they were able to note that Peter did play on a couple of tracks."

Craig: "When your mind goes back in time those days had to be amazing."

Nick Buck: "For sure. To meet Peter and to live with him was a musical dream. At that point Peter was into very much a spiritual quest. I got to hang out with Eric Clapton in his house and Pete Townshend in the studio. Looking back on it in retrospect it was fun and great stuff."

Craig: "It has often been documented about Peter's spiritual quest, is that the reason you didn't stay with him because there would not be consistent work? (Peter didn't release another solo record for nine years)."

Nick Buck: "At the time of *The End Of The Game* Peter was living in his house with his parents. He was on very much of a quest. Peter had become quite wealthy, from the days of working in a butcher shop and coming from meager means. He had a phenomenal gift of playing the guitar. He had a budding spiritual quest to understand more about his life in general. He had become wealthy in a short period of time. He had the quest for how to help mankind and why did he acquire the wealth. It was a dichotomy for him. He wanted a reason why. Why was the world the way it was. Why are children starving? We had played and it was quite free-flowing and enjoyable but there was no substance. He didn't talk about wanting a band. There was even talk of John Lennon contacting Peter, but he was on the spiritual quest. Without a band to play with live it was hard for me to make a living. I went back to New Orleans for a bit and then went to California once again. Would you like to hear an antidote about Fleetwood Mac later on?"

Craig: "I certainly would."

Nick Buck: "I kept in contact with members of Fleetwood Mac over the years. At the time of the recording of the *Rumours* album I got a call from Mick Fleetwood. He was at the Record Plant in Sausalito, California and asked if I wanted to come down and check things out. I ended up playing on a *jam* that I am uncredited on, but it is released on the *Rumours* reissue CD with bonus tracks. The song is called *For Duster (The Blues)*. I have to send Mick a letter and tell him if I could be credited on that it would be a nice gesture. At one point I almost became a keyboard-player for Fleetwood Mac. Lindsey Buckingham and Stevie Nicks wanted to keep it a five piece."

Craig: "When a fan hears the word uncredited it was understood in the 1960's and 1970's, it wasn't uncommon that a record company didn't want their artist helping a competing label. In the case of a reissue CD why would you not receive credit?"

Nick Buck: "We had gotten out of contact for each other. The legality of it is if they use your name they have to have a release. Since I wasn't contacted they did the right thing legally."

Craig: "There could have been a change of musical history. If you joined Fleetwood Mac, Hot Tuna would have needed a different keyboardist for *Hoppkorv*, and most likely SVT would never have been formed."

Nick Buck: "That is right, it could have all been different."

Craig: "Besides the work with Peter and Country Joe, once you return to California there were opportunities to play on the Papa John Creach self-titled solo record and Peter Kaukonen's *Black Kangaroo*. How did these come about?"

Nick Buck: "I came back to California to be a session-player. I toured with Quicksilver and got to appear on the Hot Tuna record *Burgers*."

Craig: "When you made the appearance on the *Burgers* album from 1972 were there talks even then about you joining the band on the road?"

Nick Buck: "There was the possibility of Jorma incorporating that path for a person to be playing the keyboards. At that point the Airplane was still going, there wasn't a good deal of time before they split but they were still were going."

Craig: "How did you feel the *Burgers* album turned out?"

Nick Buck: "It comes with a lot of wonderful styles and songs. It is a great atmosphere of music and musicianship. Soon they would move on to what Jorma called "The Metal Years.""

Craig: "When you were in the studio for the *Burgers* sessions did Jorma and Jack take suggestions from the other musicians?"

Nick Buck: "Since they had a style and knew mine the point would be to play a track and see where I could add an idea. Jorma would have an idea in his mind. They were looking at what instrumental pieces would resonate with them musically. We then would play it back and refine it, play it back, and refine it again. Finally we came up with the part that hit the button."

Craig: "Do you recall any songs left off *Burgers* and any tunes that were changed significantly?"

Nick Buck: "I kind of knew where you were going with that. I don't recollect anything I was on that didn't make the final master for the record. Remember this is going back a number of years ago. I don't remember specific edits or songs being chopped down. Hot Tuna played a lot live. There was always jamming."

Craig: "What other things were you doing after *Burgers*?"

Nick: "Jack, Jorma, and I stayed in touch. I would play on *Yellow Fever* and *Hoppkorv*. I did sessions in California and played with bands. I kept myself busy. I played with Merl Saunders (Well known keyboardist in the San Francisco scene) son Tony and carried on what I was doing. That was playing live and session work too."

Craig: "What memories do you have of Papa John?"

Nick Buck: "He was a great guy and really talented. He was an accomplished fiddle-player and always accommodating. Joey Covington helped with the stardom. He brought him to the Airplane from Los Angeles. Once he got known, Papa John had this glow about him from the accolades of success. He may have struggled for thirty or forty years and found success later on in life. Playing with Papa was a nice memory from a nice time. When Grunt Records got formed it seemed it was all the musicians that knew each other and played with each other. I remember when we were doing the *Burgers* record and Carlos Santana was three houses away. Everybody would *jam* and there was always something going on at the Airplane House. Papa John's record is a snapshot of the group of musicians that were around."

Craig: "What were your impressions of playing with Peter Kaukonen and did you play on live shows with him in support of the LP?"

Nick Buck: "I don't remember Peter touring much behind the record. We shared a house for a period of time. At that point in time he was with Jacky Kaukonen. I played with him a lot. He is a very talented player. Nothing happened out of the ordinary when we were recording the record, but it was fun playing my parts. It was a good experience."

Craig: "How were you told you would fit in nicely for *Yellow Fever*?"

Nick Buck: "Jorma had the song *Bar Room Crystal Ball*. I had been playing some synthesizer and Jorma wanted that sound. We may have played around a bit a couple of times before he called. That is a great song Jorma wrote. I loved being part of the song."

Craig: "Did anything interesting come about during the recording sessions?"

Nick Buck: "I don't remember anything not making it to the end goal. There may have been recordings in the studio of playing and jamming. I don't recall that."

Craig: "What do you recall about playing with Sammy Piazza and Bob Steeler in the studio and live?"

Nick Buck: "They were different types if drummers with different styles. Both are equally great in their own right. They had their own style and the band had their own flavor at that time. There is a different oral presence. You can listen to the records and hear it. Sammy is from Texas. The band then had a looser and dustier electric combo sound. When they moved into the period with Bob it was very defined and thicker and heavier."

Craig: "When you were doing the session for *Bar Room Crystal Ball* did Jorma bring up any talk of taking you on the road?"

Nick Buck: "It was always intimated that something could or may happen. It wasn't brought up as a formal piece but it was understated that it could happen one day. I don't know what finally turned the key. It may have been on *Hoppkorv* the addition of the keyboards to a fairly great degree. That album may have finally made the decision the right thing to do. I think I played on five songs. I suggested during the recording of *Hoppkorv* to do *Bowlegged Woman, Knock Kneed Man*."

Craig: "That was a great suggestion. I'm glad you brought that up. It is often assumed that Jorma and Jack picked all the tunes on that record. Do you recall anything during the sessions of note?"

Nick Buck: "It seemed the right tracks were picked. Harry Maslin who produced David Bowie, was the producer on the record. He came in with the reputation of doing some substantial things and being a buttoned up producer. I remember vividly in the studio he wasn't prone to having Jack and Jorma play for hours. He wanted to capture a specific genesis and spark. He thought that jamming around took away energy from the record. I remember vividly that Jack and Jorma were playing some song and Harry turned down the monitor and didn't listen to it. When they stopped he went back to the producing of the album."

Craig: "Did that cause conflict?"

Nick Buck: "If you bring the person on in this case Harry, you want him to bring what he can to create the record. He would sometimes say We are done for the night" or "I'm not hearing what I need to hear and we'll pick it up tomorrow."

Craig: "During the sessions for the record did any of these songs come up for consideration, *Thunderbolt Song*, *Snow Gorilla*, *Bright Eyes*, *I Don't Know*, *Wolves And Lambs*, *Jack's Tune*, *Killing Time In The Crystal City*, *Lost In Time* and or *Swamp Life*?"

Nick Buck: "Those songs came about later on at the rehearsals (The most noted one was 7/77 in Jorma's basement)."

Craig: "In 1977 Hot Tuna played ten shows before you joined the band on tour. How come you weren't there for all the performances?"

Nick Buck: "If I remember correctly there were two separate tours in 1977. I had to learn not only the songs from the album but all the others they were going to consider playing live."

Craig: "Did Jorma ever mention why they didn't have you start the first leg of the tour?"

Nick Buck: "That never came up. I didn't ask about that either. Maybe Jorma realized that he wanted to expand the sound. They may have thought the latest record had other textures to it and why not try."

Craig: "The first show you played was at the Old Waldorf, San Francisco on 5/7/77. How long before that show did you rehearse?"

Nick Buck: "It was a matter of weeks. It may have been a month. We got together and played. At first it was the body of music they had. When they liked the idea of *Bowlegged Woman, Knock Kneed Man*, I started to write *Snow Gorilla* and *Bright Eyes*. Jorma had *Killing Time In The Crystal City*. You also want to explore all areas of sonic power. Maybe there is something new and undiscovered you can kind of find. That could be a great addition to a song that already exists, an intro, or an ending. The process is you rehearse and touch on a lot of pieces of music. The way you would play that on stage is to make up different set lists based on how you feel. You may put something in there that only got rehearsed twice, but you feel good about it. You have to keep yourself fresh and not bored."

Craig: "How was it the first night on stage for you?"

Nick Buck: "It was great. To go through the period of history to have gone through with them and then to play live was phenomenal."

Craig: "Does anything stand out on the tour that was immensely funny or strange?"

Nick Buck: "Jack would walk around back stage with a white rabbit hat. Bob Steeler had a problem every time he ordered room service at a hotel. They can be notoriously slow to begin with. He would order room service then shower and get dressed and the food wouldn't show up until we were leaving the hotel. It happened it seemed every place we went on the tour."

Craig: "I know the feeling. I'm still waiting for room service from a 1985 interview I did at one of the hotels Bob had trouble. How did you deal with the grind of touring?"

Nick Buck: (Nick laughs). "I looked at it as what you have to do. The starving musician had to worry about getting to that point. I always made the best of it. It is what it is. It is my job and I do the best at it I could."

Craig: "What songs from the 1977 tour did you enjoy performing?"

Nick Buck: "I loved playing *Funky #7*, *Bar Room Crystal Ball,* and *Killing Time In The Crystal City*. I loved the songs from *Burgers*. There were a lot of great songs to play. *Snow Gorilla* was great to play, as was *Bowlegged Woman, Knock Kneed Man*."

HOT TUNA   Jack Casady, Bob Steeler, Nick Buck
           seated Jorma Kaukonen

GRUNT RECORDS
Manufactured and Distributed by RCA Records

**Photo by kind permission of Mike Somavilla.  From the Mike Somavilla collection.**

**Photo may not be reproduced without written consent from Mike Somavilla.**

**Photographer unknown.**

**Thank you BMG .  This is a promo picture from circa 5/77.**

Craig: "When you started to play with Hot Tuna live did you have any trepidation how the fanatical fans would accept you?"

Nick Buck: "I didn't have any trepidation. I was cognizant of what I was getting into. It didn't bother me. I didn't try to step on anybody."

Craig: "I found the audience took to you as part of the band quickly."

Nick Buck: "I felt so. I had a history with the band. I played on three records. I didn't show up out of nowhere. They had seen my name. My name and contributions weren't unknown to them. I tried to enhance what the guitar brought to their music."

Craig: "Did you ever have conversations with Jorma, Jack and or the record company why they never opened the vaults and let out the tunes we talked about you rehearsing, as well as the *Party Song* with Jack doing background vocals?"

Nick Buck: "I wasn't privy to those discussions. I can only think that it has to be about money. If money is to be made the record company will be there. If not they don't want to get into a labor of love to remaster the material and even to find it."

Craig: "When it got to be 11/26/77 and you had finished the late show at the Palladium, New York City did you have any inclination that would be the last Hot Tuna gig until 1983?"

Nick Buck: "We played that show and I looked at that as a non event in terms of nothing bad had transpired. I saw Jorma and his wife after the show and everyone said goodbye. I believe Jorma was telling me he would soon go speed skating. It was goodbye as if talk to you real soon. There was never anything formal. I don't remember any harsh words. As a break after the tour I took a train ride across the country. A couple of weeks later I got a call from Jack. It seems almost odd but I remember that is how it happened."

Craig: "When Jack called you did he talk about anything that may have happened during the speed skating trip?"

Nick Buck. "No he didn't. The only thing he told me was the band wasn't getting back together again and would I want to come over and play some music. I told him yes. We never dwelled on the break up."

Craig: "Did you call Jorma to see if everything was okay?"

Nick Buck: "Jorma often communicated with me by letter. There wasn't anything about a break up."

Craig: "Did you and Jack start to discuss the groundwork for SVT?"

Nick Buck: "Yes it was something like we had gotten together and played. Jack and I knew that we needed other players. We got a hold of tapes of different bands. Jack liked the sound of one tape from a Marin County (California) band called Air Play. We went to see them at a club in Marin. Jack and I liked the band. We talked with the drummer and the guitar-player. Air Play was kind of disintegrating. At that time there were a number of showcases for bands. A showcase was a regular gig at a club, but there would be record company executives present. It gave them an opportunity to perform their music in front of important people. Air Play had a few showcases and nothing resulted from them. Brain Marnell on guitar and Bill Gibson on drums were available."

Craig: "What made you and Jack decide to have a complete change in musical style?"

Nick Buck: "Jack had built up a musical history on open-ended jamming. Jack wanted to try the evolution of a player to find different contexts and different structures. It wasn't having an allegiance to the Ramones sound.

SVT didn't sound like that. We didn't sound punk or new wave. It was a desire to try a different playing style. Brian's forte was to write the shorter pop songs. Brian was a good player but wasn't a virtuoso soloist like Jorma."

Craig: "When the band got together did you and Jack talk about having an albatross around your necks, because the Hot Tuna fan wanted one style and the new wave and power pop fan would have liked to only see younger musicians on stage?"

Nick Buck: "We understood the path we were crossing. As players you play with the people you want to. In Jack he is one of the top five rock bass-players in the world. He may be the best. We had hoped that there would be an embrace to let the musician stretch out and do something different. Look at an artist like Neil Young and how many permutations his musical career has taken. An artist is an artist. We knew the Hot Tuna fan wouldn't like the fact we didn't have long hair and the new wave fan would have liked our hair to be spiked. At the end of the day you have to say the heck with it. The band had enough quality in the musicianship and desire to make our own fan base."

Craig: "Did you consider adding any short Hot Tuna songs or 1960's covers to get some of the older fans at least interested in the band?"

Nick Buck: "I know what you're saying but we felt if we were going to do this, we had to do it all the way."

Craig: " You played on the two 1979 singles, *New Year/Wanna See You Cry* and *Heart Of Stone/The Last Word* as well as the 1980 *Extended Play* record. Why did you leave before the 1981 album *No Regrets*?"

Nick Buck: "I thought of that for awhile. The band was having a bit of a hard time. In my mind I don't have one thing that becomes the reason. A time comes when things start to wear down. Maybe there weren't going to be enough keyboard parts, but it was time."

Craig: "We should get in a plug for the 2005 reissue of the *No Regrets* album. There are bonus tracks and you appear on those. Was the departure from SVT amicable?"

Nick Buck: "Brian came over and pleaded with me to stay. I reached the limit and didn't want to continue."

Craig: "After leaving SVT, you played on the Roy Loney & The Phantom Movers record *Contents Under Pressure*. (Roy was a member of the Flamin' Groovies. They were a San Francisco area band from circa 1965. Their sound mixed English Rock, raunchy riffs, and a bit of blues). How did that come about?"

Nick Buck: "I went back to playing sessions. I played with Roy and I formed a band called the Innocent. I went back to doing what I was doing before." (Nick wanted to bring out that there is another Nick Buck! The guy is a drummer from Europe. Nick actually can play the drums but he is not the person on the Angelic Upstarts albums or those by the Whiskey Priests).

Craig: "What were some of the other things you did that may have been overlooked?"

Nick Buck: "I did session work for a country artist Doug Myers. I play in a blues band with Curtis Lawson. The guitarist is Drake Levin. He played with the great sixties band Paul Revere & The Raiders. "

Craig: "Do you have a desire to play with any San Francisco friends, if a promoter interested in the music and not only money puts together something for the 40th Anniversary Summer Of Love celebration?"

Nick Buck: "Certainly I would be interested. A guy you know Mike "The Fan Man" Somavilla called me about the Spencer Dryden benefit (5/22/04 Slim's, San Francisco) a few years ago. I ended up being part of the performance. That threw me back into the mix. I got to see Pete Sears, Greg Douglass, and Peter Kaukonen. That got me back into the networking for social sessions."

Craig: "Wasn't it great to help Spencer out?"

Nick Buck: "It was. As mentioned he and I were roommates at the Airplane House. He was one of those guys regardless of musical stature that treated the up and coming artist the same as the band with the number one record. I was happy to contribute to Spencer personally and musically. It is a shame in the evolution of our paths I never got to play with him."

Craig: "It would have been great if you and Spencer were on the same stage at a Dinosaur's gig. I know that you have a busy schedule this week, so one more question and you'll be on your way. Would you and Jack consider releasing any of the live SVT shows, maybe even with bonus material?"

Nick Buck: "That isn't a bad idea. If somebody could take the time to approach the different labels, it would be nice to have the music out there for Brian's family." (Brian passed away in 1983).

Craig: "I'll give Mike Somavilla a call and see if you and Mike could talk for a bit about that. Nick, it was even more fun than I hoped it would be talking about Hot Tuna, SVT and the session work. Thank you for your time and may the family always be well."

Nick Buck: "Thank you Craig: "If you need anything let me know. I think I can get a package out to you this week for the book."

# Craig Chaquico- Jefferson Starship.

Craig: "Thanks for being able to take time out after a recording session today. I've looked forward to hearing your recollections of over thirty years in the music business."

Craig Chaquico: "Thank you Craig. I hope to remember that far back."

Craig: "Why don't we start with the story of the often forgotten but very enjoyable record from 1973, Jack Traylor & Steelwind, *Child Of Nature*. David Freiberg (Keyboards) is on the LP and there was heavy moral support from Grace and Paul. The title track is very strong. What do you remember about that time of your life and the record?"

Craig Chaquico: "Let me give a funny story on how I got into the band. When I was in high school I was playing my guitar outdoors. One of my teachers had walked by and told me to see him after class. I'm thinking what did I do this time? When I went to talk with him after the class was over he pulled out a guitar. He told me that he had seen me play outside. He wanted to know if I would be interested in joining a band he had, called Steelwind. I was seventeen years of age. The California law stated that you had to be twenty one to perform in any clubs that had alcohol. I had to play on stage with a disguise. They were able to get a hold of a fake mustache for me. This wasn't one of the cheap dollar jobs. The mustache was something you would see on the set of a Hollywood movie. Sometimes the glue would start to get loose. One time I'm sipping a soft drink and I see a caterpillar in the drink. Then I realized it was the mustache. There was another time when we had some intense black lighting. The audience could see my mustache was not on straight. They were wondering what was up with that dude. At night I got to be on stage, when the day came I would ride my bicycle to school."

Craig: "Did Jack have a relationship with Paul and Grace, before the period of time where three records got released, *Baron Von Tollbooth & The Chrome Nun* (Paul and Grace), *Child Of Nature*, and *Manhole* (Grace Slick 1974)?"

Craig Chaquico: "They were friends. I'm not sure how they knew each other. In 1972 when Steelwind was working on the first set of demos the Airplane would be using the studio first, and then we would come in to record. I remember how cool Jorma and Jack were to me. They never treated me as the new kid. That continued through my playing on *Baron Von Tollbooth & The Chrome Nun*, *Manhole*, and the first Jefferson Starship record *Dragon Fly*. They always made me feel welcome. They never gave off a bad vibe. They were totally cool."

Craig: "Do you see Jack Traylor these days?"

Craig Chaquico: "There were times our musical paths crossed through mutual friends. There was an odd time from the transition of me going from Steelwind to the Jefferson Starship. When I first went with the Jefferson Starship our schedules were so different. Then with me leaving there were uncomfortable feelings. That is the way it can go with a band."

Craig: "Did you ever get either a first hand story from Jack Traylor or somebody on the inside as to why he didn't continue full throttle after the Steelwind record? If you go by sales Meatloaf's first album wasn't *Bat Out Of Hell*. As great a record as the Airplane made on their first try (*Takes Off*), the second (*Surrealistic Pillow*) out sold it by light years. It is also worth pointing out the female vocalist Diana Harris could sound at times like Grace."

Craig Chaquico: "I didn't get this first hand. This is a total guess. He may have felt man I gave this a great shot. I had two amazing people taking an interest in the record, Grace and Paul. I had a major label behind me, I've given it a shot for many years, I have a regular job. I am a teacher. He went to college, had a great education, and may have wanted to apply his skills elsewhere. I often think that I got really lucky. How many great musicians fall through the cracks? I was lucky, man. How many young kids play on a record that doesn't sell and then get asked to join a band with the heritage of the Jefferson Starship? I was lucky as hell. The main reason I went on was because I had that tremendous opportunity. Had that not happened with the Jefferson Starship I would have been in college. I would be in Sacramento, California in college and playing with a local band. Think about it, that is a hard field to rise from. You need talent, luck, and the stars to align properly. Granted if I couldn't rise to the occasion I wouldn't have lasted, but I still needed the luck to get the opportunity. If the Jefferson Starship didn't happen for me, I could have been one of those guys that never got off the ground."

Craig: "Do you have any memories from *Baron Von Tollbooth & The Chrome Nun*, and *Manhole*?"

Craig Chaquico: "I remember the first time I got asked to play on more than one song. I felt oh my God, Carlos Santana is scheduled to show up at the session. It may have been Jerry Garcia that was going to help on the record (*Baron Von Tollbooth & The Chrome Nun*) and not Carlos. David Crosby will be there and the Pointer Sisters. I get a chance to play on the same sessions as these people. I got to play the lead on Jack Traylor's song *Flowers In The Night*. There were a couple of songs Jerry Garcia was going to play the lead. I was told to be there to play the basic rhythm parts. Jerry would come in and overdub a lead. I was already on the basic track. On one session I got carried away when the solo was scheduled and started to play the lead. Jerry obviously wasn't there. I don't remember the song. Nobody cared, they can erase it later. Jerry will come in and lay down the solo. The story I heard was the next day Jerry comes in to play the solo. He did great work on the record. When it came time for the song Jerry heard my solo. The guys in the recording studio told him not to worry, they'll erase it. Jerry told them wait a minute, why not let the kid have a solo that was pretty good. I always wanted to give Jerry a high four and a half every time I saw him."

Craig: "That is a story for the book."

Craig Chaquico: "I was a kid that went to Altamont (Rolling Stones, Jefferson Airplane, and Grateful Dead performed at the Altamont Speedway, Livermore, California 12/6/69). I would get into bands with an older friend and we would drive to Winterland to see shows. We were so inspired by the bands we saw, that we would buy the records. We would practice our guitars. I embraced the lifestyle. There was a thing going on in the country where we asked questions about Vietnam. Music was a doorway. To open it and love your brother, ask questions about the environment, the government, whatever, was something I looked forward to. Then to meet musicians that walked the walk. They were trying to do the right thing. They encouraged me. The act Garcia did, and the way Jorma, and Jack encouraged me as a young kid, was walking the walk. Maybe it was different back then. Today the music business is more cut throat. There isn't as much as a feeling that the music is the way of life. Maybe back then it was like that, but the corner of the world I was in with the Airplane people, Grateful Dead people, David Crosby, and others made me feel that there was a door I could walk through. A real cool story was an article Grace showed me when the *Baron Von Tollbooth & The Chrome Nun* album got released. They thought I didn't exist, that my name was made up. The guitar parts were by Eric Clapton, or somebody else. They thought that the guy playing had a contract that wouldn't let him use his real name. That was one of the biggest compliments. I was sky high, but always stayed grounded. While I thought it was the coolest thing to play on a record, I remembered when I was in high school that if I didn't keep up the grades I wouldn't get a chance to do all this. I did have a good balance. If you are young and thrown in the limelight it could cause problems."

Craig: "There is a great track on the Jefferson Starship record *Dragon Fly* called *Come To Life*. The guitar solo is perfect, but as importantly the sound of the instrument is exactly right for the tune. What do you remember about the track?"

Craig Chaquico: "I try to be melodic and not about flash all the time. The credit for the sound of the guitar goes to Jorma's brother Peter. He played bass in the early days with the Jefferson Starship. He was an accomplished guitar-player. Peter had a few guitars and older amps. He educated me on why older guitars and older amps sound better. By the time we began to record *Dragonfly* I had saved some money to get older guitars and older amps. I started to record with that type of equipment. The engineers knew how to make the guitar sound good. Now I can produce records and I know what I learned back then. That's great you liked the sound of the song. You were the type of person we were making the records for. We wanted the best sounding album. We were not about writing hits. The motivation was to make good records. I know that before I started to record I had influences of Clapton, Hendrix, Santana, Pink Floyd, and Led Zeppelin. What was nice about working in the San Francisco scene was you had to wear different hats. There was the challenge of playing rock, folk, or the blues. *Ride The Tiger* (*Dragon Fly*) is a different sound than *Come To Life*. The entire recording was a challenge. I needed that as a growing musician. You have to think out of the box. I would sometimes go to a session and be terrified. I remember when we did *Miracles* (*Red Octopus*) with Marty Balin on the acoustic guitar, me in the lead, Pete Sears on bass, David Freiberg on keyboards, and John Barbata on drums. There was only a rough vocal by Marty without strings, or anything. Not even the background vocals were put down yet. I recorded guitar parts and was really disappointed in my playing. I wanted to go back and do it all over. Everyone in the studio was telling me to wait and let the other parts of the song come together. When we finished the song I didn't need to change anything. I didn't have to change a note from the one take. When you listen to what you've done in the studio you can be very critical about your performance. You need another musician, or producer to give input. To let you know that you can't be critical until it all comes together. Sometimes the result isn't good. That case I felt the result was very good."

Craig: "When you saw the increase in record sales and fan bass from *Dragon Fly* to *Red Octopus* did that put heavy pressure on you to have to come up with material for *Spitfire*?"

Craig Chaquico: "To the others it may have. To me it was another adventure and holiday. It was wow. I am getting to make another record and go on tour again. The record company didn't give direction and force us to do specific things. They left us alone. When we went to the studio for *Spitfire* they didn't prevent the long guitar-solo. I really loved that. We had been stretching out songs live. The band let myself and Pete Sears stretch out. It wasn't ultra long. The Airplane had stretched out songs before us. The other guys never told me they were worried. I was ready to go for it. From the very first record I was lucky that Paul and Grace were not threatened with other writers. They encouraged me to write. They asked me if I had songs to work on. They could have said "You are only a guitar-player." They never were like that. They were very nurturing. *Spitfire* was fun. Then we went out on tour. Then came *Earth*."

Craig: "What type of memories do you have playing with Papa John Creach?"

Craig Chaquico: "Way nice memories. The guy could play. I loved the solos of guitar-players. Clapton solos, or Jimmy Page solos, so when I heard a guy could riff on a violin I was going wow. On stage we would play off each other. He would play a riff, I would answer, or the other way around. On the *Dragon Fly* record there was a song *Ride The Tiger*. The guitar-solo gets high up on the neck. and gets higher, and higher. There is a lick where it is beyond the frets. There is no more fret left. I got that idea from Papa John. When we would play live he would play one lick on the violin, to show we brought the improvisation to a climax and to go back to the vocals. When he played the lick on the violin I could never top that. He had no frets. I watched him so many times I wanted to do this on the guitar. I finally figured it out. You need the amp loud and the proper tone. I use the trick to this day. Papa John would often speak in the third person and call himself Papa John. He tells me a story that sometimes he can make a mistake on stage. He tells me if you don't make a mistake you aren't exploring enough. One time Papa John made a mistake. Papa John knew he made a mistake, but so the audience wouldn't know it was a mistake Papa John played the exact same mistake again on purpose. Then he winks at me and tells me that's where jazz came from. He was such a trip. I adored playing with the man."

Craig: "What thoughts do you have on the transitional period of sound and performers starting with the 1978 *Earth* album?"

Craig Chaquico: "There were many things that happened during the transitional period. We didn't stay the same, we attracted a new audience, and we pissed a lot of people off. To me there were three distinct evolutions of the band. The first four records with Papa John, and Marty, then there were the second phase with Mickey

Thomas, and the third phase with *We Built This City*, the more pop sounding of the three. The second phase there was a traumatic experience. We were in Europe and Grace had some personal troubles. When you have that type of horsepower it isn't always easy to keep it on the road. We had to play the Knebworth Festival, Herts, England, on 6/24/78. There are a hundred thousand people and no Grace. Tom Petty was on the bill and Devo, we were one of the headliners. One of the key players isn't there. We had to perform without her. Marty handled the vocals incredibly well. The show went off without any problems. Marty told us when we get back to the United States we can start writing songs and I'll be there for you guys. To back up a few days because Grace had spun out she couldn't perform at the Loreley Festival, Wiesbaden, Germany, on 6/17/78. It is a gorgeous venue. We are sitting back stage on stones that were centuries old. We are near the Rhine River, old castles, and there is a little old railroad track running. I'm thinking what an adventure. I travel around the world, I play in front of people that may not even all speak English. I could tell them stories through my guitar. I was in heaven. It turns out that Grace couldn't make the gig. It looked like we would reschedule. People backstage started to cry. This wasn't because they were fans of the band. They knew there was going to be a riot. The story I heard later was the promoter had gotten a bad reputation by selling tickets and promoting American bands, but when the people showed up the band wasn't there. There were local bands playing. I was like man we are getting to get our asses kicked. John Barbata and I are looking at each other and thinking we don't need to be here when the announcement is made. David Freiberg tells us that he would make the announcement. Later we heard there was a group of radicals that were looking to start trouble. David tells the crowd we are sorry we can't play, but we will play a free concert. When the promoter translates, he left off the part that we would come back for a free concert. He didn't want to have to pay the band. There was gasoline used to set the stage on fire during the riot. Where that came from I'll never know. I'm told that this made all three of the major network news in the United States. We lost most of the equipment. The vintage guitars I had were all gone. I lost a Sunburst 1959 Les Paul. A guitar-player will cry when they read that in your book. I lost an original Gibson Firebird. All that up in smoke. Recently at an auction the 1959 Sunburst Les Paul went for three hundred-fifty thousand dollars. It wasn't worth it back then, but still was super rare."

Craig: "Even back then it was worth that to you. You had created history on the guitar."

Craig Chaquico: "These were my babies. John was the same way picking out on his drums. John Barbata would try two hundred cymbals to pick out one. That is why he is such a great studio head. He taught me so much about not only the way you play, but how to make it sound. After the riot gig we had to go rent equipment from a local music store. It was kind of funky. Let me point this out, even when Grace had problems she was a super kind person. She had a heart of gold. Even when Grace went a bit crazy the audience liked it. It was sort of early Alice Cooper (Well known musician, known for outrageous stage acts and the major hit *School's Out*)."

Craig: What happens when you finally get back home?"

Craig Chaquico: "It turns out Marty didn't want to go on. We have to audition a singer. Mickey Thomas had good recommendations. He shows up for the audition. He auditions by singing a song I wrote called *Rock Music* (It would later go on the *Freedom At Point Zero* album). I still have the original demo of that. He nailed it on the first try. He had the right range. I had seen Mickey perform. Now we hire Mickey, but the band wants a girl singer. My friend Eric recommended we try Nicolette Larson (She had a major hit with Neil Young's song *Lotta Love*). It didn't fly. They all thought she was a great singer, but didn't fit in for what we wanted to sound like."

Craig: "The suggestion of Nicolette Larson isn't that far fetched. She could really sing. Maybe the band felt that the style wasn't the right fit, but she had a solid voice."

Craig Chaquico: "The credit goes to my friend Eric. He is a music freak. Maybe people were hoping Grace could have been ready. We also needed a drummer. John Barbata had gotten into a serious car crash. This was catastrophic. There was pain and suffering. It was not an easy transition."

Craig: "Pete Sears told me that the guy that the record company thought was second best was Jess Roden. (Some of his many appearances are on a Mott The Hoople record *Wildlife* and playing with two of the Doors in the Butts Band, John Densmore, and Robbie Kreiger)."

Craig Chaquico: "I remember Jess. I remember really liking him. I wasn't privy to the record company meeting about Jess. What was funny Mickey is offered the job and not sure he wants to take it. I was one of the people that had to talk to him, to get him to sing with us. I told him dude you are playing nightclubs and yes cream will rise to the top, but you can make records and play larger venues. I'm telling him we have a great drummer with Aynsley Dunbar (Frank Zappa and Journey) and you'll like the producer. Finally he agrees. It was fine for Mickey to sing with Elvin Bishop (*Fooled Around And Feel In Love*), we offered a chance to leap over some of the hurdles he would face."

Craig: "Did you ever get the story from Marty why he decided not to go on with the band when the band returned home?"

Craig Chaquico: "I never have. It is very possible that with all that went down Marty needed a break. Look at his career. He has written amazing songs, he's played with top bands, he had royalty checks still coming in. Maybe a time came when he was asking himself if he really needed to put up with all the baggage that can go with being in a band. Marty was great on stage. He had the voice, the persona, and the songs. Behind the scenes he was never loud. It could have been time for a rest. It is possible that if we waited longer he may have gotten back in the fold. A funny Grace note. She heard a song from the *Freedom At Point Zero* album on the radio and didn't know it was us. She told us that she would sing with that band in a minute. She attended one of the early shows. She came in a disguise. We got a permit to play at Golden Gate Park, San Francisco. The local officials were afraid that the park would be damaged. That was unfair. The Grateful Dead, and Jefferson Starship fans care about the quality of life, they help clean the parks. We needed a way around the red tape. I have a friend that I taught how to play Frisbee. She became a champion. There was a Frisbee tournament in the park. The people running the tournament had a permit for a local band. Guess who is a local band? That would be the Jefferson Starship. We got to play in the park. That was thanks to Laura Engle. She was also my manager when I started the solo records. Things come around in circles."

Craig: "Any interesting stories from the *Freedom at Point Zero* sessions?"

Craig Chaquico: "I have one that is my favorite. *Jane* started off as a more keyboard oriented song. I suggested that the guitar be more prevalent. I wanted to leave a big hole where the guitar would be. It was right for the long solo, even though it was a pop song. The first time I played it was at a nightclub. Huey Lewis (Massive record sales and hits from the 1980's including *The Heart Of Rock And Roll* and *The Power Of Love*) was there. He was always a cool hang. I played him a rough mix of *Jane* in his old car and he played me a rough mix of one of the first songs he ever did. I told him dude that sounds good. I hadn't thought of that story in years. It was nice that he saw our song go on the charts and we saw his career skyrocket. Now the story takes a turn. The manager of the band wanted the guitar-solo cut. Radio had changed. The solo has to be shorter. The band backed me up. The manager and the band got along. In this case we didn't agree. The producer told the manager that we should try it the way the band wants. The manager takes out a stop watch and times the solo. He wanted me to find one song on the radio that had a solo that long at the time. The one I finally found from about that time was Foreigner's song *Hot Blooded*. The solo on that tune was one second longer. To this day I cherish every moment. I was so glad that the band backed me. The icing on the cake was years later I met the lead guitarist (Kirk Hammett) from Metallica (1980's metal band). This was at the Bay Area Music Awards. Backstage he tells me how much he loved the song *Jane*. At the time there weren't enough guitar songs on the radio and he loved the fact there was a long solo."

Craig: "When the Jefferson Starship had people coming and going, was there a falling out with Paul Kantner?"

Craig Chaquico: "There was of sorts. As the record company wanted a change in style for the first time there were some arguments in the band. We never had this happen before. There were strong personalities and a shift of direction. I always got along with him, and always liked, and respected him very much. I have to thank Paul and Grace for giving me the chance in the music business. Then there became the issue of the name. Now we go to court and that isn't the publicity you want for the band. Now we have two bands using the name, Mickey's and Paul's."

Craig: "Were any overtures made to you to be part of any of the great reunion gigs Paul put together with former musical associates, such as Jack Traylor and Darby Gould?"

Craig Chaquico: "There was contact from a mutual friend, if I would be interesting in playing some shows with the Jefferson Starship. Until there could be a resolution of two bands using part of the name I wasn't interested. A mutual friend asked if I would play with Mickey's Starship and I gave the same response. If there was one band, and many original players, it would be cool to do that. It would be hard to do it without Grace. She deserved so much credit for what she gave to the band. She deserved to be treated well by everyone."

Craig: "How did you finally reach your saturation point with the band?"

Craig Chaquico: "Mickey wanted to have more of a pop sound. If it could have been more rock, it may have been able to continue. David Freiberg leaving brought tears to my eyes. He felt the time was right. It isn't uncommon that a lead singer will take control of the band. Management normally supports that. A lead singer has a strong personality and a healthy ego. Public speaking is the hardest thing. I respected Mickey's chops, but he wanted to go pop. Was he right? We did have three number one songs within fourteen months. More energy went to Mickey. When he was with Elvin Bishop, he was the singer in the Elvin Bishop band. Now he wanted it to be known that he was part of the Jefferson Starship. Mickey forgot that two of the number ones had Grace on the record. Then the record company wants us to hire studio musicians for the next record, because there would only be Mickey and myself. To top it off the record company wants him to pick all the songs. The want different people on the studio record and on the road. It was finally time to go. I could deal with less guitar, but hardly any was tough to take. I left and decided to try something where the guitar is important to the sound. I form a band called Big Bad Wolf. Grunge music is now coming in. The timing was terrible. Labels didn't want the killer lead vocalist, mixed with the guitar solos, the way *Jane* sounded for example. I stuck with the project for maybe a year. We did get the record out in Japan. Every American record door was closed. This was so frustrating. My job is music. This was a tough time. Now my wife is pregnant, I don't have a job, or a place to go. Now that my wife was pregnant I thought I would play acoustic. This way I am not too loud around my wife. I started to record some acoustic songs at home. Near the end of the Big Bad Wolf period I talk with Ozzy Ahlers. He is a keyboard-player that is well known in the San Francisco area. He played with Jerry Garcia for instance. He helped with Big Bad Wolf. One night we ran into each other and he asked what was happening and I did the same. He told me that he had a session scheduled for tomorrow with Joe Satriani (Played with Mick Jagger, briefly replaced Ritchie Blackmore in Deep Purple, and has released multiple guitar oriented albums). Then he tells me Joe can't make it. I tell him I know a guitar-player that is available. The next day I go into the studio with Ozzy. I always wanted to be in a band with him. As it turns out he is on all my solo records. He is working on the music for the Gumby movie. It's going to be clay animation. When Gumby plays the guitar its me."

Craig: "Was Poky (Gumby's friend) there hopefully?"

Craig Chaquico: "Poky and the Blockheads were there. The Blockheads were bad guys. My son loved this when he was four. I asked Ozzy if he would be interested in working on an instrumental record. We wanted to create without pressure. We didn't have a label. We passed our demos out and the answer was no. One label hears too much jazz, the other too little. Then they wanted blues to sound like Robert Cray (Blues guitarist, worked with Eric Clapton). Finally we come across Higher Octave Records. They liked the demo the way it was. All they wanted us was to remix a few things. It was really well received."

Craig: "I remember the first time I checked out the record *Acoustic Highway* in 1993, I was wondering what I would think. Then I put on the title track and *Return Of The Eagle*. I must have listened to both of them fifty times. The CD was crafted so well."

Craig Chaquico: "Oh man. Thanks so much. That is so nice to hear. We got so many people turning us down. We finally got encouragement to continue to make music. It became the number one new age album of the year in Billboard (Music trade paper)."

Craig: "It was cool for the older fans that you did a completely different version of *Find Your Way Back*, on the follow-up CD *Acoustic Planet*."

Craig Chaquico: "There are some Jefferson Starship roots somewhere in the record. I wrote that on a acoustic guitar. I used to play that at some of the sound checks for the new age concerts. Thank God that Laura Engle was there at the beginning to make it happen. One other piece of nostalgia, on the first tour we did for *Acoustic Highway*, John Cipollina's (Quicksilver Messenger Service) brother Mario played bass for us. Obviously David Freiberg had played with Quicksilver Messenger Service in the past. The first Quicksilver album was the first record I ever purchased."

Craig: "You recorded a great version on the 1997 CD called *Once In A Blue Universe* of the tune Dave Mason did with Traffic (Steve Winwood) and on his own *Feelin' Alright*. You also have a version of *Somebody To Love* on the 1999 *Four Corners* album. How did you decide on those two cover tunes?"

Craig Chaquico: "I don't normally play covers that aren't my own. I started to fool around with *Feelin' Alright* during a sound check. It sounded good to put on the set list. For my wife we did Simply Red's hit song *Holding Back The Years*. For *Somebody To Love* you can't tell it is the same song. I wanted to do something different for such a great tune."

Craig: "Any stories of interest about your change in styles, from the Jefferson Starship to the work with Higher Octave Records?"

Craig Chaquico: "A couple comes to mind. When I was younger I had my heroes on the wall, Clapton, Hendrix, Jeff Beck, and Jimmy Page. As I got older I realized the real heroes were my parents. By them going to work each day they were able to support a family. I often wondered if I could ever do that. My dad loved the saxophone. I am proud in his honor to play music with a saxophone. My dad thought all the rock guitar I played was only a phase, from Steelwind to the Jefferson Starship. Now he is smiling from heaven with the albums I'm putting out. The first time my dad ever saw me play outside of the Jefferson Starship was at a theater with a great saxophone-player Richie Elliot. It was the first time he saw my name in lights. He wanted me to do records with Richie Elliot, and with saxophone. He was a saxophone-player. I got nominated for a Grammy and dad passed away before the show. He passed away on Valentine's day. He had a great life. My parents were together over fifty years."

Craig: "I am so sorry. I know what you went through. My mom passed away in December of 2003. Dad and mom were married fifty-four years. I feel for you."

Craig Chaquico: "I'm getting teary eyed. I did get to record a song with Richard Elliot. On the 1996 CD called *A Thousand Pictures*, the tune was *Autumn Blue*. That was for my dad. Now he can smile with the phase of music I'm playing. Here is another story for you when I was getting successful with the new style of music. When I got established in the cool jazz market, I'm asked to listen to a specific song and guess the guitar-player. I am going through my head of people that play cool jazz, or something close to it. My first guess is the jazz guitar-player Peter White. That wasn't right. I throw out a bunch of other names. I can't come up with the musician. I'm told that it is Slash from Guns 'N' Roses, but he is using his real name Saul Hudson. The song was a hit on jazz radio. I can't believe it was Slash. A couple of years later a radio station in Los Angeles wants to have a festival at the tennis stadium where U.C.L.A. is located. They wanted myself, Lee Ritenour, Peter White and some saxophone-players. In other words they wanted the jazz, or new age sound. Since it was a big hit on jazz radio they wanted Slash to do his song. Slash tells the promoters that he doesn't have somebody that he can play with. The people he knows as musicians don't know the tune. They tell Slash look at the line-up. See if any name may know the song. Slash saw my name on the list. He tells the promoters if Craig will learn the tune he'll play the song. I was able to get Slash to play the festival with his top hat and long hair. The night of the show Slash comes out on stage and we play the song in front of ten thousand jazz fans. The song was *Obsession Confession*. Here you have the combination of oil, and water. It was really cool. It was going to be on some movie. One of the real cool moments was meeting Slash's mother backstage. She had tears in her eyes. I was proud that I could help make her proud."

Craig: "Are you seeing more of the older fans coming to check you out as the years go on?"

Craig Chaquico: "I am seeing more of the older fans and many new ones. When I first started playing cool jazz Grace did such an assume thing. She came to see one of my shows. Her being there as a friend gave us so much credibility. I'm glad that anybody likes what I'm doing."

Craig: "How often are you going on the road these days?"

Craig Chaquico: "There are times if we go out with other cool jazz bands as a package it could be fifty to sixty shows. If it isn't part of a package it is a lot less. I am taking it easy right now. I need a break. I don't want to make the same record again. Maybe I'll go back to the sound of the 1993 *Acoustic Highway*."

Craig: "I hope we all see some new music from you in the not too distant future. Thanks for all the stories you shared and the best of luck with any new project. It was a pleasure to finally get to interview you. Let me get in some plugs for people to see the things you are up to these days. They can go to www.craigchaquico.com and www.higheroctave.com."

Craig Chaquico: "Thank you very much. It was nice remembering that far back. Best of luck with the book and let me know if you need any other information."

## Joey Covington- Hot Tuna and the Jefferson Airplane.

Craig: "Thank you Joey for giving us a look at your music background. You have had such an interesting and dynamic career. Let's start prior to 1970. Talk about your work as a drummer, singer, and songwriter."

Joey Covington: "I've been recording since I was sixteen. I had local releases in Johnstown, Pennsylvania and later with a Pittsburgh band called the Fenways; (*I'm A Mover* and other singles) who were predicted to go national. I was also in a band with Jimmy Greenspoon in L.A., who went on to Three Dog Night, and I had been jamming with Papa John Creach since 1967. I recorded *Boris The Spider* (A cover song from the Who) with a song I wrote on the B side, produced by Kim Fowley (Known for his work with Frank Zappa, Hollywood Argyles, the female rock band the Runaways, and Kiss among others), and released on Original Sound Records. My cover of *Boris* is still getting airplay! I found it on a few radio station play lists on the internet recently. I formed the band Tsong in L.A., with Mickey Rooney Jr., and we were signed to MGM Records.

Craig: "Did you and Jimmy Greenspoon have a name for the band?"

Joey Covington: "The band was never formally named because as we were about to get going Jimmy left to join Three Dog Night."

Craig: "When was it first brought to your attention that Spencer Dryden would be leaving the Jefferson Airplane?"

Joey Covington: "I became aware of that in 1968."

Craig: "Prior to Spencer leaving you had done live performances with Hot Tuna. How did you first get to know Jorma and Jack?"

Joey Covington: "When Marty brought me in the mix for the Jefferson Airplane in 1968, Jorma and Jack were already planning to try their own thing, and immediately got me involved in forming Hot Tuna, via *jams*. I have tapes of the first *jams* we did, dated October 1968, and these *jams* lead us to playing live shows, which led me to bringing Marty Balin into Hot Tuna to sing."

Craig: "Was the original plan for you to be with the formation of the Hot Tuna project or to be part of both bands?"

Joey Covington: "Originally I was supposed to go into the Airplane in 1968; the Hot Tuna project got going, and diverted the original plan at the time of me going right into the Airplane. It wasn't really a set plan with Hot Tuna, it evolved, and we all went with the flow of it. I was recording with and playing live with the Airplane in 1969. I first met Jorma and Jack in Los Angeles, 1968. Marty came to hear me in L.A. and invited me to their show at the Whisky A-Go-Go. Soon after that Jorma and Jack invited me to *jam* at RCA Studios, in L.A. I did gigs with Jefferson Airplane starting in 1969, either double drumming with Spencer, or drumming without him. Spencer still did live shows but not always. I drummed for Jefferson Airplane without Spencer on Aug 2, 1969 at the Pop Festival, Atlantic City, New Jersey. A broken leg prevented me from drumming for the Airplane at Woodstock."

Craig: "How did you break your leg?"

Joey Covington: "Some stories are better off left berried in the past."

Craig: "What was Spencer's reaction to the performances with double drummers?"

Joey Covington: "Spencer liked the idea of the few shows we did with two drummers."

Craig: "In 1984 you were on a well produced TV program, Setting The Record Straight.  It had a segment with you and Papa John Creach, as well as one with Jorma and Papa John.  You told a funny story the first time you ever met Papa John Creach was at the Musicians Union in Los Angeles.  Is it true that when you asked him what he did for a living he told you "I saw wood."

Joe Covington: "Whatever is on my website or Papa John's website is true.  I learned that day that fiddle-players s*aw wood*."

Craig: "What was the reason for you leaving the Airplane in 1972, before the final tour?"

Joey Covington: "I left because I wanted to do my own solo record.  Prior to the Airplane I was in other bands and had cut a record as a solo artist (*Boris The Spider*). So the answer is I left the Airplane for the same reasons the Airplane ended.  Everyone wanted to do their own thing as artists. The sessions for my record started when they were finishing *Long John Silver* and planning the last tour etc.  At the same time I also had told Paul Kantner I couldn't do his Jefferson Starship project."

Craig: "What was your best memory from the final Airplane tour?"

Joey Covington: "My best memory of the last Airplane tour and record was that was part of the deal with RCA. the Airplane had to deliver a certain amount of albums of Jefferson Airplane product, in order for everyone to continue with their solo projects, and Grunt Records.  If not for that there probably wouldn't have been a last tour, or a *Long John Silver* album, or a *Thirty Seconds Over Winterland*.  Everyone by then wanted to do their own projects and had started them."

Craig: "Please talk about some of the session work you did in 1971 with Papa John's first record (Self-titled) and Peter Kaukonen on *Black Kangaroo*."

Joey Covington: "I put the whole record together for Papa John without taking producer credits (Which I could have easily have done).  I selected most of the songs for him including *Somewhere Over The Rainbow*, which Pops did not want to do. I called in the players and Roger Spotts, Pop's friend to arrange the tunes.  Oddly enough the song I wrote for him was the only one that charted, *Janitor Drives A Cadillac*.  I did *Black Kangaroo* as a favor to Peter, as the drummer I introduced him to bailed. The guy actually was the drummer I had found to replace me in my band Tsong; when I left to go with the Airplane Family.  Plus Peter and I were good friends, so I naturally I would come through and lay down drum tracks for him."

Craig: "What are your final memories of Papa John?"

Joey Covington: "I was there in the hospital with him and it's too personal to go into.  The eulogy I wrote is posted on Papa John's website."  http://www.joeycovington.com/papa.htm.

(I respect greatly Joey's wish to keep the memories private.  I know what it was for my family when my mom passed away.  Joey wrote a magnificent tribute to Papa John).

Craig: "Do you feel you got the credit you deserve as the most diverse drummer of the Airplane and Tuna family?"

Joey Covington "When I was playing with Airplane and Hot Tuna I got the credit.  Ralph Gleason (Music critic for the San Francisco Chronicle and was an editor with Rolling Stone) always gave me great reviews at the time.  I'm a journeyman drummer.  I started at ten and went through all styles, and played with all sorts of bands.  It's possible the other Airplane drummers were "diverse" but never talked about what else they did. What I haven't been credited with is the actual length of time I was with the Airplane Family.  November 1968 through December 1973.  Writers and press tend to go by discography released, as opposed to all the live shows during 1969, and recordings in 1969 that were done, but didn't get released.  I was still part of the family while

374

they did the last record and tour. I was recording my record so we all knew what the other was doing. Unfortunately people tend to look at album chronology and assume if someone is not on the next album they're gone from the scene. That's not how it went down. My tenure was 1968 through 1973, whether it was Hot Tuna, Airplane, Grace Slick, *Blows Against The Empire*, my solo record Fat Fandango, whatever, it was all the same business that we were in. I was part of the formation of Jefferson Starship and quit that as well, and opted for my own art. Though later on I co-wrote *With Your Love* in 1976 for Jefferson Starship; which was a hit for them."

Craig: "Did you keep up musically (Listening to and buying records) with the Airplane and Hot Tuna, after you left and right through today?"

Joey Covington: "I get all Airplane Family issues and reissues from the record company. We've all been in contact with each other over the years, so we've all been aware of what everyone has been doing."

Craig: "Do you have some favorite gigs you played during your tenures with Hot Tuna and the Airplane?"

Joey Covington: "Atlantic City Pop Festival, 8/2/69, the free concert Central Park, New York City 5/3/70, Rotterdam Pop Festival, Holland, 6/26/70, the Bath Festival 6/28/70 at Somerset in the U.K., and the Houston Astrodome on or about 7/26/70."

Craig: "In examining the Fat Fandango record of 1973, how would you break down the style of music? How did you feel about the record then and what about looking back on it over 30 years later?"

Joey Covington: "It was recorded in 1972 and released in 1973. The music was psychedelic rhythm and blues. The record won critical acclaim in Europe. There was a single released here in the States, it was getting airplay in California, but then my promo budget went to a girlfriend/singer of an RCA executive. It sold a respectable 100,000 plus copies at the time with no promo budget behind it. Fat Fandango, the record represents for me then and now my total creative expression, with no company men or producers in there changing my vision in the studio. I donated royalties to the Jacque Cousteau Society from the song *Mama Neptune*."

GRUNT
RECORDS
P.O. BOX 88387
SAN FRANCISCO, CA 94108
(415) 221-7412

Joe E. Covington's FAT FANDANGO

Jack Prendergast, Joe E. Covington, Senator Patrick Craig, Stevie Midnite

**Photograph by kind permission of Mike Somavilla.  From the Mike Somavilla collection.**

**Photograph not to be used without the written consent of Mike Somavilla.**

**Photographer unknown.**

**Thank you BMG .**

Craig: "Do you have any preference of playing live or working in the studio?"

Joey Covington: "I prefer playing live to recording. I enjoy producing music."

Craig : "Are your favorite Airplane songs to play *Lawman* and *Wild Turkey*? What is it about those two tracks that make them special for you?"

Joey Covington: "My website talks about them in terms of my personal favorite recorded drum tracks. (www.joeycovington.com). It's a drummer thing. From *Bark* I like the drum tracks I did on those songs. It has nothing to do with the melody and lyrics of the songs, or playing them live."

Craig: "Was there an agreement with the record executive Harry Jenkins if you could write a hit song (*Pretty As You Feel*), he would send you to meet Elvis Presley?"

Joey Covington: "The story of my meeting Elvis is too long to talk about now and I'm most likely saving it for my own book. I was flown to one of his Las Vegas Hilton shows late January 1972 and got to spend some quality time with him."

Craig: "Often overlooked is the great work you did with the San Francisco Allstars. What was it like working with people such as Greg Douglass (Steve Miller Band and Hot Tuna), John Cipollina, (Quicksilver Messenger Service) Pete Sears (Jefferson Starship and Hot Tuna) and Merle Saunders (Jerry Garcia)."

Joey Covington: "They're all great players; we jammed over the years prior, so we all liked playing together and we were all extended family, and friends, and on the same page for years. It was totally organic the way it came about."

Craig: "How did the project get started?"

Joey Covington: "A New York agent, John Shur called me about putting a group of all-star players together for some east coast tours. I called the guys and we went for it. The line-up changed for each tour depending who was available. Mario Cipollina, David Margen, and Buddy Cage were on one tour."

Craig: "What are your feelings as to why when Hot Tuna reformed in 1983 and the Airplane in 1989 they did not use any drummer previously associated with the band(s)?"

Joey Covington: "Skip Johnson (Grace Slick's ex-husband and Jefferson Starship lighting engineer) and Grace had Paul Kantner call me to be a part of the 1989 Airplane reunion. I don't want to talk about why I did not ultimately do the record or tour. As for the Hot Tuna reunion in 1983, I was involved in the San Francisco Allstars. I don't know where Hot Tuna was at musically or what material they were doing, so what drummer they'd choose would depend on the music."

Craig : "When they had the Los Angeles screening for the Jefferson Airplane 2004 DVD called *Fly*, what was it like being in the same room with Jorma, Jack, Grace, Bill Thompson (Jefferson Airplane manager) , and Pat (Maurice) Leraci (RCA liaison and master of the studio machines for Jefferson Airplane)?"

Joey Covington: "It was like we just saw each yesterday. It was fun though we've all seen each other over the years, it wasn't all together in one place."

Craig: "You have a new release LAuren, (That is the correct spelling) *Hideout Is A Crook's Best Friend*. That was also a track on the Fat Fandango record. Talk about the CD."

Joey Covington: "I co-produced this project with a friend of mine. I was approached to produce some of the songs from my catalogue. LAuren chose the songs (and CD title) she wanted to do, plus two Marty Balin songs.

She chose the songs she felt best represented where she is at as an artist.  Some are completely new versions of songs that Marty and I used to do live until we quit Hot Tuna and walked with them.  A few new versions from Fat Fandango, a rock 'n' blues version of *Pretty As You Feel*, and some songs that were never recorded, or done live previously. It was cool to produce, because I was able to bring the songs to another level with new ideas and approaches."

Craig:  "The two Marty Balin songs are *Emergency* and *You Wear Your Dresses Too Short*, which LAuren calls *I Wear My Dresses Too Short*.  The website is  www.lalauren.com and is well recommended to check out!  Talk about the great charity work you did playing with Bo Diddley in January of 2006."

Joey Covington:  "I've known Bo for a while and we've always wanted to play together.  Bo's from Mississippi where Katrina hit.  A guy in Florida called us to do the benefit. The City of Islamorada in the Florida Keys sponsored it, to benefit their sister city in Mississippi.  We played some of Bo's hits and mostly his new material.  We played two hours, one hour longer then planned, no rehearsals!  It was great and rocked the crowd.  Bo is a charismatic performer. What can I say, Bo Diddley is a legend!  Who wouldn't want to help those people in need and play with a legend!"

Craig:  "What drummers do you enjoy listening to?"

Joey Covington:  "I grew up on Cozy Cole (Jazz musician that played with but not limited to Jelly Roll Morton, Cab Calloway's Orchestra, and Louie Armstrong's All-Stars) and Joe Morello (Jazz musician that played with but not limited to Stan Kenton's Orchestra and the Dave Brubeck Quartet).  I like Michael Shrieve (Santana, played with Steve Winwood in a band called Go, and progressive keyboardist Klaus Schulze), Mitch Mitchell (Jimi Hendrix), Charlie Watts (Rolling Stones), Hal Blaine (Maybe the most noted session drummer in the world.  Some of his credits include the Beach Boys, the Monkees, Elvis Presley, and Simon & Garfunkel), and Bernard Purdy (Jazz and rhythm and blues musician that has played with but not limited to James Brown Louie Armstrong, and Aretha Franklin).  How can I forget Billy Cobham (Jazz musician that has played with but not limited to Miles Davis and the Mahavishnu Orchestra)."

Craig:  "Anything that you would like to plug before we end things?"

Joey Covington:  "The new CD I produced of singer LAuren, available via my website and LAuren's website. You can go to www.joeycovington.com  and www.lalauren.com."

Craig:  "Thank you Joey for sharing some time with us today."

Joey Covington:  "Thank you."

# Greg Douglass- Hot Tuna.

Craig: "Good morning. Thanks for being part of the book."

Greg Douglass: "Thank you for remembering me."

Craig: "Early on you were in a band the Virtues that became Country Weather. How were you able to get into venues such as the Fillmore West, San Francisco and the Avalon Ballroom, San Francisco and be able to open for major acts including Ten Years After and Jeff Beck?"

Greg Douglass: "There were two things. We had a great manager Bob Strand. He had wanted to be the next Bill Graham (Legendary promoter), the guy was a gold metal swimmer and had that competitive mentality. He went for everything as if it were a swim meet. Bob thought why play crappy little venues when you could play the Fillmore West. He befriended the people at both the Fillmore West and the Avalon Ballroom. The Avalon Ballroom was actually the first place we played. In the 1960's those were the places to play. We got into the Avalon Ballroom playing a show with Lester Flatt and Earl Scruggs (Two of the most noted bluegrass performers ever). The Sons Of Champlin (San Francisco band from the 1960's that were well liked by Marty Balin) were on the bill as well. We got booked because they liked the name Country Weather. When they heard us sounding more like Blue Cheer (San Francisco heavy rock band from the late 1960's, that was known for their cover version of *Summertime Blues*) than Flatt and Scruggs, they weren't too pleased. Word did get out we were a pretty good band. This helped Bob to get his foot in the door at the Fillmore West. When we were on we were great. I don't want to denigrate the bands ability. We could play."

Craig: "What prevented the band from getting known throughout the country?"

Greg Douglass: "The main problem with Country Weather was not having strong enough material for the entire nation. The San Francisco bands all had something to bring them attention. It's A Beautiful Day had *White Bird*. The band Cold Blood (Played rock, soul and funk sounding music) never made it outside the Bay Area, but they were a great band. We didn't have a hit single. We had great tunes. The song *Fly To New York* was excellent. Had we recorded a live album things may have been different. Craig, I don't think we translated well into vinyl."

Craig: "Did either the manager or anybody the band could trust ever suggest to stick to your roots, but come up with one three minute pop song for the national exposure?"

Greg Douglass: "We tried that route later on in the game. We weren't able to come up with anything that would be the killer single. Steve Derr the other guitarist in the band started to write some pop songs. The songs didn't hit home. The band didn't have a great singer. Dave Cater and I were good singers, but we didn't have a killer single, or killer singer."

Craig: "Did you ever consider getting a lead-singer?"

Greg Douglass: "We talked about that at one time. At that point the idea didn't get well received. The band stayed around until 1971 or maybe 1972. The first two or three years were terrific. We got to travel all over California. The last two years the horse was already dead. We were together about five years. I got to work on a session for Terry Dolan (Known for his band Terry & The Pirates. He worked with Greg Douglass, John Cipollina, and Nicky Hopkins, to name a few). The song was *Inlaws And Outlaws* (The title is correct) and the album was *Too Close For Comfort*. That gave me the confidence to forge ahead. The corpse was dead in Country Weather and I finally decided to smell it."

Craig: "In 1972 when you formed Mistress (Power trio) did you have to wrestle with your conscious about the risk of having another band without the commercial sound?"

Greg Douglass: "It wasn't that tough. I was so ready, ready to showcase my modest talents. I wanted to get out and make a name for myself. My songwriting partner in Mistress Brian Kilcourse had real good talent, but we needed a lead-singer. The record executives and the audience wanted a lead-singer. That being said we put together an excellent album. The album *Free Flyte* finally saw release in 1996."

Craig: "Didn't you use Mallory Earl who engineered and or produced several Hot Tuna records?"

Greg Douglass: "Mallory basically put the entire thing together. Mallory was working at Wally Heider Studios in San Francisco. That was a big studio at the time. The Airplane, Hot Tuna and it seemed everyone was recording there. Mallory liked my playing and liked me as a person. He tried to shoehorn me into session work. Mallory helped me play on the Link Wray album (*Be What You Want To)*. Mallory heard Mistress and came up with an idea, we would go into the studio during off hours and record. We got a fully polished album, as if we had recorded it quote "the right way." It could have cost thousands of dollars, if not for Mallory. We started to shop the record around to different labels and unfortunately just like with Country Weather we got passed on. To be honest I thought the album would sell. I then had one of those talks with myself. I decided that I had proved myself as a guitarist, but needed to get out and play with somebody I could learn from. I got a call to work with Van Morrison."

Craig: "How did you get involved with Van Morrison?"

Greg Douglass: "The San Francisco music scene has a lot of cross-pollination. I was working with John Cipollina. We had done work with Terry Dolan. John's brother Mario was working for a band called Sound Hole. Van had seen Sound Hole play at a club called the Lions Share in San Anselmo, California. Van wanted Sound Hole to be his back up band on the road. There was a problem with their guitarist Brian Marnell (SVT). Van may not have liked his playing. I got the call to see if I wanted to tour with Van."

Craig: "How long were you on the road with Van?"

Greg Douglass: "It was very brief. I believe we played three months. Van is notorious for changing musicians. After the three months it wasn't as if everyone got fired. Van is a great guy. I didn't see any of the moody or temperamental sides. On the tour he was very grounded."

Craig: "I'm glad you were with him during a productive series of shows. Any funny stories working with Van?"

Greg Douglass: "We were playing a concert and a guy in the front row was smoking. Van got pissed off. Van told the crowd if the guy didn't stop smoking he would leave the stage. The guy stops smoking and Van goes back to singing. On the encore Van comes out smoking an unfiltered cigarette."

Craig: "You played on the 1973 Link Wray (Famous for his unique guitar sound during the 1950's. His song *Rumble* was an early rock and roll classic) release *Be What You Want To*. What do you remember about the record?"

Greg Douglass: "I wasn't aware of his legendary accomplishments until later on, but I still was really knocked out to be playing on his record. When I walked in Jerry Garcia was there. He was part of the record. It was an experience to be around that much talent."

Craig: "Did you get to fool around with the tune *Rumble*."

Greg Douglass: "We didn't play it in the studio, but I play it today. They didn't even let Link play much guitar on the record. The original plan was for him to play on a couple of songs. Link was very laid back. He thought he was a sloppy guitar-player. I told Link embrace your slop dude. The guy can play!"

Craig: "Let's go to 1974, how were you contacted to be part of Hot Tuna?"

Greg Douglass: "Mallory Earl was the broker of the deal. He was producing the Hot Tuna record *America's Choice*. Jorma apparently was concerned about performing some of the songs live with only one guitar. At the time as they say in show biz I was between jobs. I was working in a factory. I was living with my in-laws, I come home from work one day and my father in-law tells me that somebody named Jockey Kickiepoo called. I tell him I'll call Jockey back. I don't know who this is. I dial the number and ask who I'm talking with? The guy says "This is Jorma Kaukonen." Jorma wanted to see if I would go over his house. He told me they were thinking of adding another guitarist. I go over his house and basically all afternoon we sat around and picked on acoustic guitars. Then later we played electrically. It was a really good day."

380

Craig: "Was Jack at the house?"

Greg Douglass: "Jack wasn't there."

Craig: 'The first show you played with Hot Tuna was 3/3/75 at Margarita's Canteen, Santa Cruz, California. How close to that date did you get offered the job?"

Greg Douglass: "It had to be the fall of October 1974 when I passed the audition. Jorma then went on vacation for a couple of months. This gave me time to learn the songs. There were very intricate picking styles and numerous tunes to learn. When Jack came back from Sweden we rehearsed a couple of times. Once Jorma was done with his vacation we rehearsed as a band with Bob Steeler."

Craig: "What were your first impressions of Jack and Bob?"

Greg Douglass: "With bands factions form. With the Hot Tuna band you have Jorma who is the top of the food chain. You then have Jack, and you have Bob, and myself. Bob is a great guy and a great drummer that really found his footing later on. Jack is one of the all-time innovators of the instrument. I had trouble latching on to what he did. He had that bond with Jorma. It was evident early on. When it worked it was great and when it didn't it wasn't anyone's fault. I liked Jorma very much. I didn't bond with Jack."

Craig: "During the rehearsals did you bring a song to try out called *I Ain't Holdin*. (Thanks to Mike Somavilla for the information about the song)."

Greg Douglass: "Jorma wrote the lyrics. I take that back. The lyrics were written by a real character Steve Mann. (Friend of Jorma. The title of *Mann's Fate* is from Steve's last name. Steve has done numerous sessions, including Sonny & Cher and for the glam-rock band Sweet). This is funny. I had a song with Mistress called *Paul*. I had a guitar riff that I wrote and felt it was very strong. I tried to use the same riff on *I Ain't Holdin* but it never really flew."

Craig: "Did you attempt to bring any other tunes into the band?"

Greg Douglass: "We attempted two of my finger-picking instrumental songs. For whatever reason they didn't work out. It was Hot Tuna and not my band. I didn't try to get my material into the band."

Craig: "The day you shook hands with Jorma and got the gig, did he give you an exact job description?"

**HOT TUNA**

GRUNT
RECORDS
P.O. BOX 2287
SAN FRANCISCO, CA 94109

(l to r)  JACK CASADY, JORMA KAUKONEN, GREG DOUGLAS & BOB STEELER

**Photograph by kind permission of Mike Somavilla.  From the Mike Somavilla collection.**

**Photograph not to be used without the written consent of Mike Somavilla.**

**Photographer unknown.  This is a promo picture.  Thank you BMG .**

**Notice a couple of mistakes that weren't attended to?  <u>The first is the spelling of Greg's name.</u>  It should be Douglass and not Douglas.  <u>The second is the way the names aren't lined-up!</u>  Circa spring 1975.**

Greg Douglass: "No they kind of let me do my thing. Sometimes I thought it would be to play rhythm and other times to play lead. Jorma and Jack became increasingly unhappy with my rhythm. He wanted me to provide bedrock for their sound. There were times they had a point. I wasn't the rhythm player than as I am now. The leads at the beginning I wasn't discouraged, but as time went on there were rumblings from Jorma's first wife (Margareta)."

Craig: "The last show you played with Hot Tuna would be on 7/26/75 at the Music Inn, Lenox, Massachusetts. How far before that did you sense they may make a change?"

Greg Douglass: "Craig, by the time of that show the writing was on the wall and my days were numbered. All of a sudden I was the social outcast. It got pretty ugly. I would have preferred when it was evident that things weren't happening to have Jorma walk up to me and tell me that. It can be difficult to fire somebody. I've had to do that, it isn't easy."

Craig: "How did you get the news that when the tour picked up again, Hot Tuna would go back to a trio?"

Greg Douglass: "I was getting the feeling that was the last show. I called Jorma and asked what was going on. Jorma tells me that he is busy and will call me back. Later in the day I got a call from Jack. He told me that he had bad news, they decided to go back to being a trio. I did my share of bad things back then. I used drugs, I did drink, and that doesn't help your playing, or attitude. That isn't the case now, I am clean. My behavior entered into the picture as well. In retrospect I would never have done those things if I could go back."

Craig: "Once you part ways with the band did you have any contact in the future, either pro or con?"

Greg Douglass: "After the Hot Tuna thing fell apart, I was hanging out with John Cipollina in a band Raven and had reformed a new version of Mistress. BAM (Bay Area Music Magazine) had first started. I was one of their first interviews and they asked me about Hot Tuna. I was fired a few months before and still self-righteous about the whole thing. I think I called Jack the amazing groove less bass-player and called them reptiles. I was pissed off. Apparently Jorma and Jack had read the interview. I was going to see Dr. John (Famous New Orleans style keyboardist) and Hot Tuna was on the same bill. I got a call from someone in the Hot Tuna organization that told me they didn't think it was a good idea for me to show up. Now as a middle-aged man talking I can tell you it made me a stronger person. When you survive that type of bull sh_t it makes you better. It made me a better player because I sat down with a metronome for maybe a year and worked on my timing. It made me a much better rhythm-player. Then after that I rolled up every drummer's ass for not having good time. Ultimately it was a huge favor getting fired because it led to playing with Steve Miller."

Craig: "Does it surprise you that once Jorma and Jack part ways with many musicians it seems to be removed from their memory banks. Sammy Piazza has never played one minute with them since he left, Bob Steeler played three times with Jorma but not entire shows, and you haven't played even a note with them."

Greg Douglass: "It is hard for me to say. I saw Jorma about fifteen years ago. I opened for acoustic Hot Tuna. I was a little nervous, I hadn't spoken word one to them all these years. Jorma walks in and I go up to him and extend my hand. I say how are you doing you f_ckin' piece of sh_t. Jorma starts to laugh and says I'm glad you mellowed with age. We shake hands and that broke the ice."

Craig: "It would have been even nicer if Jorma had you sit in for one song."

Greg Douglass: "It wasn't going to happen. I knew that going in. He actually got pissed off after my set. I played *Police Dog Blues* and Jorma tells me he wanted to play that song. I don't know man, I can't speak for those guys. I am glad I don't have to work for them anymore. I went on to work with some other interesting attitudes. It seems that when you work with that much talent the attitude comes with it."

Craig: "How did the process of you playing with Steve Miller unfold?"

Greg Douglass: "I got to know Lonnie Turner who worked with Steve Miller (Bass) when I worked with Terry Dolan. Lonnie and I hit it off. He played me a copy of the *Fly Like An Eagle* album. I asked where are all the guitar-solos? He told me Steve Miller wanted to do the record as a trio. Lonnie had some words left over from his days playing with Dave Mason (Traffic). He had the song *Jungle Love*. I still had the riff to the song that started out as *Paul* and then *I Ain't Holdin*. Lonnie brought the riff to Steve. He loved it. Steve needed a kick ass rock and roll song and that definitely fit the bill. I had never met Steve. I think we did three takes of *Jungle Love*. We edited takes two and three together. That was it man. The entire thing took maybe a half hour. I instantly got my guitar sound and after we got the track Steve went in and cut the vocal. The entire song was done in two hours and that is unheard of man."

Craig: "Did the success of *Jungle Love* enable you to be on a three song video shoot for European TV including *Jungle Love*, *Jet Airliner*, and *Rock 'N' Me*?"

Greg Douglass: "At that point there weren't music videos. In Europe they would use them as promotional tools in the movies. Before a movie would start they would play the song. I got a call from Steve Miller's road manager to play on *Jungle Love*, because it was going to be one of the singles from the *Book Of Dreams* album. When I got down there Steve was very affable. Steve told me as long as I was there to play on the two other songs. I knew *Rock 'N' Me*, but I never heard *Jet Airliner*. I was going to have to learn it on the fly and then perform it. That was a little weird, but my adrenaline was soaring at that point. I did a really good slide-solo on *Jet Airliner*. Later on that day Steve came to my hotel room and told me he liked what I did and would I be interested in touring with him?" That day *Rock 'N' Me* had just gone to number one on the singles charts. Talk about a good day."

Craig: "During the Steve Miller period you had a very serious accident to your hand but made a miraculous recovery. Can you talk about how you were able to play again so quickly after going through a plate of glass and what did the surgeon tell you about the length of time it would take for you to be able to play the way you had before?"

Greg Douglass: "There wasn't a time table. He did think it would be several months. I went into the hospital and the gravity of my injuries became very evident. It just so happened that night the best micro-surgeon in the world was on duty. His name was Roland Minami. This guy was so amazing that I gave my son the middle name of Roland to honor the doctor. Dr. Minami finds out that I am a guitar-player and he tells me what he is going to do. The surgery was four to five hours. Everybody was very supportive. Steve Miller flew the band out to see me at my house. He gave me financial support by getting me an advance on a song I had written. I get through the surgery, but now I become very motivated to get back on the horse. When the cast came off I couldn't hold a pick. I devised a way to stabilize my thumb and play. I needed to play for spiritual and financial reasons. Three months later I was back on the road."

Craig: "Did you get back the feeling in the hand?"

Greg Douglass: "It feels like I am wearing rubber gloves. If I hit the spot where there is scar tissue it hurts like a mother. Except for that I'm doing fine."

**(Greg went through a horrible three months, from the surgery through the rehab and any recollection of the accident is still painful for Greg. That is why I didn't belabor the subject).**

Craig: "Things get back on track and 1978 comes around, what happens with Steve Miller?"

Greg Douglass: "Steve just stopped working. He was tired and needed time off. That was that. At that point I hooked up with Peter Rowan (Played with Jerry Garcia on the *Old And In The Way* record, and is a well known guitarist, and mandolin-player). We toured Europe together and that expanded my musical knowledge. I learned about bluegrass and reggae. It was a fantastic experience."

Craig: "How did the association with Greg Kihn (Had a few hits including *The Breakup Song (They Don't Write 'Em)* and *Jeopardy*) come to fruition?"

Greg Douglass: "I was still working with Peter. I got a call from I believe Richard Corsello an engineer, that Greg Kihn was changing guitar-players and would I be interested in an audition? I went down and found out they had auditioned many players. I got the gig and it was a great three years with Greg. We toured like crazy. We all got along well. The first song we cut was *Jeopardy*. It was a great period in my life."

Craig: "The interesting thing about Greg Kihn's audience was the diversity in the ages. He was one of the few people in the 1980's to bring in the power pop fans, but also those that liked the music of the 1960's and 1970's."

Greg Douglass: "There were the people that grew up with the Yardbirds, Rolling Stones, the Beatles, and later Tom Petty, well Greg was a huge fan of those bands. I think that was why there were a good number of older people at the shows. He also liked the Ramones, Television, and the Clash from the new wave scene. He loved playing covers live. We may play a Rolling Stones song early and finish with a song by the Clash."

Craig: "Is it true after playing with Greg you went two years without touching a guitar?"

Greg Douglass: "I had gotten too much into drugs and Greg had to let me go. I did some construction work and then landed a job with AT & T selling long distance phone services for five years. I stopped playing guitar. I needed to reinvent myself. I put on a suit everyday and made it to work. I started to get clean. In 1992 AT & T did me the great service of letting me go, as part of the down sizing. I started to play guitar as therapy. I started to write songs as well."

Craig: "Is that how the record from 1992 *Maelstrom* came about?"

Greg Douglass: "I pieced that together from various sessions over the years. I moved to the San Diego area and fell in love with the region. I also fell in love and married. I put together a cassette tape of *Maelstrom* and released it. (It has since come out on CD from Taxim Records in 1993). I started to write a lot more songs and got back into my craft."

Craig: "On the 2000 CD *The Natives Are Restless* you do a wonderful cover of the Beatles song *I Feel Fine*. How did you end up using that particular one?"

Greg Douglass: "I'm always experimenting with Beatles songs. They lend themselves so well to finger-picking. I always tried the song in a specific key and it didn't resonate to be recorded. I tried it another key and it worked great. Sometimes it's trial and error. Any time I could record a Lennon and McCartney tune that is a good thing."

Craig: "We have to get in the plug for your very informative website, www.gregdouglass.com. There is a nice historic background and terrific information. Greg, it was such a pleasure to be able to talk about the Hot Tuna days and the great things before and after. I hope you continue to make superb music. As I told you last week it would take at least the entire day to go through all the musical details of your career. Thank you for your time."

Greg Douglass: "Thank you Craig. If you need anything else for the book please contact me. I look forward to being able to read it."

**While Greg changes his guitar strings please enjoy a brief bio (Next page),**

**courtesy of Greg and his close friend Mike Somavilla.**

**Mike Somavilla wrote the bio and the contents have not been altered.**

**Thanks Mike.**

# GREG DOUGLASS

Guitarist Greg Douglass is one of the best kept secrets from the San Francisco Bay Area music scene of which he has been part of for over the last 40 years. From 1966 - 1973 Greg was a member of Country Weather who played all throughout California and the Pacific Northwest, in addition to being regular performers at the Fillmore Auditorium and Winterland Ballroom for Bill Graham and at the Avalon Ballroom for The Family Dog where rock n roll impersario Chet Helms gave them their first "Real" start in the San Francisco music scene.

Country Weather soon caught the attention of Bill Graham, who decided to book their career and he immediately signed them to his Millard Agency. Prior to leaving CW, Greg would lend his services to the country rock band Appaloosa with John Coinman, (who later became the musical director for the film "Dances With Wolves"). Country Weather's long lost recordings were finally released as a double LP on RD Records in Switzerland in 2005.

In 1973, Greg and the drummer from the "Weather" Bill Baron formed the short lived band Mistress with Brian Kilcourse (Bass and Vocals), their album that they recorded at the world renown Wally Heider's Studio in 1973 was produced by Mallory Earl who also produced Hot Tuna.

Although their album was never released in time to save the band from breaking up in 1974, it did finally see the light of day under the title "Free Flyte" on compact disc when Taxim Records in Germany released it in 1996. Other unreleased Mistress recordings were released on RD Records in December 2005 entitled *New Ground* which featured Chuck Burgi on drums on 2 songs, he replaced Bill Baron prior to the break up of the band.

By the time the mid 70's hit and since, Greg has played virtually every style of music and it's because of this versatility that he has become a very much in demand recording and touring artist working with Steve Miller, Greg Kihn, Hot Tuna, Thomas Jefferson Kaye, Van Morrison, Terry & The Pirates, Problem Child, Peter Rowan, Gene Clark, John Cipollina, Link Wray, Tom Fogerty, Country Joe McDonald, Raven, Eddie Money, Steve Douglas, Tom Johnston, Kathi McDonald, Danny Kalb and Duane Eddy just to name a few.

One really interesting release was "Prehistoric Raven" by Boyd Albritton. This CD released in 1998 was actually recorded in 1975 in Studio C at Wally Heiders in San Franciso (the same studio used by CSNY, Jefferson Starship and Mistress among others) and featured members of the Jefferson Airplane, Hot Tuna, Terry & The Pirates, Quicksilver and many others, most notably were Nicky Hopkins, Greg Douglass and Sammy Piazza, but also featured among others Skip Olson and Hutch Hutchinson. As for the album title it is a reference and a nod to the band Raven that John Cipollina had in 1976, which also featured several of the same members.

After years of remaining on the sidelines helping others refine and define their music, Greg released his first album-CD "Maelstrom" on Taxim Records in 1993 with a stellar cast featuring Norton Buffalo, Steve Douglas, Nick Gravenites, Doug Harman and Peter Rowan.

Greg appears on well over 60 different releases. He Co-wrote the smash hit "Jungle Love" with Lonnie Turner for Steve Miller and played on Greg Kihn's hit song "Jeopardy", just to name a few highlights. Greg's hit song "Jungle Love" was in the trailer for the movie "The Animal" starring Rob Schneider, which was released in the summer of 2001 and it was used in a several episodes of the television show "Everybody Loves Raymond."

Although best known as an electric, rock-n-roll and blues guitar player, Greg is also equally known for his impressive and inventive acoustic, finger picking style and techniques that are reminiscent of John Fahey, Jorma Kaukonen and Leo Kottke, which are showcased on his CD "The Natives Are Restless" recorded in 2000.

Greg is presently living in Southern California where he plays with the Fabulous Pelicians and has played with the I.R.S. (International Rock Show) which features members of Badfinger, Huey Lewis & The News, Jefferson Starship and others. He also teaches guitar to about 60 students a week, has had 2 guitar instructional DVDs released, one electric and one acoustic and he is currently working on a new CD.

# Michael Falzarano- Hot Tuna.

Craig: "It's nice to have the opportunity to speak with you."

Michael Falzarano: "My pleasure."

Craig: "Can you fill the readers in how you first met Jorma?"

Michael Falzarano: "In the late 1970's I moved to San Francisco. My wife to be was already living there. She had become friends with Jorma and his first wife Margareta. When I got out there I was introduced. We became best friends. This was before we started to play together. Around 1978 or 1979 when Hot Tuna wasn't together Jorma and I started to play. Jorma and I were working on some projects. He had done Vital Parts and some solo tours. As we got into the 1980's an agent had come by and asked if Jorma wanted to get Hot Tuna back together. He wanted to gage the interest of going back out on the road. That's pretty much what happened. Jack came by the studio and they started to work together again. Jorma asked me if I wanted to be part of the Hot Tuna project. I jokingly said what I am getting myself into. I did say yes. The rest as they say is history."

Craig: "When the agent came by with the idea did the entire process happen quickly, or did there have to be some patching up of previous issues?"

Michael: "When you say patching up, I'm not so sure there was any patching up that needed to take place. The agent spelled everything out for the guys. He talked with Jack and the next thing I knew Jack came by the studio. We had a brief conversation. It was casual. The attitude was to give it a shot. It wasn't oh my God, I don't know if we can do this. It was you've been doing your thing and I've been doing mine, let's get together."

Craig: "How did Jorma and Jack decide to go outside the Airplane, Hot Tuna, and Jefferson Starship family for the drummer Shigemi (Shig) Komiyama?"

Michael Falzarano: "Things are not as deep or complex as people make them out to be. It was very simple. Jorma and I were working together. Bob Steeler the Tuna drummer of the 1970's I believe was still playing with the punk band the Offs. When the time came to get a drummer Jorma had been playing with several. Either he didn't want to use them or for whatever reasons they weren't right. Jorma asked me if I knew any drummers. I told him I knew Shigemi Komiyama, from the band the Phantoms. He was a rock solid drummer. He played real well. I told Jorma that he would get the job done and work for Hot Tuna. This was both musically and personally that he would fit. Jorma tells me to bring him in and we'll check it out. Things worked out. People often put a great deal of weight on how things happen. There are times it is nature taking its course."

Craig: "When Hot Tuna was ready to play again did you have any conversations with Jorma about specific roles? In 1975 there was miscommunication with Greg Douglass, regarding what he would or wouldn't do on stage."

Michael Falzarano: "With Jorma I have worked with him and known him for going on thirty years. It was casual. He came to the table with songs. What happened before we went on the road Jorma had written a bunch of songs. When they finally got back I spent time learning a bunch of Hot Tuna tunes. I knew many, from bands I played with years back. I was familiar with many, but still refreshed myself with several of the tunes. I came to the rehearsal armed with a bunch of Hot Tuna songs. Jorma felt at that time he wanted to do something new. He wanted to concentrate on the new material he had written. Jorma also liked my material. We even toyed around with doing some SVT songs! That didn't materialize. It wasn't a kind of thing where I said I have to have five songs a night, or three songs a night. The way it happened was one of us would say I really like that song, let's play that one. I almost had to convince him to add some Hot Tuna songs."

Craig: "Was Jack okay with the set not being Hot Tuna specific?"

Michael Falzarano: "Yes he was. You have to remember that Jack had also come from several years of other things. He had SVT and worked with other people. He was open-minded. There was nobody insisting on certain material. Maybe that was good. The tour had problems with some people coming to hear Hot Tuna songs played the way they sounded in the 1970's.  The people remembered them a specific way from six years ago.  Jorma and Jack had moved on somewhat to a different degree.  They wanted to play some other tunes.  Their hope was the audience would come along with them.  The audience didn't.  They wanted to hear what they wanted to hear."

Craig: "The first night of the tour was 10/17/83 at Livingston College, New Brunswick, New Jersey.  Prior to the first reunion gig how long did the band rehearse?"

Michael Falzarano: "This was organic.  There wasn't much rehearsal.  Jorma and I played together.  Jorma, and Jack played together forever.  I had played with the drummer.  Three or four days before the tour, we played four hours per day."

Craig: "It must have come together easily."

Michael Falzarano: "Sometimes when you do it that way it can sound fresh.  You don't want to spend several weeks rehearsing and then everyone is on each others nerves."

Craig: "On the opening night you performed one of my favorite songs of yours, *Dogs Are Dirty*.  After the first show it got dropped.  How was it decided to take it off the set list so quickly?"

Michael Falzarano: "As far as that tune goes I don't remember the thinking at the time.  With Jorma over the years there are many songs we tried just for fun.  There are so many songs.  Jorma has hundreds of songs, I have hundreds of songs.  At that time I wasn't looking to add my material.  I wanted to play the Hot Tuna tunes.  Jorma was the one pushing to go forward.  As far as the one song goes it sounded fine.  I played it for years.  There wasn't a discussion about it.  I suggested we bring songs in such as *I See The Light* and *Rock Me Baby*.  There was an element of the audience that only wanted Hot Tuna."

Craig: "I'm curious if over the years you found this to be true.  People that went to see the 1983 tour that didn't like it at the time appreciated it more as the years went by.  They would listen to a tape and be told to pretend this is a new band.  Don't think Hot Tuna 1975-1977, think new group 1983."

Michael Falzarano: "I would have to say that is true.  I know many friends and fans that come to see me play live, were very opposed to anybody being on stage with Hot Tuna, but Hot Tuna members from the 1970's.  They also had opposed material not being from Hot Tuna.  Those same people have become some of my staunchest fans now.  At this point they are behind me one hundred percent.  I get people telling me that they want to apologize for not liking me in 1983.  Today most people are pretty open about the 1983 shows.  I understood their point of view.  I would feel the same way.  If I saw a band that I loved I want to hear the songs that I loved.  The majority of the audience did come around and come on board.  There were some audiences that would have liked it only to be Jorma and Jack."

Craig: "When New Years Eve 1983 came around and it was the last night of the tour had any discussions taken place about the future of Hot Tuna?"

Michael Falzarano: "There was no discussions about we are not going to do this.  The 1983 experiment was for a short run, have fun, and get it back together.  We all worked after the tour.  The time wasn't right for Jorma and Jack to be Hot Tuna again.  In 1986 it would be."

Craig: "Did you design the sleeve for the Jorma solo record *Barbeque King*?"

Michael Falzarano: "I did.  I was doing art stuff since I was a kid.  Jorma's wife at the time Margareta was an artist.  She showed me some of her stuff and I showed her some of mine.  She was encouraging me to do it.  She wanted me to take a shot at it.  I thought I should do this and get some of my art out there.  I had made posters and several ended up in poster art books.  The record company needed the art work done.  I agreed and we put together.  In those days with vinyl you could see the art work."

Craig: "I'm with you.  A dinosaur like myself enjoyed the great album covers and sleeves."

Michael Falzarano: "The sleeve was to be in color, but they did it in black and white."

388

Craig: "In 1995 Jorma released one of his most underrated works, *The Land Of Heroes* album. You were a big part of the recording. What are your memories?"

Michael Falzarano: "That was a great time for us. We had been working together for a long time. Relix Records wanted another album. Jorma wanted to do it in Nashville. Once again we didn't go there with a master plan. I suggested a bunch of songs that we could do. He wanted to do a couple of my songs. He wanted to do *Judge, I'm Not Sorry*. We played that in concert before. *Re-Enlistment Blues* was a song he really wanted to do. Jorma had played the tune when he was younger. I suggested to him *Trial By Fire* (Jefferson Airplane song). *Do Not Go Gentle* was an instrumental he was playing. *Follow The Drinking Gourd* was a traditional song we were playing in concert."

Craig: "Jorma was performing it as far back as 1962."

Michael Falzarano: "That is right. It was interesting with *Banks Of The River*. Jorma and I were talking about the first song we ever played. Jorma thought his was *Banks Of The Ohio* and mine was *Hang Down Your Head Tom Dooley*. Both of those were murder ballads. Jorma suggests I write a murder ballad. For *Dark Train* I was on the fence with calling it *Dark Train*, or *Black Train*. Jorma thought *Dark Train* was the much better title. I enjoyed the making of the album. Obviously as time went on I would have done things differently. That is the nature of what happens when I make CD's. I would want to tinker a bit."

Craig: "You find you want to change something fairly often?"

Michael Falzarano: "I do. Once you hand something in there is no turning back. You are getting better at what you do and the song has already been created. Now you hear what you rather have done. Now you have future knowledge and can look back. I also think of how it could be recorded. That is because I produce a lot of music. On that album there were production qualities I would have done differently. Overall the three records *The Land Of Heroes*, *Too Many Years*, and the *Christmas With Jorma* record were excellent recordings. *Too Many Years* is one of my favorites."

Craig: "That was a great effort. The song that the Rolling Stones recorded *You Gotta Move* (Written by Reverend Gary Davis) came out brilliantly. What was it like in the studio with Jorma and Pete Sears?"

Michael Falzarano: "When you work with those two it is always nice. They are world class musicians. It was fun making the record. Some of the songs we were playing in concert *Fools Blues* and *Nine Pound Hammer*, we would fool around with backstage and I suggested recording it. *Gypsy Fire* was being played live too."

Craig: "You were also performing *Home Of The Blues*."

Michael Falzarano: "I had heard that on a soundtrack to some movie. I remembered the song as soon as I heard it. I thought that would be good to record. Jorma and Jack I believe played that song in the Triumphs (Circa 1959). We would play *You Gotta Move*, every now and then. Jorma was experimenting with the lap steel guitar."

Craig: "There was also *Man For All Seasons*, which took on the name *Junkies On Angel Dust*."

Michael Falzarano: "As I remember I think it was the record company saying that they didn't want the name *Junkies On Angel Dust* to appear on the album. They wanted it changed to *Man For All Seasons*. I thought the song would be a cool thing to do."

Craig: Did the Memphis Pilgrims project start in 1987?"

Michael Falzarano: "That would be correct. It was ten years after the death of Elvis Presley."

Craig: "The album you did with them *Mecca* has some quality tunes that Hot Tuna had performed, *I Was The One*, *Love Gone Flat*, *Just My Way*, and *Judge, I'm Not Sorry*. The time frame between the beginning of the band and the release of the record was rather long. What was the thinking behind the decision?"

Michael Falzarano: "What was happening at the time you have to remember I put the band together as a one time thing. It was going to be a birthday bash for Elvis. Some of the original players went on to do their own thing. You also had in 1989 the Airplane reunion. Shortly there after when the Airplane tour ended Hot Tuna was offered a record deal by Epic. We went into the studio to record *Pair A Dice Found* for Epic. It wasn't during the period I was thinking I would wait. I actually got sidetracked. Not sidetracked, but working with Jorma. In 1990 Hot Tuna went on the road for an extended period of time, right up to 2003. I had met Harvey Sorgen, and had jammed with some of the other guys in Woodstock, New York. About 1996 I had gotten the players, had gotten some money saved for the project, and had gotten the record deal. I went ahead and finally made the record."

Craig: "Often overlooked was the Memphis Pilgrims material had the ability to shine both on stage and in the studio. Not a lot of records coming out in the 1990's could say that."

Michael Falzarano: "Thanks."

Craig: "The press really took a liking to the whole idea."

Michael Falzarano: "It was a great project. Had I had more time to devote with it, and tour with it, I could have done more with it. Hot Tuna was working the entire decade. When Tuna wasn't on the road, I worked with Jorma, and other people. The other guys in the band had many projects going. There wasn't the time I wished."

Craig: "On the Hot Tuna release of *Pair A Dice Found* there is a wonderful cover of the Barry McGuire hit single *Eve Of Destruction*. How did the Hot Tuna version come about?"

Michael Falzarano: "We had pretty much finished the album. We had all the songs we wanted. Somewhere in the recording process of the album the record company wanted us to do the cover version because we went to war in Iraq the first time. I don't know if they demanded it, or suggested it strongly. The version is pretty good. I enjoyed the result."

Craig: "What were your recollections of working with Hot Tuna in the studio, compared to the live gigs."

Michael Falzarano: "Jorma and I had done a bunch of demos. The record company liked it. I was doing the Memphis Pilgrims. Kenny Aronoff was going to be the drummer. Lenny Underwood was going to take care of the keyboards. (Predicated on their respective schedules). Somewhere along the way they started to record. They were having trouble getting the thing going. Originally I didn't think of being part of the record. I had things going on. When they called I went to the studio to check out what was going on. I noticed it was such a big room that everyone was isolated. The drums may be 300 feet from the keyboards. The first thing I did was suggest all of us get out to the main room and play together as a band. We could get a feeling of playing together and not laying bricks one at a time. Some of the tunes on the album are played live with the first take used. You get a good energy that way. *Love Gone Flat* with the exception of the vocal, we did it in one shot. I called out the changes to the guys and away we went. You never can catch the live energy of a show. For some of the songs we captured it pretty well. Then the record comes out and it wasn't what all the Tuna fans wanted. The fans were used to the heavy metal (1975-1977) sound. At first the record company loved it. Later on they didn't get behind it."

Craig: "An event that wasn't the fault of the record was the death of progressive rock radio. Without the free-form stations to give the songs airplay it couldn't possibly get the attention of the public."

Michael Falzarano: "Eventually we played many of the tunes in concert. They went over very well. They rocked out."

Craig: "One that certainly fit the bill was *Ak-47*."

Michael Falzarano: "That became a staple of the band."

Craig: "When you were recording the *King James Sessions* there was an interesting story going around of a haunted studio. First on a more serious note you being a New Yorker, can you talk about the songs on the record that dealt with the September 11th tragedy?"

Michael Falzarano: "On that album there were three songs that were written in regard to the 9/11 situation. Those songs are *New Season*, *These Colors Don't Run*, and *Last Train Out*. They are a trilogy of songs for me. *New Season* came to me the next day. I was feeling dark. The three songs came to me within a week. I had written that one. The next week I was driving out to Jorma's Ranch. He lives ten hours from me. I like to stop at truck stops and talk with the truckers. I was getting a cup of coffee. One of the bumper-stickers read "These colors don't run." I was talking to a trucker about that. As I was driving down the road the song came to me. The first song was about feeling bad. I was only a couple of miles from the Twin Towers that day. *These Colors Don't Run* was the other side of the coin. I am human, I am pissed off. I oppose war and don't believe what we are doing in Iraq. I didn't agree about going in the first place. The other song is *One More Round*. It is more or less about the firemen and the workers that went into the area a week after 9/11. They had to go there every day. It is a tune of a boxer looking for strength, to go one more round. The guys and I talked with them needed their God to give them strength to do this one more day."

Craig: "You also put a tribute to your friend Allen Woody from Government Mule on the record *Last Train Out*."

Michael Falzarano: "Allen and I were good friends. We had many mutual friends. It was a shock when he passed away. I was in Italy at the time. A friend had a castle that was seven hundred years old. I was sitting there strumming the guitar. The bridge of the song was inspired by my stay in Italy."

Craig: "Where does the haunted studio story come in?"

Michael Falzarano: "I am not sure if it is, or isn't, but a good friend and excellent guitar-player Kenny Kearney had just purchased the store in Brooklyn (King James Music). Upstairs there were two giant empty rooms. We thought this would be perfect for recording. After the recording sessions were over people claimed to have heard stuff rattling and that type of thing. As it turned out there was somebody that either died there or was killed many decades ago. Is the flat haunted? I don't know."

Craig: "Bob Steeler (Hot Tuna drummer 1974-1977) and I were attempting to remember a couple of dates that he played with Jorma in Colorado somewhere between 1992-1994. Do you recall when he sat in with you guys?"

Michael Falzarano: "He did play with us twice. I want to say both times may have been Denver. I think it was Jorma, Pete, and myself. Could have been between 1992-1995. If it were a Tuna gig I would have remembered it more clearly. He definitely played almost an entire set the one time (Either first or second), and played with us again the second. I don't recall the exact specifics. Bob is a great guy and a great drummer."

Craig: "The respect is very well earned. Bob played his heart out, often pounding the skins three to four hours per night. The excitement has taken off for you with the New Riders Of The Purple Sage reunion. How did your involvement come about?"

Michael Falzarano: "I have been playing with Buddy Cage on and off for five to eight years. The drummer Johnny Markowski and the bass-player Ron Penque have played together in Stir Fried. David Nelson and Buddy Cage had obviously played in the New Riders. The stage was set. How it all came about Johnny and Buddy were playing golf and talking about doing fun cover things such as Hot Tuna, New Riders, my stuff, fun things. Ron thought why not do it as a New Riders reunion. First when Dave Nelson got contacted he wasn't sure. I then got a call and it was Buddy. He told me that they were thinking of a New Rider's renaissance and would I be interested. I said sure, who else is involved? Then it came down to David Nelson."

Craig: "What about John Dawson?"

Michael Falzarano: "Dave called John. He is living in Mexico. He isn't in the best of health for touring and lives about four hours from an airport. John gave his blessing. He thought it would really cool to keep the memories alive. We booked five shows on our own. They all sold out. We then made a tentative agreement to keep on doing it. I called up a friend at Blue Mountain Artists and told them what happened. We came in and the agency took us on. They booked us a tour. Then they booked us through next year."

Craig: "What venue was the first of the five you played?"

Michael Falzarano: "The Rain Desert, Danielson, Connecticut on 10/5/05. It held one hundred people. We needed a place that would be a family party. If we sucked we didn't want people to throw things. David Nelson didn't come in until the day before. We had one rehearsal with him only. The next show was in New Jersey. We sold out and there were two hundred people that couldn't get in. We knew we were on to something good. The band jelled. We sounded great. It got better and better. The songs are great."

Craig: 'How is the tour set up to keep the band playing enough, but not have you gone from the family's long spells at a time?"

Michael Falzarano: "For the summer we can play four shows, come back home for a week, and then go out again for ten days. When the summer ends it will lighten up some. For summer maybe fifteen shows a month."

Craig: "What I'm impressed with is the new generation of fans."

Michael Falzarano: "We see fans that were too young for the original band. We are getting the old and new."

Craig: "You have done work with a terrific musician Professor Louie (Friends with the Band and played with the Memphis Pilgrims). He is a legend around the Woodstock, New York area. When you get together do you call him Professor Louie or Aaron Hurwitz?"

Michael Falzarano: "When I first met him I called him Aaron, but everybody else is calling him Louie. I don't get it. Since he is Louie to everyone else, I started to call him Louie as well. A cool piece of information is that the name Professor Louie was given to him by Rick Danko of the Band."

Craig: "Any chance with the New Riders on the road and Hot Tuna as well you will play with Hot Tuna again?"

Michael Falzarano: "The door is always open. We have some shows booked together this year. If the opportunity presents itself and Jorma asks me to sit in for a song or two sure. We are on nothing but the best of terms."

Craig: "It has been a pleasure to listen to the great stories of the past and I know with the New Riders you will be created many more for the future. Thanks so much. Before you go I want to let the readers know how they can find out all the musical projects you have going on. Michael's website is www.michaelfalzarano.com, the New Riders site is www.nrps.net, and the Memphis Pilgrims can be found at www.memphispilgrims.com."

Michael Falzarano: " Thank you Craig. If you need anything else for the book let me know."

# Barry Flast- Jefferson Starship.

Craig: "Thanks for being part of the book. How are you today?"

Barry Flast: "Thanks for having me. I'm doing great."

Craig: "In circa 1964 did you play with a band the Long Island Sounds?"

Barry Flast: "I wasn't in the original line-up. I came along around 1966."

Craig: "Your history starts to build nicely after the Long Island Sounds. Can you talk about what came next?"

Barry Flast: "I was in a band that played a lot in the Village (A part of New York City) called the 6th Avenue Express. We patterned ourselves after the Blues Project (Al Kooper, and Steve Katz were part of that band, and would leave to be part of Blood Sweat & Tears). We worked at the Bitter End and the Night Owl very frequently. We played parties and dances as well."

Craig: "Did you have any record company interest?"

Barry Flast: "The closest brush with fame if you will was working for a guy Kal Mann. Kal had something to do with the starting of Cameo/Parkway Records. He also wrote a good deal of Chubby Checker's hits after *The Twist*. Kal was the father of a girl that some of the guys of the 6th Avenue Express had gone to summer camp with. His daughter Betsy told Kal about us. Kal had us go into New York City and record a bunch of songs he was writing for an anti-Vietnam rock opera. We thought we would be off and running and the big time would be next. Nothing ever came of the session. There was another brush with success. The singer in the band was Eric Bibb. His dad Leon was a well known folk singer (Early 1960's). We had always hoped that would be another in. It wasn't meant to be."

Craig: "It is getting near college time and you will meet somebody that will have a terrific career."

Barry Flast: "I go off to Boston University. I was in a group the Tom Swift Electric Band. Billy Squire (Popular singer and guitarist in the 1980's that had many major hits, including *Everybody Wants You* and *In The Dark*) was in the same college dorm as me. We were able to become a house band at the legendary Boston club called the Psychedelic Supermarket."

Craig: "That was one of the most famous clubs on the east coast. Cream did at least one show there."

Barry Flast: "That's right. We opened for Cream."

Craig: "All the money given to Boston University was worth it for being on the same stage as Cream. When you worked with Billy Squire did you sense that he had something that would give him a name in the rock and roll section of the record stores one day?"

Barry Flast: "Absolutely, even then you could see he was a wonderful guitar-player. Our dream was to make the big time. At the time our hopes and aspirations were behind our singer Tom Swift. Tom Swift was his real name."

Craig: "During this time frame had you met Bob Steeler (Hot Tuna drummer) yet?"

Barry Flast: "Bob and I would first meet in California years later. I made it through two years of college. I found that music was a real aphrodisiac and I wanted to pursue it full-time. I went back to New York City. I needed to find a job. I landed a job as a gofer for a recording studio. After a few months I did a demo after hours with one of the engineers Peter Granet." (He had numerous engineering credits over the years including Papa John Creach, Emerson, Lake & Palmer, and Kansas).

Craig: "Peter has had some career. The acts that he has been an engineer are ultra diverse."

Barry Flast: "Too numerous to count. Nothing came of the demo, but one day I'm walking by the Waverly Theater in New York City. I run into one of the former members of the Long Island Sounds. His name was Mike. He tells me he has a job as a staff songwriter for the Alfred Grossman Company. Mike tells me that he was happy to see me, because I would be perfect for the demo they were going to record. I go into the studio and sing on the demo. It was there I met Sam Gordon, who was from the publishing end of the business. We hit it off at once. Sam told me that I was a great singer, and piano-player, but wanted to know do I write songs? I told him that I have been writing for years. Sam wanted to hear some of my songs. He tells me to come up to his office next week and to play some of the tunes for him. The next week I go to his office and play some of the songs. He then signs me on the spot to a songwriter and staff writer position. I got paid a weekly salary to work nine to five."

Craig: "At this juncture of your career did you write a song that you hoped Janis Joplin would record *One Night Stand*?"

Barry Flast: "That happened either December of 1969 or January of 1970. Sam had a tip sheet for the artists that were going to record. This way publishers would know if the artists would need material. Sam would come to me and tell me to write a song for Johnny Mathis (Immensely popular male vocalist from the 1950's and 1960's who had several hits including *Chances Are* and *It's Not For Me To Say*), Andy Williams (Immensely popular male vocalist as well from the 1950's and 1960's, who had a popular TV show for a number of years) or Cher. One day he tells me that Creedence Clearwater Revival is going to make a record. He wanted me to write a song for John Fogerty. I knew that Fogerty writes his own stuff, excluding some traditional tunes. I didn't tell Sam that. He tells me the theme of the song should be about being on the road and being with many different women. I told Sam since I hadn't been on the road it may not be what he wants. Sam told me to take a crack at it anyway. A couple of days later I give the song to Sam. He thought it was too poppy. That was the end of that. However a month later we are going into the Record Plant studio in New York City. Todd Rundgren and John Siegler who played bass with Todd in Utopia were sitting in the studio. Norman Smart who played on the Ian & Sylvia (Canadian folk music) record *Great Speckled Bird* was there as a drummer. We had to record a couple of songs for Sam. Todd is playing the guitar and I am on piano. We finished the two songs Sam wanted recorded. It was time for a lunch break. Sam leaves the studio for an hour. I turn to Todd and ask what he thought of a song I had written called *One Night Stand*. Todd liked it so much he told me that "We should record the song while Sam is having lunch." The engineer roles the tape and records the song. Sam gets back to the studio and I ask him to check this song out. He told me that it sounded really good. He was curious what made me record it. I told him Todd thought it would be a good idea. Sam thought it sounded much better with a band than it originally sounded in the office. Sam wanted to add a few touches. He had Todd play a solo and brought in a couple of female singers. When it was finished Sam is really excited about the thing. Sam brings the song into Albert Grossman's office. Albert tells Sam it was perfect and would be great for Janis Joplin. I don't know what Albert was thinking because when Janis first heard the song she thought it was way over the top. Janis did not want to have anything to do with the song. Clive Davis (President of CBS Records at the time) thought it would be a hit. Clive went as far to think it would be the biggest hit for her since *Piece Of My Heart*. Clive wanted anything that would kick her career in the butt. The next move is sending Todd Rundgren to California. The plan is to have Todd with the Butterfield Blues Band convince Janis the song would be right for her. Todd would produce and the Butterfield Blues Band would back Janis up. Who thinks of these things? Janis cuts the tune and sings the song as if she were reading a recording contract. She couldn't relate to the lyrics and did not have much feeling behind her effort. About a week later Todd comes back to New York. We go into Sam's office. There is Todd, Sam, and I listening to the version Janis recorded. To a man we each conclude she didn't give a sh_t. Todd said "She didn't give a sh_t and that was the best I could get out of her." The version goes to Davis. Clive fires off a letter that I still have to this day. He said she needs to re-cut the demo and make it more like the kids demo version. I thought that was very flattering. I will always remember the letter. Janis had a reaction that was for all of us to go f_ck ourselves and she ran off to the Amazon with Joe Namath (Famous pro football quarterback). When she resurfaced she went to Toronto to put together the Full Tilt Boogie Band. That was the end of my song."

Craig: "Until 1983."

Barry Flast: "*Farewell Song* (Live and studio unreleased material) comes out. My tune is on it. They put the version on the LP with the Butterfield Blues Band. The song got to be a Top 10 most played on the Album Oriented Rock (AOR) play lists for the better part of the year. The reviews from Cream, Rolling Stone, and Crawdaddy all singled out that song. Columbia Records didn't want to put out a single because Janis was dead."

Craig: "That is a shame with all that went into recording the song. There is nothing wrong with releasing music from somebody that passed away, if it is getting positive reviews. In fact it could only help stimulate her catalog of records and that in turn makes money for the record company."

Barry Flast: "I know, what can you do? It is possible her family didn't want it released. Here's the thing too man, her manager Albert Grossman better protected his clients than anybody. If she didn't want the song to come out he would do his best to honor her wishes."

Craig: "How did you get to record with Paul Stookey from Peter, Paul, & Mary?"

Barry Flast: "There was a guy from Australia named Gary Shearston. He was brought over to the United States by Paul Stookey. Gary had a very unique sound of folk and psychedelic music. Originally I was going to be part of his band. He had some troubles and went back to Australia. When he came back to New York he called me that he was in the studio and there was one song that needed a piano. He wanted to know if I would help out. I said certainly. We put down the track but Gary isn't happy. He wants me to rehearse with him in Rye, New York. He tells me he isn't happy with Paul producing him."

Craig: "Did Gary have trouble being satisfied with people he worked with?"

Barry Flast: "Let's put it this way, we recorded his album five times. Warner Brothers Records spent $200,000 on the project. Here is how Albert Grossman protected his clients. He had a clause in the contract that if Gary didn't sign off that the record is okay for release, Warner Brothers couldn't make it available to the public. It gave Paul Stookey an opportunity to record a solo record. Albert Grossman had structured the contract where the last four records would include three solo (One for each member) and the final would be a Peter, Paul & Mary album. Peter tells the guys from Gary's band that we were too good to not get something out of all this. He wanted to know if we would back him on his record *Paul And...*, since Gary had split to go back to Australia."

Craig: "How did you end up on the record by Poco (Country and folk band that had Timothy Schmit who would later play with the Eagles) called *A Good Feelin' To Know* in 1972?"

Barry Flast: "This is where the theory about six degrees of separation comes into play. The producer of the album Jim Mason worked as the producer on the Paul Stookey album. They needed a keyboard-player. I caught a break because the famous session musician Larry Knechtel was touring with Bread (David Gates)."

Craig: "How do you end up in California?"

Barry Flast: "My wife at the time (Not my current wife) and I needed to get away from her parents. We were looking to leave New York. I was becoming friendly with the blues musician Nick Gravenites. Nick told me if I move out to California I could be the keyboard-player in his band. I go out to California and Nick and I play exactly one show at the Lions Share in San Anselmo, California. The next week he fires me. I am three thousand miles away from my real home and I have no job."

Craig: "What was his reason for getting you out to California and then letting you go?"

Barry Flast: "He told me that keyboards don't work in a blues band."

Craig: "Since he has been playing guitar forever wouldn't he have known that prior to the performance at the Lions Share?"

Barry Flast: "The entire thing was bizarre. Not much is going on for a couple of years. In the summer of 1974 I get a call from the booking agent of Kingfish. Julie Simon tells me that the band was booked to play a month of shows at a club called The Tides in Juneau, Alaska. They had two weeks remaining, there was an accident, and one of the members had died. I don't know how she got my number, but I was real glad. I went to Alaska and it started a good run for over thirty years. I didn't get treated very well by Kingfish. I assumed that they would cover my plane fare both ways. I went up to Alaska on a one way ticket. When we are going home they inform me I have to pay for my own ticket. Basically the two week salary went for the plane ride home."

Craig: "It must have been appalling at the time, but when you think of it now it could make a rock laugh. You do them the favor but you can't keep any money that you earned."

Barry Flast: "On the ride home I tell Dave Torbert (Bass-player) if you guys want to hire me I have to actually make money. Dave didn't take kindly to my comments. A month later they hired Bob Weir."

Craig: "On the plus side by making Dave upset you helped the San Francisco scene."

Barry Flast: "If I hadn't made an issue about getting paid I may have gotten the gig and maybe they don't hire Bob."

Craig: "Is the rumor true that he had to pay cab fare on the way home from the first gig?"

Barry Flast (Barry laughs at the joke). "One door closed and another opened. I get home and get a call that Stuart Houston (Known as Boots) is looking to put together a band to promote the singer Kathi McDonald (Performed with Big Brother & The Holding Company). By the way Pete Sears played on the record from Kathi called *Insane Asylum*. He couldn't tour with her because he had commitments for the Jefferson Starship. We spent a month or so rehearsing. That is how I met Bob Steeler. We were going to back her up on the road."

Craig: "What type of impression did Bob Steeler give you?"

Barry Flast: "He is one of the most charming and funny human beings you'll ever meet. We got along great. Bob and I used to *jam* on his music. His music was both jazzy and artsy. One afternoon Neil Schon (Guitarist for Santana and Journey) comes by one of our rehearsals. By the way the song I had hoped Janis Joplin would record *One Night Sta*nd was going to be part of the Kathi McDonald tour. Kathi was singing the f_ck out of it. I don't know why Neil was at the studio that day. He was hired to play on one or two songs. He was acting like the boss of bosses. Neil listens to a couple of tunes. Neil and Kathi walk off for a few minutes. When she comes back she calls off the rehearsal. She told us that she wasn't feeling well. A week goes by and Bob Steeler calls me. He lets me know we were fired."

Craig: "What reason did they give Bob?"

Barry Flast: "I don't know what they told Bob, but Boots told me that Neil was unimpressed with the band."

Craig: "Did you and Bob try to start your own project."

Barry Flast: "Bob and I tried to form a band with a singer Richie Martin. We rehearsed for a long time, but nothing happened. Bob then got the gig with Hot Tuna."

Craig: "There is an interesting story about John Cipollina helping Kingfish out."

Barry Flast: "I had gotten a call that Kingfish needed a keyboard-player. I asked if I would get paid this time. We were rehearsing at John Cipollina's studio for a gig at Winterland in San Francisco. Robby Hodinott the lead guitar-player was having some personal issues. It was time for the sound check and he isn't there. Matthew Kelly from the group got a hold of John Cipollina to help us. John comes to the gig with a girl he was working with named Pam Tillis. (Daughter of country music star Mel. She has put out many country albums of her own). Robby finally shows up. We played the gig with the two guitarists and the female singer."

Craig: "As we fast forward to the Jefferson Starship needing a keyboard-player was it the manager Michael Gaiman that called, or Paul Kantner?"

Barry Flast: "It was Michael. I have to say Michael has been responsible for some of the most memorable gigs I had ever gotten. He helped me get the Dead Ringers (Grateful Dead tribute band that released a live album in 1993 on Relix. Tom Constanten the former Grateful Dead keyboard-player and Dave Nelson from the New Riders Of The Purple Sage were on the recording) gig. Michael may have helped with seventy-five percent of the work I got."

Craig: "Originally you were filling in for Tim Gorman."

Barry Flast: "I had done at least six shows filling in for Tim in 1994 to begin with and was around until June of 1995. It was about forty shows over that period. Tim was going off to Los Angeles to work on a movie. I may have even played a show or two in 1993. Wait one moment please. My first gig was a private show for Glaxo on 5/21/94 in Raleigh, North Carolina. One interesting show was when Prairie Prince couldn't make it and Trey Sabatelli (The Tubes) and I played together. Darby Gould was still the lead singer then."

Craig: "Did you have to audition for Paul?"

Barry Flast: "No I didn't have to. Michael had put in the good word. To my dieing day I will feel cheated about never having gotten to rehearse with the Jefferson Starship. I didn't have the luxury of learning the tunes the way a normal musician does. In a rehearsal situation you can talk about things. I was given a tape and told to learn Tim's parts and play them that way."

Craig: "What was it like getting to play with somebody you admired as much as Paul Kantner?"

Barry Flast: "I was on cloud nine. I was a huge Jefferson Airplane fan. Every time the Airplane played the Fillmore East in New York I was there. I thought Marty was the greatest singer. The Airplane vocals were tremendous. I loved Country Joe for the political songs and Quicksilver Messenger Service for the guitars."

Craig: "As the Jefferson Starship tour went on could you tell if Paul was on the fence if he wanted you to remain a member or not?"

Barry Flast: "I knew it from almost the moment we did the acoustic tour. Paul always wanted me to play louder. Paul plays very loud. The old joke on a scale of one to ten he is on eleven. He told me that they were looking at a different direction, because our styles were different."

Craig: "What songs stood out for you as the most enjoyable to play during the forty shows?"

Barry Flast: "From the Airplane days I loved doing *White Rabbit, Lawman, When The Earth Moves Again,* and *We Can Be Together.* From Paul's' post Airplane music I loved *I'm on Fire, Shadowlands* and *The Light.* He also did a fabulous poem called *The Radiance Of Mirrors.* I enjoyed working with Prairie Prince. He was the best drummer. Prairie is so creative, so different, and so unique. He is also the nicest guy."

Craig: "You were part of a Great Society reunion of sorts for the 35th anniversary of the Summer Of Love, in San Francisco. What was it like to play with three of the members of the band that performed when Grace Slick was part of the group?"

Barry Flast: "It was a blast. We had Darby Slick playing the lead guitar, his son Jor on rhythm, and vocals, Peter van Gelder on the saxophone, I was on keyboards, Paul Lamb a friend of Jor's was on bass, another friend of Jor's named Jimmy Sage was the drummer, and Jerry Slick didn't want to play drums, so he played rhythm-guitar. People may have told you that there were two female singers, but there were three. Elizabeth McGill, her mom Allison Prival, and Tessa made up the female singers."

Craig: "How many songs did you get to perform?"

Barry Flast: "I happen to have the set list with me. *White Rabbit*, and *Sally Go 'Round The Roses* were sung by Tessa. Darby played an original called *I Don't Want To Fall In Love*, Jor played an original called *I Love You More*, Darby did an original called *Seven Years*, and the last song was *Somebody To Love*. The final tune Elizabeth and her mom did the vocals."

Craig: "Sounds like it was fun. It was nice to see if only for a day the Great Society reform as part of the Summer Of Love celebration."

Barry Flast: "I'm glad I was a part of it. Do you want the tape of the show?"

Craig: "Let me think of that for one second. How fast can you get it to me? You got to play with David Freiberg on the Quicksilver Gold album, Live At The Avalon Ballroom, San Francisco 10/11/03. You also were on the Live At The Little Fox Theatre, Redwood City, California 6/13/03 (David isn't on that one)."

Barry Flast: "David showed up to some of our gigs to sing *Pride Of Man*. It was great to work with him. A funny story the sound person would never turn me up. He thought that the keyboards weren't a part of the Quicksilver sound. He forgot about the people that played with them over the years, such as Nicky Hopkins, Pete Sears, and Michael Lewis."

Craig: "Before we end the interview you are hosting a great internet interview program Artists Archives. The readers can go to www.hbnnews.com. You are going to have a wealth of people to talk with."

Barry Flast: "My wife suggested that I do the show as a tour of my press book. I am going to start at the beginning and that meant an interview with Paul Stookey. I interviewed Pete Sears and there will be many more on the horizon. I get to play rarities from the artists I interview. It is turning out very well."

Craig: "Barry thanks very much for the stories today and the best of luck with the radio show."

Barry Flast: "Thank you Craig. Best of luck with the book. If you need anything let me know."

David Freiberg- Jefferson Airplane and Jefferson Starship.

D A V I D  and  M I C H A E L A

**Photograph by kind permission of Mike Somavilla. From the Mike Somavilla collection.
Not to be reproduced without the written consent of Mike Somavilla.
Photographer not known. A rare photo from 1963 of David and his partner Michaela Conga.
The mention of Michaela's last name is equally rare!**

QUICKSILVER MESSENGER SERVICE

RON POLTE    54 MARTHA AVE
SAN FRANCISCO   415 585-2455

*Capitol*
RECORDS

WEST POLE AGENCY
585 2271

**Photograph by kind permission of Mike Somavilla. From the Mike Somavilla collection.**
**Not to be used without written permission from Mike Somavilla. Photographer Ron Polite.**
**This is a promo photo courtesy of Capitol Records and the West Pole Agency.**
**David Freiberg, in his days with the Quicksilver Messenger Service. From left to right:**
**John Cipollina, Gary Duncan, Greg Elmore, and David Freiberg (Front). Circa late 1960's.**

Craig: "David thank you for taking time before the sound check. It is great to see you a full-time member of the Jefferson Starship."

David Freiberg: "You're welcome, Craig. It's nice somebody wants to talk with me and at my age it's great to see me anywhere."

Craig: "That is funny. There are many that want to speak with you. How is your wife Linda Imperial feeling?" (Linda is a terrific singer and a current member of the Jefferson Starship. She has had a very successful singing career. Please go to www.lindaimperial.com for an update on her health and the latest musical happenings).

David Freiberg: "She is doing fine. Thank you for asking."

Craig: "Going way back, before Quicksilver Messenger Service, you were in a male-female folk-rock combo called David & Michaela (From 1962-1964). Is it true that Paul Rothchild, the house producer of Electra Records at the time had an interesting comment about the band's folk-rock sound?"

David Freiberg: "He told me that right now the sound is on its way out. The Beatles are in but he didn't think they would last. I remember hearing them for the first time and thinking these guys sound pretty good. Years later I ran into Paul and reminded him of his comment. He didn't say anything and walked away."

Craig: "He was a bit off base on the Beatles, and on the mark with the Doors."

David Freiberg: "It appeared that way."

Craig: "As you look back on the music from David & Michaela, could it have been marketable and do you remember the last gig you played with Michaela?"

David Freiberg: "We didn't write our own songs. I wasn't happy with the stage act. It is possible it could have been marketable. CBS Records had us cut a demo in one afternoon. I never got a copy. The last performance was the night the Beatles first played on the Ed Sullivan Show (2/9/64)."

Craig: " David, you were part of a historic night! You didn't get a copy of your own demo?"

David Freiberg: "No. The entire thing was done rather quickly."

Craig: "That is a shame, because we have seen over the years that some bands have been able to release archival material and it has made the fanatics happy. Often times, those who were afraid of it seeing the light of day are surprised by the positive response; they became their own worst critic."

David Freiberg: "A musician should be his own worst critic always."

Craig: "The highly celebrated debut record by Quicksilver Messenger Service came out in May of 1968 (Self-titled). We'll talk about the legendary track *Pride Of Man* in a minute, but there is another great tune you and Gary Duncan wrote called *Light Your Windows*. The entire record was a marvelous effort."

David Freiberg: "Thank you. The credit must go to the entire band. As a unit Gary, John Cipollina, and Greg Elmore made the record what it was."

Craig: "You are always giving the credit to others, but the fans know very well you were equally responsible for the warm reception of the LP. Is it a special feeling after all these years that your version of *Pride Of Man* from the Quicksilver Messenger Service days is considered the definitive?

David Freiberg: "As a matter of fact we will perform it tonight. It is flattering to be remembered for the song all these years later."

Craig: "When you look back at the session work you did on the David Crosby record *If I Could Only Remember My Name* (1971), it must have been an amazing experience to have had so much talent assembled in the studio. Between those that played and those that gave moral support, it was an Airplane, and Grateful Dead festival."

David Freiberg: "Now at my age I think of the title as the truth. Jorma, Jack, Grace were lending support from the Airplane side, and from the Grateful Dead there were the two drummers Mickey Hart, and Bill Kreutzmann. To top it all off Jerry Garcia played guitar."

Craig: "David is it factual the way you got involved in the final Jefferson Airplane tour was while helping on the 1972 Mickey Hart album *Rolling Thunder*, Grace Slick and Paul Kantner did a session."

David Freiberg: "I had known Paul since either 1962 or 1963. With Marty gone from the Airplane they wanted a male voice to provide harmonies. They also had me bring along the song *Blind John*. We performed that on the 1972 tour."

Craig: "There is a fantastic live version from the 9/3/72 Hollywood Bowl show (Please see page 206). At the end of the song in a real deep voice you say *"Big Bad John"*, which was the 1961 hit for Jimmy Dean."

David Freiberg: "It's been so long, I didn't remember if it were Paul or me."

Craig: "Is it possible to see the song in the set some time down the road?"

David Freiberg: "The song doesn't exactly fit what we are doing at the moment. It is rather basic."

Craig: "David hums a few bars rather well I might add! There is a record from 1973 that never got the credit it deserved. Jack Traylor & Steelwind, released *Child Of Nature*. You played keyboards and Craig Chaquico was the bands lead guitar-player. Were you able to see even in his formative stages that Craig would become a highly respected musician in the rock and roll world shortly (Jefferson Starship)."

David Freiberg: "When you saw him play as far back as 1973 there was something special about his ability. It wouldn't be long before we both became part of the Jefferson Starship."

Craig: "In 1975, Quicksilver Messenger Service did a reunion record *Solid Silver*." What were your thoughts on the album?"

David Freiberg: "It was okay. There is one track I really like, *Gypsy Lights*."

Craig: "Since progressive rock radio was still alive then I found it helped those who were first discovering the band to go back into the catalog. They were then able to experience the first release, or *Happy Trails*."

David Freiberg: "Some good came out of it. It wasn't the best work of the band."

Craig: "Being involved in the Jefferson Starship at the time did you regret that you couldn't split yourself in two?"

David Freiberg: "My place was with the Jefferson Starship. As a matter of fact I wasn't even in the studio when the *Solid Silver* record got the final mix."

Craig: "Would you have liked to do some live shows in support of the record?"

David Freiberg: "The idea was to make one studio album. John Cipollina may have done some live shows. He had a bunch of things going on."

Craig: "In 2003 you were able to be part of the Quicksilver Gold live CD, called *Live At The Avalon Ballroom 10/11/03*. Barry Flast (Formally of the Jefferson Starship and has done numerous projects with Kingfish) told me that you came to some of the gigs and performed *Pride Of Man*. You were able to play with a former Jefferson Starship member and Mario Cipollina (Brother of John Cipollina, who played with the Quicksilver Messenger Service, and passed away 5/29/89). Mario played bass on some of the Quicksilver Messenger Service reunion album *Solid Silver*."

David Freiberg: "It was a really good band. Joli Valente (His dad Dino was the writer of the song *Get Together* and a member of the Quicksilver Messenger Service. Dino passed away 11/16/94) did the lead vocals, Gail Muldrow (Played with the Jerry Garcia Band) was on guitar, Ed Michaels (Played on Marty Balin's 1991 solo record *Better Generation*) played the drums, and you mentioned the other two guys."

Craig: "When you look back at the Jefferson Starship conquering the charts and concert halls with *Red Octopus*, what goes through your mind?"

David Freiberg: "It makes me realize how fortunate I have been in this business. No matter how long you have been playing rock and roll you can never expect a record to sell infinite copies."

Craig: "How did you get involved with Paul and the current Jefferson Starship?"

David Freiberg: "Paul called me for the *Intergalactic Reunion* (Paul put together several shows over the past few years where former Jefferson Starship members and friends play together), sometime I guess in 2005. Things worked out and I was asked to join the band."

Craig: "It's great to see the energy still coming from you and Paul."

David Freiberg: "I am sixty eight years old."

Craig: "I wanted to verify that before we finished. You graduated high school in 1956."

David Freiberg: "Yes I did. Seems like a long time ago."

Craig: "Paul McCartney wondered if he would be loved when he is sixty four. You and Paul Kantner are still being loved as well. Can we get a couple of more years with David being on the road?"

David Freiberg: "I'll do this as long as it is still fun. Right now it still is fun."

Craig: "Isn't it nice that the songs get changed and you can have some fun in each city?"

David Freiberg: "We performed *Ohio* (Crosby, Stills, Nash & Young) in Ohio. "Four dead in Ohio. Four dead in Ohio."

Craig: "You did a fantastic cover of the Beatles song *All You Need Is Love*, 2/14/06 at the House Of Blues, Atlantic City, New Jersey. How did that come about?"

David Freiberg: "For the Atlantic City Valentine's Day gig, we rehearsed it once during the sound check. We even got Paul to play on it. He's never at the sound check, so he had no say. I couldn't think of something for Detroit. Maybe a Motown song."

\*\*\*\*\*\*\*\*\*\*\*\*\*\*\*\*\*\*\*\*\*\*\*\*\*\*\*\*\*\*\*\*\*\*\*\*\*\*\*\*\*\*\*\*\*\*\*\*\*\*\*\*\*\*\*\*\*\*\*\*\*\*\*\*\*\*\*\*\*\*\*\*\*\*\*\*\*\*\*\*\*\*\*\*\*\*\*\*\*\*

Craig: "What about the Rare Earth hit *Get Ready*?"

(After a sudden silence, I realized that wouldn't be happening anytime soon).

Craig: "What is it like working with the younger members of the group, Diana and Slick?" (Younger in terms of age to David and Paul). Before I could get out another word David chimed in.

David Freiberg: "Don't forget Prairie Prince. It is fantastic working with Diana. She is an excellent vocalist. The entire band is a real unit. It's nice."

Craig: "David, thank you again for your time. I hope things continue to go well for you, your wife, and the band."

David Freiberg: "Thank you Craig, nice talking with you."

**Photograph by kind permission of Don Aters and may not be reproduced without his written consent.**

**From the Don Aters collection.**

**Don Aters photographer.**

**Chet Helms and David Freiberg 4/9/05 Avila Beach Resort, Avila Beach,**

**California from a Jefferson Starship concert.**

## Billy Goodman- Roadie, Road Crew Manager, writer, solo artist, played with Jorma Kaukonen 1989-1990, and Hot Tuna 1989.

Craig: "Billy thanks for giving me some of your time. From roadie to writer, and even time to play with Jorma and Jack, it's been a long ride thus far."

Billy Goodman: " Yes it has Craig. Thanks for contacting me."

Craig: "How did you first become a roadie for the Jefferson Starship?"

Billy Goodman: "I was in the Goodman Brothers Band for seven or eight years, with my brother Frank, and Steve Kimock (Zero and the Other Ones). In or around 1980 the band disbanded. I got sober. I had been drinking very heavily. For two years I was out of the music scene. I was working construction, but had become friendly with Skip Johnson (Former husband of Grace Slick). One night we were out for dinner in San Rafael, California. The subject came up that he needed a guitar tech for the Starship. I told him I'm a guitar tech. I wasn't really, but I didn't like working construction. He didn't believe me and the job got filled by someone else, but six months later he needed a roadie for Paul Kantner. Somehow I finagled my way into that opening."

Craig: "For those on the outside what is a day in the life of a roadie?"

Billy Goodman: "Depends on the band and if the musician has a lot of quirks or not. Paul Kantner was eccentric. One of the responsibilities I had was to bring Hydrox cookies to Paul's hotel room. Mind you not Oreos, but Hydrox with a half gallon of cold milk. That isn't a normal procedure in the day of a life of a roadie, but that was fine with me. The road crew would get to the venue in the wee hours of the morning, having driven from the previous city the night before. You would sleep on the bus and the rigger would go in first around eight in the morning. The light guys would go in around nine, the sound guys go in about ten thirty, and the guys that worked directly with the band would start around noon. I would roll in about eleven. I had an hour to take care of personal things and then I would wait for the stage-hands to get the gear out of the truck. The back-line gear is the amps, guitars, and drums. The band would fly from gig to gig. We had our own night liner tour bus for the road crew and production. Since the band would fly they would go to the hotel after the show and go to the airport in the morning. After the equipment was set up the band would normally come for a sound check around four-thirty. We would eat dinner, do the show, and tear down the equipment in the reverse order. The back-line crew was known as the champagne roadies because we would go in last for the load-in and were the first ones to finish at night . It was a nice job. We would take a shower before we got on the bus and away we went to the next city. A big part of the job was to take care of the personal needs of the musician you were assigned. Paul for instance was writing a book at the time. There was a trunk with his manuscript in it that had to get to his hotel room every night. I was the kiss of death roadie, because the people I worked for would always end up out of the band in a year or so. Don't ask me why. I was over the years a roadie for Paul, Pete Sears, David Freiberg, Peter Wolf (Jefferson Starship-keyboards. He played on the 1994 album *Nuclear Furniture*), and always kept an eye on Grace in case she needed something."

Craig: "How was the road crew treated by the band?"

Billy Goodman: "We were tight. It was a family but bottom line was you were a personal valet."

Craig: "Did the person you were the roadie for surprise you with the information they shared?"

Billy Goodman: "I think that's normal. Paul wasn't that way, but Grace and I were tight, we were friends outside of the band scene as well."

Craig: "Did you ever get confused as to what city you were in?"

Billy Goodman: "We would put a sign on stage for the band. This way they knew where we were playing. That way the singer talking to the audience would know what city they were in. There were a few embarrassing moments."

Craig: "Did you have a new found appreciation for the musicians on stage, being around the band each day?"

Billy Goodman: "In the Starship Grace was the only one I was a little awe struck by. The rest of the guys were just good musicians with a good gig as far as I was concerned. They were well taken care of and they did their jobs well. Mind you I was a big fan of the Jefferson Airplane. I loved the old Airplane music. I was also a big Quicksilver fan and was glad to be working alongside David Freiberg, but to be in the presence of Grace Slick was like being in the presence of Elizabeth Taylor, or some other classic Hollywood film star. She had an aura about her and was always special to me."

Craig: "What are your other memories of working with Paul?"

Billy Goodman: "Paul was very protective of his family. If the police had a situation with one of the road crew members for instance, Paul would just stop a show in the middle of the song until he knew everything was cool. He was like a biker in that way."

Craig: "Paul often got misunderstood. When he does interviews they can often be short. It isn't that he is being rude, he answers the questions in shorter sentences than some of the other contemporaries. He is very funny and very articulate."

Billy Goodman: "Paul was a ballsy guy and intelligent. As a matter of fact, all the musicians in Airplane were really intelligent, politically aware, funny, and astute. I didn't know Spencer Dryden, but I heard he was a cool guy. I absolutely loved his drumming."

Craig: "You had a great experience where you would come out and play one song with the Starship. How did this come about?"

Billy Goodman: "We were rehearsing at Hun Sound in San Rafael. There was a switch that went on where the keyboard-player would play the saxophone and the bass-player the keyboard. This was on *Stranger* (*Modern Times*). I was leaning over an amplifier trying to figure out what to plug in, I was inept at my job, but told good jokes. Somebody asked who is going to play the bass? Grace looks at me from the corner of her eye and says "Goodman will do it." I love her for that."

Craig: "Did this lead to you playing it on stage?"

Billy Goodman: "Yeah, every night. Usually it was the fourth song in the set. As soon as the song before was done Pete Sears would hand off the bass to me. I put it on, went directly out to the center, the spotlight came right on me for a couple of moments."

Craig: "Did any of the band members announce your name after the song?"

Billy Goodman: "No, but Grace would fool around with me during the song. Pinch my butt, that kind of thing. It was fun, they were cool people, and it was a good song."

Craig: "As time went on did you see Mickey Thomas's ego getting larger?"

Billy Goodman: "No more than anyone else. In show business it's normal to be a little ego centric if you're doing well." Mickey was actually pretty quiet, but once he got started he was extremely funny. Donnie Baldwin was witty too."

Craig: "When did you first find out that the Airplane wanted you for the 1989 reunion tour?"

Billy Goodman: "About a month before. I had moved to Philadelphia, written a book, *So You Wanna Be A Roadie*, that was published by Pollstar, recorded my first solo album, and was starting my folk/blues career, if you can call it that. I didn't intend to do any more work as a crew guy, I wanted to play."

Craig: "Isn't it so that when you finally decided to be a roadie for the Airplane reunion tour it was to take care of Jorma and Jack?"

Billy Goodman: "That was the bait. Skip Johnson knew I was a big Hot Tuna fan. Their first LP had a big impact on me and the people I was hanging out with. It introduced us to Reverend Gary Davis's music, and I loved Jorma from *Bless Its Pointed Little Head,* and *Volunteers.* I told Skip I wasn't going to do the Airplane reunion tour, but here he was on the phone with somebody saying "Yeah, Goodman will do it." It must have been Grace or Bill Thompson. I kept telling him I'm not going. Then Skip tells the person on the phone that I should be the roadie for Jorma and Jack. That sealed the deal plus I needed money to move to Baltimore, where I wanted to study with a blues musician named Philadelphia Jerry Ricks, who had played with Son House, and Mississippi John Hurt. I never ended up moving to Baltimore, but went to New York City instead."

Craig: "Did Jorma know before the tour started how good of a guitarist and singer you were?"

Billy Goodman: "No way. It wasn't until the very last day of the reunion tour (10/7/89, March For The Homeless, Washington, D.C.), that I went downstairs with my guitar and told Jorma ok, I listened to you play the entire tour, how about listening to me play a song. I remember I played a song by Blind Ted Darby known as *I Never Cried.* It was a great country blues piece that had everything. It was melodic, had intricate finger-picking in open G tuning with a high lonesome vocal. I think it was a big surprise for Jorma that I played the same kind of music that he did. That's when he asked me if I would go on the road with him for the electric Hot Tuna tour that was coming up."

Craig: "Did Jorma tell you how he liked it?"

Billy Goodman: (Laughs). "Jorma was a man of few words. He may have said "Wow that was good", or something like that. A funny story concerning Jorma and Jack. I had a buddy Paul McDowell who was the Hot Tuna crew chief forever. He started with the Airplane and did all the big years with Hot Tuna. I heard from Paul that Jorma and Jack were the evil twins when it came to their drummers and roadies. In other words they were really hard on them. So the first day they showed up for dress rehearsal I purposely stayed on the bus. Finally I was dragged to the stage. I turn to Jorma and Jack and I'm like what do you guys want? Well, they want to get set up and play some. But I just went out of my way to give them a dirty look and make it appear I had better things to do than take care of these two clowns. The fact that I stood my ground with them made them kind of like me I think, but it wasn't long before they had me running around. On that first day I wanted to make some kind of impression in order to survive the tour."

Craig: "When Jorma told you he wants you to play some solo shows and some Hot Tuna gigs was it a feeling of adulation?"

Billy Goodman: "I told him please don't offer me the job as a musician if I am going to end up as a roadie. The job description was to play electric bottle-neck slide guitar and be crew chief. When it came time for the electric Hot Tuna tour little did I know that Peter Kaukonen was coming along as well. I really liked Peter, but there wasn't room for both of us. I played electric until the dates in Philadelphia, because that was my home town at the time. I had told all my friends that I was in the band you know. I played the 11/30/89 Chestnut Cabaret show in Philadelphia and then I bowed out. To make it up to me Jorma asked if I would like to play some shows with him as a duo. That was a big deal for me. Jorma was a living legend, he still is. It was a big deal for me."

Craig: "What impressed me about your live playing were the older Tuna fans that don't like to see any Tom, Dick, or Sally on stage, really enjoyed how you performed. They really thought *Sweet Home Chicago* was right on."

Billy Goodman: "All my guitar playing is in open tuning, so I don't step on anybody's toes."

Craig: "When the last show with Jorma ended in 1990 was it difficult to come down from the mountain. You sat in also a couple of times in 1995 with Jorma as well."

Billy Goodman: "I had hoped the 1990 shows would go on forever. I did sit in with Jorma in 1995."

Craig: "Is it true that Jorma encouraged you after the 1990 tour to pursue your own music, because you were a good person, and a fine musician?"

Billy Goodman: "Well, I don't think he ever alluded to me being a good person, but I do think he liked my sound. He encouraged me to pursue a folk and blues career. He thought I had the ability for making my own way."

Craig: "You have done some terrific albums that can be purchased at www.billygoodman.com, how did you get to the point of recording your own records?"

Billy Goodman: "I left the roadie gig, wrote the book, and bought some studio equipment. I moved to Philadelphia to try to get managed by Cornerstone Management. At the time the Hooters were really hot in Philadelphia. There was a guy called Tommy Conwell (Tommy Conwell & the Young Rumblers). I wanted to be next in line from Cornerstone Management. I was a huge fan of Tommy Conwell. Cornerstone never did pick me up. I was making a lot of demo tapes with full production. I wanted to make a tape for my sister for a Christmas present and that was how I ended up recording my first album. I put two mikes up in my room and began to record. I kept erasing the tracks after I finished them so I could save the tape for the next song. In my head it was just a Christmas present, but when it was done I knew it would make a good album. I decided to go into the studio to recreate it but I found as many artists do that you can't recreate spontaneous moments like that. I went scrambling back to the takes that I had recorded for my sister but had erased all but one. I had to master the album from a cassette. That was a hard lesson. That was also the album where Grace Slick finally told me that I had found my sound. The title was *Walk This Street Alone*. There is even a police siren that can be heard on the song *Billy The Kid*. The microphones picked up the sound from outside my bedroom window. There is a record executive who heard that cut while he was visiting a friend in Holland. He's always looking for good cover versions of Dylan songs and that's why my version of *Billy The Kid* ended up on *May Your Song Always Be Sung – The Songs of Bob Dylan Vol. 3*." I think the siren got him."

Craig: "Billy before we wrap things up I want to make sure the readers can purchase the wealth of material you have released at your website www.billygoodman.com."

Billy Goodman: "Everything that I've recorded can be found there."

Craig: "You have recorded excellent renditions of the Little Feat song *Willin'*, the song the Rolling Stones covered on *Beggars Banquet* from Robert Wilkins called *Prodigal Son*, and some songs the fans will recognize from Hot Tuna shows, as well as your own compositions. The CD's are highly recommended, not only for the guitar playing, but for Billy's strong voice. Billy, it was a pleasure and best of luck with any future endeavors."

Billy Goodman: "Thanks Craig, it was fun."

## Tim Gorman- KBC, Jefferson Airplane keyboard-player on the 1989 tour, Wooden Ships, and Jefferson Starship.

Craig: "Tim, it's a pleasure to be able to talk about your musical career today."

Tim Gorman: "Thank you for the nice words."

Craig: "You appeared on the Spinners (Famous rhythm and blues band) album *From Here To Eternally* in 1979. What led up to you getting session work with a major artist?"

Tim Gorman: "I was working on my master's degree and got a call from a recording studio in Seattle, Kaye-Smith. Danny Kaye (Famous entertainer especially in the 1950's) was a co-owner. When I finished my education in Portland it was only about ninety miles to Seattle. It was at the time the only state of the art recording facility in the northwest. The famous rock band Bachman-Turner Overdrive recorded there. Some of the Led Zeppelin album *Houses Of The Holy* got recorded there. Heart did the record with the song *Barracuda* (*Little Queen*) at Kaye-Smith. Heart now owns the studio. They call it Bad Animal. I was hired to be a keyboard-player and arranger. During that time period I played with a number of bands in the Seattle and Portland area. One band was called Ramm (The spelling is correct). Myself and two of the background singers in the studio were also trying to get publishing deals. There was a punk band that was nine pieces called Pleasure. They actually ended up on Fantasy Records. I played on a couple of Pleasure albums and singles. The recording studio got purchased by Thom Bell (One of the main influences of the Philadelphia soul sound). I got a songwriting deal with them. Thom gave me a great arranging background. He gave me knowledge of the pop music field and how to write a song. He gave me a wealth of education, he was a great keyboard-player, and a great man. The publishing deal wasn't all that good. A couple of the background singers got better deals through Eric Kronfeld. Eric was a business manager and an attorney. Kelly Harland one of the background singers suggested to me I send Eric my tape. My tape got in the hands of Glyn Johns (Legendary producer and engineer. His credits include the Rolling Stones, the Who, and Eric Clapton). Word got back to me that he really enjoyed my keyboard playing. Kelly Harland, a guy named Bill Lamb, and myself had one week to form a band that sounded like Toto (Famous for the song *Hold The Line*). They wanted it to be professional studio musicians the way Toto was, but also be a band. Toto had received the largest advance of any unsigned band. The contract would include the record deal and pretty much all the session work you could handle. The three of us were put together with three British musicians. We were sent to London. That included the drummer Henry Spinetti (Worked with George Harrison, Paul McCartney, Bill Wyman, and Roger Daltrey). Henry's brother Victor played the director role on the Beatles film, A Hard Day's Night. In a week all six of us got to get an album together by having songs from our own catalog. The way it worked if you found a contract on your bed in your flat (An apartment) on Friday you were in. When I got home on a Friday the contract was on the bed."

Craig: "That signaled the birth of the band Lazy Racer."

Tim Gorman: "That's how Lazy Racer was born. Glyn thought it would be best for the band to work in an atmosphere that would be isolated but stimulating. We went to work in Nassau in the Bahamas. The studio was very famous, Compass Point. As a matter of fact it is still there. At the time it had one room. You would share the studio on twelve hour shifts. Emerson, Lake & Palmer did the *Love Beach* album there. Bob Marley & The Wailers (Legendary reggae band) recorded there. The name of the band comes from a lyric from the song on the first album called *Keep On Running Away*."

Craig: "Did you consider other names?"

Tim Gorman: "The Repeaters but somebody mentioned that could make us sound like a bunch of farts. Then we changed it to Lazy Racer."

Craig: "When you look back on the two Lazy Racer records (Self-titled from 1979 and *Formula 2* from 1980) what prevented wider appeal?"

Tim Gorman: "When the band was formed in England we were used to seeing videos on television. America hadn't had this yet. The first record came out and we had a Top 40 hit in Europe with *Keep On Running Away*. Glyn Johns told us we have to go out and play live. That will create a future. Somebody at the record company gave us a choice. They told us to go out on tour or take advantage of this new thing called the music video. We decided to make the videos. We ended up having to go from England to Los Angeles. There were no live performances of the band. That held it back."

Craig: "Did the opportunity to play on the 1982 Who record *It's Hard* come about because of your association with Glyn Johns?"

Tim Gorman: "Here's a good story for you. Kenny Jones was actually the first drummer in Lazy Racer. (When Keith Moon drummer for the Who passed away on 9/7/78, Kenny was named the replacement). We became very good friends. I lived in his house for awhile. I was there the day the phone rang from the Who office to ask him to come in and play. I always heard from other drummers why Kenny Jones? They would tell me they could do that. Why should he get to be the drummer for the Who, once Keith Moon died? They always thought they could do that gig. The big truth is they can't do that gig. People don't know the relationship Kenny had with Keith. Keith and Kenny were very close friends. Keith always wanted it to be that if anything happened to him Kenny would get to drum for the Who. When Kenny joined the Who he introduced me to them socially. Glyn introduced me as well. Pete Townshend told me backstage one night that he had heard the second Lazy Racer album and really enjoyed it. The way the Who gig happened was I took a vacation to see my parents in San Francisco. The phone rang and Glyn Jones tells me I can have the Who gig if I want it. The only thing is I have to let them know right now. There won't be an audition, they want you. I told Glyn it is an absolute yes. The next few weeks I walked on air."

Craig: "How did the door open to work with the Rolling Stones?"

Tim Gorman: "While Lazy Racer was making the second album I got to meet the Rolling Stones. This was through Ian Stewart (Played piano with them). I got to work on *Emotional Rescue* and *Tattoo You*. Mick Jagger and the guys had me play the Wurlitzer Piano on *Emotional Rescue*. A few months later I got a call to go to Paris. Billy Preston (Legendary piano-player. His credits include the Beatles, the Rolling Stones, and Bob Dylan. Billy passed away on 6/6/06) was sick.

Craig: "How did you first get contacted to work with the Stones?"

Tim Gorman: "That happened in a very serendipitous way. The Stones were recording at the same studio as me, Compass Point. One night three in the morning Ian Stewart comes to where I was staying and wants me to come to the studio. Ian liked my piano playing. When we got there the Stones were standing with a bunch of cocktails in their hands. They basically wanted a piano-player. It was their off time. They had finished for the evening. They asked me to play standard tunes. The next night Ian invites me to the studio again. This time Mick asked if I would play the Wurlitzer Piano on the song *Emotional Rescue*. There was no audition. They needed another keyboard-player."

Craig: "What are the differences between being in the studio with the Who and the Stones?"

Tim Gorman: "The process is different. I can only tell you what I saw. On the Stones song *Neighbors* from *Tattoo You* we played that live on the sound stage in Paris. We did fourteen to sixteen takes of the song and they were about twelve minutes long! We rocked the house. I played the Hammond B-3 on that cut. Jagger is in the center and is literally writing the lyrics on the spot. He had the chorus. The things he liked he marked down on a music stand. He gave it everything he had. We all did that. How they were going to splice this into a three minute song or so I had no idea yet. These were very long *jams* with vocals interjected every once in awhile. With the Who, Pete Townshend told me "Come to the studio with the best demos you can and bring them to the studio." That way the band or the producer can't really tell you what to do if you show up with a really good song. His demos for the series he put out called *Scoop* are amazing. *Athena* was the first song we cut for *It's Hard*. His demo sounded like a record to me. The song was beautiful, even as a demo. I came up with the brass part that is in the middle. Pete had a process that was more locked down and had less improvisation. The Stones did it the other way. Keith Richards can *jam* on some changes forever and is totally happy. Townshend live is more free-wheeling. I never knew on a solo how long Pete would go. The Who did a more organized process and the Stones more open."

Craig: "When you were with the Who did they get along or are some of the stories the fans have heard true?

Tim Gorman: "During *It's Hard* things were very good. Even live except for a couple of points where John Entwhistle's bass (Passed away 6/27/02) volume bothered Roger, things were fine. I think when we recorded the album it may have been under three months."

Craig: "Did Roger or Pete play any jokes on each other?"

Tim Gorman: "There was a funny bit on the song *Cry If You Want*. Townshend being a great lyricist wanted a tongue-twister for Roger. Pete tells me "Today is the day we do Roger's vocal on *Cry If You Want* and I'm selling tickets." Pete knew the song was a ball buster. Pete did that on purpose. Roger found out and being the professional that he is did it in two takes."

Craig: "How do we go forward from 1982 to the day you became part of the KBC Band?"

Tim Gorman: "After I got done with the Who tour I got a call from John Hiatt (He has recorded since 1974 and his song *Sure As I'm Sittin' Here* was a Top 20 hit for Three Dog Night. John Hiatt played in a band Little Village with Nick Lowe, Ry Cooder, and Jim Keltner). I played with him for two years. There was talk of the Who doing a tour or record. It never happened. Hiatt couldn't give it away in America, but in Europe the houses were packed. I got to meet Nick Lowe and Elvis Costello who were big fans of John."

Craig: "When you got the call about KBC were you in Europe or the United States?"

Tim Gorman: "I was in California. I got a call from Paul Kantner. I rehearsed with him in San Anselmo, California. The band started in 1985. I guess by 1986 the record was recorded and released."

Craig: "When Paul spoke to you the first time did he mention what caught his attention about your playing?"

Tim Gorman: "I am not very sure about that. The first phone conversation was very brief. It is possible that he got my number from one of the San Francisco music critics. Scott Matthews was a friend of Paul Kantner's. Scott and I played together with John Hiatt. Maybe it came from that camp. Scott was a drummer and very well known in the Bay Area."

Craig: "Did you audition for Paul Kantner?"

Tim Gorman: "I don't know if they had other people in mind or not. I did have to play. When I walked in the door it was so embryonic. Marty's rehearsal place was called The Church. It was a Church. The Church was in San Anselmo, California. At first things were fairly nebulous. Paul gave me lyric sheets to the song *America* on the second or third rehearsal. The first draft the band played of the song was six pages on computer paper. It wasn't even in bold print! It was six long pages basically of poetry. It was very good. I was impressed by his lyric writing. I was a fan of the Airplane. I was proud to be there. Over the next three to six months it jelled together fairly quickly. We got out playing even when we were rough at first, the audiences liked what we did. We did a lot of benefits and good causes. It meant very much to me and I know to them too."

Craig: "When you arrived for the first time how many people in the band had been selected?"

Tim Gorman: "I may have been the last guy to sign up. Marty Balin, Paul Kantner, and Jack Casady obviously were there. Keith Crossan (Saxophone), Slick Aguilar (Guitar), and Darrell Verdusco (Drums) I believe were already on board. I thought having played with the Stones and the Who, I had at least gotten to some level. The only thing I asked was to be treated as a member of the band and not a side-man. The Stones and the Who always treated me as a member. That threw the guys at first. It got put right. They did embrace the philosophy."

Craig: "The live shows must have been fun for you with so many non album tracks played."

Tim Gorman: "They were really good the live shows. The old stuff was great, and the new stuff had a lot of the free-wheeling, with a bit of psychedelic thrown in. We did get a major record deal. Thank God for the live gigs. It showed we can work together and work well."

Craig: "It is a shame we never got the second KBC album to happen, but at least the band helped lead the way to the 1989 Airplane reunion. How did you find out the Airplane would be using keyboards for the live dates?"

Tim Gorman: "In 1988 John Entwhistle from the Who had a solo tour. I went out as part of the band for about a year and a half. I got back from the tour and one day Grace and Paul called. They had finished the recording of the reunion album. I knew Kenny Aronoff, because John Mellencamp opened some shows for the Who. Kenny was obviously his drummer. Grace told me she remembered me from the KBC days. I always had a good relationship with her. They were honest that they asked David Paich first (Played on the reunion record, was a member of Toto and is one of the most sought after studio musicians). I really wanted to do this. Everyone in the Who camp was very envious when I got the Airplane gig. David Paich had some other commitments and couldn't play on the tour."

Craig: "Let's recap the resume. Rolling Stones, Who and Jefferson Airplane. Not bad. You must be so proud to have performed with three bands of that magnitude. It was earned."

Tim Gorman: "I am proud. It is a wonderful thing. Thank you, that was very kind."

Craig: "Did the time spent with the KBC Band make you feel part of the Airplane the second you were given the job?"

Tim Gorman: "Very much so. Having played with KBC really made me feel as I was with the Airplane band and not a side man. I had met Jorma a couple of times before the 1989 tour. As it turned out when the tour started Jorma, Jack, and I became thick as thieves. Jorma and Jack had their own Hot Tuna warm-up area and it had an upright piano. I wish somebody had recorded the stuff we used to play before the shows in that room. We had a couple of hours to loosen up. We played ragtime standards, they weren't Airplane, or Hot Tuna songs."

Craig: "When you say ragtime, would that mean you may have done a version of Scott Joplin's (One of the most famous ragtime pianists ever) famous *Maple Leaf Rag*?"

Tim Gorman: "Yes those kind of things. I would start a song on the piano and they would join in. I also love old country music and Celtic music. We played Floyd Cramer's *Last Date*. (Floyd Cramer was a legendary piano-player, known for his session work in Nashville). Jorma would always show me something. I was a big Hot Tuna fan and loved Jorma's ragtime guitar style. The music we would play together before the show would transcend to the stage. The three of us were well warmed up and jelled well on stage."

Craig: "What songs did you enjoy performing with the Airplane?"

Tim Gorman: "*Today* definitely. As a slower song or one that is medium in tempo, I loved the harmonies and playing the piano to that. I liked *Crown Of Creation* because it was a bombastic rocker. I loved the funny twists and turns in the song. It isn't long, but a lot gets said in a short time period. Although not an Airplane song, *America* from KBC was great. Paul did a great job with how the guitar parts should sound. Another one would be *Wooden Ships*."

Craig: "Where did you first rehearse with the Airplane?"

Tim Gorman: "I was told we would rehearse one week at the Roosevelt Theater in Milwaukee before the first show in Milwaukee."

Craig: "When you were rehearsing in Milwaukee do you remember any songs that you tried but didn't get played live?"

Tim Gorman: "We tried *Fast Buck Freddie* (Jefferson Starship-*Red Octopus*) and for some reason it didn't work. We also rehearsed two months at Frank Zappa's place Joe's Garage in Burbank, California before rehearsing in Milwaukee. We really got it together in Burbank."

Craig: "Did it surprise you *Miracles* got performed on the Airplane reunion tour?"

Tim Gorman: "Not really. I think people expected a Jefferson evening. I thought it was a good idea to appeal to certain age groups that may not recognize all the Airplane things."

Craig: "There are different stories as to how many shows the Airplane could have played on the 1989 tour. Were there firm dates if the band wanted to continue after the final show, 10/7/89 March For The Homeless, Washington, D.C.?"

Tim Gorman: "There were soccer stadiums booked for South America. There were halls booked for Japan as well. Toward the end of the tour there was some sort of disagreement how to go about all of that. Jack and Jorma had firm dates to play. They didn't want to cancel. Management tried to make it work out. Grace and Paul wanted if possible the dates to stay and Jorma and Jack had commitments. It fizzled out. That's how I remember it."

Craig: "Would you have liked the tour to continue?"

Tim Gorman: "Kenny Aronoff the drummer and I wanted it to keep going. The tour was going very well. Most of the time the attendance was real good. I remember selling out Radio City Music Hall in New York twice. Bill Graham wanted to go for a third night, but we couldn't get an open date. I learned about booking shows on the tour. If you consider the rising costs of concerts and the competition for the dollar, the Airplane did great. You had months where the Stones, Who, Airplane and Peter Gabriel would be playing concerts. The consumer has to make a decision if they could afford to see one of those shows, or maybe two. There is pressure on tour when other acts are going after the same dollar. We did well and it came down to the members not being able to agree."

Craig: "What were your feelings on Paul Kantner's unique idea for the 1991 Wooden Ships tour that often would only have Paul and yourself performing?"

Tim Gorman: "It was a wonderful way to see America. We played all over the place. Since it was normally Paul and I, or Paul, and Slick Aguilar, and I, we could fit everything into a rental Cadillac. We didn't have a driver. It was us that did the driving. There was something very Americana about that. I got to see my country that way, and not with a private jet, or tour bus. It was the Simon & Garfunkel folksy approach."

Craig: "I got the same feeling when you were talking about seeing the country, the first thing that came to mind was the Simon & Garfunkel song *America*."

Tim Gorman: "That was the soundtrack in my brain. We drove on some of the worst roads ever. We traveled eight or nine hours to a show. They were very rewarding shows for both of us. We could stretch things out."

Craig: "What were your impressions of playing with Wooden Ships compared to the Jefferson Starship?"

Tim Gorman: "The band was bigger (KBC) and we could pull out songs from every direction. The gigs were wonderful. I loved playing *The Other Side Of This Life*. I loved the extension. *America* was great too. I think it actually got played better by the Jefferson Starship than the KBC Band. *Wooden Ships* was great to perform with the Jefferson Starship."

Craig: "How did you like playing with Darby Gould and Diana Mangano?"

Tim Gorman: "It was great. It was great to see all that young energy. It was great that the female element could redirect the band in a slightly different way. I mean the way they would sing the melodies and make up their own styles. Each was very different and very good."

Craig: "What was it like playing with Papa John Creach?"

Tim Gorman: "I always loved playing *Somewhere Over The Rainbow* with Papa John. That was a real treat. Papa John was a wonderful guy."

**JEFFERSON STARSHIP**

L-R (Front Row): Paul Kantner, Jack Casady & Tim Gorman
(Back Row): Prairie Prince, Slick Aguilar, Darby Gould & Papa John Creach

**Photo courtesy of Mike Somavilla. From the Mike Somavilla collection. Photograph may not be reproduced without the written consent of Mike Somavilla. Photographer unknown.**
**This is a promo photo courtesy of**
**Variety Artists. Jefferson Starship circa 1993.**

Craig: "Is there a song that you liked playing live that somebody in the band wasn't that wild about?"

Tim Gorman: "I really liked to play the Paul Kantner song *Girl With The Hungry Eyes*, both with KBC and the Jefferson Starship. Paul wasn't that crazy about the tune. The audience gave it a great reaction."

Craig: "Did you finally have to leave after 1995 because of the outside commitments?"

Tim Gorman: "Yes. If I didn't play live I was in the studio. That's a bigger part of my life that is a little known thing. I always did session work when a tour ended. For instance I redid all the music to the Popeye cartoons. My friend from Devo (Well known new wave band that were almost robotic in their approach to music) Mark Mothersbaugh had helped me get that gig. I worked on Braveheart and Titanic. Now the studio has become a full-time gig. After 1995 I got more offers to use my musical degree. I couldn't resist it. The Jefferson Starship wasn't going to be making studio records. The studio is a real holy ground thing for me. The main reason my wife Susan was ailing at the time. She had a very serious disease and I had to spend more time at home. (Much to the sorrow of us all Tim's wife passed away in 2003). This way by working at home I could take care of my wife. Those were the reasons I left. It wasn't that I didn't want to play with the band. I loved the band and the people. I consider these people my best friends. It had nothing to do with the band or the music. It was a personal situation that had to be taken care of. It was the right time to make the jump."

Craig: "What is going on these days for you with live shows?"

Tim Gorman: "I am playing with the Greg Kihn Band. (Had a few hits including *The Breakup Song (They Don't Write 'Em)* and *Jeopardy*). Greg is going to do concerts this summer. We play six to eight gigs each summer. I have been doing that for eleven summers."

Craig: "You put out an album in 2004 *Celtic Loop*. Can you talk about how that came to fruition?"

Tim Gorman: "I wanted to see if I could mix the traditional Scottish melody lines with a stronger rhythmic element underneath it. Looping seemed to be a good new thing to me. You have newer technology coupled with old world chords."

Craig: "If the readers go to www.taymusic.net they can check out the CD as well as a project with Kirk Casey called Parallel View. The CD is titled *Every Day*. There is talk for a CD to be released in 2007 as well. You and long time friend Kirk Casey are also involved in music for the Sims games, numerous television commercials, and productions for corporations. If any of your fans are interested in buying the music or having you involved in their projects, visit the website for complete details. Thank you for spending this time with me. It was great to get the information on your involvement with the Who, Stones and Airplane Family. I hope the studio work keeps you busy forever."

Tim Gorman: "Thank you very much. I wish you the best of luck with the book. Be well."

**Darby Gould- Jefferson Starship.**

**Photograph by kind permission of Thom Dyson and Darby Gould**

**from the Thom Dyson and Darby Gould collections.**

**Photograph may not be reproduced without the written consent of Thom Dyson and Darby Gould.**

**Thom Dyson photographer.**

**From a Jefferson Starship show 8/1/04 Arnold Field, Sonoma, California.**

Photograph by kind permission of Thom Dyson and Darby Gould

from the Thom Dyson and Darby Gould collections.

Photograph may not be reproduced without the written consent of Thom Dyson and Darby Gould.

Thom Dyson photographer.

From a Jefferson Starship show 8/1/04 Arnold Field, Sonoma, California.

**Photograph by kind permission of Thom Dyson and Darby Gould**

**from the Thom Dyson and Darby Gould collections.**

**Photograph may not be reproduced without the written consent from**

**Thom Dyson and Darby Gould.**

**Thom Dyson photographer.**

**From a Jefferson Starship show 8/1/04 Arnold Field, Sonoma, California.**

Craig: "Thank you Darby, for giving me the time today."

Darby Gould: "You're welcome Craig."

Craig: "Is this fact or fiction, in 1986 Rob Brezsny (World Entertainment War) heard you performing at a softball game and you were singing material from Janis Joplin to Whitney Houston?"

Darby Gould: "That is partly true. There was an after party and he heard the band I was with at the time called the Same, performing in the garage."

Craig: "When he approached you did he have the astrology column that he was known for?"

Darby Gould: "He was writing his astrology column and he had a band that the Same had opened for called Tao Chemical."

Craig: "Did Rob use the name World Entertainment War when you first started singing with his band?"

Darby Gould: "He had a demo tape with a lot of spoken-word. He was trying to form a band at that time. I can't remember if he had that name in mind or not. I had never done original songs before. The bass-player and drummer sold me. I never sung a note at my audition and was offered the job."

Craig: "What did the other members of the Same think when you decided to pursue the opportunity with Rob?"

Darby Gould: "I'm not sure we were even together. It was the summer that I graduated college 1986 and all this went down. Some of the members of the band had moved on when they graduated."

Craig: "Do you agree with the words that are often used to describe World Entertainment War- Tribal Funk Folk Music?"

Darby Gould: "That's a pretty good description. We were pulling from the college scene and the alternative scene."

Craig: "The first major label release was in 1991 *World Entertainment War* on Popular Metaphysics Records/MCA (MCAD-10137). What made you stick with the project that long?"

Darby Gould: "I was always in an active band and always was a performer. We did have an independent recording in 1989- *Televisionary* on Infomania Records - Santa Cruz CA, before MCA released the second album. We did one on our own. In fact we used Sandy Pearlman's studio for the independent release."

Craig: "Sandy is well known in the music circles for having produced Blue Oyster Cult."

Darby Gould: "That is correct."

Craig: "What were the audiences like for the World Entertainment War shows?"

Darby Gould: "I would think a sample of the crowd would represent the whole sound of the Bay Area at the time. We were from Santa Cruz. There was a bit of everything in the audience."

Craig: "What was the furthest show you performed from the Bay Area?"

Darby Gould: "We played in Vancouver. We did some gigs in Oregon and Washington too."

Craig: "When the band started to get some recognition, was Rob's involvement with the astrology community a positive, negative or neither on the group?"

Darby Gould: "Rob's a writer and always had a pen and pad. He would be writing thoughts and rhymes. Sometimes there were words in his head for song lyrics. The music was first but the astrology was also his money!"

Craig: "How did Paul Kantner first become aware of your vocal ability?"

Darby Gould: "His daughter China was friends with a band Psychefunkapus that I had done some work with. The way it is in the Bay Area is everybody seems to know everyone else. His daughter had a copy of the World Entertainment War independent album and she passed it on to Paul."

Craig: "When you were growing up did you listen to the American bands of the sixties and seventies?"

Darby Gould: "Oh yeah. I am a huge music fan. I am a collector and archivist; I listened to the radio and had a huge record collection. When I was in high school I went into collectable record shops with my list from the Rolling Stone Collector's Guide. I would seek out their picks with five stars. My mom and dad had a couple of Airplane albums. I grew up on the Beatles. My brother was a music fan as well."

Craig: "I had worked in a few collectable record shops when I was much younger. The kids today don't know what vinyl is."

Darby Gould: "I take a lot of pride in my albums."

Craig: "What was next for you on the resume?"

Darby Gould: "I was still with World Entertainment War, but formed my own band Blind Tom. I was writing for the first time. All that was going on when Paul approached me. He had written some acoustic songs and wanted to have a project with different women singers. Grace Slick and Ronnie Gilbert of the Weavers were two of the women. Then Paul decided to go electric."

Craig: "How did the two groups World Entertainment War and Blind Tom take the news when you had the opportunity to play with Paul Kantner?"

Darby Gould: "They were always happy for me when something came up. As far as World Entertainment War the band was at the tail end of things. Blind Tom unfortunately struggled the entire time. That was tougher when they were working on songs without me. They were my long-time friends."

Craig: "What type of music did Blind Tom play?"

Darby Gould "Blind Tom was heavy rock. My influences were Ian Gillan (He is the lead singer of Deep Purple and most noted after Rod Evans the original was let go) and Paul Rodgers (Free and Bad Company)."

Craig: "The first performance you had with Paul Kantner, was it near the end of a Wooden Ships show in San Francisco, summer of 1991? Didn't you sing on the last seven songs?"

Darby Gould: "It was The Great American Music Hall on August 7, 1991. That is where my initial memories of performing with Paul are from. I had never been to that place. I remember the Jefferson Starship rehearsing around that time at the I-Beam in San Francisco. We also performed a live show in that time period from the I-Beam."

Craig: "When you first started rehearsing with Paul, and during the first few live shows, was there a fine line of emulating Grace Slick but still being Darby Gould?"

Darby Gould: "I wanted to sing the songs correctly as far as her parts were concerned. My voice is similar to hers, but I wanted to have my own voice style. As time went on I got more comfortable with the entire situation. In the beginning I didn't want to sing *Somebody To Love* or *White Rabbit*. It was enough for me to try this out in front of a lot of the older fans. I didn't want it to be about me sitting in for Grace. Being a music fan and critic myself, I wouldn't have wanted to see that."

Craig: "You received plenty of accolades for your rendition of *Lawman*. How did the song become part of the set list?"

Darby Gould: "As I got more comfortable I thought what would be a good *Grace* song to sing. I thought that would be a great one to do. After you do it five hundred million times night after night you get your own niche of it. Grace told me she liked the way I did it!"

Craig: "She knows a bit about hearing a good vocalist. That was nice of Grace. When did you first meet her?"

Darby Gould: "I met her at the Haight Street Fair in 1992. She was there for a Jefferson Starship show. I was sick as a dog. I got through it. During the performance I remember looking at her during *Lawman*. She gave me the thumbs up!"

Craig: "That had to be a special moment. One of the most noted female voices expressing her approval of your ability."

Darby Gould: "It was."

Craig: "How did Paul first start thinking about the idea of two female singers?"

Darby Gould: "I never had a conversation with him about that. I still had things going on with Blind Tom and was torn between the two bands. I came back from vacation and Diana was in the group."

Craig: "The first show you performed with Diana was it good, bad, strange, or a combination?"

Darby Gould: "It was strange and good. The two of us knew about each other but never mingled together. Once Diana came on board I still was involved with the Jefferson Starship for about another year or so. As a gig it was great. She is the flip-side of me. Somebody made an analogy of her being a feline and I being a punk. She is the hip star child and I am the rocker. Nobody could ever be Grace."

Craig: "When you decided to leave the Jefferson Starship, was there vacillation between staying and going?"

Darby Gould: "In a perfect world for me I would do everything. I was in three bands including the Jefferson Starship when I started and was willing to make a commitment to all of them. With Blind Tom unfortunately there were ties there that were personal. There was a big shadow hanging over that. It was a personal endeavor to do something not being in the light of a famous band. I wanted to see where that could take me. Unfortunately we never got it as far as we wanted it to be. One of the reasons we were promoted sometimes as Darby of the Jefferson Starship. We were getting booked with hippie bands and that wasn't what we were all about. As far as the Jefferson Starship I was stepping in for Grace, but not Grace. I always felt I wasn't a main member of the band."

Craig: "Did it feel like any show could be the last one?"

Darby Gould: "I went on for a year but I also knew it wasn't fair to Diana. I couldn't hand pick dates. I needed to make a decision. It would be unfair to not know what I would be doing if they were scheduled to play."

Craig: "You did get to go to Japan the beginning of 1995."

Darby Gould: "I drew it out a long time. Right before the Japanese tour I wrote everyone a letter. I then had to face them all for two and one half weeks."

Craig: "When you stepped off the stage for the final commitment, were the members supportive of your decision?"

Darby Gould: "They needed to know that somebody could be there for all the shows. I wanted to try to do something on my own. I also needed a real job with health benefits and was committed to somebody in Blind Tom. I had never left a band."

Craig: "I have to go back for a moment to Psychefunkapus. The self-titled album came out in 1990 on Atlantic Records (82063-2). You are on one track *Movin.'* The name is tremendously cool. One of the guys in the band was named Atom Ellis. Psychefunkapus came about because you had known China Kantner."

Darby Gould: "They were great. China turned Paul Kantner on to us. Psychefunkapus and World Entertainment War were often on the same bill. We all played together and jammed together. It was very much like the San Francisco scene of the sixties. I would jump on stage and perform with them. I am pretty sure I recorded vocals with them, before I sang with them on stage."

Craig: "How does it feel to you being in a recording studio as compared to performing live?

Darby Gould: "I like the recording studio because I work very quickly. I love hanging out and working on stuff everyday is a blast. The only thing I ever had a problem with is trying to capture the same energy as the live shows. It is very hard for me to not have the band there. It makes trying to feel the same energy difficult. Here I am by myself with music blasting in my ears. Live is much better for me. When I say I love working in the studio a lot of times it is backup bits. These could be commercials, or whatever. When I am in a studio, I try to plead as much as possible to have the band members there. With World Entertainment War it was hard getting them there with me. I think to myself I'm not feeling the love. I still think that way now. I could have done that with much more zest if the band had been there. The band is the music. It isn't just me! I started out being petrified of the studio. It would have been nice to have the lights turned off and nobody see me. I would have my dog in there. I needed to feel safe and confident."

Craig: "In 1995 you appeared on the Jefferson Starship album *Deep Space Virgin Sky*. There was a version of a song you performed with World Entertainment War."

Darby Gould: "Yes, *Dark Ages*. Paul really loved World Entertainment War."

Craig: "In 1996 you were in a band the Blackouts."

(Darby laughs for about thirty seconds).

Darby Gould: "I don't remember if Blind Tom had reached the end or not. It was a job basically. They were a cover band. They were too far from me. I wasn't going to commute to Santa Cruz again. They did promote the band with me in it. They promoted it as Darby Gould of the Jefferson Starship. I didn't think that was right. On our first gig there were people there that thought this was my new band. That was clearly not the case. I was singing covers."

Craig: "What type of cover tunes did the band do?"

Darby Gould: "Alanis Morissette, No Doubt, and even some Sly And The Family Stone. It was a typical cover band. I didn't want it promoted as Darby Gould of the Jefferson Starship. They promoted it like that even when I had left the band."

Craig: "What came next for you?"

Darby Gould: "When I first left the Jefferson Starship I hooked up with an eleven piece band. They have four women singers. When one can't make it, I fill in."

Craig: "What was the name of the group?"

Darby Gould: "They are called Big Bang Beat. The drummer is Trey Sabatelli. He would sit-in for Prairie Prince when he couldn't make a Jefferson Starship gig. I still sub for any of the women in Big Bang Beat from one to ten times a year. I was able to get studio work through them."

Craig: "In February 2005 you were part of the forty year celebration of Paul's Jefferson Airplane and Jefferson Starship music. How far in advance were you contacted about doing at least one if not more shows?"

Darby Gould: "I am contacted often. I will sing with Paul at any show that I can make. The hard thing is to have time on the schedule. My daughter is the number one priority."

Craig: "How did it feel to be back on stage with the band?"

Darby Gould: "It was great. Everyone made me comfortable."

Craig: "How was it to sing with Diana in 2005?"

Darby Gould: "It was wonderful to sing with her. For us we both have a lot in common. We are friends outside of the band."

**Photograph by kind permission of Don Aters and may not be reproduced without the**

**written consent of Don Aters.**

**From the Don Aters collection.  Don Aters photographer.**

**10/14/05 Jefferson Starship live at the Colonial Theater, Keene, New Hampshire.**

Craig: "Will you appear on any shows in 2006?"

Darby Gould: "So far no.  The schedule doesn't permit.  Things could change."

08/11/2006

**Photograph by kind permission of Don Aters and may not be reproduced without the**

**written consent of Don Aters.**

**From the Don Aters collection.  Don Aters photographer.**

**As a wonderful treat for the fans the schedule did change.**

**Darby was able to sing with the Jefferson Starship in 2006.**

**The photo is from the 8/11/06 performance at B.B. King's, New York City.**

**Darby Gould is on the left, Bobby Vega in the middle, and Slick Aguilar on the right.**

Craig: "Are there any websites or causes you would like to plug?"

Darby Gould: "I am hoping to have my site www.workingclassrocker.com updated in the near future. There isn't a site to plug, however I wish that all people research the importance of health benefits, and the differences in policies, and companies. This is a problem that faces many people on a daily basis. I wish everyone could have health benefits and afford them."

Craig: "Thank you very much for the time today. I hope things continue to go well."

Darby Gould: "Thank you."

(Thank you to Darby's site www.workingclassrocker.com for the catalog numbers of the recordings discussed).

Bob Harvey- Jefferson Airplane.

Flyer by kind permission of Bob Harvey. From the Bob Harvey collection. Not to be reproduced without the written consent of Bob Harvey.
If ever you needed something to predict the future creation of the J.A. here you go.
Playing separately (but within two weeks of each other) Bob Harvey with the Slippery Rock String Band, Jorma Kaukonen (Billed as Jerry), and Paul Kantner circa summer 1964 at The Shelter, San Jose, California.

Craig: "Bob, thank you for talking with me this evening."

Bob Harvey: "You're welcome."

Craig: "Let's start in the past and work our way forward. You were in a group the Slippery Rock String Band and Marty Balin was playing with the Town Criers. (You can hear one of the Town Criers recordings, *Hellbound Train*, on the various artists CD San Francisco Live. Released 11/18/97 on Prophecy 12010). Is it true you two met at the legendary bar the Drinking Gourd in San Francisco?"

Bob Harvey: "That is correct."

Craig: "Did you two talk about the possibility of forming a group?"

Bob Harvey: "No, we actually never spoke. I overheard Marty and Paul Kantner talking as I was walking off stage for a break. The Slippery Rock String Band was performing that night. As I passed their table I heard their conversation about wanting to form a folk-rock band. I introduced myself and told them I could play bass. The next thing I know I'm invited to their apartment to discuss the matter further."

Craig: "What solidified your decision to leave the Slippery Rock String Band and go into uncharted waters?"

Bob Harvey: "There was so much more glamour in the folk-rock scene. At the time everybody was talking about it. There were those that were against it. Look what happened at first when Bob Dylan went electric."

Craig: "They were the same people that claimed to be so open-minded; yet the first time they heard something different (Bob Dylan plugging in his guitar), they booed."

Bob Harvey: "Another reason I wanted to take the chance on the folk-rock opportunity, I was in aw of Marty's singing ability. I walked away from everything."

Craig: "When you told the band about your decision, were they supportive or bitter?"

Bob Harvey: "They told me "You will never make it." I went out and got a bass. I worked on simple timings."

Craig: "When you joined the Airplane were you around thirty at the time?"

Bob Harvey: "I was born in 1934. So yeah that would be the case. I was a little past thirty."

Craig: "It was common in the 1960's to hear "Don't trust anyone over thirty"; did you ever feel awkward about your age difference with the other Airplane members?"

Bob Harvey: "No, I didn't look thirty. I always looked younger than I really was. I hadn't said anything about my age during my introduction to the group. Had anyone asked I may have lied."

Craig: "Look what many do to their resumes."

Bob Harvey: "Exactly."

Photo by kind permission of Bob Harvey. From the Bob Harvey collection. Not to be reproduced without written consent from Bob Harvey. Photographer unknown. It doesn't get much better or rarer. This could conceivably share the title of the rarest J.A. photo ever with the Tim Lucas gem, found before the copyright page . From circa 8/13/65-9/26/65 the Jefferson Airplane (Excluding Jorma) outside The Matrix, San Francisco, California. From left to right: Paul, Jerry Peloquin, Signe, Bob Harvey, and Marty. Jorma was on his way. When you consider the age of the photo, the number of years it has been uncirculated, and Jorma's image missing from a group shot, this is a magnificent contribution by Bob Harvey, for the J.A. fan.

Craig: "You played a bunch of concert dates with the Airplane. Did you keep set lists of any of the live performances from August 13, 1965 at The Matrix in San Francisco, to October 16, 1965 at Longshoreman's Hall, located in San Francisco?"

Bob Harvey: "I don't have any documentation or memory as what we played. I had a song turned down for being too country called *Poor Girl*. I dedicated it to my wife at the time Jo. We were breaking-up."

Craig: "Nothing comes to mind in terms of cover versions or songs the band never released?" (There was a song that David Crosby, who played with the Byrds and later on Crosby, Stills, Nash & Young, had written, *Flower Bomb*, but Marty didn't like it. Bob has performed the tune for forty years).

Bob Harvey: "When I was out of the band I didn't follow the activities for about a year. After that I was allowed to go to the Airplane House and Marty would leave tickets for me at various venues. After I left and this may be shallow that was the most pain I ever felt in my entire life."

Craig: "At the time of your departure from the group and even years later, do you have the same feeling Pete Best had when he was replaced in the Beatles?" (Pete Best was the drummer that Ringo Starr took over for). Would there always be the *what if* question?"

Bob Harvey: "At the beginning yes. A time would come when it got me on the road to writing. When I started to write I felt I was on fire. I started to walk around with a journal in my hand and write lyrics. I would also put down what I was thinking. I even started to draw. The second most pain I ever experienced was in 1977. I moved to Seattle. My journals were at a friend's home that burnt down. I lost all the recorded history of the past twelve years."

Craig: "I am so sorry to hear about the damage your friend suffered and your loss of over a decade of work. There are those that tell an untrue story about Jorma Kaukonen having something to do with the change of bass-players. Isn't it a fact that the record company was responsible?"

Bob Harvey: "Absolutely. RCA was putting up the contracts and money. The condition would be the band goes to an electric sound."

Craig: "How were you told about the changes?"

Bob Harvey: "Things happened in stages. I went with Jorma to the place in Santa Clara, California where he bought all his equipment. We picked out my first electric bass. It was a Rickenbacker."

Craig: "When the record company felt they needed a more experienced electric bass-player did they tell you what was going on, or the band members?"

Bob Harvey: "The individual members let me know what was going on. Jorma would be playing electric guitar and the bass would not be the old fashioned stand-up."

Craig: "During the transitional period did you and Jack Casady ever cross paths?"

Bob Harvey: "I never saw Jack. The first time I ever did was on 10/30/65 Harmon Gym at the University of California at Berkeley. I showed up with my bass in hand and the only band member there was Skip Spence. Skip said "Oh, you didn't get the word that Jack is playing.""

Craig: "Wasn't that originally going to be your final performance with the group?"

Bob Harvey: "I was promised that even though I was on the way out I could do that gig."

Craig: "When you decided to approach the members of the Slippery Rock String Band about becoming part of the group once again was there animosity toward you?"

Bob Harvey: "They were diplomatic. They may have had inner animosity because I walked away from them and left them hanging. They had tried out a bass-player or two and they didn't work out. They were glad to get me back. The bass playing fit with what they were doing and I had the vocal harmonies. The animosity did come out later when Slippery Rock broke up."

Craig: "Slippery Rock released a single in 1967 that got a bit of a cult following on Dome Records called *Tule Fog*. Did you play on the recording?"

Bob Harvey: "I sang on that. I was the lead vocalist."

**Photo by kind permission of Bob Harvey. From the Bob Harvey collection. Not to be reproduced without the written consent of Bob Harvey. Photographer unknown. The Slippery Rock String Band from Denver circa 1967. Let's have Bob Harvey tell you a bit about the photo. "Left to right is the announcer, then Chuck McCabe on five string. He now lives in Los Gatos and runs Woodshed Productions. Next is Lee Chaney, guitar flat picker "Lightnin' Leroy," who sold a country comedy song to Ray Stevens (Famous for mixing country music with zany novelty songs). I think it was called *Old Fred*, about a dog named Fred who was a good old dog, who even did the dishes and drove the pickup into town for staples. Lee also wrote a song called *Sally Brought Him Home*, a comic look at his own life and meeting up with his wife Sally, who made him settle down, and they now operate a sewing machine store in Old Hickory, Tennessee. In the picture after Chuck and Lee is me with my bass, and then Mike Mindel the former owner of The Shelter in San Jose. Mike lives in Colorado and runs a real estate appraisal business."**

Craig: "Did you guys think that the tide turned and you had a chance to reach the next level?"

Bob Harvey: "It was my fault we didn't. I wanted the band to go rock and roll. In the end I broke up the band."

Craig: "When I listen to your material over the years it greatly impresses me that your voice has stayed in such strong condition."

Bob Harvey: "Thank you. It isn't anything I did that I can take credit for. I will take the compliment."

Craig: "In 1968 you were involved for a short time with Holly Mackerel. What a great name! Paul Williams, who wrote *We've Only Just Begun* for the Carpenters and *An Old Fashioned Love Song* for Three Dog Night was part of the project. The two of you didn't see eye to eye. Was that because Paul wanted too much control over the vocals and the musical direction?"

Bob Harvey: "Yeah. The point was I had three songs going for that album. First one got cut and then a second. The last song I wrote for the album was *Wild Flowers*. We did between ten and twelve takes. Then I got told that I sang great harmonies and wouldn't be able to take the lead vocal. I was hurt, very hurt. It was the last straw. First they cut me off from playing bass and then the song contributions kept getting cut down. I walked away from the album. On retrospect it was stupid."

Craig: "Some looked at it that way, and others thought you were a person that held your beliefs, and felt that your contributions would have been beneficial to the sessions."

Bob Harvey: "I'll buy into that."

Craig: "As the 1970's started you got to act in a couple of movies. The titles were *Commune* and *Hard Ride To The Movies*. How did you make the transition to acting?

Bob Harvey: "That is correct. I played Charles Manson in *Commune*. The films were low budget. Jack Genero was the director. I answered an ad. As the film got going we had one of the Mothers Of Invention (Frank Zappa's band) get involved with the musical side of things."

Craig: "That is cool. Which member of the band?"

Bob Harvey: Don Preston."

Craig: "He is very talented, both on the keyboards and bass."

Bob Harvey: "That is correct."

Craig: "You would then get involved with a publication Mother Trucker magazine. Later they became American Trucker" How did that unfold?"

Bob Harvey: "The market needed something for the owner-operator trucker. I started out driving, got involved in advertising sales, and editorial content. When I moved to Seattle I even stayed with them for awhile as the west coast correspondent."

Craig: "I hope you could clarify something for the readers. At age fifty five you were called as a Naval Reservist for the 1990's Gulf War. How did it come about that the armed forces needed you?"

Bob Harvey: "I had served previously. I had called to find out what the formula would be if you had served a certain amount of time in the past. The fact is if you have a skill they are looking for they can find a place. I had a journalism background and I was allowed to go back."

434

Craig: "Something positive came of this. While in Saudi Arabia you met Brian Fowler. One day the two of you would become part of the band San Francisco Blue. (The name coming from his roots in San Francisco and blue is for bluegrass).

Bob Harvey: "We started to play together in Saudi Arabia."

Craig: "Good fortune would happen in 2000. You and Brian put out a record under the name San Francisco Blue, called *Idiot's Vision*. It was nice that you stayed true to your roots. You played guitar, sang, and used the acoustic bass. How would you describe the music on the record?"

Bob Harvey: "While there is the bluegrass and folk element, Brian Fowler has a lot of psychedelic influences. Even though he plays bluegrass he's totally into Hawkwind. His head has always been into Hawkwind. (Hawkwind is a band that has been around in various line-ups since 1970. They are a mixture of psychedelic, progressive, and avant-garde).

Craig: "The feedback was rather positive on the CD. It led to a live album release. What performance was taped for the album?"

Bob Harvey: "*Live On The Cartersville Express*. That is located in Cartersville, Georgia."

Craig: "You had a fascinating gig in 2004 when one of the acts on the bill was Nik Turner from Hawkwind. Where was the show held?"

Bob Harvey: "That was in a college town in Cullman, Alabama. That would have been sometime in October of 2004. It was pretty wild and a lot of fun."

Craig: "You parted ways for a bit with Brian and in 2001 released a terrific charity single (*Comes A Time*). You were tied in nicely with the Salvation Army. Could you please tell us about the song?"

Bob Harvey: "In 2001 I suffered a heart attack. It was a life changing experience. After the operation I had a very difficult recovery. I began to have a problem being around food. Eating would cause a bad reaction. I lost a lot of weight and that was in addition to the weight I lost before the surgery. The surgeon didn't seem to have the same concern I did. I went to my regular doctor and he worked to see what the problem was and got me off the medication that was hurting my system."

Craig: "I am sorry to hear about the ordeal. How are you doing now?"

Bob Harvey: "I am fine, thank you. After September 11th the meaning of the song changed."

Craig: Do you still have a nice deal for the consumer if they send five dollars or more to the address on your website (Salvation Army) you will send them a copy of the single?"

Bob Harvey: "I am a man of my word. If they send five dollars or more to the Salvation Army I will send them the single."

Craig: In 2004 you started to play with Brian again. He had a band Jones Avenue. They put out a record *Folk Art*. Are you part of the release?"

Bob Harvey: "Wow. I am not sure. It is possible. I did practice, rehearse, and play with them. Maybe I am."

Craig: "Another nice event in 2004 was your involvement in the CD tribute to Skip Spence. A bunch of artists were asked to celebrate his work in the band Moby Grape. (Moby Grape was a west coast band that was formed around Skip after leaving the Airplane). Can you speak about the song *Hurting For People*?"

Bob Harvey: "We were going to different record companies and producers and we are sitting in Phil Spector's hallway in his house. The security guards didn't want us to move. Finally after about an hour Phil comes walking by. He doesn't say a word and goes into his office and has us play, even though he closed his door."

Craig: "That's why they called it the Wall Of Sound." (That was the name for the production technique that Phil liked to use in the studio).

Bob Harvey: "Later on we ended up at a place where they were filming the show *Big Valley* and one of the people on the set made comments about the length of our hair. An actor told us not to worry about that because he was a nothing employee, that was so low on the food chain he was hurting for people. The actor turned out to be Charles Bronson. I became a fan for life at that moment. He was very down to earth, a really nice person. His words gave me an inspiration for a song. Skip Spence grabbed Paul Kantner's guitar and I started to write some lyrics, with the title being *Hurting For People*."

Craig: "Did the two of you ever record the song?"

Bob Harvey: "No we didn't. That is a shame."

Craig: "How awful! For the archives that would have been one amazing treasure. Tell us about the record coming out next under the band name Georgia Blue."

Bob Harvey: "The title of the CD is *Hurting For People*. There will be steel guitar, fiddle, and mandolin."

Craig: "If the rest of the record is anything like the track you sent me in advance, the vocals and production are superlative."

Bob Harvey: "Thank you Craig."

Craig: "Will there be some live dates to go with the project?"

Bob Harvey: "For sure. We will play at Lizzy's in Georgia and I am looking at a places in Tennessee and Northern California."

Craig: "Would you like to get a plug in for the websites that have great information on your music and where it can be purchased?"

Bob Harvey: "Thank you. www.sfblue.co.uk and the second is http://www.georgiablue.us. There is also the one of the record companies, http://www.echotarecords.com/music.html."

Craig: "As the years went on, did you keep in contact with any of the Airplane members?"

Bob Harvey: "I did up until 1977. What happened was there were some unresolved issues with money that I was to get for the time I was in the band and there were also some circumstances with a former manager in the early days Matthew Katz. I was called to testify in Matthew's claim that he was entitled to money for his expenses from the early days. I am not sure how the case with Matthew turned out. After that I didn't have contact with any members until going to see Jorma with Hot Tuna play 1/15/05 at the Variety Playhouse in Atlanta, Georgia. Jorma was really friendly. We got to hang out and I spent some time on his tour bus. It was nice to see him again."

Craig: "You had one more reunion 2/16/02 with the original drummer of the Airplane, Jerry Peloquin. That must have been great to play with him again after almost four decades."

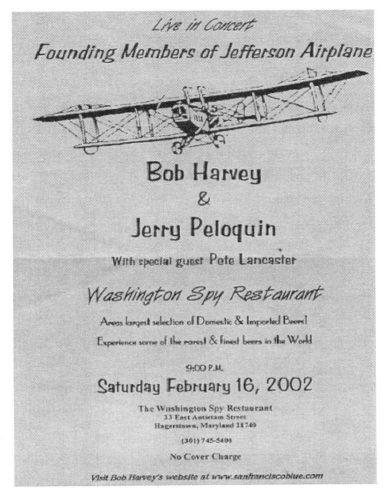

Live in Concert
Founding Members of Jefferson Airplane

Bob Harvey
&
Jerry Peloquin

With special guest Pete Lancaster

Washington Spy Restaurant

Areas largest selection of Domestic & Imported Beers!

Experience some of the rarest & finest beers in the World

9:00 P.M.
Saturday February 16, 2002

The Washington Spy Restaurant
33 East Antietam Street
Hagerstown, Maryland 21740

(301) 745-5406

No Cover Charge

Visit Bob Harvey's website at www.sanfranciscoblue.com

Both the flyer and photo by kind permission of Bob Harvey. From the Bob Harvey collection. The flyer and photo may not be reproduced without the written consent of Bob Harvey. Photographer unknown. The reunion of Jerry Peloquin (Left) and Bob Harvey (Right), at the Washington Spy, Hagerstown, Maryland 2/16/02.

**After a few moments to talk things over it is time for Bob Harvey (Left) and Jerry Peloquin (Right)**

**to take the stage at the**

**Washington Spy, Hagerstown, Maryland 2/16/02.**

**Photo by kind permission of Bob Harvey.  From the Bob Harvey collection.**

**Not to be reproduced without the written consent of**

**Bob Harvey.**

**Photographer unknown.**

438

Bob Harvey: "There was a guy that headed a Jefferson Airplane and Jefferson Starship site in Scotland. The site isn't around anymore. I can't think of the person's name, but he had asked if I would be interested in playing with Jerry. I told him if he finds the place for us to play, I'll drive to Maryland and we can have a show. We ended up being booked at a place in Hagerstown, Maryland. The venue was called the Washington Spy. That gig may have been just a moment in time, but it was an unforgettable moment. The crowd was right and the time was right. Jerry, I, and Pete Lancaster put on one of the finest shows I've ever been a part of. It was due to a very great extent to the audience, which was made up predominantly of Jefferson Airplane fans. They came expecting a great show, and showed their enthusiasm, and their appreciation. My longtime friend and collaborator Robert Gover honored me with his presence in the audience. In 1968 I wrote the music for his anti-war stage play "Us-Them." I sang five of the songs from that production that night, actually those five songs are some of my very best work ever. It was a most memorable occasion."

Craig: "Did you perform any Airplane era songs, and what style of music did you play?"

Bob Harvey: "We performed my music, which was bluegrass. We did *In The Midnight Hour* (The Airplane played this live in the early days. It was made popular by the Rascals and Wilson Pickett) and the song that the Youngbloods had such a big hit with *Get Together*." (The Airplane did this tune as well. It was written by Dino Valente of the Quicksilver Messenger Service).

Craig: "Did you record the show?"

Bob Harvey: "We rehearsed for a couple of days, and I recorded the concert, but the equipment I used malfunctioned and we didn't get even one minute."

Craig: "That is a shame. It could have been a great gig to release."

Bob Harvey: "We did a radio interview and the experience was a lot of fun."

Craig: "Did you talk with Jerry about additional shows?"

Bob Harvey: "We did. We didn't have the money for the project. We even discussed the possibility of forming a band for a cruise ship. Although it never happened, I was glad to see Jerry and play in front of a lot of old fans."

Craig: "One final question, do you have any of the recordings from The Matrix, San Francisco with the Airplane band that you were part of?"

Bob Harvey: "At one time I had all the shows. Through moving, and things getting lent out, and lost, I have been left with nothing."

Craig: "That is terrible. It would have been great if the vaults could have been opened for all of us to hear. Thank you very much for your time and best of luck with the new record. I hope there are many more to come. As importantly congratulations on fifty years of making music."

Bob Harvey: "Thank you Craig. That was very kind."

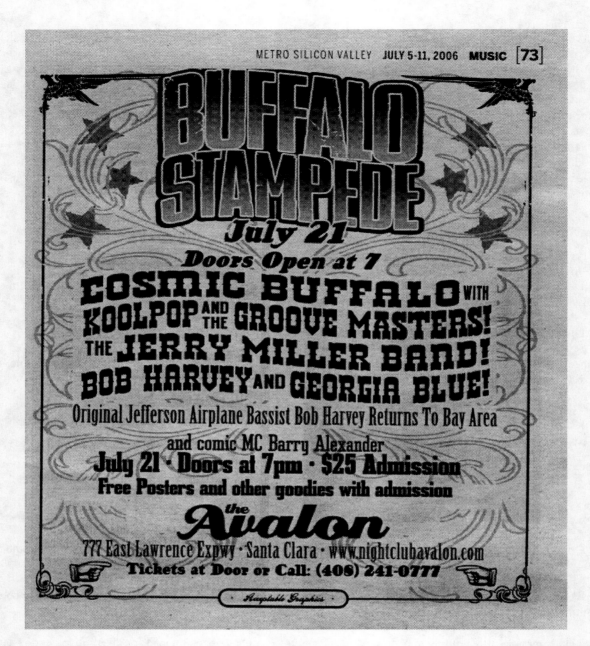

Flyer by kind permission of Paul LaBonte, Bob Harvey, and Mike Somavilla.  From the Paul LaBonte,

Bob Harvey and Mike Somavilla collections.  Courtesy of Paul LaBonte, The Avalon,

Santa Clara, California.  Special thanks to Paul LaBonte.

The flyer is not to be reproduced without the written consents of

Paul LaBonte, Bob Harvey, and Mike Somavilla.

This is a promotional flyer, for the 7/21/06 show with

Bob Harvey and from Moby Grape the great Jerry Miller.

# Paul Kantner- Jefferson Airplane, Hot Tuna, Jefferson Starship, KBC Band, and Wooden Ships.

**(Please note Paul played two shows with Hot Tuna 4/3 and 4/13/69, at The Matrix, San Francisco, California. The next time he would perform with them would be on <u>certain dates</u> starting 5/27/87 at the Great American Music Hall, San Francisco, California, and ending on 8/1/88 at Pier 84, New York City).**

Craig: "Thank you for joining me today. Before we get started, how is your back feeling?"

Paul Kantner: "It acts up every once in awhile. If I give it about eight weeks I'll be fine. Thank you for asking."

Craig: "There has been a tape that has floated around for years, allegedly released by RCA Records Circa 1965-1966 to promo the band. The story goes it was sent to radio, and TV stations, newspapers, magazines and record shops. Do you recall such a tape? The reason it appears to be fraudulent is a curse is heard at the very end. For those times it would seem hypocritical for a record company that censors the artists not to censor themselves."

Paul Kantner: "I don't recall such a tape. That doesn't mean it couldn't have happened. We didn't have a lot of contact with them. We made a few records for them, but didn't bother much with them. Record companies didn't have a clue, so we pretty much ignored them. They could do what they wanted and we did what we wanted. In the end it all sort of worked out. We didn't pay attention to them to much."

Craig: "After the recording of the first album *Takes Off*, could you have accepted if the album was a complete failure, because you would have been able to realize the dream of so many, to play in a rock and roll band and see your creation in the local record shop?"

Paul Kantner: "We never viewed ourselves as a success and still don't really. We were a minor blip on the radar that had some good local color going. That's all I needed, frankly. Nobody ever expected any success. We didn't go into music for that. It was the thing to do. It was the thing to do in those times. How it got successful was always amazing. We accepted it on that level but didn't worry about it. We did what we wanted to do and got away with most of it."

Craig: "When you were recording the first album, was it shocking to you that the record company actually wanted the line changed from *Let Me In*- "Don't tell me you want money", to "Don't tell me it's so funny?" It makes one shake their head."

Paul Kantner: "That was sort of silly. It meant nothing. It was good that they wanted to censor the thing. They chose all the wrong things. By the time we got to *Baxter's* (*After Bathing At Baxter's* the third album), we gave them things to censor so they would ignore the more serious stuff. Which they couldn't comprehend in the first place."

Craig: "Was it disheartening because you were facing a restriction on creativity?"

Paul Kantner: "Any artist thrives on censorship. That goes all the way from the past to the movie of *The Da Vinci Code*. If I were a public relations guy for *The Da Vinci Code*, I would hire Christians to come picket."

Craig: "Bad publicity is better than no publicity?"

Paul Kantner: "Publicity is publicity. Censorship to an artist is always a boom to the artist. Short of execution, censorship is a boom to almost all good artists. That is from Galileo on. (Galileo Galilei was a famous astronomer and mathematician)."

Craig: "When the second record *Surrealistic Pillow* was starting to take shape in the studio, did the band feel a certain amount of pressure to equal or surpass the previous work?"

Paul Kantner: "We felt no pressure. Look at the third record *After Bathing At Baxter's*. Marty may have felt some pressure. He has written about being expected to produce. For myself, I felt no pressure. I never had that problem. I never wrote anything that was particularly commercially successful anyway. I had no need to follow-up with it. Marty on the other hand did. He felt it thoroughly. It sort of wrecked him for awhile."

Craig: "How were your ears in terms of listening to a finished album and knowing how it will sell, or what song could make a strong single?"

Paul Kantner: "I wasn't good at that. Not at all and I couldn't care less. It wasn't my job. You do what you do. You don't pay attention to that kind of stuff. None of my business. I couldn't care less."

Craig: "When Skip Spence left the band (He would be part of Moby Grape) if Spencer Dryden hadn't been offered the job, were there other drummers you considered?"

Paul Kantner: "Spencer filled in nicely right away."

Craig: "Was he one of, if not the first choice?"

Paul Kantner: "He was the first."

Craig: "When Signe left, if Grace had not agreed to join the band where there other choices you had in mind?"

Paul Kantner: "Fortunately Grace filled that opening nicely as well. Timing was everything in those days. It worked out nicely, I would think. There weren't any singers any better than Grace on the horizon. Grace was my particular fascination. There wasn't a better singer in San Francisco, Janis (Janis Joplin) included. There weren't any better singers that could have filled that spot in our band."

Craig: "If Signe had stayed would the records have been less esoteric, or would she have had to adapt to the changing times?"

Paul Kantner: "Signe was a real good singer. Grace was a real good person. Grace made her own place in the band. That's all I needed. I have always been fond of women singers, such as Grace. Signe was very accomplished in her own way and Grace was very unique."

Craig: "Countless fans and musicians, have always admired your ability to choose a great female voice. With Signe, Grace, Darby Gould, and Diana Mangano, (The last two from the Jefferson Starship) you couldn't have filled an opening any better."

Paul Kantner: "Oddly enough Craig, they almost picked me. I didn't go out looking. They found us. Excluding Signe, the other three found us. I can tell a good singer when I hear one. So could you. There aren't that many good ones honestly. I have had luck with the four, Signe, Grace, Darby, and Diana. It is better than finding seventy-two virgins. Forget the virgins, give me a few good singers and I am in seventh heaven."

Craig: "Do any of the live concerts you've played stand out for positive reasons?"

Paul Kantner: "They were all enjoyable. I don't put one over the other. Touring is a path, not a stop-over kind of thing."

Craig: "The philosophy is a given tour is a marathon and not a quick sprint?"

Paul Kantner: "Exactly, exactly!"

Craig: "Can you talk about seeing the song *Martha* to fruition. The unused versions from the studio such as the instrumental and the rehearsal with you directing the band are fascinating."

Paul: "That song always produces, what is the word? I can't think of the word. You can do anything you want kind of a song."

Craig: "On 11/1/68 at the Schuyler Hotel, 57 West 45th Street, New York City (The band performed on the roof), can you verify that there was another song played besides *The House At Pooneil Corners*?"

Paul Kantner: "That was fun. It got our manager arrested. We did play *Somebody To Love* first. We may have even done *Crown Of Creation* had the festivities not ended, but I am not sure."

**Paul Kantner- Short and fun flight facts:**

**Middle Name- Lorin**

***Blows Against The Empire* received a highly respected science fiction prize called the Hugo Award.**

**The first non-Jefferson Airplane album (Excluding *Blows Against The Empire*) that Paul is credited on is David Crosby's- If I could Only Remember My Name, released 2/22/71.**

**Which member of the Grateful Dead did Paul lend a hand with vocals on his 1972 LP?**

**A) Jerry Garcia**
**B) Mickey Hart**
**C) Bob Weir**
**D) Non of the above**

**The answer is (Drum roll please) Mickey Hart's Rolling Thunder.**

**We now return to our regularly scheduled interview.**

Craig: "The live footage of *The House At Pooneil Corners* was fascinating. Not only from the musical sense but the reaction by various demographics."

Paul Kantner: "I don't think anybody captured anything but *The House At Pooneil Corners*."

Craig: "That was the case. The song and some footage after the final notes are all that has surfaced. There was a tune *J.P.P. McStep B. Blues* that you performed live only a few times with the Airplane and twice tried an arrangement for inclusion on a studio album. Once on its own and the other time coming out of *Wooden Ships*. In both cases it didn't make the final cut. It ended up on the real good posthumous release from 1974 *Early Flight*."

Paul Kantner: "We had better songs. That was our thoughts at the time. It ended up being secondary."

Craig: "Would that be because in the vinyl record days you would be lucky to get forty minutes on an album?"

Paul Kantner: "Exactly. There were times you were looking at thirty-eight minutes for the entire record. We thought we had better songs. It isn't a bad song. It's fine I'm saying, but just thought we had better. It's a nice song."

Craig: "In late March of 1972 did you work on a song called *Revolutionary Upstairs Maid*?"

Paul Kantner: "It was a page from one of my ex-girlfriends. It was one of those that never got out. It may develop one of these days."

Craig: "When you performed the final show on 9/22/72 at Winterland, San Francisco, did you have an inkling that it would be seventeen years before the band reunited?"

Paul Kantner: "We didn't think of that. It was one of those things that either it will happen or it doesn't. In the mean time the view was to not even think about it. If it raised its blessed pointed little head (Paul almost got a triple word score for attempting to get in the correct title of the first live album) some of us will take notice and some will take less of a notice."

Craig: "When the 1989 reunion came about how did the band decide to go away from using an Airplane, Hot Tuna, or Jefferson Starship drummer?"

Paul Kantner: "Spencer Dryden was still in disfavor because of his behavior. We wanted a strong drummer and somebody (John Mellencamp) presented Kenny Aronoff. He is an extraordinary wonderful drummer, sensitive to music, and sensitive to our peculiarities. That is what sold me on Kenny Aronoff."

Craig: "Kenny mentioned to me how much he enjoyed playing with you guys."

Paul Kantner: "I think we challenged him. That is always good for a musician. Take them beyond their known areas and see what they do. I thought Kenny went beyond his known areas. He went into our unknown areas and did it very well! He was exhilarating to play with. He was strong, powerful, as well as sensitive."

Craig: "The fans took to him. He got a positive response to the tour and when he performed his solo."

Paul Kantner: "He is a good musician. Totally aside he is a civilized human being. Most drummers are complete quads. With the exception of Spencer and our drummer now in the Jefferson Starship (Donny Baldwin has taken over for Prairie Prince while he performs with the New Cars). I was lucky to be in the company of good drummers such as Spencer in his day, Prairie Prince, Kenny, and a couple of others. I had a few that were crazy. They were wonder buses or trailer park trash! Mostly I have been in the company of very good civilized drummers, which is a treat."

Craig: "When the rehearsals started for the 1989 tour how long did it take for you to feel it coming together?"

Paul Kantner: "We jumped right into it. I thought it worked pretty well considering the circumstances. Everything worked pretty good. There were friction filled moments, but we got over them pretty quickly. We're not friction filled people. Generally that is. The music spoke for itself. The stuff was pretty well done for the whole tour."

Craig: "It is important that the indisputable facts are told. For those that were too young to have seen the band from 1965-1972, or those that had, but wanted a few hours to recapture the distant memories, the tour put a gargantuan smile on thousands of faces coast to coast."

Paul Kantner: "I think we captured a little bit of the past and some of the future. That's all you really ask for."

Craig: "How difficult was it picking the songs for the shows, with the wealth of material available to play?"

Paul Kantner: "It wasn't. It was very natural. It was unplanned. I got to write the sets (Paul laughs, but thoroughly enjoyed it), that was a traditional responsibility for me. Everybody sort of went along with it. They all played good. As a general rule things worked out well. I even gave Jorma a section for his own peculiar direction. I don't know if that amused or disturbed him, but he got to do his own little bit well. That worked nicely. We all got to do what we like to do. I did what I like, Grace, Marty, blah, blah, blah. I thought it worked out good, without making it a huge world tour. Let's go out and play wherever we can and see what we can do."

Craig: "*The Other Side Of This Life* was performed as an encore only on the opening night of the tour. Any reason it didn't make it to the other shows?"

(Paul seemed surprised. He told me it was one of his favorites).

Paul Kantner: "I don't have a clue, but I take your word."

Craig: "*The Other Side Of This Life* is one of the Freddie Neil songs you enjoy. Do you have recollections of meeting him?"

Paul Kantner: "I met him once. I was influenced by his music way before that. I liked his stuff. He had a twelve string guitar, which I am fond of. He had this low bass voice, which I am now singing more and more in. I am trying to learn the art of that. It is a lot trickier than the high piercing voice."

Craig: "When you played with Hot Tuna in 1988 you brought with you another one of his terrific songs *The Bag I'm In*."

Paul Kantner: "Freddie has a lot of good material."
**(We now will have a brief interlude, as Paul needs to get a glass of milk and a donut. Don't touch that dial please).**

Craig: "When the 1989 reunion came to an end what were your thoughts on how it worked out?"

Paul Kantner: "It didn't work as well as we all hoped, but it was still pretty good. I would hope for a better one sometime in the future, should we all live that long. God only knows, that we will even."

Craig: "We've lost enough musical greats. You should live forever."

Paul Kantner: "Thank you Craig."

Craig: "When you got together with the band (Less, Grace Slick) for the Rock And Roll Hall Of Fame rehearsal, (Performance was 1/17/96) did you rehearse at the Waldorf Astoria Hotel, or at the Power Station (Recording studio) in New York City?"

Paul Kantner: "As I remember we did a sound check at the hotel, most likely the day of. I am not recalling a rehearsal. Why rehearse? It's like bicycle riding."

Craig: "What was your feeling of having Spencer play with the band for the first time since 1970?"

Paul Kantner: "Spencer at the time was ill and weak. We had Prairie Prince with us just to fill in if needed. It ended up working out okay."

Craig: "At that time were fences mended with Spencer?"

Paul Kantner: "It was a little edgy. I missed Grace."

Craig: "You told the people she had back trouble, but on her book tour she mentioned that she thought old people look silly playing rock and roll."

Paul Kantner: "I was like go f_ck yourself. Ella Fitzgerald isn't too old! Louie Armstrong wasn't too old! You're not too old. I was irritated by it, but didn't let it bother me."

Craig: "One of the three songs performed at the induction was *Embryonic Journey*, but Jorma played the song solo."

Paul Kantner: "I suggested that. It's a lovely song."

Craig: "That was peerless that the band would do that."

Paul Kantner: "That's what we were all about. That was an excellent example."

Craig: During the Rock And Roll Hall Of Fame induction, you read a poem that was delivered with a lot of passion. Paul, it was a nice family moment when your son Alexander recited the poem during a Wooden Ships concert on 1/18/92, at the I-Beam, San Francisco, California. What was the title?"

Paul Kantner: "That was really nice. Off hand I don't remember the title. I can get that for you in two minutes. Craig do you know I have 1012 emails in my in box? No wonder I can't find things that easily."

(Paul was kind enough to use his computer and get the proper information).

Craig: "You have the most amount of messages of any person on the planet. It is also immensely hysterical."

Paul Kantner: "I hate deleting things. The poem was called *Get Ready* and it was by Rebecca Bockelie. She wrote it when she was eight."

Craig: "What struck me about the poem was a person that heard you read it was honestly moved by the emotion."

Paul Kantner: "It was a good poem. She was really young at the time of writing it. I have a funny one for you, from <u>Hunter Thompson</u>: (Journalist and author, who died at age 67 on 2/20/05. He committed suicide). "The music business is a cruel and shallow money trench, a long, plastic hallway where thieves and pimps run free and good men die like dogs. There's also a negative side."

Craig: "That should be in every rock and roll book ever published."

Paul: "It is funny."

Craig: "How do things stand with the other Airplane member's right this moment?"

Paul Kantner: "Jorma and I are at each others throats in our own quite way."

Craig: "Does this go back to a couple incidents in 2000? One, the time a venue mistakenly billed a show as Paul Kantner and Jefferson Airplane, and you took the blunt of the blame, without being at fault, and the second you were approached to do a commercial."

Paul Kantner: "As for the commercial Jorma abandoned that. I did not sign off on that. The other thing was a total mistake. He chose to sue. I had to go to court, without a lawyer. The judge threw it out and told us to go away and figure this out. I am still irritated with that (The part of having to go to court)."

**Photograph by kind permission of Don Aters and may not be reproduced without the written consent of Don Aters.**

**From the Don Aters collection.  Photographer Don Aters.**

**Paul Kantner circa 2005 from a Jefferson Starship performance.**

**Photograph by kind permission of Don Aters and may not be reproduced without the**

**written consent of Don Aters.**

**From the Don Aters collection. Photographer Don Aters.**

**Paul Kantner circa 2005 from a Jefferson Starship performance.**

Craig: "Hopefully on to a happier tune, what about seeing Marty with the Jefferson Starship again?"

Paul Kantner: "I am sure we will hook up with Marty again. He has some situations that preclude him from going out for any length of time. We set it aside for the moment. We have a great band with him and a great band without him. We have a kick-ass band. The players are terrific and Diana is terrific. I'm in seventh heaven on that level. When you add Marty, or David Freiberg, it is only a plus! We still have Darby join us every now and then."

Craig: "Darby mentioned to me how much she enjoys appearing with the band when she can. It is nice that over the years you have not let a falling out with a musician permanently remove them from future endeavors."

Paul Kantner: "Unless one of your friends is a child molester, you don't shut anything off. Short of child molesting and murder everything is correctable."

Craig: "One person that has been absent from the invitations the past few years is former Jefferson Starship guitarist Craig Chaquico. Did something happen to produce a cold war?"

Paul Kantner: "He overstepped his bounds and has not come back from that area. There are no details available. He went beyond civil behavior, put it that way. He hasn't chosen to correct the situation. Until he does he is out of the picture. The ball is in his court, as they say."

Craig: "Where do you get the energy at sixty-five to continue on the road?"

Paul Kantner: "You don't think about that stuff. You go on from day to day and you live. My life is music. I have a band. Whatever band I have is the band I'll play with. If there is no band available, I'll play alone. Fortunately I don't have to play alone yet. I take great comfort with the well playing friends around me."

Craig: "Do you still expect to have Peter Kaukonen perform some shows with you later in the year?"

Paul Kantner: "He is on the schedule for a few shows."

Craig: 'Before we wrap things up, have you been in contact lately with Signe Anderson to see how she is feeling?"

Paul Kantner: "I haven't spoken to her in about a year."

Craig: "Thank you so much for your time today. It has been a pleasure to have listened to your music all these years."

Paul Kantner: "Thank you, Craig."

Peter Kaukonen- Hot Tuna, Jefferson Starship, and played guitar on the Jefferson Airplane 1989 tour.

**Photograph by kind permission of Don Aters and may not be reproduced without the**

**written consent of Don Aters.**

**From the Don Aters collection.  Don Aters photographer.**

**The photo is from the Jefferson Starship 8/11/06 or 8/12/06 performance at B.B. King's, New York City.**

**Photograph by kind permission of Don Aters and may not be reproduced without the written consent of Don Aters.**
**From the Don Aters collection. Don Aters photographer.**
**The photo is from the Jefferson Starship 8/11/06 or 8/12/06 performance at B.B. King's, New York City.**

**I wanted Peter to be able to articulate the words from the fabulous CD he recorded in 2004, under less than optimum conditions called _Going Home_.** You can purchase the CD and many of his other well conceived recordings at www.peterkaukonen.com. Peter's parents had both passed away and he put the timeline of the events to words and music. It is a touching tribute to two people he loved.

My mom passed away in 2003 and I am fully aware of the traumatic experience. For anyone that has lost a loved one or two, maybe Pete wrote what most of us were thinking, but couldn't get the words to resonate. For that reason I didn't tinker with the use of small letters, question marks, periods, or commas. It needed to be from Peter's hands to our eyes.

## Peter's timeline begins:

I'd started writing material while my mother was still alive... the chronology was something like, her husband died and she was lost and bereft, wondering what she would do or who she would be.... after all, she'd taken care of him for years, most particularly through the years of his decline (due to strokes .....) remember that this is not "codependent;" it's age and generational appropriate..... well, my mother was nothing if not strong and resilient and, after a couple of weeks of despond, she decided that she'd go back to school and get her PhD. ...... _and then_, of course, she was diagnosed with pancreatic cancer and given three months to live.

Well, I'd been involved in my father's decline and death, but I really wanted to be involved with my mother .... I wanted to come out "clean," meaning, I didn't want to say or think, "if only I'd .... I wish that .... oh, why didn't I ....." etc. etc. etc. .....

I started writing material while my mother was still alive .... .why wouldn't I? I'm an artist and the things that happen, the things that make up my life, that make up life, are all grist for my musically anecdotal mill ... so I started writing with _Hospice Shuffle_ and _The Fast Slide Down_ ... I started with those because of the recording program I had at the time (Cakewalk) gave me midi (Musical Instrument Digital Interface. For an explination of what a midi does please go to: http://en.wikipedia.org/wiki/MIDI) control I'd never had before and, because of "beginner's mind," where I was unaware of what I was supposed to do nor not do, will probably never do anything like them again ..... (I also started a "journal" and now have close to four hundred single-spaced pages chronicling this journey; perhaps one day it'll see publication ...).

When I started writing I thought that I'd do a "musical tribute" to both my mother and my father but, when I was finished and looked at the material that I had, I realized that this work had really defined itself and that what I had was a musical timeline of the last year-and-a-half of my mother's life ........ because the material I had was focused on her .....

Many of the lyrics come as direct quotes from conversations that I had with her (the _End Of The Line_: "who will know what I have done? and who will love what I have loved?" or ........ _This Old House_: "the place where we all ate and slept where grandma brought me into this world ...." and I felt that some stories should be told about her previous life (_The Orient_ ...) and, because I was so involved I wanted to tell a story about me as well, hence _Motherless Child_ ......

but it wasn't as though I sat down and wrote the straight sequence of material, for the nature of the work was dictated by technology, meaning ..... I started working on an analog eight track (_Going Home_) ..... _Hospice Shuffle_ and _The Fast Slide Down_ were done with Cakewalk in a p.c., and I'd hoped to sync analog tape to the p.c.; don't try this at home, it's a nightmare and not worth it ...... other material was recorded on digital tape, sixteen channels of a dat but ..... computer crashes and one bad batch of tape destroyed or disappeared half of the songs I'd written and recorded ..... so, while I started with twenty-eight songs, I ended up with what's on disc and that's the way it is ..... there were some wonderful songs that didn't make it to disc and that we'll never hear, because they vanished into a digital hell .......

I have another chronicle of the thirty techs who didn't get my studio running, and the thirty-first who did, as well as the shaman who ...... okay, another story for another time, but the lesson here is, always back up your s_it, because if you don't ..... you will be in some very deep doodoo .......

It's hard to say how long a song took from beginning to end ...... for example, *End Of The Line?*" That took a long, long time because I had to teach myself how to play piano for it .... why did I have to teach myself piano? Because I'm not a pianist and because none of the four pianists I asked to do it came through .....

in fact, *Going Home* is keyboard driven, rather than (like *Black Kangaroo* or *Traveller*) guitar driven ..... why? Because writing on guitar pre-determines changes, licks, and melodies, and I wanted to be more flexible and do something completely different from what I'd done before .... the subject matter certainly demanded that, and so you get songs like *All Visitors* and *You Don't Care* and *Hello Dali!* ...... while there are still guitar-based songs like *Deep Blue* and the big guitars of *Midnight Morphine* ..... and I think *Angel Face* is just some wonderful guitar playing ....

But you understand, the point was to tell stories and paint pictures, not recycle the same old guitar licks ... again, it's hard to talk about changes songs went through from beginning to end ... I felt that I was very fortunate in this project, in that I had a story that I wanted to tell, and I had the time and the tools with which to do it ..... so I could let the songs tell me where they needed to go and how they needed to get there ..... and a lot of time went into crafting the lyrics, not just the music ..... I'm sorry, but I think there is some absolutely brilliant writing there .....

actually, there are some songs that I felt as though I had nothing to do with the creation of .... it was as though I were the channel through which they made themselves flesh and, when they were done, I sat back and said, where the f_ck did that come from?

*All Visitors* is such a song, as is *Hauling Ash* ..... and *All Visitors* always knocks my socks off; it reaches into my thorax and puts a death grip on my heart and I start choking up .... and it does it each and every time ..... sometimes you can get really, really lucky, and your work will come out with a depth and an edge that, even as you strive for quality and impact, you never imagined, and *All Visitors* is such a piece ......

I've never performed any of this material and doubt that I ever will .... why? Because you can't do this stuff on an acoustic guitar ..... oh, I might do "*Motherless Child,*" but I haven't yet ..... why? because I can't seem to get any gigs ...

why? It beats the hell out of me ...... I have hours of material worked up with an acoustic bass player (Michael Lindner, who played with Black Kangaroo on a '72 tour); it's lovely material and we play very well together, but ...... we can't get any action here ..... go figure... well... what else ...

I am now writing material about new twins... I have a couple of songs mixed, a lullaby which is just gorgeous, and a piece called *Sleep Deprived* which is very powerful ..... who knows when that'll be finished .... meanwhile, you can get a free download of *The Ballad Of Saddam Hussein* from my website, and you can order singles and albums from there as well ...... The real lessons of life are, nothing ever goes on schedule, and nothing ever goes as smoothly as you'd wish .......

Again, I'm glad you like *Going Home* .... Best of success with your project ......

Peter Kaukonen

Diana Mangano- Jefferson Starship.

**Photograph by kind permission of Don Aters and may not be reproduced without the**

**written consent of Don Aters.**

**From the Don Aters collection.  Don Aters photographer.**

**Diana Mangano circa 2005 from a Jefferson Starship show.**

**Photograph by kind permission of Don Aters and may not be reproduced without the written consent of Don Aters.**
**From the Don Aters collection. Don Aters photographer.**
**Diana Mangano circa 2005 from a Jefferson Starship show.**

Photographs top and bottom by kind permission of Rick Martin and may not be reproduced without the written consent of Rick Martin.
From the Rick Martin collection. Rick Martin photographer.

Photo one on the left is Chris Smith, Linda Imperial, and Diana.
Photo two on the right is Chris Smith (Hidden by the keyboard), Diana, and Prairie Prince.

Diana Mangano on the left and *The Working Class Rocker* Darby Gould on the right.

All three photos are from 10/16/05 Point Breeze Restaurant, Webster, Massachusetts from a

Jefferson Starship performance.

**Photograph by kind permission of Rick Martin and may not be reproduced without the**

**written consent of Rick Martin.**

**From the Rick Martin collection.  Rick Martin photographer.**

**Diana Mangano**

**5/5/06 Cervantes Masterpiece Ballroom, Denver, Colorado from a**

**Jefferson Starship show.**

Craig: "Diana, it is nice to talk with you. Thanks for spending some time with me today."

Diana Mangano: "You're welcome. It is my pleasure."

Craig: "A bit before October of 1993 when you joined the Jefferson Starship, you had given a demo to Paul's manager of *Lather*. How did you settle on that one?"

Diana Mangano: "It was a dare from a friend; one of those things where you don't expect anything but you go for it."

Craig: "When you first joined the band and Darby Gould was there, did it feel both strange and unique to have two female singers?"

Diana Mangano: "It was definitely weird. Darby was established and I was trying not to make a fool of myself. I needed to get settled in. The audience had their favorites that they liked seeing her perform."

Craig: "You earned the respect of the Jefferson Family fans very quickly. That isn't always easy. It says volumes about your ability as a singer, and the chemistry you created with the band and the audience."

Diana Mangano: "Thank you. That was very kind of you to say."

Craig: "When the *Windows Of Heaven* album was being recorded, was it a feeling of elation for you? Every kid wants to grow up and play for the New York Yankees or be in a well known rock and roll band. Was recording the record the dream you thought it would be?"

Diana Mangano: "I may not be answering this the way you thought. I am more of a live singer. In the recording studio there is less space. I also found that it was like the person that watches a wedding video forty times and the same thing happens each time. After a while you get a bit numb. It was nerve-racking. I also thought the record would have been excellent had we had more time. That is why Prairie Prince is so amazing. One time and everything's perfect. Every thing is about money and budgets. It would have been nice as far as the band was concerned, to work at the album for a year. I also was somewhat terrified doing the record. I am shy and reserved. I function fully at social gatherings and meeting people, but for the first time recording in that environment it took some getting used to."

Craig: "In September of 1995, a fantastic tribute to Jerry Garcia was released, *Eternity Blue*. How did you get involved in that project?"

Diana Mangano: "At the famous Seva Benefit, I don't remember the year."

Craig: "The 1994 Seva was the most noted."

Diana Mangano: "That's right. Hot Tuna was there and Bob Weir. I spoke with Henry Kaiser (Well known musician in the Bay Area that has appeared on almost one hundred records), we became friends. One day he calls me and tells me about the tribute to Jerry Garcia. It came about so fast I didn't have time to get nervous. He picks me up at seven in the morning and we are singing at eight. Some musicians can function well in the morning. I'm not one of those. I need it to be afternoon for my voice to kick in."

Craig: "You did two amazing tracks- the covers of *High Time* and *Brokedown Palace*. This further solidified your reputation as not only a great Jefferson Starship vocalist but a tremendous singer period."

Diana Mangano: "Thank you, that is very kind."

Craig: "You are welcome and it is well deserved. Did you have an input on the tracks you sung on?"

458

Diana Mangano: "Henry was very well organized. When we got there, he handed out papers with all the instructions. I was told what songs I would be doing. He is an excellent producer, very thorough and very aware of time. We knocked out the entire thing in a couple of hours."

Craig: "Talk about getting your monies worth! There is a live Jefferson Starship record that is rather underrated, *Across The Sea Of Suns* that came out in 2001. Fans have told me that they were blown away by your vocal performance on two tracks. Can you guess which ones?"

Diana Mangano: "Can you believe I never heard the record? I don't even know what is on it. I find it hard to listen to myself."

(Speaking with Diana, you can see how modest she is. Diana is very unassuming and down to earth).

Craig: "I find it hard to believe, but I hope you will check out the record one day. The two songs *Eskimo Blue Day* and *Hey Frederick* were done with such vocal expertise that I wrote down a quote from one of your fans. There's a guy, six foot plus and over two hundred forty pounds who told me, "When I heard Diana sing *Eskimo Blue Day*, I cried. I don't remember being that touched by a female voice since the first time I heard Grace sing."

Diana Mangano: "That was really a wonderful comment. We may bring back *Hey Frederick*. Last time we performed it, we didn't have enough time to rehearse it properly. It didn't come off as well as I would have envisioned. It is a really good song to do live. If we get it right, maybe it can go back in the set."

Craig: "What do the younger members of the band such as you, and Slick Aguilar, bring to the live shows?"

Diana Mangano: "I don't think of our group in terms of age. When you spend so much time traveling, rehearsing and playing, it is about family and friends. There isn't an age factor. If I were performing with a bunch of four year olds, it would be the same way. The band becomes your family. Paul Kantner and David Freiberg give the audience a wonderful music history. To have been performing so many decades, you can't help but be up for the shows."

Craig: "The fans have always appreciated that the sets are changed and there are many songs being performed that you wouldn't normally think. It must be nice having the opportunity to sing such diverse songs. *Darkly Smiling* (Great Society) for example comes to mind."

Diana Mangano: "It is nice that Paul can dip into forty some odd years of material. It gives me the opportunity to sing wonderful songs that were done by the Great Society and obviously the Jefferson Airplane. There is a wealth of fabulous Jefferson Starship material that I look forward to singing as well. It keeps things fresh for the performers and the audience."

Craig: "When I listen to the live shows of the current Jefferson Starship, I hear a consistent vocal sound. Are you able to get up for each gig because of the opportunity to make somebody forget about their troubles for a few hours? I remember when I was a disc-jockey; it was always nice knowing that even if one person listened to the station, it may make them feel good. The same holds true for the athlete or the actor."

Diana Mangano: "I hold the same philosophy, as when you were a disc-jockey. You want to reach out and touch some lives. The other night somebody came up to me after the show and told me how much it meant to them seeing the band. If you can be a positive influence on one fan, you can feel good about the night's work."

Craig: "Any chance we can see Marty Balin, on a show or two when the weather warms up? Would it be advantageous for him to be on stage for a few concerts?"

Diana Mangano: "I miss Marty anytime he is not on the tour. He has to take care of his family right now. That is the priority. It doesn't mean in the future he won't perform with us."

Craig: "During the end of one of the shows from the U.K., Slick did a nice thing. He went over to the microphone and said "Marty, we miss you brother.""

Diana Mangano: "It goes back to what we previously talked about. The band is a family and a piece is missing. In some way the piece is constantly there too."

Craig: "Diana, thank you once again for affording me this time. I realize how busy you are today."

Diana Mangano: "You're welcome. It was nice talking with you."

After we finished the interview, Diana actually took the time to ask me questions about the book I was writing and about my former days in radio. Her reputation of being down to earth is obvious, and her respect for Grace Slick is very evident.

# Jerry Peloquin- Jefferson Airplane.

Craig: "Jerry it is nice to be able to speak with you today."

Jerry Peloquin: "Thank you, Craig."

Craig: "Was your involvement in the very early days of the Jefferson Airplane stem from you dating a girl Jacky Watts, who at the time had a friend dating Marty Balin?"

Jerry Peloquin: "Jacky and Marty's girlfriend were living in the same apartment on California Street in San Francisco. Marty wanted to start a band and asked me if I played a musical instrument. I told him I did. Marty and I became the first two members of what would become the original Jefferson Airplane."

Craig: "Didn't Jacky go on to work behind the scenes for the Airplane Family?

Jerry Peloquin: "She was called a managerial assistant, but was doing a lot more. Jacky was good for the organization. She went on to marry Jorma's brother."

Craig: "She married Peter Kaukonen."

Jerry Peloquin: "She managed their offices. My memory isn't clear on the sequence of dates. She didn't stay married to Peter. She is married to somebody else, that I believe is named Randy Sarti and is involved in the travel business."

Craig: "Did you or Jacky bring in the early manager of the band Matthew Katz?"

Jerry Peloquin: "I brought in the manager Matthew. I met him through Stu Goldberg. Stu owned a store called Marina Music. It was located on Union Street in San Francisco. One step off from the Drinking Gourd."

Craig: "The famous bar in San Francisco."

Jerry Peloquin: "Stu and I were roommates. We were living on Asbury. He knew Matthew because he liked the fact that Matthew was a guitar aficionado. He in turn introduced me to Matthew. That's how it happened."

Craig: "Was Matthew looking for a specific opportunity in the music business?"

Jerry Peloquin: "Matthew was kind of a promoter. He had written a book on Amelia Earhart. (In 1928 became the first woman to fly solo across the Atlantic). He was very intellectual. He had a band that I believe was called the Tripsichord Music Box, (A mixture of psychedelic and rock with some dark arrangements. The group formed in 1963 under the name of the Ban. In 1967 they changed the name. Thank you to http://www.answers.com/topic/the-tripsichord-music-box for the info about the Ban) after Moby Grape."

Craig: "Do you believe the story that Matthew and Skip Spence wanted to form the band Moby Grape around Skip, this way he could play guitar and not drums, and be more of a central focus?"

Jerry Peloquin: "I don't have first hand information on that. I have heard that."

Craig: "When the Airplane first started, what was your feeling as to the possibility this could be the real thing? Did you think that ego and personality conflicts could be the downfall?"

Jerry Peloquin: "It is easy to have second guesses. It is easy to sit back here and say something else. At the time I had a job. I came from a working class family in the Boston suburbs. I served four years in the Marines. I was a professional musician. To these guys it was a cultural phenomenon. I knew something was going to happen. I looked at the Byrds and Dylan. There was a sense of pregnancy in the air. Something was going to happen. I didn't get a sense of anything but happiness with the band, until the last month."

Craig: "With the *Counter Culture* movement of the 1960's were there people in the music scene that weren't happy you had served the country four years?"

Jerry Peloquin: "You have to remember the times. I had to keep it a secret."

Craig: "When the group got to the line-up that you were a part of, was it pre-planned that you would have a female singer Signe Anderson?"

Jerry Peloquin: "It is my recollection that Marty thought verbally and physically this was his band. Marty had a couple of guys he knew that had some money. They were willing to invest in a club. It is my recollection that Signe came in through the Drinking Gourd. Marty and Paul met there. That was a club that pre-dated The Matrix. I am thinking that there may have even been a bass-player before Bob Harvey. He didn't last long. He was a red-headed guy that worked for United Airlines. I can see his image. He had a crew-cut. I wish I could remember the guy's name."

Craig: "That at least narrows it down some. (Jerry laughs). Can you tell the readers if this is urban legend or a fact? You were rehearsing one afternoon for a night performance and in the middle of *In The Midnight Hour*, (The Rascals and Wilson Pickett were known for their versions) Paul Kantner was unhappy with the drum beat. The song got stopped and this lead to a slight altercation."

Jerry Peloquin: "Let me give you as clear as I can my recollection of that set of events and how they happened. I was the only one in the band that had a job. I was working for an optical company. I believe it was in San Francisco but may have been San Mateo. One day we are rehearsing and Paul broke his glasses. I brought the glasses in to be repaired and I gave them to him. I'm telling you this to show what it led up to. About two weeks after, I'm talking to a friend of mine and he says to me "Did you know that during the day when the band is rehearsing at The Matrix, Paul is bringing in other drummers?" I said what. I was a lot younger then and full of outrage. I got off work and went to the club and confronted Paul. I asked is it true what I am hearing that you are recruiting people to play drums. When he told me yes, I whacked him. I said some choice words and out I went. The next night was the *RCA Audition*. I went in and talked with Marty. Marty told me that it was a lot easier to replace a drummer than to replace Paul. I told Marty then you can replace me. I then went over to a place called the hungry i (**That is the correct spelling and it is lower case letters**. A legendary 1950's and 1960's club in San Francisco, that gave early exposure to many comedians) and played two weeks with Nina Simone. (She was a jazz and rhythm and blues artist known for her one Top 20 hit *I Love You Porgy*)."

Craig: "Didn't take too long to get a new job. Was it surprising to you that Marty put business over friendship?"

Jerry Peloquin: "It did and didn't surprise me. Marty was very business like. He was very interested in the business side of music. Although there was talk about smile on your brother, ("*Let's Get Together*") it was always about money. That is my opinion and that is how I read them. Well Marty anyway. The other guys I didn't know all that well. I couldn't make those comments. I certainly could about Marty. He was very professional. I say that with a certain amount of respect."

Craig: "After you left did you have further contact with the band?"

Jerry Peloquin: "In 1968 or it may have been 1967 I got a call from Jacky Watts. Spencer Dryden wasn't feeling well. The band had seen me play in New York and they are wondering if I would like to come back and play. I got on a plane and flew to San Francisco. I meet with Jacky. I don't remember the details, and I don't remember what was said, but I got a bad feeling. I decided to go back to my own band."

Craig: "If you had told Jacky that you are interested in playing with the band again, would it have been for a few gigs or as a replacement for Spencer?"

Jerry Peloquin: "At the time I wasn't thinking of it that way. I had a band called Wings. We recorded a record for ABC-Dunhill. There were a lot of things going on in my musical and professional life that made me think that I didn't need to do this. There were drugs everywhere in the *San Francisco Scene*. I was never a big druggie. I am no saint but as a drummer the first thing that goes is your meter. That is your main purpose. You have to hold a beat. You can't have five people dictate what a rhythm should be. You have to hold it together. You have the drummer and the bass-player is right on top of them. The drums and the bass set the feeling and the mood for any piece. The first person to get replaced is the drummer and the second the bass-player. That's the way it is. The drummer is always paranoid."

Craig: "When the second album from the Airplane came out did you have a feeling that Pete Best had." (The drummer replaced in the Beatles by Ringo Starr). The *what if* question?"

Jerry Peloquin: "I wasn't there with Grace Slick. That was Grace's band. She changed the character. It wasn't the same band that I played with before *Takes Off*. That was more a cultural phenomenon than a musical one. Grace brought a real point of view and an edge that they didn't have previously."

Craig: "To you the second phase of the flight wasn't something you experienced first-hand."

Jerry Peloquin: "I had seen Grace in clubs but didn't know her."

Craig: "You took a positive view when you digested things."

Jerry Peloquin: "Look at how other bands have had changes in sound. I'm glad that I did what I did. I feel bad on retrospect I lost my temper. I felt betrayed. I was feeling a sense of comradery before. I helped build The Matrix. I built it with my hands and I worked all day and then worked all night. I demonstrated a good deal of loyalty. I did feel betrayed when other drummers were being rehearsed. I am not sorry I did it, but I am sorry I lost my temper. There also was another time that I had contact with the band. There was the court case I had to testify that you are aware of."

Craig: "Yes, you and Bob Harvey were asked to take the stand in the case with the former manager Matthew Katz."

Jerry Peloquin: "Yes, that is correct. I testified for Matthew. I didn't see Bob Harvey at the trial. I was there one day. (Both Jerry and Bob Harvey didn't want to get into the results of the trial)."

Craig: "When the Airplane days ended, you had a great musical odyssey playing with so many people. Why don't we get into your live resume. This is really impressive. You performed with Chad Mitchell (Known for a sound close to the Kingston Trio and Peter, Paul, and Mary. Had a cult-following in the 1960's), Jose Feliciano (Folk-rock and jazz artist that is well known for his cover of the Doors hit *Light My Fire*. Jose was fairly popular in the 1960's and 1970's), Tim Buckley (Had a cult following for his mixture of Folk-rock, psychedelic and improvisational music in the 1960's and 1970's), New York Electric String Ensemble (Released a self-titled record in 1967 with classical songs played in a jazz style), Paul Winter Consort (Had a cult-following in the 1960's and 1970's for the mixture of jazz with sounds from around the globe), and the 1968 band called Wings."

Jerry Peloquin: "One of the guys in the band (Wings), Jim Mason was a co-writer of *I Dig Rock And Roll Music* for Peter, Paul & Mary. There was also Oz Bach who was a bass-player with Spanky And Our Gang (*Sunday Will Never Be The Same*) and Steve Knight who played with Mountain. (Leslie West was the guitar-player and *Mississippi Queen* was one of many well known songs from Mountain). I am forgetting another kid. Jack McNichol was his name. I can't leave out Pam Robins."

Craig: "She was part of the 1960's folk band Serendipity Singers (Often compared to the New Christy Minstrels. A mixture of folk, pop, and a good time sound gave them a nice following in the 1960's). What happened with the project?"

Jerry Peloquin: The bass-player Oz was an insane human being. One day he went insane. When he freaked out so did the record company. Then the wheels came off the band."

Craig: "Who holds the rights to the material? It would be good to have the music available today."

Jerry Peloquin: "I am not sure about the rights. I do have a copy of the music from Oz's widow. My son is a drummer and loves the music. I have been thinking about a way to put it out. It may be public domain at this point."

Craig: "Please see about getting released and I can write the liner notes."

Jerry Peloquin: "Sure."

Craig: "We know at this point you had a short stay with Nina Simone. What other tales of the road do you have for us?"

Jerry Peloquin: "I worked with Tim Buckley, and then Chad Mitchell, and then Wings. It gets a bit confusing. I think that was the order. After that I played with the New York Electric String Ensemble. Then it must have been Jose Feliciano and finally Paul Winter Consort. There was a brief stint with Paul Simon's brother Eddie Simon."

Craig: "Where did you perform with Eddie Simon?"

Jerry Peloquin: "We played a couple of nights in Queens, New York City. It didn't work out. He also was in Wings for a bit and got replaced by Jim Mason."

Craig: "How long did you play with Tim Buckley?"

Jerry Peloquin: "I played either three or four months. With Chad Mitchell I played about one year. I also did stand-in. If a drummer were sick, I filled in."

Craig: "Did playing with Tim and Paul Winter give you a feeling of artistic freedom because of the diversity and complexity of the music?"

Jerry Peloquin: "Certainly Paul Winter was the most interesting. He had Brazilian drums, and interesting percussion stuff. I always liked hand drums. It gave me a chance to play the congas. Now it seems everyone is playing them."

Craig: "When you played with Tim Buckley was it during a time when his head was in the right place?"

Jerry Peloquin: "Yes it was. His head was in a good place and he was playing in a time when you could do a fifteen minute solo. He was willing to take chances musically."

Craig: "Did you take full advantage of the improvisational sounds of Tim Buckley."

Jerry Peloquin: "I wasn't that type of drummer. If you listen especially to Wings, I was very clean and very good at keeping time. Being flashy wasn't my style. I looked at a percussionist as giving a platform so other people can work. The drum should provide a foundation. I always believed that. It was a lot of fun and I got a chance to play different instruments. With Paul Winter he liked anything different."

Craig: "When you reflect on the sixties do you feel that there were those musicians that weren't true to what they wrote or sung about?"

Jerry Peloquin: "There are those where it was a charade. It was about money and always will be about money. The story of helping our fellow man wasn't always followed. I didn't see a lot of that. There were people that followed the right way and others that were following a human trait of greed."

Craig: "Was there a roundabout connection with you and somebody that played with Janis Joplin?"

Jerry Peloquin: "I worked with Peter Albin, (Bass-player) who was with Janis Joplin during the Big Brother & The Holding Company days. He had a brother Rodney. Rodney was a terrific banjo-player. I played with Rodney. Before known as Big Brother they had a real cool name, the San Andreas Fault Line."

Craig: "That could be one of the best 1960's names ever."

Jerry Peloquin: "It was a cool name."

Craig: "What year did you make the change and cut back on the live performances and go back to school. Did that also mean less session work?"

Jerry Peloquin: "I was more of a live performer. I did have one opportunity for session work. When we were working on the Wings album I met session drummer Hal Blaine. (He has played on 150 songs that made the Top 40). He tells me chuck the band and work with him. I got all the work I can handle. I made over six figures last year. You know what I said?"

Craig: "How soon is the next flight?"

Jerry Peloquin: "I told him no. I am going to stick with the band because we will make it. (There is a lot of laughter from Jerry). That was a masterful demonstration of snatching defeat from the jaws of victory."

Craig: "Although now you can look back and think the decision wasn't the best, doesn't honesty and loyalty count for something?"

Jerry Peloquin: "I can't say that I hadn't looked for a dollar. Many are called and few are chosen."

Craig: "You have an impressive educational background."

Jerry Peloquin: "I have an under-graduate in engineering and a master's degree in structural design. Currently I do organizational and industrial psychology. I had trained for this for a number of years. I was in Chicago with Chad Mitchell and I was playing at a club. I checked out a great local blues band. I can't remember the name now. I went up to the guys in the band and we started to talk. I found out during the day one of the musicians was driving a folk-lift. It hit me like a ton of bricks. This could be me twenty years down the road. I quit music. Hung it up. Went to the University Of Chicago and got the degree."

Craig: "Bob Harvey who you played with in the early Airplane days tells a great story of having a reunion with you on stage in 2002. Can you tell us your remembrances of the one night show in Maryland?"

Jerry Peloquin: "It was kind of strange. First Bob tells me that he would be in Hagerstown, Maryland, and would you like to have a drink. Then he asked if I still had my drum set. I told him no, but my son plays and has a kit. He tells me to bring my son. I am coming across Route 70 to meet him and my cell phone rings. Some radio jock from a Hagerstown station is on the line. He tells me that Bob Harvey is in his office and we end up having a phone interview. We get to the club the Washington Spy. I tell Bob that I haven't played in twenty years. The old story is if you don't play in one day you know it, two days your friends know it, and three days everyone knows it. I told Bob I have no chops left. I thought if I used brushes nobody would know the difference. The next day we played and the place was packed. We played three sets. When I was done I could not move."

Craig; "Bob Harvey told me the worst thing. The show got taped but not one minute came out. It would have been such a great night to release for all to hear. There were even the two Airplane era songs in the set *Let's Get Together* (A big hit for the Youngbloods, written by Quicksilver Messenger Service member Dino Valente) and *In The Midnight Hour*."

Jerry Peloquin: "I was looking forward to a copy of the show. It would have been great to have captured the moment."

**Photo by kind permission of Bob Harvey. From the Bob Harvey collection.**

**Photo may not be reproduced without the written consent of Bob Harvey. Photographer unknown.**

**Jerry Peloquin during the reunion with Bob Harvey at the Washington Spy, Hagerstown, Maryland**

**2/16/02. For a larger photo of Jerry as well as more photos and the flyer of the show please see the**

**Bob Harvey interview.**

Craig: "Did you keep any of the Airplane rehearsals or shows from the 1965 era?"

Jerry Peloquin: "Recording equipment was expensive back then. I don't have anything. I have pictures. In fact one is the night before the opening of The Matrix."

Craig: "You have been so kind talking with me today. Thank you. Is there any project of yours you would like to plug?"

Jerry Peloquin: "Grameen Foundation, at www.gfusa.org. The site talks about micro-finance and micro-enterprise. The readers can learn about helping to stop global poverty."

Craig: "Thank you for the great historical view on things. It was very nice speaking with you."

Jerry Peloquin: "You are very welcome. Any further information you need, please let me know."

## Sammy Piazza- Hot Tuna.

Craig: "It is a pleasure to be able to discuss the wonderful contributions you've given to the music industry."

Sammy Piazza: "Thank you for the comment."

Craig: "There have been rumors over the years on the 1969 Quicksilver Messenger Service album *Shady Grove*, you had done some uncredited work. Is this a rock and roll fable?"

Sammy Piazza: "No, I didn't have anything to do with the record. I came out to California in July, or August of 1969. In 1968, and 1969 I was working in Texas with Jimmy Vaughan (Guitar-player known for his work with the Fabulous Thunderbirds. Jimmy is the older brother of Stevie Ray Vaughan). We had a band called Texas. Doyle Bramhall Sr. was in our band. He wrote a bunch of songs for Stevie Ray. Originally we were called the Chessmen. We had been playing in Texas for a couple of years. We came out to California to get out of Texas. The band disbanded in California, but that was what brought me there originally. Jimmy Vaughan, and I went back to Texas. Before he started to play again he went on to a regular job. I started to play with a trumpet-player named Phil Driscoll. We played hotels, and did songs like *Walk On By* (Big hit for Dionne Warwick), and *MacArthur Park* (Richard Harris had a major hit with the song). I got sick of that by August 1970. I moved out to California and started to *jam* with a band called Dry Creek Road. There was a concert with Pink Floyd and Leon Russell. Dry Creek Road was one of the opening bands. Jorma, Jack, and Will Scarlett came down to fill in the blank space between Leon Russell and Pink Floyd. At that point they didn't have a drummer. They had played The Forum the night before. (Please note the only verified performance by the J.A. at The Forum, Inglewood, California was on 10/31/69. Sammy has a terrific recollection of his musical history). That is how I met Jorma and Jack. Three days later, and I think it was a Wednesday, Jorma calls me. They were going to New York to start a three week tour. Jorma wanted to know if I would be interesting in playing the shows starting <u>around</u> 11/7/69. Jorma wanted me to go by the Airplane House and ask Jacky Watts (Former wife of Peter Kaukonen and an office manager for Hot Tuna) for some bread. There would be a ticket waiting for me. I met them in New York. We rehearsed in a hotel room and that was about it."

Craig: "The rumors all these years were way off about Quicksilver."

Sammy Piazza: "To show you how way off, I first met the guys from Quicksilver at the time of the reunion record *Solid Silver* (1975). A friend of mine Skip Olson was playing bass. He is no longer living. That is really the way I met Gary Duncan. When I was in Hot Tuna we didn't hang out with Quicksilver. Most of the hanging was with the Grateful Dead and the New Riders Of the Purple Sage. There were different musical camps."

Craig: "It is amazing how history gets turned around. Most documentation has your first gig with Hot Tuna on 1/10/71 at the Fillmore West, San Francisco. You were playing shows two months earlier."

Sammy Piazza: "I remember Grace Slick being pregnant. I remember there would be bands like the New Riders, and Brethren (Rusty Young was in the band. His credits include Buffalo Springfield and Poco). What would happen is between the New Riders set, and the Airplane, Hot Tuna would perform. At that point we had a harmonica-player, Will Scarlett. We may play forty five minutes before the Airplane. In November it was Thanksgiving week. I started to play at the Fillmore East, New York City in late November 1970. When the New Riders were done we would go out and play. There were really five of us. I can't forget Papa John. Bill Graham was there. What was funny is Bill, and I were born on the same day. January the 8th. Elvis Presley was born the same day. David Bowie too! Bill was helping me set up my drums. We get to talking. He asked when I was born. I told him in 1945, he told me he was born in 1938. When Bill heard Hot Tuna in November, he decided this would turn out to be something. One of the shows from New York I kept the program that had Brethren, Taj Mahal (Well respected blues, and jazz musician), and Hot Tuna. Taj Mahal had three people in his band play tuba. Hot Tuna played many of the colleges. We were all over the place. That is when it started as Hot Tuna the band as a headliner."

Craig: "Did Jorma and Jack tell you why they didn't use Joey Covington on all the shows? (In 1969, and some of 1970 Joey would be part of the Hot Tuna line-up, and sometimes Marty Balin as well)."

Sammy Piazza: "It was a political thing. This isn't taking away anything from Joey's drumming, but there were political issues behind the scenes. Marty had done shows, the guys went to Jamaica. That turned out to be a big bad trip. I was kind of the new guy. I came out to California and was playing the drums since I was fourteen. I knew what I was doing. I had been playing fifteen years professionally. That's why we sounded so good. In the hotel room rehearsal I had a pair of brushes and a record album. The band was able to play in the hotel room. Jack had an acoustic bass. This was reasonably close to what would be electrified on stage. We went over the endings and some of the songs. Joey was into singing. He wanted to sing as well as play. There was a big split in the Airplane that was already starting, but I didn't know about this. I didn't care to know about this. The guys liked that I was an exceptionally good musician. Joey was a good musician too. I fit in better, because I wasn't part of the friction that was going on. This could be money, musical selections, even how they acted on stage. They wanted to break away and play the electric blues, with some country. Here's a good story Craig. The Airplane played a gig in Wilkes-Barre, Pennsylvania. It was at the Armory. It was funny because I went back there twice with other groups. At that point Jack bought a stereo for his mom, as a gift. Jack's mom is in the Washington D.C. area. This was on a Saturday night. He wanted to know if I wanted to drive with him to give the stereo to his mom. We drove to D.C. When we got there it was early in the morning. Before we got to the apartment his mom lived, Jack took me to the house he grew up in. He drove me to the gas station where Jorma worked the graveyard shift. Jorma would bring his guitar to work. Jorma would sit there and play. At that time it wasn't self-service. (Sammy does a great impression of Jack Casady). I got a tour of Washington, D.C. It was great to see where Jorma and Jack grew up. Then we went over to meet Jack's mom."

Craig: "Jack talked about his mom being his best friend, at the Rock And Roll Hall Of Fame inductions on 1/17/96."

Sammy Piazza: "She was a great lady. We then drove to New York. We got there about 8:30 on Sunday night. It was like he took me home to meet mom. It was good. We got to know each other. What was funny was we stopped in some little gas station off the interstate. We wanted a cold drink. This big guy with a beard comes up to the car. Jack had gotten out getting the drinks. The guy asked me if that was Jack Casady that got out of the car? I told him it was. He runs up to Jack and hands him some hash in tinfoil. Jack dressed the same on and off stage. The headband, glasses, boots, and jeans. Jack gets back to the car and laughs. He tells me "You have to be careful with what these people give you." Nobody recognized me."

Craig: "You had a nice opportunity to play on a couple of Papa John Creach albums, the self-titled and *Filthy*. What are your memories, of Papa John?"

Sammy Piazza: "Let me back up for one moment. I am going to tell you something that nobody else has published, or printed ever."

Craig: "Can I now start to sign autographs?"

Sammy Piazza: (Sammy laughs). "The Jefferson Airplane *Bark* album has a song *Feel So Good*. We would often close the Hot Tuna shows with the song, before the encore. What happened was they were recording that album in the studio. The studio was Wally Heider Studios in San Francisco. Hot Tuna was doing some recording. I was going down there every night. I was in and out. Joey Covington had his drums set up. That was downstairs in Studio A. Upstairs was Studio C. It isn't a big building. There were two studios upstairs. One was Studio B and the other Studio C. Bill Kreutzmann the drummer for the Grateful Dead and I were really good friends. At the time the other Grateful Dead drummer Mickey Hart had left the band. Kreutzmann had his drums upstairs. I went to talk with him. We got along well, because he was a good drummer, and a nice guy.

We would talk drums. He was a regular guy. It is about midnight. Joey Covington had left. The Airplane had finished up with whatever they needed to do. Grace was there and wanted to play piano. Jorma and Jack were there as well. Jorma wants to do *Feel So Good*. Michael Shrieve (Santana) happened to be there. We became fast friends after he came off the road with Santana. Michael had listened to the first Hot Tuna record (Self-titled from May of 1970) and didn't know I was in the band. The first Tuna record did not have drums. Michael was in the studio because Santana was going to start recorded an album. Everyone is mulling around. Jorma again suggests *Feel So Good*. I get them to bring the drums down. Joey's were set up and already had microphones. Kreutzmann's drums were brought down. He had a regular set. We didn't get any credit for this. Listen to the song. You'll hear two drums. That is Shrieve and I playing the parts. Shrieve is the prominent sound. You'll hear me mixed in. You are the first person that I am telling this."

Craig: "That is tremendous. Thank you. Did you both do the parts in one take?"

Sammy Piazza: "One take. One take only. Shrieve and I are on the same level musically. We both had a jazz background. We both had a conventional grip, not like Ringo Starr. Pull out the album and you'll hear the two drummers. When I heard how into the music you are, I wanted you to get the story. I knew you would be interesting in something like that. Shrieve would call me up and I would hang out at some of the Santana sessions. It was fun. Neil Schon (Journey) was in the band. Those were the innocent days. That was before music became a corporate conglomerate. Jorma, Jack, and I, would hang out all the time. The way it ended was sad. Jorma called me five years ago and told me he was sorry for what he did. It was all about the money and the advances paid by the record company. When they decided to go back on the road they hired Bob Steeler for much less money."

Craig: "We'll get into the parting of the ways in a bit."

Sammy Piazza: "Jorma and Jack talked about the good old days. When they played The Matrix, San Francisco they would get just enough money to have a steak. They were living hand to mouth, before it happened big for them."

Craig: "It was reinforced while I was writing the book, that there were truly those that would have played for nothing. It was about helping to change the world and loving your neighbor. There was also the segment that didn't believe that for one second. It was always about the dollar."

Sammy Piazza: "It all became about money when the record companies had to put out so much and there was pressure on the artist to make it a profitable venture. Jack wanted me to play in the Airplane. One day I'm with Bill Thompson, Jorma, and Jack on a plane. Jack wanted to know if I would like to play in the Airplane. I said sure. Jorma, Jack, and Thompson on sitting on the three front seats of the plane. I am in the back. They are talking about me. Jack tells them he wants me to start playing in the Airplane. Jack was sick of the personalities clashing. Jorma was adamant that it not happen. I'm thinking sh_t, I could have dug that. Jorma kept saying no. He didn't want me to get involved with the things they were dealing with. They were going to make a break. Jorma didn't want me to be part of what they were going to get away from. They knew I was real. They were down home guys, and I was too. We got along on those terms. It wasn't that I was so special, but we got along, and played well together. Jorma didn't want me to be part of all the factions. When we first started to play Jack tells me "Let Jorma and me play the hot licks." I played what I felt. It sunk in with Jack that was the way it should be, we didn't overshadow each other. You had asked me about Papa John. The wife that I have now has been with me over thirty years. We would all hang out together. We were all friends. He got a chance to do his own record. On the first one I got to play brushes. I played on *Somewhere Over The Rainbow*. Papa John would tell us the songs and we'd play. It was great. Do you know how the Airplane song *Wild Turkey* got the name? Every once in awhile Jorma would buy a bottle of Wild Turkey. We wouldn't drink much of it. Jack liked to buy Blue Nun. We never got completely nuts, because you couldn't play. People would throw things on stage. All we wanted were towels and ice water. Jorma warned me whatever is thrown on stage look the other way. You never know what it is. That happened all the time, especially on the east coast."

Craig: "Do you recall if you played on any of the sessions from March of 1972, through May of 1972 at Wally Heider Studios? Those included *Eat Starch Mom* as an instrumental, the never released Paul Kantner song *Revolutionary Upstairs Maid*, and *Trial By Fire* with Jerry Garcia on pedal steel guitar."

Sammy Piazza: "By the way I have ninety percent of all the live shows I ever played with Hot Tuna on tape."

Craig: "I'll be over for dinner."

Sammy Piazza: "I don't recall playing on those sessions. I can tell you that *Trail By Fire* got written after I gave Jorma a Christmas present. We used to give each other crazy presents. One year I gave him a ten gage Magnum shotgun. They were legal then. After that he wrote *Trial By Fire*. I never heard in the studio the sessions with Jerry Garcia. We did play it on stage. There is a line in the song "With a ten gage shotgun at my head." With *Eat Starch Mom*, Jorma would come up with different riffs. On the Hot Tuna album *The Phosphorescent Rat*, the song *Easy Now*, Jorma used to play that to warm up. I said that was a fun song to play. We recorded it. Jack was going to write some words to it. Jack never wanted to be a songwriter. The money is there. Back then it didn't matter. In 1973 Jack came to the studio one night with a digital watch. You pushed a button and it gave the time digitally in red numbers. He paid nine hundred dollars for it. That is way before you could get it for twenty dollars. *Revolutionary Upstairs Maid*, I was not part of any sessions, or rehearsals. That was the whole deal. They kept me away from the friction. Jack wanted me in. They got John Barbata through David Crosby. I wasn't there, but Jorma told me the next day. They had a big Airplane meeting. Sometime before *The Phosphorescent Rat*. Jack never gets upset. Certainly not outwardly. In the meeting he told Paul he didn't want to play with him again. The dividing camps were feuding. Jorma didn't want me to have to take sides. If I had come in to the Airplane It would look like I'm against Paul. We didn't hang out, but I always got along with Paul, and Grace. When Joey Covington left, Barbata came in. Paul got him from David Crosby. John Barbata is a damn good drummer. He tuned his drums real well. He was used to playing in the studio. We used to make the studio work around a Hot Tuna record. I'm a producer. There is a basic way to do things, even with the digital way of doing recording. Now I produce a country band. They are going to be real good. I believe *Surrealistic Pillow* was cut in eleven days. If somebody knows what they are doing, you can get the best out of everyone. If you start producing yourself, or use people that are more known for a live gig, you don't get good results. I would have liked the drums a bit louder on the Tuna records."

Craig: "How was it doing the studio records with Tuna?"

Sammy Piazza: "We structured things enough in the studio to know we were making a record. We worked for tempos, but it had the live feel."

HOT TUNA    L-R   JACK CASADY, PAPA JOHN CREACH, JORMA KAUKONEN & SAMMY PIAZZA

**Photograph by kind permission of Mike Somavilla. From the Mike Somavilla collection.**

**Photograph not to be reproduced without the written consent of Mike Somavilla.**

**Photographer unknown.**

**Thank you BMG.**

**This is a promo photo for the *Burgers* album circa 1972.**

Craig: "Did anything get left off the *Burgers* album that you recorded?"

Sammy Piazza: "Everything that we worked on got put on the LP. *Sunny Day Strut* did come later, near the end of the sessions. Here is a good one. We were always renting things from Studio Instrument Rentals (S.I.R.). They were on call twenty-four hours a day. If you listen to the song, I'm overdubbing kettle drums. That is highly unusual. Not common for Hot Tuna. That was Jack's idea. I overdubbed some high-hat drums on *Been So Long*. The single version of that tune has the high-hat and we overdubbed some percussion. It didn't get out there that much, but it has more on it."

Craig: "There is a song on *Burgers*, called *Highway Song*. I have heard over 300 Tuna shows, and never one live version. Did you ever play the song in front of an audience?"

Sammy Piazza: "I got tapes of that. Jorma did a duet in the studio with David Crosby. I can remember it as being the third or forth song of the set on some nights. The reason I remember playing it live is one day we did a show and I had talked with Jorma about a more up-tempo version. He had told me that he didn't think he could pick it that fast. We were in the Aragon Ballroom, Chicago, with John Hammond Jr. (Blues musician with a devote following in the 1960's), Howlin' Wolf (Legendary blues musician, most noted in the 1950's, and 1960's), and Papa John's dad. I remember that because of the people around us."

Craig: "What are your memories from recording *The Phosphorescent Rat*?"

Sammy Piazza: "I think of *Corners Without Exits*. Here is the deal. When we decided to make the record I mentioned that I have more energy in the afternoon, than at night. We weren't busy, or sleeping every afternoon. Jorma and Jack always wanted to do it at night. We split it, two afternoons, and two nights. The engineer Mallory Earl was great. He had an arranger Tom Salisbury, he was real good too. He was a real arranger. Educated in Milan. He was a hot shot arranger. That is where the string parts came from. Jorma wanted production on it. It was diverse. *Easy Now* came as a warm up song for us live and we decided to put it on a studio record."

Craig: "Any material left off *Phosphorescent Rat*?"

Sammy Piazza: "Yes, I got one. I can't think of the title. The first song we did Papa John was on it. It may have been a Reverend Gary Davis song. Papa John is on the tune. They fired him after that got recorded. They got Papa John out of the band because Jorma's first wife Margareta wanted him out. She felt that he was getting more applause. It was a bunch of you know what. There is no reason for it."

Craig: "Did Jorma ever consider friendship and telling his wife this is not the best idea I've heard?"

Sammy Piazza: "Jorma had an expression, "A man has got to do what a man has got to do." He had no choice."

Craig: 'Do you recall the last show you played with Hot Tuna? The documented date 11/18/73 at the Orpheum Theatre, Boston, doesn't seem right."

Sammy Piazza: "It may have been a benefit at a bowling alley. Maybe it was a giant room for a party. No, that is not correct. Wait a moment. The last one I played was in Stanford, California. Albert King (Legendary blues musician) opened the show, he had four horn players, and a one armed trumpet-player. That was when I told the guys we'll see each other on Monday for the band meeting. This was December of 1973. The show was on a Friday, or Saturday night. I came to the office at 2PM for the meeting. We were going to have gigs booked in Paris and all over Europe. Jorma's dad was a diplomat for the government. He had secured some kind of pass to play in Czechoslovakia. We had a big three week tour planned. It was going to start the end of January 1974. We were going to London and Paris. Jorma and Jack had gotten into speed skating. They were going to go to Europe two and a half weeks before me. I didn't want to speed skate, because you can break your leg and play guitar. Can't do that with the drums. I got to the office and Jacky Watts is there with an assistant. Bill

Thompson is on the phone with the door closed. He opens the door and tells me to come in. He gives me a check for an advance on *The Phosphorescent Rat* album for $13,000. He gave me another check for a tour we had just done. I should have known something was up. On the last part of the tour we were eating at separate tables. Bill tells me that Jorma is leaving tomorrow and is going to Europe. The tour is off and the band is broken up. Later I found out that RCA Records had hired a guy from Buenos Aires, Argentina. He was instructed to look over the books. He looks over the books and sees the Jefferson Airplane was advanced almost two million dollars and owe two albums. Then he sees that Hot Tuna is part of the Airplane group, as are Marty, Paul, and Grace. The guy wanted everything stopped. He wanted everything stopped except for the Airplane members to cut two albums, to get the money back for the record company. They didn't want to get rid of me musically. Now it was becoming a separate thing. I was going to Church. I never told them to go. I was playing at an Afro-American Church in Oakland, California. I had heard some fabulous singing. I went over there and got a Sunday gig. They broadcasted it on the radio. I liked it. Hey, I'm a Christian. It was cool and I played with a big Church. Between the record company wanting two albums from the Airplane members, and Jorma, and Jack unsure about me going to Church, a change was decided. Let's call it like it is. I'm sixty-one man. I got plenty of money, but I never saw exactly what the contracts were. I know they got more. They are Hot Tuna. About five years ago Jorma told me he was sorry and didn't have beliefs then. He mentioned that he was another person. Now things are different. What happened was I wrote him and chewed him out. We were having some email conversation. It got a lot off my chest. That may not have been the right thing, but I did it. Jorma did tell me now he does have spiritual beliefs. That's why when they reformed in 1983 I was never asked to come back. I was playing in Stoneground (Rock and blues band that had Pete Sears at one time)."

Craig: "From the day you parted with Hot Tuna , prior to the conversation with Jorma five years ago, had you had communication with Jorma and Jack?"

Sammy Piazza: "I ran into Jack when he was working on the KBC record. Gary Duncan (Quicksilver Messenger Service), and I were working on *Piece By Piece*. Here's how that came about. Gary and I were dock workers. When I got out of Stoneground, Gary called me up and said "If you need some bread my wife's aunt owns a freight service. It's hard work, but I can get you into the union. It will be you, and me, and three other guys." At that point he wasn't doing anything. I got hurt there. I slipped a disc and needed an operation. I told Gary that we should get some money for a musical project and I had a good engineer. His name was Bob Olhsson, who did the Marvin Gaye, *What's Going On* album. He was great. He worked for Motown and knew what he was doing. Bob picks the equipment, and we leased it, and built a studio. I produced the entire thing. I arranged the entire thing, listened to everything that went on there, and Gary wrote the majority of the songs. We couldn't do it without each other. I mean Gary, Bob, and I. We were fortunate, and blessed to have Bob. We had W. Michael Lewis, the guy that wrote the original theme to the TV show Cops, play the piano parts. Most of the stuff was live. We spliced a couple of things. Now my forte is production. I went to Fantasy Studios to make some safety copies of the album. I saw Jack there. We had always gotten along. I saw Jorma at The Stone in San Francisco. This was 1986. He played acoustically that night. We talked for a bit. I didn't vent on him until 1998. We talked about light stuff in 1986."

Craig: "Are you surprised that Jorma hadn't asked you to sit in on a song or two after you left Hot Tuna?"

Sammy Piazza: "You just hit a nerve. The only thing that really pissed me off was when Hot Tuna was playing the Fillmore, San Francisco, I got tickets. I asked for Sammy, plus six. We go backstage and Harvey Sorgen was the drummer. He was a nice guy. When they played their set, I never got asked to sit in. This was 6/15/97. It pissed me off. It was before the summer Further Festival tour. Pete Sears was there. I know him real well. He's a great guy. I don't know Michael Falzarano that well. I kept waiting for Jorma to bring me up. It never happened. It wasn't that big of a gig. That flew in my face. I don't hold anything against them. I wanted a chance to play. I told Jorma are you afraid of the past being brought up? That's the way I took it. I forgive, but that doesn't mean I have to like it. They could have negotiated with me about the money, before things came to a head. The three of us Jorma, Jack, and I can play. I was offered the drumming job to be in ZZ Top, before I came to California. I wanted to get out of Texas. When Billy Gibbons had a band the Moving Sidewalks

(Popular in Texas. Jimi Hendrix liked them) in 1968, we knew each other. The Chessmen played with Jimi Hendrix, when I was in the band. Jimmy Vaughan and Jimi Hendrix traded wa-wa peddles. I knew Stevie Ray Vaughan when he was twelve. The people thought Jorma, Jack, and I were an electric trio. We were a jazz-band, in the sense that Jack plays jazz. He has the feel. I used to be over Jorma's house everyday. We got along great. It was a fun thing. I lost a good friend. It hurt, not knowing why. One of Jack Casady's best friends is Mitch Mitchell (Played with Jimi Hendrix). Mitch and I became fast friends. We play very similar styles."

Craig: "What drummers do you enjoy listening to?"

Sammy Piazza: "I like Mitch Mitchell, Michael Shrieve, Joe Morello (Jazz musician that played with but not limited to Stan Kenton's Orchestra, and the Dave Brubeck Quartet), Gene Krupa (One of the most famous jazz drummers ever), Art Blakely (Jazz Messengers), and Ginger Baker (Cream). I saw Cream in Dallas in 1968. When he played the solo on *Toad*, it wiped everyone out. Those were the guys that I listened to over and over."

Craig: "I wish your schedule allowed us to talk for days. It would have been nice to talk about some of the other musical projects you have been a part of, and the record company, and studio you are involved with. Gaff Music has some quality artists, such as Henry Kaiser (Well known Bay Area guitar-player), Ian McLagen (Small Faces), and Tom Constanten from the Grateful Dead. The readers can go to http://www.gaffmusic.com/, and check out the interesting core of musicians on the label. You also own a large company Alpha Omega, which specializes in pre-employment screening. The website can be seen at http://www.sammypiazza.com/. Thank you so much for the insights into the Hot Tuna situation of 1974 and the good times as well. I hope things will always be excellent for you."

Sammy Piazza: "Thank you very much. If you need some pictures for the book let me know. May you have good luck with the book."

# Pete Sears- Jefferson Starship and Hot Tuna.

PETE SEARS

**Photograph by kind permission of Mike Somavilla.
From the Mike Somavilla collection. Photograph not to be used without the
written consent of Mike Somavilla. Photographer unknown. A promotional photo. Year unknown.**

**Photograph by kind permission of
Don Aters. From the Don Aters collection. Photo may not be reproduced without the written consent of
Don Aters. Don Aters photographer. Year of photo unknown.**

Craig: "Thank you for the opportunity to speak with you today."

Pete Sears: "You're welcome Craig. I look forward to the conversation."

Craig: "Since we have a wealth of material to talk about, why not start at the beginning and work our way to the present."

Pete Sears: "I'll remember what I can."

(Pete laughs for a few seconds).

Craig: "One of the earliest bands you were involved with was called Sons Of Fred and you played bass. What are your recollections of the group?"

Pete Sears: "We started out as a semi-professional band. I was in a school band playing guitar. Sons Of Fred needed a bass-player. The members asked if I were interested in playing bass. The bass-player was about to leave."

Craig: "Didn't the group have the terrific experience of recording in Abbey Road Studios (E.M.I. at the time)?"

Pete Sears: "We got a backer for the band. They bought equipment for us. Before you knew it, we were a full-time professional band. We were able to tour all around the U.K. We actually played between six and seven nights a week. The travel conditions were a bit rough. We used to sleep in the back of an old van. The van would break down all the time. We often got to the gig at the last possible moment. We had to set up in the dark many times. Although we had a backer, the funds were not exactly plentiful. It was great experience. We toured, we learned, and we had fun. We released five singles that were done at E.M.I. Studios. There was a marvelous U.K. TV program called Ready Steady Go Live. The band performed on the show. Another TV show that we appeared on was Thank Your Lucky Stars. The band played a lot of rhythm and blues music live. The singles were original. One of the rhythm and blues tunes the band did was a version of *Walking The Dog* (Written by Rufus Thomas. Two very well known versions were by the Rolling Stones and Aerosmith). As often happens in the music business, the band eventually fizzled out. To answer your question about Abbey Road, it had to be late 1964 or maybe very early 1965. It was obviously still E.M.I. The experience was great. I was young and able to record in a studio that the Beatles had."

Craig: "Did you ever get introduced to George Martin (Engineer for the Beatles)?"

Pete Sears: "Off hand no. It was fascinating to have been in the same place the Beatles had recorded *Please Please Me*."

Craig: "Did you keep the music for your own personal archives?"

Pete Sears: "There is an interesting story about that. A few years ago my wife's niece is visiting with her boyfriend. He was twenty-one at the time. He was asking me about the bands I played with in England. He actually heard of the Sons Of Fred. Not only that but he owned all the singles and I didn't have copies of them! He sent me a copy of the singles on tape. I put them on a CD for my collection. I wanted to track down the other members to make sure they get copies. We weren't bad. We always played in tune."

Craig: "Normally if somebody is under the age of thirty, they wouldn't listen to anything older then yesterday. Maybe there is hope yet to preserve 1960's music."

Pete Sears: "It was very cool."

Craig: "The next stop on the Pete Sears train was the Fleur de Lys. What are your memories from that period?"

476

Pete Sears: "To be honest, I don't remember how I met those guys. They needed a keyboard-player. I played the piano. I was never heard. The equipment was very antiquated. I couldn't even hear myself. Even the purchase of an electric piano didn't help. The last gig we did, the piano fell off the stage and on the floor!"

Craig: "There were great moments. Didn't Jimi Hendrix play on a session with the band?"

Pete Sears: "That is true. Let me tell you how that happened. Phil Sawyer was our singer at the time. The guy was a terrific talent. He even had a stint in the Spencer Davis Group. We were over at Eric Burdon's (The Animals) house. Chas Chandler (The Animals) was there too. We are hanging out and Chas walks in the living room with a guy that seems to be very nice. It turns out that was Jimi Hendrix. Some time passed, and we were recording a song called *Amen*, and after it is finished Jimi Hendrix came in and did an over-dub. This is all going down late 1965 or early 1966."

Craig: "Was Gordon Haskell, later to be in King Crimson part of the group?"

Pete Sears: "Yes he was. In fact he was there after I left. He is a great friend and Gordon still tours Europe playing guitar. Some rock and roll book mentions I have a copy of *Amen*. That isn't true. If anybody out there does please get in touch with me."

Craig: "There have been stories that Jimmy Page not only produced some of the recordings from Fleur de Lys, but played guitar on at least one tune. From your recollections of the sessions is that true?"

Pete Sears: "Jimmy Page did produce some of the sessions. I don't recall him playing any guitar. I had heard those tales as well over the years. Even after I left, if something like that transpired I would have known."

Craig: "The band had two songs that have been talked about for years. The cover of the Who's song *Circles* and a track titled *Mud In Your Eye*. Why didn't the record company release the songs the second Jimmy Page gained fame?"

Pete Sears^: "You would have thought that would have happened. It is possible they are sitting in some studio to this day or lost! I don't even know how to track that stuff down. It is a pity. It must be since 1966 hearing an acetate, (A single of the recording was pressed at the time for the band members to listen to. In those days not many people had reel to reel decks and or cassette players) that I even have listened to the song. The lost Fleur de Lys acetate I refer to was of the song "*Amen*" that Jimi Hendrix overdubbed on. I am fairly certain I had already left Fleur de Lys and joined Sam Gopal Dream by the time Jimmy Page showed up as producer. I once played bass on a Roy Harper (English singer-songwriter, guitarist, and close friend to Jimmy Page) album recorded at Abbey Road and Jimmy Page is featured on another track - that has been my only connection with Jimmy through the years. Playing on the same album, but not together. Fleur de Lys was a good band. It was a fun time, but the chapter came to an end. We had a memorable show in London. The band was opening for rhythm and blues artist Eddie Floyd (*Knock On Wood*) and we were sitting in the dressing room and Brian Epstein (The manager of the Beatles) walks in. He wished us luck on the performance. What a nice guy. It was tragic his life ended so early."

Craig: "There was another memorable moment when the band went to see Pink Floyd and you were impressed."

Pete Sears^: "It has to be some point in 1967. The band is in what would be referred to mod clothing. Seeing them on stage had a profound affect on me. I couldn't speak for the other band members. There was something about how free, cool, and wonderful they were. Right after that Mick Hutchinson formerly of the Sons Of Fred, calls me up. He was playing with Sam Gopal. They were surrounded by strange people, poets, and those looking for greater musical improvisation. I went to meet Mick and it clicked. There wasn't any vocalist. The Electric Garden Club later became the Middle Earth Club, was a venue that we would play and sleep there after. We didn't have a real place to stay. We called the band Sam Gopal's Dream. We played strictly Indian style ragas (Defined as color or moods), with Sam on tabla, Mick Hutchinson playing ragas on guitar, and me playing bass and B3. However, as you say, I was impressed with Pink Floyd when I first heard them at the Marquee Club in London. It was a fresh, experimental approach to music, and Sam Gopal Dream certainly captured some of the essence and spirit of the times, personified by Pink Floyd. The record company Virgin wanted to sign us, if we would add a vocalist to the line-up. We did a show filmed by the B.B.C. that had Traffic and Pink Floyd on the bill. I would love to find the footage."

Craig: "Didn't a second Jimi Hendrix moment occur after that?"

Pete Sears: "We were at the Speakeasy in London. I am playing with my head down and I look up because there is another guitar-player on stage. Jimi plugged in and played several songs with us."

Craig: "Please tell me somebody recorded that and it is sitting in your living room."

Pete Sears: "There was a guy at the bar. He had a reel to reel machine. It was recorded. Once again a piece of history has been lost. Nobody remembers what happened to the tape."

Craig: "This is brutal. All the great people I get to speak with and they tell me about some of the most amazing moments that aren't preserved for all to experience."

Pete Sears: "You are right. It is brutal. It is horrible. That was that! It was fun having played with Jimi again. Jimi told me a great story about not wanting to play the hits. He wanted to play the blues."

Craig: "When you turned down the opportunity to hire a vocalist and record Sam Gopal's Dream, did the United Kingdom have independent labels?"

Pete Sears: "I don't recall at that time the independent labels being around. Our problem was there were many experimental bands that had some sort of vocals."

Craig: "Did you consider a compromise, hire a singer that would add some flavor to the extended *jams*?"

Pete Sears: "We did think about it. We should have done it. Mick kept asking me to give the vocals ago. I wasn't a singer. I would love to hear the music now. There was one gig that we performed after not sleeping for almost a week (Or at least it felt that way). Mick is yelling about political situations into the microphone. It was an early version of punk rock. We finish the gig and it wasn't the serious playing we normally did. About five in the morning the manager tells us that there was a buzz going around about the band. There were several major labels that watched us play. We are thinking of all nights. It couldn't have been that bad, or Jimi would not have gotten up to play with us."

Craig: "If only every moment in time could be captured. In 1969 you moved to the United States. One of the earliest progressive rock radio disc-jockeys Tom Donohue and yourself. were involved in a band called Silver Meter. Can you talk about that please?"

Pete Sears^: "Sam Gopal's Dream broke up for a bit. I did some work with Steamhammer (Blues mixed with rock). They used to back blues guitarist Freddy King (He passed away 12/28/76). I wanted to get to the states really bad. I saved some money up. I got a ticket. I came over to the states with five bucks in my pocket. I looked up a friend in Santa Monica, California named Leigh Stephens (Blue Cheer and Silver Metre). There was a rehearsal room on the Santa Monica Pier. We rehearsed about three months. We met Tom Donohue. We did one album and I kept a tape of a live recording from the Fillmore in San Francisco. During the live gigs we sometimes played two Elton John songs. He was first starting out."

Craig: "Do you recall which two tunes from Elton you performed?"

Pete Sears^: "We did *Country Comfort*. I later did that with Rod Stewart. The other one was *Sixty Years On*. Silver Metre was going to do another record. Something happened with Tom Donohue. I am not clear on the details. The money wasn't there. I went back to England and I did another album with Stoneground. It didn't seem right. Very slick and too produced. I wasn't happy with it. The interesting thing was the first album I did with them didn't get released. I thought that was much better, and more indicative of our sound, and direction. I also did the second album of the four with Rod Stewart, called *Every Picture Tells A Story*."

Craig: "You first appeared on Rod's 1970 *Gasoline Alley* album."

Pete Sears^: "That is correct. I left Copperhead (John Cipollina) right before their first album to play in a band Nicky Hopkins was getting together. I went back to England to play on another Rod Stewart album, then back to Mill Valley to take possession of a house Nicky was renting me. Nicky burned out on the road experience after the Stones tour, so the band never materialized. He didn't do well on the road, because of health problems. Prairie Prince (Tubes, Jefferson Starship, New Cars, and Todd Rundgren) would also have been a part of that band. Nicky was a real good person and a talented musician. Time went on. I did work on Rod Stewart's album *Never A Dull Moment*."

Craig: "In that time period was there talk of a power-trio including you, Neil Schon (Journey), and Greg Errico (Sly And The Family Stone and Santana)?"

Pete Sears: "Sometime around 1972 I was doing session work and Neil Schon was there. Neil and I got together with Greg. We formed a group Sears, Schon and Errico. We were looking for a vocalist. We were unable to find one. The music was heavy duty. We did well on the live shows. I introduced Aynsley Dunbar (Journey) and Neil Schon at a session in Los Angeles."

Craig: "For helping to team up members of Journey, you should be compensated with some of their royalty checks."

Pete Sears: (Pete chuckles). "Nothing came of the power trio in terms of recording. In 1973 I was asked to contribute to Grace Slick's album *Manhole*. This is the first time I met Grace. Paul was upstairs in the building working on some of his own music. I had contributed to the first Papa John Creach record, but this was the first time we actual met. I did a track where Grace wrote lyrics on the spot. She called the song *Better Lying Down*. The piano part was fun to do."

Craig: "When you look back on the Rod Stewart 1974 record *Smiles* and the session work over the years for him, was he open to suggestions from other musicians?"

Pete Sears: "Rod had a production style I liked. He let it happen in the studio. He may tell me to play the piano half-way through on a particular track. Much of the music was live in the studio. I would play the piano and Ron Wood (Rolling Stones) would play the bass. Ron was a guitar-player. He was once in a band the Birds."

Craig: "The group he played with was from England, and spelled it Birds and not Byrds."

Pete Sears: "That's right. We brought in musicians from Pentangle (English-folk band)."

Craig: "Did you get to play with John Renbourn and Jacqui McShee (Both were members of Pentangle)?"

Pete Sears: "I don't remember them being on the tracks. I am sure our paths have crossed. We would drive to Rod Stewart's house in the afternoon. Each album his house got progressively bigger."

Craig: "I usually have the opposite situation."

Pete Sears: (Laughs). He would play a song for us on acoustic guitar. We would fiddle around for a bit with it. Then we go to the studio and do it. I enjoyed the sessions."

Craig: "Next for you the Jefferson Starship flight begins. When you first met Grace was Grace in the studio the same persona as live?"

Pete Sears: "She was pretty out there. She had amazing focus on the tune and the lyrics. Her personality was amazing. She helped define the 1960's generation. She also was part of an important type of rebellion. The rebellion against problems with civil rights, Vietnam, etc."

Craig: "When the recording was over for the Jefferson Starship album *Dragon Fly*, did you get the feeling the band was on the verge of something special?"

Pete Sears: "The album felt great. I was in England and Paul, Grace, and David Freiberg had called me several times about being part of the record. The Rod Stewart album went longer then anticipated. Studios were broken down and every problem was going on. We finally finished. I wasn't sure if I wanted to be in the Jefferson Starship project. I came over from England to meet Paul and Grace. They had a limo waiting for me at the airport. They had a beautiful house overlooking the ocean. We even wrote a song on the spot called *Hyperdrive*. We hit it off really well."

Craig: "Paul continues to play *Hyperdrive* in the past couple of years."

Pete Sears: "That is great. Around the time I met Jorma during the *Quah* album recordings. I didn't see him again until the Hot Tuna days."

Craig: "We'll get into that a bit later. It seems if you had doubts of contributing to the Jefferson Starship, they had to dissipate after the album was completed."

Pete Sears: "It was clear that they were not going to carry on as the Jefferson Airplane. That is why the name change. I wasn't even asked to learn any Jack Casady bass parts. They wanted it to be known that it was another band."

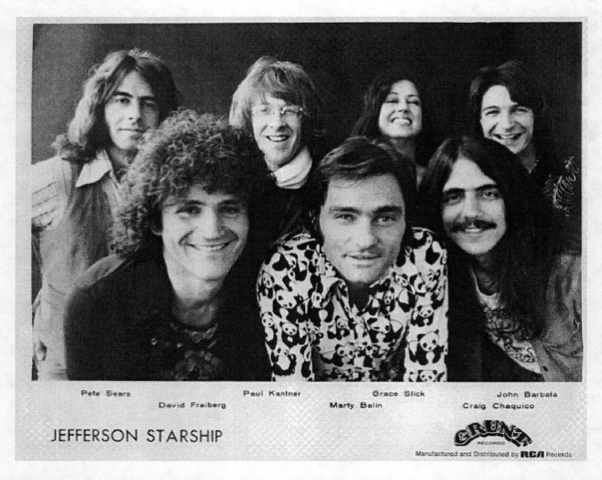

JEFFERSON STARSHIP

Pete Sears · David Freiberg · Paul Kantner · Grace Slick · Marty Balin · John Barbata · Craig Chaquico

**Photograph by kind permission of Mike Somavilla. From the Mike Somavilla collection. Photograph may not be used without the written consent of Mike Somavilla. Photographer unknown. This is a promo photo circa 1975. Thank you BMG .**

Craig: "When *Red Octopus* was completed, could you and the band members sense that something rather special and intense would be happening soon?"

Pete Sears: "I couldn't predict anything. I can't speak for the others. I knew it was a good album. I felt good about the material. I was not thinking in terms of hit singles or sell-out tours. It felt good. The album felt right. We had good production. It did feel special, but I couldn't say it would sell as well as it did."

Craig: "What was it like working with Papa John Creach?"

Pete Sears: "What a great guy. A wonderful man. Always a gentleman. Very inspiring person to play with. I loved playing on the song from his first solo record *The Janitor Drives A Cadillac*."

Craig: "That was great that you and Joey Covington were part of the only hit single he had."

Pete Sears: "I didn't realize that. That's cool. His rendition of *Somewhere Over The Rainbow* was absolutely unbelievable. When we played *Hyperdrive*, the fiddle was unbelievable. I enjoyed his presence and working with him so much. He enjoyed driving his Cadillac around. A real character and a total pleasure to work with. We were a good live band!"

Craig: "With the success of *Red Octopus*, what were Grace and Paul's reaction to the original Airplane fan base?"

Pete Sears^: "I can't speak for them. They were part of the Airplane. I wasn't. To me it was a new band. There were enough good reviews about the record and our live playing. People that came to the shows enjoyed it. We weren't trying to be any group but the Jefferson Starship. I had joined a rock band called Jefferson Starship that only played two or three "Airplane" songs, including "*White Rabbit*" and "*Somebody to Love*." It was great to play these songs with Grace - she was an amazing vocalist. I never thought about the Airplane at that time. Playing with Jefferson Starship in the seventies was, as far as I was concerned, a moment in time, relatively unrelated as an entity to what came before, or after. The material was mainly drawn from Paul and Grace's solo projects. The audiences were fantastic, and the band improvised and took the music out to the edge a lot. It wasn't until the eighties that the band had to play the music from the albums note by note. It was a pleasurable experience. We had a sense of rebellion. We had crazy rock things such as ten minute bass-solos."

Craig: "When you recorded *Spitfire*, did the success of the previous record put an albatross around the neck of the musicians?"

Pete Sears: "Yes, when you come up with a record that sold the way *Red Octopus* did and had received such accolades, the pressure was there. It was there first from the record company. The spirit of the band was terrific. We kept that up through the 1970's. Maybe one could argue there were too many writers. The band had a sound. That gave the band an identity. We kept the identity. Not everyone will like all songs. We were experimental. We were diverse and not looking for a formula. For better or worse, it was an honest band. We were writing extremely high. We sold out County Stadium in Milwaukee (Former home of the Milwaukee Brewers baseball team)."

Craig: "Then the 1980's come and ruined the musical universe."

Pete Sears: "Things changes so much. We had people working with us in the recording studio that were trying to get the same sound as when they worked with Heart. I had wanted to bring in singer Jess Roden in 1979. (He played with ex-Doors members John Densmore and Robbie Kreiger in the Butts Band, and has done numerous session work). He had a bluesy voice. That is where I was at. I had him come to California to audition. The record company wanted a voice that better blended in with the harmonies. It is a shame. Jess is a fine singer."

Craig: "Why does a band allow a record company to be so out of touch with what the group is about? Especially with the strong personalities within the group?"

Pete Sears: "It's a good question. I honestly don't know. The band was originally set-up as an equal entity. Through the 1970's it was very much that way. It worked well. In the 1980's the record company pressure began. You did what they did or you got dropped. Contracts had clauses about producers, sounds and so on. There were record companies looking for a Journey sound. Paul was always forward thinking. He didn't see anything wrong with moving ahead of the sound. What happens also is a gradual process. It doesn't turn around the entire one hundred eighty degrees overnight. When you are part of an organization you find that all these things like bad decisions are not all at once. In the very early 1980's we were still a good band. I liked the song *Jane*. I thought the piano part was a good thing. What surprises me is why did we allow the awful video of *Winds Of Change* out? The video had nothing to do with the lyrics. Some production company didn't even know the vision of the band. It was becoming an L.A. (Los Angeles) thing, but not in a good way. It slowly sunk deeper and deeper. We didn't sell the way people may have thought. We had more airplay but that didn't mean more success. My wife Jeanette and I were deeply involved in Central American politics. We tried to help refugees from Guatemala in the Bay Area. We were doing fundraisers. The record company had a stack of cassettes they wanted us to check out for hit song material. I had this tune called *"One More Innocent"* that I wrote with my wife and the record company felt it was too much of a downer. The new rule was no politics. The band was the Jefferson Starship. It was always a platform for politics. In the 1970's at least anybody for better or worse could say what they want. It was an attraction of the band. We weren't that type of band. We weren't good at it. We alienated many of our fans. I still do get a few people that come up to me today and tell me the 1980's was their favorite period of the band!"

Craig: "I went to school with a great doctor that will give them help. It'll be expensive and long. Does Mickey Thomas have any idea how many of the fans to this day are still appalled by that period of the band?"

Pete Sears^: "I have to say there are certain age groups that love that time. I couldn't stand the songs but there is a base for it. The songs were well crafted and Mickey is an excellent singer. It wasn't for me. We were playing live one night and there was either a bass or keyboard part. I notice that the stage had a park bench. Mickey is lying on the park bench. It may have been during the song *Sara*. I am thinking to myself what am I doing here? I am a rock and roll musician. I have to honestly stress that there is something for everyone. There is a group that enjoys that. I didn't. I was at great odds with that. When I left the Starship it wasn't on the best of terms. There were musical and personality clashes. The record company and the other band members wanted us to dress in suits! I drew the line there. There was even suggestion to make the solos the same every performance. They wanted to go from the days of ten minute bass-solos to every performance sounding like the record. When I left the band my income level plunged. I had to get out and play again. I played a bit with Frank Marino the guitarist from Mahogany Rush (Frank Marino worshipped Jimi Hendrix. Mahogany Rush had a cult following in the U.S.A. during the 1970's), and Aynsley Dunbar. It was a short bit. We should have kept it going. The record company wanted a singer. I didn't need to hear that."

Craig: "In 1988 you did a terrific record *Watchfire*. You have often referred to the album as ecological awareness. Tell us about the album."

Pete Sears: "As mentioned previously throughout the 1980's my wife and I were involved with the situation in Guatemala with the civil-war. There was terrible genocide in the country. Villages wiped off the face of the earth. My wife's mother was living there. We got this first hand. We had connections in the past helping with the earthquake. My mother-in-law had to be air-lifted out of the country. She was very vocal about what was going on. There were safe-houses in the Bay Area. I organized a drive for aid. These people needed food and clothing. Since the policy of the record company had changed when I was in the end of the tenure with the Starship about the political material not allowed on the albums, I wanted to get the word out. Producers thought the story was too much of a downer. I went into the studio with Mickey Hart (Grateful Dead) and some African drummers. We recorded the song *One More Innocent*. We created a non-profit video company to send out videos to TV stations that would make people aware of what was going on. We used the message of human rights violations along with footage of me in the studio. Having been sick of the direction the Starship went, for the record *Watchfire,* I did it all live in the studio. There were a few vocal over-dubs. Jerry Garcia helped out

482

with the project and Mickey Hart was a help. It was a reaction to the way things were recorded in the 1980's. I am not saying it was better. I will say it was different and a breath of fresh air."

Craig: "Was it a sense of pleasure and relief to be able to record an album without the pressure of a three minute song or a hit single?"

Pete Sears: "It was a sense of relief. I didn't record it with the thoughts of having a record label come to me. Holly Near's (Folk music) label Redwood were the nicest people. It was incredible to work with them. The album went on to Grateful Dead Records in 1996 and now I am starting to remanufacture it once again. Another great thing about *Watchfire* was bringing Jerry Garcia and David Grisman (Old And In The Way) together for the first time in fifteen years. That period was a heavy period. Jerry had asked me to play piano on his first solo record. I was with Long John Baldry (British singer that performed British blues and folk) at the time and couldn't make it. It was a shame. What a guy Jerry was. He did so much to help people behind the scenes."

Craig: "In 1992 you became part of Hot Tuna with Michael Falzarano (Memphis Pilgrims) and Harvey Sorgen (Memphis Pilgrims). How did that incarnation of the band come about?"

Pete Sears: "This was interesting. I hadn't seen Jorma in several years. He had showed up to about three Jefferson Starship shows to say hello. In 1992 I was helping with the SEVA Benefit. There was a benefit with Hot Tuna, John Lee Hooker, and some other people. I volunteered to play the solo piano at the after party. I was playing my piano off in the corner. I wasn't looking up. I get a tap on my shoulder and Jorma is standing there. Jack is there too. They were very friendly and nice. It was good to see them again. They let me know that they were recording a live album at Sweetwater, (*Live At Sweetwater* and *Live At Sweetwater 2*) and if I wanted to sit in to bring a piano. Their stage is real small. There weren't drums at that point. I sat up behind the band with Jorma, Jack, and Michael. Jorma asked me to play on every track. Even though there were songs I had no idea what they were. It was a lot of fun. Some of the happiest times were playing with Hot Tuna. Jorma let me share in the musical environment. The supportive role can be as exciting as the solo role. Almost every song there was a part where you could do what you want. There were no ego trips. It was good music and good people."

Craig: "Was the experience enhanced that they were not interested in making studio albums? You didn't have to worry about the record company holding you to three minute songs, or telling you what to write about? If you wanted to play *Walking Blues* for ten minutes you could."

Pete Sears: "It was great. It was like that with the Jefferson Starship in the 1970's. When I played the blues with Nick Gravenites, (Famous blues guitarist and blues song-writer) it was that way. You went out and played. That was all there was to it. This was the same opportunity. Hot Tuna was back to the feeling of playing the blues. Jorma created a great feeling."

Craig: "Did you like the fanaticism of the Hot Tuna fans in New York, New Jersey, and California?"

Pete Sears: "New York was great. I loved the crowd. They were hardcore Hot Tuna fans. I loved them all over the country. The fans were very supportive. I was walking into an existing situation. The fans were very open to a new sound. They embraced a keyboard in the band."

Craig: "You were respected because to the fan, you were part of the scene. It wasn't as if some outsider was getting a job that didn't know the roots of the music."

Pete Sears: "I had always had a strong admiration for these players. The way Jorma and Jack played the songs were fantastic. I enjoyed Jorma's guitar playing so much that I went out of way to play in a supportive role. I didn't want to come in with my own agenda. I wanted to blend in."

Craig: "There must have been a lot of special memories from the Japanese shows of 1997. You were able to make an album, *Live In Japan*. The stage didn't allow enough room for drums, but at least you were on the record."

Pete Sears: "What was nice about it, the album you here is how it happened. We didn't rerecord any part of it. The audience and the performance were strong. After about sixty seconds of listening to it back, we realized we could release this."

Craig: "Were you surprised at the crowd response to the shows?"

Pete Sears: "There is a great appreciation for the blues in Japan. They had a bar in Japan that had an incredible selection of blues albums on vinyl. They would play the blues as people sat at the bar. The club in Yokohama was so packed that the band had to climb through a window to get to the stage."

Craig: "1998 saw another live recording being released *And Furthurmore*. What was it like playing on the Further Festival shows?"

Pete Sears: "They were great. The band enjoyed it very much. We got to go all out and play electric. The band went for broke and played the Hot Tuna style blues. I got to meet the band Los Lobos and become friends with the guys. I always admired their work. Bob Weir had Ratdog perform. The Hot Tuna fans loved the full blast electric shows."

Craig: "That goes back to the 1975-1977 shows when the walls would shake. At the end of the three to four hours, the fans were as tired as the band. When Jorma had talked about recording a new sound with Blue Country Heart (Jerry Douglas, Béla Fleck, and Byron House), how were you told about the change in direction?"

Pete Sears: "We had a long run. It was actually the longest run of the band. Jorma was talking to a record company and had an idea of doing something different. Michael Falzarano and I felt that the era of that formation of Hot Tuna would close. It is traditional for Hot Tuna to change. It is part of the order of things. To me it wasn't a surprise. There were no hard feelings. I had my band the Dawn Patrol. Near the end it was very expensive for Jorma. We began to use a bus and paying the band and the expenses added up. If he goes out with Jack only it is cheaper. The entire process was very painless. It was a great period of my life."

Craig: "You had done some work with a band Zero in 1994. They received a break when Robert Hunter (Lyricist for the Grateful Dead) got involved and the style became more improvisational. You were on the CD they called *Chance In A Million*. How did you get to be part of the project?"

Pete Sears: "I was with Hot Tuna at the time. When we weren't playing, I did some work with them. One of the highlights was trading parts back and forth with Nicky Hopkins on the song *Mercury Blues*. (Written by K.C. Douglas. Three popular versions came from Canned Heat, Steve Miller, and Meatloaf). I am glad I got a recording with Nicky."

Craig: "In 2006 there were some reunion shows with Zero. One of the concerts you were a part of in Colorado had former Grateful Dead member Donna Godchaux perform with Zero. How were these shows put together?"

Pete Sears: "Donna was an old friend of the band. I have known her for years. My first allegiance is to the Flying Other Brothers. I have to keep an open schedule for any events that may transpire with them. In this case I had the free time. It is always great to play with Steve Kimock from Zero. Donna was ill with a cold when she appeared, but she came along and sang fantastic. They plan to have more shows and most likely it will be with the keyboard-players revolving in and out."

Craig^: "I have to mention to the readers something that you did, that was award winning, "Fight In The Fields." An original score about Cesar Chavez and the Farm Workers Union. The program aired in April of 1997."

Pete Sears: "That one really sticks outs. I heard a couple of days ago that the documentary is getting a new lease of life. It has been picked up by a Spanish Television station. I am not sure at this point if it is in the U.S.A. or south of the border. I got a call from the producer that they needed a music cue-sheet. I'll find out more soon. I'm glad I still had it."

Craig: "In 1999 you were on one of my favorite live albums And *Love Will See You Through* (Phil Lesh-Grateful Dead). Jorma, Phil Lesh, and you combine for some hot rock and roll. The idea that you guys could play songs ranging from *Good Shepherd* to *Dancing In The Street*, must have been fun as well as musically satisfying."

Pete Sears: "There are some spontaneous *jams*, and there was great enjoyment playing the songs. I had a Hammond B3 and it was great using it on stage. I felt very good about the freshness. Jorma and Phil had a good time. Thank you. It was real and had some really good stuff."

Craig: "In 2001 there was a great album you released called the *Long Haul*. I had two songs jump at me the first time I listened to it, *Brother John* and *Meadway Rag*. What do you recall about the *Long Haul*?"

Pete Sears: "It was a labor of love. When I make a solo record it is never with the intention it will sell. I try to make it the best album I possibly can. I wanted a folk and blues thread to everything. It is music I love and grew close to. I worked hard on the order of songs to make sure it will flow. I enjoyed it when it was finished. *Brother John* was about an old friend John Cipollina (Quicksilver Messenger Service) who passed away. I am glad you liked the track. *Meadway Rag* is about the emergency war housing where I grew up in London. There weren't enough houses to go around because of the war. They were pre fabed modular homes. There were rows of them. The house was on the road to Meadway. That is why I named the tune *Meadway Rag*. I loved that style of music. The Dixie-land sound was always great to listen to."

Craig: "In the early part of 2006 you released an instructional video on playing the piano. How did that opportunity present itself?"

Pete Sears: "I taught a bit here and there at Jorma's Fur Peace Ranch in Ohio. I thought why not. A couple of young guys that started a company called Icons Of Rock came to me. I tried to do it from the beginning to go as far as they want to go with it. It was a lot of fun."

Craig: "The readers can go to http://www.petesears.com/ and check out the instructional video and your activities on the website."

Pete Sears: "Thanks!"

Craig: "You are involved in a short and long term project with artist Andreas Nottebohm called *Black Hole Studio, Musical And Visual Art*. Tell us about this."

Pete Sears: "I know him many years. He has a three dimensional technique of painting that jumps out at you, the images are astounding. We came up with the idea that he will have a series of his work with prints. Each print will have a CD with a twenty minute piece of music. This will take several years. I am using radio signals from outer space. There is no confinement here. We will release this as one body of work. The project will take at least another year and it will be in the art world and not the music world. There is nothing commercial about this. It is out on the edge."

Craig: "On a completely unrelated note, did you do a studio session for Mick Jagger's brother Chris? What is often forgotten Mick has a brother, and Chris has put out several albums. Mick often contributes background vocals."

Pete Sears: "I did. In England around 1973 I was asked to do session work. I haven't talked to him since. When I came to the states, I lost touch with a lot of good people from England."

Craig: "You were able turn the clock back on 10/29/05 for the opening ceremony of the Jerry Garcia Amphitheater, McClaren Park, San Francisco, California. How did it feel appearing with the Jefferson Starship?"

Pete Sears: "There wasn't any rehearsal. I went for it. The spirit of the band is still there. It is like the 1970's. It was fun."

Craig: "How long was it since you played *Hyperdrive*?"

Pete Sears: "I think it was the 1970's. I didn't even know if I remembered it and I helped write the song. It worked out great. The band Paul currently has is full of wonderful people."

Craig: "I couldn't let you go without talking about the exciting work with the Flying Other Brothers. How did you get involved with them?"

Pete Sears^: "The groundwork was already there with Roger McNamee. I recommended the Flying Other Brothers ask Barry Sless to join on guitar. I love Barry's playing, he brings a great dimension to the band. I had already been a member of the FOB's since I left Hot Tuna in 2002. There are three albums *52 Week High* (I did a session), *Secondary,* and *IPO.*"

Craig: "Was there a natural growth from the first record to the second?"

Pete Sears: "Yes. I am really excited about the *jam* sessions and playing off each other. This is very strong. I am singing a version of the Grateful Dead song *Stella Blue* on some of the live shows. When Brent Mydland from the Grateful Dead passed away (7/26/90), Jerry Garcia had a box of songs he wanted me to learn. I wasn't a singer. I have taken lessons since then. I feel *Stella Blue* is a tribute to Jerry."

Craig: "Do you have tour dates set for the entire country?"

Pete Sears: "We are doing more and more dates. We have played Alaska, and we plan to play more festivals. We have a new agency and they plan to get behind the latest music we have written."

Craig: "Why don't we get a plug for the terrific site from the Flying Other Brothers. The readers can go to http://www.flyingotherbros.com and check out the latest happenings of the band. They can also enjoy some samples of the music."

Pete Sears: "Thanks for the plug."

Craig: "It is well deserved. Before we end the conversation, you are always so proud of the work of a band you play with Dawn Patrol. Fans can go to http://www.petesears.com/ and click on a link to find information about the group. Lastly congratulations to your mother-in-law on the book Blood In The Cornfields being published. Her name is Bonnie Dilger and I hope it is very successful. Pete, there isn't enough time in a month to cover your career. It was a pleasure to speak with you. Thank you for enlightening all of us on your fabulous musical journey."

Pete Sears: "Craig, thank you for the plugs. It was nice talking with you today."

486

## Darby Slick- Great Society.

Craig: "Welcome Darby, it's nice to have you share some history with the readers."

Darby Slick: "Thank you."

Craig: "When the Great Society formed did you have preconceived notions what you realistically wanted for yourself?"

Darby Slick: "When we first got together we wanted to play in front of people. It was a very different line-up. My other sister-in-law Jennie Piersol was the other female vocalist. Both Grace and Jennie were excellent singers. Grace was playing rhythm guitar and I was playing guitar. Jerry Slick was on drums but we needed a bass-player. Jennie quit the band. I believe she was having a child. That led to David Miner and Bard Dupont. Bard obviously was not a bass-player and we fired him. I brought in my friend Peter van Gelder. Peter wasn't a bass-player but he was a real musician. Peter was a saxophone-player and could play the keyboards too. I knew he would pick up the rock and roll bass fast."

Craig: "Do you remember the first song you wrote for the band when Jennie was a member?"

Darby Slick: "It was a song about surfing. I don't know if I ever named the tune."

Craig: "Do you remember the hook or any lyrics to the song?"

Darby Slick: "Craig, the song did have a name, *When I Get You Down To The Ocean*. It was surfing stuff with a boy and girl theme. (Darby sings what he remembers and real well too). "When I get you down to the ocean, there will be a commotion, all the surfers there will pearl when they see you are my girl, they've had their eyes on you so long."

Craig: "One for the archives. Nice job with the vocals!"

Darby Slick: "Thanks Craig."

Craig: "What proud moment do you remember from the Great Society days?"

Darby Slick: "A proud moment was our version of *Sally Go 'Round The Roses*. We made it very much our own sounding song. Our deal when we did cover songs was to try to make them our own and not make it sound like the original record. A few years after we had played the song I went to Chess Records in Chicago. A great place, that was famous for Chuck Berry, Muddy Waters (Legendary blues musician), and the Rolling Stones. I was there doing some recording work and I ran into one of the writers of *Sally Go 'Round The Roses* (Zell Sanders was the writer Darby met. The other writer was Abner Spector). Zell was so complimentary how we had done the song. You could see the joy in his eyes."

Craig: "What were your feelings in 1968 when the two live albums were released posthumously? (*Conspicuous Only In Its Absence* and *How It Was*)."

Darby Slick: "I have a bunch of reactions to those records. The most negative would be the promises that were broken to us. We were told it would truly be a collector's item and then it got turned around and sold to Columbia Records. We all had an agreement that Grace wouldn't be pushed above the band and they did that. The third and the most upsetting for me was the tapes for the record were taken from The Matrix, San Francisco. It wasn't a bad place but the quality wasn't the same as if Wally Heider Studios, San Francisco. had come out and recorded the band. To make up for that they sped up the master recording. All the songs are sped up but not the same. It is kind of randomly. The tape recorders were run at different speeds. About four or five years ago I bought a multi speed tape recorder and I put all the songs on the two records to the proper speed. The records sounded wonderful to me.  No wonder I hated it at first.  The other is a chip I've had on my shoulders all these years.  I've gotten better about that.  When Grace decided to leave she found it necessary to say that the Great Society weren't good musicians because we had fiercely loyal fans that she didn't want to upset.  Grace liked the fact that the Airplane was signed already to RCA and we didn't have a contract.  I was thinking of leaving too.  There was instability in the band.  She jumped at the chance to be successful.  What remains is this, I challenge anybody to listen to the first Jefferson Airplane record, listen to the first Grateful Dead, and compare it to our live records and tell me we weren't as good as the other bands.  I believe on a simple technical level we were as good as anybody else.  That's my story and I am sticking to it."

Craig: "How did you feel when the album of studio recordings materialized in 1995 called *Born To Be Burned*?"

Darby Slick: "I don't have any problem with the album.  The qualities that were there then are there now."

Craig: "There is some terrific material on the CD.  Not only the song *Free Advice* but *Father Bruce* and *Girl* to name only three."

Darby Slick: "Okay."

Craig: "If you look at the total picture the Great Society is one of the most underrated bands of that era."

Darby Slick: "I have to agree with you.  The famous critic Ralph Gleason (Music critic for the San Francisco Chronicle and was an editor with Rolling Stone) got it.  He got it very well.  He wrote glowingly about us."

Craig: "Why did the story about the musicianship get perpetuated all these years?"

Darby Slick: "When Grace wrote a book in 1980 (*Grace Slick: The Biography*) she perpetuated the story about the musicianship.  I wrote my book in 1991 called *Don't You Want Somebody To Love: Reflections of The San Francisco Sound*.  I got to tell my story.  (Darby's book is available by going to www.amazon.com).  When Grace wrote the later book in 1999, *Somebody to Love? : A Rock-and-Roll Memoir*, she sort of set the record straight about the musicianship."

Craig: "When Grace made the decision to leave the band from your recollection did any members attempt to change her mind?"

Darby Slick: "She had only told Jerry Slick until it was a done deal.  Jerry wanted to be noble about it and not get in the way of her career.  At this point we were a four person band and Peter van Gelder and I had both thought of living in India.  We meant it.  Peter stayed between a year and a half and two years and I stayed only five months.  I wanted to experience what it was like back home when *Somebody To Love* became a hit."

Craig: "What was your reaction the first time you heard the Airplane studio version?"

Darby Slick: "I hated it.  The Great Society had a double time feel to it.  It was funk.  The Airplane put a rock and roll feel into it.  I also was not impressed with *White Rabbit*.  I understood you had to radically cut down the beginning.  We used to play that song for fifteen minutes.  We had three major solos in the song."

Craig: "The version on *Conspicuous Only in Its Absence* is almost four and one half minutes before the vocals first appear."

Darby Slick: "The version they took for the record was actually a short one.  If we were playing a show with several people on the bill and only had a few minutes left, we couldn't stretch it out.  We liked to close the shows with *White Rabbit*.  If we got to a point where there would be only a few minutes left before *White Rabbit*, we had to play a short *Somebody To Love*.  There were Fillmore shows in San Francisco where we would play the song fifteen minutes and the people would go nuts."

Craig: "What was your reaction to the Airplane albums with Grace going from *Surrealistic Pillow* to *Long John Silver*?"

Darby Slick: "To be honest with you these weren't records I bought. The Airplane was the least favorite San Francisco band to me. That was multiplied when Grace left the Great Society. I don't know if you are aware that I am in a drug and alcohol recovery program (Darby has been sober for over eighteen years). Part of that is looking at the past. Looking at what we call your side of the street. I told Grace this later that she not only made the right decision but was absolutely justified to leave. I didn't feel that way at the time. It's kind of like the situation where you are dating a woman and she leaves you for a guy you think is a moron. You think she left me for this guy. To me the Airplane weren't that good of a band. Years later I would hear songs Signe Anderson sang on the first album and actually like them. I thought Signe did a great job at the KBC Band show that was a special event."

Craig: "11/27/85 Bill Graham Productions" 20th Anniversary Thanksgiving Party, Fillmore Auditorium, San Francisco, Signe and Spencer Dryden appeared on two songs."

Darby Slick: "She did a great job on *It's No Secret* and *Plastic Fantastic Lover*. It was a fun show."

Craig: "Was it a bizarre situation that after Grace went to the Airplane she still was married to your brother Jerry, and you would have to see each other in social circles, and shopping at the local stores?"

Darby Slick: "We all made nice. In fact when I got home from Calcutta, India, I went to see Grace and Jerry at the hungry i (That is the correct spelling and it is lower case letters. A legendary 1950's and 1960's club that gave early exposure to many comedians) in San Francisco. I even slept over their house that night. I still had those unresolved bitter feelings in me."

Craig: "After coming back from India you played in a band called Hair. What are your remembrances?"

Darby Slick: "I was really into funk when I got back to America. I liked songs like the Box Tops doing *The Letter* or the Soul Survivors hit *Expressway To Your Heart*. Hair the band was before the musical of that name. I put together a multi-racial band because I wanted to get into funk. We played a lot of cover songs and it wasn't about being popular. It wasn't for a career move, it was for the enjoyment of the funk music. I think we lasted until the end of 1968."

Craig: "After Hair dissolved what came next?"

Darby Slick: "I did some recording in Chicago and I wrote stuff for Sesame Street (Famous children's television show)."

Craig: "Before we get to the solo records, are you credited for inventing the fretless guitar?"

Darby Slick: "I invented it and my son Jor designed it. The idea is when you play a note it doesn't just last two seconds, there is sustain. This happened in the early 1990's. I used it on stage for my gigs with Big Brother & The Holding Company in the 1990's."

Craig: "When you played with Big Brother And The Holding Company for a bit in the 1990's were you allowed to bring any of your own songs with you?"

Darby Slick: "Sam Andrew from the band didn't want me to change the sound of the group. I wanted us to play *Somebody To Love*. The crowd would have eaten that up."

Craig: "All one can say is boo hiss. That would have been terrific to go along with their strong stage material."

Darby Slick: "Sam is a friend and I respect his decision."

Craig: "On the 1995 CD *Sandoland* you got to play with your son and use the fretless guitar."

Darby Slick: "It was wonderful. I like my son's songs better than the ones I wrote. It was very gratifying. I enjoyed playing with him in a live environment."

Craig: "Is the title of the record the name of the place where the cartoon character Speed Racer lived?"

Darby Slick: "It actually is a place where he raced in one episode. It was my son that wanted the title to be *Sandoland*. That was fine with me."

Craig: "The 1998 release *King Of The Fretless Guitar* saw a cover of the Jimi Hendrix song *Red House*. How did that come about?"

Darby Slick: "I thought it would be worth giving away the royalties to take the challenge and stand up as far as the guitar goes. Jimi is still my favorite guitar-player. I think Jimi would like the version. I wanted the critics to confirm I was going up against Jimi Hendrix. The reviews were good. One publication said something like "He dares to take on Hendrix and pulls it off." I made the cut."

Craig: "The two albums can be purchased by going to the Taxim Records website, www.taxim.com. On 10/20/2002 at the San Francisco Civic Center, San Francisco, for the 35th Anniversary Summer Of Love, there was a Great Society reunion of sorts. Yourself on lead-guitar, your brother Jerry (Did not want to play drums. He played rhythm-guitar), Peter van Gelder (Sax), as well as some others including your son Jor on rhythm-guitar and vocals, Barry Flast (Formerly of the Jefferson Starship) on keyboards, Pete Lamb on bass, Jimmy Sage on drums, Allison Prival on vocals, Elizabeth McGill on vocals, and Tessa on vocals. What were your thoughts of that day and did you rehearse anything that you didn't bring to the stage?"

Darby Slick: "My son Jor was in contact with the people. Joli Valente the son of Dino from the Quicksilver Messenger Service helped greatly as well. My son and Joli were in contact with the promoters. We had three days to rehearse. What we rehearsed was what we played."

Craig: "Besides the sound problems were you happy with the performance?"

Darby Slick: "The sound may have had everything to do with me not being happy. The drummer may not have been able to hear me play."

Craig: "Was there consideration to ask former Great Society members David Miner and Bard Dupont to perform with you?"

Darby Slick: "My son handled the line-up for the most part. I'm not in contact with those guys. Neither of them stayed in music as far as I know."

Craig: "What does the future hold for Darby Slick?"

Darby Slick: "I would like to play shows with the fretless guitar. I would like to go around the country and perform. I also got a call the other day about the possibility of having the Great Society play several dates."

Craig: "Hopefully it was a realistic discussion."

Darby Slick: "In the music business most aren't. We shall see. Craig, when you brought up the book it reminded me that I have to buy a copy."

Craig: "You don't have a copy of your own book?  That is farcical."

Darby Slick: "I find if somebody needs a copy I give one away."

Craig: "As happy as I am that we were finally able to talk, it is even nicer how you have stayed clean for all this time.  Be healthy forever.  Darby thanks and I hope the fans get to see the Great Society play again.  Please buy several copies of your book."

Darby Slick: "Thank you Craig.  Thank you for the plugs."

# Jerry Slick- Great Society.

Craig: "Jerry it is a pleasure to be able to get first hand insights on not only Grace Slick but the music of the Great Society. Thank you for your time today."

Jerry Slick: "Thank you."

Craig: "Today we finally get a chance to separate some fact from fiction. Did the band get together because you and Grace were inspired after having seen a live Jefferson Airplane performance?"

Jerry Slick: "There was some influence by the Airplane I think, but more primarily by the Beatles. The truth is Darby was the instigator of getting a band together. The story always is told that Grace and I were responsible. The three of us were basically playing together. As a result of the Beatles we decided to give the idea of a band our attention. Darby also was influenced by Keith Richards from the Rolling Stones. He liked Keith's guitar style. Yes we went to see the Airplane, but it was not our favorite type of music."

Craig: "Once the three of you decided to pursue the idea of a band how long did it take to get the other members David Minor and Bard Dupont?"

Jerry Slick: "I'm not clear on the exact date. We didn't have that overall picture. We were thinking it would be kind of fun to do. Our idea was to not give a sh_t if we were commercially successful or not. We were snotty rich kids. It seemed to all come together quickly. When Bill Graham promoted his first show at the Calliope Warehouse 924 Howard Street Loft, San Francisco, California on 11/6/65 there must have been about one thousand people there. It went on all through the night. The next day Darby called me up and made his case for exploring the idea of a band. We didn't play that night, but it was a public showing of the energy from in and around San Francisco, soon after we got our first manager John Carpenter. I don't recall how we got together with him. John was friends with David and Bart. I should point out that one of the real reasons Grace went to join the Airplane was she got tired of singing solo with the Great Society. Grace loved the harmonies of the Airplane. She felt they were also more sophisticated with their vocals and harmonies. David was more of a soul singer. There voices didn't match for the harmonies. The primary reason for Bart getting into the band was his great hair. He had a great Beatle haircut."

Craig: "Once the band was in place how long did it take for you to write material worthy of being performed?"

Jerry Slick: "We were bound and determined to play only originals. When we first started we had eleven songs. The total time of the stage show was about thirty-three minutes. Tom Donohue (One of the first progressive rock disc-jockeys and manager of bands) owned a nightclub in North Beach, California. It was called Mothers Nightclub and it was a psychedelic club. One evening he had a cattle call of bands. This may have been for either the club or a record company. We show up and after about three seconds of hearing Grace they were real interested in us. There may have been a crowd of ten there."

Craig: "Did it take long to get the tunes to sound the way you wanted for the stage? The Great Society is one of the bands from the 1960's that should have gotten more credit for the original compositions."

Jerry Slick: "It didn't take too long. We had a limited set with eleven songs. If the songs are well structured it is the Beatles influences. Grace and Darby were influenced by that sound and arrangement. We didn't want to mess around with more complex songs until we were confident in the eleven we had decided to play."

Craig: "Peter van Gelder remembered one of the forgotten cover tunes the band performed, Bob Dylan's *It's All Over Now, Baby Blue*. Do any come to your mind?"

Jerry Slick: "Craig, the Airplane could have done our song *Free Advice*."

492

Craig: "That would have been tremendous because they would have ended up performing both sides of the Great Society's single *Somebody To Love* (Called *Someone To Love*) and *Free Advice*. I asked Marty Balin if Grace suggested any songs to the Airplane besides *White Rabbit* and *Somebody To Love*. He told me *Sally Go 'Round The Roses*."

Jerry Slick: "Did they ever perform that?"

Craig: "Unfortunately they didn't. It wasn't they didn't like the song, it was not a match for the band."

Jerry Slick: "You had asked me about cover tunes that we did and that were forgotten. Tom Donohue who acted as a manager later on wanted very much for us to cover a song written by John Denver called *Leaving On A Jet Plane*. We turned him down. Donohue was looking for the more universal appeal."

Craig: "Could you imagine if the band had said yes? History could have been completely rewritten because Peter, Paul, & Mary may never have gotten the opportunity to record their version."

Jerry Slick: "Grace did not want to sing the song. She wanted to have nothing to do with it. Tom Donohue also wanted Grace to sing a couple of Peggy Lee (Popular female vocalist in the 1960's) tunes. They would have been jazz standards. None of us wanted to have anything to do with that. For one thing Grace had no interest in singing these songs. One reason that we weren't that interested in singing the songs Tom suggested was we weren't confident at that point playing our instruments. If you play an original you could better get away with a mistake. When it is a popular standard you may not know what you are listened to while working on the arrangement."

Craig: "Did the band consider any Beatles songs?"

Jerry Slick: "The reason we didn't we wanted to focus on the originals. A couple of covers were thrown in as filler for the lack of original material we had at the time."

Craig: "There are two songs that the Great Society performed that to me are close in sound and equal in brilliance *Darkly Smiling* and *Grimly Forming*. It is a similar situation with the Airplanes' *The Ballad Of You and Me And Pooneil* and *The House At Pooneil Corners*. In the case of the Airplane everyone loves *The Ballad Of You and Me And Pooneil* and *The House At Pooneil Corners* is just another song. With the Great Society *Darkly Smiling* is one of the most well respected tunes from the band and *Grimly Forming* is forgotten. Why is that?"

Jerry Slick: "The truth is I don't recall all of the parts of the two songs. I would have to go back and listen to the two songs. It is coming back to me. *Grimly Forming* was a song Peter had a lot to do with. *Darkly Smiling* was kind of a folk-rock song. Peter and Darby had started to play around with more odd time signatures. I recall *Grimly Forming* is more intellectual. Even when Peter had joined the band Darby was already getting into the Indian music. Peter wanted to avoid the folk-rock sound with his songs. One has to be careful with Raga Rock (A term that first came about in the 1960's that would define rock and roll albums with Indian influences). It isn't very good rock and it certainly isn't real Indian music. The best example of Raga rock going nowhere is the Paul Butterfield Blues Band doing *East-West*. That thing is so lame. They are great Chicago blues musicians, but had no understanding of the real Indian music."

Craig: "It is amazing you took that song as an example. 1/8/67 Webster Hall, New York City, Mike Bloomfield (Guitar) and Mark Naftalin (Keyboards) joined the Airplane on stage for *East-West Jam*. They both were from the Paul Butterfield Blues Band."

Jerry Slick: "It may have been fun for them. I have to admit for me I have fun playing the blues, but not to listen to them. To *jam* on *East-West* for one time is fine. They issued an entire album of *East-West* and I thought it was a real low level for them. I bet I should get back to your question on *Grimly Forming*. It was based on a stranger vibe. It may have been harder for the fan to digest. *Darkly Smiling* is more of a singer's song as well. The meter flows better. Diana Mangano started to sing the song with the Jefferson Starship and that helped perpetuate the popularity. I understand she sings it rather well."

Craig: "She does a great version. Paul Kantner deserves credit for allowing songs on stage that he was never a part of. Can you elaborate why the studio material you recorded never got exposure while the band was together? The great label Sundazed put it out posthumously in 1995 as *Born To Be Burned*."

Jerry Slick: "The same thing was true with our single *Somebody To Love/Free Advice*. That was about the time things fell apart with Tom Donohue. He swore up and down the single was released. As far as we could tell the single had limited distribution. That severed our relationship. We would have a new manager named Howard Wolf. I think Howard got the band the contact with Columbia."

Craig: "Is it definitive that had the band not broken up you did have at least one offer to record from Columbia?"

Jerry Slick: "Yes that is true. I don't remember the specifics. This was the time when the record companies were signing up all the bands in San Francisco. The bar got raised because the Airplane had signed for a good chunk of change."

Craig: "It is a shame that numerous bands of the 1960's had to end up being rediscovered later on and not discovered at the actual point in time. The record collector and the musicians should be happy that there are the retro labels helping to preserve the magic of that era."

Jerry Slick: "That is a great thing about the digital age we live in. Today everything seems assessable. I am thinking now that the guy that had all the records from The Matrix, San Francisco was Pete Abrams. He recorded everybody that would get on stage at The Matrix. Through Pete and a lawyer partner that he had we got signed up by Columbia. I believe we had signed a paper that gave him the rights to the material performed at The Matrix. It isn't totally clear at the moment. I don't know if he thought in terms of a long range plan or was only interested in the music at that moment. He may have wanted to archive the stuff. He did have some legal hassles because Big Brother & The Holding Company didn't want material released from the club."

Craig: "Did you feel being the closest to Grace that her stage persona was three hundred-sixty degrees different than her personal? When I look back at the Great Society and the Jefferson Airplane on stage she talks about counter-culture and rebellion. She attended a college, married at a young age, and lived in a nice residence."

Jerry Slick: "To me it wasn't so much on stage and off stage. I think the attitude was she always felt she was on stage. When I first met her she had been performing all her life. The real difference between the two Graces isn't on or off stage. The two Graces are about being sober or non sober. Most of the stage persona was fueled by alcohol. There was a good deal of her personal life that was also fueled by alcohol. I could remember that Grace loved to argue. To Grace arguing was entertaining and recreation. Grace liked to provoke people at parties to argue. I have to admit I didn't know how much she liked to drink. She loved to provoke people and argue. At a party she would take on somebody and become devils advocate. It can be sadly easier to be a rock star with alcohol. There is no question about that. It is the nature of the beast."

Craig: "There have been several musicians that have told me she was uncomfortable on the stage."

Jerry Slick: "That is correct. She was drinking to break down the inhibitions. Grace talks now about not wanting to perform. My instincts think that is because she has gotten off the alcohol."

Craig: "Do you recall when Grace got offered to take Signe Anderson's place in the Airplane, how long she thought about the decision?"

Jerry Slick: "The decision came down pretty quick. It was the right time. The Great Society wasn't getting along. Grace did talk with me about what she should do. I read recently that was the last time she listened to my opinion."

Craig: "Some feel the last time she listened to any opinion."

Jerry Slick: "Probably so. We talked about it briefly. I was ready to not be a full-time musician. It was easy for Grace to leave that situation and be able to sing with an established band. She would get to sing harmonies and as far as she knew she was getting away from the fighting that was going on in our band."

Craig: "If you looked Grace in the eye and told her that the decision to join the Airplane was all wrong and would hurt a lot of people what would she have done?"

Jerry Slick: "She would have said no. If I had been really firm about the choice she wanted to make she would have rejected the offer to join the Airplane."

Craig: "When you look back on the music the Great Society played live and in the studio, do you have some favorite songs?"

Jerry Slick: "I like the sound of my drums on *Everybody Knows*. *Somebody To Love* is up there in the Top 10 of three chord rock songs. *White Rabbit* from a musician's point of view is a killer. The form and chord changes are so powerful. It is an outstanding song. The last performance we played we did a Miles Davis song. I liked the time signature. I can't remember the title. We had another guitar-player Oscar somebody."

Craig: "That is funny, he is always known only as Oscar. His name is Oscar Daniels."

Jerry Slick: "He added a big chunk of power. Oscar had a big strong solo voice. When Peter played the horn Grace would play the bass. I remember that on all our tunes when Peter didn't play the bass. Grace could play the drums too."

Craig: "Grace was known to play the recorder very well."

Jerry Slick: "Here's a story about that. In the Great Society she played the recorder pretty often. We were at a club in North Beach and there were a number of jazz clubs in the neighborhood. One night standing at the door was Herbie Mann (Played the flute and was very well known in the jazz circles during the 1960's and 1970's) and he told Grace if she ever got that thing in tune he would be glad to play with her."

Craig: "When Grace went to the Airplane did you follow the band out of curiosity?"

Jerry Slick: "The Airplane stylistically was not my favorite band. Jack Casady is one of the best pop music bass-players in the world. Jorma is an excellent musician. I did buy some albums to see what Grace was doing. Excluding a couple of records I didn't pay much attention."

Craig: "What type of relationship if any do you have with Grace today?"

Jerry Slick: "The last time I spoke with her was in the 1980's. Grace was working on a book and Barbara Rose was helping her. Barbara came over a couple of times to interview me for the book. One time Grace came over. We chatted for a couple of hours."

Craig: "The band you played with after the Great Society had a very offensive name the Final Solution. When you look back at the name wasn't it in awful taste?"

Jerry Slick: "At the time I'm not even sure I knew what it meant. The name sure was in bad taste. The band never talked politics. The guys weren't racist. Sometimes people do things for shock value. I wasn't there when they took the name. I can tell you first hand that sometimes bands take names for odd reasons. The Great Society took the name as a joke on Lyndon Johnson."

Craig: "For the 35th anniversary of the Summer Of Love (10/20/02 Civic Center Plaza, San Francisco) you were able to have a Great Society reunion of sorts in San Francisco, with you, Darby Slick, and Peter van Gelder."

Jerry Slick: "I played rhythm guitar and no drums. We had some other musicians with us. From the Great Society days we performed *White Rabbit, Sally Go 'Round The Roses* and *Somebody To Love*. Darby's son Jor on rhythm-guitar and vocals, Barry Flast (Played with the Jefferson Starship and Kingfish) on keyboards, Jimmy Sage on drums, Paul Lamb on the bass, and three female singers Elizabeth McGill, her mom Allison Prival, and Tessa."

Craig: "Why don't you tell the readers what you have done after giving up music full-time?"

Jerry Slick: "It was a continuation of what I had done prior to the Great Society. I went to film school in college. I started to work in commercials but the band thing started. I gave that up. After playing with the Final Solution I went back to what I do best cinematography. I freelance these days. Slick Film will work with corporations. We do commercials as well."

Craig: "Thank you very much for the first hand account of the Great Society days and the insight regarding Grace Slick. May you have continued success with Slick Film."

Jerry Slick: "Craig, it was my pleasure. Let me know if you need any other information for the book."

## Bob Steeler- Hot Tuna.

Craig: "Thanks for being here today. It's been hard to track you down."

Bob Steeler: "You're welcome. It's been crazy. Between the day gig and the painting at night, one day goes into the next."

Craig: "I'm glad that you can relax tonight. Not too long ago your musical past was brought to the present. A record company that releases unbelievable psychedelic music from the 1960's and 1970's put out a record you did circa 1969/1970, with Think Dog, called *Dog Days*. (Think Dog had two albums worth of material that never saw the light of day. The record company released the second album, and on vinyl only. There may be a CD release in the works). Can we categorize the music as British underground (The band was from America), and psychedelic, and what do you remember about the group?" (You can purchase the record by going to www.psychedelic-music.com).

Bob Steeler: " You could call us psychedelic and British underground. I got a forty dollar royalty check for the album recently, from one of the members of the band Lynn David Newton. The music was good. The guys wanted to sound like the Beatles. They put heavy effort into songwriting. The only thing I didn't like about the band was when some of the material sounded like it came from a circus."

Craig: "How soon after Sammy Piazza's final gig with Hot Tuna did you find out about the opening for a drummer?"

Bob Steeler: "There was a sequence of events that took place from my recollection. I was in California with Kathi McDonald's Band (She had played with Big Brother & The Holding Company). Her producer David Briggs wanted the band to sound like the Who. We were fired almost immediately. We may have been together three weeks. I hung out. I met this girl and her best friend was Michael Casady's wife. Michael is obviously Jack's brother. Michael was doing road work for Hot Tuna. Michael's wife went to see Hot Tuna sometime in 1974. It may have been in a place called the Lions Share, San Anselmo, California. (The date would have been 7/5/74) She told Jorma, and Jack they sounded great, but needed a drummer. She told them about me. The next day Jorma gives me a call. He told me that he heard I was a good drummer and wanted to know if I would be interesting in coming down to play with him. I told him sure. The next day I go to Jorma's house. We played two and a half hours. He asked if I wanted to play the next night, at Bimbo's 365 Club, San Francisco. Hot Tuna played five and a half hours (7/7/74). That was the beginning. I played with the combination of Hot Tuna and Jorma five years."

Craig: "How difficult was it to learn the songs in one day?"

Bob Steeler: "I like improvising more than anything else. I play songs better when I don't know them thoroughly. The are fresher when they are new. You end up concentrating very hard. I noticed for example with Tuna, Jorma and Jack would come back from speed skating. When we would play the first time after the vacation it was fresh. When we played the Knebworth Fair Festival, Hertfordshire, U.K. (8/21/76), I hadn't seen Jorma and Jack for three months. We went on the stage without rehearsing and we played cold. We were the only band to get a good review that day. We were cooking, it was something else. Jorma and Jack were paying attention. I was paying attention beyond what we normally do. Once you know the material you aren't nervous about it. You're comfortable when you play. I love to improvise. I grew up listening to first rock and roll, then I got into be-bop immediately. I played with jazz bands in New York City. That was awesome. I learned how to improvise. That's how I learned to do it. That's what I like to do. That's why that stuff doesn't scare me. I don't know how to read music. I'm not expected to know the songs cold. The pressure is off too. How well could I know a tune I never heard before. After I hear it once I know it."

Craig: "Did you listen to Hot Tuna's music prior to joining the band?"

Bob Steeler: "No, not at all. I was not a fan at that time. When they started I wasn't a fan of folk-music. I was listening to Jimi Hendrix and Led Zeppelin. I also listened to be-bop. I liked more intense harder music. As I got older I started to like and appreciate folk-music more. The finger picking style is really cool. I'm into it now."

Craig: "When you first were told you had the job with Hot Tuna did Jorma tell you that although the crowd will give the accolades to Jack and I there will be plenty of ways that you can showcase your talents?"

Bob Steeler: "They never tell you that they'll give you solos, or anything like that. Guys don't do that. The fact they wanted me to play with them was all I needed. They had confidence in me and liked what I did. Typically musicians don't qualify things to others. If they do it doesn't keep the air fresh. I don't mean they don't tell you where to put an accent on a beat, I mean the playing style. All I needed for my own benefit was they wanted me. They didn't even correct anything about my playing for a month. Jack would have suggestions here and there. They didn't like when I played too many cymbals. Having played jazz I liked the cymbals. Not to crash on the cymbals, but to play logger-rhythms. They were more used to a straight ahead approach. Some of the stuff I did initially was confusing."

Craig: "How long was it before Greg Douglass's first appearance with you guys on 3/3/75 at Margarita's Canteen, Santa Cruz, California, that you knew a second guitarist would be in the line-up?"

Bob Steeler: "They did not discuss stuff with me. I think Jorma told me that he heard Greg was a good guitar-player and he wanted to play with him. He showed up and he was part of the band. I thought he was doing real well. He is a good player. He is a shredder. Which is a different kind of style from Jorma. He plays more like Joe Satriani (Played with Deep Purple for a short time in 1994, when Ritchie Blackmore left. Besides his own work he toured with Mick Jagger's band). Greg Douglass can play. He is a real good player. Some of his styles took away from the bare-boned blues style that Jorma plays. I don't mean to say that Jorma doesn't play other things, or doesn't play complex things. Jorma plays many things that are complex. Jorma's style comes from more rudimentary play. Jorma isn't putting out fast scales all over the place. That wasn't his focus."

Craig: "Is there truth to the story Greg wanted to play a lot of lead guitar and Jorma didn't want to share the solos?"

Bob Steeler: "I don't recall if there was any discussion to Greg getting to play leads."

Craig: "If you had to give Greg Douglass's role a title when he was hired what would you have said?"

Bob Steeler: "Second guitar-player. The situation is interesting. One of Jorma's many strengths is his very strong rhythm playing. He is as good as anybody on the planet. He is so good it's ridiculous. His lead playing is great too. The way he plays rhythm is terrific. As time went on Greg was playing more solos that resembled the guitar hero, or the heavy metal side. It was Jorma's trip. I could see he was in a position he wasn't wild about."

Craig: "Was the parting between Jorma and Greg amicable? When he walked off the stage at the Music Inn on 7/26/75 in Lenox, Massachusetts, did he know that was the final gig?"

Bob Steeler: "I never saw a goodbye. I may not have known that was his last show. I don't think it went down as goodbye. Did the change take place in the middle of a tour?"

Craig: "The next show would be the 6th of September."

Bob Steeler: "I honestly don't know. I would tell you. I don't remember. It isn't always easy to tell why things happen. Stuff is going on all the time in a band. Did you know Jorma's wife at the time Margareta was not only an incredible artist but wrote incredible poetry. Man she could write. The way she could write she could have helped out with some of the songs. Jorma had a beautiful house at the time. When you walked into his house you had a fantastic feeling of space. It was a very cool house. It really was. She was a very talented woman."

Craig: "People can check out the website of her artwork at www.margaretakaukonen.com. Did you feel the fans took a liking to Greg? The 1975 shows with the band as a four piece are legendary."

Bob Steeler: "From my point of view at the beginning he was definitely accepted. Jorma and Jack liked him. One of the things is as a hired gun you have to wonder where you stand. I remember when I first got the gig with them my girlfriend's best friend comes over and tells me " Be careful Hot Tuna doesn't fire you." Here I just got the gig and hours later I have to be careful not to be fired. From the first day I got the gig I had this huge note of paranoia hanging over me. It made me worry."

Craig: "Thankfully the Tuna fan had you during the best days of the band. When it was time for you to go into the studio and record your first record with Hot Tuna (*America's Choice*) was it a good experience?"

Bob Steeler: "It was very strange. The producer (Mallory Earl) was working by the hour. I thought that was bizarre. He wanted everything to take as long as possible. I wasn't crazy about that. We also played so loud that I had to ask for headphones to hear myself. When I asked for the headphones I was told they wouldn't make any difference. I said I want them anyway. I insisted on the headphones. It was a different trip than anything I was used to."

Craig: "How did you feel the songs turned out?"

Bob Steeler: "The songs were not my best takes by any means. By take three I am pretty much done. I have my best energy on the early takes. On some of the songs they weren't looking for a good take for two or three days. After you play a ten minute tune five times you forget where you are with it. It's hard to play something for fifty minutes. It was hard for me. I didn't know if I were in the bridge, or the second chorus. We did some long *jams* too. Once after one take it was so good the people in the control room were jumping up and down. The take was so good it was insane. Then the producer tells us that we almost got it. I tell him that was the best I got. It can't get better. Then I remember he is working by the hour. I wanted it to take as little time as possible. As a drummer energy is consequential. You need to use as little energy as possible. After you play a ten minute tune five or six times you aren't warmed up, you are beat. We are playing as loud as we can play. Forget about the music, it was physically demanding. I was using the biggest sticks I could buy, to simply hear myself play."

Craig: "Did things improve in the studio for *Yellow Fever*?"

Bob Steeler: "It got better for me. I was used to it. I got them to give me headphones. I could hear myself, the mix was good, things were okay."

Craig: "During the sessions for *Yellow Fever* there was a second guitarist used John Sherman. What made Jorma bring in an outside source? Couldn't he have done the overdubs as needed?"

Bob Steeler: "Jorma could have done that. Think about the facts if all Jorma did was overdub, it gets to be like talking to yourself. You could be the greatest guitar-player in the world but somebody else can help you get fresh ideas, and a different sound. John had a good style. He didn't have the chops of Greg Douglass. He had a fantastic style and great sound. That can be more important than the chops."

Craig: "When did you find out Nick Buck would be joining Hot Tuna on stage for some of the 1977 tour?"

Bob Steeler: "Probably when he showed up to play. We jammed a couple of times. At which point I didn't ask a lot of questions. I was a hired gun and did what they wanted me to do. I played the best I could possibly play all the time. I always gave it my best. My primary concern was to give a good accounting of myself.

Sometimes adding a musician could be a social thing. It gives them somebody else to play with and hang out with. That isn't a bad thing."

Craig: "How did you get along with Nick Buck?"

Bob Steeler: "We got along okay. He is a good musician, and I got along with him."

Craig: "What was your reaction to having a keyboard-player on stage?"

Bob Steeler: "I couldn't care one way or the other. I love keyboard-players. My best friend is a keyboard-player."

Craig: "During the rehearsals for the 1977 tour you had a terrific bunch of new songs to consider playing live. Three of them *Bright Eyes*, *Snow Gorilla*, and *The Party Song* (Jack sang background vocals), would be performed live, what are your memories of the tunes?"

Bob Steeler: "On the *Party Song* we all got to sing."

Craig: "Did Jorma think the other songs from the rehearsals weren't strong enough for a live performance?"

Bob Steeler: "Jorma didn't discuss that. Basically in those days he felt we will cross that bridge when we get to it. We didn't plan things. Jorma sometimes would ask what I wanted to play. Normally it was up to Jorma and Jack. They didn't plan stuff. I wasn't aware of it anyway."

Craig: "To this day do you have several Hot Tuna songs that are your favorites?"

Bob Steeler: "I can tell you right now. *Funky #7* and *Trial By Fire*. *Trial By Fire* is one of the greatest tunes ever written."

Craig: "How did you like *Invitation*?"

Bob Steeler: "I didn't like *Invitation*. It was okay. I liked *Feel So Good*. I liked that one."

Craig: "How about *Baby What You Want Me To Do*?"

Bob Steeler: "Yup. I loved that one. *Sunrise Dance With The Devil* is one I loved to play. To me *Invitation* was a normal rock song. It sounds like things other people do. The changes were normal. The other songs were more sophisticated."

Craig: "When it got to the last show of the 1977 tour on 11/26/77 at The Palladium, New York City (Late show), did you know it was the end of Hot Tuna as we knew it? (Thankfully I was there)."

Bob Steeler: "I didn't. Not long after I was told by Jorma that the band had gone as far as it could. Jorma and Jack would pursue separate projects."

Craig: "When you got the news that Jorma would be playing with you only what was your first reaction?"

Bob Steeler: "I knew Jack wasn't going to be in the band. Jorma and I went out and we played. It wasn't that strange to me. I had done duets before. Not long ago I played with a saxophone player for one hour. It didn't scare me."

Craig: "What did you think when Jorma played Hot Tuna material acoustically, but electric you guys were playing the *Happy Go Lucky Space Rats Go Underwater*?"

Bob Steeler: "I like change. I liked to do new stuff. I didn't know where it would go, but it was interesting. The road crew didn't like it."

Craig: "In July of 1979 Jorma made the band a trio, with the addition of Denny Degorio on bass. (The group was called Hidden Klitz). How did that come about?"

Bob Steeler: " Denny came through me. We were playing in a punk band toward the end of the time I spent with Jorma, called the Offs."

Craig: "Soon after Jorma formed White Gland (August of 1979), how come Danny O'Brien was the drummer, and you had left?"

Bob Steeler: "The time had come where I didn't want to cruise along on somebody else's trip. I wanted to do something where I had more influence. I didn't make money, but I had fun in the punk scene. I played with Flipper on their first couple of gigs. I played with Johnny Thunders (New York Dolls). I also played with Wayne Kramer (MC5). Although he wasn't punk I played with Edgar Winter." (Brother of blues legend Johnny Winter. Edgar plays the blues, funk, and rock and roll. He had a major hit with the song *Frankenstein*).

Craig: "When 1983 came around and Hot Tuna finally reformed were you surprised that you were not asked to play drums and they used Shigemi Komiyama?" (Jorma also brought in Michael Falzarano to play guitar and handle some vocals).

Bob Steeler: "Not really. Sometimes when you leave a band (When I left to do my own trip in 1979), the other people can feel betrayed. I would have. We never had bad words. Things were fine. Jorma and I even jammed three times after I left in 1979. I have nothing but great memories to have played with Jorma and Jack."

Craig: "On 7/18/85 you played one song with Jorma at Nancy's Whiskey Pub, New York City. A song that the Temptations and the Rolling Stones made famous, *It's Just My Imagination (Running Away With Me)*. Was that planned?"

Bob Steeler: "No it wasn't. The only time it was planned was in Colorado. Jorma, Pete Sears, Michael Falzarano, and myself. The sound system was so awful I couldn't hear. I ended up playing backwards the entire tune. I don't remember the date, but I believe it was between 1992 and 1995. As for the Nancy's Whiskey Pub performance, I am not sure if he asked me to sit in, or I went to hear him play, and then he asked me to go on stage. I may have asked. I don't know what happened."

Craig: "It is great that if you never play together again, at least you did make music with Jorma after 1979."

Bob Steeler: "It was great."

Craig: "If given the opportunity would you have played with Jorma and or Hot Tuna again on a steady basis?"

Bob Steeler: "I absolutely would have played with Jorma, or Hot Tuna again."

Craig: "You've had a heavy amount of activity the past ten years. Can you catch the readers up with Steelhead, America's Choice, and Chameleon?"

Bob Steeler: "Steelhead was a group that had influences from the Grateful Dead to Metallica (Started in the 1980's as a metal oriented band). We did a great version of the Grateful Dead's *Franklin's Tower*. We played *War Pigs* from Black Sabbath. Much of the music was funk-rock. When we changed bass-players we weren't able to capture the strength of the previous one. I played with them from about 1995 until 2000. America's Choice (Plays Hot Tuna material in superlative fashion) is a band I should record with. The two other guys John

Zabecki on guitar and Steve Austin on bass, compliment each other really well. John is an amazing finger-picker. The cool thing about playing with them is I didn't need to rehearse, I already knew the tunes."

Craig: "How many shows do you do a year with America's Choice?"

Bob Steeler: "We play six or so. If time permitted it would be more. Chameleon got its name from the Herbie Hancock (Jazz keyboardist) album *Head Hunters*. I started with them around 2004. I am not a member. I play when they need a drummer. I also do work with some guys in the band. I don't like to use the term smooth jazz, because it doesn't do justice to all they can play, and myself as well."

Craig: "You had once mentioned to me that you would like to record some of your own material and release it. You wanted to play piano on the songs. Are the plans still in the works?"

Bob Steeler: "They are. I am attempting to get a home studio set up. It has been the studio from hell thus far. Once I have it installed properly and am able to be comfortable with the features I want to get a bunch of material recorded. Until the studio is set up properly I can't go ahead with the project."

Craig: "Once you have the studio in working order and the songs recorded would you consider selling the material through a website for your fans, and at the live gigs?"

Bob Steeler: "I would like to make it available."

Craig: "You may have some great archival tapes that could be of interest as well. You can look at a four decade history of the music you have helped create. The Tuna fans would love to see the product available."

Bob Steeler: "Thanks Craig. This is all possible. I want to do it right."

Craig: "Are you still actively painting?"

Bob Steeler: "I am. There are paintings I do for myself. There are projects for other people. It can be the same as music. Some projects are really interesting and others can be tedious. For instance if somebody wants you to paint a thousand blades of grass. There isn't any improvisation on that one."

Craig: "That's why we need you as active behind the drums as possible. Especially if it is for a power trio. Bob it's always great to spend time with you. The fans can visit the Bob Steeler website at www.bobsteeler.com. I understand you will be updating it soon. Thanks so much for helping out with the book. When things settle down with the studio installation I look for some great rock and roll, blues, funk, and jazz from the big man on the big machine."

Bob Steeler: "Thanks so much Craig. I'll be sure to let you hear the tracks when they are recorded. Let me know if I can answer anything else for the book."

Jack Traylor- Steelwind with David Freiberg and Craig Chaquico, and contributed to Sunfighter, Baron Von Tollbooth & The Chrome Nun, and Manhole.

Craig: "Thanks for offering your assistance with the Steelwind information. How are you feeling?"

Jack Traylor: "My pleasure Craig. I had the flu bug for about two weeks, but am doing much better now."

Craig: "How did you first become acquainted with Paul Kantner?"

Jack Traylor: "Around 1961 I was playing at a coffeehouse in Palo Alto, California. It most likely was called The Insight. Paul had stopped by a few times and one night he asked if I could show him some guitar stuff. It was soon after I took an eight year hiatus from music. I didn't play from 1961-1969. I was teaching during that period."

Craig: "How did you get involved in Paul Kantner's 1971 *Sunfighter* album?"

Jack Traylor: "In 1969 I wanted to start performing again. I thought music would be a viable exit from teaching. When Paul was getting ready to record the *Sunfighter* record he talked with me about the song *Earth Mother*. Paul liked the tune and put it on the record."

**Jack Traylor & Steelwind**

(L to R) Jack Traylor, Diana Harris,
Denny Virdier, Skip Morairty & Craig Chaquico

Photograph by kind permission of Mike Somavilla. From the Mike Somavilla collection. Photograph not to be reproduced without the written consent of Mike Somavilla.
Photographer unknown. This is a promotional photo.
Thank you BMG.

Craig: "In 1973 Steelwind released *Child Of Nature*. You had Craig Chaquico on the LP, as well as David Freiberg. There also was a terrific singer Diana Harris that was part of the group."

Jack Traylor: "Diana was great. We had a singer before her named Francis, that didn't work out. I'm glad we got Diana, she was excellent."

Craig: "Do you have memories how the band got along?"

Jack Traylor: "For the most part we got along fine. We were friends."

Craig: "Another record that you were part of was from 1973, *Baron Von Tollbooth & The Chrome Nun* with Grace Slick and Paul Kantner. You got to sing your song *Flowers Of The Night*."

Jack Traylor: "It reminded me of family. The group that I knew sticking together to record an album. I liked that Jerry Garcia and David Crosby were walking around the studio. I also enjoyed the fact that once the Jefferson Starship was about to be born there was more importance placed on the lyrics. That may not always be important for the live shows, but in the studio it was nice that the words were an important part of the songs construction."

Craig: "In 1974 you had a co-writing credit on the Grace Slick album *Manhole* (*Epic # 38*) with Paul and Grace."

Jack Traylor: "Craig, I don't remember that. Maybe I contributed some parts of the song, but nothing is clear at the moment. It could have been something we did at Paul's house."

Craig: "Although Steelwind didn't top the charts, it was a wonderful record. Why didn't you continue in the music business to see if the next album could have caught more attention?"

Jack Traylor: "Sometime either in 1973 or 1974 Steelwind opened a show for King Crimson (Progressive rock band that once had Greg Lake and is always led in any incarnation by guitarist Robert Fripp) at the Academy Of Music, New York City. I looked out from the stage and in the first four rows were fans no older then twenty-two. At the time I was thirty-eight. I thought to myself is this what I want to do for the rest of my life? I loved to perform and write but didn't like the business side of things. You have people that hang on to musicians and then the politics of recording."

Craig: "What was it like opening for King Crimson?"

Jack Traylor: "Robert Fripp was the only person of any group we opened for excluding the Jefferson Starship that asked if he could do anything for us. Robert wanted to make sure we were comfortable and happy. The Jefferson Starship did that because we were friends and I like to call them family. What Fripp did was be a gentleman. He was a real nice guy."

Craig: "Some would say you caught Robert on an unusual day. When you were in Steelwind could you sense that Craig Chaquico was going to do something special in the music industry?"

Jack Traylor: "I could sense it at an early age. He may have been fifteen the first time I heard him. Craig had excellent technique and talent. There was not a doubt he would make a name for himself."

Craig: "Once you decided to leave the music business did you stay in contact with the people that you had played with?"

Jack Traylor: "I didn't pay attention to the business. By not being involved on a daily basis I lost touch with a great deal of people."

Craig: "Before you were contacted to be part of the Intergalactic Reunion show on 4/5/03 at the Marin Center Exhibit Hall, San Rafael, California, can you remember the last time you and Paul Kantner had spoken?"

Jack Traylor: "It may have been 1993. He had lost my phone number."

Craig: "The gig from San Rafael had such great moments with Signe Anderson and Spencer Dryden being part of the festivities, as well as you, Darby Gould, and Tim Gorman, to name a few. What are your memories of that night and how did you get contacted?"

Jack Traylor: "The memories are fantastic. I got an email from somebody telling me they were a fan and would I be interested in participating. I didn't know the person. I told them if I'm contacted by Paul Kantner I would be honored to perform. I then get a call from Michael Gaiman (Jefferson Starship manager). Since I don't follow the music business I didn't know Michael. I told Michael have Paul call me. A few minutes later Paul Kantner was on the phone and we talked about the show."

Craig: "How much preparation did you have for *Earth Mother*, *Flowers Of The Night* and the grand finale of *Volunteers*?"

Jack Traylor: "I practiced ten days before the show a good amount each day. I had a concern how my songs would go over."

Craig: "How was the fear alleviated?"

Jack Traylor: "I was walking back stage and Slick Aguilar the guitarist was playing *Flowers Of The Night*, I could tell by his interpretation and ability the song would sound fine. Slick is a truly good person and an excellent musician."

Craig: "How was it to see David Freiberg after such a long period of time?"

Jack Traylor: "It was wonderful. David is such a good person. Talking with him that night was terrific."

Craig: "When you hit the stage does anything come to mind that you were thinking?"

Jack Traylor: "The first thing was not to have a senior moment and forget everything. I did get out a good line, welcome to the antique road show."

Craig: "Not only didn't you have a senior moment you were able to win the crowd over."

Jack Traylor: "I loved the fact that there were people of all ages in the audience. I saw parents with their kids, and hippies, as well as people in business clothing. There were all ages there."

Craig: "That is the beauty of timeless music. The Jefferson Airplane and the spin-off bands have created such everlasting sounds that people can grow old with the music and pass it down to the next generation."

Jack Traylor: "I hope it stays that way. It was a great night for me."

Craig: "Have you been in contact with Paul Kantner about any other reunion concerts?"

Jack Traylor: "He told me he had some ideas. Nothing is firm at the moment but you never know."

Craig: "I hope that the fans see you on stage again in the near future and more importantly take care of your health. I'm glad you are feeling better."

Jack Traylor: "Thank you.  Craig remember the guys in the book are friends of mine, so be nice to them."

Craig: "The music of your friends has been an important part of my life for over thirty years.  My goal is to talk about the legendary rock and roll and keep the plane flying.  Thanks for spending some time with me today."

Jack Traylor: "You are welcome.  I hope the book works out fine for you."

# Peter van Gelder- Great Society.

Craig: "It's nice to be able to talk with you."

Peter van Gelder: "Thank you."

Craig: "How were you first informed that the Great Society wasn't happy with Bard Dupont's bass playing, and they were looking for a different musician?"

Peter van Gelder: "I was back east and had received a call from Darby Slick. Darby and I were very good friends. He explained that the band needed somebody with more musical ability and that would take the instrument seriously."

Craig: "Did you have any contact with Bard Dupont?"

Peter van Gelder: "I never did."

Craig: "Did you have to think about the decision?"

Peter van Gelder: "I had a jazz background, but I had never been in a band. I thought it would be a fun and interesting opportunity."

Craig: "How did they break you into the group?"

Peter van Gelder: "I believe it was at the Fillmore Auditorium, San Francisco. The band had to alternate the bass-player. When I got there they let me play on two songs. They saw I could handle the job, but took the bass away from me because I didn't know their full repertoire. (Peter laughs)."

Craig: "Did you have preconceived notions of what you wanted from the Great Society?"

Peter van Gelder: "I didn't look at the band as a commercial enterprise. I was enjoying playing, but didn't think of record contracts, or full scale tours. In 1966 I was blown away with the popular music scene. I could listen to the Airplane, Grateful Dead, and the Blues Project (Included Steve Katz, and Al Kooper, later of Blood Sweat & Tears)."

Craig: "How plentiful were the live gigs?"

Peter van Gelder: "I am not exactly sure on this, but I believe John Carpenter was a friend of the Airplane's first manager Matthew Katz. John got us weekend gigs."

Craig: "When you started to play with the Great Society did you feel the band had comradery, or in fighting?"

Peter van Gelder: "There was tension. Jerry Slick was more into the commercial success. The others wanted self expression, without compromise. They wanted to create a sound and not have a sound created for them. I think of Paul Revere & The Raiders (In the 1960's and 1970's they had many Top 40 hits, including *Kicks* and *Indian Reservation* (*The Lament Of The Cherokee Reservation Indian*), as having a sound created for them."

Craig: "After hearing Grace a few times live, could you foreshadow great things to come?"

Peter van Gelder: "I wasn't sure she would be a star. I did sense she had style, was a revolutionary, and truly loved music. She took the Great Society very seriously."

Craig: "If you look over documentation of songs the Great Society performed, is there a cover tune that has gotten overlooked?"

Peter van Gelder: "The Bob Dylan song *It's All Over Now, Baby Blue*, we did a good version. Dylan is the man of the century. You could do a Dylan cover and the audience was okay with it, they identified with him."

Craig: "Why did David Miner leave the group?"

Peter van Gelder: "He felt the tension had reached a boiling point. There were egos and arguments. You have the normal pressures of a band. Trying to secure a record deal, playing enough live shows, and which songs are best to do."

Craig: "There is a story that two weeks after David quit the band he tried to get his job back. Is this true, or another example of rewriting history?"

Peter van Gelder: "I heard that as well. From what I recall, that didn't happen. I do not remember David requesting to rejoin the Great Society."

Craig: "David's place was taken by Oscar. Since 1966 he has only been called Oscar. Does he have a real name?"

Peter van Gelder: "His name was actually Oscar Daniels. He was a real good flamingo-guitarist. Oscar was a good friend of the band. Unfortunately he would end up with drug problems."

Craig: "How did the band receive the news that Grace was going to the Jefferson Airplane?"

Peter van Gelder: "Her husband told the band. It was rather matter of fact. It may have been after a rehearsal."

Craig: "Did the Great Society have at least one record contract on the table when the band broke up?"

Peter van Gelder: "We did. As often happened in those days the deal wasn't a good one. Howard Wolf the manager had negotiated a contract. It wasn't going to be that good for the band."

Craig: "Do you have any regrets that the Great Society wasn't able to record a studio record, when the band was together?"

Peter van Gelder: "For me I didn't think about that. I don't know how the others would answer the question. I can listen to the two live albums that were put out after the band broke up." (*Conspicuous Only In Its Absence* and *How It Was,* were released in 1968).

Craig: "When the band disbanded did you keep up with how Grace was sounding with the Airplane?"

Peter van Gelder: "I went through a period where I didn't listen to any western music for twenty-five years. The one exception was Jimi Hendrix, he was a genius."

Craig: "We'll get into your study of the sitar in a moment. Did you have contact with Grace and the others after the group broke up?"

Peter van Gelder: "I think I spoke to Grace one time. I don't remember the year she was in the recording studio and I called to see if I could drop by with my daughter. She told me that would be fine. Darby and I played sitar together from about 1969-1974. We did a bunch of shows as well. Somewhere between 1995 and 1997 Jerry, Darby, and myself tried to play together. Nothing happened with it. It couldn't get off the ground. In the summer of 2003, or maybe it was 2002, (10/20/02 Civic Center Plaza, San Francisco) Jerry, Darby, and I played a Summer Of Love concert with multiple artists. We played *White Rabbit* and *Somebody To Love*." (They also played *Sally Go 'Round The Roses* and some others. Please see the main section of the book for the complete set list and the musicians in the band).

Craig: "You are an accomplished sitar-player. Can you fill the readers in on the interesting story of going to India when the Great Society broke up to study with Maestro Ali Akbar Khan?"

Peter van Gelder: "In the mid-sixties I went to India. It took two months to get there. Flying was too expensive back then. Darby, and I sold our equipment, and decided we would both go. We didn't travel together. Darby got there first, and after not seeing me, he returned home. I studied the sitar under Maestro Ali Akbar Khan. I am also an instructor of the sitar at Ali Akbar College of Music in San Rafael, California." (Peter didn't want to be braggadocios, but his credentials also include the University of Chicago awarding him a Professional Development Fellowship in 1989).

Craig: "When did you get your first sitar?"

Peter van Gelder: "The first one I bought was in 1969. I purchased another in 1989."

Craig: "I hope as a gift to keep up the new sitar every twenty years, you receive one in 2009. What does a sitar cost?"

Peter van Gelder: "You can pay five hundred dollars for a less expensive one. They can go from one thousand dollars to twenty-five hundred dollars. Craig, can I ask you a question about Grace?"

Craig: "Please feel free to ask me anything."

Peter van Gelder: "Do you think when Grace was in the Airplane, she was stifled as far as a songwriter goes?"

Craig: "One of the strengths of the band was having four people that could write, and sing. Those would be Marty, Paul, Grace, and Jorma. This was also an albatross, because in the days of vinyl LP's you were limited to usually under forty minutes. If each member wanted to contribute several songs, it could cause a great deal of conflict. As Jorma's playing stretched into longer compositions, if you put a blues song on a record, you may have to remove somebody else's track. There was no way to split the pie fairly. You never hear people bring up the fact that the Airplane never put out a double album. I hope the readers will visit your website http://www.petervangelder.com, and learn about your proficiency, and admiration for the sitar. Are you playing with any specific musicians at the moment?"

Peter van Gelder: "I play with Manose. He is from Nepal and very proficient on the flute."

Craig: "Peter, thanks so much for your insight on the Great Society. Best of luck with any future projects."

Peter van Gelder: "Thank you. Best of luck with the book."

## Jefferson Family Friends:

## Peter Albin- Big Brother & The Holding Company with Janis Joplin remembers Spencer Dryden and Janis Joplin.

Craig: "Thank you for talking with me today."

Peter Albin: "It's a pleasure."

Craig: "When Big Brother And The Holding Company was in the formative stages, did you switch from guitar to the bass to accommodate your friend Jim Gurley?"

Peter Albin: "I had actually switched before Jim joined the band as a guitarist."

Craig: "How did you pick the bass as an instrument prior to the Big Brother days?"

Peter Albin: "I had a bluegrass background. The bass was instrumental in the sound. It's possible at this point I haven't picked up a guitar in twenty years."

Craig: "It seems strange to hear that, since you did play both bass and guitar (Peter is being modest. He would switch instruments on stage and was rather good on the six string). When the first Big Brother & The Holding Company album was near completion did you get the feeling that you had been part of a record that could hold its own then and for years to come?"

Peter Albin: "At that time no. There was a specific sound the band had live and was searching for on the record. The budget was very limited in the studio. We were given twelve, maybe thirteen takes per song. It was twelve, because thirteen was thought to be unlucky. There were parts we wanted to correct when the album was completed. A couple of times I felt the band had sped up during a take and I wanted the best possible result."

Craig: "Was that one of the reasons you wanted to get out of the contract from the label and sign with a larger one (Which was done) for the *Cheap Thrills* album?"

Peter Albin: "There were other factors too. Our deal with them which we were told was standard for the time, had them take a large percentage of the publishing royalties and there wasn't the upfront money other bands of the time had received. The record company liked to release a bunch of singles from an album first, to see how those would sell. Sometimes if the singles didn't achieve enough income they wouldn't release the record."

Craig: "Where did Chet Helms fit in during this period? Is there any involvement with the band?"

Peter Albin: "Not as a manager. We had to let him go because of the amount of time he needed to spend with the promoting of the Family Dog Dance Concerts. If you look at the early posters, we were playing for a Chet Helms promoted concert almost every weekend."

Craig: "Were there hard feelings about having to make a change in managers? (Chet knew Janis from college days, and helped to formulate things at the start)."

Peter Albin: "It was almost a relief to him. It would have been impossible to have given the proper time allocations to both the promoting of bands and the managing of Big Brother."

Craig: "When the Cheap Thrills album came out, we always hear about the sterling vocal on *Summertime*, or the timeless *Piece Of My Heart*, but a tune that is overlooked was *Combination Of The Two*. It is an example of a great band, creating something that should have been elevated to a higher pedestal."

Peter Albin: "Thank you. I like the tune too."

510

Craig: "When you first began to play with Janis in the live environments and in the studio, were you able to sense that there were inner demons, and if not dealt with a rocky road would be the path ahead?"

Peter Albin: "There was a time before she had come to San Francisco for good that she was clean for a year and a half. When we were in the studio she had a great idea what she wanted to do and was able to execute it properly. The same on stage."

Craig: "What are your recollections of the music scene circa 1967 and 1968?"

Peter Albin: "I don't remember playing too much with the Jefferson Airplane. We were booked often with Country Joe & The Fish and Quicksilver Messenger Service. I always admired the Airplane's music, both live and their work on record. When we did play with the Airplane it was very enjoyable."

Craig: "From 1965-1972 between shows that Big Brother and the Airplane were on the same bill and those that you attended as a fan, how many times would you have seen the Jefferson Airplane on stage?"

Peter Albin: "It would have to be pretty close to twenty-five. A time that we played with the Jefferson Airplane that stands out is Tribal Stomp #1. Chet Helms promoted the show, at the Avalon Ballroom, San Francisco."

Craig: "When I spoke with Don Aters the photographer he mentioned the original pressing of the 2/1/66 Tribal Stomp poster is worth about eighty-eight hundred dollars."

Peter Albin: "I have a second pressing. The money would be nice for an original."

Craig: "Are there studio records from the Airplane that you enjoyed at the time of release?"

Peter Albin: "I loved the albums *Surrealistic Pillow* and the first one, *Takes Off.*"

Craig: "You have some fascinating stories about meeting or seeing Airplane members, before they were part of the band."

Peter Albin: "I am not good on dates. I always mention that. I am not sure on the sequence of events. My brother Rodney and I were playing folk music, in a band called the Liberty Hall Aristocrats. There was a show that both the Liberty Hall Aristocrats and Marty Balin's Town Criers appeared. Marty was terrific."

Craig: "I can give you a copy of Marty doing a great tune with the Town Criers, called Hellbound Train."

Peter Albin: "I would love to hear that."

Craig: "What other memories do you recall?"

Peter Albin: "One night Rodney and I were booked at a place in San Jose, California, the Offstage Theatre. Also performing that night was a guy named Jerry. Jorma played as Jerry Kaukonen. Then there was the time that my brother Rodney is playing a gig and I wanted to check it out. When I get to the venue the drummer is Jerry Peloquin. (Jerry would be the original J.A. drummer, before Skip Spence). I don't recall the name of the place my brother and Jerry played. Here's another Airplane meeting. There was a place in California called something along the lines of Golden Lamp, maybe Golden Lantern. I remember, it was called the Golden Lamp, located in Burlingame, California. When I walk in the place the guy that was the master of ceremonies for the evening turned out to be Bob Harvey." (**Bob Harvey was the Airplane's bass-player prior to Jack Casady**).

Craig: "As it turned out you met Marty, Bob, Jerry Peloquin, and Jorma before the Airplane first took off. You had an introduction to four of the six members before the original line-up took hold. Excluding Paul and Signe you would know the members of the band for the first incarnation."

Peter Albin: "That is right. There is one story left that you'll get a kick out of. There was a female singer in the San Francisco scene 1964 and 1965 Joanie Simms. I don't recall if she spelled the last name Sims or Simms. Her forte was more blues and Broadway show tunes.  She really liked Sophie Tucker (Ziegfeld Follies).  One day she had an audition.  She asked me to play the guitar.  We get to the place.  She sings two or three songs.  When we get off stage I notice there is a guy hidden from the light.  We walked by and there was Marty Balin.  I asked Marty what he was doing there.  Marty tells me he is putting a band together."

Craig: "Did Marty ever tell you how she did, on the audition?"

Peter Albin: "To this day I never found out."

Craig: "If she had impressed Marty maybe Signe Anderson never gets to sing.  The entire history of the San Francisco scene could have been altered."

Peter Albin: "That is true.  I hadn't thought about that."

Craig: "Any recollections of Skip Spence?"

Peter Albin: "I liked the guy.  He was funny.  I enjoyed his music as well."

Craig: "We will obvious discuss Spencer Dryden in a few minutes.  There is always history being rewritten and those that were nowhere near the events claiming to be on site.  Today we can go right to the source.  Would it be fair terminology that Janis left Big Brother because she wanted to go solo after *Cheap Thrills*?  If the language is correct, isn't that strange, because unlike Bob Dylan for example who could perform with an acoustic guitar, and harmonica, she would need musicians to perform live, or record in the studio."

Peter Albin: "Yea, yea it wasn't always clear.  It seems that she was getting advice from friends and family, that she was the main attraction of the band and could do better on her own.  There were those in her inner circle that were telling her she would make more money, have more fame, and could play with a larger group of musicians.  There were names being thrown around such as Mike Bloomfield (Paul Butterfield Blues Band and Electric Flag) and Nick Gravenites (Mike Bloomfield and Electric Flag).  Remember please I am recalling this information from what I ended up hearing."

Craig: "If Janis were alive today and admitted that everything the friends and family told her she believed to be true, wouldn't that discredit the entire theme of the 1960's, to put peace and love and unity over money and individual accolades?"

Peter Albin: "Did that hurt us at the time?  Sure it did.  There were some people that were feeding her incorrect stories.  One was that I was getting a larger share of the pie, than she was.  We set up the group as an equal enterprise.  We all got the same amount of money and expenses.  I would never have taken more than the other members, nor would I have been offered more."

Craig: "When the news was given to you and the band that she was going to take a different musical path how did you find out?"

Peter Albin: "I believe that she called all of us.  That took guts."

Craig: "Once Janis left to follow a new direction, how long before things would be okay between Big Brother and her?"

Peter Albin: "I am not the best on dates.  I think in 1969 I was playing with Country Joe in Detroit, Michigan, and Janis was booked there too.  It could have been Cobo Hall, Detroit 5/10/69.  We talked for a bit.  I also remember going to a couple of parties at her home around that time.  At the 4/4/70 show at the Fillmore West, San Francisco, she got on stage with us (Big Brother).  It may not have been the Fillmore.  The title is a bit fuzzy, but it was either *Eagle Rocking Blues* (Reverend Gary Davis) or *Eagle Rock* (Junior Wells)."
(Thank you to http://www.officialjanis.com/dates_1970.html for having the exact date.  The site wasn't sure on the venue.  Please visit them for a live history of Janis).

Craig: "You played briefly with Country Joe & The Fish the first time. What made you decide to work with him and why was it relatively short?"

Peter Albin: "I was filling in for a tour. Big Brother was also reorganizing and thinking what we wanted to do next."

Craig: "In October of 1970 Big Brother released *Be A Brother*. Kathi McDonald was the female singer in the band. I always thought the record should have received better attention. The tracks *Sunshine Baby* and *Joseph's Coat* were terrific."

Peter Albin: "There were many good tracks. We weren't able to get the airplay for *Be A Brother* or the next album, *How Hard It Is*."

Craig: "I hope the fans that come see the band today can experience the two albums."

Peter Albin: "We offer them at the concerts, as part of our merchandising package."

Craig: "The 1971 release *How Hard It Is*, offered some nice material as well. *Nu Boogaloo Jam* and *Buried Alive In The Blues*, sounded great on the album."

Peter Albin: "There is an interesting story with *Buried Alive With The Blues*. Originally we did a version in the studio that had Mike Finnigan sing the lead vocals. Mike is a well known session guy that plays the keyboards and sings. He has done work with Crosby, Stills, & Nash, Stephen Stills solo, David Crosby solo, and a bunch of others (Ringo Starr and Dave Mason, to name a couple). The take with Finnigan was excellent. His manager decided that if we were going to use it, Mike would have to be treated as if he were part of the band, and get a bigger cut. Somewhere there is a terrific version buried."

Craig: "It makes the title of the record even that much more appropriate. Didn't it register in Mike's mind that if he consents to letting his vocal version be used it could only be beneficial to him?"

Peter Albin: "You would have thought so. I guess you'll have to ask Mike."

Craig: "You would turn up a couple of more times with Country Joe in the next few years and also play with two other bands."

Peter Albin: "I worked with him 1971-1973. I believe in 1978 too. In 1975 I was in a band called Grits. (The country-rock group and not the jazz-free-form band). In the years 1975 through 1977, I played with the Out Of Hand Band. The joke was always we were the out of work band."

Craig: "You went through a long period of time where you didn't make music the main focus."

Peter Albin: "The time came where I needed a break. For many years I was involved in a managerial capacity for a wholesale distributor."

Craig: "Do you remember how the Dinosaurs were formed around 1982?"

Peter Albin: "I am not that clear on how it all came together. I do know we never rehearsed."

Craig: "Is it true that Spencer Dryden wasn't the first drummer? You had a gig scheduled and the original drummer was a no show?"

Peter Albin: "That sounds right. I can't remember the name of the first drummer. In the music business people come and go all the time."

Craig: "Did your friend from Country Joe (Barry Melton) give the name Dinosaurs to the band, because of some stage banter he had with a fan?"

Peter Albin: "Yes that is correct. Somebody yelled out for us to play a certain song. Barry told the fan that we are just a bunch of old dinosaurs."

Craig: "Why did it take six years before an album would be released?"

Peter Albin: "The interest wasn't strong enough for a studio record."

Craig: "What about an independent label for a live CD, or mail order?"

Peter Albin: "At the beginning when Robert Hunter played with us, the Grateful Dead Heads would come to the shows. They would tape the performances. As they passed around the different shows, it got harder for us to do that."

Craig: "What were the Dead Heads thoughts of the band?"

Peter Albin: "They were used to more diverse set lists. They didn't like the fact we would play many of the same songs over and over."

Craig: "Why did Robert Hunter leave?"

Peter Albin: "He got tired of the road. He also mentioned that there were back room politics that seemed to go on with most bands."

Craig: "He was replaced by another person that had an association with the Grateful Dead, Merl Saunders (Jerry Garcia, Keith, and Donna Godchaux)."

Peter Albin: "Merl had done a lot of session work and fit right in."

Craig: "What was it like playing with Spencer Dryden?"

Peter Albin: "Spencer took an active role in the financial end of the band. His original goal was to have a Dinosaurs show as a special occasion and not be playing clubs all the time. As it turned out we did end up playing the clubs."

Craig: "What were your feelings on his drumming?"

Peter Albin: "Spencer was a fun guy. I was surprised when we started to play that he had gotten into the punk rock style. I was used to his percussion approach from the Jefferson Airplane days. It was a shame he was replaced in the Airplane. He would use a crash and mod style from the punk movement. Sometimes he would play a backwards beat. This may have been a result of a hearing problem. If he played the punk style he wasn't depending on percussion, or more complex rhythms."

Craig: "Did you know that Spencer had trouble hearing?"

Peter Albin: "Not until we began to play together. It would often take waving our hands in front of his face to gain his attention."

Craig: "Besides the unfortunate hearing loss did you notice any physical problems with Spencer the first few years the Dinosaurs were assembled?"

Peter Albin: "Nothing comes to mind. He may have had trouble with his hip. That is all I recall."

Craig: "Were you friends with Spencer?"

Peter Albin: "Most definitely. I had hired Spencer a couple of times, in the office world. Once was for the distribution company and the other for a music company. By the time the job with the music company became available Spencer had trouble standing and had to leave soon after starting."

514

Craig: "When Spencer was in his last year did you have contact with him in the hospital?"

Peter Albin: "In fact the last time I would see Spencer he was in the hospital. All things considered he was very lucid. He tells me when he gets out of the hospital he wants to by a Mini Cooper (Car). I told Spencer to get well and a bunch of us will get you the car. There was a really nice thing that Barry Melton (Country Joe & The Fish) did for Spencer. When it was near the end Barry got a bunch of information from Spencer to make his private affairs more easily settled and to attempt to avoid any legal hassles."

Craig: "I'm glad somebody that he trusted was there to ease the burden on any family members."

Peter Albin: "Barry was fantastic. With all the people that liked Spencer it was a shame that there wasn't a big memorial service. I always waited for something to happen, of a large magnitude."

Craig: "Glad you two Dinosaurs were close and that Barry helped behind the scenes. Speaking of Dinosaurs. When the Dinosaurs record got reissued in 2005 with one of the greatest titles *Dinosaurs/Friends Of Extinction*, one of the many bonus tracks was *No More Country Girls*, with Papa John Creach. The version had the feel of the blues song *Sitting On Top Of The World* (Written by Lonnie Chatman, and Walter Vinson. Made popular by Cream, the Grateful Dead, and Howlin' Wolf). What was it like playing with Papa John?"

Peter Albin: "He was a nice guy and a real good fiddle-player. He taught me a bunch of songs, including *Somewhere Over The Rainbow*. I also found out that the way he hurt his back was from the time he was an auto mechanic in Pennsylvania. He would always be hunched over. One time we were on a train and he had to sit in a very strange position."

Craig: "Before you have to leave I am curious on your thoughts of the two Big Brother live albums that came out posthumously. The first *Cheaper Thrills*, recorded 7/28/66 at California Hall, San Francisco. Jorma and Jack would like the fact a favorite of theirs *I Know You Rider* (Traditional song) is included. Many of the favorites are on the CD, such as *Ball And Chain*, *Down On Me*, and *Women Is Losers*."

Peter Albin: "There are many people that don't like the fact I was singing some of the songs back then."

Craig: "It gives the Big Brother fan a look at the early days and a chance to enjoy the songs in a different light."

Peter Albin: "Thank you."

Craig: "The other live recording is *Live At Winterland 4/12 & 4/13/68*. This shows the band flexing their muscles on an almost ten minute *Ball And Chain* and *Light Is Faster Than Sound*."

Peter Albin: "This one I really like. I got a chance to hear the tapes before the CD came out. It sounded good. Things weren't tinkered with."

Craig: "I want to get in a plug for the Big Brother & The Holding Company website. The readers can go to www.bbhc.com and find out all the latest news. How many live shows do you hope to do a year?"

Peter Albin: "Depending if we get two tours of Europe, we will play between fifty and seventy concerts. We've rotated female singers. Lisa Battle, Lisa Mills, and Sophia Ramos, to name a few."

Craig: "Having followed your career for a long time I'm thrilled that Big Brother is continuing and not only playing to the older fans but a new generation. Thank you for the musical insights and stay well."

Peter Albin: "Thank you Craig. Good luck with the book and please stay in touch."

**Don Aters- (World famous music photographer) remembers Chet Helms and gives us some Hot Tuna for lunch.**

Photographs top and bottom by kind permission of Don Aters and may not be reproduced without the written consent of Don Aters. From the Don Aters collection. Don Aters photographer. Top photo Jack Casady from a Hot Tuna show circa 2004. Bottom photo Chet Helms and Linda Imperial of the Jefferson Starship from the 4/9/05 Avila Beach Resort, Avila Beach, California Jefferson Starship performance.

**Photograph by kind permission of Don Aters and may not be reproduced without the**

**written consent of Don Aters.**

**From the Don Aters collection.  Don Aters photographer.**

**Circa 2006 Don Aters, Jorma Kaukonen, and Jack Casady.**

**Photograph by kind permission of Don Aters and may not be reproduced without the**
**written consent of Don Aters.  From the Don Aters collection.  Don Aters photographer.**
**Jack Casady from a Hot Tuna show, circa 2006.**

**Don Aters was Chet Helms best friend.  Nobody is more qualified to give a look at a man that never had a bad word to say about anybody.  He promoted for the love of rock and roll and not the mighty dollar.**

Craig: "Thanks for agreeing to not only remember Chet, but to let the readers know how they can try to get him into the Rock And Roll Hall Of Fame."

Don Aters: "How you doing?"

Craig: "Great, thank you. You always wanted to see Chet in the Rock And Roll Hall Of Fame, and he wanted you to finish your master's degree and teach music. Hopefully both wishes can come true."

Don Aters: "I have a bit over a year and his wish will come true. As for Chet, if fans can write a nice letter to the following address:

Rock and Roll Hall of Fame Foundation
1290 Avenue Of The Americas
New York, NY 10104

It will help greatly. They can also start on-line petitions. Their website doesn't have an email address, for the induction department."

Craig: "Let's make the letters flow. What bands did Chet enjoy seeing play live during the San Francisco scene of the 1960's?"

Don Aters: "He liked the big five. They were the Big Brother & The Holding Company, Charlatans, Grateful Dead, Jefferson Airplane, and Quicksilver Messenger Service."

Craig: "What about a couple that weren't as successful?"

Don Aters: "Jim Kweskin Jug Band, Roky Erickson (13th Floor Elevators), and Doug Sahm (Sir Douglas Quintet)."

Craig: "Doug Sahm wrote and has to this day the definitive version of *She's About A Mover.*"

Don Aters: "Yes they do."

Craig: "What made Chet a special person?"

Don Aters: "He was so well liked, that he could have somebody take him out for dinner every single night. Chet never had a bad word to say about anybody. He was always civil and a gentleman. We got to be exceptional friends the past eight years."

Craig: "There were numerous people that helped him with charity functions over the years. Did he tell you some of the guys that he could count on in at a moments notice?"

Don Aters: "The three that come to mind are David Freiberg (Quicksilver Messenger Service, Jefferson Airplane, and Jefferson Starship), Pete Sears (Jefferson Starship, Hot Tuna and the Flying Other Brothers), and Terry Haggerty (Sons Of Champlin)."

Craig: "You have a story that is typical of how a good person in the music business is often taken advantage of."

Don Aters: "There were about two hundred Family Dog (The name of Chet's promotion) posters. Chet had the copyright to one hundred fifty and fifty percent of the copyright on the rest. In the early 1970's he had to pay off a tax debt. Chet was never about money. He had to sell two hundred and fifty thousand posters for twenty-five thousand dollars. To give you an example of how a poster could escalate in value, they were first offered

518

free, then they were available for a buck, and then two dollars. The original Airplane poster is now valued at about eighty-eight hundred dollars!"

Craig: "That is awful, he didn't care about the dollar, but when he needed it he couldn't even get market value for his own property. Is there a talent Chet had that most of us wouldn't know?"

Don Aters: "He was getting very good with digital photos. I had given him some tips."

Craig: "Don, thanks for the nice words about Chet and for helping with so many of the photos about the book. I have to get a plug in for the great website you have www.haightstreetmusic.news.com. There is a tribute to Chet on the site that only you could have written properly."

Don Aters: "Thank you."

Craig: "Before you go any last words?"

Don Aters: "Please write to the Rock And Roll Hall Of Fame. Here is the address once again:

Rock and Roll Hall of Fame Foundation
1290 Avenue Of The Americas
New York, NY 10104

Every letter (Nice ones please) sent opens the door for Chet that much more."

Craig: "Thanks again. I hope you finish the masters program, and Chet looks down from heaven, with a smile the size of the Avalon Ballroom (Chet promoted shows at the Avalon Ballroom in San Francisco, and The Family Dog, At The Great Highway, San Francisco)."

Don Aters: "Thanks and best of luck with the book."

Tom Constanten- Grateful Dead, opening for the Jefferson Starship, and sitting in with them several times.

Craig: "Good morning T.C., thanks for giving me this time."

TC: "You're welcome."

Craig: "For the first question, I hope you can clarify your time in the armed forces. How did the four-year period of active duty come about?"

TC: "I had received a draft notice. I then went to enlist. The choices were either that, Canada, or jail."

Craig: "Those of us lucky enough to have been brought up in the time of a volunteer army have no idea of the decisions young people had to make during the Vietnam era. What were the advantages of enlisting?"

TC: "Had I waited one more year, I would have been five times more likely to go to Vietnam."

Craig: "When you got out of the armed forces, were there any of those in the *Counter Culture* who displayed animosity toward you for severing your time?"

TC: "I never experienced any, either with the fans, bands I played with, or musical contemporaries."

Craig: "When you left the Grateful Dead in January of 1970, did you find over the years when listening to a live show or a record such as *Wake Of The Flood* with Keith Godchaux, or Brent Mydland *In The Dark*, how you would have handled the keyboard parts?"

TC: "I do that with everything I listen to. I met Keith twice, and Brent once, and knew Pigpen (Ron McKernon) rather well, also Vince Welnick (The Tubes and Grateful Dead) and I are good friends. I never had anything but friendly camaraderie with the keyboard-players. Do I listen to something and think I could have done it differently, sure? I'll do that with anybody."

Craig: "When the mutual decision was made that you were going to pursue some other opportunities, were there regrets, either at the time and or years later, regarding leaving the Grateful Dead?"

TC: "There is no place for regrets. That is needless baggage. In fact, you never know. I could have been one of those keyboard-players who is no longer alive had I remained. Everything I went through has been a necessary component in getting me to where I am today."

Craig: "You always have such a positive view on your experiences."

TC: "Those that have so much baggage only get dragged down. I don't function well that way; I like to be in the moment and liberated to function properly. When you're playing music that is improvised, you don't want to be burdened. You can't have your thoughts or movements burdened."

Craig: "You have always been admired for not bringing personal situations on the stage."

TC: "I can get that way. I am a rack mount homo sapien human being, like any one else."

Craig: "Your level of professionalism allows you to circumvent that."

TC: "That's good. I think you should avoid that out on stage; unless of course you are making it part of your act. Then it can be done very effectively."

Craig: "Were you thinking of those in the new wave, punk or power pop movement?"

TC: "I was actually thinking of Rodney Dangerfield (Comedian)."

Craig: "That's an interesting point. If he were happy, the act would go down the tubes."

TC: "Yeah." (TC starts to laugh).

Craig: "When you were thinking of a change from the Grateful Dead, how long of a process was it?"

TC: "It wasn't long. There was an opportunity for me to write music and direct. There was a project in New York. I would be doing all original music and not music that was pre-fabricated, for me to jump in on. There was a mime troupe named Rubber Duck. Along with drummer Gary Hirsch (Country Joe & The Fish) and some others we played three weeks worth of shows. (Some of the material performed came out in 1972 under a new name Touchstone. The LP was called *Tarot* and released on United Artists UAS-5563). As far as I can tell and you can ask Phil Lesh (Grateful Dead), it was entirely friendly. It was like a family member going out and plowing another field."

Craig: "From your time spent in the late 1960's and early 1970's with the Grateful Dead, would you describe things with fellow American bands such as the Jefferson Airplane, Quicksilver, Allman Brothers, etc. as friendly, adversarial, or a peaceful coexistence, with only so much of a pie to be split?"

TC: "It was almost nothing but friendly comradery. We always had the idea there is plenty to go around. Even in the 1960's we would sing with each other. I remember Janis Joplin, David Crosby, and even Paul Kantner at a festival in Louisiana would sit in with us and Jerry Garcia would sit in with one of them."

Craig: "Great to see that there was such respect. In many vocations there is nothing but a cut-throat attitude."

TC: "Rivalry can be very serious and very hostile."

Craig: "In 1970 you had the chance to work with the Incredible String Band for their double album *U* as an arranger. They were known for their mixture of folk and electric folk, improvisational, and Middle Eastern sounds. How did the collaboration come about?"

TC: "I crossed paths with both Mike Heron and Robin Williamson a couple of times. We had mutual friends. Once Mike Heron came over the house that Pigpen and I were sharing in Novato, California. My collaboration came as a result of that visit. They were a different type family than the Grateful Dead, but are every bit as lucid and luminiferous."

Craig: "TC", I'm glad that I have my dictionary handy. Luminiferous is the transmitting of light."

TC: (Chuckles).

Craig: "A few years later, you had the experience of teaching at SUNY Buffalo and the San Francisco Art Institute. What were your thoughts the first day you walked into class and would be spreading knowledge and not performing it?"

TC: "To be sure professoring (A new word by TC) and performing are not the same, but not all that different."

Craig: "How did the jobs come about?"

TC: "They both came about by people in the music departments that knew who I was and what my qualifications were. When I walked into the class everybody knew who I was and what I was about. I didn't have any proving to do. I was able to get straight to the business of talking about what I wanted to talk about. That was history and methods of music, usually."

Craig: "Did any of your students go on to record in a band or star on Broadway? Were there people the average guy or girl on the street would know their names?"

TC: "Not the average person. Many did go on to get degrees in music and professorships of their own."

Craig: "Is there a feeling of accomplishment when your knowledge can be transmitted to a student?"

TC: "It certainly isn't unpleasant. It isn't a goal you can plan. It comes about by attending to your business and doing it well."

Craig: "Having not been the most eager person in a classroom, I always found that I was more motivated if there was something being taught by somebody I respect. Did you ever get any vibes that the students were more in tune with you because of your reputation?"

TC: "Sometimes it can work out that way; but the way I play it is they listen to what I have to say because it is accurate and corresponds to what is really happening. I don't have to show anybody a certificate of certification; I don't have any! It is purely on the validity of the musical material I am talking about. I had some students that hadn't a clue who I was."

Craig: "That is fascinating. If you look at the time they were taking the courses, even if they weren't fans of the Grateful Dead, you would think they would know a little something about the band."

TC: "Just a year ago, I read an interview with a former student of mine who got a doctorate from Duke University and he talked about the fact that I had never mentioned I was in any band or anything. The validity of what I say is what works. I don't have to parade any set of credentials."

Craig: "1993 saw a rather enjoyable album *Morning Dew*, the follow up to the 1992 *Nightfall Of Diamonds*. How did you decide to record what became one of the finest renditions of the song?"

TC: "The pieces weren't so much selected to be on the album as each one having a cluster of reasons for being there."

Craig: "Getting into some of the wonderful covers on the recording, how did you decide to use the Beatles, *I've Just Seen A Face*?"

TC: "That was almost a collision of songs. I was doing the two handed bumachuck (Another TC word) part from *Wooly Bully*, from Sam The Sham And The Pharaohs and trying to fit the Beatles medley onto that. First it started out as something like a piano etude. Then I decided to alternate the hands in a rhythmic pattern, not unlike a drummer would. It turned into to something else and seemed to work on stage occasionally."

Craig: "You work on one part of the plumbing and something else gets fixed."

TC: "That happens often."

Craig: "Another song that got great feedback was the cover of the Jefferson Airplane's *Lather*. What were your recollections of that piece and the cover of a traditional song *John Barleycorn* that was such a big part of Traffic's (Steve Winwood) career."

TC: "Both those pieces struck me as songs I would like to play on a harpsichord. They had that mystic sort of feel. That is from the music by itself, not even thinking about the words. I wanted to explore it on that level."

Craig: "One of the constants that people loved about the record was the mixtures of your own pieces and the covers that tie together in a nice bow. Were you as happy with it in 1993 and today in 2006 as your fans were?"

TC: "There are always things you look back on and say I could have done it better. It is just as well as you didn't get to. I thought we put good energy into it at the time and we were all pretty much on the same page as what we wanted to do. Don't forget there was a factor helping to make it better, and that was the audiences. From performing songs in concert over a number of years, I wanted to select those pieces that work out the best. I think everything mitigated in the direction to make it work better."

Craig: "For all of us who have had the pleasure of hearing the album, hats off."

TC: "Well, thank you very much."

Craig: "The album released on 1994 with Jorma Kaukonen, *Embryonic Journey* had a unique twist, eleven versions of the song. I always felt it was a shame that it got put out as a limited edition. Are there takes that weren't put on the album?"

TC: "It gets you to start thinking because there are stories like that behind many albums. Some of the amazing groups and performers like the Beatles, Bob Dylan and the Grateful Dead have alternates that will come out, but not every album has a story like that."

Craig: "How was it decided by you, Jorma, and Relix Records to release the album of the various takes?"

TC: "It was for my solo album *Morning Dew*, that Relix put out and they asked Jorma to help with some of the particles and there was a session to do a track of *Embryonic Journey*. Supposedly we were to get one track of it; I think the last one. I found a take I liked and said to release that one. Somebody at Relix decided to release a whole string of them. None of the tracks were curiously flawed, as often happens in the studio. The tangents you go off on can be fun also."

Craig: "I remember being thankful to get a copy because of its limited pressing. Did Jorma have the same positive feelings about the record, you did?" The chemistry was blended so well. This is one of Jorma's signature songs. If I am not mistaken the first one he ever wrote to be recorded."

TC: "That sounds about right. We had a lot in common and the chemistry was immediately there. Maybe it was the 1960's Haight-Ashbury or the Viking connection. His family is from Finland and mine is from Norway. Musically it was quit compatible. We don't do things the same way, and we don't play the same instruments."

Craig: "What is a difference that comes to mind?"

TC: "I asked him specifically and he told me he plays it (*Embryonic Journey*) pretty much note for note each time, which I certainly do not do. There will be crooks and nannies from one version here and there that will not be in another one. That's part of what makes those takes different. Listen to the album again and you won't hear him vary it much."

Craig: "It is interesting that the song selected *Embryonic Journey* is not one of the improvisational songs for which Jorma is typically known. A song such as *Walking Blues* or *Baby What You Want Me To Do* allows Jorma much more freedom."

TC: "He can also improvise in the Reverend Gary Davis songs as well."

Craig: "You get a lot of interesting feedback with the work you and Bob Bralove (Keyboard-player with Stevie Wonder and a sound designer) perform. The band is called Dos Hermonos. Can you talk about the concept?"

TC: "For the avant-garde jazz, it's like being in Da Vinci's laboratory. We also have done work with Vince Welnick as a psychedelic keyboard trio. Bob through his computer methods, hooks up the keyboards through the video, so what you see is also what you hear, and there is a video culet for every different piece. There is also different audio for each piece; but calling it a piece can be rather loosely, because they are very highly improvised. I find it very enjoyable to perform in an arena, where improvisational music plays such a big part, and you can jump into the deep end of the pool." **(Please note Vince Welnick passed away after the interview with TC).**

Craig: "When you reflect on how you have played with so many different musicians and various genres, it is pretty special."

TC: "One of the things I learned from the 1970's is to never tell someone you can't do something."

Craig: "It seems a shame that there are always people that are out to squash dreams and not encourage them."

TC: "It is an absurd business that way."

Craig: "Getting to the present, over the past couple of years you have performed some exceptional shows with the current version of the Jefferson Starship, both being on the tour with them and at times playing on a few songs. How did this come about?"

TC: "In some marvelous little room in the Vatican, somebody said lets get this little kid a job. One thing leads to another and there I was. I am really grateful for it. It is a lot less dysfunctional than the Grateful Dead sound in my day. It's a nice family. We have done every configuration; I even did some shows, with Country Joe (Country Joe & The Fish) this last tour."

Craig: "The fans really look forward to how you rework and mix some of the classic songs such as *Amazing Grace* with *House Of The Sun* (A traditional song, made popular by the Animals and covered by many), and *All Along The Watchtower* (Bob Dylan) with *Werewolves Of London* by Warren Zevon."

TC: "You want to give people something to think about."

Craig: "Do you think touring with the Jefferson Starship will continue?"

TC: "I am on for a lot of the shows this summer. I am ever so happy about that. The formula seems to be working and to mention athletics, if your team is on a win streak, keep the same line-up."

Craig: "Isn't it nice with the current version of the Jefferson Starship, the songs Paul Kantner is pulling out of the hat? There are plenty with improvisation and Diana Mangano is handling the vocals so well."

TC: 'Oh, yes! Everyone is happy on the bus."

Craig: "Things come full circle. In 2006 you are playing with some of the contemporaries from the 1960's."

TC: "Forty years earlier."

Craig: "As Paul Kantner gets ready to celebrate birthday number sixty five, its forty years earlier and forty years later. I hope you have forty more years of your brilliant work to offer us. Thank you so much for affording me this time today."

TC: "Thank you, you're most welcome."

**A quick note please.** The great Jefferson Family publication Holding Together (Steve Rowland) has a song by song review of the album by Touchstone with Tom Constanten called *Tarot*. Please email Steve and ask about issue #33. He can be reached at steveg.rowland@btinternet.com.

# Dennis McNally- Grateful Dead Publicist and author.

Craig: "I appreciate being able to speak with you. My deepest sorrows on the passing of Vince Welnick."

Dennis McNally: "Thank you. It's been a tough couple of weeks."

Craig: "As a person that has been connected to the Grateful Dead for so long, I'm hoping you can give the readers a story and insight on the band members that have left us too soon. Why don't we start with Vince and work our way backwards. We can save Jerry Garcia for last."

Dennis McNally: "Starting with Vince, my favorite story was when the Grateful Dead sang the national anthem opening day in Candlestick Park, San Francisco 1993. The Grateful Dead had a thirty year career and never once sang the national anthem. In 1993 the San Francisco Giants had almost left the city. Jerry Garcia wasn't a big sports fan, but he was a fan of San Francisco. The Giants were part of his childhood, players like Willie Mays and Willie McCovey. Jerry said okay. Vince immediately said that he would draw up the charts for an arrangement. He put it as an arrangement straight to the sons of the pioneers. He convinced Bob Weir and Jerry Garcia his co-workers to rehearse. They went out and did a beautiful job and thanked him for it. Keep in mind many famous musicians had not done the best of jobs with the national anthem. The Grateful Dead weren't known for their harmonies, but because of Vince's meticulousness we managed to pull it off. The Dead owed him a gold star for that day. It was sweet. In general Vince was very vulnerable. As soon as you knew him it was clear that he was vulnerable. He was flat on his back and he was the first to say that, before the Dead selected him. The Dead had saved his life, he bought into that. When Jerry passed away, he was devastated. That's Vince."

Craig: "Did Vince feel that most of the fans made him feel part of the family?"

Dennis McNally: "To give you an idea how they made him feel welcome on the first concert there were fans passing around bumper stickers that read "Yo Vinnie."

Craig: "What are your remembrances about Brent Mydland?"

Dennis McNally: "I watched Brent's first show. I wasn't an employee of the band. When I became part of the daily workings of the band, Brent had been around five years. Brent was extremely vulnerable. He was a fragile guy. He didn't feel an internal self-confidence. He always had self esteem issues. He took that out in self destruction behavior. One time I witnessed him smashing a beer bottle on a table in the hotel room. He looked up and grinned, like this was so cool. It was so not cool to me. There is something intrinsically bad about vandalism. On a more positive level I watched him especially around the time 1984-1989 to grow as a musician. He had three of the best tunes on the album *In The Dark*. I have one lasting image of Brent that I try to cherish. He had a lovely little music box lullaby song called *I Will Take Your Home*. There was a tour where for weeks on end he would come early and practice that song over and over. One time in particular and I believe it was live, his young daughter sat next to him when he played the song for her. It was one of those moments where you say aw, and add the w several times. It was a sweet moment."

Craig: "How old was the daughter at the time?"

Dennis McNally: "I believe between six and eight. She was a very sweet little girl."

Craig: "What about something special that you remember about Keith Godchaux?"

Dennis McNally: "I wasn't an employee yet. I saw him play three or four times. He was a great piano-player. He refused to play anything else. That was one of the reasons the band had trouble with him. He didn't want to give the variety that the band had asked. This isn't a great story but a visual thing. In 1977 the Jerry Garcia Band organized a show for Greenpeace. In 1977 Greenpeace was cutting edge. They took their ship the St.

James Bay to get in the way of whales and whalers. In San Francisco they held out a cup to the rock and roll community to help them gas up. I remember Paul Kantner and Garcia kicked in some. The Jerry Garcia Band did a show on Fisherman's Wharf, they played on a flatbed truck. The dressing room was the interior of a crew van, the Metro Van. I remember seeing everyone sitting in this empty truck. Keith is there looking like an unmade bed. He was not what you called meticulously groomed. Keith is wearing sloppy clothing and a very ugly jacket. I don't know what about that distressed me (laughter) but it was very ugly. That sums up my memory of Keith. Each of these three guys in a row had a terrible vulnerability. In each case the band selected the member for purely musical reasons, but didn't realize the price for playing with the Grateful Dead. It worked for Bruce Hornsby because he doesn't have self esteem issues and has a life apart from the Grateful Dead. Brent's death devastated Jerry more than he ever let on in public and more than he even knew himself."

Craig: "You got to see Pigpen perform one time is that correct?"

Dennis McNally: Yes that is correct. Since I didn't have a first hand introduction, the best thing is if you want a first hand account to get that from somebody that talks about him in my book." (Dennis has written a must read for any Grateful Dead fan, *A Long Strange Trip: The Inside Story Of The Grateful Dead*). It is mentioned in the book how what you see is not always what you get. Pigpen may have had a rough looking exterior but Jerry Garcia always talked about his heart of gold. In the fall of 1968 Pigpen had a girlfriend Vee Bernard that had a stroke. Pigpen encouraged her not to take the easy way out and to work harder with physical therapy. After having her hair cut short for surgery and treatment options Vee would wear a wig. Pigpen one day took her around the Haight-Ashbury district to show her many girls have short hair. This gave her the confidence to dispose of the wig.

Craig: "What about Jerry Garcia?"

Dennis McNally: "One sports story about Jerry Garcia. Jerry was not all that involved with sports. He once said he didn't need the additional heartbreak that comes with following sports. He did pay attention. One Sunday in the fall we get into a van in Philadelphia. Jerry got in right behind me. There is a black cloud over his head. He was pissed. I'm making small talk, and asked if saw the San Francisco 49'ers (Pro football) game? He growled yeah. I asked if he seen the game until the end? He said no. What had happened was the 49'ers had sucked that day. This was when they were pretty much great every game. Well not every game. On the last play of the game Joe Montana had thrown a short pass to Jerry Rice, who got by three guys for an eighty yard touchdown. When I told Jerry that he lightened up. When Jerry accepted the invitation from the San Francisco Giants we got there about ten in the morning. We do a sound check. We have about two hours to kill. Tony Bennett is going to sing *I Left My Heart In San Francisco*. Jerry, and Tony had met several times over the years. They schmooze for a bit. I spot three or four old San Francisco Giants. Former Giants- Orlando Cepeda, Willie McCovey, Willie Mays, and Gaylord Perry. I go over to Willie McCovey and introduce myself. As a kid Jerry idolized him. Willie is a gentleman, a great guy, he was more then happy to go over to Jerry Garcia. Bob Weir had idolized Gaylord Perry. They're hanging out, and that was fun. Finally I go over to Willie Mays. I say Mr. Mays, can I introduce you to Jerry Garcia. He says no. Willie Mays is notoriously grumpy. Jerry watches this and starts to laugh. Jerry had people sucking up to him all these years. If there was one thing he didn't need was more people awed by Jerry Garcia. Jerry thought that was one of the funniest things he had ever seen. Every so often he would run into somebody that had no idea who he was, and Jerry liked that."

Craig: "One of the many pleasant things of working on my book was hearing how the San Francisco musicians were not in competition with each other. I never sensed that from some other forms of music. Why do you think the bond was formed with the groups from San Francisco in the 1960's?"

Dennis McNally: "Musicians are all dealing with the same issues. If you see things in a finite way that there are only so many gigs, therefore we have to beat out this other band to get the gig, there will not be a comradery. In San Francisco in the 1960's the elite which were the Airplane, Big Brother And The Holding Company, Quicksilver Messenger Service, and the Grateful Dead, they quickly had their own theme and their own momentum going. They didn't need to have competition. I remember when the Bammies (Bay Area Music

Awards) gave awards after *In The Dark*, Jerry had to show up alone and accept them. Jerry couldn't fathom that. He couldn't ever get used to music being individual. Jerry luckily missed out on the gene of competition. That's why he never played solo, he always played with other musicians."

Craig: "Of the big four bands that were mentioned a minute ago, the Airplane had gotten a record deal first. Did any of the Grateful Dead members talk about the Airplane in the early days?"

Dennis McNally: "The Airplane had ambition. The Dead saw the Airplane as organized, they had a real business structure, and they had a manager. First it was Matthew Katz, then Bill Graham, Marty Balin had business sense. Marty put the band together to create a sound. Marty had a clue. The Dead perceived themselves as happy hippies, that hadn't a clue. The Dead didn't pursue a record deal. They had to be wooed by Warner Brothers. Jerry was cynical of the record business. Jerry had a wide knowledge of what the industry had done to African-American musicians. The Airplane had a vision. They started to play in 1965 and several months later they are starting to record. That was their world. Jerry's point of view was that he hung out with Jorma since 1962 and he was an old friend. Jerry had seen Paul Kantner around. The Dead's perception was the Airplane was the band that was organized. The ironic joke of all time is Jerry helped the Airplane with the recording of *Surrealistic Pillow*."

Craig: "Spiritual adviser."

Dennis McNally: "Spiritual adviser, he gives them the title of the album, rearranged *Somebody To Love*, plays some uncredited parts, and you know has something to do with their commercial success. Mind you only something, but he did have something to do with them being the leading American band in 1968. That was determined by how much you got paid per show. The possible exception could be the Beach Boys. Come to think of it by 1968 Brian Wilson had flipped."

Craig: "I believe we can go a year back. Brian flipped when the Beatles released *Sgt. Pepper's*."

Dennis McNally: "There you go, by 1968 the Airplane is the number one band in America at the gate and the Grateful Dead are shuffling along. Financially the Dead is barely making it. Which was okay with them. They were doing okay. If you compare yourself to other bands it was clear who was in charge."

Craig: "What were Jerry's thoughts on Jorma and Jack, as you started to see them play live over the years?"

Dennis McNally: "They were two great musicians, two great players. Jerry had great respect for them. Jerry thought they were game (A favorite adjective of Jerry's). The Airplane was a band more closely associated with blues based song structures and the Dead frequently would leave the planet. In 1996 during the Further Festival Tour, Hot Tuna frequently opened the show. I frequently would hang out with Jorma. The show would end with a *jam*, two, maybe three songs. There were different guitarists that would play on different nights. On one of the shows the song *Playing In The Band* comes up. Jorma is asked to jump in. Jorma looks up and says "Mama didn't teach me to play notes in no tens." The tempo is in tens. With all respect to a great musician, Jorma is more conventional in time signatures. The Grateful Dead and the Airplane liked each other as people. They could *jam* together on songs that were conventional, because you have to have common ground. At any rate there was a constant and well earned respect for the Airplane. These are old friends. When we get near Ohio on tour, Bob Weir tells me to call Jorma. Respect and friendship!"

Craig: "What else do you remember about the Further Festival?"

Dennis McNally: "One of the Further Festival shows was like six hours. It started at four in the afternoon. The temperature was around ninety degrees. There were times the shows started at noon. That meant there were a couple of hundred people in the facility. When Hot Tuna was done there was a whole lot more. The fact is Jorma is starting a show that was very well sold in front of almost nobody. I never saw him complain. It was clear he was there to play music. Not only did he play his set, but stuck around for the entire show. Most musicians would be gone already. That type of maturity and wisdom and fineness is Jorma."

Craig: "What do your sources tell you about any celebrations for the 40th anniversary of the Summer Of Love?"

Dennis McNally: "I'm the wrong person to ask. I didn't jump up and down for the 30th anniversary. I have no idea what is planned."

Craig: "Based on the tone of your voice would that mean you are of the belief to let memories be memories?"

Dennis McNally: "Pretty much. The bands are gone. I can't imagine the Jefferson Airplane having a one day reunion. Besides that as a historian the Summer Of Love was a phrase invented by merchants. The Summer Of Love in 1967 was after the media had destroyed the Haight (Haight-Ashbury Street, and vicinity). The Haight was gone by spring. That summer you are talking about a bunch of high school kids fleeing Omaha. The real Summer Of Love was the summer of 1966. The Haight-Ashbury scene was not about high school kids, it was about people in their twenties. They were experiencing their freedom in a modest profile. There were a couple of thousand people in an urban neighborhood. They had a wonderful time. They had wonderful art. The big party called the Be-In got the attention of the media and it was all over. The Summer Of Love 1967 is really the death nail of the real Summer Of Love."

Craig: "What recollections do you have about Chet Helms and Bill Graham?"

Dennis McNally: "I knew them both well and respected both of them for their different contribution. In some ways they are two sides of a coin. I greatly respected Chet. I spent a long time in this business. If you go into it for money, you will fail. It is also true that if you can't pay the bills you can't continue. In the late 1980's he did a show that may have been financed by Bill at the Greek Theater. There were great bands, it sold out, and great vibes. He announced the next year that he would do two days in Monterey. It was a catastrophic failure. You can't think if you had success at the Greek Theater in Berkeley where everyone could get to that you would have the same results when you increased the difficulty by being in Monterey. Chet had a fantastic intuitive understanding of music, but didn't always make good business decisions. Bill Graham had less musical intuition, but had bigger musical ears. He got Otis Redding because bands told him to get Otis Redding and he listened. Bill did run the business to his own personal profit. At the same time he had Cecil Taylor (Jazz), and the Yardbirds. Bill Graham had Woody Herman (Jazz) and the Who on a bill. There was the Grateful Dead with Miles Davis (Jazz). So you know, say what you want about Bill that he may have been a bully at times, difficult, and conniving, but he created the entire concert production industry. He gave his customers a good product. Bill was a guy that would yell at Jimi Hendrix if he felt Jimi mailed in the performance. He complained if the Grateful Dead were on stage late. Bill was an actor. He always wanted to be an actor. I worked for him in 1983 when he established the beginning of his archives. I was using a typewriter in the office, Bill's door is open. He gets into a screaming match on the phone with an agent. It was virtuosic, it was stunning for the abuse, the volume, and the stress level. It blew my mind that somebody could scream that long and that hard. I was impressed. The phone conversation ended. He steps out of his office and is looking around the room. He basically was searching for applause. He had a smirk, as if I showed him, and he went back to his office. He wasn't all that mad with the guy, he demonstrated what he could do. That was an element of Bill."

Craig: "Dennis, it is greatly appreciated that we could talk under the circumstances of Vince Welnick's passing. Thank you and I hope the readers will check out your book, *A Long Strange Trip: The Inside Story Of The Grateful Dead*. I'm sorry that time prevents us from covering the Dead's history."

Dennis McNally: "Thank you Craig. Best of luck with your book."

# Jerry Miller- Talks about Skip Spence and Moby Grape.

Craig: "Thank you for being able to give the readers an insight on Skip Spence and the wonderful music you both created in Moby Grape."

Jerry Miller: "My pleasure. I'm sorry that I couldn't retrieve your original messages. I haven't learned how to use any form of voice mail on this phone."

Craig: "As long as you feel good and can still play the guitar, you can have somebody else write down your messages."

Jerry Miller: (Jerry laughs) "Thanks man."

Craig: "When Moby Grape was first starting did Skip Spence ever confide to you which side of the story is true about him going to Mexico in 1966, when he was in the Airplane? Some believe he told then manager Matthew Katz, while others claim he disappeared without any band member or staff personnel being aware of his activities."

Jerry Miller: "The entire time I knew Skip, it never came up. I am sorry to say I never got the definitive answer. It was one of those things that you couldn't be totally surprised if he didn't inform the band, or the manager."

Craig: "As you were writing and recording the first Moby Grape album how did it feel working with Skip? Did he have a personality that was conducive for creativity with the band, or could you foreshadow that something is not right? "

Jerry Miller: "I found he had a good personality, but he was pretty wild. At times a little bit crazy. I didn't even know he was a musician the first time I saw him. I walked in to the place we were supposed to meet. There is a guy sitting with a wild and crazy look on his face. I didn't know he was such a good musician yet. As time went by I found out. He was kind of schizoid."

Craig: "If you look at even early pictures of him with the Jefferson Airplane and Moby Grape there are times that you can see in his eyes a person that could have mental health issues."

Jerry Miller: "He could flip-out real easy."

Craig: "When the album got finished did you and Skip feel there could be some problems with management and the record company that could prevent the band from getting the proper support?"

Jerry Miller: "Even before the completion of the first album we knew there would be problems. We knew there would be trouble. We needed to do our own thing."

Craig: "What was your reaction when the record company decided to release several singles at once, which defeated the purpose of somebody going out and purchasing the album?"

Jerry Miller: "I thought then it was kind of crazy. I still feel it was crazy. The should have put only *8:05* (That is the title) and *Omaha* as the single. That would have made it easy for the record label and radio stations to push just the one single. It would have made a lot more sense."

Craig: "When you and Skip were talking about how the record was turning out on the creative side did you both feel something special can happy hear if things unfold correctly?"

Jerry Miller: "I did. We thought the record was and did turn out great. What can I say but it was beautiful. It was hard work. Good and hard work. The work that is hard, but you feel good about what you accomplished. We put a lot of hard work in that record. That was all the guys."

Craig: "There is no question about the effort you guys gave to the recording. As much as forces were attempting to destroy the terrific outcome you still managed to reach number twenty-four on the album charts. That is not an easy climb for a new band."

Jerry Miller: "Thanks. That is true what you said. Thank you again for the compliment."

Craig: "When you started to work on the second record and the direction was more toward the musicianship of the band and the songs were longer and less structured, did the record company put pressure on Moby Grape to conform to the formula of the first LP?"

Jerry Miller: "We didn't have that from the record company. The problem we ran into was not being able to stay on our coast. There would have been more continuity of what we were doing. We end up in New York. Now we are three thousand miles from home. Appeasing people outside the band was foolish. We should have recorded in or around in Los Angeles. That would have made us around the people of the band. When we went to New York it was getting to us staying in a hotel. Skip was getting crazed. Not only Skip but the whole band. We got kicked out of every hotel we stayed in New York. We were in the studio sometimes sixteen hours a day. We were warn down. If we would have stayed out west we would have been more comfortable. We kept getting held longer and longer in New York. The project of the second album lost its theme. It was scattered and didn't have the continuity. Rather then it being an album it ended up being a bunch of tunes."

Craig: "The title *Grape Jam* was appropriate, because the material was spread out and not even."

Jerry Miller: "Yea that is correct. Originally as I recall the *jams* (*Boysenberry* and *Black Currant*) weren't even going to be on the record. David Rubinson (Producer by trade) wanted it included. Craig, I have some news for you."

Craig: "I am all ears."

Jerry Miller: "Yesterday I talked to one of the former band members of Moby Grape, Peter Lewis (One of the guitarists). Bob Mosley (Bass) and Skip Spence's son Omar are playing together right now. Now we are having talks!"

Craig: "That is fantastic. I hope for all of us who admired your music that if it works out you guys will be free of any drug and or management issues. Make sure that you are always in the talks with the three guys."

Jerry Miller: "I am in the talks. I am! The news gets better. Don Stevenson as well is talking with them."

Craig: "What is your gut feeling on how this could turn out?"

Jerry Miller: "I'm feeling good about it. We are thinking of doing this and doing it right. One of the possibilities is to do something with Alvin Lee (Ten Years After) back east. It is too early to get excited."

Craig: "Are we finally over the days of having to go to court, if you want to use the name Moby Grape for the new project?"

Jerry Miller: "Absolutely. No more court for us! We got everything back. There is one more appeal if he (Matthew Katz) wants to continue with the court system."

Craig: "Does that mean even on the worst scenario if you have to go to court one final time until the trial is over you can use the name Moby Grape, without interference from any outsider?"

Jerry Miller: "Yes we can. Yea, we can use the name if we desire."

Craig: "That is great. You guys went through so much to be able to play under the name you felt comfortable with. The best scenario is you continue to make great music and don't have to worry about anything but the band members getting along."

Jerry Miller: "Thank you. This may be the longest running music lawsuit in history. Skip and Bob Mosley (Bass) made up the name."

Craig: "Is Omar staying away from bad influences?"

Jerry Miller: "Omar is a number one Christian boy. The pre-requisite is if we do this it has to be without the baggage. We are hanging out with upright citizens."

Craig: "Are the travel logistics a problem for you guys?"

Jerry Miller: "With air travel the way it is today it is not a problem. We may use Marin County, California to get together. We had a three-way conversation with Sony and a potential manager. The offer was nice. We want to have something good to offer before we go on the road. That will take a lot of rehearsal. We want to have great new tunes."

Craig: "Do the other guys want to record first and then tour?"

Jerry Miller: "As a matter of fact Peter Lewis feels that way. We need to be around fresh people. I hope we learned from the past. This can be fun to play music. Omar not only does his own stuff, he does Skip's material, and writes for the Church. I try to play on weekends."

Craig: "When Skip suffered the breakdown in New York City and ended up being confined to an institution for six months, did a particular event lead to the tragedy of him destroying a hotel door with an axe? The story turned even sadder when he wanted to use the weapon on the band members."

Jerry Miller: "Something definitely happened. He bumped into these people. Very strange folks. I don't know if you would call them witches or trolls. They were obviously into something and they were messing with him. I guess the heavy drugs. I would assume. He went from being a jolly guy with a beard to having shaved, wearing a leather jacket with no shirt, and having an axe. He was sweating like a pig. He got into something with these people. They were packing (Carrying guns) and everything. These trolls or whatever they were influenced him."

Craig: "When he was confined to Bellevue Hospital in New York did the band members visit him?"

Jerry Miller: "I didn't go visit him. I felt there was no point in us hanging out. We had it at this point. David Rubinson went. I don't remember if Peter Lewis did or not. It may have been we all went home. It was loony back then. Skip had really flipped."

Craig: "Did you get to see him soon after his release?"

Jerry Miller: "We saw him when he came back out to Santa Cruz. He was riding a Triumph motorcycle."

Craig: "Did you find that although he couldn't turn the clock completely back at least he was better by getting away from the evil influences?"

Jerry Miller: "No, it was all different. When we saw Skip there were a lot of possibilities we could do. There was an offer for a Canadian tour. There was an offer for an American tour as well. They wanted the entire band. That meant very specific members. Once the whole band wasn't available it changed everything for all of us. The four of us would play on the west coast and do different things. Skip had a lot of disappointment even on his return. His family wasn't happy with him. You never knew what he went through during the six months. When he came back out to the west coast he was still cool, but more into another world. He would stop in his tracks and start laughing. He did that before, but not as radical."

Craig: "When Skip and you would talk music, did he look over his shoulder at the Jefferson Airplane?"

Jerry Miller: "He did like being where he was. He liked Moby Grape. It gave him a good chance to write. He was a brilliant writer. The contest was really between the five of us. We all played and wrote. We had families to support.

We didn't hang out all that much until it was time for work. The management situation was real bad. One night we were playing in Cleveland, Ohio. There was nobody there to pick us up. Skip is wearing a beautiful blue suit. He goes into a phone booth to find out what we are supposed to do. He went crazy in the phone booth. He started to spit and it landed on the beautiful suit. He got along with the Jefferson Airplane members as far as I could tell. He never had any bad wishes toward them as a band, or as people. The guy that was cool that I met at Skip's funeral was Spencer Dryden. As sick as Spencer was he made it there. As I recall he was the only Airplane member I saw at the funeral. I had a nice chat with him. What a nice guy. Spencer was so sick, that it was an effort to walk. That was big time to make it all the way there."

Craig: "When people want to know what type of person Spencer was your story says volumes. What is fascinating about his appearance at the funeral Spencer didn't play in the band with Skip."

Jerry Miller: "Spencer was a good man. Skip would have really liked that. Skip liked pretty much everybody, until he got pissed off."

Craig: "What are your personal remembrances of the Airplane?"

Jerry Miller: "Basically they were a lot different than me. I had come from playing clubs, as did Mosley and Stevenson. We were playing the Dragon A-Go-Go in San Francisco. We had played places before that as well. We were doing covers from the Beatles, Rolling Stones, and Righteous Brothers. We also played Sam And Dave. We had all those tunes ready and we were real disciplined. We wore the same suits and played ten sets a night!"

Craig: " Ten sets! I get exhausted watching a Yankee game. Did you keep tapes of any of the performances?"

Jerry Miller: (Jerry laughs). "There aren't any tapes of any of that. It was cool. We had bass, drums, guitar, saxophone, and keyboards. It was a small band that could sound like a big band. We heard about what was happening at the Avalon Ballroom and decided to check it out. Looked like a nice game. We could be good at this. We could have more fun."

Craig: "I have to ask you about the Bob Mosley story of joining the Marines. Wasn't it strange that they would want a guy in the mid-twenties playing in a rock and roll band?"

Jerry Miller: "Craig, man to this day I don't understand the events. He was twenty-six. There was a lot of monkey business going on at that time with experiments. Who knows what made him do that. Things did get crazy for him. I can't see how he wanted to join the Marines and not play Woodstock. As I recall he didn't serve any years. He got in and got right out. I don't think he made it through basic training. He decided he made the wrong move. I could have told him that off the bat."

Craig: "There is an album that Moby Grape had to put out under the name of the Melvilles (1990). It is one of the most overlooked rock albums (*Legendary Grape*). It finally saw the release on CD with bonus tracks in 2003. Since you were going through who had the rights to the name, it first got released on tape only (500 or so copies were made). There are three tracks that are worth listening to forever, *All My Life*, the cover of Chuck Berry's *I'm Talking About You* (Called on the record *Talk About Love, I'm Talking About You*), and *Bitter Wind In Tanganika*. What are your remembrances of the material?"

Jerry Miller: "Thanks for that. Yes it is pretty cool. Bob Mosley gets credit for the Chuck Berry cover. We couldn't use the name Moby Grape on the original 1990 release. What was more frustrating we would get together and rehearse and get a good gig. If we tried to use the name Moby Grape there would be an injunction from the former manager. The promoters did not want to get involved. We had to come up with something. We had to play around with the name. We tried initials from the group members as well."

Craig: "It is always horrible that the people that are able to make quality music, which few of the population can, have outside circumstances dictating the road the band takes."

Jerry Miller: "It is a shame. As for the album you are talking about it is a good piece of work. We spent a good amount of time on all those tracks."

Craig: "The first thought I had when hearing the songs was a Moby Grape fan will get great pleasure in the music and not simply purchase the recording because they previously enjoyed what you guys had released."

Jerry Miller: "It was enjoyable. I liked doing it. A couple of weeks ago I pulled out a black and white video tape of me, Peter Lewis, Don Stevenson, Bob Mosley, a piano-player, and one other guitar-player, from The Backstage, Seattle, Washington. It was around 1988 or 1989. I was amazed how good that was."

Craig: "I'd like to see the tape from back then, as would all the other Moby Grape fans."

Jerry Miller: "The video recording was dark. We could kick some ass."

Craig: "Is the Jerry Miller on the Jay Geils 2005 release *Geils Plays Jazz*, yourself?"

Jerry Miller: "I don't recall being there. I hope I would remember. You never know. It is somebody else. It is another Jerry Miller. When I lived in Cape Junction, Oregon, it was a little town. There were four Jerry Millers. Robert Plant is a good friend. When I was living in Cape Junction, he calls the wrong Jerry Miller. He got on the phone with a guy that owned a brewery. Jerry Miller who owned the brewery had never heard of Robert Plant, Led Zeppelin, or Moby Grape. They get to talking and the guy gets to put in a Steel Head Brewery in Europe."

Craig: "I hope Robert Plant finally tracked you down without having to spend more money."

Jerry Miller: "He did. He is a great guy. It isn't talked about how Robert Plant helped Skip Spence with his expenses from the hospital. He paid his bill."

Craig: "That is a wonderful story. Robert Plant is on the tribute record for Skip called *More Oar*."

Jerry Miller: "Skip was a genius man. How the songs went together on his record called *Oar*. The way he did it was to put maybe the number one song with the fifth. It is very intricate and crazy."

Craig: "Isn't it sickening that so many of our heroes went through hell to get to heaven?"

Jerry Miller: "It's true, isn't it. Craig how is Paul Kantner doing?"

Craig: "We were able to do the interview for the book this week. He is fine, excluding back problems that come and go. He told me that it can be about eight weeks before the discomfort goes away. I wished him a fast get well."

Jerry Miller: "If he needs the number of my doctor let me know. He fixed me up real good. I couldn't even walk before the surgery in 1991. I can now lift an elephant, but would not."

Craig: "Please stick to lifting Gibson and Fender guitars only."

Jerry Miller: "There you go buddy."

Craig: "Jerry thanks. I appreciate your time and the great possibilities we could have with a Moby Grape reunion. Stay well and keep in touch."

Jerry Miller: "You're welcome and let me know if you need anything."

**Mike Somavilla-** Quicksilver Messenger Service historian, founder of Crest Of The Wave Productions, and organizer of the benefit for Spencer Dryden.

Craig: "Mike, thanks for joining me today. You always have both historical and hysterical stories to tell."

Mike Somavilla: "You're welcome, thanks for having me."

Craig: "Why don't we start off with how Crest Of The Wave began and how it ties in with some of the Airplane Family members."

Mike Somavilla: "It started as a vehicle to promote Terry & The Pirates (Terry's unreleased album from 1972 had Spencer Dryden, Greg Douglass, and John Cipollina of Quicksilver Messenger Service, to name a few. Warner Brothers Records had even issued some test pressings. To this day there is a cloud of mystery as to why the project didn't come to fruition). I was a big fan of this band. I met John 10/4/83, when he was in Nicksilver. That was the band with Nick Gravenites (Famous blues musician, firmly entrenched with San Francisco musicians). At the end of the concert that night I asked if Terry & The Pirates had a business manager or agent, or somebody that I could talk to about your music. There are some records I am having difficulty finding, and I hope they could help me out. John writes down a phone number, and address on a piece of paper, but no name. The next day after work I decided to make the phone call. The person picks up on the other end, and I say hello, I would like to get some information on Terry & The Pirates, can you help me? The person on the other end says well this is Terry Dolan, what can I do for you? That was the springboard. We had a great conversation. I wrote him a letter asking about some other things and at the tail end if there was a Terry & The Pirates fan club. I asked if not, could I start one. He wrote back one month later and told me of course you can start one. Crest Of The Wave was built to help promote everything Terry & The Pirates were associated with. The name of the company came from a Rory Gallagher (Well respected guitar-player with and without his band Taste. Rory passed away 6/14/95) song *Crest Of A Wave*. On his 1971 album *Deuce* he had the song *Crest Of A Wave*. I'm a big fan of Rory. I decided to change the title a bit, and there you go. Although *Crest Of A Wave* was formed as a vehicle for everything Terry & The Pirates, it later included anything Cipollina was involved in as well. When I moved to the Bay Area it was expanded to include many of the musicians that were part of the scene."

Craig: "As the company also turned into an avenue for getting record deals for many of the Bay Area musicians, how did you first begin to make the proper contacts, and have the knowledge of the industry?"

Mike Somavilla: "Mainly it was meeting the people. I would tell them what I was doing. I let them know if they needed my help in any capacity, I was available. Most told me they had older recordings that they would want shopped. They gave me a shot at it. There were never trust issues. The people I worked with were part of a large family of bands."

Craig: "How did you find the specific labels that would be interested in your services?"

Mike Somavilla: "Just from my own buying habits as a collector. I saw which ones would be right for a particular sound. Taxim Records for example I knew about because Terry Dolan had done a record deal with Line Records several years earlier. At the time Line had the same guy that was running Taxim. When I heard about him through a distributor I was buying Lime Records from he told me that Hans had a new label. I contacted Hans and told him that I can offer you a bunch of great music. I listed some of the things I had available. One of those was a Greg Douglass record called *Maelstrom*. The first deal I ever got was for Greg, with Taxim Records. Then I heard about a label in France that were big Cipollina fans. I contacted them, and they jumped at the chance to release Terry & The Pirates, *Too Close For Comfort*. They also released Problem Child. That was another band that John had with Greg Douglass. I knew we had live recordings, but no studio recordings. I felt it was worthy to try to get a record deal for all this lost music."

Craig: "When did you first secure the record deal for Greg Douglass, *Maelstrom*?"

Mike Somavilla: "Let's see, that came out in 1993. I think it was late 1991. It was a matter of transferring the old tape we had with just Greg, which was recorded in 1987 at David Hayes' studio. Taxim wanted to see about adding some other musicians. They wanted it to be a fuller album. I then went about contacting some other people. Unfortunately Jerry Garcia's people turned us down. They never responded is more likely the way it happened. I had the same problem getting a hold of Jerry as some of the Airplane folk. The gatekeeper didn't want to pass the information on."

Craig: "Didn't that surprise you that they didn't get back to you?"

Mike Somavilla: "I just felt they thought Garcia was too important for this."

Craig: "I had a great discussion about that with Marty Balin and his dad. Managers, agents, and publicity reps are not playing guardian to a minor. When somebody reaches the age of eighteen let them decide what they want and not what the employee thinks they want. Were you also responsible for landing record deals for Darby Slick (Great Society), Pete Sears, and the former roadie that played with Jorma, and Hot Tuna, Billy Goodman?"

Mike Somavilla: "Darby I did get a record deal. Pete I helped in the sense that there were all these mistakes in his bio. I had gotten an advanced copy of his cassette *Watchfire*. With that was the advanced bio, and press release. I'm reading through it and see all this misinformation and mistakes. I contacted the label to ask if they realized the errors. Somebody there asked me why does it matter? I told them if you print misinformation it will be kept getting passed on that way. Each writer will not have the facts. It needs to be cleared up. They called Pete Sears and told him they had talked with me and I made suggestions. They wondered what they should do. Pete told them to change it! A few days later at the CD release party I told him that I hope he didn't feel I overstepped my bounds. He told me not at all, and thanks. The same thing happened on the *Long Haul* release. I'm reading the bio, and am thinking here we go again. There were names misspelled, names spelled correctly, and then the next line incorrectly, facts were left out, and it was a mess. Pete calls me at midnight, and we spent the entire overnight hours correcting the misinformation. As for Billy Goodman, I met him through Jorma. I book the Bruce Latimer Show, a Bay Area TV show. Billy was there with Jorma, and he had heard I had European contacts, and asked me about them and I gave him a list of names. Billy wound up getting signed to Taxim Records, although not directly from my initial connection. As for Darby Slick – I ran in to him at a benefit concert for Stanley Mouse (Considered one of the Top 5 poster artists from San Francisco) , which led me to getting him a record deal for the CD *Sandoland*. His son Jor is on the record and Sandoland is the place where Speed Racer (Famous 1960's cartoon) raced."

Craig: "Maybe Racer X makes an uncredited appearance. There are two stories with Airplane Family members Greg Douglas, and David Freiberg that are hilarious. Can you share them with the readers please?"

Mike Somavilla: "Again as with John Cipollina, when it comes to Greg Douglass I want anything these guys recorded. When Greg was about fourteen, he was in a band called the Statics. By chance I tracked down one of the guys in the band. I asked if he had any old recordings, and he did. After he gave it to me he thought maybe he shouldn't. He was jokingly referring to me blackmailing him with this. I said to the guy Jim Gammon the trumpet-player, if I blackmail anyone it would be Greg. I transfer the thing to CD, and send Greg a copy. I didn't put a name on it. I told him to check it out, and bugged him for a week to listen to it. When he finally listened to it, he was shocked. He leaves a message on my machine about one of the songs on the CD called the *Surfin' Clod*. He wrote this tune about a spastic surfer that gets on the board backwards, the guy can't surf to save his life. Later on in the message he tells me if he finds the recording on any European compilation he will kill me. As for David, the song was the recording of the *Star Spangled Banner*. Quicksilver Messenger Service had recorded the song for the Committee, which was Howard Hesseman's (Actor from the television show WKRP In Cincinnati) comedy troupe. The committee wanted a rock version of the *Star Spangled Banner* to play at their performances. As the story goes and this is allegedly how it happened, the Charlatans passed on it. The deal was they would get paid an ounce of pot, and one hundred bucks to play a rock version of the song. They played it so well they got a hundred bucks, and two ounces of pot and they were asked back in December to play at their Christmas party. I was on the hunt for this recording for years. I contacted many people in the Committee, including Howard, it was all to no avail. Several years later at a bachelor party of a friend I met a guy that had a copy; he had worked for KMPX-FM radio (San Francisco) at the time and made himself a dub. He thought if anybody should have a copy it was me, because I was such a hardcore Cipollina fan. During the rehearsals for the 30th anniversary of the Summer Of Love I'm talking with David Freiberg, and told him how I finally found a person that has a copy of the Quicksilver version of the *Star Spangled Banner*. David says to me "Oh why would you want to go and do that for?" I said to him "David it's historical, it's hysterical, it's Quicksilver's very first recording" and David just sort of rolls his eyes and shakes his head and says to me "Mike, I was there, you weren't, it wasn't recorded very well, people were banging on this or beating on that and sonically it's not going to be that good", but he also understands that it is me who he's talking to and just accepts my crazy passion when it come to Quicksilver. David is a very humble man, he just doesn't understand why anybody would care or place any importance in this music after all these years. What's more, he doesn't take all this fascination with Quicksilver too seriously either."

Craig: "When I spoke with David, he couldn't understand why I would be interested if he had a copy of the David & Michaela CBS demo. That is one of his many strong points. He doesn't have the ego attached to his head. On a serious note, you did a wonderful thing for Spencer Dryden. Can you expand on that?"

Mike Somavilla: "I knew Spencer through the Dinosaurs and met him in 1987. I knew he was having some medical problems and I was asked by Steve Keyser (John Cipollina's manager) to work on a benefit for him and I thought it was a great idea. I made some phone calls. I knew there wouldn't be any trouble to get musicians, but first I had to get a venue. At first I met up with a lot of resistance. I called the Fillmore Auditorium, in San Francisco. They wanted eighteen thousand dollars for the rent. I told them "Guys if we pay you that much money how is it a benefit?" I called other venues and they weren't responsive either. Chet Helms gave me some invaluable information that proved to be quite useful as well. I also called Pete Sears to get him involved (Pete was playing with the Flying Other Brothers at the time and they were a big part of the whole night). I had started the ball rolling booking some of the artists for the night and brought in Pete, he brought it all together, and boy did he. Pete's one of the most generous people I know. He donated boundless energy and time to this cause and found some key people to play for Spencer to boot. Kathy Peck (Part of the all girl band the Contractions and more importantly Executive Director and Co-Founder, H.E.A.R.- Hearing Education and Awareness for Rockers. Thank you to http://www.audiologyonline.com), Steve Keyser, and I helped gather goods and services for the auction and raffle. In all through everybody's endeavors we made thirty-six thousand for Spencer, just through the concert, and auctions. This doesn't count private donations."

Craig: "Wouldn't the Fillmore be a place that would welcome somebody with Spencer's resume?"

Mike Somavilla: "I was a little surprised, but not totally. Remember none of the old guard was left from BGP (Bill Graham Productions). It is now part of a corporation Clear Channel. The people that were part of Slim's had no qualms about coming to the rescue. Craig, I want to point out that besides the great help from Pete Sears, Roger McNamee (Flying Other Brothers) was incredible for his support."

Craig: "What did Spencer say to you?"

Mike Somavilla: "He told me that he didn't have the words to know how to say thanks. I told him you just did. I was glad to have helped him and to be a part of this incredible evening. I called Bill Thompson (Jefferson Airplane manager) because I couldn't get anywhere with R.I.A.A. (Recording Industry Association Of America) or BMG (Record Company) in getting Spencer replacement copies of his gold album awards he had with the Airplane. Bill took a hold of it and got the gold albums for Spencer and I got to be one of the presenters on stage. It was a great moment."

Craig: "Spencer had such a quality about him. He always did things behind the scene that went without publicity. When Skip Spence passed away, Spencer was the only Airplane member at the funeral. At the time Spencer had some physical problems. Let's not forget that Spencer didn't even play with Skip!"

Mike Somavilla: "Spencer was a great guy!"

Craig: "Thank you for the list of musicians from the performance. On the bill from the Airplane Family were, Pete Sears, David Freiberg, his wife Linda Imperial (Jefferson Starship), Peter Kaukonen, and Nick Buck. Mike it is always great to hear your stories. This time it was even better, because you were able to put a smile on Spencer Dryden's face, when he needed it. Thank you so much. I'm glad that Crest Of The Wave is doing well. When I talk to Greg Douglass I'll ask if Hot Tuna ever considered playing the *Surfin' Clod*."

Mike Somavilla: "Thank you. I wish you well on the book."

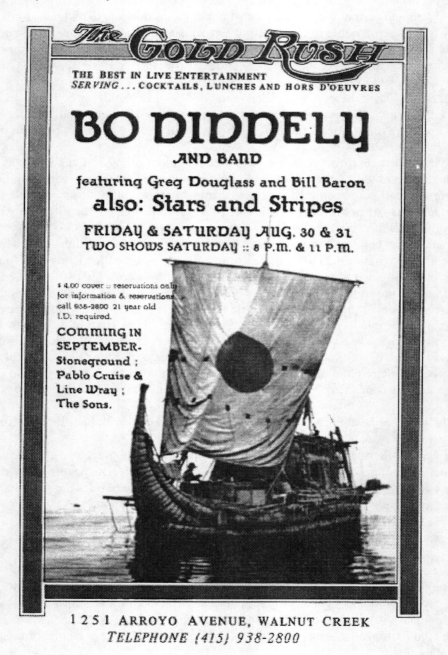

**Flyer with kind permission of the Melody Peters and Mike Somavilla collections. One more goody from the vault. Greg Douglass as part of Bo Diddley's band, from San Francisco 8/30 and 8/31/74. Notice the incorrect spelling of Diddley! Not to be reproduced without the written consent of Melody Peters and Mike Somavilla. From a 1974 concert produced by Bob Strand. Thank you Bob as well.**

# NAMES FOUND UNDER THE CIRCUS TENT
## (WELCOME BACK MY FRIENDS TO THE INDEX THAT NEVER ENDS)

539

541